A HISTORY OF MODERN P

A History of Modern Political Thought

The Question of Interpretation

GARY BROWNING

OXFORD
UNIVERSITY PRESS

OXFORD

UNIVERSITY PRESS

Great Clarendon Street, Oxford, OX2 6DP,
United Kingdom

Oxford University Press is a department of the University of Oxford.
It furthers the University's objective of excellence in research, scholarship,
and education by publishing worldwide. Oxford is a registered trade mark of
Oxford University Press in the UK and in certain other countries

First Edition published in 2016

Impression: 2

Published in the United States of America by Oxford University Press
198 Madison Avenue, New York, NY 10016, United States of America

British Library Cataloguing in Publication Data

Data available

Library of Congress Control Number: 2016936523

ISBN 978–0–19–968228–7 (hbk.)
978–0–19–968229–4 (pbk.)

Printed in Great Britain by
CPI Group (UK) Ltd, Croydon, CR0 4YY

Preface

Some books write themselves. This one did not. The idea came to me one weekend in blazing hot sunshine. I was to write a book that would get to grips with the question of interpretation by reviewing the modern history of political thought in the light of several interpretive paradigms. I wrote out ideas in a whirl of activity and then collected them and myself in rewriting them. By the end of the next month and the sunshine I had sent my ideas to Oxford University Press. I let them settle there. The rest is history or at least a number of years of unremitting industry. It has not been an easy book to write. I worked with my initial inspiration and continued to work through my imaginative sense of what was to be done. Imagination combined with perspiration as I read and re-read texts and contexts to get a sense of what was to count in the intellectual reach of interpretive schemes. How is a particular political thinker to be included and examined? I worked hard to nail interpretations of thinkers that would cohere with what I wanted to say about wider interpretive schemes. Days came and went along with particular interpretive trails. In the end I had something resembling a book and then it was a case of reconstructing the resemblance to take account of alternative trails. The resulting study emerged slowly along with my own interpretive standpoint. I realized quite early that I wanted to develop a synoptic perspective. It would be dialectical and would testify to the legacy of Hegel and Marx. Who knows if the resulting work is a part of the Hegelian tradition? Certainly it represents a continuous if critical reflection on Hegel's ideas and in particular his conception of the history of philosophy that was inspired in part by encountering Oakeshott at an impressionable age and reading through all of Collingwood's writings. Yet it also reflects working with deconstruction. My enthusiasm for the history of ideas was reinforced by reading Skinner many years ago and by devouring Gadamer in a night or two way back in the 1970s. So the book has many sources of inspiration and represents a concern to be integrative and dialectical in interpreting ideas. Nothing of any note is a mere mistake and must be recognized and worked with.

The history of ideas is in part a work of mourning for the dead. Derrida is instructive on this. In revisiting the dead, their spirit is rekindled and so my thoughts are engaged by the dead who have gone but continue to speak. In the last five years I have lost many who mattered and who continue to matter as their spirits stay close. I am thinking of Conal, my son, who would have appreciated the concentration that I have put into this book even if he would have been clear and honest in his assessment. I am also thinking of my mother,

Myra, who read my first book as a labour of love which must have been hard labour and of my father, Frank, who softened in his last years in a way that has lent itself to a reinterpretation of his and my life. Monty too deserves a mention as he sought fruitlessly for a happiness that was beyond his capacity. They all suffered from mental frailty either at the end of things or in ways that troubled what should have been years of growth and enchantment but they all showed me that illness and suffering can be interpreted in multiple ways and should neither be denied nor dismissed.

I would also like to thank friends and colleagues who have helped with the writing of this book. My wife, Raia, has been wonderful. She knows what is involved and shares many of my convictions. She has been a constant help and guide in enabling me to make use of time and in talking over aspects of my argument. My daughter Eleanor shows a wonderful spirit of vitality and warmth. Andy Kilmister read a draft and provided invaluable and considered criticism. Doerthe Rosenow and Victoria Browne read chapters and I have presented papers on Derrida, Foucault, and Gadamer to audiences at Oxford Brookes and Brunel University. Anne-Marie Kilday and Tina Miller at Oxford Brookes have been supportive and Nick Hewlett has been a great friend through this project and beyond. Dominic and Olivia at Oxford University Press have been patient and supportive.

Contents

1

Introduction

Titles serve as a way of introducing texts, signposting what is to be read. Of course, signposts can be misleading, because their directions have to be interpreted. The title of this book guards against misinterpretation by registering its interest in the nature of interpretation. This book reviews ways in which the history of modern political thought can be interpreted and shows how distinct styles of interpretation have been applied to selected modern political thinkers. Interpretation in the history of political thought is controversial. There are seemingly endless disputes over interpreting a thinker in this way or that. Marx may be labelled a determinist, a social scientist, a class warrior, or a philosophically inclined normative theorist. Likewise Machiavelli is represented in multiple ways. He has been an evil ideologue, a realist, a proto Marxist and a conventional Renaissance republican. There is also more general debate on the nature of the enterprise. Its contestability is revealed in disputes over its relations to the disciplines of philosophy and history. Klosko, in *The Oxford Handbook of the History of Political Philosophy*, observes that 'the history of political philosophy spans two different disciplines, history and philosophy. In working in the area, it is essential to keep the two separate.'[1] This separation, however, cannot be taken for granted, because political thought takes place in time and some but not all of its historic forms may be styled philosophical. Indeed, Dunn, in a landmark methodological essay, 'The Identity of the History of Ideas', argues strongly for combining the two disciplines in the history of political thought. As he remarks, 'both historical specificity and philosophical delicacy are more likely to be attained if they are pursued together, than if one is deserted for the other at an early stage of the investigation.'[2] A theme of this book consists in its engagement with the ways in which past forms of political thought raise historical and

---

[1] G. Klosko, 'Introduction', in G. Klosko (ed.), *The Oxford Handbook of the History of Political Philosophy* (Oxford, Oxford University Press, 2011), p. 1. See also J. Pocock, 'Theory and History: Problems of Context and Narrative', in J. Dryzek, B. Honig, and A. Phillips (eds), *The Oxford Handbook of Political Theory* (Oxford, Oxford University Press, 2006), p. 169.

[2] J. Dunn, 'The Identity of the History of Ideas', *Philosophy*, vol. XL111, no. 164, 1968, pp. 85–104.

philosophical questions. Historical contexts distinguish past political concerns from present ones, while philosophical presumptions about these past concerns can be questioned in the light of present theoretical and political considerations. The interpretive interplay between past and present and between theory, politics, and history is a theme of this book's engagement with interpretation.

A determination to get to grips with the contestability of interpretation in the history of political thought explains the rationale of this book. It is a book of two parts. Its opening part reviews general interpretive approaches to the subject and the succeeding part analyses selected modern political theorists. The two parts go together. A sign of their compatibility is conveyed by our dual analyses of Hegel and Marx, who elaborate general schemes of interpretation and seminal substantive theories of modern politics. If Hegel and Marx reveal the affinity between substantive social and political theory and wider frames of interpretation, this book more generally shows how generic schemes of interpretation frame analyses of particular political theorists. Individual studies of past theorists are structured by general interpretive assumptions. These assumptions may or may not be presented in particular acts of interpretation. A commentator, say, may offer a convincing view of Bentham's notion of utility, without delivering a general analysis of the status and accessibility of past ideas. In this book exemplary general schemes of interpretation are examined expressly. The rationale for doing so is that they matter, and the ways in which they do will be justified in the course of the ensuing argument. These general schemes offer ways of constructing and assessing past political thinking. They do so in distinguishable and in some respects contrary ways, which allow for distinctive and sometimes conflicting interpretations of particular theorists. Hence the discrepancy between images of Marx and Machiavelli that was flagged at the outset is in part to be explained by the multiple ways in which interpretation may be conceived. An indisputable feature of the history of political thought is its sophisticated practice of reinterpretation, so that judgments on past thinkers are subject to continuing modifications. This continual process of reinterpretation tends to be ignored in standard general texts that furnish seemingly definitive if condensed summaries of past thinkers. Reflection on the question of interpretation shows how the process of reinterpretation is neither contingent nor arbitrary but derives at least in part from the character of interpretation itself.

The interpretive schemes that are reviewed in this book do not exhaust the repertoire of its notable forms, but serve to highlight how explanatory strategies repay attention. They frame the ways in which particular interpretations are conducted. The selected schemes consist in the dialectical teleology of Hegel and Marx, the historical analyses of Collingwood and Oakeshott, the contextualist turn of the Cambridge School and affiliated authors, the textual and discursive deconstruction of Derrida and Foucault, and Gadamer's hermeneutical interpretation of horizons, past and present. These schemes are not readily commensurable, because they assume selective positions in reviewing past thinkers. Hegel and Marx see past thought as bearing upon the present, and assimilate its forms as component elements within their own theoretical systems. Collingwood and Oakeshott insist upon the autonomy of historical understanding and yet connect their own political theories to ongoing traditions of political thought. The contextualism of the Cambridge School announced itself in opposition to preceding forms of commentary, which omitted reference to the historical contexts in relation to which past thinkers formulated their theories. In contrast Derrida and Foucault interpret past texts against the grain of what their authors intended, assuming that authors do not set the agenda for interpreting how flows of language or forms of discursive practice are to be understood. Gadamer takes past and present to provide interpretive horizons that are adjusted reciprocally in a process of interpretation that yields an outcome that neither replicates the past nor reflects the prejudices of the present.

The changing formulations and distinguishable features of these interpretive schemes are reviewed in the following chapters. To interpret particular past thinkers in the light of one of them is to view thinkers from a certain angle that foregrounds or accentuates what is ignored, underplayed, or opposed in alternative interpretive styles. What they entail is abstract without attending to how they operate in practice. Hence in chapters 8 to 18, reviews of several modern political thinkers will be conducted which draw upon the previously outlined interpretive perspectives. This focus upon particular modern political thinkers is of intrinsic value in that it reckons with notable theorists of modern politics. Yet it also highlights what is at stake in interpretation, because past thought is not simply there, waiting for our uncomplicated access to its ideas. It is accessed by processes of interpretation that are framed in distinct ways. There is no better way of appreciating what is involved in these frames of interpretation than in reviewing how they make sense of actual past thinkers. In reviewing the impact of the Cambridge School's challenge to preceding assumptions, Gunnell argues that reflection upon its transformation of the study of particular thinkers such as Machiavelli, Hobbes, and Locke provides an ideal register of its value.[3] Analysis of how generic ways of interpreting ideas impact upon interpreting particular thinkers is undertaken rarely and one of the features of this study is that it contributes to this relatively neglected analysis of political thought.

The second part of this book reviews modern political thinkers, and assesses the pros and cons of the interpretive perspectives that are reviewed in the preceding section. The analysis of individual modern political thinkers

---

[3] J. Gunnell, 'History of Political Philosophy as a Discipline', in G. Klosko (ed), *The Oxford Handbook of the History of Political Philosophy*, pp. 60–75.

incorporates biographical, textual, and contextual commentary so as to convey the character and provenance of their thinking. Its critical edge is sharpened by considering interpretations of their thought that draw upon the interpretive schemes, which are reviewed in the first part of this book. Hence, Machiavelli is reviewed by engaging with the interpretive commentaries of Skinner and Pocock, who are exemplary representatives of the contextualist Cambridge School. Their commentaries have altered presumptions about Machiavelli by alerting readers to the intellectual pedigree of his thought and to the historic political concerns to which his writings were addressed. A focus upon Oakeshott's stylish construal of Hobbes as a distinguished contributor to a traditional form of political philosophy is supplemented by reviewing Collingwood's endorsement of Hobbes's justification of centralized legitimate political authority along with Foucault's contrary but not disconnected dismissal of it. Locke's political thought is scrutinized by appraising Dunn's historic study, which reads Locke in the light of his assumed contextual specificity, and which runs counter to re-readings of Locke as prefiguring liberal argument and to Dunn's own second thoughts on the subject.[4] The paradoxes underlying Rousseau's political thought are foregrounded by Derrida's deconstructive textual analysis, which critiques his retrojection of an idealized and purportedly uncivilized state of nature by observing his resort to the very aspects of civilization that are deprecated in its formulation. Kant's international political theory is examined by reviewing Hegel's early and trenchant critique of its Enlightenment contradictions and by analysing its ambiguous critique by Foucault and Derrida. Subsequently Hegel's political thought is interrogated by reviewing its early and radical Marxist critique and by considering complaints against its alleged metaphysical closure that are offered by French post-structuralism and Gadamer's Heideggerian hermeneutics. Multiple traditions of Marxist analysis of Marx are analysed in the spirit of Gadamer's hermeneutics to show how the passage of time and changing interpretive contexts allow Marx to assume a multiplicity of guises. At the close of the twentieth century Derrida's deployment of a reconstructed Marx to counter neo-liberal orthodoxies of international order reveals how a past thinker can be re-construed under the impact of subsequent events. Bentham's political thought is examined by focusing upon Foucault's reading of Bentham's proposed Panopticon as the central exhibit of a wider picture of disciplinary power. The relevance of J.S. Mill to the present is assessed in the light of Collini's contextualist portrayal of his Victorian moralism and

---

[4] See J. Dunn, *The Political Thought of John Locke: An Historical Account of the Argument of the 'Two Treatises of Government'* (Cambridge, Cambridge University Press, 1969). For his later thoughts on the subject see J. Dunn, 'What is Living and What is Dead in the Political Theory of John Locke', in J. Dunn, *Interpreting Political Responsibility: Essays 1981–1989* (Princeton, Princeton University Press, 1990), pp. 9–25.

Skorupski's invitation to perceive his ongoing relevance. The status of Nietzsche's radical critique of modernity is assessed by examining how Foucault, and Derrida appropriate it to their own radical agendas. Finally, the politics of Simone de Beauvoir's *The Second Sex* is revisited by attending to its Hegelian credentials and by relating hermeneutically its exposure of the oppression of women to preceding forms of political thought.

In reflecting upon the interpretation of these political thinkers, the distinctive credentials of interpretive schemes are demonstrated. Past political thinkers are revealed to be more than museum pieces awaiting exhibition. Rather, political thought is constructed and reconstructed in the light of alternative interpretive assumptions and changing contexts. Interpretive schemes yield individual and contrary results. Past theorists are identified as reflecting unfamiliar assumptions that have receded from view, yet they are also shown to speak to current issues. Mill is a case in point and the pros and cons of conflicting views on his contemporary relevance will be reviewed in due course. The Conclusion of this study addresses issues that arise in the course of its successive analyses of interpretation. It defends interpretive pluralism, because alternative schemes of interpretation are shown to yield positive outcomes when their perspectives are applied to particular theorists. The dependence of the insights that they provide upon their distinct perspectives renders them incommensurable so that there is no knock-down argument to establish the superiority of one over the others. Textual interpretation cannot be encapsulated either by the reconstruction of a past author's intentions as exponents of the Cambridge School would have it or in the deconstruction of authorial perspectives as post-structuralists insist. An author's intentions bear upon their doctrines in ways that contextualist interpretation reveal, yet alternative interpretive perspectives show how texts can reflect rather than express a discursive practice or how they can be entangled in unintended contradictions arising out of their privileging particular ideas.

While embracing interpretive pluralism, this study is critical of the reflexive explanations of their interpretive practices that are offered by individual schemes of interpretation. They are shown to harbour blind spots in their reflexive interpretations of what they are doing that militate against their monopolistic explanatory claims. They aspire to but do not deliver autonomous sufficient forms of explanation. Our Conclusion goes beyond—without denying—an interpretive pluralism in setting out a relational, more inclusive account of interpretation that is developed out of the preceding critical review of several interpretive styles. A dialectical perspective is defended that revisits the interpretive holism of Hegel and Marx while abandoning their self-styled certainties, particularly over the imagined teleological end of history. Our commitment to dialectical holism recognizes the internality of the relations obtaining between the component parts of the interpretive process. There are no externalities to interpretation in relation to which it can be measured.

There is neither an underlying identity to political practice nor an actual record of the past thought of theorists such as Hobbes or Marx. The practice of politics, political thought, and the history of political thought are all interpretive activities, which preclude the idea of objects that are external to interpretation. Interpretive insight is not to be achieved by aligning interpretation to an external reality but rather by relating interpretations and components of interpretation to one another, so as to frame a cohesive coherent interpretation that respects the interplay between the elements constituting the interpretive process. Our summative conception of interpretation in the history of political thought is framed by a critical dialectical review of the several schemes that are reviewed previously. It is critical and inclusive in that it respects a plurality of interpretive perspectives, including continental and Anglophone, contextual and deconstructive, and develops a dialectical holistic conception of interpretation by reflecting upon their practices. Given the inherently interpretive character of political thinking, present forms of political thinking resemble past forms so that dominant conceptions of the present do not supersede past ones on account of a superior alignment to enduring political realities. Present forms of thinking establish their credentials by comparison with rival and past forms and by interpreting present political constructions that emerge out of preceding conditions.

PLAMENATZ AND THE NATURE OF POLITICAL THOUGHT

General interpretive schemes differ radically from one another but they share at least one thing in common. They hold that interpreting the history of political thought requires an express view of interpretation and its procedures. Their reflexive approach to the subject contrasts with the general run of standard histories of political thought in the nineteenth and early twentieth centuries, which line up a number of historic theorists without analysing overly the process by which the line-up is constituted. There are canons to the right and canons to the left, but no-one seems to care too much about the interpretive framework by which they are positioned. In a historical review of the subject Farr observes, 'Line-up canon and tradition came to be conceived as existing "out there" or "back then," not literary artifacts of a genre. They appeared as natural kinds or found objects that the historians of political thought were humbly narrating.'[5] There are many surveys of the history of

---

[5] J. Farr, 'The History of Political Thought', in J. Dryzek, B. Honig, and A. Phillips (eds), *The Oxford Handbook of Political Theory*, p. 230. For a relatively recent and engaging example of the

political thought, which assume past texts to represent successive components of a canon yet they attend neither to how individual texts are to be analysed, nor with the inter-relations between them. Redhead's *From Plato to Nato* and Williams' *Political Theory in Retrospect* are serviceable examples of this kind of text, which provide successive summaries of past thinkers but beg questions about how the history of political thought is to be interpreted.[6]

Plamenatz's multi-volume study, *Man and Society* serves as a paradigm of a text that assumes analysis of past political thinkers is to be conducted with a minimum of fuss. Questions pertaining to past and present, to continuities and discontinuities, to the interpretive authority of authors, and to the inter-play between texts and contexts are neither addressed nor determined. *Man and Society* is dated both by its gendered title, by its breezy acceptance of the manifest relevance of past theorists to the present, and by its presumption of an untroubling amenability of texts to theoretical analysis. In his celebrated article, 'Meaning and Understanding in the History of Ideas' (1969) Skinner disparages a merely textual study of the history of ideas. The passage of time has persuaded Skinner to rework his original article for its inclusion in a retrospective collection of essays so as to soften its polemical tone. Yet ironically the original version remains relevant to an historical appreciation of how Skinner challenged the practices of commentators on the history of political thought by defending a specifically historical form of analysis. The article announces a new style of doing the history of political thought by denouncing standard practice, which it takes to be sub-standard.[7] Skinner considers a merely textual approach to distort its presumed purpose in explaining past ideas by imagining it can 'consider and explicate a determinate set of "fundamental concepts" of "perennial interest"'.[8] Skinner conducts a polemical assault on unreflective commentaries, concentrating his fire upon those who unthinkingly either assimilate past texts to present concerns or

genre, see G. Williams, *Political Theory in Retrospect: From the Ancient Greeks to the Twentieth Century* (London, Edward Elgar, 1992).

[6] B. Redhead (ed), *From Plato To Nato* (London, BBC Books, 1985); G. Williams, *Political Theory in Retrospect*. In the Introduction to their commentary on political thinkers, Boucher and Kelly do not profess their text to be historical because it does not specify the historic development of ideas but rather elaborates on the ideas of selected past thinkers. See D. Boucher and P. Kelly, 'Introduction' in D. Boucher and P. Kelly (eds), *Political Thinkers* (Oxford, Oxford University Press, 2005), p. 16.

[7] See the original version, Q. Skinner, 'Meaning and Understanding in the History of Ideas', in J. Tully (ed.), *Meaning and Context—Quentin Skinner and His Critics* (Cambridge, Polity Press, 1988), pp. 57–89. See also my subsequent comments in chapter 4 on the article, Skinner, the Cambridge School, and Contextualism. Pocock highlights the seminal role of Skinner's original article in J.G.A. Pocock, 'Quentin Skinner: The History of Politics and the Politics of History', in J.G. A. Pocock, *Political Thought and History—Essays on Theory and Method* (Cambridge, Cambridge University Press, 2009), pp. 128–9.

[8] Q. Skinner, 'Meaning and Understanding in the History of Ideas', in J. Tully (ed.), *Meaning and Context—Quentin Skinner and His Critics*, pp. 57–89.

relate them to allegedly universal questions. Plamenatz serves as one of the authors whom he has in mind, and is duly criticized in a footnote to the essay.[9] In his Introduction to *Man and Society*, Plamenatz subscribes to an unproblematic, unreconstructed sense of the unity between past and present forms of thought. In reflecting upon the character of past theories he observes, 'They are ways of looking at men and society which are of perennial interest.'[10] While his methodological observations are elliptical, they are memorable. He warms to the idea that Hobbes's synoptic philosophy possesses an evident cross-temporal power, and he is happy to assert that a concentrated reading of a text of any consequence will yield the meaning of its doctrines. He declares, 'No doubt Hobbes is a special case. We can get more of his meaning by merely reading what he wrote than we can say of Machiavelli's or Montesquieu's or Burke's. It is a matter of degree. But even in their case, we learn more about their arguments by weighing them over and over again than by extending our knowledge of the circumstances in which they write.'[11]

Given his interpretive recipe of meditating upon past texts, Plamenatz can be labelled a textualist but he operates without delivering a considered critical justification of his methodology. In so doing he is to be distinguished from those who offer a considered defence of the primacy and value of concentrating upon texts. For instance Strauss, the celebrated American scholar of the history of political thought, invests texts with an authority that warrants their close scrutiny due to their intimation of profound truths that are not disclosed expressly on account of their authors' recognition of the need to sidestep persecution and unsympathetic readers.[12] For Strauss the value of classical and pre-modern texts turns upon their insistence on a universal truth, which is subsequently abrogated by modern forms of historicism and relativism. A modern descent into subjectivism and relativism undermines the integrity of personal and public life and is a baleful consequence of the wrong road that has been taken with the advent of modernity. The relevance of the classic texts of political theory is clear; either, like Plato's *Republic* they convey a timeless truth or, like Machiavelli's *Prince* they insinuate a disturbing and immoral compromise with the ways of the world. The urgency and foreboding menace of Strauss's justification of the relevance of the great texts of political theory stands apart from Plamenatz's more measured and less elaborated sense of their continuing contribution to political thinking.[13] Plamenatz neither assumes a decisive and retrogressive break in historical understanding nor

---

[9] Ibid., p. 38.

[10] J. Plamenatz, 'Introduction', in J. Plamenatz, *Man and Society* (London, Longmans, 1963), p. xxvi.

[11] Ibid., p. xvi.

[12] See L. Strauss, *Persecution and the Art of Writing* (Chicago, University of Chicago Press, 1988).

[13] See J. Plamenatz, 'Introduction', in J. Plamenatz, *Man and Society*, p. xxv.

attributes esoteric strategies to past thinkers. He merely assumes that past texts convey meanings of perennial relevance that can be ascertained by a clear-headed scrutiny of texts on the part of a disinterested analytical commentator. His reading of past texts presumes no arcane knowledge of how they might have been composed, nor elaborate contextual understanding of what authors might have been trying to do in the light of their current political situations. What Marx and Engels might have been trying to do in writing *The Communist Manifesto* or Mill in composing *On Liberty* do not require consideration; the first is a revolutionary document that declares its principles openly and the second is an analysis of the political freedom that is to be enjoyed by an individual. Principles and arguments supersede particular circumstances and their pros and cons can be identified by close textual analysis. Plamenatz makes few presumptions about the purposes underlying past texts and is silent on the ways in which they might be read. He carries little academic baggage save for an enthusiasm for texts, a determination to see their continuing relevance, and forensic skills to be applied to their analysis.

For Plamenatz the meaning of a piece of past political thinking is to be established by a reading of doctrines that retain their validity over time. Past political thought is resumed in a subsequent interpretation without recourse either to an accompanying parade of historical scholarship or to a general exploration of how preceding texts are to be interrogated. The point of reviewing past political doctrines is exhibited by their manifest relevance to the contemporary world, which, in turn, testifies to their susceptibility to contemporary interpretation. This message is clear if undertheorized. It is not altered unduly by Wokler's commentary on Plamenatz's approach in a posthumous edition of *Man and Society*. Wokler's respect for Plamenatz as both a teacher and a political theorist is evident in his endorsement of his practice of textual analysis. He offers a plea of mitigation for Plamenatz's omission of contextual explanation in that exigencies of publishing are held to have induced him to concentrate on texts and to exclude supplementary contextual analysis.[14] Plamenatz is observed to have been aware of what historical scholarship might offer in furnishing accounts of the contexts in which ideas are framed, but also to have recognized with some plausibility that philosophical interpretation might be conducted as a discrete activity. Wokler maintains that Plamenatz had analysed some of the less philosophical thinkers in the light of their historical contexts, showing a facility in relating their ideas to their provenance in particular contexts. Yet this historical contextual material was sacrificed, because of the constraints imposed by the organization of the

---

[14] R. Wokler, 'Introduction', in J. Plamenatz, M. E. Plamenatz and R. Wokler *Man and Society: Political and Social Theories from Machiavelli to Marx: Hegel, Marx and Engels and the Idea of Progress*. Revised edition (London, Longmans Group, 1992), p. ix.

text as a whole. References to historical circumstances pertaining to political ideas that were shaped most evidently by contextual influences were excised from *Man and Society* because there was insufficient space to include them while adhering to the two-volume format of the text.[15]

Ironically, given that Skinner and the Cambridge School highlight how the intentions of past authors are integral to the meaning of texts, the intentions of Plamenatz in writing *Man and Society* have not been considered by historically minded critics. Just as the meaning of *The Communist Manifesto* depends in part on ascertaining how Marx and Engels envisaged its role in promoting the Communist League, so the point of *Man and Society* derives from Plamenatz's sense of how it might impact upon current political science. Wokler urges that Plamenatz's enthusiasm for analysing the ideas of past political philosophers arises out of his perception of how they might counteract the inadequacies of the contemporary positivist turn in current social and political science. Traditional political thought might provide an antidote to a current exclusive focus upon empirical political behaviour.[16] Likewise Philp, in his Introduction to the publication of Plamenatz's posthumously published lectures of 1975 on Machiavelli, Hobbes and Rousseau that were to be delivered in Cambridge, sees persisting value in Plamenatz's analytical skill, which holds up in the light of subsequent scholarship. He recognizes how Plamenatz's approach was directed against the contemporary turn to positivism in philosophy.[17] The historic texts of political philosophy are valuable for Plamenatz because they analyse the values that inform political conduct. Philp and Wokler appreciate how Plamenatz employs his analytical skills to criticize past theoretical explorations of values. Wokler urges that the philosophical arguments of past thinkers are pitched at a sufficient degree of abstraction to justify Plamenatz's view that their meaning was 'not determined solely by the circumstances that occasioned their production.'[18]

Skinner disparages reading past theories in the light of present convictions, because it abstracts ideas from the past contexts in which they were formulated, and tends to assimilate them to unrelated interests and circumstances of the present. He is clear in rejecting the assumption of perennial ideas whereby ideas are insulated from historical circumstances. Neither Plamenatz nor Wokler and Philp elaborate on how the contemporary use of past ideas might be justified. Plamenatz himself has little to say on how ideas might be relevant to very different contextual circumstances. Plamenatz's practice has, however,

---

[15] Ibid., p. xi.

[16] Ibid., p. ix. See also J. Plamenatz, 'The Use of Political Theory', vol. III, no.1, 1960, pp. 37–47.

[17] See M. Philp, 'Introduction', in J. Plamenatz, *Machiavelli, Hobbes and Rousseau*, eds. M. Philp and Z. A. Pelczynski (Oxford, Oxford University Press, 2012).

[18] R. Wokler, 'Introduction', in J. Plamenatz, M. E. Plamenatz and R. Wokler *Man and Society: Political and Social Theories from Machiavelli to Marx: Hegel, Marx and Engels and the Idea of Progress*, p. xi.

been defended by others. For instance, Bevir imagines that it makes sense to talk of perennial problems and perennial issues in the history of political thought, when they are considered at a high level of abstraction. In an article on contextualism, he submits, 'Yet, if we can couch past beliefs at a sufficient level of abstraction, we can often make them relevant to our concerns and even problems that have persisted more or less perennially throughout history.'[19] The devil, of course, is in the detail and in calculating whether the relevance that accompanies abstraction is achieved at the expense of the more concrete features that would render a political theory of interest to any age. The ways in which the ideas of past thinkers have been drawn upon by commentators from succeeding periods is reviewed in subsequent chapters and the relevance of the past to the present is justified in particular forms of interpretation.

Skinner himself recognizes how understanding past thought historically can stretch our sense of conceptual possibilities in the present, because the differences between past and present alert us to what is contingent and changeable in past and present conceptual forms. This process of conceptual stretching is another way of perceiving the relevance of past thought when framed at a sufficiently high level of abstraction. For instance, Plato's conception of justice, which takes a just order to reflect psychical differences between individuals, may be related to a modern notion of distributive justice that justifies an unequal distribution of wealth because of differences between the capacities of individuals.[20] In any event, while Plamenatz's position on reading past texts might well be defensible, his own defence was insufficiently articulated and indicates more general deficiencies in his approach. Most notably he did not reflect sufficiently on the processes of interpretation. He did not consider expressly either the extent to which historical scholarship might be required or if a greater suspicion of the apparent meaning of texts might be warranted. He assumes that authors are in control of what they write and that a commentator can recover what the author conveyed and yet it is by no means clear that this is uniformly the case. Moreover, he assumes that philosophical texts are the unproblematic sites of political thought, whereas Foucault points contrariwise to the role of discourses in endowing authors and texts with their meanings. While one might appreciate Philps's considered reflection on Plamenatz and Wokler's empathetic reconstruction of the enduring value of Plamenatz's *Man and Society*, its omissions point to the imperative of reflecting more explicitly upon the process of interpretation.

---

[19] M. Bevir, 'Contextualism', in G. Klosko (ed), *The Oxford Handbook of the History of Political Thought*, p. 22.

[20] Of course inequalities in distributive justice may be justified by many reasons and an inequality of capacities is only one means of doing so.

HISTORY OF POLITICAL THOUGHT:
THE QUESTION OF INTERPRETATION

If Plamenatz's *Man and Society* indicates a value of past texts in compensating for the exclusion of normative values from prevalent ways of doing social science, it suffers from presuming an uncomplicated access to its object of study. It presumes that past political thought can be assimilated without the paraphernalia of historical scholarship. It ignores the difficulties involved in reading a text without reference to an author's intentions and its contextual setting and yet assumes that interpretation is a matter of recovering the meaning of arguments in their intended form. Plamenatz's presumptions are questionable, precisely because they beg questions of an interpretive strategy that is neither shared nor explored. The question of interpretation is fundamental to the history of political thought. It requires an answer. Interpretation is implicated in all aspects of the subject. It is integral to all social practices. Taylor, following Heidegger, observes generally how human beings are self-interpreting animals, remarking that 'the human animal not only finds himself impelled from time to time to interpret himself and his goals, but that he is always already in some interpretation, constituted as human by this fact. To be human is to be already engaged in living an answer to the question, an interpretation of oneself and one's aspirations.'[21] To be in the world is to practise interpretation, but the defining character of the history of political thought is its intensive practice of interpretation. In attending to the object of its analysis, the way it is to be understood and its significance are all to be interpreted. Assessments are to be made on what is to be interpreted, the texts that are to be read, and the past and present contexts that bear upon investigations. General interpretive schemes are distinguished by how they respond to these interpretive questions.

On the face of things a focus upon texts as objects of explanation appears to be relatively uncontentious. After all, deconstructionists, contextualists, and hermeneuticists look to texts, even if they perceive them in distinctive ways. A commonsensical view holds that interpretation begins with texts, which are then to be interrogated by alternative interpretive strategies. Hobbes's *Leviathan*, Machiavelli's *The Prince*, and Hegel's *Philosophy of Right* are objects to which historians of political thought standardly turn when they attend to their subject. Yet things are not entirely clear-cut. Not all texts that are consulted were published by their authors. Hence if the study of political thought is to track authorial intentions then there might be reason to reflect on what is happening. Perhaps some eligible and routinely interpreted texts might

---

[21] C. Taylor, 'Self-Interpreting Animals,' in C. Taylor, *Human Agency and Language: Philosophical Papers 1* (Cambridge, Cambridge University Press, 1985), p. 75.

be excluded from discussion. For example, Marx's 'Economic and Philosophical Manuscripts' and *Grundrisse*, Hegel's *Philosophy of History* and *Lectures on the History of Philosophy*, Foucault's *The Birth of Bio-Politics* and *Society Must be Defended*, Collingwood's The *Idea of History* and *The Idea of Nature*, Oakeshott's *Lectures in the History of Political Thought*, and his *Notebooks*, which are all invoked and interpreted in this book, might be regarded with suspicion. None of them were published in their authors' lifetimes, and hence the case for reading them as expressing their authors' intended contributions to political thought cannot be taken for granted. Moreover, interviews with Derrida, Skinner, and Foucault are referenced later in this book along with autobiographical and literary writings of Beauvoir. Doubts might be raised about their status. How do they compare with other writings that were prepared carefully for publication, such as Hegel's *Philosophy of Right*, Oakeshott's *On Human Conduct*, Marx's *Capital*, and Foucault's *The Order of Things*? Questioning is to be welcomed, because it registers the interpretive agenda. Nothing is to be taken for granted or to operate as a fact without it being interpreted in the light of overall questions about how a body of political thought is to be construed.

In this book unpublished texts and interviews are considered along with texts that were intended for publication. In considering past political thinkers and general interpretive schemes judgments are made on what constitute relevant texts to be appraised by interpreting them in the light of a wider assessment of past thinkers and interpretive positions. On this and other issues judgments are made holistically. The classic hermeneutical principle of interpretation relates part to whole and whole to part so that a passage in the bible is related to its wider context and book of the bible is assessed in relation to the bible as a whole, and in turn books of the bible and the bible as a whole are interpreted in the light of specific references.[22] Hence if Collingwood's (still) unpublished manuscripts raise questions that affect a reading of aspects of his philosophy then their contribution to an interpretation of these issues is taken into account.[23] On the other hand, if an interview is considered either to be unrevealing or to be guided by an interviewer along a path that misrepresents

---

[22] See H-G. Gadamer, *Truth and Method* trans. J. Weinsheimer and D. Marshall (London, Sheed and Ward, 1975), pp. 174–6.

[23] See the comments in chapter 12 on the contrast between what is expressed in Collingwood's published and unpublished writings. There the focus is upon contrasting views on Hegel and the differences are interpreted as relating to Collingwood's sense of how his comments might be received by his readership. There are other ways in which a contrast can be identified between what is said in his published and unpublished material. The contrast calls for interpretive judgment on the part of the commentator and I have outlined my reasons for attending to the unpublished material in G.K. Browning, *Rethinking R.G. Collingwood—Philosophy, Politics and the Unity of Theory and Practice* (Basingstoke and London, Palgrave Macmillan, 2004), pp. 1–27.

an author's thought then it is not to be taken into account. The way forward is to rely on express and holistic interpretive judgment.

Critical interpretive judgment also comes into play when assessing how a text is to be considered. A text may be imagined in a variety of ways. It may be seen to constitute, reflect, or distort political thought. For instance, Foucault concentrates upon discourses not so much for what they might exemplify about texts, but to show how their constituent features are exemplified in texts. What matters primarily for Foucault is the discourse rather than the text, which in turn explains his deprecation of the role of authors. An author's own understanding of their place in the scheme of things is subordinated to the scheme of things. For instance, in *The Order of Things* Marx is allocated to a modern episteme to which he would not have imagined himself to subscribe.[24] Foucault subordinates authors and their intentions to discourses, which he himself constructs so as to highlight discontinuous practices and ways of thinking. Contextualists tend to align past thinkers with traditions or discourses to which they subscribe intentionally. Hence Skinner relates Machiavelli to the traditions of humanism and neo-Roman republicanism, which he is shown to use in developing his republican ideas. Yet in relating thinkers to more enduring discourses or languages of thought, Pocock is prepared to align thinkers with what he takes to be a Machiavellian moment, which is a style of thinking in time that is not embraced expressly by past theorists.[25] In analysing discourses Foucault allows for texts that are more practical than the reflective texts of great philosophers. He shows the discursive roles of more technical guides to practices such as manuals associated with psychiatry, medicine, sexual therapy, and punishment. His focus on texts that rehearse conditions and procedures of practices reflects his interest in concrete and institutional operations of discipline and power rather than in conventional notions of centralized political power that are conceptualized abstractly in standard texts of political philosophy. Foucault is unconventional in his interpretive practice in stretching the notion of politics beyond a centralized horizon.

Derrida concentrates on philosophical texts, and yet he reads texts as not saying precisely what their authors might intend. Hence his deconstructive interpretation of texts imagines them to operate in multiple disordered ways that do not express authorial intentions, the recovery of which is the interpretive priority of contextualists such as Skinner. Notoriously, Marx takes texts of political thought to operate as distortive ideological reflections of class interests. How is the meaning of a text to be decided in the light of these distinct possibilities? How are we to choose between construction and deconstruction? Judgments have to be made but they should be made in the

---

[24] M. Foucault, *The Order of Things* (London and New York, Routledge, 2002), pp. 283–5.
[25] J.G.A. Pocock, *The Machiavellian Moment: Florentine Political Thought and the Atlantic Republican Tradition* (Princeton, Princeton University Press, 1987), pp. 1–85.

light of critical analysis of interpretive schemes and their application in specific examples of interpretation. To anticipate what will be shown later both constructive and deconstructive readings can be productive. Reading Rousseau in the light of Derrida's deconstruction allows us to appreciate the paradoxes that occur when theory coerces language to make claims that subvert its own operations. No-one can read Derrida on Rousseau and not learn something of the contortions of Western thought in trying to make essentialist claims on what is natural and what is supplementary. Equally, Rousseau's own intentions in stretching the way we think to show the alienation in modern society and the unacceptability of inequality cannot be denied. Constructive studies that highlight the intentionality of authors enable us to consider what Hobbes and Locke were trying to do in framing analyses of legitimate central political authority and yet deconstructive Foucauldian operations that subvert authorial perspectives so as to cast doubt on the very project of legitimating centralized authority register political concerns that bear upon past and present. Our subsequent review of interpretation will recognize the countervailing merits of contrary interpretive styles, while also identifying their explanatory limits.

If texts of political thought are susceptible to multiple forms of interpretation then the study of contexts is equally susceptible to a plurality of interpretive styles. The historic political contexts in which past thinkers are situated condition how they conceive of politics and how they evaluate political priorities. Yet what constitutes a context in which past political thinkers are situated is itself a matter of interpretation. Politics change over time. As Hegel ruminates, 'There is nothing new under the sun, but this is not so with the sun of Spirit.'[26] Hegel himself affirms the historicity of political philosophy by maintaining that political thinking is determined by the public political cultures in which thinkers are situated. Oakeshott and Collingwood follow suit in locating past thinkers in historical contexts that frame the particular political vocabularies by which their thinking is conducted.[27] Again, in dismissing ahistorical readings of philosophy, economics, and politics, Marx relates thinkers to their social and political contexts, but instead of imagining political cultures as constituting relatively unified contexts to which political philosophies can be correlated, he diagnoses social and political contexts to be beset by contradictions that motivate and distort the production of ideas.[28]

---

[26] G.W.F. Hegel, *The Philosophy of History* trans. J. Sibree (New York, Dover Press, 1956), p. 63.

[27] R.G. Collingwood, *An Autobiography* (Oxford, Clarendon Press, 1978), pp. 53–76; M. Oakeshott, *Lectures in the History of Political Thought* ed. L. O'Sullivan (Exeter, Imprint Academic, 2006), pp. 31–45.

[28] This is what is at issue between Hegel and Marx. See chapters 12 and 13.

In explaining past political thinking contextualists concentrate upon local and immediate ideological contexts to which thinkers respond in formulating ideas to achieve determinate purposes. Thinkers do things with ideas that are framed in the discursive styles of the day. Contexts are connected internally to the beliefs and intentions of past thinkers in that a thinker's ideas and purposes constitute how they perceive their situation. In contrast, Foucault imagines discursive contexts to shape ideas without past thinkers being reflexively aware of their impact. Alternatively an explanatory context can be invoked which has less to do with the situation of a past thinker than with that of the interpreter. For instance, Derrida re-reads Benjamin and Marx in the light of subsequent events so as to provide new insights on past and present forms of thought, while Foucault's genealogical deconstruction of the idea of punishment is inspired by a radical critique of its present practices. To insist upon a particular form of context is as reckless as dictating how contexts are to be construed given the range of contextual interpretations that can be offered. The ways in which texts and contexts are construed depends upon how they are to be interpreted, and an interpretation of interpretations can recognize interpretive diversity as well as developing a dialectical and integral interpretive conception of how texts, contexts, and their interpretation can be configured coherently in the history of political thought.

CONCLUSIONS

In Gadamer's hermeneutics no advance stipulations restrict what is to count as relevant to an explanation. Everything is to be decided by a dialogical and open process of interpretation. Its paradigm is that of a conversation in which all contributions are to be welcomed in an open discussion, during the course of which truth emerges. The study of past thought resembles a conversation in that differing standpoints are taken into account and its outcome is not reducible to the activity of a single party. Evidence of past forms of thinking is elicited by an interpreter, who is situated in the present but is open to the influence of the past. As in a conversation, past and present perspectives contribute to the process of working through the meaning of the ideas in question. The past is accessed from the vantage point of the present, but past thought constitutes a distinct horizon of understanding that influences the emerging depiction of the past so that history is the product of an interplay between past and present perspectives. In later chapters Gadamer's more elaborated account of interpretation will be criticized, because he tends to privilege authorial perspectives and to neglect a close scrutiny of the conflicted traditions that shape the prejudices of the present. Yet his insistence on the open and multifaceted character of interpretation harmonizes with the multiplicity of ways in which past thought is interpreted. Certainly, the hermeneutical recognition of the necessarily changing vantage points of interpretation provides a frame for appreciating the phenomenon of reinterpretation. The history of political thought allows for an ongoing reinterpretation of past thinkers because the circumstantial and interpretive horizon of the present alters and so accordingly do perceptions of the past. Gadamer's hermeneutics is not conceptualized as integrating opposing styles of interpretation but our projected dialectical exercise of achieving an integral and summative interpretive framework is consonant with a hermeneutical commitment to interpretive inclusivity. In his review of the ongoing history of reappraisals in the history of political thought, Ball is instructive in recognizing how interpretation is central to the enterprise. He observes, 'The decision to interpret or not to interpret is not an option open to human beings, but a requirement that comes so to speak, with the territory of being human.'[29] For Ball, interpretative engagement is inspired by present circumstances and is directed at preceding interpretations. He remarks, 'the seminal works of political theory are kept alive and vivid—keep their "classic" status, so to speak—only in so far as they are not worshipped at academic shrines but are, on the contrary, carefully and critically reappraised.'[30]

If text and context are open to questions of interpretation, then the interpretation of interpretations within the history of political thought must also avoid fixing limits on interpretive procedures in advance of its inquiry. Hence in ensuing chapters a plurality of interpretive schemes and a number of affiliated interpretations of particular modern political theories that draw upon these schemes will be reviewed. What constitutes interpretation and how styles of interpretation are to be related to specific acts of interpretation are delicate questions. An index of how fine judgments relating to interpretive traditions have to be made is indicated by analysis of Beauvoir's thought. Beauvoir's social and political thought is expressly innovative and diverges radically from that of predecessors, yet her thought does not represent news from nowhere, which lacks reference to preceding traditions. Beauvoir's thought is related to traditions of Hegelianism and Marxism in a manner that is at once critical and participative. Her conceptualization of the relations between women and men deploys a Hegelian notion of social recognition and she shares the historical and social perspective of Hegelianism and Marxism in that she highlights the sociality and historicity of concepts and practices. Yet her focus on conflicted relations between the sexes and the existential dimension of women's abjection challenges androcentric aspects of Hegelianism and Marx's relative indifference to conflict between the sexes. Is Beauvoir Hegelian? Is she Marxist? Or is she a critic of Hegelianism and Marxism?

[29] T. Ball, *Reappraising Political Theory* (Oxford, Oxford University Press, 1995), p. 7.
[30] Ibid., p. 29.

These questions highlight how interpretive judgments have to be made on what is crucial in a form of thinking and on how a piece of thinking is to be related to preceding traditions of interpretation.

Interpretive judgments on how Beauvoir's thought is to be connected to preceding traditions such as Hegelianism and Marxism not only affect readings of Beauvoir, they also affect how those intellectual traditions are perceived. Beauvoir may be seen either as developing traditions of critical social thought or as disrupting them by showing how they fail to deal with a significant aspect of society. What renders Beauvoir's political thought radical is that in focusing on the social construction of femininity she transforms the way in which the subject of politics is to be conceived. Instead of identifying politics with acknowledged public institutions, she identifies the political in practices of private life and in the ways in which the sexes are socialized into adopting exclusive forms of behaviour that mark out their differing public futures. Hence her thought underlines how the identification of the frame or object of politics is a matter of interpretation. A transformation of the inter-pretive horizon of the political changes the ways in which politics are to be conceived in the present and the past. An analytical account of politics in the present cannot assume that there is an uncontestable object of politics, and yet such assumptions are standardly made in contemporary texts on politics.[31] Beauvoir's reading of politics in both the present and past can also be invoked to reinterpret preceding theories of politics including those of Hegelianism and Marxism, by critiquing their assumptions about the family, work, and political practices. In his review of conceptions of men in political theory, Carver observes how in the retrospective light of a present that is informed by subsequent feminist and masculinist studies, Marx's relative silence on issues of gender, masculinity, and conflict between the sexes appears to detract from his account of society. Carver observes, 'with the best will in the world, and whether reading "with the grain" or against it, there are considerable difficulties in either adjudicating on Marx as an authority worth reading in, say, feminist theory, gender studies, or in simply finding material to cite that would constitute any very impressive contribution, one way or another to contemporary debates ... This "lack" is in itself grounds for considerable criticism.'[32] Beauvoir's critical interpretation of the situation of women in modern society challenges notions of politics in the past and present and shows how there are no fixed elements in processes of interpretation. Objects

---

[31] See the comments in a later chapter on standard analytical texts on political philosophy by Miller and Swift. See A. Swift, *Political Philosophy—A Beginner's Guide for Students and Politicians* (Cambridge and Malden MA, Polity, 2001) and D. Miller *Political Philosophy: A Very Short Introduction* (Oxford, Oxford University Press, 2003).

[32] T. Carver, *Men in Political Theory* (Manchester, Manchester University Press, 2009), p. 205. See also C. de Stefano, *Configurations of Masculinity: A Feminist Perspective on Modern Political Theory* (New York, Cornell University Press, 1991).

and styles of interpretation change and perceptions of past politics and its interpretations, in turn, are subject to continuous transformation.

If this book takes the question of interpretation to be integral to the history of political thought, inspiring its reflection upon a plurality of interpretive styles, then it is also selective in its procedure. For one thing it is selective in focusing upon certain styles of interpretation and also in reviewing a particular set or canon of modern political thinkers. It focuses upon modern political philosophers, though the philosophical credentials of Beauvoir have been queried, albeit on sexist grounds.[33] Why political philosophers? Collingwood agrees with Foucault in recognizing that political thought can take place at many levels so that a selective focus upon political philosophy requires justification.[34] Political philosophy is focused upon here because its abstract and general level of thinking allows for possibilities of its relevance stretching beyond the immediate circumstances of its generation.[35] Whereas Tawney or Crosland might press or relax the case for social equality due to the circumstances obtaining in determinate contexts, Marx's analysis of capital is more likely to retain a currency amongst future generations. Marx's aim is to provide a general account of the systemic operation of capital, which explains the motion of things and persons under capitalism. Insofar as the logic and rules of this systemic operation remain largely intact, notwithstanding ongoing technological and social developments, then the relevance of Marx to the analysis of political power is assured. The selection of a particular set of political thinkers makes no special claim to provide an exhaustive understanding of modern politics other than that it furnishes a wide range of theoretical insights into modern politics and society and allows for critical interpretive engagement with a number of styles of interpretation.

Our selective approach to the history of modern political thought is more tendentious in its concentration upon the Western tradition of political thought, which leaves alone non-Western political thought. This selective attention reflects the interpretive expertise of this particular commentator and the interpretive opportunities that are afforded by the recursive interpretations of modern Western political thought. Modern Western political thought has spawned a multiplicity of interpretations reflecting general

[33] See the comments on Beauvoir and the philosophical canon in M.A. Simons, 'Introduction', in M.A. Simons (ed), Feminist *Interpretations of Simone de Beauvoir* (University Park, Pennsylvania, The Pennsylvania State University Press, 1995), pp. 6–9.

[34] See R.G. Collingwood, 'Political Action', in R.G. Collingwood, *Essays in Political Philosophy* (Oxford, Clarendon Press, 1989), pp. 92–100.

[35] See R.N. Berki, *The History of Political Thought* (London, R.M. Dent, 1976). Note also Kelly's arguments for the overlaps of schemes of interpretation in P. Kelly, 'Rescuing Political Theory from the Tyranny of History', in J. Floyd and M. Stears (eds), *Political Philosophy versus History?* (Cambridge, Cambridge University Press, 2003), p. 31.

schemes of interpretation that allows for an intensive critical engagement
with the question of interpretation. The intensity of this interpretive
engagement invites critical reflection upon processes of interpretation that
can enable considered judgments to be made about political thought and
its interpretation. This study neither supports a sense of Western superiority, nor suggests that the West can be treated in isolation. It shows Western
thought to have spread beyond any natural geographical borders. The
thoughts of Locke, Mill, Kant, and Hegel are invested with colonialism
and the global reach of political issues is recognized by many theorists
such as Kant, Hegel, and Marx who are not standardly taken to be global
theorists.[36] The history of Marxist interpretation is instructive in the several
ways in which the world, imperialism, and neo-colonialism shape its interpretive practice. For example, Derrida's critical re-reading of Marx in the
light of a proclaimed neo-liberal world order shows how a politics of
economic exploitation and class power militate against Western claims of
liberal cosmopolitanism.

Our focus on Western political thought is intended neither to fix the object
of political thought, nor the ways in which the political is conceived. There are
no fixed reference points in the history of ideas; interpretation is not to be
constrained. Just as feminist ideas demand a rethinking of past androcentric
doctrines in their rethinking of the constitution of politics, so non-Western
political thinking can inspire a similar radical rethinking of past and present
political thought. The ways in which it might do so are prefigured in the
history of the impact of feminist thought, which has subverted interpretations
of politics that were taken to be fixed and natural rather than historical and
cultural.[37] This book might have been constructed in alternative ways, reflecting alternative interpretive assumptions. Yet its concern is with the notion of
interpretation, and in engaging with interpretive theories of interpretation it
addresses the question of how the question of interpretation has been interpreted. In reviewing the application of interpretive theories to selected modern
political theorists in the Western tradition it recognizes how modern politics
have been interpreted in a plurality of ways. It shows how theorists can be
followed along their intended routes, but also how theories can be deconstructed to reveal subversive and more contestable notions of politics. The
interpretation of the history of political thought shows how interpretation
determines all aspects of political thought so that nothing is to be taken
for granted and the history of political thought is a history of changing

---

[36] See G. Browning, *Global Theory from Kant to Hardt and Negri* (Basingstoke and New York,
Palgrave Macmillan, 2011), pp. 22–82.
[37] For an example of a feminist re-reading of political thought see D. Coole, *Women in
Political Theory: From Ancient Misogyny to Contemporary Feminism* (Hemel Hempstead:
Harvester Wheatsheaf, 1993).

interpretations of politics and theory.[38] Political theory is not invented on a deserted and desert island, or if it is, then a refugee on the island has a past that is connected with an historic political world, so that any message in a bottle that a refugee might dispatch reflects an interpretation of the past and will itself have to be interpreted.

---

[38] See T. Ball, *Reappraising Political Theory*, pp. 6–10.

Part I

Interpretive Schemes

2

Hegel and Marx

Political Culture, Economy, and Ideology

INTRODUCTION

Hegel and Marx establish a dialectical reading of the history of political thought. Systematic connections are made between political theorists and the background conditions within which they operate, and between these theorists and the dialectical synoptic theories by which they are interpreted. They connect theorists to one another and to the social and political frameworks of the societies in which they developed their ideas. All theorists and theories lead to Hegel and Marx, and the ideas of Hegel and Marx, like the theories preceding them, are explained as emerging out of the specific social and political contexts in which they are situated. Hegel and Marx imagine themselves as occupying a temporal position that allows them to make summative judgments on the course of history. Their teleological theories of history maintain that the end or telos of history explains the course of events. Hegel and Marx may be said to undertake grand theory and, justifiably enough, have been construed as devising paradigmatic grand narratives.[1] 'Grand narratives' is a phrase that is coined to highlight and undermine the designs of theory to provide overarching explanations of historical development. Lyotard follows in the footsteps of others, such as Adorno and Berlin, who, in the immediate aftermath of harrowing, inhumane events, argue against large-scale philosophies of history, which aim to supersede the contingencies of the historical condition.[2] While teleological narratives raise issues over how the contingency of events is to be respected, and whether or

---

[1] J.-F. Lyotard, *The Condition of Postmodernity* trans. J. Van Den Abbeele (Manchester, University of Manchester Press, 1979), pp. 31–7.
[2] See T. Adorno, *Can One Live After Auschwitz?—A Philosophical Reader* trans. R. Livingstone and others, ed. R. Tiedemann (Stanford, California, Stanford University Press, 2003) and I. Berlin, 'Historical Inevitability', in I. Berlin, *Four Essays on Liberty* (Oxford and New York, Oxford University Press, 1969), p. 43.

not a single line of historical development can be sustained, they do provide a way of uniting aspects of history. Historic political theories are construed as representing more than merely local unrelated phenomena, but appear as playing a role in a larger scheme of historical development that leads to the present.

Hegel and Marx imagine historic forms of political thought to reflect the contexts in which they are situated and to occupy a position in a more general scheme of historical development. These contexts are cultural and material frameworks, which shape all features of society in historical periods. Hegel sees the political culture of an epoch as framing the thought and practice of a people, so that socio-economic activity, political structures, religious practice, artistic imagining, and philosophical speculation all exhibit a common cultural form. For Hegel, public culture and philosophical thought reflecting upon forms of culture develop in the modern world so as to achieve a systematic recognition of the freedom and universality that underpins the entire process of development. Political philosophy, in this perspective, is interpretive but the scope and determinants of interpretation are provided by the basic character of a political culture and by the ongoing development of philosophy, which culminates in Hegel's own system.[3] The value of Hegel's standpoint allows for recognition of a past political theory's relationship to historical social and political structures and Hegel's own systematic procedure provides a yardstick to measure theoretical sophistication. Differences between culturally diverse ideas are accommodated along with a supervening unity that is furnished by a holistic dialectical interpretation of the process. While Hegel's perspective is capacious and perceptive, it harbours blindspots. For instance, it imagines past political cultures to be holistic in their values, and recessive and minority concerns are ignored. Likewise, a past philosophy is presumed either to anticipate or contribute to Hegel's system in its method and form, whereas theories in reality cannot be assumed to be so readily commensurable in their methods and interpretive aims.

For Marx, production and historic forms of organizing production configure forms of social activity, in theory and practice, and the development of forms of production is ultimately related to the possibility of achieving communism, a system of production that supersedes classes and exploitation. Hence political philosophy reflects the underlying structure of production and, in particular, the interests of classes which occupy differential positions in the productive structure of a society and determine the goals of theories. Social and political theories either construing the social and political world in particular ways, or arguing the case for specific policies, are ideological in reflecting class interests. This perspective tends to reduce the interpretive

---

[3] G.W.F. Hegel, *Lectures on the History of Philosophy*, vols. 1–3 trans. E.S. Haldane and F.H. Simpson (London, Paul, Trench and Trubner, 1892), see vol. 1, Introduction, p. 1.

aspect of a political philosophy to the economic conditions of its production. However, there are many ways of interpreting Marx's sociological and political thought, and while some interpretations take Marx to be a reductionist, whereby past political philosophies are epiphenomenal or functional expressions of technology or material interests, other versions, notably Hegelian and Gramscian formulations, allow for a relative independence of thought from the material production and development of a society's needs.[4] Whatever the details of an interpretation of Marx's perspective on ideas, Marx's interpretive standpoint links past forms of thought to social and economic interests and to determinate forms of production. Hence, a theorist, such as J.S. Mill, may hold a manifest interest in individual liberty, but this interest is at least compatible with the presumption of a capitalist society and the existence of classes, holding differing economic interests, and exerting differential forms of power.[5] Marx's interpretive framework allows him to make connections between ideas and material interests, and to recognize that ideas are related to their historical contexts. Hence it makes sense to consider Aristotle's justification of slavery in relation to the contemporary institution of slavery in Greek society, rather than to deliberate upon its relevance for societies that have largely dispensed with slavery. It appears as a particular normative commitment that is generated by a specific form of social organization. In general, Marx offers a way of recognizing the contextual generation and relevance of political ideas, while also relating them to the bigger picture of social and political historical development. However, Marx tends to assume that class interests underlying ideas and arguments are what counts and yet on the face of things, theoretical explorations of, say, gender by Mary Wollstonecraft and international peace by Kant, are not reducible to issues pertaining to social class.[6]

Critics of the interpretive schemes of Hegel and Marx disavow their determination to see an overall directionality and general explanation of history. These critiques are to the point. One-dimensional readings of history are questionable, because they detract from the openness of history and the multiplicity of factors that are involved in its development. While Hegel and Marx provide a means of observing continuities in history, their interpretive

---

[4] See for instance, A. Gramsci, *Prison Notebooks*, vols. 1–3 trans. J. Bottigieg (New York, Columbia University Press, 2011); H. Marcuse, *Reason and Revolution: Hegel and The Rise of Social Theory* (London, Routledge, 1955); S. Avineri, *The Social and Political Thought of Karl Marx* (Cambridge, Cambridge University Press, 1968); B. Ollman, *Dialectical Investigations* (London, Routledge, 1993).

[5] See K. Marx, *Capital*, vol. 1 trans. S. Moore and E. Aveling, ed. F. Engels (Moscow, Progress Publishers, 1969), pp. 483–5.

[6] See M. Wollstonecraft, *A Vindication of the Rights of Woman* (Harmondsworth, Penguin, 1994); I. Kant, *Idea for a Universal History with a Cosmopolitan Purpose* in *Kant's Political Writings*, ed. H. Reiss (Cambridge, Cambridge University Press, 1991), pp. 41–53.

schemes tend to underplay gender, the environment, and ethnicity. Hegel overrates the role of the state while Marx overemphasizes production at the expense of wider cultural issues. It is worth pausing, however, before dismissing Hegel and Marx as relics of a reckless modern era, in which theorists were incautious and allowed the pursuit of systems to supersede recognition of the diversity of historical phenomena and the irreducible contingencies that limit generic forms of explanation. Hegel and Marx exercise caution in framing their theories of history. They are aware of the pitfalls of philosophical ambition and they assimilate more modest forms of empirical historical explanation into their general interpretive narratives. Moreover, their generic teleological explanations were framed either to be retrospective in their operation in the case of Hegel, or else, in the case of Marx, to provide the impetus for political action by revealing phenomena actually evident in the record of the past and in aspects of the present. If the plausibility of their theories of history suffers from the extent of their reach, they nonetheless relate past to present in ways that make interpretive sense of the inter-connections between theory and practice and between past and present.

HEGEL

The focus for Hegel's interpretations of past political thinkers is the political culture in which a thinker is situated. Hegel understands theorists to theorize from within the orbit of a particular culture and in the light of preceding and contemporary ways of conceiving of politics, society, and philosophy. Hegel is a philosopher who takes history seriously and who emphasizes the sociality of human beings. To imagine thinkers as developing ideas about politics in isolation from their location in historic cultures is fanciful. Hegel imagines history, politics, and philosophy to be inter-related in that political theories are developed in determinate historical contexts and are related to one another by successive political theories responding to preceding ones. He takes his own philosophy to represent the consummate way of thinking through these relations systematically. Hence he holds that history, politics, and philosophy are connected systemically, just as the past and the present are inter-related. Philosophy is practised in an historical context, and ultimately history is to be understood philosophically as a medium in which reason is operative. Political culture constitutes the frame in which social life and the development of ideas, including historical consciousness and philosophical awareness, take place. Political thought, from this perspective, is historically determined and is intelligible philosophically as an historical product.

The Preface to the *Philosophy of Right* highlights Hegel's views on the historicity of political thought. He observes, 'When philosophy paints its grey on grey then has a form of life grown old. By philosophy's grey on grey a form of life cannot be rejuvenated but only understood. The Owl of Minerva raises its wings only at the falling of the dusk.'[7] He also rehearses a sense of the dependence of political philosophy on the record of history in maintaining, 'What is rational is actual and what is actual is rational'.[8] Hegel is against ideologues, like Fries, who urge their preferences without reference to what is actually the case and what can be expected in the light of prevailing circumstances.[9] In the *Philosophy of Right* Hegel elaborates on his historical understanding of political thought and provides a rationale for its validity in his comments on Plato. He recognizes the pedigree and acuity of Plato's philosophizing and his political thought, but he also maintains the dependence of Plato's thought on an historic political culture. He signals how, in important ways, Plato's political thought is not relevant to modern society because it does not and cannot include provisions for individuality and freedom, which were not established in Greek political culture, though there were signs of its yet unrealized demands. He observes, 'In his *Republic* Plato displays the substance of ethical life in its ideal beauty and truth; but he could only cope with the principle of self-subsistent particularity, which in his day had forced its way into ethical life by setting up in opposition to it his purely substantial state. He absolutely excluded it from his state, even in its very beginning in private property and the family as well as in its more mature form as the subjective will, the choice of a social position and so forth.'[10] In the *Philosophy of Right* Hegel contrasts the complex notion of community that is realizable in the modern states with the traditional and unmediated unity of the Ancient Greek state. On this reading, the political philosophies of Plato and Hegel are significantly and necessarily different as they are theorizing different objects of political association, the Ancient polis, and a modern state encompassing the freedoms of civil society.[11]

Hegel's reading of Plato in the *Philosophy of Right* is supplemented by an elaborated commentary on Plato and the *Republic* in his *Lectures on the History of Philosophy*. At the outset of these lectures Hegel acknowledges that the history of philosophy may appear as 'the spectacle of ever recurring changes in the whole such as finally are no longer even connected by a common aim.'[12] However Hegel urges that philosophy cannot rest content with a narrative of the history of philosophy which does not establish a systematic unity. He observes, 'In history, so, likewise in science, and especially in philosophy do we owe what we are to the tradition which, as Herder has put it, like a holy chain, runs through all that was transient, and has

[7] G.W.F. Hegel, *Hegel's Philosophy of Right* trans. with notes by T.M. Knox (Oxford, Oxford University Press, 1969), p. 13.
[8] Ibid., p. 10.   [9] Ibid., pp. 5–6.   [10] Ibid., p. 185.   [11] Ibid., pp. 14–36.
[12] G.W.F. Hegel, *Lectures on the History of Philosophy*, vol. 1, p. 3.

therefore passed away.'[13] Hence in his *Lectures on the History of Philosophy* Hegel establishes that there is coherence to the historical narrative and the unity is provided by the progressive achievement of truth. It is a developmental unity, however, that allows for difference along with coherence and progress. Differences arise out of the divergent schemes of philosophizing that are undertaken in differing historical contexts. Plato's *Republic* is taken as a prime example of the contextual differences, which underlie the progressive development of philosophy. Hegel remarks on the local contextual inspiration of the *Republic*, 'When we thus study the content of the Platonic Idea, it will become clear that Plato has in fact represented the Greek morality according to its substantial mode for it is the Greek state-life which constitutes the true content of the Platonic *Republic*'.[14] Hegel interprets Plato's *Republic* to be a reassertion of the traditional, hierarchical form of rule in the Greek polis, and its tone of intemperance is taken to reflect the contemporary threats to which it was subject. More generally Hegel takes Plato to be an idealist, who perceives thought to be central to reality and its explanation. He interprets Plato as contributing to his own sense of objective idealism, whereby the rational is taken to be fundamental to reality. He observes that, for Plato, 'What is real is rational.'[15] Hegel recognizes the philosophical significance of Plato's objective idealism in establishing a tradition of an idealist conceptualization of reality, to which Hegel himself subscribes. Like Plato, Hegel is an idealist, who takes the world to be rational. Idealism in this light has nothing to do with subjectivism but is a determination to perceive the world as rational, and to recognize the rational order underlying its appearances.[16] Hegel's interpretation of Plato as an objective idealist underlies his reading of Plato as supplying a rational system explaining reality, consisting of a Logic (*Parmenides*), a Philosophy of Nature (*Timaeus*), and a Philosophy of Spirit (*Republic*). Hence, for Hegel, Plato's politics are different from how many commentators have envisaged them. Plato is neither a radical innovator who is committed to a utopian scheme of political change, nor a pessimist who paints a picture of a political fantasy but in reality is apolitical.[17] Hegel takes Plato in his political philosophy to be rehearsing the underlying order of a traditional form of politics, which provides order and hierarchy and allows no room for individual freedom.[18]

---

[13] Ibid., vol. 2, p. 2.   [14] Ibid., p. 95.   [15] Ibid.

[16] See G. Browning, *Hegel and the History of Political Philosophy* (Basingstoke and New York, Palgrave Macmillan, 1999); G. Browning, 'Hegel's Plato: The Owl of Minerva and a Fading Political Tradition', *Political Studies*, vol. xxxvi, 1988, pp. 476–485; G. Browning, 'Plato and Hegel: Reason, Redemption and Political Theory', *History of Political Thought*, vol. viii, no. 3, 1987, pp. 377–393.

[17] For alternative interpretations that take Plato's politics to be either radical and utopian or apolitical see K. Popper, *The Open Society and Its Enemies*, vol. 1 (London, Routledge, Kegan & Paul, 1945); L. Strauss, *The City and Man* (Chicago, University of Chicago Press, 1964).

[18] G.W.F. Hegel, *Lectures on the History of Philosophy*, vol. 1, p. 3.

Hegel's interpretation of Plato's *Republic* constitutes a perceptive reading of the dialogue. It situates its authoritarianism in a traditional mode of politics, and it relates its disregard for individualism and subjective freedom to the traditional practice of politics in Ancient Greece, in which individual freedom is not a well-established value. Indeed, Hegel argues that individuality and particular forms of freedom associated with individuals, such as rights of the person and property rights, were absent from the political culture of Ancient Greece, and only emerged in modernity, subsequent to the actual experience of politics to which Plato had access. Hegel's reading of Plato is plausible and allows us to put his hierarchical ideal state into a historical political context. Certainly, it possesses the interpretive advantage over rival interpretations of recognizing how Plato is motivated to protect society from forces of innovation and change. Hegel's Plato, however, is questionable. It abstracts from features of Plato's text to present a generalized argument that Plato is reasserting authority and hierarchy and in so doing it underplays notable aspects of the *Republic*. For instance, it ignores its radical espousal of equality between the sexes amongst the political elite and its provision of innovatory educational institutions that would provide philosophical training for future leaders. Hegel's interpretation of Plato's politics only works at a high level of abstraction, which omits its references to innovatory social reforms. This one-sided review of Plato's political thought intimates that Hegel's general interpretive standpoint of aligning political philosophies to the prevalent norms of a political culture is questionable. Why must a thinker only consider the conditions of politics within the limits of what is sanctioned in the prevailing culture? There is no logical or historical reason why a thinker cannot think out of the box of current conceptions. Hegel's inclination to read political philosophy as mirroring contextual assumptions smacks of limiting the political imagination so as to fit with a schematic generic reading of historical development. Likewise, Hegel's synoptic interpretation of Plato's philosophy as constituting a system consisting of Logic, Nature, and Spirit distorts Plato's thought by abstracting from its dialogical and artistic form, which resists the determinacy that Hegel assigns to it. Doubts over Hegel's enterprise are compounded by his view on the relations between theory and practice that are expressed in lectures on political philosophy. In his lectures Hegel conveys a more critical standpoint of the status quo, intimating that his overt interpretive standpoint in his published writings perhaps reflect an accommodation to political power.[19] Moreover, Ware has identified an ambiguity in Hegel's interpretive standpoint. He points out how Hegel's view of philosophy as comprehending a culture retrospectively in the light of its complete expression of its features before its demise can be

[19] See G.W.F. Hegel, *Die Philosophie des Rechts: Die Vorlesung von 1819/20*, ed. D. Heinrich (Frankfurt, Suhrkamp Verlag, 1983), p. 48.

construed as foreshadowing the collapse of a regime rather than as reinforcing its structures.[20]

Notwithstanding the tensions within Hegel's interpretive standpoint, his interpretation of Plato's politics reveals how his conception of the history of political philosophy can yield insights. Hegel's own political philosophy is predicated upon his historical reading of modernity. His historical perspective allows him to identify key features of modernity in his social and political theory. Society and politics, for Hegel, are not to be subjected to fantasies or imagined without reference to their actual development. Hegel takes political thought to be linked to analysis of actual politics, rather than allowing for idle speculation and the specification of abstract principles. He recognizes the importance of rights in enabling individual freedom, and yet he dismisses their abstract specification as idle unless the concrete conditions of actual practice allow for their formulation and maintenance.[21] Hegel also identifies features of modern society, such as the market, civil society, personal morality, contracts, and state sovereignty that collectively promote freedom to be development signalling historical progress.[22] He is surely right to align theory to historical practice and to highlight how modernity allows for new and distinctive concepts of social and political life to be deployed.[23] Moreover, Hegel's engagement in philosophy is conducted in an historical spirit. *The Phenomenology of Spirit* is a wide-ranging critical engagement with the historical conditionality of systematic philosophy and within this review he invokes a variety of historical phenomena and identifies enabling and disabling aspects of modern moral life.[24]

Hegel's synoptic perspective recognizes the historical development of public culture, which supports philosophy and social and cultural developments in politics, art, and religion. Hegel's system is historically oriented, but it is misleading to maintain that Hegel merely imposes an a priori historical scheme upon recalcitrant phenomena, just as it is misguided to label him an historicist in the Popperian sense of framing laws to explain historical events deterministically.[25] If Hegel is an historicist, he is so by virtue of his recognition of historicity as an inescapable dimension of all human activities rather than by framing general laws of historical development. Hegel exercises care to avoid simply reducing history to the requirements of a philosophical

---

[20] See R. Ware, 'Hegel's Metaphilosophy and Historical Metamorphosis', in *History of Political Thought*, vol. 17, no. 2, 1996, pp. 253–279.

[21] G.W.F. Hegel, *Hegel's Philosophy of Right*, pp. 37–75.

[22] Ibid. See in particular the closing comments at pp. 216–23.

[23] See G. Browning, 'What is Wrong with Modernity and What is Right with the *Philosophy of Right*', *History of European Ideas*, vol. 29, no. 2, 2003, pp. 223–239.

[24] G.W.F. Hegel, *The Phenomenology of Mind* trans. J.B. Baillee (London and New York, George Allen and Unwin Ltd, 1973).

[25] K. Popper, *The Poverty of Historicism* (London, Routledge, 1996), p. vii.

standpoint. He envisages philosophical history as completing but not super-seding other forms of history.[26] Hegel explains a philosophical approach to history by showing how non-philosophical approaches underpin and invoke philosophical history. Non-philosophical forms of history provide a record of what has happened and offer empirical insights into the development of freedom, but lack understanding of the overall meaning of history. This lack entails that there is a gap between past and present, and an explanatory hiatus between the historian as agent of historical understanding and the past as object of historical study. Hegelian philosophical history draws on non-philosophical history and at the same time supersedes it by recognizing the role of human freedom and rationality in the course of human history, and so past and present are united by the recognition of the continuity provided by the development of freedom on the part of rational individuals. For Hegel, historical understanding emerges out of the freedom that is marked by the advent of political associations. Historical narratives arise out of the need to establish forms of identity in the wake of the formation of non-naturalistic, political forms of association.[27] Historical understanding is correlated to the freedom of human agency that informs political associations. It registers free actions and their consequences, but the meaning and extent of freedom is not fully comprehended in particular empirical or pragmatic studies of history. The centrality of freedom is only fully realized in philosophical history, which presupposes the historical development of freedom and conceives of freedom as underlying all human activity. Hegel's rational philosophical history, which is enabled by the development of the history of philosophy, outlines the progress of freedom in political culture.

Philosophical history, for Hegel, unites the present world of the historian with the past, which is the object of historical understanding. Hegel observes, 'Because we are concerned only with the idea of Spirit—and we regard the whole of world history as nothing more than the manifestation of spirit—when we go over the past, however extensive it may be, we are really concerned only with the *present*.'[28] A reciprocity between past and present, between historical method and its object, emerges in philosophical history. Hegel observes, 'To him who looks at the world rationally, the world is rational in return.'[29] Hence, philosophical history interprets freedom teleologically. Hegel conceives of the course of this historical development to consist in the expansion of freedom from the arbitrary freedom of a single individual under oriental despotism to the universal achievement of freedom in modern North European states. Hegel remarks that 'the Orientals knew only that *One* person is free; the Greeks and Romans that *some* are free; while we know that all

---

[26] See G.W.F. Hegel, *Lectures on the Philosophy of World History. Introduction: Reason in History* trans. H.B. Nisbet (Cambridge, Cambridge University Press, 1975), p. 24.
[27] Ibid., p. 10.   [28] Ibid., p. 89.   [29] Ibid., p. 18.

humans are implicitly free.'[30] Hegel identifies the modern state's system of public law, protecting individual rights, and its orchestrated social and political institutions allowing for the institutionalization of a people's freedom to register the universal freedom that has been achieved in modern Europe.

Hegel's interpretation of the historical development of politics and of its theoretical conceptualization shows historical sophistication and a rationale for imputing progress to the course of Western history. His reading of Plato's political philosophy indicates how his approach allows for a contextually informed appreciation of a past theorist. In succeeding chapters we will also show how his interpretation of Kant reflects a sensitivity to the problems of Enlightenment theory and practice. Hegel identifies the divisions in Kant's philosophy between reason and the world, morality and desire, and the state and international order as reflecting inherent tensions within the Enlightenment. Hegel's reflection on Kant, like his reading of Plato, is instructive. His reading of, and sensitivity to, the historical sociality of human identities is also invoked and used by Beauvoir to highlight the predicament of woman. Our subsequent chapter on Beauvoir testifies to the ongoing influence of Hegelian modes of thinking. However, Hegel's thought and his way of interpreting preceding political theory raise issues of interpretation. Hegel's holism neither allows for discordant features within a political culture nor for an appreciation of dissident and minority expressions of cultural and political life. Original inhabitants of the New World are either ignored or regarded as merely recessive. Nascent forms of feminism are disregarded, nationalists are deprecated, and populism condemned.[31] The political imagination is not limited to dominant public norms. If Plato could imagine a form of sexual equality, then Hegel is not justified in ignoring the claims of feminism. Moreover, to imagine an end to history, in which the development of freedom is necessarily achieved, appears to rest upon a paradoxical unity of freedom and necessity. Its rationale resides in the thought that freedom is implicit in the very notion of human agency, so that its development and practical recognition is a logical outcome of this inherent capacity. For Hegel, realizing freedom is an achievement that warrants a sense of finality, due to its concordance with the conceptual conditions of agency. It is this strong sense of the centrality of freedom to human experience which underlies Hegel's argument for the necessity of freedom. McCarney draws upon it thoughtfully in explaining and justifying Hegel's concept of an end of history.[32] Yet to consider history as following a necessary pathway to the realization of freedom remains

---

[30] G.W.F. Hegel, *The Philosophy of History* trans, J. Sibree (London, George Bell and Sons, 1956), p. 26.

[31] For a discussion of Hegel on original peoples, see W. Conkin, *Hegel's Laws—The Legitimacy of a Modern Legal Order* (Stanford, California, Stanford University Press, 2008).

[32] J. McCarney, *Hegel on History* (London, Routledge, 2010), pp. 65–83.

highly controversial and underplays the possibilities of human action. After all, European civilization in the mid-twentieth century sustained unbearable forms of racism and genocide and its present susceptibility to environmental catastrophe reinforces caution over the notion of a benign end to history. Again, global inequalities, colonial legacies, and the lack of effective forms of international democratic governance threaten and compromise the experience of freedom.[33]

Hegel's assumption that history exhibits a unitary directionality is problematic in that it ignores the multiplicity of meanings that can be ascribed to historical events and undervalues their sheer contingency. To ascribe a necessary direction to world history, which culminates in the political freedom of modern European society is to condense a multitude of occurrences into a single frame of meaning. Hegel's narrative omits significant forms of activity and ways of thinking, which bear upon subsequent lines of development and human identities, including the rise of feminism, divergent sexualities, global inequalities, migration, nationalism, climate change, secularism, the persistence and revival of fundamentalism, the ubiquity of capital, the commodification of art, the loss of community, and the fate of original peoples. Again, Hegel's perspective on the historical conditionality of philosophy is disputable. It is engaging and ambitious. Philosophy does develop within the context of changing political cultures and may be seen as progressing by reflecting upon preceding philosophies. Hegel makes sense of Plato and of Kant by relating them to historical cultural conditions. Yet more needs to be said. Philosophy is practised in divergent styles. Plato's use of metaphor and imagery is deprecated by Hegel, when it is arguably central to his sense of the ultimate yet mysterious significance of the Good and the forms.[34] Hegel's aim of including all preceding thought in his own philosophical perspective strains against the sheer diversity of content and style that is exhibited in historical development.

MARX

Marx is a systematic theorist, who follows Hegel. Like Hegel, Marx is a dialectical theorist. It is true that Marx critiques Hegel and talks of turning Hegel upside down and of developing a form of materialism to counter Hegel's

---

[33] For a discussion of Hegel and international political theory, see G. Browning, *Global Theory from Kant to Hardt and Negri* (Basingstoke and New York, Palgrave Macmillan, 2011), pp. 42–61.

[34] On Plato and form, see I. Murdoch, *The Fire and the Sun—Why Plato Banished the Artists* (Oxford, Oxford University Press, 1977).

idealism. But he tends to overlook what he has in common with Hegel. Perhaps his very proximity to Hegel's thought rendered the similarities difficult to see. What unites Marx and Hegel is a common determination to frame and connect concepts systematically so as to highlight the connections between social phenomena. In the *Grundrisse*, where Marx sets out his mature methodology, he remarks on how social reality is not a world of discrete things. He designates it to be relational and adds that relations 'can be expressed, of course, only in ideas.'[35] Marx develops an inter-related set of concepts to capture the inter-relations between elements in the social world. This system of concepts encompasses the historical world from which the present has emerged and also points to the future, in which communism will supersede the contradictions of capital and pre-capitalist societies. Marx, like Hegel, understands the present in terms of its emergence from the past. The past bears upon the present, is comprehended by a theoretical perspective that is formulated in the present. Past and present, for Marx, are united in terms of their roles in the narrative of historical development. Marx's concentrated critique of capital is accompanied by a narrative of its development, and analysis of the conditions of its reproduction and its ultimate demise. Capitalism is engendered via contradictions in a preceding mode of production and is to be replaced by communism, a form of society, which can deliver the generic capacities of human beings to produce freely and universally. This framing of capitalism by a pre-capitalist past and by a projected communist future represents a teleological reading of history. Like Hegel, Marx interprets past thought as arising out of determinate historical contexts, which determine social and political thought in a particular period. Marx follows Hegel in adopting a realistic perspective, in taking account of present realities and historical developments. To imagine and urge possibilities that are not latent within present empirical conditions is to be utopian,[36] Marx's concentrated critique of capital is accompanied by a narrative of its development, the conditions of its reproduction, and its ultimate demise. Capitalism is destined to be replaced by communism, a form of society, which can deliver the generic capacities of human beings to produce freely and universally. This framing of capitalism by a pre-capitalist past and by a post-capitalist communist future represents a teleological reading of history, in which the end of communism provides the interpretive frame to identify and assess the present alienated and fractured condition of society. Marx differs from Hegel by taking production and the class interests arising out of the productive process to be the determining elements in the contexts of past thought, the process of historical development and the character of politics of

---

[35] K. Marx, *Grundrisse* trans. M. Nicholas (Harmondsworth, Penguin, 1974), p. 164.
[36] See K. Marx and F. Engels, *The Communist Manifesto* trans. S. Moore, in K. Marx, *Political Writings*, vol. 1, *The Revolutions of 1848* (Harmondsworth, Penguin, 1973), pp. 92–5.

contemporary society.[37] The systematic character of Marx's reading of past and present entails that he connects past thought to the historical conditions of its production, to the possibilities of the present, and to the interpretive power of his own theory to frame the conditionality of past thinking and present-day analysis. While contradictions distort the operations of production and theorizing in the past and present, they are imagined to be susceptible to Marx's own formulation of a coherent account of historical development that allows for a unified way of perceiving past, present, and future.

The German Ideology plays a significant if controversial role in any account of Marx's theory of the history, and more specifically in a review of his interpretation of ideas and the history of political thought. The text is controversial in that Carver and Blank, in the light of archival research, argue that the manuscripts that have been taken to constitute the work, were not only left unpublished by Marx and Engels, but, in fact, were never envisaged as forming a single connected piece of work.[38] This research, which highlights the role of subsequent editors in presenting the text, reinforces doubts about reading its material as straightforwardly conveying a set of doctrines about materialism and history.[39] Nonetheless, the various pieces of writing on the Young Hegelians by Marx and Engels, which have been taken to constitute *The German Ideology*, continue to provide the most express account of how Marx interprets the history of ideas. As Arthur suggests, the 'Chapter on Feuerbach' still offers an important account of Marx's theory of history.[40] It highlights the role of the mode of production as the site for incubating historical change, imagines large-scale historical change to be generated by contradictions between the forces and relations of production occurring at critical conjunctures, and takes ideas to be generated by material class interests forged in the productive process. Marx and Engels, however, warn against treating their generic statements on history as providing a key to historical interpretation and urge that attention should be paid to actual empirical developments.[41]

---

[37] For a convincing account of the radicalism of Marx, see T. Smith, *Dialectical Social Theory and Its Critics* (New York, State University of New York Press, 1993), pp. 36–138.

[38] See T. Carver and D. Blank, *Marx's'German Ideology' Manuscripts—Presentation and Analysis of the 'Feuerbach Chapter'* (Basingstoke and New York, Palgrave Macmillan, 2014); T. Carver and D. Blank, *A Political History of the Editions of Marx and Engels's 'German Ideology' Manuscripts* (Basingstoke and New York, Palgrave, 2015); and T. Carver, 'The German Ideology Never Took Place', *History of Political Thought*, vol. 31, no. 1, 2010, pp. 107–27.

[39] For an account of the disjointed character of the manuscripts and the need to read them in relation to their contexts, see G. Browning, '*The German Ideology*: The Theory of History and the History of Theory', *History of Political Thought*, vol. xiv, no. 3, 1993, pp. 455–73.

[40] C. Arthur, Review of T. Carver and D. Blank, *Marx's' German Ideology' Manuscripts-Presentation and Analysis of the 'Feuerbach Chapter'* and T. Carver and D. Blank, *A Political History of the Editions of Marx and Engels's 'German Ideology' Manuscripts*, Marx and Philosophy: Review of Books, 22 May 2015.

[41] K. Marx and F. Engels, *The German Ideology* trans. S. Ryazanskaya (Moscow, Progress Publishers, 1976), p. 53.

The most well-known passages in *The German Ideology* deal with the status and interpretation of ideas, and are contained in the manuscript on Feuerbach. In tendentious language, ideas are declared to be phantasms of the human brain, reflecting passively material forces. Marx and Engels remark, 'The phantoms formed in the human brain are also necessarily sublimates of their material life-processes which is empirically verifiable and bound to material premises. Morality, religion, metaphysics, all the rest of ideology and their corresponding forms of consciousness thus no longer retain the semblance of independence'.[42] The reductionism that is implied in this statement is continued in their identification of the ruling ideas of an epoch as representing the illusory claims of the class that dominates the process of production. Marx and Engels urge, 'the ideas of the ruling class are in every epoch the ruling ideas, i.e. the class which has the ruling material force of society is at the same time its ruling intellectual force'.[43] Hence political ideas of an epoch may claim to express universal truths, but in reality dominant ideas reflect the interests of dominant classes. For instance, in bourgeois society freedom and equality may be trumpeted by Bentham, but these values are linked to the interests of capital, which demands individual workers to be free to sell their labour.[44]

The brusque dismissal by Marx and Engels of the efficacy of ideas and their reduction of ideas to the material interests of class have to be interpreted in context. Throughout these manuscripts, Marx and Engels are engaged in polemical dispute with Young Hegelian theorists, whom Marx and Engels stigmatize for exaggerating the role of ideas.[45] In consequence, the apparent reductionism of Marx and Engels at least in part serves as a polemical riposte against the alleged significance and independence of ideas. They critique the exaggerated importance that is granted to ideas by the Young Hegelians and cast scorn on the baroque formulations of their intellectual schemes. The dismissal of ideas and the promotion of material factors as playing the countervailing crucial role in historical development are component parts of their aggressive response to the claims of contemporary intellectual opponents. In their elaborated engagement with the ideas of the Young Hegelians, however, Marx and Engels take ideas seriously, and the manuscripts offer extensive critiques of the ideas of Stirner and Bruno Bauer as well as of Feuerbach. In the course of these discussions Marx and Engels interpret ideas as responding to and reinforcing economic interests, but the process of reinforcement and the form in which ideas are examined intimate how ideas are not seen as automatic responses to historical circumstances. Political ideas are illusory as well as instrumental in promoting interests and hence it makes sense to attend to the

---

[42] Ibid., p. 42.   [43] Ibid., p. 67.   [44] Ibid., p. 68.
[45] For analysis of the polemical context of the text, see G. Browning, *The German Ideology*: The Theory of History and the History of Theory', pp. 455–65.

ways in which ideas are distortive and illusory. Ideas are not simply reduced to economic circumstances.

Marx and Engels highlight how the prevailing economic conditions provide the context that allows for the profusion of ideas that are articulated by the Young Hegelian theorists. The retarded character of German economic development engenders an overproduction of ideas in modern Germany. The frenzied and eccentric engagement with ideas is a sign of the lack of significant economic activity and development in Germany.[46] The peculiar circumstances of Germany, its lack of the progressive development of capital, and the bourgeoisie allows scope for elaboration of ideas which are abstractions that are not determined precisely by material interests.[47] Marx and Engels, in critiquing Young Hegelian ideas, show how ideas are shaped by social and economic circumstances and emphasize aspects of their own ideas. For instance, they show how the radical individualism of Stirner abstracts from his social context only to express in risible form his social and economic marginality.[48] In so doing they also emphasize how their own theoretical perspective embraces the inter-relations between individuality and sociality. They also contrast their own empirically based reflections upon history with those of Stirner, whose highly elaborate teleology is critiqued.[49] In critiquing the radical egoism of Stirner and the critical criticism of Bauer, Marx and Engels point to the social and economic circumstances which condition the generation and role of ideas. Criticism and individualism arise out of and relate to a social context. They observe how the ideas of honour and loyalty are significant in a feudal hierarchal context, but warn that it would be a mistake to abstract these ideas from their setting to accord them an independent role.[50] The analysis of the role of ideas by Marx and Engels in the manuscripts that are assembled in *The German Ideology* is ambiguous. They assert the dependence of ideas on material contexts and maintain that dominant political ideas represent the interests of ruling classes in particular epochs. In so doing they recognize how the role of ideas in society is not confined to the express intentions of their authors and how an interpretation of the ways in which they may reflect and promote partial interests can contribute to historical understanding. They observe, for instance, how ideas of freedom and individuality fit with capital and a society that favours market freedoms over feudal hierarchies.[51] Their assertion that ideas can simply be reduced to economic circumstances and interests, however, is problematic in that any particular description of interests and circumstances cannot accommodate the plurality of ways in which they can be discursively delineated and evaluated. Marx and Engels in their detailed and elaborated analysis of the ideas of the Young Hegelians implicitly recognize that ideas cannot be reduced to

---

[46] K. Marx and F. Engels, *The German Ideology*, pp. 208–11.   [47] Ibid., p. 142.
[48] Ibid., p. 53.   [49] Ibid.   [50] Ibid., p. 68.   [51] Ibid.

circumstances, and their reductionist rhetoric reflects the character of their polemical debate with rival Young Hegelian theorists.

Throughout his writings Marx employs his critical interpretive scheme for understanding ideas by engaging in close and critical readings of past and contemporary forms of thought to reframe misaligned ideological readings of economic and political conditions. In chapter 13 of this book, Marx's critical and revealing reading of Hegel is reviewed. Marx's critique of Hegel shows how political ideas can be evaluated by assessing them in terms of the social and economic realities to which they relate, and in so doing demonstrates contrasting features of his own thought. In his early 'Economic and Philosophical Manuscripts' Marx develops a powerful critique of capitalism by critiquing the assumptions of contemporary political economists. The work is notable because it provides a holistic and multifaceted critique of capitalism, in which the operations of capital are taken to constitute so many interconnected ways of alienating the proletarian wage-labourer. Marx does not invent a set of concepts for understanding the operations and features of capitalism that he invokes. Rather he modifies concepts that he draws from the writings of political economists, such as Smith, Ricardo, and James Mill. Marx develops a novel critical perspective by examining the wider implications of labour, the source of value, operating as wage-labour under capital. He urges, 'Let us now rise above the level of political economy and examine the ideas developed above, taken almost word for word from the political economists, for the answers to these two questions: (1) What is the meaning, in the development of mankind, of this reduction of the greater part of mankind to abstract labour? (2) What mistakes are made by the piecemeal reformers, who either want to *raise* wages and thereby improve the situation of the working class, or, like Proudhon—see *equality* of wages as the goal of social revolution? In political economy *labour* appears only in the form of *wage-earning* activity.'[52] Marx, in the 'Economic and Philosophical Manuscripts', constructs a critique of capital on the basis of the observations of political economists but he alters the way in which capitalism is to be identified by observing the historical and social implications of the development of wage-labour. He identifies how the wage-labourer in a society that is predicated upon the assumption of private property is alienated from the conditions and products of production while the competitive privatized system also alienates them from fellow human beings and from their own generic capacities as freely producing human beings.[53] Marx's synoptic theoretical perspective allows him to use the work of political economists while also indicting them

[52] K. Marx, 'Economic and Philosophical Manuscripts', in K. Marx, *Early Writings* trans. R. Livingstone and G. Benton (Harmondsworth, Penguin, 1975), p. 289.

[53] See B. Ollman, *Alienation—Marx's Conception of Man in Capitalist Society* (Cambridge, Cambridge University Press, 1971).

for their ideological partiality in neglecting to recognize the alienating conditions to which proletarians are exposed under capital. Likewise in the 'Economic and Philosophical Manuscripts' and notably in *The Poverty of Philosophy*, Marx critiques the abstract character of Proudhon's reformist ideas, which due to their individualistic formulations of society rehearse bourgeois concepts and assumptions.[54]

Marx's theoretical system is directed towards the goal of communism, which serves as a telos of historical development, and underpins the radical revision of the assumptions of bourgeois theorists and reformers, who take the current practices of capitalism as universal procedures. In contrast, and in line with a perceived directionality of history, Marx highlights the conditionality of modes of production and the class-affiliated character of social and political thought. In *The Communist Manifesto* critical-utopian socialists and communists, such as Fourier and Owen, are stigmatized for framing socialist ideas which do not align their visions with the actual development of the proletariat and its consciousness.[55] Contrariwise, Marx's commitment to communism is predicated upon the proletariat developing a revolutionary consciousness. Class consciousness is necessary if the proletarian class is to assume a revolutionary role in the historical process. Marx's interpretation of ideas highlights their historicity. Ideas of authority, rights, individuality, and state forms are aligned to particular historic modes of productions. Ideas of political economy emerge with and support capital, private property, and markets. Marx's conceptions of communism and proletarian revolutionary activity depend upon grasping and acting upon a comprehension of the directionality of history. Marx's interpretation of past political ideas in abstracting from the intentions of authors, and in many cases from the details of ideas and texts, allows for a concentration upon how ideas function in social life. In subsequent chapters we will examine how Macpherson, a twentieth-century Marxist political theorist, interpreted Hobbes and Locke by focusing upon how their political theories are aligned with the economic structure of emerging capitalist society. But Marx's focus upon a supervening narrative of how ideas contribute to a supposed overall directionality of history that encompasses past forms of social organization and future developments is problematic. A sense of the directionality of history tends to coerce ideas into a supervening scheme so that, for instance, the energy and imagination of utopian socialists is undervalued and the relevance of gender to past and present thinking about politics is underrated. The focus upon class and a communist future entails that what is deemed inessential to the underlying historical directionality is ignored.

---

[54] K. Marx, *The Poverty of Philosophy* trans. H. Squelch (New York, Cosimo, Inc., 2008), pp. 100–50.

[55] K. Marx and F. Engels, *The Communist Manifesto*, pp. 92–5.

CONCLUSION

Hegel and Marx offer related yet distinctive interpretations of the history of political thought. They develop synoptic overviews of the historical process, discerning and outlining its essential directionality and holding dialectical views of the inter-connections between their own theories and the past theories that are understood in terms of their roles in supervening schemes of historical development. The systematic, synoptic standpoints of Hegel and Marx allow them to identify past theorists as occupying particular positions in a wider scheme of historical development. The sweep of Hegel and Marx's historical imagination equips them to identify past political theorists as developing their ideas in determinate past contexts, which are also related to the present in that the perspectives of Hegel and Marx are developed by critical reflection upon ideas and historical circumstances. Hegel and Marx are also contextualist historians of political ideas, in that they relate ideas to large-scale contexts of either particular political cultures or modes of production. For Hegel, the context is provided by the political culture of an epoch, which is inclusive in constituting a framework of social and political practices in relation to which cultural developments and ideas are to be identified and comprehended. For Marx, the determining context is supplied by the mode of production, the organization of production by which forces of production are connected to relations of production, which in turn shapes the ideas of an epoch. The synoptic historical perspectives of Hegel and Marx enable them to offer perceptive commentary on past political thought. They make sense of political theory by seeing it as part of a more general process of social and political change whereby the basic structures of societies inform and inspire specific forms of theory. Their standpoints also relate past to present in that they take their own synoptic perspectives to arise out of the historical processes that their theories of history delineate, so that they can explain their own privileged positions in analysing and assessing the directionality of history.

Both Hegel and Marx use their generic conceptions of history in offering insights into particular political thinkers in ways that show their attention to the particular texts of past thinkers and are not to be dismissed as merely deriving from a generic and unitary perspective, which blocks attention to detail and singularities. For instance, Hegel is insightful in showing how Plato responds to and rehearses a traditional hierarchical society that is in the process of transforming into something different under the impact of new and discordant voices. Hegel makes sense of Plato's conservatism and his recoil from the novel challenging rhetoric of the sophists. Likewise Marx's interpretation of Stirner's thought remains perceptive in highlighting its abstractions and strained teleology even if it is partisan in its uncompromising dismissal of Stirner's perspective. Again, Hegel's reading of Kant is sharp and productive, if partial and questionable. Hegel and Marx's panoramic perspectives on the development of Western social and political structures and correlative philosophical and political ideas are productive assumptions. Moreover, their general conceptions of history are not designed to dispense with the work of empirical historians, who attend to particular circumstances. Nonetheless, the perspectives of Hegel and Marx suffer from undervaluing the diversity of ways of imagining politics and political standpoints by assimilating ideas into unitary explanatory frameworks. In Hegel's *Lectures on the History of Philosophy* all philosophies lead to Hegel's own systematic reading of modernity, and, in turn, Hegel's systematic dialectical perspective assimilates all philosophies into moments of his own system. Likewise Marx's sense of the directionality of history tends to assimilate the past, present, and future of theory and practice into Marx's own terms of reference. The upshot is that they leave theoretical remainders, which cannot be coerced into their frameworks and which complicate the big pictures, which their schemes maintain.

Questions must be raised about the theoretical schemes of Hegel and Marx. They assume that in each epoch there is a predominant unifying contextual framework or structure and an overriding directionality to the historical processes at work so that all theories and ideas within an epoch can be assigned relatively neatly to designated roles. Yet their assumptions of unity beg questions. For instance, is there a single political culture, which may be individuated unequivocally that can underpin Hegel's enterprise of relating political thinkers to a unifying contextual frame? A problem with Hegel's Plato is that Plato is a highly individual thinker, whose conception of philosophy was singular in the context of Ancient Greece. Likewise, Marx's critical reading of the ideology of individualism under capitalism highlights structural disparities of power between individuals that might be underplayed if the structures of capital are ignored yet J.S. Mill's concern with individuality raises issues of morality and social conformity that are not to be reduced to class and class conflict. Again, Nietzsche's critical scrutiny of modern culture doubtless reflects tensions in bourgeois society and yet his genealogical critiques of metaphysics and contemporary morality remain radical and timely in ways that Foucault's post-Marxist sensitivity to the capillary de-centred operations of power can detect rather than Marxist schema of class identifications.[56] Stirner's political thought can be posed as constituting a continuing question to both Hegel and Marx. While Stirner's radical individualism may be dismissed as merely a derogation from Hegel's systematic review of consciousness or as a despairing complaint of a bourgeois individual lacking social connections and historical possibilities but its normative focus upon individuality may also be turned against the generalizing frameworks of Marx and

---

[56] See F. Nietzsche, *On The Genealogy of Morals* trans. Carol Diethe (Cambridge, Cambridge University Press, 1994) and M. Foucault, 'Nietzsche, Genealogy, History', in M. Foucault, *The Foucault Reader*, ed. P. Rabinow (London and New York, Penguin, 1984), pp. 76–100.

Hegel. Given the consequences of the steady accumulation and consolidation of social and political power in late modernity Stirner's individualism is not evidently wrong-headed in its sharp rejection of the essentialisms of Hegel and Marx.

The continuing value of Hegel and Marx can be seen in the subsequent and ongoing contribution to the history of political thought by a range of scholars, who have been influenced by their ideas. Gramsci, for instance, combines Hegel and Marx in framing a dynamic view of the relations between theory and practice. For instance, he appropriates the work of Machiavelli to envisage Machiavelli's conception of the prince as a paradigm for a resourceful and politically strategic Marxist political party, which attends to strategy and tactics in a tensely balanced situation of political power blocs, which in turn reflect changing concentrations of social and economic power. Gramsci's reading of Machiavelli might appear to be anachronistic and partial in relating Renaissance politics of principalities to twentieth-century class politics. Yet he makes connections that advertise the tactical, strategic aspects of modern party politics and the continuing relevance of Machiavelli's focus on political instrumentalism.[57] Del Lucchese makes the point that Gramsci reads Machiavelli productively as employing immanent political concepts to highlight how politics is situated in historical and changing contexts, which remain relevant to a Marxist politics of revolution.[58] The Marxist political theorist and historian of political ideas, C.B. Macpherson, also employed a Marxist frame of reference to explain the ideas of the early modern English political theorists Hobbes and Locke in ways that have been challenged by rival historians, and yet contribute to ongoing debate over their ideas. Moreover, the influential, historically oriented ethics of celebrated recent and contemporary moral philosophers, Taylor, MacIntyre, and Williams entertain ideas that are drawn from Hegel and his interpretation of the history of ideas.[59]

What the interpretive schemes of Hegel and Marx highlight is the value and disputability of framing normative theories of politics and society by general readings of historical development. For Hegel and Marx, to consider theorizing about society without recognizing empirical realities and a sense of how society has developed and its concepts have evolved, is a nonsense. They stigmatize would-be reformers and utopians, who have insufficient regard for the actual identity of what they propose to change. Hegel is surely right

---

[57] For discussions of Gramsci and Machiavelli, see T. Ball, *Reappraisals in Political Theory* (Oxford, Oxford University Press, 1995) pp. 17–18 and F. Del Lucchese, *The Political Philosophy of Niccolo Machiavelli* (Edinburgh, Edinburgh University Press, 2015), pp. 160–3.

[58] F. Del Lucchese, *The Political Philosophy of Niccolo Machiavelli*, p. 161.

[59] See A. MacIntyre, *A Short History of Ethics* (London, Routledge and Kegan Paul, 1967); C. Taylor, *Sources of the Self—The Making of the Modern Identity* (Cambridge Mass., Harvard University Press, 1989); and B. Williams, *Ethics and the Limits of Philosophy* (Glasgow, Fontana Press/Collins, 1985).

to maintain that politics is an activity that takes place over time. Recognition of its historical character is crucial in evaluating political regimes. Again, Marx is right to dismiss ideological and political prescriptions that do not identify how societies have been constituted, and the direction in which they are likely to develop. However, it would surely be equally wrong to dissolve the normative into the descriptive and ideal reflection into analysis of historical circumstances. Hegel himself warned against reducing the absolute question of what is right into the relative question of the historical circumstances that brought about a state of affairs.[60] The standpoints of both Hegel and Marx are questionable, with Hegel being decidedly cautious in his published writings about superseding the status quo and Marx being overly optimistic that radical conceptual and practical innovation can depart decisively and positively from conventions and traditions. The intellectual and political imagination is not limited by what has merely been the case, but it is also liable to lapse into preceding and rehearsed formulas if it is not reflective about the role of traditions and the situated character of judgments about society and politics. The critical standpoints of Hegel and Marx contribute importantly to our interpretive resources in understanding political ideas but should not be taken uncritically.

[60] G.W.F. Hegel, *Hegel's Philosophy of Right*, pp. 16–18.

3

Oakeshott, Collingwood, and the Historical Turn

INTRODUCTION

Collingwood and Oakeshott are twentieth-century English idealists, historians as well as philosophers, who established a particular way of conducting the history of political thought. In their philosophies, they identify and review the relations between distinct forms of knowledge and experience. They subscribe to an interpretive philosophical perspective, which accommodates the constructive, purposeful aspects of individual agency with rule-bound traditions of social and political life. While the general contours of their approach to theory and practice are worked out in early works, they offer changing formulations of its relationship in the course of their careers. They explore the study of the history of ideas, by providing considered accounts of how the nature of the history of political thought is to be conducted and by offering close interpretations of particular texts. They are sensitive to the historicity of past texts and to the defining features of a specifically historical understanding of past thinkers, and yet they also allow for the relevance of the history of political thought to the ongoing practice of political thought. Their own political theories emerge out of their conceptualizations of past thinkers on the conditions of political association. Traditions of political thought, for Oakeshott and Collingwood, represent interpretations of historical political practice and inform conceptualizations of Western civilization. They distill features of these traditions into their own substantive political theories. Their interpretive approach to the history of political thought recognizes the impact of past contexts upon particular political theories, but imagines traditions of theorizing as connecting forms of political thinking across time and as informing present contributions to its practice.

What distinguishes Collingwood and Oakeshott from predecessors and many of their successors is their expertise as practitioners in the discipline of history, which informs the originality and force of their analyses of its epistemological conditions. Their theoretical understanding of history acknowledges how the practice of history developed in the nineteenth century so as to constitute a distinct and recognizable form of knowledge, the features of which were amenable to philosophical analysis of their roles and epistemological status. They recognize the autonomy of historical understanding, separating historical knowledge sharply from the procedures of natural science. In *Experience and Its Modes* (1933) Oakeshott identifies the natural sciences in terms of the construction of hypothetical laws by scientists to establish regularities in the processes involving natural phenomena. History is distinct from the natural sciences, in that it is not interested in generalizations and hypothetical laws. Instead it focuses upon change and particulars, constructing contingent historical events from occurrences, so that explanation is provided by the contextual specification of occurrences.[1] Integral to Oakeshott's conception of historical understanding is the construction of the historical past on the part of historians by establishing and interpreting evidence and discriminating the role of purposeful actions of historical agents in events. Likewise, Collingwood distinguishes the enterprise of historical understanding from that of the natural sciences. While the natural sciences presume and hypothesize the regularity of occurrences, he understands historical understanding to focus upon the rethinking of thoughts that are entertained in particular past human actions and so historical explanation is presented as a form of rational explanation of past conduct.[2] The distinctiveness of historical explanation from that of natural science is underlined by Collingwood in his historical analysis of the several ways in which the notion of cause has been employed in explaining phenomena. The idea of cause is shown to be susceptible of differing explanations and the meaning that is assigned to causal explanation is held to accommodate reasons for action as well as the regularity of law-like processes.[3]

In distinguishing the presuppositions of the discipline of history, Oakeshott and Collingwood are at one in highlighting the viability and autonomy of historical understanding. In so doing they distinguish the past from the present. Historians, for Oakeshott, construct the past from evidence that is assembled in the present.[4] The past represents a paradox in that all experience is present experience, but the peculiarity of historians is that they construe the present as offering evidence of past experience. Historians, in imagining

---

[1] M. Oakeshott, *Experience and Its Modes* (Cambridge, Cambridge University Press, 1933), pp. 86–169.

[2] R.G. Collingwood, *The Idea of History* revised edition, edited by W.J. van der Dussen (Oxford, Clarendon Press, 1993), pp. 282–302. This edition will be cited throughout, save where the previous edition is cited when one of its features is highlighted.

[3] R.G. Collingwood, *An Essay on Metaphysics*, revised edition, edited with an Introduction by Rex Martin (Oxford, Clarendon Press, 1998), pp. 285–344.

[4] M. Oakeshott, 'The Activity of Being an Historian', in M. Oakeshott, *Rationalism in Politics and Other Essays* (London and New York, Methuen & Co, Barnes and Noble Books, 1962), p. 153.

the past, take the past to be distinct from the present, and a mark of the integrity of the historical past is that it is not to be compromised by associations with the present.[5] Oakeshott recognizes the singularity of this historical attitude to the past, observing how it differs from a practical attitude to the past, which is assumed easily in everyday life, for instance in a lawyer's surmising of what has happened in a case involving a client, or in a politician's appeal to the past to justify a policy.[6] In practical affairs, the past is invoked precisely because it can serve an interest in the present, whereas the historian concentrates upon determining what happened in the past for its own sake. Likewise, Collingwood identifies a defining feature of historical understanding to be that the historian establishes and scrutinizes evidence in the present to imagine a past that differs from the present. The enterprise of the historian is captured in the memorable if controversial phrase, the 'rethinking of past thoughts'.[7] The phrase has been construed by commentators as implying an empathetic identification with past actors on the part of the historian.[8] However, Collingwood conceives of the recovery of past thoughts by the historian to be a rational procedure, which depends on the interpretation of evidence. The formulation implies that past thoughts can be rethought and so intimates a continuity between past and present. It is a form of continuity, however, which at the same time acknowledges change in that the historian's situation is different from that of the historical actor, whose thought is recovered by the historian.[9] The context of the thought is therefore different and Collingwood recognizes that the past which is recovered by historians consists of unique events that are not to be merged with the present. The moral value of the study of history resides precisely in its capacity to show how actors deal with unique situations that are distinct from and insusceptible to general rules.[10]

In understanding the history of political thought, Oakeshott and Collingwood imagine a process of double interpretation. Past political thinkers are envisaged as interpreting and engaging with past historical contexts. In turn they are interpreted by an historical examination of the ways in which their thinking springs from determinate past forms of political association and related contextual conditions. Oakeshott's posthumously published *Lectures*

---

[5] Ibid., p. 95.

[6] See M. Oakeshott, 'Present, Future and Past', in M. Oakeshott, *On History and Other Essays* (Totowa, New Jersey, Barnes and Noble Books, 1983), pp. 1–45.

[7] R.G. Collingwood, *The Idea of History*, pp. 282–302.

[8] See M. Bevir, *The Logic of the History of Ideas* (Cambridge, Cambridge University Press, 1999), pp. 9–10.

[9] R.G. Collingwood, *An Autobiography* (Oxford, Clarendon Press, 1978), pp. 106–29.

[10] R.G. Collingwood, *The New Leviathan Or Man Society, Civilization and Barbarism Essay*, revised edition, edited with an Introduction by David Boucher (Oxford, Clarendon Press, 1992), pp. 119–25.

in the History of Political Thought analyses past political thinkers by reviewing them in the light of the forms of political experience from which their thought arises. For instance, in considering Plato and Aristotle, Oakeshott examines the political experience of the Ancient Greeks, analysing the vocabulary and structures of their politics along with their images of the world. In interpreting Aristotle, Oakeshott remarks, 'The book called the *Politics* is a work in which Aristotle is reflecting upon the experience of the ancient Greeks, and particularly upon what they regarded as their greatest achievement, *polis*-life.'[11] Likewise, Collingwood interprets past political thinkers by taking their doctrines to constitute responses to questions arising out of and about their political contexts. In *An Autobiography* he criticizes contemporary Oxford philosophers for misinterpreting past philosophers as furnishing answers to current questions, rather than as responding to questions that arose from their historical situation. Collingwood devised a logic of question and answer to focus upon what past historical actors were doing in thinking and acting in their past situations. For Collingwood, situations or contexts provide the settings in which past thinkers develop their thinking. Hence the history of political thought, for Collingwood, involves the interpretation of past forms of thinking, which were engaged in interpreting and attending to past political situations.[12]

The affinities between Collingwood and Oakeshott and their reciprocal respect for one another are acknowledged in Collingwood's discussion of Oakeshott in *The Idea of History* and in Oakeshott's review of Collingwood's posthumous *The Idea of History*. Oakeshott commends Collingwood's appreciation of the development of historical studies and his recognition of the autonomy of history as an academic discipline.[13] He respects how Collingwood approaches his analysis of the nature of historical understanding by reflecting upon the practice of historians rather than by imposing upon the study of history an external conception of its identity. In his review of *The Idea of History*, however, Oakeshott remarks critically on what he takes to be Collingwood's late dissolution of philosophy into history.[14] The question of Collingwood's understanding of the relations between history and philosophy in his later works is controversial, and in this remark Oakeshott reflects the opinion of Collingwood's literary editor, Knox.[15] In fact, Collingwood

---

[11] M. Oakeshott, *Lectures in the History of Political Thought* (Exeter, Imprint Academic, 2006), p. 116.

[12] For an account of the logic of question and answer, see R.G. Collingwood, *An Autobiography*, pp. 53–76.

[13] M. Oakeshott, Review of R.G. Collingwood, *The Idea of History* (1947), in M. Oakeshott, *Selected Writings*, vol. 3, *The Concept of Philosophical Jurisprudence* (Exeter, Imprint Academic, 2007).

[14] Ibid., p. 199.

[15] See T.M. Knox, 'Editor's Preface', *The Idea of History* (Oxford, Clarendon Press, 1946), p. xxv.

maintains the separate character of the two disciplines throughout his career, observing, for instance, in his late text *An Autobiography* that philosophy determines the epistemological and metaphysical status of historical understanding.[16] In reflecting on the course of his intellectual career Collingwood declares in *An Autobiography* that he has been motivated by trying to achieve a rapprochement between the two disciplines.[17] This aim does not entail the dissolution of philosophy into history, but on the face of things, it distinguishes his approach to the relations between history and philosophy from that of Oakeshott, who maintains the discrete character of modes of experience.[18] Indeed, this difference between them is intimated in Collingwood's criticism of Oakeshott's conception of history, for Collingwood maintains that Oakeshott, in his account of history in *Experience and Its Modes*, fails to show that history is necessary in experience.[19] Collingwood maintains that history and historical understanding bear upon disciplines such as philosophy and art, in that the characters of philosophy and art change over time and hence require to be understood historically. In his late *An Essay on Metaphysics* Collingwood observes how metaphysics reflects upon and colligates the absolute presuppositions of historical epochs, and in *The Principles of Art* he considers art as an expressive activity and observes how art in the twentieth century was degenerating into an entertainment.[20] Similarly, in his last publication, *The New Leviathan*, he outlines an ideal liberal polity and a related conception of Western civilization by reviewing and reflecting upon the principles that are exhibited in the historical development of mind, politics, and Western civilization.

Apparently, Collingwood's recognition of reciprocal ties between philosophy and history and his historically oriented analyses of art, metaphysics, and politics differ from Oakeshott's insulation of disciplines from one another. Yet Collingwood maintains the autonomy of history from philosophy and other disciplines even if he emphasizes the role of history in tracing the development of theoretical disciplines. Moreover, while Oakeshott separates history from other disciplines, he recognizes that philosophical speculation is undertaken in specific historical contexts and acknowledges the historical development of philosophy. The upshot is that there are clear affinities between Oakeshott and

---

[16] See R.G. Collingwood, *An Autobiography*, p. 77; for an expanded discussion of the relations between philosophy and history in Collingwood's late works see also G. Browning, *Rethinking R.G. Collingwood—Philosophy, Politics and the Unity of Theory and Practice* (Basingstoke, Palgrave Macmillan, 2004), pp. 27–51.

[17] R.G. Collingwood, *An Autobiography*, p. 77.

[18] See M. Oakeshott, 'The Activity of Being an Historian', p. 37; see also M. Oakeshott, *On History and Other Essays*, pp. 1–45.

[19] R.G. Collingwood, *The Idea of History*, p. 159.

[20] R.G. Collingwood, *An Essay on Metaphysics*, pp. 29–32; R.G. Collingwood, *The Principles of Art* (Oxford, Clarendon Press, 1938).

Collingwood. These affinities are evident in their approaches to the history of political thought. They both take the history of political thought to consist in historical traditions of inquiry, which are to be understood by locating theoretical contributions to these traditions in determinate historical contexts. They also imagine their own theories of political association as arising out of traditions of political thought and reflection upon historical conditions. Their approach to the study of the history of political thought highlights two features. On the one hand, they recognize the autonomy and procedures of historical understanding. Hence, Oakeshott and Collingwood attend to the historical contexts in which past theories are situated. On the other hand, Oakeshott and Collingwood in *On Human Conduct* and *The New Leviathan* compose substantive theories of politics, which articulate the conditions of an ideal political association. In so doing they combine philosophy and history in ways that are not specified clearly. They invoke historical traditions of inquiry and historical political developments in framing their own theories of the state while warning against importing present notions into historical accounts of the past. The past is distinct from the present but in their own theorizing they recognize continuities between past and present in intellectual traditions and in their own debts to past thinkers.

COLLINGWOOD

Collingwood was a philosopher as well as a professional historian. As a practising archaeologist and historian he knew history from the inside, as it were, as well as possessing the philosophical turn of mind to identify and reflect upon its underlying principles. In *An Autobiography* he reviews his intellectual career and maintains, 'My life's work hitherto, as seen from my fiftieth year has been in the main an attempt to bring about a *rapprochement* between philosophy and history.'[21] Just what is meant by a rapprochement between philosophy and history is questionable and Collingwood identifies the relationship between the two in different ways at different points in his career. However it is specified that one of its implications is that the study of political thought should invoke an historical perspective. He makes this clear in *An Autobiography*. There, Collingwood reports on his isolation from other philosophers at Oxford due to his historical approach to the subject. This approach was reflected in his commitment to a logic that correlates doctrines to the actual historical questions to which they are addressed. This logic of question and answer was directed against the affiliation of his colleagues to

[21] R.G. Collingwood, *An Autobiography*, p. 77.

propositional logic and epistemological realism. Propositional logic imagines that propositions can be separated from supporting contexts of meaning and realism stands for a separation of knowledge from the process of acquiring it.[22] Collingwood took refuge from the prevailing philosophical orthodoxies by teaching the history of philosophy, and in so doing attending to the actual questions that are asked by past philosophers and to the particular answers that they gave to these questions. This practice differed markedly from that of contemporary realists. Realists, according to Collingwood, either assumed that the history of philosophy represented a series of answers to the same universal questions, for which there were 'right' answers, or merely took the history of philosophy to be the antiquarian exercise of recording what doctrines were composed at certain points in time.[23] Collingwood asked himself the following questions while teaching the history of philosophy. 'Was it really true, I asked myself, that the problems of philosophy were, even in the loosest sense of that word, eternal? Was it really true that different philosophies were different attempts to answer the same questions?' In answering this latter question, Collingwood concludes, 'I soon discovered that it was not true; it was merely a vulgar error, consequent on a kind of historical myopia which, deceived by superficial resemblances, failed to detect profound differences.'[24]

In delivering a critique of realism Collingwood reveals that his sense of what was at issue between himself and the realists and confirmation of his own standpoint were highlighted by his consideration of the history of political thought. He recalls reflecting on the political thought of Plato and Hobbes. He asked himself the question of whether or not the evident differences between their political theories amounted to contrasting theories of the same thing, namely the state. In his *An Autobiography* he asks a question, which is fundamental to an understanding of the issues to be faced in the history of political thought. He poses the question, 'Can you say that the *Republic* gives one account of "the nature of the state" and the *Leviathan* another?'[25] He reflects that the realists would maintain that the question is answered easily. Plato and Hobbes provide different accounts of the state but they are united in addressing a common subject matter, namely the state. Collingwood, however, takes this answer to be mistaken. Plato reflects upon the Ancient Greek polis and Hobbes theorizes the character of the absolutist state of the seventeenth century. While realists take Plato and Hobbes to be engaged in a common enterprise in theorizing about a universal object, Collingwood, who is aware of the historical differences between the Ancient polis and the modern state, argues that it is misleading to imagine Plato and Hobbes as focusing upon a common object. He concludes that Plato and Hobbes, as political theorists, are engaged in theorizing about an object that is in some sense the same and in

---

[22] Ibid., pp. 33–42.   [23] Ibid., p. 60.   [24] Ibid., pp. 60–1.   [25] Ibid., p. 61.

some sense different. While a realist would imagine the sameness to be their attention to a universal, 'the state', which is conceived differently by Hobbes and Plato, Collingwood imagines that the unity of their activities consists in the continuity of history, whereby they are theorizing about the continuously developing subject of politics. The differences between them are constituted by their focus on different elements of an historical process, namely the Ancient polis and the modern state. Collingwood observes, 'Pursuing this line of inquiry, I soon realized that the history of political theory is not the history of different answers given to one and the same question, but the history of a problem more or less constantly changing, whose solution was changing with it.'[26] Collingwood maintains that the study of political thought is an historical enterprise, in that different theorists at different points in history will furnish different answers to questions about changing conditions of political society. Unlike Plamenatz, but like Hegel and Marx, he recognizes that changes in political conditions shape the ways in which political thought is undertaken. Unlike Hegel and Marx, however, he conceives of the processes of history to be insusceptible to a general theoretical perspective, which can assign to particular political theories determinate roles in promoting a discernible directionality of history. Collingwood's posthumously published *The Principles of History* highlights how he imagines history to be a contingent process, and in identifying it to be a process without a supervening goal, he distinguishes his conception of history sharply from the teleological theories of Hegel and Marx.[27]

In the conception of political thought that is outlined in his *Autobiography* Collingwood emphasizes how past and present are distinct and yet connected. His philosophy of history explains the nature of historical understanding by analysing how past and present are related by the historian's construction of historical knowledge.[28] In the essay, 'History as Re-enactment of Past Experience' (1936), which was published by the editor Knox as one of the metaphysical epilegomena to *The Idea of History*, Collingwood sets out his distinctive doctrine of historical understanding as consisting in the re-enactment of past thinking.[29] Collingwood maintains that historical understanding, in contrast to scientific explanation of natural phenomena, which establishes laws recording the regularities in their movements, concentrates instead on what he terms the inside of actions, the thought processes that are expressed in human activities. Historical understanding consists in the interpretation of past thought and action by rethinking what agents aimed to do and to think in past situations in the light of the critical evaluation of the available evidence.

---

[26] Ibid., p. 61.
[27] See R.G. Collingwood, *The Principles of History and Other Writings in Philosophy of History* (Oxford, Oxford University Press, 1999).
[28] See R.G. Collingwood, *The Idea of History*, pp. 205–82.
[29] R.G. Collingwood, *The Idea of History*, pp. 282–302.

As Dray maintains, Collingwood takes historical understanding to represent a form of rational explanation, in which the rationality of past action is explained by the historian's re-enactment of the thinking involved in the conduct of past agents.[30] This character of historical explanation assumes that there is continuity and discontinuity between past and present. Relics of past events are available in the present, and can be scrutinized by the historian to serve as evidence for past events. It is the historian's interpretation of present phenomena that reconstitutes the past and so realizes continuity between past and present. Collingwood maintains that the notion of historical truth assumes that the same thought can be rethought on different occasions, though there is difference as well as sameness involved in its rethinking, in that the contextual circumstances of the present ensure that a recovered past thought forms part of a different repertoire of thoughts that are maintained by the historian.[31]

In 'History As Re-Enactment of Past Experience', which is published as an epilegomenon in *The Idea of History*, Collingwood asks the question if, in rethinking a thought of Plato's, the historian's thinking is identical to Plato's. He concludes that it is both identical and different, remarking, 'What is required if I am to know Plato's philosophy is both to re-think it in my own mind and to think other things in the light of which I can judge it.'[32] Collingwood's recognition of the differences and connections between past and present allows for past theories to be understood in terms of how they are framed historically as answers to the questions of past thinkers and for their evaluation in the light of subsequent knowledge and questions. For Collingwood, history is not a process where progress can be established by subordinating past thought and action to the requirements of a present perspective.[33] But he does allow for progress by the prospect of a political thinker superseding a preceding thinker by rethinking the doctrines of a previous political thinker in the light of a subsequent context. He remarks, 'Philosophy progresses in so far as one stage of its development solves the problems which defeated it in the last, without losing its hold on the solutions already achieved.'[34] Collingwood's posthumously published *The Idea of Nature* reviews cosmological ideas historically, showing how successive ideas on nature reflect changing cultural and intellectual assumptions. He also shows, however, how past ideas are assimilated successively by succeeding thinkers, who thereby make progress in cosmological thinking.[35] In a series of

---

[30] See W. Dray, 'R.G. Collingwood and the Understanding of Actions in History', in W. Dray, *Perspectives on History* (London and Boston, Routledge and Kegan Paul, 1980), pp. 9–26.

[31] R.G. Collingwood, *An Autobiography*, p. 77.   [32] Ibid., p. 301.

[33] See R.G. Collingwood, 'Progress As Created by Historical Thinking', in R.G. Collingwood, *The Idea of History*, pp. 321–34.

[34] Ibid., p. 332.

[35] R.G. Collingwood, *The Idea of Nature* (Oxford, Clarendon Press, 1945), pp. 174–7.

unpublished notes on cosmology, Collingwood worked out his own first-order cosmology, which built upon preceding ideas, notably those of Hegel, in developing a metaphysical conception of nature.[36]

Collingwood's attitude to past ideas is not univocal. He respects the autonomy of historical understanding and insists upon the distinction of the past from the present, which demands an appreciation of the differences between past contexts and questions from those of the present. At the same time he views an engagement with the past to involve a critical assessment of its assumptions. Historical continuities link past ideas to present modes of thinking, as the present emerges out of past activities. Collingwood's final publication, *The New Leviathan*, reveals how he invokes past ideas in developing a political philosophy, which sets out the order of an ideal liberal polity and a conception of liberal civilization.[37] Central to Collingwood's elaboration of the conditions of an ideal formulation of European civilization is his sense of it as representing an historical achievement. Likewise he imagines the component aspects of a liberal polity and civilization, namely mind, morality, political association, and civilization along with barbarous reactions against civilization to be historical. His analysis is conceived expressly as an historical undertaking.[38] Liberal civilization, however, is not construed as a necessary teleological goal of the historical process and the force of barbarism's contemporary challenge to civilization in the form of fascism emphasizes its historical vulnerability.[39] The rationale of Collingwood's analysis is to make sense of the principles of a liberal civilization, so as to establish their coherence, and in so doing reinforce commitment to them at a parlous historical moment. The danger to civilization is acute in that Collingwood diagnoses all its component parts, including metaphysics and art to be jeopardized by a tendency to misrecognize its principles. Metaphysics is vital in revealing the underlying presuppositions of a civilization just as art is integral to the capacity to express emotion, and the prevalent tendency to abandon metaphysics and to substitute amusement or propaganda for art undermines intellectual and emotional capabilities.[40]

Collingwood shows how all aspects of civilization have developed historically and he traces the emergence and evolution of practical forms of social life, such as the family and legal and political institutions. In adverting to this historical development he observes how the role of women in the family and in the wider web of social and economic life has changed, so enabling women to participate as equals in a liberal society. His analysis of mind includes a

---

[36] R.G. Collingwood, 'Notes Towards a Metaphysic', Collingwood Manuscripts, Bodleian Library, Dep. 18.

[37] R.G. Collingwood, *The New Leviathan* (Oxford, Clarendon Press, 1992), pp. 212–342.

[38] Ibid., p. 61.   [39] Ibid., pp. 375–91.

[40] See R.G. Collingwood, *An Essay on Metaphysics*, pp. 49–80 and R.G. Collingwood, *The Principles of Art*, pp. 94–104.

dialectical appraisal of moral thinking, which examines the coherence and rationality of various moral forms, such as utility and strict adherence to moral rules. He concludes that the most coherent form of morality requires a commitment to attend to the particularities of unique situations and to apply rules appropriately in those contexts. He sees this form of morality as being underpinned by the development of historical studies, which focus on the rationality of unique actions.[41] Collingwood also explores the theories of a number of past political thinkers, who contribute to the historic identity of liberal civilization by framing theories that either promote liberalism or undermine its credentials. Collingwood disparages the tradition of German political theory, arguing that Kant, Hegel, Marx, and Nietzsche, in responding to an illiberal German political context, fail to recognize and support the political conditions of freedom. In contrast he appreciates theorists of classical politics, namely, the social contract theorists, Hobbes, Locke, and Rousseau. He admires how these social contract theorists emphasize the constructive activities of individuals in addressing and overcoming perceived problems in social interaction. He urges, 'the great merit of the classical politics is that it knows life to be dynamic or dialectical.'[42] Collingwood's interpretation of social contract theory is interesting even if it is conducted at some distance from the classic texts of Hobbes, Locke, and Rousseau. He considers the notion of a social contract to be metaphorical in representing political activity to be constructive and deliberative. He takes it to convey how naturalistic behaviour is transformed by political construction to allow for amenable political conditions conducive to free and rational conduct.

Collingwood's praise of English social contract theorists and his critique of German political theory is puzzling in that in his unpublished writings on moral life he critiques social contract theory due to its limited account of free human agency, and takes the notion of freedom that is worked out by Kant and his successors (notably Hegel) to be the touchstone of a specifically modern and fulfilling sense of human identity.[43] The puzzle is most likely to be explained by the contemporary context of the Second World War. Collingwood imagined *The New Leviathan* to serve as a support for the English war effort and in this context, valuing English liberal philosophy over what is denigrated as German illiberal philosophy makes some sense even if it is at odds with much of what he wrote on other occasions and is unimpressive historically and philosophically as an interpretation of traditions of thought. In subsequent chapters, Collingwood's reading of Hobbes and Hegel will be examined more closely, and the question of interpretation will be seen to be complicated by the way in which an historian of political thought, such as

---

[41] R.G. Collingwood, *The New Leviathan*, pp. 119–24.   [42] Ibid., p. 259.
[43] See R.G. Collingwood, 'Lectures on Moral Philosophy: 1929,' Collingwood Manuscripts, Bodleian Library, Dep. 10.

Collingwood, might approach a tradition of political thought in ways that are overdetermined. This in turn raises doubts over whether an act of thought is ever determined by a single reason so that it can be rethought by focusing upon a determinate intention. If Collingwood's *The New Leviathan* raises questions over its interpretation of particular theorists, its overarching theme of providing a convincing account of liberal politics and civilization in the light of its historical development demonstrates how Collingwood is prepared to combine present-day theorizing with historical analysis of past political theorizing. This project shows how Collingwood's conception of history allows for a combination of philosophy and history, by tracing continuities and discontinuities and yet this rapprochement between philosophy and history is not explored in detail by Collingwood. The interplay between past and present at work in *The New Leviathan* is inspired by Collingwood's recognition that theorizing about politics demands an appreciation of the historical development of politics just as analysis of the past depends upon interests that are generated by subsequent developments. However, the extent to which present-day theory and historical understanding of past phenomena may be seen as independent of one another is underexplored.

OAKESHOTT

Like Collingwood, Oakeshott was a philosopher and an historian, who reflected philosophically upon the nature of experience and was a distinguished historian of political thought. His expertise in the history of political thought is exemplified in the lecture series in the history of political thought that he gave at the London School of Economics and Political Science in the 1960s. These lectures, which have now been published posthumously under the title, *Lectures in the History of Political Thought*, differ from preceding lecture series that were devoted to specific texts and theorists in that they highlight the contexts in which historic texts of political theory are situated. They are expressly historical in character and set out a rationale for explaining political thought historically. They disclose Oakeshott's understanding of the contextual inspiration for political thought in that he relates historic theories of politics to the concrete traditions and forms of political experience of distinct types of political regime. Hence Oakeshott outlines the political experience of the Ancient Greeks and Romans, the nature of medieval government, and the character of a modern European state to serve as contextual references for the political thought of Ancient, medieval, and modern theorists. The lectures reflect Oakeshott's understanding of the dependence of political thought upon the historical conditions of political practice and his approach to the history of political thought relates theory to concrete forms of political experience.[44] At the outset of the lectures, Oakeshott remarks, 'History I take to be a mode of thought in which events, human actions, beliefs, manners of thinking are considered in relation to the conditions, or the circumstantial contexts in which they appeared.'[45] He distinguishes such an approach from a scientific one, which would invoke general laws of conduct to provide a causal understanding of past phenomena. Oakeshott's historical approach is designed to render past events, beliefs, and actions more intelligible by relating them to similar kinds of things rather than to record the regularities with which they occur. The thought is that considering ideas in the wider context of a political culture enhances understanding without either explaining their necessity or justifying them in a general or normative sense.[46]

In his *Lectures in the History of Political Thought* Oakeshott is also at pains to highlight how his enterprise disavows a teleological conception of the progress or regress of political thought over time. He emphasizes the distinctness of particular forms of past thinking to the extent that he denies the efficacy of a continuous history of political thought. He observes, 'But although this is to be an historical study, I want to avoid the appearance of putting before you anything like a continuous history of European political thought.'[47] In relating past political thought to the actual public culture of past political situations Oakeshott follows the lead of Hegel, whom he admires, but he is against the teleology of Hegel that maintains a developmental continuity in the history of political thought. Oakeshott opposes the idea of a continuous history of political thought because he attends to the distinctiveness of past forms of political thinking, which derive from past circumstances that are different from the present. Oakeshott argues against assuming the history of political thought to represent a series of ideas that are retrojected onto the past without reference to their local sources of inspiration. Rather, he relates political ideas to the political cultures within which past political thinkers were situated.[48]

To understand Greek political thought, Oakeshott sets out the political experience of the Greeks, analysing the conditions of their political experience, and more specifically their political vocabulary and images of the world. He then reviews the political thought of Plato and Aristotle by relating their thought to the political culture of Ancient Greece, taking them as sifting and criticizing the current general beliefs about politics so as to render them coherent.[49] Similarly, Oakeshott imagines modern thinkers to be operating within the context of the emergence of the modern state. He recognizes

---

[44] M. Oakeshott, *Lectures in the History of Political Thought*, eds. T. Nardin and L. O'Sullivan (Exeter, Imprint Academic, 2006).
[45] Ibid., p. 31.   [46] Ibid.   [47] Ibid., p. 32.
[48] Ibid., p. 42.   [49] Ibid., p. 73.

characteristics of the modern European state such as its composition of legally free human beings, its univocal centralized and sovereign authority, and its interaction with other similar states as informing the theories of modern political thinkers. In characterizing forms of modern political thinking, he identifies an interpretation of the state, which, in relying upon organic and nationalistic formulas, suffers from an incapacity to register the constructed and free nature of the association of individuals in a modern state. In contrast, he recognizes how Calvin, Hobbes, Locke, Rousseau, and Mill, amongst others, have provided interpretations of the state as an association of individuals, who associate together freely to achieve purposes of various kinds.[50]

Oakeshott's *Lectures in the History of Political Thought* reflects his view of history as a constructive activity, which imagines the past to be different from the present, and is separate from philosophy, science, or the practical needs of the present. In *Experience and Its Modes* (1933) Oakeshott argues for the insulation of modes of experience from one another. Modes of experience, save philosophy, namely history, science, and practice arrest experience in organizing it from a particular and limited perspective, while philosophy thinks through the conditions of experience completely, observing the limits of the other modes. Hence history is different from scientific or practical experience and removed from philosophy. It is neither linked to present philosophizing nor to current practical matters. In 'The Voice of Poetry in the Conversation of Mankind', an essay in *Rationalism in Politics*, Oakeshott reformulates the relations between the modes of experience, imagining that they relate to one another conversationally rather than independently or dependently. The character of the imagined conversation is somewhat indeterminate, though it is conceived as a conversation in which no voice is dominant.[51] In 'The Activity of Being and Historian', another essay in *Rationalism in Politics*, Oakeshott observes a sharp divide between the study of history and other ways of imagining the past. Oakeshott insists that the past of the historian is different from the practical, scientific, and aesthetic attitudes to the past. A practical attitude to the past looks to the past to resolve issues in the present and hence assimilates the past to present concerns. The historian in contrast studies the past for its own sake and respects its distinctness from present concerns.[52] Oakeshott is categorical in his recognition of the historian's appreciation of the separation of past from present interests. Hence

---

[50] Ibid., pp. 418–19.

[51] See M. Oakeshott, 'The Voice of Poetry in the Conversation of Mankind', in M. Oakeshott, *Rationalism in Politics and Other Essays* (London and New York, Methuen & Co, 1962). In his posthumously published *Notebooks* Oakeshott sketches plans for producing a text that rehearses a conversation between a number of interlocutors representing differing styles and activities in life. See M. Oakeshott, *Notebooks: 1922–86*, ed. L. O'Sullivan (Exeter, Imprint Academic, 2014), pp. 307–70.

[52] M. Oakeshott, 'The Activity of Being An Historian', pp. 168–75.

Oakeshott is insistent that philosophy should not determine the direction of historical inquiry. Philosophy can review the postulates of historical understanding, but it is not to impose a pattern upon its narratives of the past, just as the demands of practical political life are not to dictate to the historian an account of the past, which is not justified evidentially.

Notwithstanding Oakeshott's conception of the separation between distinct ways of imagining experience, Oakeshott allows for connections between philosophy, political practice, and history, even if the three worlds are specified in distinctive ways. In his celebrated 'Introduction to *Leviathan*' (1946), Oakeshott presents a broad characterization of the history of political philosophy by identifying it in terms of three traditions. The three traditions are the rational natural tradition, the tradition of will and artifice, and that of rational will.[53] What Oakeshott has to say on this score is elliptical and yet suggestive for it outlines the links between philosophy, politics, and history. His identification of traditions in political philosophy presumes philosophical expertise in that political philosophy is conceived as a distinct and highly abstract form of reflection on politics.[54] This philosophical recognition of the character of philosophical argument accords with his remark in his *Lectures in the History of Political Thought* whereby he maintains that a presupposition of the inquiry is an identification of styles of political thought that involves distinguishing explanatory from practical forms of thinking.[55] In the 'Introduction to *Leviathan*' Oakeshott expands upon the nature of the three designated traditions of political philosophy by highlighting what he takes to be their textual masterpieces. Plato's *Republic* is held to be the masterpiece of the rational natural tradition. Hobbes's *Leviathan* is representative of the tradition of will and artifice and Hegel's *Philosophy of Right* is exemplary in the tradition of rational will. Oakeshott's identification of traditions in political philosophy unites distinct political philosophies historically by observing their adherence to common if developing conceptual standpoints. Hence, Oakeshott sees history as bearing upon philosophy and shows how the disciplines of history and philosophy are connected with one another. Likewise, he imagines that each of these traditions of political philosophy is aligned to practice in that each develops in relation to practical historical circumstances. The focus upon will in the will and artifice and rational will traditions reflects a modern emphasis upon freedom and individuality which is distinct from Plato's assumptions about the natural order of things. This alignment of philosophy with historical conditions of practice is not to say that Oakeshott either imagines that philosophy is to prescribe what is to be done in practical life, or that philosophical ideas can be reduced to practical interests. Its alignment

[53] M. Oakeshott, 'Introduction to *Leviathan*', in M. Oakeshott, *Hobbes on Civil Association* (Oxford, Basil Blackwell, 1975), p. 3.
[54] Ibid.   [55] M. Oakeshott, *Lectures in the History of Political Thought*, pp. 42–3.

with practice enables its understanding of practice but does not furnish it with a recipe for political action. Oakeshott's conception of the ways in which modes of experience are related is finely balanced. On the one hand, he insists upon their independence throughout his career and yet the metaphor of a conversation between experiential activities allows for a relationship between them. In an article 'Practical Life and the Critique of Rationalism', Smith rightly remarks upon Oakeshott's determination to isolate philosophy from practical considerations. He remarks, 'The central thrust of *Experience and Its Modes* is to protect philosophy and the other modes of experience from the blandishments of praxis. "A philosophy of life," Oakeshott avers, "is a meaningless contradiction." Life—practical experience—and philosophy—the quest for intellectual coherence—remain fundamentally inimical to one another.'[56] Certainly, for Oakeshott, political philosophy is not an ideology aiming to impact upon practice. In a posthumously published essay, 'Political Philosophy' Oakeshott observes, '[W]e must expect from political philosophy no practical conclusions whatsoever.'[57] Yet Oakeshott aligns political philosophy to particular historical contexts and understands political philosophy as arising out of practical experience and as developing historically. His own substantive political philosophy, which is set out in *On Human Conduct* is self-consciously aligned to the development of the modern state and to a particular tradition of political philosophy.

In *On Human Conduct*, a classic work of substantive political thought, Oakeshott employs a new vocabulary to specify the conditionality of political association, which is derived from reflection upon the development of the modern European state.[58] The work is divided into three inter-related sections: (i) On the Theoretical Understanding of Human Conduct; (ii) On the Civil Condition; and (iii) On the Character of the Modern European State. The opening section undertakes a theoretical exploration of the character of human conduct by analysing its component conditions of agency and social practice. Oakeshott distinguishes the character of a practice from that of a process. A practice is constituted by the contingent beliefs of its human participating agents, while processes are composed of natural phenomena, which are to be understood by scientific hypotheses explaining the generic recurrence of patterns amidst change. Insofar as the three essays are mutually instructive, the relationship between social practices and their constituent reflective agents is held to demonstrate how individuals are equipped to participate in a scheme of social and political cooperation, which Oakeshott

---

[56] S. Smith, 'Practical Life and the Critique of Rationalism', in E. Podoksik (ed.), *The Cambridge Companion to Oakeshott* (Cambridge, Cambridge University Press, 2012), pp. 131–52.

[57] M. Oakeshott, 'Political Philosophy', in M. Oakeshott, *Religion, Politics and the Moral Life*, ed. T. Fuller (New Haven and London, Yale University Press, 1993), p. 153.

[58] M. Oakeshott, *On Human Conduct* (Oxford, Oxford University Press, 1975), pp. 185–326.

designates as civil association. Civil association, for Oakeshott, represents an ideal mode of political association, in which individuals are imagined as agreeing to procedural rules of behaviour, which regulate but do not determine the conduct of individuals. These rules do not prescribe particular forms of conduct because they depend upon individual interpretation of their application to particular circumstances. The rules shape but do not direct their actions, and hence allow for individuality and freedom. Oakeshott's analysis of the postulates of the human condition and his related construction of a paradigmatic form of civil association is followed by the third essay that reviews the historical formation of the modern European state, which exhibits intimations of the form of civil conduct that is theorized in the preceding section, under the title, 'On Civil Association'. Hence the elaboration of his own political thought is shown to develop out of his historical understanding of the development of European politics.

In tracing the history of the modern European state, Oakeshott distinguishes between two historic forms of political association, a *societas* and a *universitas*. A *societas* is a form of political association, which constitutes what Oakeshott designates the civil condition. In a *societas* individuals recognize the authority of a set of general laws, which provide a framework of order that allows them to pursue their own independently formulated activities. It is a free association of individuals, who are united by their common commitment to establish a cooperative social framework that allows individuals to undertake their several self-chosen purposes and activities. A *universitas*, on the other hand, is committed to achieving a common collective goal. Its members are unified by their resolve to achieve a common purpose. Oakeshott takes both forms of society to be discernible in modern European history, just as Collingwood recognizes that European history incorporates the development of a liberal society along with a barbarian revolt against it. For Collingwood, the individual freedom of a liberal civilization is threatened by the barbarism of fascism, while for Oakeshott, prospects for the development of civil freedom are compromised by the contemporary strength of collectivism. In his account of the modern European state, Oakeshott refers to several political theorists, who have framed historic theories of a political association, which favour one or other of his designated paradigmatic models of political association. His commentaries are economical but incisive. For instance, he identifies Machiavelli tellingly as a theorist of a form of *societas*. Likewise, Hobbes is perceived to be theorist of a *societas*, while Bentham is the subject of a masterly footnote that identifies him to be an energetic advocate of a *universitas*.[59] His brief but compelling analysis of Hegel as a theorist of a *societas* interprets Hegel to be a political theorist, who, in framing an authoritative political philosophy,

---

[59] Ibid., p. 169.

attends carefully to the experience of agents, social practices, and states in the modern world.[60]

Oakeshott's *On Human Conduct* is an intricate analysis of the nature of human conduct, the character of an ideal civil association, and the development of the modern European state. The component elements of analysis go together in that human beings are shown to be reflective and free agents, whose possibilities for undertaking self-chosen individual actions are enhanced by their subscription to a civil association, which in turn is shown to be intimated in historical development. While Oakeshott imagines historical understanding to be autonomous, his philosophical exploration of the conditions of political association is predicated upon an historical reading of modern European history. Oakeshott's carefully contrived philosophical account of a state that allows for individuality and freedom and his antipathy towards collectivism shape and in turn reflect his reading of European political history. His substantive political thought is constructed in the light of preceding historical explorations of the civil condition, and his political philosophy reflects his reading of the political experience of modern Europe and the political theorizing of philosophical predecessors, notably that of Hobbes and Hegel, which in turn reflected upon the history of the modern state.

CONCLUSION

Oakeshott and Collingwood are practising philosophers and historians, who bring their expertise to bear upon the study of the history of political thought. They are united by their understanding of history as an autonomous discipline, which operates in ways that are distinct from scientific and philosophical forms of explanation. They understand the activity of history to represent the collection and interpretation of evidence in the present to explain past situations and actions. They recognize how the historicity of the past distinguishes it from the present, and they are alert to the problems of importing present assumptions and purposes into the study of the past. Hence they take the history of political thought to constitute an enterprise, which identifies the particularities of past contexts. Notably, it recognizes different styles of past theorizing that relate to the different forms that have been assumed by past political associations. They take issue with the idea that past political theories should be interpreted as constituting so many ways of interpreting a common object of inquiry, namely the state. Forms of political association differ over

---

[60] Ibid., pp. 257–63.

time and the state is a shorthand formula, which obscures differences between the Ancient Greek polis, a medieval realm, and a modern European state.

In respecting the autonomy of historical understanding Oakeshott and Collingwood reject the standpoints of Hegel and Marx, who attribute a supervening directionality to history.[61] They are alike in repudiating large-scale theories of history, which assume that an overall teleological development may explain the component aspects of history, including its multiple forms of political thought. Oakeshott and Collingwood are aware of the practice of historians and appreciate how the principles of historical understanding are flouted by imposing a grand pattern on its development. The differences between Hegel and Plato, say, on political thought, are not to be subordinated to their supposed roles in promoting or retarding social and political progress. If Collingwood and Oakeshott attend to the discontinuities between past and present, they also perceive continuities in the history of political thought. They identify traditions of thinking about politics and they frame their own conceptions of politics in the light of historical social and political practice and in relation to preceding political philosophies. They see themselves as participants in liberal traditions of political philosophy, which presume the prior expression of liberal political practice. Their substantive theories of politics are also enlivened by their perceptions of dangers to liberal traditions from collectivism and fascism. Collingwood, in aiming to engineer a rapprochement between history and philosophy, is happy to combine history with philosophy in composing his own political philosophy, even if he was neither entirely clear nor consistent on the precise nature of the roles to be assigned to each discipline. In *An Essay on Metaphysics*, for example, he imagines that metaphysics is to represent the study of the series of absolute presuppositions that have been assumed in the course of history, while in some of his unpublished writings he allows a pronounced role for first-order philosophical speculation.[62] Oakeshott is insistent on the divisions between the varieties of experiential standpoints but still construes the history of political thought to involve connections between history, practice, and philosophy. In an article on Oakeshott and Dunn, 'Scepticism in Politics: A Dialogue Between Michael Oakeshott and John Dunn', Tseng recognizes that Oakeshott simultaneously perceives connections between history and philosophy while insisting upon their independence from one another. He remarks, 'Oakeshott surely agrees that to establish a philosophical theory of civil association, a historical examination of a modern European state is helpful, but he simultaneously contends

---

[61] See R.G. Collingwood, *The Idea of History*, pp. 122–6.

[62] For an extended discussion of the different ways in which Collingwood imagines metaphysics, philosophy, and history in Collingwood's published and unpublished works, see G. Browning, *Rethinking R.G. Collingwood—Philosophy, Politics and the Unity of Theory and Practice*, pp. 1–27.

that <u>political philosophy can only be communicated but never united</u>, if we want to avoid the dreadful mistake of *ignoratio elenchi*.'[63] Tseng identifies the connections to be communicative but while Oakeshott might agree that the relations are conversational, it seems that these relations between the disciplines structure the conversation rather than allowing for the independence of the interlocutors.

The work of Collingwood and Oakeshott in the history of political thought has been influential. They have exerted an impact upon the Cambridge School and contextualist approaches more generally. Skinner acknowledges the influence of Collingwood and Pocock recognizes that of Oakeshott.[64] Oakeshott and Collingwood's respect for the autonomy of historical understanding lends itself to a contextual historical approach to the study of the history of political thought. Oakeshott's identification of past traditions of political philosophy highlights the role of the historian in recognizing the conceptual languages of past thinkers in ways that anticipate Pocock's analyses of past languages of political theory. Collingwood's logic of question and answer, whereby thinkers, in framing theories of politics are to be understood as responding to particular historic questions reflecting past contexts, inspires Skinner's focus upon what past thinkers intended to do by writing a particular text.[65] If Collingwood and Oakeshott recognize the significance of the application of an historical perspective to the study of past political thought that focuses upon historical contexts, they also allow for the reciprocity of past and present. Their own substantive theories of politics are developed by reflection upon the historical development of politics and the continuity of traditions of political thinking. They are both concerned to trace the history of political associations that allow for individual freedom and their work in political theory and in the history of political thought is influenced by their perception of threats to rational political order that are posed by fascism and collectivist ideologies. While Oakeshott and Collingwood are committed to a view of history that recognizes the distinctness of past political thought their practice of the history of political thought is far from unequivocal in that they connect past thought to present theoretical and practical concerns. They are influential theorists of the history of political thought, who register the ambiguities to which the

---

[63] R. Tseng, 'Scepticism in Politics: A Dialogue Between Michael Oakeshott and John Dunn', *History of Political Thought*, vol. XXX1V, no. 1. Spring 2013, p. 160.

[64] See Q. Skinner, 'The Rise of, Challenge to and Prospects for a Collingwoodian Approach to the History of Political Thought', in D. Castiglione and I. Hampsher-Monk (eds), *The History of Political Thought in National Context* (Cambridge, Cambridge University Press, 2001), pp. 175–8; see also J.G.A. Pocock, 'Time, Institutions and Action: An Essay on Traditions and Their Understanding', in J.G.A. Pocock, *Political Thought and History—Essays on Theory and Method* (Cambridge, Cambridge University Press, 2009), pp. 187–216.

[65] Q. Skinner, 'The Rise of, Challenge to and Prospects for a Collingwoodian Approach to the History of Political Thought', pp. 176–7.

subject is liable. They are informed and thoughtful guides to past political thought. Yet it is by no means clear that Collingwood's formula for understanding the past as rethinking past thought allows for the ambiguities of his own thinking. Likewise Oakeshott's concern to insulate the historical past from contaminating practical and philosophical influences is complicated by his own tendency to interweave philosophy, history, and political practice. Perhaps in undertaking the history of political thought, we should be prepared to admit the multiplicity of meaning that past thinkers entertain as well as allowing for a plurality of ways of interpreting their thought.

4

Quentin Skinner, the Cambridge School, and Contextualism

INTRODUCTION

The question of how are we to conduct the history of political thought is now asked in large part due to the activities of what has become known as the Cambridge School. In the English-speaking world, the challenge to orthodoxies in the study of the history of political thought, and notably to the practice of reading texts without considering their contexts, was posed in Cambridge. Quentin Skinner is a key figure in the ensuing critical interrogation of a practice which had lined up great political thinkers in a canon and then set out their doctrines without much ado. Cambridge scholars and affiliated adherents to contextualism insist upon the application of historical scholarship to the study of the history of political thought, so that past political ideas are not simply dusted down and presented for public inspection and current enlightenment. Rather, they are imagined to be the products of thinkers who aim to exert an impact upon issues and practices that arise out of their particular historical contexts.

In considering the history of the Cambridge School, Skinner acknowledges the role of Laslett, the Cambridge historian, whose scholarly re-reading of Locke altered perceptions of how Locke, and political thinkers more generally, might be interpreted. He also recognizes the work of John Pocock and John Dunn in making methodological and substantive contributions to a contextual conception of the history of political thought.[1] Subsequently students of Skinner, Dunn, and Pocock and members of the wider community of historians of political thought have contributed to the development of a style of interpretation that is associated with the Cambridge School.[2] In this chapter

---

[1] Q. Skinner, 'The Rise of and Challenge to and Prospects for a Collingwoodian Approach to the History of Political Thought', in D. Castiglione and I. Hampsher-Monk (eds), *The History of Political Thought in National Contexts* (Cambridge, Cambridge University Press, 2001), pp. 175–7.

[2] The impact of methodological reflections on political theory is covered in later chapters of this book. For a discussion of the students of Pocock and Skinner, see D. Boucher, *Texts in Context: Revisionist Methods for Studying the History of Ideas* (Dordrecht, D. Reidel, 1985).

the Cambridge School is analysed initially by reviewing the thoughts of Pocock and Dunn, and then Skinner's methodological essays are reviewed. Consonant with the Cambridge School's recognition of the historical character of ideas, the changing formulations of their ideas are noted. Skinner's article, 'Meaning and Understanding in the History of Ideas' (1969) is taken by Pocock to have served as a point of departure in the study of the history of political thought and to have offered a manifesto of a new approach by offering a polemical critique of standard works in the subject.[3] The sharpness of its polemical tone is subdued in a later revised formulation of this essay, but its cogent articulation of the claims of a contextualist, historical interpretation of texts remains compelling and continues to frame thinking on past political thought.[4] To show the broader reach of contextualism, Collini's approach to intellectual history is also reviewed. He shares with the Cambridge School an emphasis upon situating thinkers in past contexts and in avoiding anachronisms.

DUNN, POCOCK, AND SKINNER

Laslett revised conventional readings of Locke's political thought by applying historical scholarship to his texts. In attending to the circumstances in which the *Two Treatises of Government* was composed, he altered perceptions of what Locke was doing in writing the text. By researching the library and correspondence of Locke in the light of the wider political context, Laslett argued persuasively that much of the text was written some time before its date of publication. To alter the dating of the text is also to alter the specification of its context, and to modify the perception of the purposes for which it was written, thereby transforming appreciation of its political role.[5] Laslett's commitment to historical scholarship was embraced by Dunn and Pocock, who adopted what came to be known as a Cambridge style of undertaking the history of political thought. The debt to Laslett is acknowledged by Dunn in the Preface to his own highly historical reconstruction of Locke, *The Political Thought of John Locke*. In a footnote in his methodological essay, 'The Identity

---

[3] J.G.A. Pocock, 'Quentin Skinner: The History of Politics and the Politics of History', in J.G.A. Pocock, *Political Thought and History: Essays on Theory and Method* (Cambridge, Cambridge University Press, 2009), p. 128.

[4] See Q. Skinner, 'Meaning and Understanding in the History of Ideas', *History and Theory*, vol. 8, 1969; the original version of the article was reprinted in J. Tully (ed.), *Meaning and Context—Quentin Skinner and His Critics* (Cambridge, Polity Press, 1988), pp. 57–89. The revised version is a chapter in Skinner's retrospective essays, Q. Skinner, 'Meaning and Understanding in the History of Ideas', Q. Skinner, *Visions of Politics*, vol. 1, *Regarding Method* (Cambridge, Cambridge University Press, 2002).

[5] See the editorial introduction to J. Locke, ed. P. Laslett, *The Two Treatises of Government* (Cambridge, Cambridge University Press, 1963), pp. 3–16.

of the History of Ideas' (1968), Dunn thanks Laslett and Skinner for 'the several years of discussion on the subject'.[6] In this landmark article Dunn begins by stating bluntly the criticisms to which the practice of the history of political thought is liable on the part of both historians and philosophers: 'In short (the history of political thought) is characterised by a persistent tension between the threats of falsity in its history and incompetence in philosophy.'[7] On the one hand, historians are liable to critique how the history of political thought is conducted because of its reification of general terms such as rationalism and empiricism, which do not perform any reliable work in historical analysis. On the other hand, philosophers are justifiably suspicious of the mere elaboration of historical doctrines, which are not put to the philosophical test. In the light of these plausible critiques, Dunn acknowledges the temptation for the historian of political thought to concentrate on one or the other of its disciplinary concerns and to opt for either an historical or a philosophical line of inquiry. Dunn maintains this temptation is to be resisted. He urges, 'What I wish principally to argue in this paper is that the costs of such self-abnegation are much higher than is normally recognised; that the connections between an adequate philosophical account of the notions held by an individual in the past and an accurate historical account of these notions is an intimate one; that both historical specificity and philosophical delicacy are more likely to be attained if they are both pursued together, than if one is deserted for the other at an early stage of the investigation.'[8]

In arguing that a philosophical interpretation of a text has to go hand in hand with its historical reconstruction, Dunn concentrates upon clarifying the historical interpretation that is to be offered of past political thought. He warns against using the language of resemblance to unite different theorists and counsels against constructing categories to connect thinkers and ideas, which ignore the actual practice of thinkers doing things.[9] In emphasizing what past thinkers were doing in constructing doctrines, Dunn is at one with Pocock and Skinner. In a footnote to his argument that thinkers should be seen as doing things with words rather than setting out doctrines without motivating purposes, Dunn cites Austin in urging that the context in which authors have written is important for interpreting what they were trying to do and for establishing the truth criteria to which they were aiming to conform. He warns against a hasty concern to render past thinkers relevant to present contexts, which will inevitably distort an understanding of what they were aiming to do, even if interest in a past political philosophy might be inspired by present philosophical interests.[10] In subsequent revisionary reflection on the history of political thought, Dunn acknowledges the validity of Gadamer's insight into

---

[6] J. Dunn, 'The Identity of the History of Ideas,' *Philosophy*, vol. XL111, no. 164, April 1968, p. 104.

[7] Ibid., p. 85.   [8] Ibid., p. 86.   [9] Ibid., p. 87.   [10] Ibid., p. 98.

the inter-related character of past and present interests, which renders a sharp separation between past and present unacceptably realist.[11] In later methodological writings, Dunn continues to recognize the historicity of past texts and the priority of reading them historically to ascertain the contextually related purposes of their authors. Yet he also allows for the relevance of past ideas to present forms of political analysis. In a retrospective survey of the Cambridge School and the history of political theory, he acknowledges the ongoing value of the canon of Western political theory, while also identifying the priority of an historical understanding of the authorial purpose of a past text, because it allows a text to be read 'the right way up'.[12]

Like Dunn, Pocock acknowledges Laslett's influence, dating the genesis of the 'Cambridge method' to be in the period 1949–50, when he became aware of Laslett's work.[13] Subsequently, Pocock has exerted a continuous influence on the Cambridge style and on the wider academic world. His influence is conducted primarily by substantive scholarly studies, which investigate particular languages or discourses of past thought, for example in The Ancient Constitution and the Feudal Law: A Study of English in the Seventeenth Century and The Machiavellian Moment. His substantive historical studies have been combined with a series of methodological essays. His seminal methodological essay, 'The History of Political Thought: A Methodological Enquiry' (1964), interrogates the very idea of undertaking a history of political thought.[14] In the essay, he establishes an intellectual frame for conceiving of the history of political thought, which continues to inform his approach. He remarks on how political thought exists at different levels of abstraction, with the most abstract level of political philosophy constituting a traditional philosophical investigation of ideas. The historian is deemed to be capable of determining these levels of abstraction. Pocock maintains, 'It is perfectly possible, by the ordinary methods of historical reconstruction to determine the level of abstraction on which a particular piece of thinking took place.'[15] Like Oakeshott, he endows the historian with the task of determining the categories by which investigation takes place. Throughout his career, he sees it as the task of the historian to focus upon particular styles of thinking, which are related to wider historical discourses or languages of political

---

[11] J. Dunn, 'Introduction', Political Obligation in Its Historical Context—Essays in Political Theory (Cambridge, Cambridge University Press, 1980), p. 3.

[12] J. Dunn, 'The History of Political Theory', in J. Dunn, The History of Political Theory and Other Essays (Cambridge, Cambridge University Press, 1996), p. 26.

[13] J. Pocock, Political Thought and History—Essays on Theory and Method (Cambridge, Cambridge University Press, 2009), p. vii. See also J.G.A. Pocock, 'Present at the Creation: With Laslett in the Lost Worlds' International Journal of Public Affairs, vol. 2, 2006, pp. 7–17.

[14] J. Pocock, 'The History of Political Thought: Methodological Enquiry', in P. Laslett and W.G. Runciman (eds), Philosophy, Politics and Society (2nd Series) (Oxford, Blackwell, 1964).

[15] Ibid., p. 186.

thought. A major theme of the essay is to criticize a tendency for historians of political thought to prioritize an abstract level of philosophical thought and to substitute philosophy for history. In contrast, Pocock prefers to deal with political thinking as a series of interventions, by which thinkers aim to achieve determinate objectives. He observes, 'The historian is interested in men thinking about politics just as in them fighting or farming or doing anything else, namely as individuals behaving in a society, whose recorded behaviour can be studied by a method of historical reconstruction, in order to show what manner of world they lived in and why they behaved as they did...'.[16] He imagines past thinkers as using political ideas or as debating in a particular language of politics. He remarks, 'Any stable and articulate society possesses concepts with which to discuss political affairs and associates these to form groups or languages.'[17] Pocock's substantive historical studies reconstruct the development of languages of political thought. Hence he analyses ways in which the idea of the ancient constitution and the vocabulary of the common law are used and in his imaginative tour de force he reviews the enduring engagement with a Machiavellian moment, the maintenance of political structure over time, which reaches from Renaissance Italy to the American Revolution. He tends to trace long-term continuities in the history of political thought by following the continuing employment of particular languages or discourses of political theory.[18]

In later methodological essays Pocock reaffirms his style of doing the history of political thought as interpreting conceptualizations of politics in relation to linguistic and discursive political contexts. In 'The Concept of a Language', he observes that '[w]hen we speak of "languages" therefore, we mean for the most part, sub-languages; idioms, rhetorics, ways of talking about politics, distinguishable language games of which each may have its own vocabulary, rules, preconditions and implications, tone and style.'[19] For a time, and under the influence of Kuhn, the historian of science, Pocock employed the term 'paradigm' to capture the conceptual and linguistic contexts in which he identified political thinkers to be operating. However, in his retrospective introductory Preface to an edited collection of methodological essays, he admits to the misleading associations of the notion of a paradigm. A paradigm, for Pocock, tends to close the context due to its implication of a single encompassing conceptual frame for thinking, when, in reality,

---

[16] Ibid., p. 194.   [17] Ibid., p. 195.

[18] See J.G.A. Pocock, *The Ancient Constitution and the Feudal Law: A Study of English Historical Thought in the Seventeenth Century: A Reissue with Retrospect* (Cambridge, Cambridge University Press, 1987); J.G.A. Pocock, *The Machiavellian Moment: Florentine Political Thought and the Atlantic Republican Tradition* (Princeton, New Jersey, Princeton University Press, 1987).

[19] See J.G.A. Pocock, 'The Concept of a Language', in J.G.A. Pocock, *Political Thought and History—Essays on Theory and Method*, p. 89.

alternative languages of politics co-exist and individual thinkers are never absorbed by a particular discursive context.[20] In an essay on Skinner, he declares, 'It is the diversity of languages, reflecting the diversity of problems, with which the historian of discourse remains concerned.'[21] Pocock's recognition of the openness of conceptual contexts is instructive. It is at odds with Bevir's critique of his work that takes him to assimilate historic thinkers into a determinate conceptual discourse, and so to underplay reflective agency.[22]

Skinner acknowledges the role of Pocock, along with Dunn and Laslett, in establishing and developing the distinctive methodological framework of the Cambridge School.[23] Skinner himself has been to the fore in posing questions about the identity of the history of political thought and in articulating a particular methodology. Central to Skinner's methodological stance is to focus upon the past questions that past thinkers sought to address and to avoid retrojecting present assumptions on to past theorists. His article, 'Meaning and Understanding in the History of Ideas' (1969) called into question prevalent ways of undertaking the history of political thought and set out an agenda for what might be achieved. Its own historical significance is captured in Pocock's observation, 'In 1969, Skinner published an essay, "Meaning and Understanding in the History of Ideas", which came to be the manifesto of an emerging method of interpreting the history of political thought.'[24] The article assumes the guise of a manifesto due to its rhetorical force in critiquing prevailing assumptions and in its resolve to present a decidedly historical approach to the subject. In a retrospective collection of methodological essays, Skinner revised the language of the original article, softening its rhetoric. Given the impact of the polemical language of the original version, however, it will be focused upon and cited in this account of the Cambridge School.[25] In the original version of the article Skinner casts his argument in a polemical tone by highlighting what he takes to be two misguided approaches to the study of the history of political thought.[26] The two countervailing yet

---

[20] See J.G.A. Pocock, 'Preface' in J.G.A. Pocock, *Political Thought and History—Essays on Theory and Method*, pp. vii–xvi.

[21] J.G.A. Pocock, 'Quentin Skinner: The History of Politics and the Politics of History', p. 138.

[22] M. Bevir, *The Logic of the History of Ideas* (Cambridge, Cambridge University Press, 1999), pp. 216–17.

[23] Q. Skinner, 'The Rise of, Challenge to and Prospects for a Collingwoodian Approach to the History of Political Thought', in D. Castiglione and I. Hampsher-Monk (eds), *The History of Political Thought in National Context*, pp. 175–7.

[24] J.G.A. Pocock, 'Quentin Skinner: The History of politics and the Politics of History', p. 128.

[25] The original article is Q. Skinner, 'Meaning and Understanding in the History of Ideas', *History and Theory*, vol. 8 (1969); the revised version is Q. Skinner, *Visions of Politics*, vol. 1, *Regarding Method*. The revised abridged version also concentrates upon critiquing the textual approach. Unless indicated otherwise, this book cites the original version of the article as it was reprinted in J. Tully (ed.), *Meaning and Context: Quentin Skinner and His Critics*.

[26] The critique of contextualism is omitted from the revised version, along with the account of how agents are linked to ideas: Q. Skinner, *Visions of Politics*, vol. 1, *Regarding Method*, p. 3.

misguided perspectives consist, on the one hand, in a reliance upon supposedly 'autonomous' textual analysis and, on the other hand, upon a reductionist contextualism. If the former assumes that texts can be read without reference to contexts, then the latter assumes that contexts determine ideas without reference to the activities of authors. Both underestimate the work of disciplined historical imagination that is required to interpret what a past political thinker is doing in developing and expressing ideas. Past thinking can neither be assimilated to present-day assumptions nor reduced to what fits with an independently specifiable context.

To repudiate a view that imagines texts can be read without reference to the intentions and circumstances of their authors he identifies a series of mythologies to which a narrowly textualist approach is subject. Mythology arises out of imagining texts as rehearsing 'timeless' truths rather than in engaging with their character as historical products. Skinner remarks, 'I do wish, however, both to insist on the various ways in which to study simply what each classic writer *says* is unavoidably to run the perpetual danger of lapsing into various kinds of historical absurdity, and also to anatomize the various ways in which the results may in consequence be classified not as histories at all, but more appropriately as *mythologies*' (emphasis in original).[27] Multiple mythologies derive from commentators projecting on to historic texts requirements and principles that derive from their own preconceptions of the nature of 'classic' political ideas, rather than from historical analysis.

Skinner exposes and condemns the mythology of doctrines, by which past thinkers are presumed to possess a standard repertoire of concepts and doctrines. This standard repertoire does not arise out of a historically sensitive reading of the text, but derives from what the commentator, in a different historical situation, assumes to be an appropriate set of concepts. This mythology occurs in a variety of unfortunate guises. Lovejoy presents a distinct if acutely unhappy version in that he assumes the history of ideas to represent a succession of exemplifications of unit ideas, such as plenitude, which remain uncontaminated by the particular contexts in which, periodically, they are articulated.[28] In other styles of commentary the misleading identification and cataloguing of doctrines assumes other forms. Inappropriate standard doctrines may be assigned to past thinkers by their casual references to topics. Past thinkers may be criticized for either omitting to mention an imagined standard doctrine or for referring to it in a non-standard way. Praise or blame is bestowed by a formula, which does not depend upon interpreting the historical thinker's own concerns but on the anachronistic terms of the commentator. Skinner observes how Shakespeare has been held to be sceptical

---

[27] Q. Skinner, 'Meaning and Understanding in the History of Ideas', p. 32.
[28] See A. Lovejoy, *The Great Chain of Being: A Study of the History of An Idea* (New York, Touchday, 1960), pp. 3–24.

over an inter-racial and interfaith society, and Plato has been criticized for failing to take account of public opinion. And, of course, the question of whether or not Shakespeare or Plato could have held such opinions is an historical one, which is not even posed.[29]

Another form of mythology arises from a commentator concentrating their own critical powers on rendering past political thinkers' ideas coherent, when it is by no means clear a priori that thinkers have prioritized coherence over other qualities. The interpretive premium that is placed on the theoretical coherence of past arguments is not justified. The priority assigned to coherence underpins commentators' search for an underlying unity to sets of ideas, even when, like Marx, theorists developed ideas over a long period, in collaboration with others and in many distinctive contexts.[30] The fact that a thinker might have changed their mind is not allowed to intrude upon the design of unifying the diverse writings of Rousseau and Machiavelli.[31] The movement between the texts of theorists is stilled, textual silences are filled, and their contradictions resolved by philosophical readings that owe more to the intellectual sophistication of commentators than to the purposes and reflective schemes of the past. Skinner reasons, with some plausibility, that coherence might not have been at the top of past agendas. Equally plausible is his view that its claim to interpretive priority is to be investigated rather than merely assumed.

Skinner identifies prolepsis as another mythology that undermines authentically historical interpretation of past ideas. Prolepsis imagines a piece of thinking to anticipate subsequent forms. It reflects the presumption of Whig historians to read the past backwards and so to undermine the enterprise of understanding the past in its own terms.[32] Hence, Skinner observes how Popper's construal of Plato as a totalitarian is to misconstrue Plato and perhaps to misperceive totalitarianism. He diagnoses Popper's reading of Plato as a 'totalitarian party politician' to be an anachronistic misrepresentation, deriving from Popper's own antipathy to subsequent forms of totalitarianism.[33] Likewise, Talmon's historical survey of *The Origins of Totalitarian Democracy* tends to say more about his own reading of the twentieth-century world of totalitarianism than about Rousseau's notion of the general will, which is formulated in the eighteenth century.[34] Skinner also diagnoses a series of ways in which current attitudes distort readings of preceding forms of thinking by their exhibition of the mythology associated with parochialism. Parochialism assumes many idioms but it consists essentially in misplacing

[29] Q. Skinner, 'Meaning and Understanding in the History of Ideas', p. 35.
[30] Ibid., p. 42.	[31] Ibid., pp. 39–42.
[32] See H. Butterfield, *The Whig Interpretation of History* (London, G. Bell and Sons Ltd, 1951). Butterfield was a Cambridge historian, who supervised Pocock's doctorate. He maintained interests in the philosophy of history, the history of science, and historiography.
[33] Q. Skinner, 'Meaning and Understanding in the History of Ideas' p. 40.
[34] Ibid., p. 44. For a specific reference to Talmon, see fn. 99 of Skinner's text.

current assumptions. The prevalent attribution of influence as a way of establishing causal explanations of past ideas is critiqued by Skinner as reflecting a connection that is in the mind of the commentator rather than in the alleged recipient of influence.[35] The tendency to identify past ideas under a contemporary conceptual scheme, for example, in reading Locke as an advocate of 'government by consent', constitutes another example of a misleading form of parochialism.[36]

The moral that Skinner draws from his review of these mythologies is clear. Standard approaches to the history of political thought subvert rather than deliver an historical understanding of the past. The antidote to the abuses resides in the formulation of an appropriate methodology for interpreting past thinkers. In framing his own methodological scheme, Skinner draws on the linguistic philosophy of Austin and of the later Wittgenstein.[37] In so doing, he does not align himself with logical positivism, which is implied by Bevir's review of Skinner's contextualism and its philosophical antecedents.[38] To the contrary, in drawing upon the later Wittgenstein's identification of meaning with linguistic usage and the social construction of concepts, Skinner opposes a positivist reduction of meaning to empirical verification and to conceptual essentialism. For the later Wittgenstein, there is no formulaic way of drawing boundaries between the meaningful and the nonsensical as logical positivists would have it. Meaning depends on diverse language games and practical forms of life. Likewise Austin, in focusing on how words are used and what can be done with them, attends to different forms of meaning such as illocutionary and perlocutionary forms that depend on linguistic performance and its interpretation. In framing a methodology for the history of political thought Skinner rehearses Austin in highlighting the significance of what authors are doing in formulating and expressing ideas. The point of what they are doing, the illocutionary force of their words, expresses their intentions, and these intentions cannot be grasped by a mere reading of their texts. For instance, if their intention is for a text to be read ironically, it is insufficient to establish the semantic meaning of their arguments; a recovery of their

---

[35] For a more sympathetic account of influence, see G. Browning, 'Agency and Influence in the History of Political Thought: The Agency of Influence and the Influence of Agency', *History of Political Thought*, vol. 31, no. 2, 2010, pp. 345–66.

[36] Q. Skinner, 'Meaning and Understanding in the History of Ideas', p. 36.

[37] Ibid., pp. 59–61.

[38] See M. Bevir, 'Contextualism', in *the Oxford Handbook of the History of Political Philosophy* (Oxford, Oxford University Press, 2011). See in particular Bevir's comment on Skinner, 'Like Laslett, he took Weldon to have shown that much of political argument was vacuous. Again like Laslett, he associated Weldon with the work of Ludwig Wittgenstein, who at the time was generally placed alongside Ryle and J.L. Austin and so was read as offering a kind of linguistic version of logical positivism', p. 15. This reading of Skinner, Austin, Ryle, and the later Wittgenstein is odd. None of them were logical positivists. Indeed, arguably all of them were highly significant critics of that doctrine.

intended meaning is required. The intentions of authors that are expressed in texts depend upon aspects of the contexts to which authors are responding.[39]

Skinner observes how the illocutionary force of texts, what authors are trying to achieve in their writing, is often ignored. Skinner's substantive studies of Hobbes and Machiavelli focus upon this dimension of their work.[40] For Skinner it is neither sufficient nor even possible to establish how the doctrines of Hobbes and Machiavelli are to be taken without relating them to how they express or respond to current conventions and attitudes. The force of the arguments of Hobbes and Machiavelli turns upon how they intend to impact upon their contextual situations, hence the need to establish how they imagine their interventions to be operating. Rather than marvelling at Machiavelli's originality or shuddering at his inhumanity, Skinner relates him to prevailing conventions and currents of political argument to register how he contributes to contemporary politics. Skinner aims to disclose what Palonen in his book, *Quentin Skinner*, terms politicking, which is the process of exerting an impact upon the political world.[41] Skinner concludes, 'Meaning and Understanding in the History of Political Thought', by observing how the study of past texts is not of direct relevance to current issues and thinking. Past thinking about politics is absorbed in past issues and styles of thought, and their value to the present is indirect rather than direct. It resides in their difference from the present rather than in conveying universal truths. In disclosing multiple and distinct beliefs about politics, they extend our imaginative horizons rather than confirm prevailing ideas.[42]

In subsequent methodological essays Skinner responds to critics and engages with other styles of conceptualizing the history of ideas. In the process he recasts and modifies his ideas. In 'Motives, Intentions and Interpretation', a late essay that draws upon preceding articles, Skinner defends critical inquiry into the intentional meaning of texts against its critique by forms of post-modern literary criticism. He observes the critique of intentional meaning that is maintained by Foucault and Derrida, who oppose deferring to the authority of authors. He confronts and repudiates the notion of the so-called intentional fallacy whereby meaning is held to be equated to and misaligned with intentions.[43] Skinner reviews the critique of intentions from a number of angles,

[39] Q. Skinner, 'Meaning and Understanding in the History of Ideas', p. 61.

[40] See, for instance, Q. Skinner, 'The Ideological Context of Hobbes's Political Thought', *Historical Journal*, vol. 9, 1966, pp. 286–317; Q. Skinner, 'Conquest and Consent: Thomas Hobbes and the Engagement Controversy', in *The Interregnum: The Quest for a Settlement, 1646–1660*, ed. E.G. Aylmer (London, xxx, 1972), pp. 79–88; Q. Skinner, *Hobbes and Republican Liberty* (Cambridge, Cambridge University Press, 2008); Q. Skinner, *Machiavelli* (Oxford, Oxford University Press, 1981).

[41] K. Palonen, *Quentin Skinner: History, Politics, Rhetoric* (Cambridge, Polity Press, 2003) pp. 5–6.

[42] Q. Skinner, 'Meaning and Understanding in the History of Ideas', p. 67.

[43] See Q. Skinner, 'Motives, Intentions and Interpretation', in Q. Skinner, *Visions of Politics*, vol. 1, *Regarding Method* (Cambridge, Cambridge University Press, 2002), p. 90.

identifying differing meanings of meaning. He observes how the concept of meaning can refer to the semantic meaning of a text, a text's effect upon readers, and its intentional meaning. It is this latter form which Skinner takes to depend upon interpretation of an author's intentions. To clarify the sense in which he takes intentional meaning to be valuable, he distinguishes the illocutionary sense of intention from that of a motive. For instance, a motive for writing a text, such as the desire to earn money, may be external to what is in the text. In contrast, how a text expresses an intention of its author, for instance, in its character as a critique of a particular style of politics, is internal to the text and contributes to the way it is to be read. In justifying the recovery of authorial intentions, Skinner makes clear that he is not taking intentions to be private matters. They are, as the later Wittgenstein suggests, publicly accessible.[44] Hence in his recent study of Hobbes's account of liberty, Hobbes's intentions in reformulating his account of liberty are held to be expressed in *Leviathan*.[45]

In 'Interpretation and the Understanding of Speech Acts', an essay in *Visions of Politics*, vol. 1, *Regarding Method* (1992) that reworks the earlier 'Reply to My Critics', Skinner returns to methodological themes. He observes how he focuses upon illocutionary acts and forces in establishing how authors intend their texts to be read. He cites Austin, Strawson, and Wittgenstein as philosophical sources of his conceptualization of intended meaning.[46] He emphasizes how the recovery of authorial intentions is integral to establishing the intended meanings of texts. He acknowledges that intentional meaning is one amongst many forms of meaning and is not to be construed as operating so as to exclude other forms.[47] Nonetheless, he argues for the recovery of intended meanings, which he takes to be crucial in situations where there is uncertainty over how an author intended a text to be read. Skinner recognizes how this is a demanding task in complex cases, such as interpreting Plato's dialogues, but the very debate over how the dialogues are to be read underlines its significance. Where the conventions governing formulations of intentions have lapsed, then their historical recovery along with authorial intentions is both requisite and arduous. In arguing for the significance of intentional meaning, Skinner observes that he is not prioritizing the role of the author in interpreting a text, even if he is assigning responsibility to authors in endowing texts with meaning. Intentional meaning is to be accessed primarily by recovering the argumentative contexts informing the production of texts. He expressly observes that the role of the historian of political thought is to be

---

[44] Ibid., p. 97.

[45] Q. Skinner, *Hobbes and Republican Liberty* (Cambridge, Cambridge University Press, 2008), pp. 124–78.

[46] Q. Skinner, 'Interpretation and the Understanding of Speech Acts', in Q. Skinner, *Visions of Politics*, vol. 1, *Regarding Method* (Cambridge, Cambridge University Press, 2002), pp. 103–7.

[47] Ibid., p. 113.

concentrated upon the recovery of discourses in the sense that this project is maintained by Pocock.[48] In so doing he explains how in following what he construes to be a Collingwoodian notion of intellectual history in recovering intended meanings of authors, he is not to be understood as empathetically re-entering the minds of past thinkers.[49] Intentions of past thinkers are to be recovered by interpretation of publicly available evidence, even if occasionally there may be insufficient evidence to explain what was intended in expressions of thought. For instance, he takes Derrida's example of the impossibility of assigning an intentional meaning to the surviving fragment in Nietzsche's manuscripts, 'I have forgotten my umbrella', as representing an example of what might not be recoverable. This example, for Skinner, however, does not rule out recovering intentional meanings in standard cases where there is more evidence to be acquired.[50]

The illocutionary force of Skinner's methodological writings point in at least two directions. On the one hand, it is set against what is taken to be ill-considered textual and contextual interpretation of historic texts and, on the other hand, it supports a particular way of undertaking the history of political thought. Skinner's methodological assumptions underpin his own substantive studies of past political thinkers and languages of political thought. In early essays he sought to locate Hobbes in political controversies of his day, and to move commentary away from generic views of Hobbes, which are derived from the imputed coherence of his texts.[51] He produced a large-scale text on early modern political thinkers, *The Foundations of Modern Political Thought*, in which he applies his methodological reflections by relating texts to discursive contexts in the development of thought in early Modern Europe. He observes how the circumstances and languages of religious conflict and social development promoted changes in the vocabularies of politics and in ways of considering politics. In his narrative, Skinner accommodates minor as well as major thinkers, extending the range of what constitutes political thought, and in the course of his text he traces what he takes to be central to the development of the modern state, namely the notion of state sovereignty.

In reviewing *The Foundations of Modern Political Thought*, Black observes how it shows us 'the "intellectual matrix", and provides new insights, in some important cases, into the real meaning of "great texts."'[52] However, the sharpness of Skinner's identification of the emerging profile of modern

---

[48] Ibid., p. 120.   [49] Ibid.

[50] Ibid., p. 121. It is worth pointing out that Skinner takes his argument here to counter Derrida's sense of the undecidability of interpretation yet Derrida's argument is not disposed of by this recourse to the availability of evidence.

[51] See Q. Skinner, 'The Ideological Context of Hobbes's Political Thought', *Historical Journal*, 286–317.

[52] A. Black, 'Skinner on the "Foundations of Modern Political Thought"', *Political Studies*, vol. XXV111, no. 3, 1980, p. 452.

political thought is questioned. Moreover, Black suggests that Skinner tends to relate thinkers to local contexts when the complexity of political thought resides in the multiple discursive connections between thinkers and a variety of contexts, immediate circumstances, and preceding contextual traditions.[53] Black questions the imperative that texts are to be interpreted without reference to subsequent contexts. He notes how Skinner's methodological injunction against reading the past in the light of a subsequent perspective is at odds with Marsiglio's evident intention to influence readers outside his immediate context.[54] In a characteristically jaunty critical review of Skinner's text, Minogue questions the propriety of the very project of tracing the foundations of modern political thought in the light of Skinner's methodological assumptions.[55] To consider foundations appears to commit to a teleological perspective, in which the foundational is only realized in the context of what has ensued. Indeed, in a subsequent interview with Petri Koikkalainen and Sami Syrjamaki, 'Quentin Skinner on Encountering the Past', Skinner acknowledges that the title was unfortunate in that it committed him to writing teleologically. He notes, 'My own book is far too much concerned with the origins of our present world when I ought to have been trying to represent the world I was examining in its own terms so far as possible.'[56]

Skinner's monograph on Hobbes, *Reason and Rhetoric in the Philosophy of Hobbes* (1996) offers an innovative reading of Hobbes as well as exhibiting a critical awareness of the rhetorical dimension of past political thought. In this monograph, Skinner attends closely to Hobbes's engagement with prevailing notions of rhetoric, arguing that Hobbes's scientific treatment of politics is designed to replace traditional forms of rhetorical argument. However, Skinner also recognizes how Hobbes reckons that this project requires the deployment of traditional rhetoric so that *Leviathan* employs the very rhetorical arguments that he critiques so as to maximize its ideological impact in the public sphere. Hence Skinner observes and explains Hobbes's employment of figurative and holistic language in *Leviathan*, which conflicts ostensibly with its own formal assessment of rhetoric.[57] Palonen considers that Skinner's recent engagement with rhetoric allows for a more evident focus upon the persuasive style of political argument than in his preceding more analytic mode of dealing with performative aspects of speech acts.[58] In his retrospective article in *Visions of*

---

[53] Ibid., p. 454.   [54] Ibid.

[55] K. Minogue, 'Method in Intellectual History: Quentin Skinner's *Foundations*', in J. Tully (ed.), *Meaning and Context: Quentin Skinner and His Critics*, p. 184.

[56] Q. Skinner interview with Petri Koikkalainen and Sami Syrjamaki, 'Quentin Skinner on Encountering the Past', Finnish Yearbook of Political Thought [Redescriptions Yearbook of Political Thought Conceptual History and Feminist Theory], no. 6 p. 53.

[57] Q. Skinner, *Reason and Rhetoric in Hobbes's Leviathan* (Cambridge, Cambridge University Press, 1996).

[58] K. Palonen, *Quentin Skinner: History, Politics, Rhetoric* (Cambridge, Polity Press, 2003).

Politics, vol. 1, *Regarding Method*, 'Retrospect: Studying Rhetoric and Conceptual Change', Skinner reflects upon how his concern to understand conceptual change incorporates explanation of how states of affairs are re-described in innovative evaluative terms.[59]

Skinner continues to engage with Hobbes, but in the wider context of the conceptual history of liberty. Skinner holds that many of the theorists of politics in the English Civil War and its aftermath employed a neo-Roman or republican notion of liberty, which is at odds with the explanatory dichotomous model of liberty that was devised by Berlin in the twentieth century. Skinner perceives how the notion of republican liberty has a long pedigree and can be traced to preceding republicans, notably Machiavelli. He considers that its recognition can contribute to a broadening of the conceptual range that is associated with the idea of liberty.[60] In *Hobbes and Republican Liberty* (2008) Skinner reviews Hobbes's formulations of the idea of liberty in his political writings as his responses to republican or neo-Roman conceptions. He explains, 'My purpose in the following essay is to contrast two rival theories about the nature of liberty.'[61] He reads Hobbes in *Leviathan* as devising and operating with a negative view of liberty to oppose the contemporary formulations of republicans. In so doing Skinner rehearses his view of the history of political thought whereby past texts are seen as forms of intervention within distinct ideological contexts. He maintains, 'As will already be evident, I approach Hobbes's political theory not simply as a general system of ideas but also as polemical intervention in the ideological conflicts of his time. To interpret and understand his texts, I suggest, we need to recognise the force of the maxim that words are also deeds.'[62]

The focus of *Hobbes and Republican Liberty* is upon how Hobbes reacts to contemporary republican arguments to frame an original and politically oriented view of liberty. Skinner concentrates upon historical battles with which Hobbes is engaged. But he also reflects upon the continuing influence of the negative view of liberty that is devised by Hobbes. He observes, 'If we focus moreover, on his (Hobbes's) basic belief—that freedom is simply the absence of interference—we find it widely treated as an article of faith. Consider for example the most influential discussion of freedom in Anglophone political theory of the past fifty years, Isaiah Berlin's essay, "Two Concepts of Liberty".'[63] Clearly, *Hobbes and Republican Liberty* expresses

---

[59] Q. Skinner, 'Retrospect: Studying Rhetoric and Conceptual Change', in *Visions of Politics*, vol. 1, *Regarding Method*, pp. 175–88.

[60] Q. Skinner, 'A Third Concept of Liberty', *Proceedings of the British Academy*, vol. 87, 2002.

[61] Q. Skinner, *Hobbes and Republican Liberty* (Cambridge, Cambridge University Press, 2008), p. viii.

[62] Ibid., p. xv. The maxim is Wittgenstein's, see L. Wittgenstein *Philosophical Investigations* trans. E. Anscombe (Oxford, Oxford University Press, 1958), p. 146.

[63] Q. Skinner, *Hobbes and Republican Liberty*, p. 213.

Skinner's dissatisfaction with contemporary formulations of liberty that tend to favour the centrality of a negative view. He sees the retrieval of republican argument as reviving a currency, which is not to be undervalued by the current dominance of a liberal negative view that is traced to Hobbes. He concludes his study of Hobbes's argument against neo-Roman views of liberty by observing, 'But it is still worth asking if he won the argument.'[64] Connections between past argument and present assumptions also inform Skinner's review of forms of Ancient and Renaissance rhetoric. In the closing essay of his *Visions of Politics*, vol. 1, *Regarding Method*, 'Retrospect: Studying Rhetoric and Social Change', Skinner focuses upon argumentative strategies that aim to be balanced and persuasive rather than certain and beyond debate. These strategies are explained contextually but they are also seen to conflict with contemporary forms of analytic philosophy, which aim to provide watertight unyielding accounts of concepts. In the essay, Skinner makes clear his aversion to contemporary neo-Kantian projects that aim 'to halt the flux of politics by trying definitively to fix the analysis of key moral terms.'[65]

The Cambridge School has exerted a significant impact upon the study of the history of political thought in emphasizing its historicity and in insisting upon locating past political thinking in appropriately past contexts. However, the School accommodates different emphases amongst its contributors and its major figures have developed their thinking about the history of political thought in different ways. What unites them is their commitment to historical scholarship and to revealing the past contexts relating to past texts. Pocock tends to recognize and explain continuities in history by attending to languages of politics that persist over long stretches of time. Dunn has recognized the value of past texts in enlightening us on contemporary questions of politics, but maintains that historical scholarship is required to explain how they are intended to be read. Skinner's recent work on the history of neo-Roman liberty recognizes the persistence of a notion of liberty across differing cultures and epochs. His reading of Hobbes as arguing against republican liberty and as advancing an innovative account of negative liberty also relates to present arguments about liberty. It is true that Skinner's interpretation of Hobbes situates him in debates of his own time and harmonizes with Skinner's determination to resist the anachronistic temptation to read the past backwards from the present. Yet Skinner's own concern to stretch the notion of liberty can be seen to emerge from a present dissatisfaction with prevailing models of liberty, notably Berlin's, which excludes republican formulations. In

---

[64] Ibid., p. 216.

[65] See Q. Skinner, 'Retrospect: Studying Rhetoric and Conceptual Change', in Q. Skinner, *Visions of Politics*, vol. 1, *Regarding Method*, p. 177. Relatedly Skinner observes how Rawls's comments on the common good in *A Theory of Justice* reflect his allegiance to a particular and contingent moral tradition. See Q. Skinner, 'The Paradoxes of Political Liberty', in D. Miller (ed.), *Liberty* (Oxford, Oxford University Press, 1991), p. 199.

his Introduction to *Visions of Politics*, vol. 1, *Regarding Method* (1992) Skinner recognizes that his work in the history of political thought is intended as 'a contribution to the understanding of our present social world.'[66] He presents this enlargement of understanding as indirect rather than direct in that its contribution is to be seen as a kind of exorcism of the bewitching concentration of particular conceptual formulations about politics in the contemporary world by which alternative and past notions are excluded.

If the Cambridge School accommodates a variety of styles and changing formulations amongst its practitioners, then a number of other practitioners of the history of political thought can be considered to subscribe to affiliated contextualist styles. Stefan Collini adopts a related approach though he eschews conceptual schemes or methodological programmes and hence distances himself from any distinct methodology in intellectual history, even though he allows for an affinity to the methodological approach of Skinner, Pocock, and the Cambridge School. Indeed, he questions the utility of identifying himself with any distinct school of intellectual history. He recognizes that many intellectual historians like himself, who have been associated with Sussex, might acknowledge an affinity with one another, yet he himself does not imagine that these sentiments are sufficient to warrant the designation 'school'.[67] Collini is also committed to an inter-disciplinary perspective, which makes him wary of imagining the study of the history of political thought as constituting a distinct form of historical explanation that is independent of connections with other disciplines.

Collini's affinity to the Cambridge School lies in his commitment to contextualism and to the procedures of historical explanation. Like Skinner, he is unbending in his opposition to anachronism and guards against allowing the assumptions of the present to distort conceptions of the past. In his own reflections on the nature of intellectual history, Collini takes it to consist in the recovery of past thought by identifying its appropriate contexts. In characterizing the attitude to the past of the intellectual history of the group of Sussex intellectual historians to which he has been connected he highlights their contextualism and resistance to the prejudices of the present. He remarks that 'the informing spirit of much of this work (of intellectual history) has been the attempt to recover past ideas and re-situate them in their intellectual contexts in ways which resist the anachronistic or otherwise tendentious and selective pressures exerted by contemporary academic and political polemic.'[68]

---

[66] Q. Skinner, 'Introduction: Seeing Things Their Way', in Q. Skinner, *Visions of Politics*, vol. 1, *Regarding Method*, p. 6.

[67] S. Collini, 'Introduction', in S. Collini, R. Whatmore, and B. Young (eds), *Economy, Polity and Society—British Intellectual History 1750–1950* (Cambridge, Cambridge University Press, 2000), p. 13.

[68] Ibid., p. 14.

CONCLUSION

The contextualism of the Cambridge School has exerted a considerable impact upon the study of the history of political thought. Skinner, Pocock, Dunn, and Laslett before them, have produced exemplary historical scholarship, which has sharpened interpretive perspectives on past thinkers and themes and inspired a welcome self-consciousness over method. Their emphasis upon the contexts in which past thinkers have operated shifts attention away from the present and onto the actual circumstances in which thinkers were situated and hence allows for appreciation of what past thinkers were doing in producing political theories. This contextualism is evident in the work of related intellectual historians such as Collini. Skinner's focus upon recovering the intentions of past thinkers is useful in pointing to the active role thinkers play in using ideas and combats a prevalent tendency to reify ideas and so to misconceive how they are framed and deployed by particular thinkers in specific ways. Likewise, Pocock broadens the scope of inquiry by focusing on discourses in which ideas are articulated. The Cambridge School's express focus on retrieving past circumstances, conventions, languages, and intentions is clear and is in pointed contrast to the easy assumptions of the similitude between past and present, which have informed standard commentaries that have been criticized by its members. The value of contextualism appears most clearly in specific interpretations of particular thinkers and themes, and later in this book contextualist interpretations of Locke, Machiavelli, and Mill will be reviewed.

Central to the contextualism of the Cambridge School is its sharp separation of the past from the present. Their recognition of the distinctness of the past is of a piece with the standpoint of Collingwood and Oakeshott and is emphasized in Collini's related contextualism. Yet, the project of attending to the past is a present activity, which doubtless is motivated by scholarly historical concerns but cannot be determined exclusively by such considerations. The past is not easily circumscribed for interpretive purposes. Past ideas and texts have to be identified and individuated and contexts require specification. Ideas and contexts are not susceptible of precise and unyielding identifications of their identity. Ideas are relational and contexts, as King and Derrida observe, are infinite.[69] Any attempt to close down ideas and contexts highlights the role of the interpreter in deciding to focus on 'this' rather than 'that', and this process of fixing interpretations will depend upon the interpreter. Skinner tends to focus upon the immediate local discursive contexts in interpreting past ideas, interpreting thinkers as engaging with immediately available

---

[69] P. King, 'Historical Contextualism Revisited', in P. King, *Thinking Past a Problem* (London, Routledge, 2000), pp. 213–27; J. Derrida, *Of Grammatology* (Baltimore, Maryland, Johns Hopkins University Press, 1974), p. 260.

concepts and forms of expression. However, it is by no means clear that thinkers of considerable philosophical ambition such as Hegel are not influenced directly by preceding philosophers of another epoch, with whom they imagine they are conducting an argument.[70] The criteria of individuating what is to be explained depend upon interpretive formulations of the present as much as upon a focus on the past. Pocock's identification of a past language of political discourse is evidently a product of his own capacity for imaginative conceptual construction as well as a facility in sifting and evaluating evidence. 'The Machiavellian moment', for example, is a construction, which does not represent the determinate thought of any particular past thinker. It is constructed from the present so as to explain aspects of the ideas of a variety of thinkers from differing epochs and represents the interests as well as the conceptual ingenuity of a skilled historian.[71]

Present conceptions enter into interpretations of the past, just as past ideas bear upon the present. Skinner's identification of a neo-Roman view of liberty in early modern Britain avoids interpreting the history of political thought in terms of current views of liberty, yet his dissatisfaction with Berlin's dichotomous reading of liberty underlies an interest in a form of liberty that might challenge contemporary orthodoxy. If present-day interests can intrude into analyses of the past that are focused upon seeing the past in its own terms, then a more general denial of the relevance of the past to the present is also questionable. In *The Political Thought of John Locke* Dunn avers that Locke has nothing to say on politics to future generations. This observation has been repudiated subsequently by Dunn himself, who acknowledges it to be ill-considered.[72] The remark might well have been ill-considered but it reflected an historic sense of the priority the Cambridge School assigned to retrieving a past context of a thinker and to avoiding anachronistic judgments.[73] In truth Skinner has recognized inter-relations between past and present throughout his career and indirect benefits that a study of the past can bring to present forms of understanding. He has maintained consistently that historical scholarship can free actors in the contemporary world from assuming that dominant conceptions of the present are either fixed or universal.

In an interview in *The Art of Theory—Conversations in Political Philosophy* (2014) Skinner emphasizes how he takes the study of the past to be important

---

[70] There is some evidence that Hegel did regard the Ancient Greeks in this way. See comments on Plato and Aristotle in G.W.F. Hegel, *Lectures on the History of Philosophy*, vol. 2 trans. E.S. Haldane and F.H. Simpson (New York, Humanities Press, 1955), pp. 1–234.

[71] J. Pocock, *The Machiavellian Moment: Florentine Political Thought and the Atlantic Republican Tradition*.

[72] J. Dunn, 'What is Living and What is Dead in the Political Theory of John Locke', in J. Dunn, *Interpreting Political Responsibility—Essays 1981–1989* (Princeton NJ, Princeton University Press, 1990), p. 24.

[73] J. Dunn, 'Introduction', in J. Dunn, *Interpreting Political Responsibility—Essays 1981–1989*.

to the present. He remarks, 'The reason for studying the past is that, as my
great mentor in Princeton [Clifford] Gertz always used to say, "These guys are
meant to be working for us!" I think that's a really fine remark. We are
trying to find out what these guys think and we're trying to take it on their
terms. We're trying to reconstitute their world. But of course we hope that
will illuminate our world, and if it doesn't we're not going to publish
our results because they're not going to be important.'[74] For Skinner the
illumination that past thinkers can offer consists in the indirect impact that
a focus on the past offers in broadening our sense of the range of possibilities in theory and in politics. It goes along with a focus of attention upon
retrieving past attitudes and ideas and seeing things from the viewpoint of
the past rather than the present. In his retrospective Introduction to his
methodological essays in *Visions of Politics*, vol. 1, *Regarding Method* he
entitles the Introduction, 'Seeing Things Their Way', which betokens his
sense of the distinctness of the past.[75] Skinner's recognition of the political
point of studying past thought is accompanied by his denial that there are
perennial questions and problems in political thought, which past thinkers
might be thought of as addressing. He emphasizes the distinctness of the
past from the present, which rules out such universality even if it allows for
an indirect relevance.

In questioning Skinner's disparagement of the idea of perennial questions in
political thought, Boucher makes the point that past political philosophers
standardly assume that they are framing theories for the future as well as for
their own time in that they presume they are addressing universal questions.[76]
To deny such a possibility is implicitly to engage in a critique of what
they intended to be doing, and perhaps demands a more elaborated critical
engagement with their intentions than is offered by contextualists. There seems
to be no good reason why commentators on past texts should not engage with
the philosophical and political questions that are posed by past thinkers. To see
the past as inherently related to the present would seem to demand it. Moreover,
Bevir and Parekh, amongst others, have urged that there are in fact perennial
questions to which political philosophers may be seen as responding, if the
questions and responses are framed at a sufficiently high level of abstraction.[77]
Shorten urges questions pertaining to political thought might persist for a
considerable period. He remarks, 'Whatever might constitute a question (of
political thought) might remain so for a considerable-yet-finite period of time,

[74] Q. Skinner interview with Tersa Bejan, 'Quentin Skinner on Meaning and Method', *The Art of Theory—Conversations in Political Philosophy*, November 2011, www.artoftheory.com, p. 9.
[75] Q. Skinner, 'Introduction: Seeing Things Their Way' in Q. Skinner, *Visions of Politics*, vol. 1, *Regarding Method*, pp. 1–8.
[76] D. Boucher, *Texts in Context: Revisionist Methods for Studying the History of Ideas*, p. 45.
[77] B. Parekh and R.N. Berki, 'The History of Political Ideas: A Critique of Quentin Skinner's Methodology', *Journal of the History of Ideas*, vol. 34, no. 2 (April–June 1973), pp. 163–84.

so that no pull of linguistic contexts would preclude any given attempt to answer that question from having sufficient "abstraction" for it to be capable of speaking to a later audience.'[78] Certainly, it is not self-evidently true to maintain that the substantive political theories of Hegel and Marx are irrelevant to contemporary social and political issues. Arguably, contemporary capital persists in maintaining the same logic of large-scale instrumentality, commodification, and self-reproduction to which Marx drew attention. If anything, as an unholy alliance of football fans and global traders might acknowledge, the logic has become more pronounced. Again, Hegel's analysis of the constitutive recognitive relations between social subjects remains relevant to and informs the work of contemporary social theorists of recognition, such as Taylor and Honneth.[79] While Dunn, in his historical study of Locke, *The Political Thought of John Locke*, was trenchant in his denial of the contemporary relevance of Locke's ideas, subsequently he has recognized the ongoing significance of past political ideas.[80]

In focusing upon the historical identity of past ideas, the Cambridge School and related contextualists tend to assume that the past constitutes an object that can be recovered by the application of appropriate forms of historical scholarship, which are uncontaminated by anachronistic and distorting formulas bestowed upon it by the present. While worries over how present concerns tend to distort interpretations of the past are genuine, it is a mistake to presume that ideas and texts are susceptible of unambiguous intentional analysis. In 'Meaning and Understanding in the History of Ideas', Skinner recognizes that complex pieces of political thought such as Plato's dialogues pose problems of interpretation, even before issues over the availability of source material are raised.[81] Moreover, more recently and particularly in interviews, he has acknowledged a greater scepticism over historical understanding and has recognized the significance of Gadamer's hermeneutical reading of historical interpretation depending upon the interpretive horizon of the present.[82] Nonetheless he maintains an historical orientation, referring in the retrospective essay introducing his methodological essays to the significance of situating past thinkers in historic contexts that make sense of their projects. In reviewing his approach he maintains, '[M]y work is as historical as

---

[78] R. Shorten, 'How to Study Ideas in Politics and "Influence": A Typology', in *Contemporary Politics*, vol. 19, no. 4, 2013, pp. 361–78.

[79] A. Honneth, *The Struggle for Recognition* trans. J. Anderson (Cambridge Mass., MIT Press, 1996); C. Taylor, 'The Politics of Recognition', in A. Gutmann (ed.), *Multiculturalism: Examining the Politics of Recognition* (Princeton: Princeton University Press, 1994), pp. 25–73.

[80] See J. Dunn, *The Political Thought of John Locke* (Cambridge, Cambridge University Press, 1969). For Dunn's later views see J. Dunn, 'The History of Political Theory', in J. Dunn, *The History of Political Theory and Other Essays*, pp. 11–38.

[81] Q. Skinner, 'Meaning and Understanding in the History of Ideas', p. 107.

[82] See Q. Skinner interview with Petri Koikkalainen and Sami Syrjamaki, 'Quentin Skinner on Encountering the Past', p. 50.

I can make it.'[83] Derrida and post-structuralists more generally engage in a more radical scepticism over the possibilities of recapturing past ideas through historical recovery of the past intentions of authors. Skinner admits that the recovery of intentions represents only one way of explaining meaning. However, for Derrida it is insufficient merely to allow for the possibility of forms of explanation other than that of intentional authorial ones. Authors are not sovereign, they are unreliable narrators. While Derrida's suspicion of authors might be overplayed, it remains true that authors' intentions can be seen to be insusceptible of coherent formulation, but rather are enmeshed in tensions and strains that point to other ways of interpreting them. Derrida's deconstruction turns upon his disruption of the presumption of a universal truth that is maintained by past (and many present) Western philosophers. Skinner, and contextualists more generally, tend not to engage with the large claims of past political philosophers in concentrating upon local and particular discourses. They do not, like Derrida, question the logic of past forms of thought. There seems to be no compelling reason why the history of political thought should ignore the expansive claims of past theorists and thereby refrain from entering into philosophical debate with past modes of thought.

In succeeding chapters the interpretive strategies of Skinner and Pocock will be analysed further by reviewing how they are put to work on Machiavelli to reveal a Machiavelli who is different from preceding perceptions of him, which focus upon his imagined immorality and skullduggery. Skinner and Pocock review Machiavelli in the light of past forms of republicanism upon which he drew and of prevailing political practices such as advising princes. In doing so they show how he used and developed Renaissance concepts of time, fortune, and virtue. The upshot is that Machiavelli appears more intelligible and less outrageous than standardly portrayed, even if something of Machiavelli's originality appears to be underplayed. We also review Dunn's classic study of Locke, *The Political Thought of John Locke*, which Skinner has acknowledged to be the path-breaking text of the Cambridge School.[84] Dunn highlights how Locke responds to the intellectual and political contexts of his time rather than ours, and succeeds in offering a plausible and historically sophisticated reading of Locke's political thought even if subsequently he has revised his estimate of its ongoing relevance. The contextualist approach is also shown by reviewing Collini's historical understanding of Mill's moral and political thought. It disposes of images of Mill that are drawn from outside of his local context. It shows how abstracting

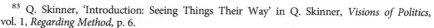

[83] Q. Skinner, 'Introduction: Seeing Things Their Way' in Q. Skinner, *Visions of Politics*, vol. 1, *Regarding Method*, p. 6.
[84] See Q. Skinner interview with Petri Koikkalainen and Sami Syrjamaki, 'Quentin Skinner on Encountering the Past', p. 39.

Mill from his Victorian context is to miss out on his moralism and espousal of unfashionable radical causes. While these studies of past political thinkers have much to offer they raise interpretive issues about appraising the significance and individuality of past theorists and about the nature and appropriateness of contextualism.

5

Derrida

Deconstructing the Canon

INTRODUCTION

Texts, for Derrida, demand interpretation. Their meaning is not clear-cut and they do not register what authors mean to say. What an author means to say is always liable to say more than is intended. The conceit of metaphysics is that there is an objective, universal truth that orders what is to be known, and which can be transmitted neatly in philosophical texts. Yet the truth is that truth is what is expressed in language and is susceptible of multiple interpretations. In this chapter, Derrida's practice of deconstruction, his subversion of metaphysics along with its implications for the study of the history of political thought, and his own interpretation of past political thought will be reviewed. His analyses of Marx, Rousseau, and Nietzsche, which will be developed in subsequent chapters, are signposted. Derrida's deconstruction of texts is at odds with hermeneutical studies that presume meaning can be elicited by recovering the thought of past authors in the light of the contexts in which they were situated. As Dienstag observes, 'He [Derrida] opposes the hermeneutic practice of discovering or presuming continuities and instead sought to focus on their opposite. Deconstruction emphasizes discontinuities both within texts and between texts and their readers.'[1] Derrida shows how texts can yield contradictions and tensions, which are neither intended nor understood by their authors. They reflect blockages that can be detected as arising from the pressure that is exerted on the part of authors to fix meanings within them. This is not to say that deconstruction is the only way to read texts, as Derrida's practice itself is not exclusively deconstructionist and on occasions authors are to be taken at their word.

---

[1] J.F. Dienstag, 'Postmodern Approaches to the History of Political Thought', in G. Klosko (ed.), *The Oxford Handbook of the History of Political Philosophy* (Oxford, Oxford University Press, 2011), p. 43.

Derrida refuses two sorts of interpretations of authors and ideas that have been common in the history of political thought. First, he rejects a summative view whereby all ideas are judged according to a universal standard of truth.[2] Western philosophy, for Derrida, suffers from a logocentrism, which imagines truth to be ascertainable by an objective register of meaning.[3] Philosophy presumes a foundational truth. If there is such a foundational perspective, then all ideas can be seen in its light. The light shines on a single form of truth. But this form of truth runs into problems because there is no single formula of truth. While Derrida is an opponent of the supposed universality of Western metaphysics, he is also suspicious of neat and final interpretations of texts. Authors may know what they say, but they always say more than they know. The fluidity of meaning, which flows from texts, reflects a resistance to closure that challenges any particular interpretive scheme. Language, for Derrida, is open and resists determinate resolution. Authors might intend to say this or that in their texts but the dependence of 'this' on 'that', the endless associations of signs with other signs, complicates the determinacy of any intended meaning and opens texts to alternative interpretations.

These two sorts of refusal are associated. The claims of Western metaphysicians to establish a final, determinate truth are compromised by the indeterminacy of the linguistic ways in which they make their claim. Metaphysics purports to provide objective criteria supporting its truth claims, which supersede associational meanings that are generated by the play of linguistic signs. For Derrida, however, language is not an instrument, serving an extralinguistic metaphysical purpose. It neither represents an external reality, nor serves as a transparent medium for the expression of inmost thoughts. The constitutive signs of language are internally related to one another, rather than deriving their meaning from an external outer reality or from an internal inner dimension. Representation of an external reality and the expression of an inner self neither impart meaning to nor limit the operations of language. They are activities that are undertaken within language and so there is no extra-linguistic determination of what is to count as truth. The ideal of speech as revealing the presence of truth explains its metaphysical priority over writing, but Derrida takes this presumption to be unsupportable. Relatedly, for Derrida, 'there is nothing outside the text.'[4] Texts do not admit of an 'external' or 'internal' resolution of their meaning, whether a resolution is imagined as a context to which the text is reduced or as an intention to which an author is committed. Texts are composed of signs, the meanings

---

[2] For such a view, see L. Strauss, *What is Political Philosophy? And Other Studies* (Glencoe Il., Free Press, 1959).

[3] J. Derrida, *Of Grammatology* trans. G.C. Spivak (Baltimore, Maryland, Johns Hopkins University Press, 1974), pp. 10–11.

[4] Ibid., p. 158.

of which depend upon their multiple associations and inter-relations, so that there is no single universal truth but an interplay of meanings and a multiplicity of interpretations. In 'Structure, Sign and Play in the Discourse of the Human Sciences' in *Writing and Difference*, Derrida intimates how his refusal to accept the rules of metaphysical discourse intimates his acceptance of the play of signs within language. He concludes, 'There are thus two interpretations of interpretation, of structure, of sign, of play. The one seeks to decipher, dreams of deciphering a truth or an origin which escapes play and the order of the sign, and which lives the necessity of interpretation as exile. The other, which is no longer turned towards the origin, affirms play and tries to pass beyond man and humanism, the name of man being the name of that being who, throughout the history of metaphysics or of ontotheology—in other words, throughout his entire history—has dreamed of full presence, the reassuring foundation, the origin, and the end of play. The second interpretation of interpretation, to which Nietzsche has pointed the way, does not seek in ethnography as Levi-Strauss does, the 'inspiration of a new humanism'.[5]

Derrida's interpretation of interpretation opens up interpretive possibilities and resists closure in the history of political thought. It challenges the traditional claims of political philosophy to reveal universal truths, in that Derrida denies its claims to close the play of signs and the multiplicity of meanings. There can be no final interpretation of democracy or freedom, because what they mean turns upon their relations to changing and multiple conceptual idioms. Again, Derrida is against privileging the author's perspective in interpreting texts of political thought. An author, like Hegel, might imagine that he offers the final word on inter-personal relations or on historical development, but history discloses a continual reworking of how sexuality and gender relations are to be conceived. Likewise, Derrida is sceptical over claims that contexts can supply conclusive material in establishing the meaning of political theories. A context, for Derrida, is not a limit outside the interplay of signs, like a sub-conscious drive imposing on conscious agency, hence it does not foreclose debate on what a text might mean. Given that a context is part of the linguistic field in which a text operates, it cannot be separated from the play of interpretive possibilities to establish itself as a definitive cause outside of the play of interpretation. Derrida's contribution to interpreting past political thinkers is to open up interpretive possibilities and to foreclose on closure. In doing so he, and his interpreters such as Norris, accept the conditional utility of scholarly interpretations of thinkers, which allow for an authorial voice and contextual determination. Norris maintains plausibly that it is wrong to assume that 'deconstruction entails a complete

---

[5] J. Derrida, 'Structure, Sign and Discourse in the Human Sciences', in J. Derrida, *Writing and Difference* trans. A. Bass (London, Routledge & Kegan Paul Ltd, 1978), p. 292.

disregard for authorial intentions.'[6] Derrida, however, challenges the finality
of these forms of interpretation, even if he himself occasionally reads a text
in terms of its manifest content and the imputed designs of its author, when
an author such as Nietzsche or Benjamin anticipates his own perspective.
Generally, Derrida's relentless deconstruction of authorial and contextual
standpoints tends to undermine rather than allow for alternative styles of
interpretation, and underplays what texts and authors might have to offer.

METAPHYSICS, LANGUAGE, AND WRITING

Western metaphysics is a language of universal truth that has been conducted
in many idioms. Plato's *Dialogues*, for Derrida, establish the priority of
presence. The spoken word purports to supersede writing because it allows
for the ideal of presence, direct communication of a truth, which is uncontaminated by the indirect formulations of writing. Participants in Plato's
dialogues, save for some of the later ones, engage with Socrates, who, as critic
or seer, yields the standards and incarnates the presence, whereby the ideas
of the dialogue are judged. Plato admonishes reliance on writing, because
it deflects from the truth, which is to be presented by a presence that is
independent of ancillary statements in writing.[7] Where Plato subscribes to
the notion of a universal rational order external to and responsible for the
permutations of thought and language, Descartes and Rousseau turn inwards
and imagine truth to be the transparent reflection of self-consciousness. In
another guise, teleological theorists ascribe a supervening rational meaning to
historical development so as to locate truth on a linear chronological scale.
These distinctive metaphysical idioms suffer from similar internal disorders,
which are liable to deconstruction. Plato's objective order of reason is correlated to its cognition, but that relation complicates and compromises its
independence. The inner self is a ruse and a mystery as much as a revelation,
and raises questions over discriminating the authentic expression of the
self in the stream of self-consciousness. Moreover, the reporting of self-
consciousness relies upon the very discursive conventions, against which the
turn inwards and away from the world was directed. Finally, the absorption of
historical events into the embrace of a teleological narrative deprives events
of the contingency by which they are constituted. In an interview Derrida
explains how his approach refuses the moment of Hegel's dialectic, which

---

[6] Note the multiple ways in which Derrida examines Rousseau's *Essay on the Origin of
Languages*, J. Derrida, *Of Grammatology*, pp. 168–265; See also C. Norris, *Derrida* (London,
Fontana Press, 1987), p. 112.
[7] J. Derrida, *Of Grammatology*, pp. 18–27.

absorbs preceding terms via an assimilative, critical dynamic. In so doing Derrida refuses to assimilate the contingent and the particular into a circle of philosophical discourse. He observes, 'If there were a definition of *differance*, it would precisely be the limit, the interruption, the destruction of the Hegelian *relève* wherever it operates.'[8]

In *Of Grammatology* Derrida undertakes a generic and historical critique of metaphysics and in so doing deconstructs the metaphysical quest for universal meaning. The opening section of its part one is entitled, 'The End of the Book and The Beginning of Writing', in which Derrida identifies an end of an epoch, where speech is privileged over writing and he signals the advent of another age, in which writing is to assume primacy. How is this to be understood? Derrida disturbs the conventional priority that speech is assigned over writing, taking it to be coincidental with the impetus in Western philosophy to establish absolute knowledge. Philosophy and speech converge upon a sense of presence, whereby truth is realized without following the chains of signifiers along which truth eludes finality and resolution. The closing of the page on the book, however, vitalizes writing and the endless play of signifiers, and dispels the illusions of presence and philosophical speculation. Contemporary innovative forms of writing, such as cybernetics, which are removed from speech, combine with the destructive philosophical operations of Nietzsche and Heidegger to foreshadow the demise of Western metaphysics.[9] In the opening section of *Of Grammatology* Derrida offers a compressed history of Western metaphysics, which runs from Aristotle to Hegel by way of Christian theology. In all its guises concepts are imagined as operating beyond the play of signifiers. Aristotle conceives of language as articulating thoughts inside the mind; Christian theologians perceive God as determining the conceptual architecture of the created world. Descartes establishes certitude by inward interrogation of self-consciousness, and Hegel traces the movement of thought beyond conceptual interplay towards a terminus of truth. Within this narrative Derrida identifies Rousseau to be pre-eminent in announcing a form of confessional truth, whereby philosophy accesses an inner authenticity. In *Of Grammatology* he concentrates upon deconstructing Rousseau's analysis of language so as to highlight his own deconstructive strategy. Derrida, like his predecessors, Nietzsche and Heidegger, acknowledges how his deconstruction emerges from an internal examination of metaphysics. He remarks, 'The hesitation of these thoughts (here Nietzsche and Heidegger's) is not an "incoherence": it is trembling proper to all post-Hegelian attempts and to this passage between two epochs. The movement of deconstruction does not destroy structures from the outside.'[10]

---

[8] J. Derrida, 'Positions: Interview with Jean-Louis Houdebine and Guy Scarpetta' trans. A. Bass, in J. Derrida, *Positions* (London, Continuum, 2004), p. 38.

[9] J. Derrida, *Of Grammatology*, pp. 10–26.   [10] Ibid., p. 24.

Derrida interprets metaphysical truth to imply a privileging of the spoken word and a concomitant deprecation of writing. Metaphysics is aligned with 'presence' and a direct experience of truth. Truth is to be expressed directly and without indirect contrivance and elaboration. Writing works differently; it allows for the considered reflection of the author. It employs conventions and devices, which distances authors from direct experiential apprehension of the truth. Derrida rejects the notion of an external truth that is to be accessed by language and refuses a priority of speech over writing. Language for Derrida is non-representational, though he neither denies an external world, nor refuses to acknowledge that words are standardly used to refer to things and to express thoughts in one's head. But the outside and the inside are figures of language, and reference depends on using words. If words are constitutive rather than instrumental, then the priority that is traditionally assigned to the spoken word is questionable. If meaning depends on the play of words, then, the devices by which words are put together, and the play of words that is mediated by conventions and formulas, such as grammar and spacing, are not to be dismissed as subordinate to what words refer. Writing is primary rather than secondary. What we have is language, and the way it operates shapes how the world and language users are to be considered. There is no world outside language, to which truth might be aligned. Our inmost thoughts may be profound, but they do not supersede linguistic expression, for they are enabled and delivered within a language that allows for their expression. If philosophers pursue a holy grail of truth that resists and supersedes the constraints of language and expression, then what they seek is as mythical as the holy grail of Christian mythology. Derrida rejects the notion of a determinate, foundational truth, just as he breaks with the idea of speech as the basis of language. Writing, for Derrida, takes priority. The opposition between writing and speech, however, is to be superseded. It is of a piece with other dichotomies, which elevate one side of a conceptual pairing so as to generate a determinacy at odds with the play of language. Just as the truth of Plato's ideas, in its independence from sensuous phenomena, is to be rejected, so the privileging of speech as the vehicle for an objective truth is to be denied.

Writing for Derrida is not divorced from speech. They both configure the world and our thoughts and they do so by connecting signs and expressions in multiple ways. Connecting devices, including spacing and grammar, are associated with writing but they inform speech, so Derrida concludes that speech is a form of writing, and that writing is not to be classified as a degenerate form of speech. In *Of Grammatology* Derrida deconstructs the ways in which Saussure, Levi-Strauss, and Rousseau privilege speech over writing and shows how their arguments betray the dependence of speech on writing. The history of political thought, in the light of Derrida's deconstruction of metaphysics is neither a progressive Hegelian achievement of the truth, nor a series of conceptual explorations of political truths by canonical authors. Authors and universal truth do not frame the contents of political thinking; rather language and writing admit a play of meanings to which texts are susceptible. Derrida's resistance to standard readings of texts, whereby they are interpreted to be expressions of their authors' intentions or as so many ways of exploring a universal truth, opens up the scope of interpretation to register unintended features and conceptual tensions. If Derrida releases interpretive possibilities, he downplays hermeneutical readings. The final word is not left to authors even if Derrida allows for a double reading of texts, whereby a scholarly interpretation of authorial conceptions is supplemented by a deconstructive reading.[11] Derrida himself can be interpreted as intending *Of Grammatology* to be read in the light of his own sense of the end of metaphysics, and yet he does not reflect upon this possibility of an implicit teleology influencing the framing of its argument. His introductory narrative on the history of metaphysics culminates in the death of the book and the primacy of writing. It is a linear narrative in which the questionability of metaphysics and the play of signs in writing are prominent themes. The upshot is that the reader receives a reading of history, in which contingent developments are construed as symptoms of a definitive end of metaphysics. If the notion of the end of metaphysics is to lead the reader to the play of multiple meanings rather than to a closure of possibilities, then, perhaps, we should not take Derrida at his word. We might question the ways in which he structures his argument. Doubtless the death of metaphysics is a narrative that makes sense of the historical questioning of the series of conceptual formulations of a determinate truth outside the play of signs. However, the texts of classical metaphysics exhibit a range of styles and undertakings, which is not captured without remainder in Derrida's narrative. Plato's dialogues represent a quest for truth, but as Murdoch and Strauss in divergent styles intimate, the search is never closed and the conversational interplay between characters opens up multiple possibilities.[12] The *Parmenides*, for instance, casts doubt on the language of forms or objects of truth if they are to be envisaged as existing outside of the phenomena to which they refer.[13] Again, Rousseau imagines nature to constitute a pointed and yet unsustainable contrast with civilization and yet the contrast allows for a sharp critique of civilized practices that supersedes the unreality of nature.[14]

---

[11] Ibid., pp. 157–64; see also A. Bradley, *Derrida's 'Of Grammatology'* (Edinburgh, Edinburgh University Press, 2008), pp. 147–8.

[12] See I. Murdoch, *The Fire and the Sun: Why Plato Banished the Artists* (Oxford, Oxford University Press, 1977); L. Strauss, *The City and Man* (Chicago, Chicago University Press, 1964).

[13] Plato, *Parmenides* trans. F.M. Cornford, in E. Hamilton and H. Cairns (eds), *The Collected Dialogues of Plato, including the Letters* (Princeton, Princeton University Press, 1961), p. 945.

[14] See the commentary on Rousseau in this chapter and in chapter 11 on Rousseau.

DECONSTRUCTING TEXTS

Philosophical truth cannot be separated from the terms in which it is established, so the meaning of texts is not to be reduced either to the intentions of authors or to independently specifiable contexts. While Skinner maintains that the death of the author is an exaggeration, Derrida conceives of the author to be inseparable from the text.[15] We cannot let the author have the final word on their text, because the author is not detachable from the text. What we have is writing. The author is disclosed in the language of the text, and its play of signs can be interpreted in multiple ways. In *Of Grammatology* Derrida recognizes how an author (Jean-Jacques Rousseau) can always say 'more, less, or something other than what he *would mean* or want to say' (emphasis in original).[16] Rather than ascribing meaning to an author, Derrida assumes that there is nothing but the text, but to say there is nothing but the text is not to imply that its language does not involve meanings that relate to a plurality of possibilities.[17] To separate text from context is the equivalent of separating the author from the text. Authors and contexts do not constitute discrete terms, by which a text may be reduced either to serving the author's purposes or to reflecting features of its context. It is a category mistake to imagine text, context, author, or reader to operate independently from one another, and to assume fixed identities by which roles can be definitively assigned. Derrida, in refusing to assign sovereign authority to an author is at odds with Strauss, who imagines authors as bearers of truths, which they can insinuate within texts.[18] His deconstructive standpoint also runs counter to Skinner's notion of a determinate context, which provides the conceptual and discursive resources for an author's intervention into a political situation.[19] For Derrida, the very imagining of truth as fixed, and secure from the interplay of signs, is a symptom of the closure of Western metaphysics. It is to be exposed by a process of deconstruction, which loosens its grip on signs as well as relaxing the rigidity of the roles that are assigned to author, reader, and text.

Derrida's practice of deconstruction interprets texts against the grain of their intended authorial meanings. Western metaphysics closes meaning by assigning determinacy to 'truths' outside the play of language and its multiple associations of signs in writing. Derrida's deconstructive easing of interpretive rigidities exposes the conceptual tensions, to which a philosophical fixing of truth is subject. Derrida's reading of Plato's dialogue, the *Phaedrus* in *Plato's*

---

[15] Q. Skinner, 'Interpretation and the Understanding of Speech Acts,' in Q. Skinner, *Visions of Politics*, vol. 1, *Regarding Method* (Cambridge, Cambridge University Press, 2002), p. 117.

[16] J. Derrida, *Of Grammatology*, p. 144.   [17] Ibid., p. 144.

[18] L. Strauss, *Persecution and the Art of Writing* (Chicago, Il., University of Chicago Press, 1988).

[19] Q. Skinner, 'Meaning and Understanding in the History of Ideas', in Q. Skinner, *Visions of Politics*, vol. 1, *Regarding Method*, p. 87.

Pharmacy is instructive. In *Plato's Pharmacy* Derrida explores the ambiguities of the word, *pharmakon*, which can mean either cure or poison, in reconsidering the story of how Thamus the King of Egypt is offered the gift of writing as a cure by the Egyptian divinity Threuth.[20] The King refuses this gift, imagining writing not to be a poison rather than a remedy, because its role in aiding memory and in facilitating the transmission of thought renders people overly dependent on its operation, thereby undermining memory and the expression of ideas. It derogates from speech and the direct authority that is demanded by the speaker of words. Derrida attends to the unremarked ambiguity of the word *pharmakon*, which thereby serves as a register of the multiple meanings that are conveyed by signs.[21]

Plato's support for speech in the *Phaedrus* is of a piece with his standard dialogical quest for an essential truth, which supersedes the interplay of words in writing and an endless transmission of significations. Socrates, Plato's principal interlocutor, points to the authority that is exercised over words by their father, the speaker of words. Paternal authority supports the authority of presence in the form of speakers, who cultivate speech to command the sovereign truth of the Good. Derrida, however, subverts Plato's patriarchal defence of the authoritative claims of speech by observing that the very notion of fatherhood is dependent upon the operation of language. Derrida follows Freud in challenging the authority of the figure of the father by remarking on how it is unfeasible to imagine fatherhood to prefigure the word and the operation of signs. Derrida deconstructs Plato's language in disturbing the presumed priority of speech over writing. He shows how the spoken word is not to be established by an extra-linguistic paternity. What we have are words and the endless chain of signifiers within language, within writing. We lack the register of a legitimating truth, outside the play of words, which might frame and legitimate metaphysics and political authority.[22]

If *Plato's Pharmacy* deconstructs the pedigree of truth and the order of metaphysics, Derrida's *Of Grammatology* undermines the deprecation of writing and the elevation of absolutist truth, holding them to constitute interrelated forms of Western philosophy's closure. Following its deflationary narrative of Western metaphysics *Of Grammatology* deconstructs the priority assigned to speech over writing in the work of three theorists, who are central to the modernist misalignment of speech and writing. First, Derrida turns to Saussure, whose structural linguistics are diagnosed as maintaining a traditional hierarchy, notwithstanding their apparent radicalism in maintaining the arbitrariness of signification. Saussure's science of linguistics appears to release the

[20] J. Derrida, 'Plato's Pharmacy', in J. Derrida, *Dissemination* (Chicago, Chicago University Press, 1981), p. 32.
[21] Ibid., p. 35.   [22] Ibid., p. 38.

fluidity of meaning from prevailing constraints, as it identifies the arbitrary relationship between signified and signifier. However, Derrida observes how Saussure assigns primacy to phonetic over non-phonetic schemes, which intimates a nostalgia for the priority of speech over writing. This intimation is confirmed by Saussure's identification of the dependence of writing on speech. His attribution of a dependent obfuscatory role to writing is reflected in his tracing of the origins of politics and violence to its development. Derrida connects his deconstructive critique of Saussure's radicalism to the association of phonetic writing with the truth regime of Western metaphysics. He observes, 'The system of language associated with phonetic-alphabetic writing is that within which logocentric metaphysics determining the sense of being as presence, has been produced.'[23]

Derrida's deconstructive techniques operate so as to subvert the apparent implications of an author's standpoint. In identifying the traces of hierarchies that are maintained by the continuing privileging of speech over writing, in Saussure's *Course in General Linguistics*, Derrida suggests the actual priority of writing in the operations of language. If hierarchical traces are to be effaced and the free play of signs is to be recognized, then difference can be thought.[24] If signs are constituted simply by their internal differences, and the form of individual signs is not to be valorized, then meaning is disclosed to be the play of signs and the sign in isolation possesses no independent frame of meaning. Hence Derrida concludes, 'Without retention in the minimal unit of temporal experience, without a trace retaining the other as other in the same, no difference would do its work and no meaning would appear'.[25] Difference is revealed to be the formation of form.[26] Derrida's vocabulary of deconstruction emerges out of his deconstructive engagement with Saussure. Language depends upon the differences between signs, so that difference and the trace represent distinctive and creative aspects of meaning. Derrida observes, 'That the signified is originally and essentially (and not only for a finite and created spirit) trace, that it is *always already in the position of the signifier* is the apparently innocent proposition within which the metaphysics of the logos of presence and consciousness, must reflect upon writing as its death and source.'[27]

In interpreting Levi-Strauss, Derrida shows the continuing impact of Saussure on contemporary structuralism. In the section of *Of Grammatology* that is entitled 'The Violence of the Letter' Derrida deconstructs the normative and theoretical assumptions of the anthropologist. Derrida offers an immanent critique of related dichotomies in *Tristes Topiques* focusing upon its opposition between speech and writing. In so doing Derrida questions Levi-Strauss's privileging of the apparently idyllic primitivism of the natives,

---

[23] J. Derrida, *Of Grammatology*, p. 43.   [24] Ibid., p. 50.   [25] Ibid., p. 60.
[26] Ibid., p. 65.   [27] Ibid., p. 75.

whom he has been studying. In Levi-Strauss's confessional account, the transmission of writing in Nambikwara is presented as a dramatic and consequential intrusion into innocent South American lives. The innocence that he attributes to Nambikwarans resonates with Rousseau's celebration of the simplicity of nature. Derrida interprets this imagined innocence to mask a reverse ethnocentrism that represents a guilt-ridden fantasy of a civilized anthropologist rather than considered analysis. Levi-Strauss takes the advent of writing as an event, which ruptures social relations, in presaging exploitation and in constituting an originary violence by which law is instituted. Given the stakes, Levi-Strauss confesses how his introduction of writing to the natives amounts to a violation of a prelapsarian utopia. Levi-Strauss accepts the burden of responsibility, because he identifies no inner cultural momentum towards writing, and its advent represents a sharp break in social relations, in that the natives possess no prior knowledge of writing.

Levi-Strauss induces the natives to draw squiggles on pages in imitation of writing, which he interprets as harmless imitation. However, his sense of the impact of his introduction of writing changes on observing how the chief affects to be able to read the writing to impress other tribes so as to enhance his prestige and increase his power. Levi-Strauss assumes that the chief's action confirms a connection between writing, politics, and exploitation. He is aghast at what he has done and his sense of responsibility derives from his assumption that Nambikwarans were unable to write prior to his writing lesson. He categorizes their tracing of intricate patterns on shells as purely aesthetic, and takes their capacity to elaborate genealogies to be quite separate from the classificatory schemes that are associated with writing. Writing, for Levi-Strauss ruptures the social world, enabling cultural and scientific progress, but also unleashing violence and law. Prior to his intervention he imagines the Nambikwarans to lack writing and to be innocent of the forms of power and violence that the chief begins to practise. Derrida, however, dissents from Levi-Strauss's account. He observes how Levi-Strauss's separation of writing from what he takes to be the tribe's aesthetic activities is unjustifiable, because Nambikwaran culture would not imagine a mutual exclusivity to divide writing from aesthetic activity. Derrida also objects to Levi-Strauss's association of writing with knowledge, culture, and violence. He takes this association to be the product of a partial interpretation of the evidence pertaining to primitive culture and the historical development of knowledge and violence. For Derrida, the originary condition of language implies a form of writing and so the development of violence is not to be attributed to writing as opposed to speech.

The centrepiece of Derrida's *Of Grammatology* is his deconstruction of the overt logic of Rousseau's critique of modern society and culture. Rousseau is taken to be crucial in the development of a modern sensibility. Derrida observes, 'Rousseau's work seems to me to occupy, between Plato's *Phaedrus*

and Hegel's *Encyclopedia*, a singular position'.[28] Rousseau draws upon his inner sensibility to imagine an idyllic, natural, primitive world, which contrasts with the perverse sophistication of modernity. He presents his critique of modern civilization by elaborating a series of demarcated and dichotomous concepts. An originary natural innocence, unencumbered by otherness and duplicity, is contrasted with the hierarchies and pretences of civilization. Innocence is lost in modernity and yet Rousseau's redemptive project is complicated by its entanglement with the sophisticated techniques of modernity that Derrida reads as compromising the dichotomies by which Rousseau operates. For a start, and in ways that subvert his emphatic endorsement of simplicity, the intricacies and indirection of writing are invoked to imitate the supposed directness of speech. Rousseau's texts are eloquent in their intimation, not of what is natural and neatly opposed to modernity, but in their modernist critique of the present via an imaginary naturalism that is never to be repossessed. Derrida takes the concept of nature to be neither natural nor primitive. It bears traces of the multiple conceptual identities of modernity. Rousseau may present the ideas of nature and civilization dichotomously, but they intimate one another, rendering their meaning ambiguous and undecidable, rather than firm and oppositional.

We will focus more squarely upon Derrida's critique of the *Essay on the Origin of Languages* in our subsequent chapter on Rousseau. In reviewing the ambivalences in Rousseau's critique of the written word and its association with pretence and alienation Derrida draws upon Rousseau's *Confessions*. The *Confessions* represents a modernist paradigm of artful self-expression, a precursor to Proust, Joyce, and Woolf. Derrida adverts tellingly to its performative contradictions. It expresses a critique of writing by means of a textual tour de force. Rousseau is aware of what is at stake, in staking his naturalist credentials on a mannered form of confessional writing, and he contrives to explain the anomaly by claiming his writing serves as a supplement that allows him to express inner feelings. Derrida observes how the notion of a supplement is stretched by Rousseau's usage. His supplement supersedes serving as an ancillary technique to facilitate expression. It supplants the role of speech in enabling Rousseau to explore a range of sensitive subjects. Supplementarity operates as more than mere form, as Rousseau's literary confessions announce his resort to a procession of supplements. The loss of his mother at birth is compensated by his adoption of a mother substitute in Madame de Warens. Likewise Rousseau's resort to masturbation serves as more than a substitute, for it allows scope for control and fantasy to supplant inter-personal engagement.[29] Supplements supplement supplementarity by superseding the original form, and hence what Rousseau appears to condemn as secondary and

---

[28] Ibid., p. 97.
[29] J.-J. Rousseau, *The Confessions* trans. J.M. Cohen (Harmondsworth, Penguin, 1976), p. 145.

removed from nature assumes a primacy that is not to be relegated to a derivative role. The pure and the natural, such as mother-love, sex, and self-expression do not function as primal residues of primitive experience but are only to be glimpsed by means of the mediation of civilization. Derrida deconstructs Rousseau's dichotomies of nature and civilization, the immediate and the mediated, and the simple and the sophisticated.

At the core of his reading of Rousseau, Derrida attends closely to his *Essay on the Origin of Languages*, observing the ambivalences in Rousseau's ostensible argument that speech is primary and the written word thwarts natural expression in underpinning the mediated, alienated character of modern civil society.[30] Rousseau's *Essay on the Origin of Languages* represents Derrida's prime example of the twisted form of Rousseau's reading of the natural and foundational. The *Essay* establishes a series of dichotomies, where one side of the dichotomy is taken to be originary and valuable while the other is designated secondary and perverted. Derrida, however, identifies tensions, which disturb the processes of dichotomization. The sharpness of Rousseau's series of contrasts between the pure and primitive and the derivative and sophisticated unravel in the convolutions of the language by which they are identified. Rousseau's search for origins and the natural foundation of pure language is a mythological device, which is a retrojection from the present rather than identification of the past. Derrida's deconstruction of Rousseau on language will be revisited in a subsequent chapter where its relevance for a reading of Rousseau's politics will be shown. Primal language and nature are imagined by Rousseau to represent inner sensibility in touch with an original purity that has been distorted by the processes of mediation and civilization. Rousseau's narrative is a regressive mythology, whereby the past is invoked to critique a present that casts individuals into restricted, mediated roles. Derrida's interrogation of Rousseau reverses the interplay between past and present. Rousseau's past is not a retrieval of a natural simplicity that represents deliverance from the present, but functions as a projection from the present. Rousseau misrepresents his own narrative of the present as a derogation from the past. Derrida's critical interpretation of Rousseau does not rely on an alternative authoritative guide to the past, but pays critical attention to the ways in which Rousseau frames his argument. In so doing it demonstrates contradictions and the process of deconstruction, which operates by examining texts without succumbing to the sovereign authority of the authors. The implication for the study of past political thought, which will be reinforced by our commentary in chapter 11 on Rousseau is that we should not take

---

[30] J.-J. Rousseau, *Essay on the Origin of Languages* trans. J. Moran and A. Gode, in J.-J. Rousseau, *The Discourses and Other Early Political Writings* ed. V. Gourevitch (Cambridge, Cambridge University Press, 1971).

authors at their word, but rather recognize how words can complicate their apparent intentions.

POLITICS

Derrida turns directly to politics in later works such as *Specters of Marx*, *Rogues*, *Philosophy in a Time of Terror*, and 'Force of Law: The "Mystical Foundation of Authority"'.[31] At the outset of the latter Derrida observes how in turning to politics he is continuing the project of deconstruction. Insofar as deconstruction implies a questioning of foundations, a disturbing of presumed stability, it involves an application to a politics of ethics and justice.[32] If metaphysical notions of law, of justice, or of the state assume that conditions of political order are maintained by universal criteria, then Derrida's deconstructive techniques destabilize their application. Rousseau's *Social Contract* and Plato's *Republic* presume problematically that reason frames political associations by means of criteria of justice, which resist disputatious frames of interpretation.[33] Derrida cites *Glas*, in which he deconstructs Hegel's imagining of the patriarchal family as a bridge between the natural and the spiritual, and the individual and the ethical, to represent an example of his direct engagement with ethical and political theory.[34] In *Glas*, he conducts a critique of Hegel by juxtaposing passages of the *Philosophy of Right* and Hegel's early religious texts, with passages from the works of Genet, the homosexual and criminal playwright.[35] Political questions, for Derrida, are not to be resolved authoritatively by recourse either to an overriding metaphysical logic or to the predetermined course of an author's intentions. Derrida undermines definitive determinate answers to standard accounts of justice, terror, democracy, and rogue states.

---

[31] J. Derrida, *Specters of Marx: The State of the Debt, the Work of Mourning and the New International* trans. P. Kamuf (London, Routledge, 1994); J. Derrida, 'Force of Law: The "Mystical Foundation of Authority"' trans. M. Quaintance, in D. Cornell, M. Rodenfield, and D. Gray Carlson (eds), *Deconstruction and the Possibility of Justice* (London, Routledge, 1992); J. Derrida, 'Autoimmunity: Real and Symbolic Suicides—A Dialogue with Jacques Derrida, Deconstructing Terrorism', in G. Borradori (ed.), *Philosophy in a Time of Terror—Dialogues with J. Habermas and J. Derrida* (Chicago and London, University of Chicago Press, 2005); J. Derrida, *Rogues* trans. P.-A. Brault and M. Nass (Stanford, California, Stanford University Press, 2005).

[32] J. Derrida, 'Force of Law: The "Mystical Foundation of Authority"', p. 4.

[33] See Plato, *The Republic of Plato* trans. F.M. Cornford (Oxford, Oxford University Press, 1945); J.-J. Rousseau, *The Social Contract* trans. G.D.H. Cole, in J.-J. Rousseau, *The Social Contract and Discourses* (London, J. Dent & Sons, 1975).

[34] J. Derrida, 'Force of Law: The "Mystical Foundation of Authority"', p. 7.

[35] Ibid., p. 8.

In 'Force of Law: The "Mystical Foundation of Authority"', Derrida distinguishes between two ways in which deconstruction may be practised. He observes, 'One takes on the demonstrative and apparently ahistorical allure of logico-formal paradoxes. The other, more historical or more anamnesic, seems to proceed through readings of texts. Meticulous interpretations and genealogies.'[36] He proceeds to demonstrate these dual ways in which deconstruction may be practised; on the one hand, by indicating the aporia or stumbling blocks in thinking of justice, and on the other hand by undertaking a critical reading of Walter Benjamin's historic text, 'Critique of Violence'. Derrida sets out three paradoxes to which justice and law are liable, and in so doing highlights ongoing dilemmas in the practice of politics and justice. First, he recognizes how the idea of justice presupposes the freedom of agents to make just decisions. But in making just decisions an agent also recognizes that rules are to be invoked and followed, which in turn raises the question of the compatibility of rules and decisions with the freedom of agency.[37] The decision of a judge, say, has to conform to a relevant legal rule but the match between rule and decision cannot be automatic because that would deny the agency of those involved in the particularities of decision-making. There must be some creative interpretive element in the judgment for the very notion of justice to be operative; it must be, 'both regulated and without regulation'.[38] The gap between judgment and rule entails that any particular judgment can be said to be legal, but its justice is always in question. Judgments are therefore undecidable in that the decision-making process is always underdetermined, and so cannot be decided upon by criteria external to the decision itself. This undecidability of justice is evident in the founding of law. The originary aspects of law by definition cannot appeal to a pre-existing legal code. What is the justice of the rule or law that is founded performatively and which manifestly cannot invoke the operation of law to secure its judgments in particular cases? This undecidable question informs all operations of the law because the justice of law can be questioned at any stage, and the sheer existence of a legal code does not constitute its justice.

The paradox of undecidability informs the operation of law in multiple ways. Decisions have to be made about the relevance of seemingly contrary rules or laws, and creative particular decisions have to be made about the law or rule in particular cases. The question of particularity cannot be answered by reference to a rule, because it is the very nature of rules that gives rise to the problem of judgment of particular cases. Derrida imagines that demands of justice supersede any determinate, finite decision. Hence he derives, by implication, an infinite 'idea of justice', which is not to be reducible to any particular manifestation, which is always underdetermined. This indetermination of

---

[36] Ibid., p. 21.   [37] Ibid., p. 23.   [38] Ibid.

particulars presumes a multiplicity of possible determinations, and this possibility of multiple finite instances, intimates the notion of an infinite horizon
of justice, which resembles a Kantian regulative idea, a messianic promise, or
an Hegelian-Marxist teleology in establishing limits for determinate decisions.
Yet Derrida draws back from committing to a sort of Kantian regulative
idea or Hegelian teleology. Kant's resort to regulative ideas is a response to
the lack of determinacy in making large-scale judgments of areas of experience
that cannot be specified determinately, and neo-Hegelian teleological frameworks order historical experience holistically according to universal criteria.
Derrida, while appreciating the attraction of such measures, denies their
relevance, because the question of justice is in the present, right here and
now, rather in the future or operating as an ideal that is abstracted from the
existential moment.

Justice, for Derrida, demands decisions without determining criteria. Justness is to be established performatively by ongoing events and decisions,
which take account of calculable criteria without being fully determined.
They are performative, either directly or in referring to the performativity of
original decisions. Derrida's formulation of the paradoxes of justice is not
designed to relieve individuals of the responsibilities of justice and to remove
the burden of making decisions in the light of calculating the circumstances,
even if those calculations cannot set aside what is incalculable. Indeed, the
demands of calculation are high and are constantly being recalculated, because
the sphere of politics is neither to be restricted to any determinate zone, such
as a nation state, nor is it to be reserved for individuals of a certain sex or
sexuality, nor even for those of a certain species.[39] What Derrida focuses upon
in his interpretation of justice is the difference between law and justice, which
is irreducible to the determinacy of a legal code. The performative aspect of
law or of a constitution highlights its mystical authority, which cannot be
related to determinate rules or the positivity of law.

In the succeeding section of 'Force of Law: The "Mystical Foundation of
Authority"', Derrida turns to Walter Benjamin's, 'Critique of Violence'. His
reading of this interpretation of law and violence from 1921 does not conform
to what may be termed standard operations of deconstruction, which undermine the constructive role of the author. Instead, it operates by framing the
political context of the text and author, indicating the fragility of the political
framework and status of law in the Weimar Republic, and thereafter explaining the rationale of the text, highlighting and commenting upon its express
meaning. Rather than undermining the role of the author, Benjamin is seen as
anticipating deconstruction. The antimonies in the operation of law and
justice that Derrida identifies provide resources for a deconstruction of law

---

[39] Ibid., p. 29.

and justice. At the last, however, in reflecting upon a counter-factual consideration of how Benjamin would assess Nazism and the final solution, Derrida suggests how deconstruction might supersede the Benjamin text.

Derrida recognizes how Benjamin's meditation on violence anticipates rather than requires deconstruction. He remarks, 'But this deconstruction is in some way the operation or rather the very experience that this text, it seems to me first does itself, by itself, on itself.'[40] Benjamin's critique of violence is not a concentrated indictment, but is critical in the same way that Kant's *Critique of Pure Reason* is a critique. He subjects violence to an analytical evaluation of its operation and foundation. Benjamin begins by observing how violence presupposes its transgression of law and justice and then reviews how law construes the operation of violence. He reviews how violence is interpreted by positive and natural law. Positive law cannot provide reliable criteria either for employing or combating violence because law operates as a means of achieving justice and justice itself is not justified by law. Relatedly natural law establishes rational ends of justice but merely assumes the justice of legal means to achieve those ends. The upshot is that both forms of justification are circumscribed and are at a loss to provide foundations. Benjamin remarks, '[I]f positive law is blind to the absolute of ends, natural law is equally so to the contingency of means.'[41]

Benjamin concludes by recognizing how the violence of law requires external justification. He observes that 'a standpoint outside positive legal philosophy but also outside natural law must be found.'[42] Benjamin's analysis of the paradoxes of legal theory and the law's incapacity to justify its monopoly on violence calls into question the entire system of law. In reviewing the justification of its operation he directs attention to the original performative declaration of law. Benjamin remarks, 'Violence crowned by fate is the origin of law.'[43] It is the performative aspect of law at its foundation that lies behind its ongoing authorization of violence. Derrida allows Benjamin's observations on the antimonies of legal theory to highlight the instability of law and to indicate the crucial role of the performativity of an originary founding violence in its operation.

In analysing the operation of law and its monopolistic claim on the legitimate use of violence, Benjamin invokes the possibility of a general strike. A general strike by its very generality calls into question law as a whole, and its monopoly on violence. Benjamin discriminates between a general strike that aims to change political conditions, but which assumes the ongoing nature of law and politics, and a proletarian general strike, which strikes at the heart of

[40] Ibid., p. 30.
[41] W. Benjamin, 'The Critique of Violence', in W. Benjamin, *Reflections, Essays, Aphorisms* trans. E. Jephcott (New York, Schocken Books, 1985), p. 279.
[42] Ibid., p. 280.   [43] Ibid.

law in demanding an overthrow of the state. The latter strike challenges the very founding authority of law in claiming that law lacks affirmative foundations. Derrida, in rehearsing the logic of Benjamin's argument, wonders if a general strike is a metaphor for the characteristic operations of deconstruction. He muses, 'Is that what deconstruction is? Is it a general strike or a rupture?'[44] Derrida answers his question by concluding that deconstruction is both a general strike and a rupture. He supports Benjamin's identification of the police in a democratic society as complicating legal operations, due to their increasing tendency to go beyond the law in making peremptory executive decisions. He suggests that Benjamin might have positively recognized their operations to be spectral in flitting between rather than within boundaries.[45] Benjamin concludes his article with an elliptical but highly suggestive distinction between mythological and divine justifications of law, which Derrida interprets to be incisive in identifying the contrary indeterminacy of law. Myth presents violence as a manifestation of fate and hence shows law to exercise power in determining the fate of particular actions and in relating outcomes to underlying processes. Divine intervention, in contrast, stands above law and particularities. Benjamin expresses the consequential and irresolvable antimony between law and justice in the following terms, 'If mythical violence is law making, divine violence is law destroying.'[46]

In a postscript to his analysis of Benjamin's 'Critique of Violence', Derrida conjectures on how Benjamin might have analysed Nazism and the final solution, while recognizing that such a counter-factual defies an answer given the contextual specificity of Benjamin's text. He imagines that Benjamin would have seen Nazism as the radicalization of evil, representing the complete collapse of communication and of the totalitarian radicalization of the state. He hypothesizes that Benjamin would have viewed Nazism as the nemesis of the corruption of parliamentary democracy, exemplifying the thoroughgoing undermining of parliamentary practice by the application of a police state. Benjamin is imagined as conceiving of Nazism and the Holocaust as the radicalization of mythical violence in its founding and conserving aspects. Nazism serves as the final solution of mythic violence which obliterates witness to its violence. It lies outside of the representation of right and of myth. Hence the very finality of Nazism invokes its other; a divine singularity. This reading of the final solution would take the collapse of the ethical to be beyond humanity. For Derrida, it suggests how a Benjaminian interpretation of violence, notwithstanding its polysemic mobility, might cast divine violence on a colossal scale, by which fate is silenced in its expiatory manifestation of divine anger. In deconstructing Benjamin at the close of his essay, Derrida suggests that a combination of the mythical and divine, of the

---

[44] J. Derrida, 'Force of Law: The "Mystical Foundation of Authority"', p. 38.
[45] Ibid., p. 45.   [46] W. Benjamin, 'The Critique of Violence', p. 297.

destructive and affirmative are required to respond to the calamity of the holocaust. He observes, 'It is the thought of the differences between these destructions [of Benjamin and Heidegger] on the one hand and a deconstructive affirmative on the other that has guided me tonight in this reading.'[47]

Derrida's interpretation of Benjamin highlights his reading of political texts and his analysis of political judgment. He insists on the undecidability of ethics and politics. Undecidability is the overt political expression of his deconstruction of texts and his disruption of meanings and the closure of metaphysics. Political questions have to be decided, but Derrida insists upon their indeterminacy. In the political texts, *Rogues* and *Specters of Marx*, he exposes the logical paradoxes that subvert finalized political judgments and how past theorists can be invoked to illuminate ongoing political questions. In *Rogues* Derrida deconstructs the assumption that states can be designated as rogue by reference to an assumed universal standard, which can never be established. Ambiguities are constitutive features of the paradoxes that Derrida identifies in democratic decision-making; paradigmatically the democratic method must determine how democracy is to be conducted, but the form of democratic participation is presupposed by, rather than determinative of, democratic participation.[48] Moreover, democracy is susceptible of infinite reinterpretation so that its form is always provisional. Derrida suggests that its indeterminacy is to be aligned with the notion of perfectability in the promise of a democracy to come, which underpins a critical form of political practice, and which is accompanied by a recognition that the promise is never to be redeemed.[49]

Rogues revisits the argument of 'Force of Law: The "Mystical Foundation of Authority"', in identifying the sense of a justification, which is promised but never delivered decisively. He is prepared to frame his interpretations of justice and democracy by resorting to a Kantian notion of a regulative idea, though again he takes care to distinguish his use of the notion from the Kantian move of imagining experience in generic transcendental terms.[50] In *Specters of Marx*, which will be examined in detail in chapter 14 on Marx, Derrida invokes Marx as a spectre to haunt the contemporary post-Marxist ideological world of a new internationalism, which reflects the constrictive assumptions of a neo-liberal Western regime. The new internationalism lays down the law on rights and political order but is insensitive to global economic inequality and to the infinite possibilities of specifying rights and considering order. The contradictions to which the new internationalism is liable renders it susceptible to Marxist critique.[51] Derrida's interpretation of Marx is a politically motivated reading, which responds to post-Marxist

---

[47] Ibid., p. 63.
[48] J. Derrida, *Rogues* (Stanford California, University of Stanford Press, 2005), p. 38.
[49] Ibid., p. 37.   [50] Ibid.   [51] J. Derrida, *Specters of Marx*, pp. 62–4.

circumstances, in that Derrida refrained from engaging with Marx when the name of Marx operated as an organizational feature of the political world. In doing so Derrida evokes aspects of Marx's texts, for instance, their messianism and spectral language, which serve as insinuating disruptions of present orthodoxies.[52] He uses Marx to critique a new liberal internationalism, which proclaims a particular reading of international order to be just without opening to multiple contrary possibilities that are conjured by the ghost of Marx.

CONCLUSION

Derrida deconstructs the canon of Western philosophy, and in so doing subverts the history of Western political thought. He denies a canon because there is no supporting frame for an underlying truth holding together diverse texts. The texts themselves do not deliver political truths that can be correlated to a non-linguistic objective order. There is no external structure to which linguistic manoeuvres can be aligned. Derrida disrupts a final redemptive truth in the historical process, and rejects a vision of the history of ideas as the recovery of an author's meaning. Derrida's practice of deconstruction is at odds with alternative formulations of methods in the history of political thought. The Cambridge School's focus upon recovering authors' intentions is upset by his observation of the fluidity of meaning, which renders authorial intentions as indeterminate as textual declarations. The context, just like a text, lacks a fixed meaning. Again, Gadamer's projected dialogical engagement with past texts assumes that horizons can be fused, when texts, for Derrida, reveal blockages and tensions rather than openness to engagement with future readers.[53] Genealogy presumes a dependence of the present upon the past while proclaiming their mutual contingency. Derrida maintains that texts do not exhibit a single determinate meaning. He observes how they do and do not operate as their authors proclaim. In reading philosophical texts, he tends to focus on textual contradictions, which reflect an authorial presumption of extra-linguistic and stable truths that are at odds with a text's form of argument. Hence, past texts of political philosophy are to be deconstructed. Rousseau's imaginative evocation of a utopian primitivism colludes with the object of its critique, the civilization of modernity. Hegel's end of history affects to close what is inherently open and undecidable, and so is undermined

---

[52] Ibid., pp. 210–20.
[53] J. Derrida, 'Three Questions to Hans-Georg Gadamer', in D. Michelfelder and R. Palmer (eds), *Dialogue and Deconstruction—The Gadamer–Derrida Encounter* (New York, State University of New York Press, 1989), pp. 52–4.

by its own formulation. Locke's natural rights are neither natural nor right, if they are to be taken as statements of a universal normative order that is external to the play of signs in language.

Derrida's deconstruction of interpretive closure is highly compatible with the ongoing multiplicity of interpretations of past political thinkers.[54] The continuous and discontinuous flows of interpretive energy, which configure and reconfigure political thinkers in ever changing forms, intimate how authors and critics are absorbed in a process of continual interpretation. The possibilities of one Marx or two, the young and the old, the philosophical and the scientific, the anthropological and the historical offer revealing but opposing closed interpretations of Marx that are susceptible to the ebb and flow of many factors, including the availability of sources, the state of play of the economy, and of relations between classes as well as more theoretical issues such as the rise and fall of forms of humanism, historicism, structuralism, Hegelianism, and rational choice theory.[55] Derrida's suspicion of closure is exemplary in its ruthless identification of tensions. It lends itself to the critical interrogation of classic texts of political philosophy. Derrida registers how the play of words is not to be resisted. The presumption of a universal truth is exposed as a misleading dissemblance. The deconstruction of Western metaphysics is a sub-text of Derrida's own texts that is formulated expressly in *Of Grammatology*, his sophisticated and notable expression of his method. Of course, the intentional deconstruction of Western metaphysics serves as a hermeneutic and self-subverting clue to the reading of Derrida's texts. Derrida's intention, which is expressly announced in *Of Grammatology*, is to deconstruct Western metaphysics. Derrida's narrative of the construction and intimations of the destruction of Western metaphysics is intentionally grand; as grand as the grandest of authorial narratives. The dismantling of the identity of Western metaphysics is an orienting frame for the disorienting practice of deconstruction. Deconstruction does not take place in an historical vacuum. Derrida is alive to the circumstances of his time. It frames his project. In *Of Grammatology* he recognizes himself to be a successor to the likes of Heidegger and Nietzsche, who have disrupted the metaphysical tropes of the Western metaphysical canon. He imagines himself to be writing at a particular time, in a context that enables his project to be undertaken. He observes how the contemporary development of formal mathematical and cybernetic languages allows for a recognition of writing's emancipation from its subordination to speech. Reference to the discursive context of and Derrida's intentions in writing *Of Grammatology* intimates how the deconstruction of

---

[54] For an account of classic texts of political thought that highlights their susceptibility to reinterpretation see C. Condren, *The Status and Appraisal of Classic Texts* (Princeton, Princeton University Press, 1985).

[55] See chapter 13.

authorial intentions is itself susceptible to a form of deconstruction. The
project of deconstruction is not immune from the intentional project of an
author doing something with words in the light of contextual circumstances.

The susceptibility of Derrida's work to contextual interpretation that allows
a role for the author indicates that deconstruction is not the only method by
which texts might be interpreted. Indeed, Derrida's own readings of Nietzsche
and Benjamin tend to interpret their writings by ways of following their
intentions. Benjamin's analysis of violence and the law is taken to be exemplary in its recognition of its indetermination, and Nietzsche is construed as
expressly undermining metaphysics in registering the multiplicities of meaning that supersede the dogmas of Christianity and humanism. While past
political theorists, who frame dichotomies to privilege their construals of the
political condition are susceptible to deconstruction, they can also be read in
ways that are not deconstructive. Rousseau's idea of nature might well be
contrived and derived from an analysis of civilization but it also serves as a
powerful critique of the idea of progress and of the inequality in the modern
social world. Past texts of political thought can be read productively in a
variety of ways. While abstract forms of speculation lend themselves to
Derridean deconstruction, reconstructing intentions of authors and attending
to the circumstances in which texts are composed can be revealing.[56] The
general truth claims of past authors warrant a critical interrogation that is
lacking in highly historical accounts. Yet past theorists tend to be doing more
than rehearsing metaphysical claims about the political arena. For instance,
Hegel may be wrong in asserting an end to history and in imagining that the
nation state has resolved the tensions of modern political experience, but his
attention to the problems and possibilities of aligning the logic of individualist
market behaviour to the claims of public political organization remains of
value in considering modern social and political forms of organization.

---

[56] Note that Derrida's practice does not sideline intentions but sees meaning as being
irreducible to authorial intentions, see C. Norris, *Derrida*, p. 13. See also A. Bradley, *Derrida's
'Of Grammatology'* (Edinburgh, Edinburgh University Press, 2008).

6

Foucault

Politics, History, and Discourse

INTRODUCTION

How are political ideas to be conceived and interpreted? In several inter-related ways, Foucault offers a way of interpreting political ideas and their history, which is at odds with standard ways of doing so. He has a distinctive way of connecting past and present, which at the same time allows for their radical distinctness from one another. He rejects teleological readings of history that unite present and past in terms of a supervening narrative of progressive development. Power and authority are seen as being exerted in multiple sites and in disjunctive ways so that he opens up the meaning of past politics in recognizing that it is not to be restricted to that of a centralized authority and the operations of the state. Individuals are not taken to be primary in the productions of historic ideas and in establishing the terms of discourse. Rather individual agency is produced by historic discourses. What distinguishes Foucault from other prominent theorists of the history of political thought is that he broadens the identity of past political thought, deconstructing conventional ways of imagining its continuities, and highlighting the constitutive role of discourses in framing political order, social practices, and the possibilities of agency. Foucault is a prolific author, who frames the past in discontinuous ways, but he maintains a consistent deconstruction of assumed identities in past thinking. Madness and punishment, for Foucault, are discontinuous due to the changing ways in which they are conceptualized and administered. Just as present discursive practices and forms of power are not set in stone but can be resisted, so discontinuities in the past can be traced and registered. Foucault's resistance to present practices is connected to his subversion of formulaic ways of seeing the past. His imaginative reading of past and present is provocative but insightful in challenging standard ways of reading the history of political thought and in responding to contemporary social and political practices.

Foucault's political attitude is oppositional. Simons notes, 'Most of Foucault's thought is posed in oppositional terms. He urges us to "refuse what we are", meaning that we should refuse to remain tied to the identities to which we are subjected.'[1] Foucault's opposition to standardized identities extends to the past and to conventional notions of politics. He imagines power as circulating, without a centralized source, so that politics in the form of power and a concomitant claim to truth, are to be encountered on a multiplicity of sites. Knowledge is neither innocent nor universal. In an essay entitled, 'Prison Talk', Foucault observes, '[I]t is not possible for powers to be exercised without knowledge, it is impossible for knowledge not to engender power.'[2] Hence the politics of resistance is not to be circumscribed and Foucault's approach to the history of ideas is aligned to his refusal to subscribe to conventional practice. The politics of refusal merges with his deconstruction of standardized notions of truth and power and formulaic ways of conceiving the past. Standardly, the historian is detached from the object of their study, taking care not to be seen to import present attitudes into the past. Foucault, however, sees his confrontation with contemporary power and its discursive frames as demanding engagement with past forms of knowledge and power. This is not to say that Foucault sees a unity between past and present. He denies its unity. For Foucault, truth is discontinuous and the very commitment to universal truths and essentialized humanism subjects individuals to the power of discursive truth regimes. Re-imagining the past so as to realize its discontinuities opens up a prospect for resisting power in the present.

Foucault's perspective allows for an original and deconstructive engagement with the history of modern political thought. It disturbs formulaic ways of interpreting political ideas and their development. Throughout his career, Foucault repudiates a universal or summative history, which might serve as a frame for a general history of political thought. He rejects the claims of Hegel and Marx to provide summative conceptions of history.[3] Foucault's radical edge is sharpened against generic and totalizing views of history. The teleologies of Hegel and Marx, which frame their readings of past political theorists, are critiqued for illicitly eliding the differences between past and present. In surveying Foucault's revisiting of desire in the context of the dialectic in ruins, Butler observes, 'Foucault contrives to unmoor the dialectic from the subject and its teleological conclusion.'[4] In contrast to teleological historical schemes, Foucault imagines history to constitute an uneven series of

---

[1] J. Simons, *Foucault and the Political* (London and New York, Routledge, 1995), pp. 1–2.

[2] M. Foucault, 'Prison Talk', trans. C. Gordon, in C. Gordon (ed.), *Power/Knowledge* (Brighton, Harvester, 1980), p. 52.

[3] M. Foucault, *The Archaeology of Knowledge* trans. A.M. Sheridan Smith (London, Tavistock Publications, 1995), p. 12.

[4] J. Butler, *Subjects of Desire—Hegelian Reflections in Twentieth Century France* (New York, Columbia University Press, 1987), p. 56.

discursive regimes of truth and power, which do not presage a unity of individual and discursive destiny in the progressive revelation of truth. The sites and methods of the operations of power, and the ways in which they are configured are radically discontinuous. Foucault's historical narratives highlight discontinuities rather than trace the past's continuity with the present. His critique of the present depends upon a contingency that denies a reconciliatory endpoint and presumes unresolvable disjunctions between past and present.[5]

If Foucault undermines the Hegelian dialectical supersession of alterity or even a Collingwoodian retrospective review of continuities, then interpreting the history of political thought becomes a matter of recognizing the disjunction between discourses that have shaped institutions, conceptual frameworks, and subjects. History is not a matter of recovering the meaning of authors by a close scrutiny of either texts or contexts, or even by relating authors, texts, and contexts. Foucault's radicalism breaks with preceding assumptions about the objects of historical understanding as well as repudiating notions of continuity in the history of political thought. If he rejects teleological narratives, he also undermines notions of continuity in political identity. Texts, like authors, do not have meaning outside of discursive frames, which determine patterns of meaning and what is to count as a text at any particular historical conjuncture. Past authors and present readers are not to be conceptualized as subjects sharing trans-historical conceptual horizons that allow for the passage of ideas between the two and the hermeneutical recovery of past thought on the part of the reader. In his essay, 'What is an Author?' Foucault observes, 'We are used to thinking that the author is so different from all other men, and so transcendent with regard to all languages that, as soon as he speaks, meaning begins to proliferate, to proliferate indefinitely. The truth is quite the contrary: the author is not an indefinite source of significations which fill a work: the author does not precede the work; he is a certain functional principle by which in our culture, one limits, excludes, and chooses ...'.[6] Authors, for Foucault, are not the determining agents of past ideas, for their texts are constituted by discourses.

In his deconstructive reading of past thought and practice, Foucault re-reads past thought in counter-intuitive ways, which disturb assumptions of whom and how we are. He destabilizes the meaning of general categories of theory and practice such as madness, punishment, discipline, sexuality, humanism, and the state, by showing how they do not operate with universal meanings that are susceptible of historically innocent philosophical analysis. Madness for instance, the subject of his initial historical work, does not set an ahistorical agenda for the ways in which categories of normal and abnormal

[5] See M. Foucault, 'What is Enlightenment?' trans. M. Henson, in M. Foucault, ed. P. Rabinow, *The Foucault Reader* (London and New York, Penguin, 1984), pp. 32–50.
[6] M. Foucault, 'What is an Author?', trans. J.V. Harari, in M. Foucault, ed. P. Rabinow, *The Foucault Reader*, (London and New York, Penguin, 1984), pp. 118–19.

people are imagined; rather, the ways in which madness is conceptualized and managed determines how people are categorized and treated. The ways in which mad people are diagnosed and handled entail consequences for how power operates in society. Mad people are subjected to the power of designated authoritative medical expertise and the bipolarity between sanity and insanity constitutes differential notions of reason and unreason, the conditions of agency, and diagnoses of bipolarity. The constructed character of madness, its contingent confinement to the margins of society, and its susceptibility to the discursive agenda of commanding medical expertise raise questions about the location and operation of power, just as the history of punishment exhibits a range of disjunctive practices, which bear upon political issues pertaining to the public operation of power and construction of forms of identity. Foucault's sense of the isomorphism of knowledge and power and the control that is exerted by modern institutions, practices and theories highlights how changing discursive practices rather than unencumbered individual agency combine to frame the objects of the history of political thought.

In a number of his texts and particularly in his late lectures on governmentality Foucault deals with authors, concepts, and texts, which figure in preceding and more conventional ways of considering politics and the history of political thought. For instance, in *Discipline and Punish* he interprets modern forms of punishment as differing from preceding styles of corporal punishment. The diminishing role of violence in inflicting punishment is noted alongside the substitution of measures that are calculated to modify behaviour through the application of instrumental and rationally calculated disciplinary techniques. These techniques are transferable to a variety of institutions and are taken to represent the development of a panopticism, a term that is derived from Bentham's Panopticon project. Bentham's Panopticon was an architectural device, which was designed to deliver economical but effective control and surveillance over multiple groups of inmates. Bentham's project is taken by Foucault to epitomize a novel and systemic form of social power that induces docility amongst its targeted populations. Foucault's conceptualization of panopticism is distinct from Bentham's own positive conception of the project. It serves as an example of how Foucault identifies ideas and political theories in ways that run counter to those that are maintained by theorists who are associated with them. Foucault offers a provocative reading of Bentham and of what he understands to represent a modern disciplinary society even if his identification of a developing panopticism might not be historically accurate. We will review the pros and cons of Foucault's interpretation of Bentham in chapter 15.[7] Foucault's capacity to reframe past political thinkers by relating them to discursive practices with

---

[7] M. Foucault, *Discipline and Punish: The Birth of the Prison* trans. A. Sheridan Smith (Harmondsworth, Penguin, 1977), pp. 195–231.

which they themselves would not have identified is evidenced in his reading of Marx. In *The Order of Things* Foucault imagines Marx as subscribing to a modern episteme, a discursive order that is presupposed in a variety of modern disciplines such as economics, biology, and philology. The upshot is that Marx's ideas are linked to forms of thinking that do not rehearse his political radicalism. While Marx might espouse a radical break with capitalism, the order underlying his ideas is taken to reflect affinities to apparently contrary or unrelated perspectives of modern theorists such as Ricardo and Cuvier.[8]

When Foucault interprets past political thinkers, he tends not to take them at their word, but relates their thought to discursive practices that he has defined. In his late lectures on governmentality, where Foucault turns his attention to how conduct is influenced by expressly political measures, he re-imagines past political thinkers by linking them to discourses that they would not have invoked as influences. In his lectures, *Security, Territory and Population*, Foucault reviews the history of past political thought, taking ideas as tracking and reflecting discursive and institutional frameworks. Foucault identifies the character of these changing discursive practices that constitute the frames by which authorial ideas are to be interpreted. Hence he interprets several modern political theorists as delineating state policy in terms of 'reason of state', a phrase that denotes an administrative, police state. A police state is a novel governmental form, which contrasts with a preceding dynastic model that informs Machiavelli's *The Prince*.[9] In *Society Must be Defended* and *The Birth of Biopolitics* Foucault perceives political theorists such as Hobbes and Rousseau to be operating in particular discursive frameworks that disturb their claims to provide generic answers to political issues.[10] In *The Birth of Biopolitics* Foucault develops a subtle reading of the ways in which neo-liberalism reflects the emergence of a developing civil society that provides the conditions for market activities and a form of enterprising individualism. He identifies how Smith, Ferguson, Hobbes, and Locke track and register differing forms of governmental organization that allow for individualism, and how German ordoliberals and the Chicago School of neo-liberalism reflect and develop subsequent neo-liberal discursive practices.[11] Foucault's general interpretive practice of specifying the discursive contexts within which

---

[8] M. Foucault, *The Order of Things* (London and New York, Routledge, 2002), pp. 283–5.

[9] M. Foucault, *Security, Territory, Population: Lectures at the College de France 1977–1978* trans. G. Burchell, ed. M. Senellart (London and New York, Palgrave Macmillan, 2009), pp. 87–115.

[10] M. Foucault, *Society Must be Defended: Lectures at the College de France 1975/6* trans. D. Macey ed. M. Bertani and A. Fontana (London, Allen Lane, 2003); M. Foucault, *The Birth of Biopolitics—Lectures at the College de France 1978–1979* trans. G. Burchell, ed. M. Senellart (London and New York, Palgrave Macmillan, 2008).

[11] M. Foucault, *The Birth of Biopolitics—Lectures at the College de France 1978–1979.*

theories are shaped and theorists operate is not evidenced in his analyses of Nietzsche and in occasional comments on Kant. Rather, in interpreting Nietzsche he focuses on a reading of texts and ideas that recognizes his originality and creativity in framing productive ways of understanding theory and practice that resonate in the present and influence Foucault's own thinking. It remains true that Kant and Nietzsche are recognized as occupying particular roles in developing webs of discourse, but the focus on Kant in the essay 'What is Enlightenment?' and on Nietzsche in several of Foucault's works, but notably in the essay, 'Nietzsche, Genealogy, History', is upon their insightfulness and continuing impact.[12] Foucault's identification of Nietzsche as a precursor of his own deconstructive project will be analysed more closely in subsequent chapters. It is worth remarking here, however, that the status of Nietzsche as a precursor to Foucault's own deconstructive project appears to release Nietzsche's ideas from their historical provenance. Nietzsche's ideas, like Foucault's theoretical practice, are presented as providing a form of truth that is apparently not itself to be reduced to the conditions of its own historical emergence.

In what follows, the several ways in which Foucault disturbs standard readings of the history of political thought will be reviewed. His early analyses of madness and the clinic, which identify the interweaving of power and knowledge in sites that hitherto had been undertheorized will be examined. Thereafter his archaeological readings of discursive structures will be reviewed so as to highlight his understanding of their historicity, which differs radically from theorists of the history of political thought such as Hegel and Marx. His genealogical inquiries into the deployment of disciplinary techniques and the development of sexuality as a discourse will highlight how he takes forms of power and conceptual schemes to be dispersed and historical rather than concentrated and generic. His late analyses of governmentality will focus upon his reading of historic political theorists. Along the way, the force of Foucault's challenge to alternative forms of the history of political thought and his unconventional understanding of the operations of power will be explored and comparisons made with contrasting styles of interpreting the political. Foucault's originality resides in his deconstruction of conventional notions of agency, texts, political power, the state, and thought so as to identify their discontinuous and heterogeneous ways of operating, which are neither reducible to the terms of past actors and authors, nor susceptible of a dialogue between past and present.

---

[12] M. Foucault, 'What is Enlightenment?', p. 42; M. Foucault, 'Nietzsche, Genealogy, History', in M. Foucault, ed. P. Rabinow, *The Foucault Reader* (London and New York, Penguin, 1984), pp. 76–101.

HISTORY, DISCOURSE, AND TRUTH

Amidst Foucault's constantly changing vocabularies and theoretical paradigms, his consistent turn towards history in a multiplicity of idioms highlights the historicity of theory and the lack of universal foundations for the conceptualization of truth and knowledge. Thought, for Foucault, does not allow for unwavering rational understanding. The scene is set by his first work. In *Madness and Civilisation* Foucault neither assumes a generic concept of madness, nor a correlative notion of an essentialist reason. An emphatic way of rejecting the purported dichotomy between reason and madness is to show the multiple formulations and treatments of madness, and to explain them as contingent expressions of discursive practices rather than to represent them as essentialist terms determining practice. Foucault destabilizes notions of madness. Madness and reason are relativized. The focus of Foucault's analysis is the transition from the Renaissance to the classical period of modernity. Whereas madness in the medieval world maintains 'mad' people as part and parcel of the community while excluding lepers, in the Renaissance the 'mad' are symbolic figures, whose strangeness renders them ambivalent marginal presences that are deemed to be capable of profound insight. The status of madness is conveyed in the mythological ship of fools, on which the mad are imagined as undertaking a spiritual journey. This ambiguous respect for the mad collapses in the classical period, in which the mad, along with other marginal types such as vagrants, are incarcerated in houses segregated from normal life. Foucault maintains that confinement took place on an immense scale, with the Great Confinement of 1656 a heightened example of a general European trend.

Following the classical period and the exclusion of 'mad' people from the rest of society by their confinement, the 'mad' return to the human community. Initially they are the objects of a moral normalizing therapy, but subsequently they are subjected to a developing discipline of professional expertise and medical techniques. Whereas early psychiatrists, such as Pinel, are standardly seen to be humanitarian, Foucault highlights the coercive, judgmental regime to which the mad are increasingly subjected. He observes, 'The asylum in the age of positivism, which it is Pinel's glory to have founded, is not a free realm of observation, diagnosis, and therapeutics; it is a juridical space where one is accused, judged and condemned, and from which one is never released except by the version of this trial in psychological depth—that is, by remorse.'[13] Foucault critiques the presumed authority and moral neutrality of the medical regime to which the insane are subjected, and highlights its disciplinary objectifying exertion of power. The operation of scientific

---

[13] M. Foucault, *Madness and Civilisation: A History of Insanity in the Age of Reason* trans. R. Howard (London, Routledge, 1999), p. 269.

authority follows from the self-identification of professionals, who treat those who are categorized as mentally ill, but it is precisely this categorization that is challenged by Foucault's historical account of the mutability of categorizations of madness. Gutting observes, 'Foucault's account seems implausible only if we continue to insist that the identification of madness as mental illness is an objective scientific discovery. His history, however, suggests that the identification was, on the contrary, introduced as a means of legitimating the authority of physicians'.[14] Foucault's destabilization of the assumptions of medical discourse is also traced in his *The Birth of the Clinic* (1963).[15] He identifies a shift in the conceptualization of disease, from a generic understanding of disease to a focus upon individual anatomical symptoms of the body. The scrutiny of the individual body takes place, and the power of the clinician is exhibited in the directed gaze, upon an individual patient's body. Foucault conceptualizes medicine and its changes in terms of power and conceptual transformation, rather than in a narrative of progress that abstracts from discursive paradigms.

Foucault's reading of the dichotomization of the mad and the rational in the modern world, whereby the mad are assigned to the abnormal margins of the population, is symptomatic of modernity's marginalization of the dissonant and different. It raises issues of power and exclusion within the political community. Foucault's Preface to *Madness and Civilisation* highlights its political implications. He observes, 'In the serene world of mental illness, modern man no longer communicates with the madman...the man of madness communicates with society only by the intermediary of an equally abstract reason which is order, physical and moral constraint, the anonymous pressure of the group, the requirements of conformity.'[16] Foucault is a constant critic of the pressures to conformity and normalization in the modern world that arise out of contingent historic social discourses and practices that demand resistance. Foucault's critique of an essentialist 'madness' and his focused analysis of changing forms of conceiving and treating 'madness' is imaginative and plausible. Gutting, however, in 'Foucault and the History of Madness' recognizes how Foucault's work has been criticized by historians for its lack of thorough evidential support.[17]

Foucault's early history of madness serves as a marker for how he undertakes histories, which disrupt the essentialization of categories and point up social practices of power and normalization that are to be resisted politically in the present. In *The Order of Things* (1966) and *The Archaeology of*

---

[14] G. Gutting, *Foucault: A Very Short Introduction* (Oxford, Oxford University Press, 2005), p. 72.
[15] M. Foucault, *The Birth of the Clinic* trans. A. Sheridan Smith (New York, Vintage, 1975).
[16] M. Foucault, *Madness and Civilisation*, p. xii.
[17] See G. Gutting, 'Foucault and the History of Madness', in G. Gutting, *The Cambridge Companion to Foucault* (Cambridge, Cambridge University Press, 2003), pp. 49–74.

Knowledge (1969) Foucault elaborates on his theoretical archaeological reading of historical processes, which allow for his historical work. *The Order of Things* consists in the study of modern thought from the end of the seventeenth century to the present. Its focus is neither on the intentional agency of thinkers and subjects nor on the background contextual influences, which are taken up either consciously or unconsciously by thinkers. What Foucault aims at revealing is the positive unconscious of knowledge.[18] Foucault reviews the formation of diverse discourses of a given period, which constitute what he terms *epistemes*. Epistemes are the unconscious forms of knowledge and rules, underlying a discourse in a specific epoch. Unlike Kantian categories of the possibility of knowledge, they represent historical, a priori sets of rules that are constitutive of knowledge at a given time. They allow for mutability and instability.

The subject of knowledge is removed from epistemic authority. Rather it is the impersonal discursive formation and the rules of operation of knowledge in any epoch that determine things. These rules determine what can be thought and said, and how things are to be understood. For Foucault, meaning is not to be equated either with the reflective activities of a human agent or with teleological progress. Foucault sets out three periods or epochs in which distinctive epsitemes are operative. An episteme that is operative until the end of the sixteenth century works with the notion of resemblance. Renaissance thought operates through metaphor, and is succeeded by the classical episteme of representation, whereby the surfeit of Renaissance figurative resemblances between items is replaced by a representative system of signs by which order is formulated and completed. The sign is severed from a corresponding object. The end of the classical period is signalled by de Sade's focus upon desire, which cannot be expressed exactly. Its obscurity and diffuseness registers the demise of the representational system of language. The taxonomical imperative of Renaissance knowledge yields before the latent power of forces that are imagined as lurking beneath the surfaces of things. In modern knowledge what matters is historicity, finitude, and in general what cannot be represented. 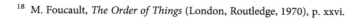 Hence in Ricardo and Marx, the activity of production, labour, is taken to be the inherent source of value that determines the phenomenal movement of prices. Hence against the grain of the self-image of Marx and Marxists, Foucault perceives Marx's categorial system to exemplify the emergent discursive order. Marx appears as a 'fish in water' in the nineteenth-century scheme of things, rather than as a dissident and ground-breaking theorist. Foucault observes, 'At the deepest level of Western knowledge, Marxism introduced no real discontinuity; it found its place without difficulty, as a full, quiet, comfortable and goodness knows satisfying form for a time (its own) within an epistemological arrangement that welcomed it (since it was this arrangement that was in fact

---

[18] M. Foucault, *The Order of Things* (London, Routledge, 1970), p. xxvi.

making room for it) and that it, in return, had no intention of disturbing, no power to modify, even one jot, since it rested entirely upon it.'[19]

The transition to the modern episteme in *The Order of Things* rehearses how Foucault understands the discursive conceptual frame of modernity. The transformation involves a change from a world in which representations are ordered economically in taxonomical frames to a world in which the source of representing is unrepresentable in a scheme of representations. Hence the modern episteme invokes forces that are situated outside the frame of schematic representability. Foucault identifies Kant as a pivotal figure, who aims precisely to identify a framework of categorical representability by transcendental analysis of subjectivity.[20] The Kantian frame, though, does not capture the historicity and finitude of the empirical material that enables representation, and so phenomenological and anthropological schemes of thought track successively the historicity of finitude in humanist teleologies of the end of history. Humanism and grand historical schemes appear to maintain an unyielding grip on thought. Foucault, however, intuits its demise, taking it to be signalled in Nietzsche's iconoclastic reflections. Foucault observes, 'This arrangement (humanism and history) maintained its firm grip on thought for a long while; and Nietzsche, at the end of the nineteenth century made it glow into brightness for the last time by setting fire to it.'[21] In his remarks on Nietzsche, Foucault seems to allow for a historical thinker to think outside of the box of prevailing discourse just as he himself anticipates independently the end of the prevailing episteme. At the very end of the work he remarks on how the essentialist notions of 'man' and 'humanism' are receding.[22] *The Order of Things* was a remarkable bestseller and a demanding read. It attracted critics unsure of how to take the determining role of epistemes and discourse, the rules of which limit what is to be thought. Foucault himself revisits his theoretical framework for archaeological analysis in *The Archaeology of Knowledge*. He replaces the notion of episteme with that of archive, so as to allow flexibility and determinacy, in that an archive informs several fields, or disciplines. However, Foucault continues to maintain that the rules of discourse are primary, and their expression by individual subjects secondary. Archives of a given period comprise the discourses underpinning fields of knowledge, such as political economy and grammar. An archive encompasses practices and social activities, and its formal rules constituting a discursive unity determine discourse. These rules are held to be rules underlying systems of dispersion, which collectively constitute a discursive formation, governing how objects are considered, how strategies are devised, and how projects are formulated. They also constitute enunciative modalities, which position individual subjects in terms of the discursive statements that they are capable

---

[19] Ibid., p. 285.   [20] Ibid., pp. 262–3.
[21] Ibid., p. 286.   [22] Ibid., p. 422.

of uttering. Foucault imagines his perspective to undermine the idea of continuity in history by destabilizing notions of the subject and meaning. He observes, 'Continuous history is the indispensable correlative of the folding function of the subject—in the form of the historical consciousness.'[23] Foucault highlights how his method serves as an antidote to teleology, observing that 'the series described (in *the Archaeology of Knowledge*), the limits fixed, the comparisons and correlations made are based not on the old philosophies of history, but are intended to question teleologies and totalizations.'[24]

Foucault rejects history as the record of a series of meaningful actions that are undertaken by individual subjects, just as he repudiates summative histories. He warns against the contemporary turn to anthropologize Marx so as to render him a humanist, but if Foucault avoids totalizing history then it is less clear that he avoids the pitfalls of schematic structuralism.[25] He aims to provide an explanation of historic discourses by uncovering the rules that govern them These rules, however, are only to be ascertained by analysing actual discourses and are likely to amount to nothing more than contingent co-existing symmetries rather than determining causes. Foucault neither offers a convincing account of discursive change, nor explains the causal and epistemological relations between formal sets of rules and material phenomena. The upshot is that his understanding of discursive formations appears unduly formal.[26] It divorces form from actual practice and the effective relations between discourses, actual ideas, and reflective agents are not established. Problems are compounded by the rhetoric of *The Order of Things*, where the discourse-breaking thought of Nietzsche appears solitary and self-inspired, anticipating Foucault's own independently formulated hints at the impending end of a discursive era. The thought of Nietzsche and of Foucalt himself are presented as independent constructions, which do not depend upon discursive structures. They lack both explanation and justification. The conditionality and operation of Foucault's own theorizing tends to lack convincing explanation throughout his career, even if *The Order of Things* is as suggestively evocative of modernity and its discursive order as *Madness and Civilisation* is incisive in highlighting issues of power.

GENEALOGY AND POWER

In *Discipline and Punish* Foucault switches his attention from formal connections within a discourse to a substantive account of institutions and practices.

---

[23] M. Foucault, *The Archaeology of Knowledge*, p. 12.   [24] Ibid., pp. 15–16.
[25] Ibid., p. 26.
[26] For a perceptive critique, see L. McNay, *Foucault: A Critical Introduction* (Cambridge, Polity Press, 1994).

His engagement with the practical world is emphasized in its dramatic opening description of the torture and public execution of the regicide, Damiens,
in 1757.[27] The opening sets up a rhetorical contrast between cruel corporeal
punishment inflicted in the name of the royal authority and a more considered,
scientific, and apparently humane form of punishment, which is recounted in
the rest of the book, and is presaged in a dry account of the activities
of prisoners at a subsequent date. Foucault, though, undermines the contrast
in that his text highlights succeeding forms of punishment, that while less
overtly cruel, are insidious and pervasive in their use of mechanisms of control
to monitor and discipline delinquents. Punishment shifts from the infliction of
bodily pain to the realignment of the soul, whereby criminals are subjected to
exacting and scientific examination of their crimes and criminal behaviour.
The springs of their actions are reviewed, analysed, and corrected, and they are
subjected to the discipline of incarceration. The disciplinary regime that they
experience is organized so that criminals are disciplined by being subject to
rigid control of the space and time that they are allotted in routines that are
designed to render them docile. The apparently more humane treatment of
criminals in modernity masks their concentrated subjugation by the imposition of a scientific disciplinary regime.

In *Discipline and Punish* Foucault dispenses with the preceding paraphernalia of formal structural analysis to adopt a genealogical explanation that
tracks the circuitous history of crime and punishment. In his essay, 'Nietzsche,
Genealogy, History', he observes how a genealogy identifies contingent
change, without assuming an origin or goal to the historical process. He
remarks, 'History is the concrete body of a development, with its moments
of intensity, its lapses, its extended periods of feverish agitation, its fainting
spells; and only a metaphysician would seek its soul in the distant ideality of its
origin.'[28] *Discipline and Punish* shows how the body serves as the site of social
discipline and the transmission of power. Power is identified expressly as
working within social practice, whereas its role was merely implicit in *The
Archaeology of Knowledge*. Foucault continues to oppose totalizing explanations. Foucault's focus on prisons is supplemented by recognition of the
simultaneous development of disciplinary mechanisms in social sites such as
medical asylums, hospitals, schools, factories, and military establishments.
These disciplinary operations assume local and multiple forms rather than
emanating from generic planning or a single set of causes. Consequently
Discipline and Punish imagines the large-scale disciplinary formations in
modern Western society to emerge by a coalescence of contingent factors.[29]
The ensuing disciplinary society applies reason and technology to control

---

[27] M. Foucault, *Discipline and Punish*, p. 3.
[28] M. Foucault, 'Nietzsche, Genealogy, History', p. 80.
[29] M. Foucault, *Discipline and Punish*, p. 216.

populations and to mould bodies, systemically rendering them docile in the process.[30] This disciplinary society exhibits local overlapping forms of control, in which surveillance and discipline are exercised so as to exclude dissonance and difference in engineering normalized individuals. What Foucault terms the microphysics of power relations are constituted by its capillary and multiple forms in modern society. Bentham's Panopticon, a multi-purpose, architectural device to exercise disciplinary control is held to epitomize the emerging disciplinary society, where societal control is maximized by the application of technologies of power. It is a highly instrumental society in which the Panopticon serves as a symbol of its operations of surveillance and control. The Panopticon is designed so as to minimize costs of security while maximizing effective control over the inmates of a prison or poorhouse.

Foucault's originality as an historian of ideas resides in his re-imagining familiar narratives from a contrary perspective. Hence the comforting liberal narrative of a progressively more humane system of punishment eliminating excess repression and cruelty is reassuring to the modern Western world. After all, it is what sets the West apart from Orientalism. Yet this story is complicated by Foucault's disconcerting genealogy. Foucault rejects a teleology of progress. His narrative reveals the incommensurability of systems of punishment, so that past brutality is not simply superseded by more humane regimes. The mechanisms of organizational control alter, and punishment assumes incommensurable forms. The regulation of docile normalized bodies succeeds the infliction of bodily torture and execution. There is no common scale. Political thinking that registers progress by measuring past and present according to generic rational schemes are revealed as partial in assuming there can be a trans-historical frame of analysis. *Discipline and Punish* displaces settled judgments on progress in regimes of punishment to disrupt contemporary attitudes. Bentham provides a rationalist account of how a liberal regime might promote maximal utility by adopting new utilitarian schemes for disciplining criminals and the poor. Foucault re-imagines Bentham's projected reforms by highlighting how they represent a concentrated regime of disciplinary power, reducing the projected inmates of Panopticon buildings to so many docile normalized subjects or rather objects.

In lectures and interviews close to the publication of *Discipline and Punish* Foucault offers more general observations on the nature of power. He talks of technologies of power that impact directly upon the body so as to exert control over biological aspects of existence. This operation of power constitutes bio-power. It operates upon populations to control their conditions of life and is conceptualized as at once productive and repressive. In the first volume of *The History of Sexuality—The Will to Knowledge* Foucault sets out a genealogical

---

[30] Ibid., pp. 195–231.

study of modern forms of sex and sexuality. He demonstrates how the development of the discourse of sexuality shapes productively the possibilities of sexual awareness and conduct.[31] In a characteristically disorienting move, he undermines the contemporary self-image of conceptual exploration of sexuality as a recent phenomenon. Standard representations of sexuality in the past are also challenged. He debunks the prevailing wisdom that the Victorians were silent on sex and sexuality, whereas the freewheeling modern era is progressive and experimental in its unfettered exploration of sexuality. Foucault identifies the Victorian era as developing an explosion of interest in sex and sexuality, generating proliferating multiple discourses that monitor and control perversions. The attention that is given to these perversions accords them status by the very disciplinary perspective that aims at their repression. These discourses are productive in framing terms by which sex is explored, even if the dominant Victorian attitude is repressive in its disciplining of sexual phenomena that are at odds with the biopolitical normalizing requirements of heterosexuality and the reproduction of procreative norms. In reviewing the mindset of nineteenth-century bourgeois society Foucault remarks, 'It did not set boundaries for sexuality; it extended the various forms of sexuality, pursuing them according to lines of indefinite penetration.'[32]

Foucault recognizes the simultaneous creative and repressive aspects of power, which produce the very vices and perversions that constitute the objects of repression. *The History of Sexuality* shows convincingly if contentiously, how the monitoring and regulating processes of normalization produce individuals who recognize themselves by means of their acquisition of normalized and conventional sexual attitudes and behaviour. His genealogy of the discourse of sexuality and sexual norms allows Foucault to conceptualize subjectivity in a way that at once makes sense of the modern self and registers processes of agency, which he had tended to ignore previously. Preceding accounts of formal structural determination of an individual's discursive repertoire of expressions or of the sheer domination of the body by disciplinary interventions tended to underplay the ways in which the self assimilates, resists, or participates in the development of attitudes and concepts. Foucault's accommodation of subjectivity in *The History of Sexuality—The Will to Knowledge* is succeeded in its later volumes, *The Use of Pleasure* and *The Care of the Self* by analysis of bodily pleasure and sexuality in classical antiquity and the early Christian World. He identifies how individuals develop an ethics of sexual activity and pleasures in classical antiquity by attending to and working on current practices. While recognizing the culturally specific

---

[31] M. Foucault, *The History of Sexuality: vol.1 The Will to Knowledge* (London, Penguin, 1978).
[32] Ibid., p. 47.

context of the Ancient World, Foucault draws on the experience of the Ancient World, notably on how individuals framed an ethics, or an *askesis* to shape their engagement in sexual activities creatively, to reflect upon how the self in his own contemporary world might resist or modify normalizing procedures.[33] Foucault's recognition of the possibilities of agency in his provisions for the care of the self in his *History of Sexuality*, which are explored further in his *Technologies of the Self*, has been welcomed by McNay. Feminists more generally, however, have been critical of his use of the masculinist practices of classical antiquity.[34] Foucault's exploration of the creative possibilities available to individuals to shape and resist sexual practices allows scope for agency which exacts a price in valorizing questionable individualistic strategies.

GOVERNMENTALITY AND POLITICS

In his late analysis of governmentality Foucault focuses upon the nature of conduct and the conduct of conduct, in which power is seen to be exercised by historically constructed forms of subjectivity. Foucault deals with the political in a way that contrasts with his earlier studies in the lectures on governmentality at the College de France. Previously, as he observes in *Society Must be Defended—Lectures at the College de France 1975–76* he had reviewed ways in which power had been exercised that are not seen as standardly political. His histories of madness, medicine, sexuality, and punishment highlight local non-state forms of power, which are outside the purview of standard political theories that conceptualize power and its operations by analysing the state and related political institutions.[35] Foucault's preceding histories stretch the notion of the history of political thought by unveiling the politics of discourses not previously recognized to be political. His lectures on governmentality change direction by analysing the changing governmental discourses of states and related institutions that are directed towards influencing the conduct of conduct.

[33] M. Foucault, *The Use of Pleasure, The History of Sexuality vol. 2* trans. R. Hurley (Harmondsworth, Penguin, 1990); M. Foucault, *The Care of the Self, History of Sexuality vol. 3* trans. R. Hurley (Harmondsworth, Penguin, 1990).

[34] See L. McNay, *Foucault: A Critical Introduction* (Cambridge, Polity Press, 1994); M. Foucault, ed. L. Martin, H. Gutman, and P. Hutton, *Technologies of the Self: A Seminar with Michel Foucault*, (Amherst MA., University of Massachusetts Press, 1989). For a feminist critique, see J. Grimshaw, 'Practices of Freedom', in C. Ramazanoglu (ed.), *Up Against Foucault: Exploration of Some Tensions Between Foucault and Feminism* (London and New York, Routledge 1993), pp. 51–72, see also L. McNay, *Foucault and Feminism: Power, Gender and the Self* (Cambridge, Polity, 1992).

[35] M. Foucault, *Society Must be Defended lectures at the College de France 1975–76*.

In analysing the technologies of governmentality shaping distinct forms of agency, Foucault reviews texts of political theorists, whose works are interpreted in more traditional histories of political thought. Foucault's reading of renowned political theorists remains unconventional. The meaning of past texts is not assimilated to authorial perspectives for texts are interpreted in the light of the ways in which they connect unintentionally to historic forms of economy, politics, society, and the operations of power. In *Society Must Be Defended* Foucault contrasts kingly central power and juridical authority with an alternative historico-political discourse in which there is a direct contest or war of domination and counter-domination. The latter implies a straightforward agonistic battle for power that is visible in the English Civil War, and more generally in early modern Europe. It is distinct from preceding ideological analyses and formulations of power in juridico-legal terms. The new politics is a departure from Machiavelli and Hobbes, who had assumed the centrality of state power and its legal expressions. Foucault observes, '[W]e think of Machiavelli and we think of Hobbes. I would like to show that they have nothing to do with it, that this (new) historico-political discourse cannot be that of the Prince's politics or, obviously that of absolute power... This is basically a discourse that cuts off the king's head.'[36] The difference between the new historico-political discourse and the preceding juridico-legal discourse is brought out by Foucault's review of Hobbes's *Leviathan*. In our succeeding chapter on Hobbes we examine Foucault's Hobbes and the dichotomy that he establishes between the two discourses. Foucault is perceptive in observing the tactical and strategic behaviour of Hobbesian individuals in the state of nature, which intimates a juridico-legal discourse but Foucault's rejection of the discourse depends upon his commitment to a historical contest for power that does not imagine the state as performing a generic role that is beyond that of partisan appeal.

In his subsequent lectures on governmentality, *Security, Territory, Population* and *The Birth of Biopolitics* Foucault reflects on historical examples of the arts of government.[37] Governmentality is a concept, which is framed so as to avoid essentializing the state or universalizing a particular frame of politics. This deconstruction of generic conceptualizations of government and politics is of a piece with Foucault's preceding approach. His late analyses of historic forms of political thought identify them within changing frameworks of governmentality, which succeed statist notions in the modern era. In *Security, Territory, Population* Foucault analyses the art of government in post-Renaissance forms of political theory. Whereas Machiavelli had focused upon how a prince might secure a principality by tightening his grip

---

[36] Ibid., p. 59.
[37] M. Foucault, *Security, Territory, Population: Lectures at the College de France 1977–78*; M. Foucault, *The Birth of Biopolitics: Lectures at the College de France, 1978–79*.

on juridical sovereignty, Foucault sees theorists of the subsequent classical age as attending to the wider administration of 'things', pertaining to the biopolitical welfare of the territory and population over whom power is exercised.

Theorists of the classical age do not concentrate upon theorizing the power of a prince in controlling his state. The point of this form of governmentality is to influence the conduct of the population so as to maximize the development of a territory. In promoting biopolitical development, power is exercised by controlling the conduct of subjects. Conduct is influenced, in turn, by pastoral processes involving institutions, notably the Church. Politics is a way of utilizing processes of persuasion and influence. Individual subjects internalize schemes of conduct. Governmentality is changeable in that it responds to and shapes the historic ways in which politics is enacted. In highlighting the historicity of forms of political power, Foucault observes, 'After all, maybe the state is only a composite reality and a mythicized abstraction whose importance is much less than we think. What is important for our modernity, that is to say, our present, is not then the state's takeover of society, so much as what I would call the "governmentalisation" of the state.'[38]

In *The Birth of Biopolitics* Foucault interprets the rise of the discourse of political economy and the concomitant idea of the conceptual separation of the 'economy' from non-economic social and political phenomena, as allowing for a new and hitherto undeveloped from of political theory, namely liberalism. Liberalism operates as a particular style of governmentality, in that it presumes and fosters a 'natural' sphere of society, where the market and purely economic operations occur. This idea of a separate or natural sphere of the economy is susceptible of multiple associations. It does not denote a primitive or prior condition to government. What is natural about market operations is neither a condition that precedes a social and political state, nor an acultural condition. Liberalism is a multivalent ideology that invokes multiple forms of rhetorical justification. On the one hand, liberal politics is aligned with, and justified by, a pre-existing juridico-political discourse, whereby the centrality of political authority is assumed. Politics is thereby focused upon the state and its authority and yet state power in this liberal discourse, is subjected to limits. Hence in Locke's proto-liberal theory, governmental power is limited by the presumption that it must be aligned to natural rights.[39] In contrast to the Lockean standpoint, a utilitarian perspective emerges, in which the rights of subjects are neither invoked nor naturalized. Rather, the interests of society are identified and asserted so as to highlight the direction that government should follow. Government in this light is about maximizing social utility, which is conceptualized in terms of

---

[38] M. Foucault, *Security, Territory, Population: Lectures at the College de France 1977–78*, p. 109.

[39] M. Foucault, *The Birth of Biopolitics: Lectures at the College de France, 1978–79*, p. 91.

biopolitical interests. Foucault maintains, 'In short, this approach consists in the analysis of government: its practice, its de facto limits, and its desirable limits . . . The question addressed to government at every moment of its action and with regard to each of its institutions, old or new is: Is it useful? This is not the original, the revolutionary question: What are my original rights and how can I assert them against any sovereign? But it is the radical question. The question of English radicalism; the problem of English radicalism is the problem of utility.'[40] Foucault interprets liberalism as imagining a realm of social interests, which are taken to be distinct from government, but which are enabled and promoted by the technologies of liberal government. Liberals theorize how government can provide conditions of security, which are central to the flourishing of market conditions. Utility, for Foucault, epitomizes liberal governmentality in promoting instrumentality and flexibility of means in developing generic, biopolitical interests, which incorporate disciplinary technologies.

Foucault's dyadic conceptualization of liberal ideology is framed by a contextual interpretation of its role in modern society and politics. Liberalism appears when markets accommodate an instrumental autonomous logic that is attached to social interests, and is theorized by the political economy of Smith. Foucault's identification of liberalism, as a distinct and context-dependent form of political logic, highlights how he locates and interprets political theorists in relation to specific historical frames or discourses. Foucault's discursive contextualism is formulated retrospectively, and identifies past political thought in ways that are distinct from those which past theorists maintain themselves. In *The Birth of Biopolitics* Foucault also rehearses an historical understanding of forms of neo-liberalism. The discourse of neo-liberalism, which was developing in the late 1970s, is related to the arguments of the ordoliberals, a group of political economists and social theorists, who were centred around the University of Freiburg, during the Weimar Republic. The dark times of inter-war Germany served as the context for theorists, who reflected on the nature of markets in considering ways to revive markets and society that were floundering under the impact of successive events, notably reparations, hyper-inflation, and depression.

The ordoliberals responded to the increasing activity of governments in intervening in economic and social affairs. While German governments intervened to counteract the contemporary threats of socialism and fascism, the ordoliberals diagnosed governmental activity as impairing and thwarting, rather than achieving its intended outcomes of protecting individuals from unemployment and fostering growth. Foucault takes the ordoliberals to perceive Nazism as concentrating prevalent features of current public policy,

[40] Ibid., p. 40.

rather than representing an aberrant and hyper-mixture of ill-assorted ingredients. Nazism demonstrates the poverty of current political strategies, and indicates the fragility of liberalism. The concoction of Keynesianism, planning, state power, the dismantling of juridical checks on state activity, and the reduction of individuals to components of a national social community are diagnosed as undermining the basis of liberalism.[41] These elements of public policy are concentrated in Nazism. Individually they pose problems, but collectively they inspired the ordoliberals to rethink radically the nature of society and liberalism. They imagined Nazism as dramatizing the defects of prevailing counter-liberal measures, which involve the application of statist technologies to the economy and society. Ordoliberals concluded that the enhancement of state power was to be reversed, because, as they maintained, market society had never been allowed to flourish. Ameliorative corrective measures reversing the trend of increasing state powers were demanded. Foucault formulates the ordoliberals' understanding of the contemporary situation as one which amounted to 'a state under the supervision of the market rather than a market supervised by the state.'[42] In re-imagining market operations ordoliberals identified competition rather than exchange as constituting the crucial principle of market behaviour. It is not enough for exchange to take place, and for governments to allow unimpeded economic transactions. Markets do not simply require governments to exercise restraint, and to adopt laissez-faire policies. Competition must be cultivated. The energizing force of competition is imagined as coordinating society and vitalizing economic activity. On this neo-liberal reading, competition is to be enabled by releasing the restraints of monopoly that arise not from market failure but from misconceived political interventions. Foucault traces historic connections between the ordoliberals and the early economic policy and founding political rhetoric of the West German state. The ordo liberals, due to the influence of its members Eucken, Ropke, and Bohm, are seen as exerting an impact upon the development of the social market economy of the post-war German Federal Republic and the European Union. Foucault also connects the ordoliberals to the anarcho-liberalism of the Chicago School due to the work of von Mises and von Hayek, who were familiar with the members and ideas of both groups.

In discussing the post-war influence of the ordoliberals upon western Germany, Foucault highlights the speech on 18 April 1948 of Ludwig Erhard, who supervised the economic administration of the Anglo-American zones of Berlin. Erhard pressed for price deregulation and the liberalizing of the economy from state control. His stated aim was to avoid anarchy and the termite state.[43] Economic freedom, as advanced in this speech, legitimates

---

[41] Ibid., pp. 112–16.   [42] Ibid., p. 116.
[43] Ibid., p. 158.

the German state so that it might operate effectively in the aftermath of an appalling immediate past, without relying on traditional historical sources of legitimation. The appeal of economic freedom in providing ideological support for the regime had the additional value of being acceptable to the USA, even if it were at odds with contemporary UK Keynesianism. Foucault understands the ensuing social market economy of the Federal Republic of Germany as employing technologies of politics that cohere with the theory of the ordoliberals and the related ideas of von Hayek. Free competition is central to its organization of society and the social system is subject to laws, which are compatible with competition. A safety net for the poor is provided but operates through social insurance, which fosters self-reliance. Laws for von Hayek and for the social market economy of the Federal Republic of Germany are not to be focused on particular planned objectives, but are framed so as to be general and non-directive, but eliminating particular forms of monopoly and impediments to individual enterprise. This emphasis upon competition as an organizing principle of society is constitutive of neo-liberalism and is introduced into France by D'Estaing following the perceived failures of French planning.[44]

The theories of the ordoliberals, von Hayek, and the practice of the emerging West German post-war state supersede preceding liberal models of how economy and politics have been imagined. Instead of laissez-faire, by which individuals are left alone to carry out their plans, society is to be structured by interventions so as to engineer the conditions of an enterprise society in which the spirit of enterprise is to flourish. Inequality is accepted, indeed everyone, equally, is to accept the conditions of inequality. A transfer of income might be enacted so as to alleviate destitution, but not to alter the conditions of competition nor to undermine self-reliance. The transformation in governmentality that is established by neo-liberalism receives an American expression. Foucault understands the background conditions of the USA to be distinct from those of Europe, due to its lack of a preceding feudal state and on account of <u>its populist ideological commitment to the flag of freedom</u> on the part of the left and right. Foucault identifies a distinctive American idiom of new liberalism that shows a concern with <u>developing human capital</u>, a theme which tends to have been neglected by the classical economists. This neglect is taken to apply even to Marx, whom Foucault sees as interpreting the very contradictions of capitalism to be tied to the reduction of labour to abstract labour, whereby qualitative aspects of labour are sidelined. American neo-liberals understand human capital as giving rise to income streams and recognize how parents are active in promoting the capital of offspring and limit the number of offspring so as to maximize their capital. Attending to the

---

[44] Ibid., p. 146.

possibilities of human capital is imagined by neo-liberals as extending to genetic engineering, and so the capacities of agency and frames of politics are taken to be historical and related to technologies of governmentality. Foucault reviews the widening range of activities that are subjected to neo-liberal analysis by Becker and others. Marriage is theorized as a formula for optimizing capital, and crime, punishment, and the legal system are shown to be susceptible to analysis, which considers their rationality in employing scarce resources to achieve designated ends, rather than as upholding moral principles. The upshot is that crime is not scrutinized by deontological or even a consequentialist frame of ethics, but via a rationality-maximizing logic of what is worth outlawing given the costs of its prohibition.

Will Davies has characterized Foucault's *The Birth of Biopolitics* as a jumbled series of lectures.[45] And Gane in his article, 'The Emergence of Neo-liberalism' critiques Foucault for failing to acknowledge the importance of the role of Mill in the history of liberalism, and for underplaying the roles of von Mises and von Hayek in promoting neo-liberalism.[46] They rather miss the point. Foucault is not aiming to provide an exhaustive history of liberalism, and he recognizes how liberalism and neo-liberalism and contemporary political thought may be understood in multiple divergent ways.[47] What he aims to do in the lectures is to interpret political economy, political ideas, and political practice in the light of his construction of historical forms of governmentality. How is his enterprise to be judged? Certainly he omits much that bears upon modern political thought and liberalism. Forms of social liberalism, notably new liberalism in England, Rawlsian liberalism in the USA, and sundry expressions of feminist liberalism are ignored. Von Hayek and von Mises are discussed but doubtless more might have been said about them. However, what Foucault does say is interesting and enlightening. He imagines liberalism as assuming a discursive identity that presumes interests as emerging in ways that are correlative to an idea of society that is distinguishable from the political organization of the state. The interests of society in this conception of liberalism are not imagined as being attributable to a set of subjects who recognize a sovereign and are the recipients of rights. They have fundamental and non-territorially defined biopolitical interests and Bentham's utilitarianism is invoked as a paradigmatic way of conceiving of these interests. The relationship between politics and society in enabling these interests is not fixed. Society is not a detachable base on which the political is erected. Thereafter, neo-liberalism shows how political technologies of an emerging

[45] W. Davies, 'A Response to Nick Gane's "Emergence of Neoliberalism"', *Theory, Culture and Society*, vol. 31, no. 4, 2014, pp. 299–302.

[46] N. Gane, 'The Emergence of Neoliberalism: Thinking Through and Beyond Michel Foucault's Lectures on Biopolitics', *Theory Culture and Society*, vol. 31, no. 3, 2014, pp. 3–27.

[47] M. Foucault, *The Birth of Biopolitics*, pp. 291–317.

governmentality can frame relations between society and the political in novel and different ways; a new subjectivity, <u>an enterprise self,</u> is constituted by the governmentality of neo-liberal political economy, just as utilitarian liberalism assumes that society is composed of and should protect selves who are intent upon <u>maximizing their interests.</u> At the close of his lectures Foucault reflects on how liberalism and its construal of the relations between society and politics are related to <u>the historical development of the notion of civil society as a sphere that is distinct from formally designated political institutions.</u> He rehearses historical conceptions of civil society and focuses upon Ferguson's classic analysis of its character. He notes how Ferguson perceives civil society to represent <u>the reciprocal interaction of nature and society,</u> to involve political leadership and to be historical in character, allowing for ongoing development. Foucault recognizes how Ferguson's standpoint fits with his own interpretation of historically developing forms of liberal and neo-liberal governmentalities.

CONCLUSION

What Foucault brings to the history of political ideas is a challenge to conventional notions of history, politics, and ideas. Ideas on politics, punishment, sexuality, power, and reason are neither to be taken at face value, nor in the terms in which they have been formulated historically. General theories of progress are also to be discounted. The past does not lead inexorably to the present. Foucault highlights the relativity of terms and he opposes interpreting ideas as straightforwardly representing the intentional views of authors. Foucault's perspective certainly offers directions in which historians of political thought can challenge received notions. The development of Western liberal ideas is accompanied by the growth of an unacknowledged disciplinary society. The king's head has been cut off so it is a mistake to identify politics with the central apparatuses of power. Foucault's specific histories highlight disturbing but significant ways of imagining institutions, ideas, and practices. In his early theoretical writings he tends to subordinate ideas and agents to the requirements of abstractly conceived forms of structural determination. His later work, however, allows for agents, while providing frameworks of analysis that contextualize ideas in novel and critical ways. If Hegel's historical teleology embraces all forms of political thinking in its supervening absolutism, Foucault smashes at the door of the absolute, reminding readers of changing and incommensurable ways in which power has been exercised. Foucault's interpretation of changing forms of governmentality allows for discrete and distinct ways of framing and understanding political ideas. Locke and Hobbes as well as Machiavelli, Ferguson, and Bentham are identified in ways that disconcert but augment our understanding of them.

Foucault's method of viewing ideas via discursive frameworks, which are constructed by him rather than representing ways in which things were understood by past historical actors, entails that it is neither easy to refute his histories nor to be fully persuaded by them. Historical evidence cannot be supplied neatly to confirm the discourses or technologies of power that he identifies. In *Discipline and Punish* Bentham's Panopticon project is not discussed so as to represent events but to highlight how we might imagine an emerging discursive idiom or operation of power. Hence the contemporary rejection of Bentham's project is not to be seen as decisive in establishing how modern society is to be understood. However, if Foucault's discursive practice does not depend crucially upon historical evidence it remains suggestive if not entirely convincing. His account of the governmentalities of liberalism and neo-liberalism captures aspects of political analysis and practice but it delibe-rately abstracts from the interweaving character of multiple forms of modern political discourse. Foucault invites us to read texts against the grain of their authors' intentions, and he operates by imagining their involvement in wider discursive contexts, which disturb Derrida's more concentrated reading of texts. Yet Derrida's deconstruction of determinate textual meanings chal-lenges Foucault's sense of texts playing a clear and precise role in the devel-opment of a discourse. Foucault's theoretical practice covers a multiplicity of practices and discourses and provides radical and imaginative ways of under-standing discursive practices and operations of power. Yet how is his theor-etical practice to be explained and justified? If Foucault maintains that authors are not to be taken as establishing the terms by which they are to be under-stood, then how are we to read Foucault? The question of the status of Foucault's own theoretical standpoint may be approached by considering Foucault's reading of Nietzsche. Nietzsche's genealogy and critique of human-ism are to be valued but it is not clear that Foucault explains the processes by which Nietzsche developed these insights. Indeed, it is equally the case that Foucault does not explain the conditions of his own theoretical achievements.

7

Gadamer and Hermeneutics

INTRODUCTION

The title of Gadamer's classic work, *Truth and Method*, proclaims its interest in truth and method and yet Gadamer sees neither truth nor method as projects to which philosophy or the human sciences should be committed.[1] Gadamer neither offers a method, nor imagines truth to represent a determinate set of rules or criteria, which are external to and detachable from the everyday process of interpreting experience. Rather, he understands truth to be integral to experience and he imagines the processes of interpretation that are maintained in human dialogue to constitute its process of development. It is a mistake to isolate and formulate rules for explaining truth, when all activities, including theoretical practice, presuppose forms of understanding of the truth. The point, for a philosophical inquiry into truth, is to attend to what is involved in this everyday understanding rather than to imagine and frame novel procedures. Understanding, for Gadamer, is always already taking place and the interpretive skills, which are being deployed continuously in every sphere of theory and practice, are constitutive of interpretive understanding. Hermeneutics, for Gadamer, is precisely the everyday practice of interpretive understanding, which renders redundant the discovery of 'method' and 'truth.' Hermeneutics operates in the very use of language, where language users interpret one another to understand and comment upon what is said. Likewise, past texts are interpreted in the light of present interpretive preconceptions, and, in turn, influence those conceptions, and hence contribute to the development of reflective traditions, which arise out of the interplay of interpretive forms of understanding. The meanings of texts depend upon the historical assumptions underpinning their expression, and their hermeneutical interpretation is undertaken in the light of the present interests and standpoints of interpreters. It is this conception of a dialogue between text and interpreter, and between past and present, which is Gadamer's definitive

---

[1] H.-G. Gadamer, *Truth and Method*. Revised Edition, translation revised by J. Weinsheimer and D.G. Marshall (London, Sheed and Ward, 1960), p. xxi.

contribution to the history of ideas, and to the character of the history of political thought. Gadamer's *Truth and Method* operates as a series of reminders of the hermeneutic practice with which we operate conventionally, rather than in specifying a set of distinctive methods for attaining a truth, which supersedes the ordinary experiential world.

Truth and Method is a big book, which deals with many subjects. Its range reflects Gadamer's notion of hermeneutics. Hermeneutics arose out of theology and interpretation of the bible, whereby the whole and parts of it were interpreted by mutual reciprocal forms of critical attention. Gadamer extended the range of hermeneutics by imagining it in the light of the Heideggerian notion of the contingency of the human world of existence, whereby selves constitute a world by their mutual interpretive practice.[2] Gadamer interprets hermeneutics to be as extensive as the operation and interpretation of language by its users.[3] The individual for Heidegger, and for Gadamer, is not the isolated individual of Cartesian mythology but a determinate being in the world, whose activities and relations are situated socially and subject to continuous interpretation.[4] Gadamer maintains, 'It is from *language as a medium* that our whole experience of the world, and especially hermeneutical experience unfolds' (emphasis in original).[5] What counts as a world is constituted by interpretive activity linking individuals to one another and to their conceptions of the world, their pasts, and projected futures. Given the hermeneutic situation of individuals then the scope of Gadamer's hermeneutics extends to the past, and to the generic operation of language as the medium in which the interpretive activity of human beings takes place. Hence, *Truth and Method* reviews interpretive activity as the condition of truth rather than focusing upon a scientific method, which imagines its methods to provide naturalistic unchanging truths, while resting upon unacknowledged interpretive activity. Gadamer attends to art and aesthetic theory, as he is alive to the truths, which are yielded by hermeneutic aesthetic interpretive creativity. He interprets the history of hermeneutics to distinguish and highlight his own interpretive practice of hermeneutics, and then more generally, he attends to the features of experience that render it an interpretive hermeneutic enterprise. Gadamer observes how meaning in language is transmitted between interlocutors and reflects on the role of prejudice in enabling individuals to orient themselves to the interpretation of meaning.

[2] For a discussion of hermeneutics see M. Heidegger, *Being and Time* trans. J. Macquarrie and E. Robinson (Oxford and Malden MA, Blackwell, 1962), pp. 352–8.

[3] H.-G. Gadamer, *Truth and Method*, pp. 381–493.

[4] There are differences between Heidegger and Gadamer, not the least of which is Heidegger's emphasis upon the existential courage of the individual who faces death. Gadamer highlights the openness of individuals to one another. For Heidegger's account of being towards death see M. Heidegger, *Being and Time*, pp. 279–312.

[5] H.-G. Gadamer, *Truth and Method*, p. 457.

Gadamer identifies how interpretive understanding is achieved by dialogue. There is never a clean slate or a *tabula rasa* in understanding. In interpreting people, their actions, and their constructed institutions and practices, interpreters presume their own perspectival horizon of understanding, which is constituted by their life-history. Interpretation, however, involves going beyond one's own horizon and engaging with others and different perspectives. Gadamer urges a fusion of horizons in conversational dialogue, in political activity, and in interpreting past texts that express historical frames of meaning. A paradigm case for interpretive dialogue is a conversation between two people that admits of adjustments and modifications on both sides as the participants alter their perceptions of what may be at issue between them. They will tend to allow for an adjustment of their horizons of understanding to accommodate the standpoint of the other. They will be enabled to develop their understanding by bringing to the discussion pre-existing views, or prejudices, but their openness in the discussion allows for change and development in their forms of understanding. Likewise, in the course of engagement with texts, artefacts, institutions, and practices individuals will start out with prejudices but are likely to modify their understanding as they come to appreciate another horizon of understanding associated with the objects of their understanding. Individuals are oriented within the world by their assimilation of tradition, but engagement with the world, notably with others and with cultural products, broadens their understanding. Traditions develop by conversation and conversational forms of interpretation.

The upshot of Gadamer's perspective on the human world of understanding is that there is neither an innocent reading of texts nor a detached naturalistic understanding of the social world. The ideal of a non-interpretive, value-free objectivity, that is dreamed of by social scientists who aspire to divest themselves of their pre-existing values and assumptions, is rejected by Gadamer.[6] He concludes *Truth and Method* by observing, 'Thus there is undoubtedly no understanding that is free of all prejudices, however much the will of our knowledge must be directed towards escaping their thrall.'[7] The point is to engage with interpretation by being open to the other's point of view and interpretive horizon rather than screening out all pre-existing interests and values from interpretive commitments. Gadamer's denial of a point of view outside all points of view is plausible, for the very notion of interpretation depends upon a world of interpretive values and skills, which it would be senseless and self-defeating to deny. The recognition of the significance of tradition in framing the standpoint of the interpreter and of the horizon of interpretation that is maintained in the subject or object of interpretation, underlines the relevance of history and historical understanding to the

[6] Ibid., pp. 3–9.   [7] Ibid., p. 490.

interpretive engagement. We are constituted by multiple and historical forms of interpretation. As Taylor remarks, 'Gadamer's argument in *Truth and Method* deals with our understanding of our own tradition, the history of our civilization, and the texts and works that belong to this. This means that what we study will be in one way or another internal to our identity. Even where we define ourselves against certain features of the past, as the modern Enlightenment does against the Middle Ages, this remains within our identity as a negative pole, that which we have overcome or escaped. We are part of the "effective history" (*Wirkungsgeschichte)* of this past, and as such it has a claim on us.'[8]

Gadamer's view on interpretation has implications for how he conceives of ideas, politics, and history. The world is necessarily a world of ideas, which are to be interpreted. Its conditionality precludes determination outside of on-going interpretive practices. Ideas are neither universal nor external to processes of interpretation. Prejudice and particular horizons of interpretation frame the ways in which ideas are understood. Likewise, politics is not an activity which is susceptible of universal analysis. Political situations are always to be interpreted and do not admit of definitive solutions. In contrast to forms of philosophical analysis such as that of Rawls, that aim to achieve definitive normative conceptualizations of political issues, Gadamer understands politics to involve dialogue, where political truth depends upon conversation and adjustment of positions in the light of dialogue.[9] Gadamer's emphasis upon communication is related to but distinct from Habermas's notion of a procedural form of justice. Habermas operates theoretically by framing a foundational and just means of dialogue. It constitutes 'the comprehensive perspective of an unlimited communication community.'[10] For Habermas, the conditions of fairness and rationality that can limit the ways in which dialogue is conducted establish generic truths to constitute basic forms of procedural justice.[11] In contrast, Gadamer's interpretation of the practice of politics does not admit of a universal form of justice, which is determined by an ideal style of communication. Rather, the sphere and style of political activity are not to be delimited, they demand critical engagement with traditions and prejudice and entering into open dialogues with others.[12] Again,

---

[8] C. Taylor, 'Gadamer on the Human Sciences', in R.J. Dostal (ed.), *The Cambridge Companion to Gadamer* (Cambridge, Cambridge University Press, 2002), p. 142.

[9] See J. Rawls, *A Theory of Justice* (Cambridge, USA, Harvard University Press, 1971). It is true that Rawls modified his standpoint in *Political Liberalism* so that he was offering a limited political conception of justice, framed by the assumptions of liberal democracy, but he continued to maintain that philosophical analysis could establish a non-controversial standpoint on justice.

[10] J. Habermas, *Between Facts and Norms: Contributions to a Discourse Theory of Law* (Cambridge, MA, MIT Press, 1996), p. 162.

[11] For Habermas's account of a discourse theoretic justification of rights see ibid., pp. 118–32.

[12] A debate between Gadamer and Habermas took place in 1967 on the nature of social science and tradition, with Habermas urging a social scientific analysis of tradition and Gadamer

Collingwood maintains that the historian can achieve an understanding of the past, which recovers past thought and purposes. Gadamer differs from Collingwood in that he maintains the interpretation of the past is inevitably to be conducted from a present, in which the historian is necessarily bringing to the work of interpretation perspectives from the present. A dialogue between past and present will ensue in which there may be a fusion of interpretive horizons, but this fusion is distinct from the retrieval of the past that is unaffected by the present. As Gadamer observes, '[T]he interpreting word is the word of the interpreter; it is not the language and the dictionary of the interpreted text. This means that assimilation is no mere reproduction or repetition of the traditionary text; it is a new creation of understanding.'[13]

In maintaining a distinctive reading of history, politics, and ideas, Gadamer also differs from other perspectives in interpreting the history of political thought. On the one hand, he connects language users in a common interpretive bond and allows for possibilities of mutual understanding between political ideas of past and present, rather than imagining that past theories are to be deconstructed in ways that their authors would not recognize. In debate with Gadamer, Derrida critiques this notion of continuity between past and present.[14] Derrida, in pointed contrast to Gadamer, questions continuity between speakers and between texts and their interpreters.[15] In commenting specifically on their approaches to political thought, Dienstag observes 'Where Gadamer wants to identify a solidarity produced by language, Derrida by contrast, wants to show how identity always hides, and indeed is based on a discontinuity.'[16] If Gadamer promises a form of unity between past and present, which contrasts with the discontinuities emphasized by Derrida, then Gadamer also differs from the Cambridge School in emphasizing differing aspects of interpretation. While Skinner has recognized positive aspects of Gadamer's approach, he is more inclined to highlight the possibilities of distortion that can arise from undue influence of present assumptions on

maintaining that a scientific perspective cannot overrule dialogical engagement in dialogue with all points of view. For a record of the debate see J. Habermas and D. Heinrich (eds), *Theorie Diskussion: Hermeneutic und Ideologiekritik*. Mit beitragen von K-O Apel, C. v. Bormann, R. Bubner, H.-G. Gadamer, H.J. Giegel, and J. Habermas (Frankfurt, Surhkamp, 1973). See also J. Mendelsen, 'The Habermas–Gadamer Debate', *New German Critique*, no. 18, 1979, pp. 43–78.

[13] H.-G. Gadamer, *Truth and Method*, p. 472.

[14] For a record of the debate between Gadamer and Derrida see D.P. Michelfelder and R.E. Palmer (eds), *Dialogues and Deconstruction: The Gadamer–Derrida Encounter* (New York, SUNY Press, 1989).

[15] J. Derrida, 'Three Questions to Hans-Georg Gadamer', trans. D.P. Michelfelder and R.E. Palmer, in D.P. Michelfelder and R.E. Palmer (eds), *Dialogues and Deconstruction: The Gadamer–Derrida Encounter*, p. 53.

[16] J. Dienstag, 'Postmodern Approaches to the History of Political Thought', in G. Klosko (ed.), *The Oxford Handbook of the History of Political Philosophy* (Oxford, Oxford University Press, 2002), p. 44.

interpretations of past political thought. Skinner insists on the priority to be assigned to historical scholarship and relating past texts to their appropriate historic contexts.[17] Gadamer does not deny the distinctiveness of the past. Indeed its distinctiveness explains why historical inquiry should aim for a fusion of horizons, but the notion of fusion implies an achieved unity between past and present not the recovery of what has gone. The potential frailty of Gadamer's standpoint is that it might legitimate the importation of present notions onto an alien past. However, he urges that historical interpretation should be alert to possibilities of misreading the evidence by assimilating the past to the present. A strength of Gadamer's position is that it explains why there is a continuous process of reinterpretation of past texts as succeeding generations reinterpret texts in the light of their own distinctive interpretive horizons.

The interpretive possibilities of Gadamer's hermeneutics are evident in his own interpretive practice, notably in his interpretation of Ancient philosophy, and in particular in his interpretation of Plato.[18] Gadamer offers a perceptive reading of Plato, and in doing so he relates Plato to his own philosophical standpoint. In his first book, *Plato's Dialectical Ethics*, Gadamer distinguishes Plato and his dialogues from Aristotle's exposition of his concepts.[19] Gadamer stresses the dialogical aspects of Plato's philosophy. He recognizes how Plato expresses lived experience in depicting Socrates engaging in dialogue with an assortment of characters and imagining truth as the product of conversational engagement. He identifies links between his own philosophy and that of Plato, in that he sees Plato's commitment to dialogue as advancing an interpretive practice that is of a piece with a hermeneutical commitment to interpretation, in which truth is a product of continuous interpretation. In his later work on Plato, Gadamer interprets the later dialogues as confirming a view of the internal relationship between the forms and the empirical world. Forms are not external to experience in that form and experiential particulars are taken to imply one another, and understanding constantly arises out of engagement with things in the world. Gadamer's own experiential dialogical notion of truth informs his reading of Plato, but it offers a view of Plato that is plausible and is supported by other scholars.[20] Gadamer's reading of Plato is influenced

[17] Q. Skinner, 'Introduction: Seeing Things their Way', in Q. Skinner, *Visions of Politics*, vol. 1, *Regarding Method* (Cambridge, Cambridge University Press, 1992), p. 3.

[18] An informative and interesting reading of Gadamer's *Interpretation of Plato* is Catherine H. Zuckert, 'Hermeneutics in Practice: Gadamer on Ancient Philosophy', in R.J. Dostal, *The Cambridge Companion to Gadamer* (Cambridge, Cambridge University Press, 2002), pp. 201–25.

[19] H.-G. Gadamer, *Plato's Dialectical Ethics: Phenomenological Interpretations relating to the Philebus* (New Haven, Yale University Press, 1991).

[20] See J. Findlay, 'Hegel and Platonism', in J.J. O'Malley, K.W. Algozin, and F.G. Weiss (eds), *Hegel and the History of Philosophy* (The Hague, Martinus Nijhoff, 1974), p. 68; H.-G. Gadamer, *The Idea of the Good in Platonic-Aristotelian Philosophy* (New Haven, Yale University Press, 1986), pp. 62–76.

by present experience in other ways. Zuckert detects in his analysis of mathematics in the *Republic* his sense of it performing a valuable service in steering potential philosophers away from the political distractions of the Cave, which resonates with Gadamer's own concern to separate himself, if only obliquely, from Nazism by concentrating on non-political subjects. In aligning Plato with his own philosophical practice, Gadamer is enabled to provide a distinctive interpretation of Plato, which also recognizes the specificity of Plato's context, notably the practices of the sophists against which the dialogues are directed. However, Gadamer tends to ignore the character and provenance of Plato's literary and historical remarks, and reads Plato schematically as outlining a particular line of thought that anticipates his own philosophy.

In the succeeding section of this chapter I will interpret aspects of *Truth and Method* in the light of the interpretive horizon of this book. The seemingly disparate parts of Gadamer's text will be reviewed so as to highlight their hermeneutic contribution to an overall view of the central role of historical understanding for interpretation and truth. *Truth and Method* develops its understanding of interpretation by means of an historical analysis of its character. Subsequently, the implications of Gadamer's hermeneutics for the history of political thought will be reviewed by focusing upon his commentary on Strauss and by considering the possibilities that are offered by Gadamer's hermeneutics to readings of political thought which highlight gender and sexuality. Gadamer himself did not focus on the history of political thought, though in his shrewd analysis of Strauss he reviews the politics of Strauss's use of classical thought and the value of his approach to the historical study of political thought. Feminists have remarked upon the pros and cons of Gadamer's hermeneutics for feminism, and the practice of re-reading the canon of political thought in the light of present conceptions of gender, sex, and sexuality will be shown to lend itself to a hermeneutic approach.

TRUTH AND METHOD

Gadamer's *Truth and Method* is a work of reflection and it reflects upon itself in the course of its argument. It urges a consonance between truth and the interpretive activity of making sense of experience. There is neither need for discovery of the truth nor for providing a distinct and neutralized method for its attainment. Truth and the experiential processes of interpretation are joined. The book follows a number of pathways, the coherence of the overall framework is not advertised and yet its rationale resides in its argument for and exhibition of a form of hermeneutics, which is taken to be central to the human world and is exemplified in key features of the text. The process of achieving interpretive coherence by a series of interlocking reviews of interpretive practices constitutes the overarching theme of the text. It demonstrates how meaning is an ongoing process of construction and interpretation by its own reflection on past texts. Part One of the book is entitled, 'The Question of Truth as it Emerges in the Experience of Art'.[21] The focus on art follows a brief critical review of Mill's naturalistic approach to social sciences, which is deficient in failing to register the interpretive aspect of human identity.[22] In contrast, Gadamer imagines art to be an imaginative, non-naturalistic interpretive form of experience. Its interpretation of experience is neither arbitrary nor external. If the rationale for analysing art is not explained, it would appear to reside in its interpretive disclosure of the truth within experience.

Gadamer's analysis of art begins by showing how the language of art is interpretive, expressing truth, allowing for interpretive practice by participants, and admitting ongoing interpretation. The interpretation of art that is offered in *Truth and Method* is delivered by the interpretive reconstruction of preceding aesthetic perspectives, which constitutes a concrete demonstration of the dynamic of interpretation underlying Gadamer's hermeneutics. Following his reading of art and the history of aesthetics, Gadamer attends to the history of hermeneutics itself. He interprets its particular historic forms and articulates his own summative view of hermeneutics. He imagines the entire human world of meaning to be hermeneutical, which is to be understood by means of a hermeneutic circle embracing past and present, and allowing for an acceptance of prejudice to inform interpretive engagements with contemporary and past forms of thinking. Hermeneutics, for Gadamer, offers an alternative and appropriate way of interpreting the human world, in contrast to the naturalistic methods, which he critiques in the opening chapter of *Truth and Method*.

Ultimately Gadamer understands art to be a social experience in which truth emerges by the processes of interpretation in which its participants and commentators engage. This conception of art is itself the product of its history and interpretation. At the outset of *Truth and Method* Gadamer observes the historicity of art and aesthetics, maintaining, 'Concepts such as "art", "history", "the creative", "worldview", "genius", "external world", "interiority", "expression", "style", "symbol", which we take to be self-evident, contain a wealth of history.'[23] His review of art in the modern world focuses initially upon Kant's analysis of art as a form of feeling. He is critical of the limits that Kant places upon art as an experience. Kant's use of the term *sensus communis* to characterize the notion of the beautiful is symptomatic of the status he ascribes to art, because it is imagined as a reflective judgment whereby universal and particular are aligned, but only by a sense that is devoid of

---

[21] H.-G. Gadamer, *Truth and Method*, pp. 1–171.   [22] Ibid., pp. 3–8.
[23] Ibid., pp. 9–10.

rational categorial backing. Likewise it represents a turn away from a preceding humanist usage, which, for Vico stood for a general tendency to adopt the right line of conduct and to see the wood from trees. Kant distinguishes aesthetic taste from moral sense, which he reserves for reason and rational categorical judgment. Kant's *Critique of Judgment*, while justifying the operations of taste transcendentally, detaches aesthetics from morality and politics, and thereby undermines the status of art and expressive artistic language.[24] According to Gadamer Kant supplies a universal register for taste but renders aesthetics subjective, isolating it from the wider web of moral and political traditions. Significantly, for Gadamer, Kant looks to individual genius rather than shared experience as the way for art to express the mystery of creativity, which is not fully susceptible of articulation. Gadamer observes, 'Through genius nature gives art its rules.'[25]

Gadamer interprets Kant's immediate successors in aesthetics as following his lead in interpreting art as the province of individual genius. Schiller and Fichte imagine art to be oriented towards the subjectivity of spirit, and individual genius. Hegel counters this subjectivity, observing the dangers in Romanticism, and identifying art with the universality of Spirit and the experience of cultural education, *Bildung*.[26] Gadamer is sympathetic to Hegel's integration of art into the wider orbit of human meaning, though he is suspicious of what he takes to be Hegel's subordination of art to philosophy.[27] Gadamer's ambivalent reading of Hegel will be reviewed in chapter 13. He takes the neo-Kantian successors of Hegel, who return to Kant and the notion of individual genius and art, as answers to a Romantic demand for a new mythology in which art displaces other forms of life. Gadamer concludes, 'Thus through "aesthetic differentiation" the work loses its place and the world to which it belongs insofar as it belongs instead to aesthetic consciousness.'[28]

Heidegger serves as a counterpoint to the disorienting individualism of Romantic conceptions of art. He envisages art as expressing inter-subjective meaning, which is explored in his lectures on art. This view of art arises out of his identification of the inter-subjective character of *Dasein*, that is, being in the world.[29] Gadamer completes his analysis of art by advancing his own interpretation of art as play, which emerges out of his preceding historical analysis. Play incorporates inter-subjective and performative aspects of art, which attest to its social and interpretive character. Art is continually developed in performance. For instance, a theatrical performance depends on a number of players. What is true of drama applies to other arts, including the

---

[24] I. Kant, *Critique of Judgment* (Oxford, Oxford University Press, 1969), p. 85.
[25] H.-G. Gadamer, *Truth and Method*, p. 55.   [26] Ibid., pp. 9–19.
[27] Ibid., p. 98.   [28] Ibid., p. 87.
[29] See M. Heidegger, 'The Origin of the Work of Art', in D. Krell (ed.), *Martin Heidegger: Basic Writings* (London, Routledge, 1978), pp. 83–140.

novel, where author and reader are complementary to one another. The notion of play allows for interpretive interplay between players and admits a role for an audience. Gadamer observes, 'An encounter with the language of art is an encounter with an unfinished event and is itself part of the event.'[30] In his essay, 'The Relevance of the Beautiful,' Gadamer recognizes that the inter-relations between aspects of a work of art should not be subverted by a virtuoso performer. He observes, 'When we become aware of an actor or singer or any creative artist as mediator, we exercise a secondary level of reflection. When the complete experience of a work of art is genuine, however, what amazes us is precisely the unobtrusiveness of the performance'.[31] Reflecting on the dialogue between past and present that is sustained in traditions of performance, Gadamer observes, 'In view of the finitude of our historical existence, it would seem that there is something absurd about the whole idea of a unique correct performance'.[32]

Gadamer interprets the history of aesthetics as disclosing the possibilities of the hermeneutical interpretation of art. The multiplicity of actors involved in the production and reception of art enact the interpretive engagement of hermeneutics. Art, to function as art, requires interpretation and open engagement by all involved. Successive generations of audiences will develop different interpretations of art and these aspects of art show its hermeneutical features. Gadamer's review of art indicates interpretive features of understanding and in Part Two of *Truth and Method* he considers the history of hermeneutics as a form of interpretation. He shows how hermeneutics figures as the medium for interpreting the human world as a whole. He observes how hermeneutics follows two pathways; theological and philological, as humanistic literature and the bible required reading and interpretation. He reports on how Luther undertakes a hermeneutic reading of the bible, which presumes the unity of the bible in interpreting its individual books in the light of its holistic identity, rather than a series of parts written by distinct authors. Schleiermacher is credited with developing a general historical form of hermeneutical understanding, taking interpretation to be coeval with understanding. For Schleiermacher texts are to be understood by means of the hermeneutic circle whereby parts are related to wholes and the notions of whole and part are seen as provisional in that they are constantly being reshaped by developing forms of interpretive understanding.[33] Gadamer is critical of Schleiermacher's tendency to identify interpretation of past texts with the psychological understanding of past authors. Gadamer regards

---

[30] H.-G. Gadamer, *Truth and Method*, p. 134.
[31] H.-G. Gadamer, 'The Relevance of the Beautiful', in H-G. Gadamer, *The Relevance of the Beautiful and Other Essays* (Cambridge, Cambridge University Press, 1986), pp. 1–56.
[32] H.-G. Gadamer, *Truth and Method*, p. 120.   [33] Ibid., p. 190.

historical hermeneutical understanding as engaging with past texts from a present perspective that excludes equating interpretation with a resuscitation of a past actor's psychological state. Empathetic identification with a past author is no substitute for interpreting evidence. He observes, 'Schleiermacher's problem is not historical obscurity but the obscurity of the Thou.'[34]

Gadamer relates how the historical school succeeds Schleiermacher's approach, with historians such as Ranke and Doyen aiming to produce a universal history by a series of particular empirical studies, whereas Hegel's philosophical historicism purports to furnish universal historical truth. Gadamer imagines Dilthey as combining the historical school's empirical breadth of study with a sensitivity that is developed from Schleiermacher. Nonetheless, he is critical of Dilthey's mere sketch of a hermeneutical grounding of human science to serve as a distinguishable method, which draws upon inductive procedures from the natural sciences. Heidegger is taken as superseding Dilthey by providing an appropriate theoretical underpinning to the practice of hermeneutics. Heidegger theorizes its character by indicating the circular form in a new guise. He takes *Dasein*, determinate human beings, to operate within a socially situated world in which they are future-oriented, but also are related to the past in that they cannot be imagined outside of inherited beliefs and cultivated orientations. Gadamer's own understanding of hermeneutics recognizes how human beings invariably harbour prejudices in maintaining traditions and in engaging interpretively with other individuals and with texts. Hermeneutics represents this engagement whereby an individual's horizon of understanding comes into contact with those of others, either directly in conversation or indirectly in interpreting texts. Gadamer imagines understanding as arising out of a fusion of horizons whereby individuals modify their standpoints in their engagement with the different horizons of others.

In elaborating on hermeneutics, Gadamer imagines language, history, tradition, and prejudice to contribute to its processes of interpretation. Gadamer's account of hermeneutics draws upon his preceding review of art and his historical analysis of the practice of hermeneutics. Hermeneutics functions in a way that is distinct from the natural sciences and is more akin to artistic insight. Art depends upon the reciprocal contributions of multiple participants in its play, insofar as they interpret, express, perform, and receive works of art. Works of art are also never complete in that successive generations, in perceiving things differently, renew ways of seeing and interpreting art. Likewise Gadamer's hermeneutics is not a delimited activity, but rather embraces the whole of humanity. To be human is to inhabit a world of meaning that is constantly interpreted and reinterpreted. Language is crucial to meaningful experience and hence to hermeneutics. Gadamer observes,

---

[34] Ibid., p. 191.

'Language is the medium in which substantive understanding and agreement takes place between two people.'[35] Without the medium of language, there would be no human world. Gadamer maintains, 'Language is not one of man's possessions in the world; on it rather depends the fact that man has a world at all.'[36] In the essay 'On the Scope and Function of Hermeneutics', Gadamer observes, 'Reality does not happen "behind the back" of language...reality happens precisely within language.'[37] Language is essentially dialogical, and participants in a conversation are continuously interpreting what is being said and discriminating between what is shared and what is distinct in their standpoints.[38] The horizons of participants' understanding are different but mutual understanding is to be achieved by a fusion of their distinct horizons. Language constitutes a shared world of meaning, which allows for individual horizons of meaning. The human world is this world of meaning. For Gadamer, meaning is constituted by language, which is shaped by the past and hence demands a historical perspective on its development. There is no absolute foundation by which a definitive form of understanding can be proclaimed. Meaning can be explored, shared, and developed by conversation, but conversations presuppose a past, which both informs conversation and is to be interpreted. Wachterhauser observes, 'History and language are the two conditions of knowledge that makes our knowing "finite"'.[39] Finite knowledge depends upon interpretive skills of human beings inhabiting a social, linguistic world that is continuously emerging from the past, and which is continuously subject to reinterpretation.

The past shapes perceptions of the present by tradition, which forms the context for individual and collective standpoints and practice. In specifying the nature of individuals and their horizons of understanding, Gadamer critiques the Enlightenment rejection of prejudice. He remarks, 'The overcoming of all prejudices, this global demand of the Enlightenment will itself prove to be a prejudice, and removing it opens the way to an appropriate understanding of the finitude which dominates not only our humanity but our historical consciousness.'[40] Understanding, for Gadamer, is always a finite understanding, which bears the marks of its situatedness, in time and in language. Individuals neither invent nor declare a world of meaning. They are socialized into a world of meaning, within which they maintain

---

[35] Ibid., p. 384.   [36] Ibid., p. 443.

[37] H.-G. Gadamer, 'On the Scope and Function of Hermeneutics', trans. G. Hers and R. Palmer, in D.E. Linge (ed.), *Gadamer, Philosophical Hermeneutics* (Berkeley, University of California Press, 1976), p. 35.

[38] H.-G. Gadamer, *Truth and Method*, p. 442.

[39] B. Wachterhauser, 'Getting It Right: Relativism, Realism and Truth', R. Dostal (ed.), *The Cambridge Companion to Gadamer*, p. 57.

[40] H.-G. Gadamer, *Truth and Method*, p. 276.

viewpoints, assumptions, and traditional forms of thinking that shape their perspectives on the world. In conversations with other language users they assume perspectives, horizons of intelligibility, which they derive from traditions. These traditions, in turn, are developed by the interplay of conversation. The past bears upon the present. Gadamer observes, '[L]inguistic communication between present and tradition is, as we have shown, the event that takes place in all understanding.'[41]

In Gadamer's perspective there is no extra-historical, extra-linguistic access to truth and meaning. The human world is a constructed and continuously reconstructed one. Ideas that have been articulated and assessed in the past set the context in which viewpoints are assumed and reconstructed in the present. As the course of the argument in *Truth and Method* discloses, interpretation of past ideas allows for the refinement of meanings and a broadening of perspectives. Past and present differ and the historian of the present cannot simply recover the identities of the past. The horizon of the present is brought to bear upon the horizon of the past and what can emerge is a fusion of horizons that constitutes a new form of understanding, which is informed by the past. Gadamer's *Truth and Method* is an immense text, which itself fuses theory and practice, and past and present in reaching an understanding of hermeneutics by interpreting aesthetic and traditional hermeneutical forms of understanding. His interpretation of the past and his practice as an historian inform his present understanding of hermeneutics just as his hermeneutical approach shapes his historic engagement with past forms of thought. The resulting circularity of understanding does not admit of a neat knock-down way of validating judgments; truth is a matter of interpretation. Interpretive understanding may go awry if assumptions of the present are too readily imported into the past and Gadamer has been critiqued on this score for rehearsing uncritically traditional assumptions. Eagleton is not alone in observing the relatively undertheorized notion of tradition with which Gadamer operates.[42]

Gadamer is explicit in relying on tradition and prejudice to orient hermeneutical inquiry and all forms of human activity and a criticism that has been levelled against him is that he does not provide resources to critique inherited traditions, which may be ideological and support inequalities of power. Habermas objected to Gadamer's hermeneutics precisely on these grounds in that in reviewing Gadamer's thought he maintained that Gadamer allows tradition to dictate to reason, rather than critiquing power relations by the

---

[41] Ibid., p. 463.

[42] Feminists have critiqued Gadamer's apparently uncritical stance towards patriarchy. For Eagleton's criticism, see T. Eagleton, *Literary Theory: An Introduction* (Oxford Basil Blackwell, 1981), pp. 72–4.

application of critical reason.[43] Habermas recognizes that ideological and systematically distorted communication requires critical reason to reveal and critique 'the experienced reality of communication distorted by force'.[44] Gadamer rejects this Habermasian reading of tradition and prejudice and responds by observing that reason cannot critique everything at once. Tradition and prejudice are ontological conditions of being in the world and reason is engaged constantly in critical reflection on these conditions, but it is always a reflection upon tradition and prejudice and cannot be dismantled by a supposed scientific reason that is abstracted from experience.[45] Gadamer takes tradition to be central to experience and it is not to be overturned by reason, even though he recognizes how tradition is to be interpreted continuously. In highlighting the centrality and reciprocity of tradition and interpretation, Gadamer is resisting the notion of the use of reason as an abstract formula to critique experiential forms of knowing. While Gadamer is right to resist the notion of a social science that is supposedly outside the frame of traditions, he might still be criticized for failing to show how traditions that support inequalities and repression require radical critique.

HISTORY OF POLITICAL THOUGHT

Maliks notes how Gadamer tended not to focus upon the history of political thought and how his hermeneutical style of interpretation has not exerted the direct impact on the subject that its expertise in the critical examination of texts might have been expected to have contributed. Maliks observes, 'One would have expected Hans-Georg Gadamer's hermeneutics to have much to contribute to the study of the history of political thought... Yet there is little impact of Gadamer's hermeneutics on the study of the history of political thought.'[46] The expectation of Gadamer's influence arises out of his way of engaging with texts. His debate with Derrida shows his distinctive style in that in contrast to Derrida he emphasizes a dialogical engagement with past authors and texts, rather than subjecting them to a hermeneutics of

---

[43] See J. Habermas, 'A Review of Gadamer's Truth and Method' in J. Habermas, *Understanding and Social Inquiry*, ed. F. Dallmayr and T. McCarthy (South Bend, Notre Dame University Press, 1977, pp. 335–63; J. Habermas, 'Systematically Distorted Communication', *Inquiry*, vol. 1, no. 13, 1970, pp. 205–18; J. Habermas, 'Summation and Response' trans. M. Matesich, *Continuum* vol. 8, 1970, pp. 124–8.

[44] J. Habermas, 'Summation and Response' trans. M. Matesich, p. 125.

[45] H.-G. Gadamer, 'On the Scope and Function of Hermeneutics', pp. 32–5. See also R. Gall, 'Between Tradition and Critique: The Gadamer-Habermas Debate', *Gelgung*, vol. 8, no. 1, 1981.

[46] R. Maliks, 'Hermeneutics and the History of Political Thought', in H. Paul and M. Kasten (eds), *Gadamer's Influence on the Humanities* (Leiden, Leiden University Press, 2012), p. 233.

suspicion.[47] Yet this goal of opening a conversation with past modes of thought does not entail that the past and past texts are to be accepted uncritically. Central to Gadamer's hermeneutics is the critical interpretive dialogue that is to be conducted between past and present just as political debate presupposes unrestricted critical dialogue between participants.

The distinctive style of Gadamer's approach to the history of political thought can be seen in his critique of Strauss in 'Hermeneutics and Historicism'.[48] Gadamer recognizes and is appreciative of Strauss's dissident stance on political philosophy, by which he opposes the contemporary faith in historicism and the subordination of thinking to a supposed directionality of history.[49] He understands Strauss's project in his numerous works on the history of political philosophy to be that of 'confronting modern historical self-consciousness with the clear rightness of classical philosophy.'[50] He is sympathetic to Strauss's retrieval of the possibility of natural law or objective rightness in opposition to a historicism that subordinates law and what is right to the dictates of an historical understanding that reveals an end to history. Gadamer perceives the problematic character of establishing an historical assumption that the present can provide a standpoint by which preceding thought can be subsumed. He notes the irony of a historicist perspective that presumes it can supersede the historicity of the very judgments on the relativity of thought that its perspective licenses. Gadamer observes, '"Historical" understanding, whether today's or tomorrow's, has no special privilege. It is itself embraced by the changing horizons and moved with them.'[51]

While Gadamer sees the merit of Strauss's critique of historicism, he is critical of Strauss's view that past thinking can be accessed in ways that are not shaped by present interests and perspectives. He critiques the idea that Strauss shares with Collingwood, which is that a past theory can be rethought in the same and 'correct' way that it was understood by the past theorist.[52] Gadamer is sceptical that there is a definitive and ascertainable thought or set of thoughts in a piece of writing that may be susceptible to rethinking. Present perspectives shape the ways in which past thought is interpreted. He agrees with Strauss that the Classical Greek polis represented a very different political association from that of the modern state but he also insists that this thought would have been inaccessible to Ancient thought.[53] Hence, for Gadamer, interpretation of the past is not to imagine a past that is divorced from the

---

[47] See H.-G. Gadamer, 'Text and Interpretation' trans. D. Schmidt and R. Palmer, in D. P. Michelfelder and R.E. Palmer (eds), *Dialogues and Deconstruction: The Gadamer–Derrida Encounter*, p. 40.

[48] H.-G. Gadamer, 'Hermeneutics and Historicism', in H-G. Gadamer, *Truth and Method* trans. Revised by J. Weinsheimer and D.G. Marshall (London, Sheed and Ward, 1960), pp. 505–42.

[49] Ibid., p. 533.   [50] Ibid.   [51] Ibid., p. 535.
[52] Ibid.   [53] Ibid., pp. 537–8.

present but to interpret it in the light of the present. Again, Gadamer appreciates particular interpretations of past thinkers that have been undertaken by Strauss but is sceptical of the latter's sense of past writers, under threat of persecution, writing esoterically to convey their 'real' meaning. For Gadamer, meaning is never simply objective at the expense of subjectivity. Interpretation is necessarily a matter of engaging with others and in this engagement there is not a simple right answer. Rather there is continuous dialogue, between interlocutors and between past, present, and future. Gadamer accepts much of what Strauss maintains on politics and its understanding. He shares Strauss's criticism of historicism and his sense that philosophical truth is not to be reduced to historical development. However, he is also critical of Strauss's view that truth resides in the uncontaminated doctrines of past theorists. This Straussian assumption runs counter to the continuous construction of historical understanding and Gadamer's sense that politics is not an activity in which timeless truths can be implemented.[54]

Gadamer's critical analysis of Strauss reveals how his hermeneutical perspective is relevant to the study of the history of political thought. For Gadamer, the reciprocity of past and present and the irreducible and ongoing interpretivist character of understanding are of particular moment in appreciating the continuing process of reinterpreting political ideas. In subsequent chapters this feature of hermeneutics will be drawn upon in reviewing how the political theories of Marx, Mill, and Beauvoir lend themselves to processes of rethinking. Collini observes how Mill's thought has been reinterpreted over successive generations and suggests that the process of reinterpretation of political theorists can be seen to conform to a standard pattern. Gadamer's sense of the continuous and illimitable processes of reinterpretation disturbs a formulaic reading of reinterpretation. Likewise analysing the history of Marxist reinterpretations of Marx underlines the openness of texts to multiple possibilities of their interpretation, which tend to jar with a Marxist correlation of textual meaning with economic circumstances. One of the ways in which Marx has been reinterpreted has been in highlighting the role of imperialism in the maintenance of capital. This recognition of the interaction of the West with non-Western states is also reflected in political theories such as Fanon's that see conflict with the West as forming an essential part of political theory. This changing frame of political theory demands reinterpretation of its character and is compatible with Gadamer's notion of the continuing interpretive activity linking past and present.

Perhaps the most evident way in which reinterpretation of texts of political thought might be related to Gadamer's hermeneutics is suggested in Lawn's study of Gadamer's hermeneutics. Lawn values Gadamer's insight into the

---

[54] Ibid., p. 541.

ways in which present standpoints continually open up new vistas on the past. As an example of these processes he cites how feminist theorists have revisited the past and discovered hitherto neglected female political theorists, who raise political issues that have been ignored previously.[55] The possibilities that are offered to feminism by Gadamer's hermeneutics have been discussed by contemporary feminists, and divergent feminist views on Gadamer are collected in Code's *Feminist Interpretations of Gadamer*.[56] While some of the contributors to this collection of essays are critical of Gadamer's relative silence on issues of power, the majority see positive possibilities for feminism in his thought. Hekman regards Gadamer's concept of a horizon to be a more helpful designation of the social theorist's position than a post-modern tendency to allow for a variety of judgmental perspectives.[57] Certainly Gadamer's identification of the interpreter's interpretive horizon that is framed by his or her relationship to a tradition allows for an appreciation of the ways in which feminist theorists operating with a revised perspective on traditional gender norms have reinterpreted the canon of the history of political thought. This process of reinterpretation has been conducted in multiple ways. Feminist theorists, such as Wollstonecraft, have been added to the canon in the light of developing interest in hitherto gendered exclusions of women from the public world. In turn this contributes to a critical focus upon the continuing construction of canons of political thinkers that reflect present interests and perceptions of the past. Likewise the political thought of past male political theorists has been re-examined in the light of a heightened consciousness of the ways in which the lives and roles of women have been presented in classic texts of political thought. For instance, Coole's *Women in Political Theory* re-examines the doctrines of seminal political thinkers from a feminist perspective, and interprets Rousseau's reading of humanity as maintaining a distorted bifurcation of qualities between men and women. The consequences of this sexual division underpin Rousseau's endorsement of (male) citizens' wholesale participation in the public world, because it depends upon the exclusion of women from that world and their labour in the private world.[58] Likewise Pateman's *The Sexual Contract* reinterprets classic social contract theory from a feminist perspective so as to highlight the subjugation of women in a prior sexual contract that corrals them in the private world and excludes them from the public world of politics. Pateman invokes the feminist concept

---

[55] C. Lawn, *Gadamer: A Guide for the Perplexed* (London and New York, Continuum, 2006), p. 128.

[56] L. Code (ed.), *Feminist Interpretations of Hans-Georg Gadamer* (Pennsylvania, Pennsylvania State University Press, 2003).

[57] S. Hekman, 'The Ontology of Change', in L. Code (ed.), *Feminist Interpretations of Hans-Georg Gadamer*, pp. 181–203.

[58] See D. Coole, *Women in Political Theory: From Ancient Misogyny to Contemporary Feminism* (London, Harvester/Wheatsheaf, 1993), p. 118.

of patriarchy to explain implications of the social contract that had been ignored by preceding commentary. She observes, 'Commentaries on the texts (of social contract theory) gloss over the fact that the theorists construct a patriarchal account of masculinity and femininity and then of what it is to be men and women.'[59]

Reinterpretation of the canon of political theory in the light of changing perspectives on the role of women and on the gendered dimension of political theorizing is not limited to revisionist analyses of how women and their roles are portrayed. Reappraisal of the representation of men in classic texts of political theory has been undertaken by theorists, who have been influenced by feminism but also by the recent development of men's and masculinities' studies. Carver's *Men in Political Theory,* for instance, provides a series of provocative reinterpretations of classic political theories by focusing on how men are portrayed within them. In re-reading Machiavelli, Carver attends to the different sorts of men and their differential forms of socialization that are depicted in Machiavelli's *The Prince.*[60] In this re-reading Machiavelli is seen to privilege politics for a certain kind of alpha male of aristocratic descent who has been trained by sport and induction into political practices to exercise power ruthlessly and subtly in ways that lesser, effeminate males could not achieve. If Machiavelli sharply distinguishes men from women he is also shown to attend closely to the production of the right sort of man for the business of ruling. Similarly, Rousseau's state of nature is interpreted as an anthropological retrojection of the present that valorizes a certain kind of fantasized male, who is tough and naturalistic rather than effeminate and civilized. In our subsequent chapter on Beauvoir, we recognize the challenge that her analysis of women as constituting the second sex represents for traditional views of the political. Beauvoir's critique of the sociological production of men and women with differential attributes and roles poses questions for the interpretation of sex and sexuality and also for what constitutes politics if sexual differentiation is achieved by means that are susceptible to political change. In recognizing the continuous reinterpretation of the past by the changing perspectives of present interpretive standpoints, Gadamer's hermeneutics possesses the conceptual resources to accommodate the radicalism of Beauvoir's challenge to conventional notions of politics. The fluidity of its interpretive position has the potential for allowing a radical historical revisionism on how past political thought might be interrogated in its light.

The interaction of subject and object in Gadamer's thought is evidenced by the fact that the subject who undertakes studies of texts is herself a historical subject whose views are both affected by the tradition in which she is situated

---

[59] C. Pateman, *The Sexual Contract* (Cambridge, Polity Press, 1988), p. 5.
[60] See T. Carver, *Men in Political Theory* (Manchester, Manchester University Press, 2004), pp. 105–30.

and by the texts that she interprets. Hermeneutics is about the fusion of horizons. The interpreter of a text is affected by how the tradition into which the text is situated is to be read and by the text itself. The horizon of the subject and the horizon of the text reciprocally affect the process of interpretation. The point is to fuse the horizons. The interpreter occupies a position in a tradition of interpretation and of political thought so she or he will influence and be influenced by the substantive political theories that are the objects of inquiry and by the traditions of inquiry to which they are attached. For Gadamer it is to be expected that interpretations change, just as notions of politics are transformed over time. The interpretation of Locke's thought in the twenty-first century will differ from an interpretation of the mid-twentieth century. No doubt interpretations will differ according to what is known about Locke's texts. Laslett's careful dating of the writing of *The Second Treatise on Government* allows for changes in how the text is interpreted. However, Gadamer recognizes that transformations in politics and society that are subsequent to the writing of a text also promote changes in interpretation. For one thing a sensitivity to gender issues alerts readers in the twenty-first century to the relative absence of express reference to women as political actors in Locke's texts. It is an absence that is now noticed and calls for review rather than to be passed over in a silent acquiescence that replicates Locke's own standpoint. The position of the interpreter, for Gadamer, is neither neutral nor to be taken for granted. The interpreter views the text in the light of their assumptions and the interpreter uses their concepts in the  process of interpreting past texts so that while a recognition of gender might not inform Locke's conceptual vocabulary it can be used to probe his texts. Interpretation is an historical exercise that involves the conceptual worlds of past and present as past political thought is constructed and interpreted from the present.

CONCLUSION

Gadamer offers a subtle reading of the circularity and revisionism of interpretation, which fits with the historical record of continually changing interpretations of texts. His interpretive approach is distinct from other methodological and theoretical perspectives on the history of political thought and his perspective offers a notable resource by which to study political thought, even if he himself did not specialize in the area. His emphasis upon the dialectical inter-relations between interpreter and interpretation, and between the subject and object of textual examination is salutary and is sensitive to ways in which human beings understand one another and to the practice of textual interpretation. Where Oakeshott divorces historical research from the practical interests of the present,

Gadamer embraces the perspective of the interpreter in the process of achieving historical understanding. The practical past is not separated from an historical past because the intimations of traditions that underlie present ideas influence the ways in which historical research is conducted. Gadamer points to what may be styled the dialectical implications of interpretation. Present and past are linked by the experiential circumstances of interpretation. Interpretation is necessarily conducted in the present, and there is no experience save that which takes place in the present. Yet Gadamer does not renounce the past in adverting to the role of the present horizon in undertaking historical interpretation of texts. The point of textual interpretation is to get at the truth of a past text. Hence Gadamer allows for the pastness of a text, recognizing how it evidences express purposes and ideas that reflect distinctive past issues and circumstances. This past horizon, however, is invoked in the light of questions that emerge in the present.

The difference between Gadamer's and Oakeshott's approaches is brought out sharply by Gadamer's recognition of the affinity between legal interpretation of past cases and historical research, whereas Oakeshott takes the work of a lawyer on a practical case involving past conduct to epitomize the non-historical past. Gadamer's approach also raises questions over the ways in which Skinner's approach has tended to formulate his contextualism. In later writings Skinner has observed the plausibility of Gadamer's recognition of the constituted character of the past, yet he imagines the primary focus of historical inquiry is upon distinct past contexts, whereas Gadamer maintains the reciprocal inter-relations of past and present.[61] Gadamer's imagining of historical understanding as involving a conversation between present and past promises to shed light on both, and in aiming to respect past constructions of ideas, Gadamer presents a standpoint that is distinct from deconstruction. However, the particular way in which past and present are taken to fuse in Gadamer's hermeneutics raises doubts over his enterprise. Gadamer takes tradition to influence how the interpreter of texts undertakes their investigation, but this notion of tradition is relatively unexamined. Gadamer's resistance to Habermas's notion of a wholesale rationalist critique of tradition is justified in that reason cannot be conceived as an instrument that is external to the experience that it examines. Yet critical questions remain to be asked of Gadamer's notion of tradition. Just what does he mean by it? Is there a single line of tradition to which the interpreter is party or are there multiple strains of tradition that inform possible interpretations? Are traditions to be embraced even where they maintain unacknowledged forms of repression? What sort of interrogation of a tradition should be undertaken? Foucault's genealogical approach is itself undertheorized but it offers a break from contemporary norms that coalesce with unacceptable forms of control by engaging more

---

[61] See Q. Skinner, 'Introduction: Seeing Things Their Way', in Q. Skinner, *Visions of Politics*, vol. 1, *Regarding Method*, pp. 1–8.

critically with antecedent practices than Gadamer's approach appears to assume. Gadamer does not appear to apply radical critique to traditions. In *Truth and Method* he shows a continuous engagement with Hegel's speculative philosophy of history while at the same time dismissing its absolutist, closed reading of history. Yet it remains unclear the extent to which Hegel and Hegelianism constitute aspects of a tradition upon which his own philosophizing and political judgments rest. In chapter 13 we will review Gadamer's interpretation of Hegel's philosophy. We will also assess the compatibility of Gadamer's approach with the multiplicity of readings of Mill, Marx, and Beauvoir in chapters 14, 16, and 18.

Part II

Interpretations of Modern Political Thinkers

8

Machiavelli

Modernity and the Renaissance Man

INTRODUCTION

Machiavelli is no longer simply a proper name; it has a more general meaning. To designate a person or an action 'Machiavellian' is either to condemn someone or to post a warning. When colleagues are Machiavellian we know what they are up to and we either bemoan their skullduggery or scurry along the corridor looking for protection. Machiavelli's name stands for political immorality or amorality. It signifies the end of the Christian medieval era and a modern reckoning with power and interests, stripped of Christian or moral associations. Elizabethan England, with its fears of Catholicism and its painting of lurid images of political depravity imagined Machiavelli to be the incarnation of an immoral pursuit of power.[1] Strauss and his adherent Mansfield follow suit by framing Machiavelli, literally and metaphorically, as a figure that symbolizes the turn against natural law and indifference towards moral evaluation of the political realm.[2] Yet Machiavelli can be imagined differently. After all he is a Renaissance man, literally and metaphorically. He is deeply influenced by Renaissance humanist scholarship. Like other Florentine scholars, he draws upon classical authors in reacting to the twists and turns of Renaissance Florence's political history in aiming to revitalize the city of Florence and its citizenry. Skinner and Pocock have contributed massively to turning the tide of perceptions away from generalized and often hyperbolic estimates of Machiavelli's alleged uniquely immoral standpoint towards a contextual appreciation of how he develops and responds to humanist scholarship and current ideological concerns.[3]

---

[1] Shakespeare is a case in point. His depiction of Iago in *Othello* is a caricature of Machiavelli.
[2] L. Strauss, *Thoughts on Machiavelli* (Chicago Il. and London, University of Chicago Press, 1958); H. Mansfield, *Machiavelli's Virtue* (Chicago, University of Chicago Press, 1998).
[3] See in particular J.G.A. Pocock, *The Machiavellian Moment: Florentine Political Thought and the Atlantic Republican Tradition* (with a new afterword by the author) (Princeton and

Machiavelli was born in May 1469 in Florence, and the city and its politics, together with the Renaissance and its humanist traditions influenced his writings. Machiavelli's reputation as a writer depends chiefly upon two works—*The Prince* (1521) and *The Discourses on Livy* (1531), which he wrote virtually simultaneously. He also wrote *The Art of War* (1521) and *The History of Florence* (1527) as well as a play, *Mandragola* (1518).[4] Italian Renaissance city states in the fourteenth and fifteenth centuries were independent and divided. Their accumulation of finance capital, supporting flourishing and dynamic economies, attracted foreign intervention into their affairs. The city states collectively constituted an uncertain environment, in which political instability arose out of the divisions within cities, between the rich and poor, and nobles and merchants, and out of the disharmony between city states and foreign powers. Fragile alliances between these elements heightened tensions as much as resolved them. Moreover, Italian city states were small-scale communities, face to face societies, in which political differences yielded intense conflicts.

These Italian city states were the primary sites of what became known as the Renaissance, which signifies literally a rebirth of interest in Classical Greece and Rome. This interest was manifested in forms of scholarship, which focused upon language, rhetoric, the arts and philosophy, artistic achievement, and a naturalistic interest in the human form and worldly pursuits.[5] Machiavelli drew upon humanistic scholarship, its literary forms and political paradigms, in developing and composing his political ideas. He received a scholarly education

London, Princeton University Press, 2003); J.G.A. Pocock, 'Custom and Grace, Form and Matter, an Approach to Machiavelli's Concept of Innovation', in M. Fleischer (ed.), *Machiavelli and the Nature of Political Thought* (New York, Croom Helm, 1973), pp. 153–74; Q. Skinner, *Machiavelli* (Oxford, Oxford University Press, 1981); Q. Skinner, 'Machiavelli's *Discorsi* and the Pre-humanist Origins of Republican Ideas', in G. Bock, Q. Skinner, and M. Viroli (eds), *Machiavelli and Republicanism* (Cambridge, Cambridge University Press, 1990), pp. 121–42; Q. Skinner, *The Foundations of Modern Political Thought*, vol. 1, *The Renaissance* (Cambridge, Cambridge University Press, 1978).

[4] N. Machiavelli, *The Chief Works and Others*, ed. A. Gilbert (Durham NC, Duke University Press, 1989); N. Machiavelli, *Discourses on the First Ten Books of Livy* trans. C. Detmold, in N. Machiavelli, *The Prince and The Discourses* (New York, The Modern Library, 1950), pp. 103–540; N. Machiavelli, *The History of Florence* (London, Routledge and Sons, 1891); Machiavelli, *Legations* (in N. Machiavelli, *The Chief Works and Others*), pp. 120–61; N. Machiavelli, *The Literary Works of Machiavelli*, ed. and trans. J. Hale (Oxford, Oxford University Press, 1961); N. Machiavelli, Mandragola (in *The Literary Works of Machiavelli*); N. Machiavelli, *The Prince* trans. L. Ricci, in N. Machiavelli, *The Prince and The Discourses* (New York, The Modern Library, 1950), pp. 4–102.

[5] See G.A. Brucker, *Renaissance Florence* (New York, John Wiley and Sons, 1969); P. Burke, *The Italian Renaissance: Culture and Society in Italy* (Cambridge, Polity Press, 1986); F. Chabod, *Machiavelli and the Renaissance* (New York, Harper and Row, 1958); J.R. Hale, *Machiavelli and Renaissance Italy* (London, English Universities Press, 1961); P. Johnson, *The Renaissance: A Short History* (New York, Modern Library, 2000); J.H. Plumb, *The Italian Renaissance* (New York, American Heritage Library, 1989).

in the humanist tradition, which looked to classical traditions and, in particular, focused on Ancient Rome. Classic Roman authors represented a discursive context, which was different from that of medieval Christian thinkers. Classical authors focused upon the realities of practical political life and upon how to develop regimes of virtue that can survive and prosper, whereas medieval Christianity, although containing many currents of thought, tended to see the world as problematic and humanity as requiring redemptive faith in an otherworldly deity.

Machiavelli was offered the opportunity to join the political administrative life of his native Florence in 1498, and he joined the republican administration of Florence, heading the Second Chancery, and serving the Council of Ten. His sensitivity to the ebb and flow of political fortunes is recorded in his writings on his diplomatic work for the Chancery. In his *Legations*, he remarks on politics and on political leaders, for example, he comments on Cesare Borgia and Soderini, whom he understands to display qualities of leadership, which anticipate the paradigmatic forms of princely virtue that he outlines in *The Prince*. The fall of the Republic in 1512, and the restoration of the Medici family to political power, in turn, led to Machiavelli's dismissal and torture following suspicion of his implication in a group opposing the incoming regime. Machiavelli survived the torture and then composed *The Prince* in 1513, which followed the format of a Florentine humanist tradition in in that it provided advice to a prince on how the exercise of true statecraft might build a strong state and achieve glory.

It is not altogether clear why Machiavelli, whose political sympathy was generally republican, wrote a tract on the exercise of princely rule. In a letter to his friend, Vettori, he bemoans his lack of purpose and his desperation to undertake political work, and so, in part, the writing of *The Prince* is evidently motivated by his concern to display his prospective utility to the Medicis, to whom he dedicated the work.[6] However, the literary care and political expertise that are displayed in the tract suggest that it serves not merely as a calling card for office, but constitutes a reflective exercise, which explores the intrinsic problems and possibilities of exercising political rule in a principality that is beset by disruptive forces. At the very least, Machiavelli appears to consider that attending to the requisite skills and operational strategies that might establish and maintain political order in a principality is a worthwhile and necessary task, when the political environment is subversive of the conditions of security and peace that enable subordinate aims and purposes to be undertaken. Given his beliefs on the periodic requirement for republics to be re-established by heroic foundational political action, then it is plausible to infer that he imagines the task of framing the art of princely rule to be valuable

---

[6] N. Machiavelli, *The Literary Works of Machiavelli*, p. 140.

in itself as well as being instrumental in allowing for the future development of an effective republican regime.[7]

The Prince shows how to provide civil order and peace, while also bringing glory both to the prince and to the city. Machiavelli follows tradition in employing the literary form of an advice book and adheres to prevailing conventions in recommending how princely leadership must display virtue.[8] He departs from tradition, however, in emphasizing that resourcefulness and flexibility serve as key elements in the exercise of political virtue. Hence, statesmen are not to be restricted by conventional moral codes. Reason of state, for Machiavelli, demands moral flexibility, and he reckons that deceit and force are requisite expedients given a realistic appraisal of the times and the character of men.[9] He remarks, 'A man who wishes to make a profession of goodness in everything must necessarily come to grief among so many who are not so good. Therefore it is necessary for a prince, who wishes to maintain himself, to learn how not to be good, and to use this knowledge and not use it, according to the necessity of the case.'[10] Machiavelli's realism in favouring political measures that harmonize with circumstances, is linked to his conception of fortune. *Fortuna* conceptualizes the experience of time, which bears upon the practice of politics. It is not construed as a force, which is unamenable to human initiative.[11] In contrast to preceding medieval views, Machiavelli, like fellow humanists, maintains that human beings may exert influence over fortune. At the same time he also subscribes to a tough-minded assessment of how the intricacies of changing events, the sheer contingencies of the circumstances of fortune, resist and thwart assimilation to human agency. Hence Machiavelli maintains that fortune is not an unmoveable force dominating humanity and is susceptible to some degree of control. He observes, 'I would compare her (fortune) to an impetuous river that, when turbulent, inundates the plains, casts down trees and buildings, removes earth from this side and places it on the other; everyone flees before it, and everything yields to its fury without being able to oppose it; and yet though it is of such a kind, still when it is quiet, men can make provision against it by

---

[7] For an account of the role of great individuals in founding republics see N. Machiavelli, *Discourses*, p. 138. For a general discussion of the relationship between *The Prince* and the *Discourses*, see J. Femia, *Machiavelli Revisited* (Cardiff, University of Wales Press, 2004), pp. 11–14.

[8] On the tradition of advice books for princes, see A.H. Gilbert, *Machiavelli's 'Prince' and its Forerunners: 'The Prince' as a Typical Book de regimine principium* (Durham, NC, Duke University Press, 1938); and for a view that highlights the distinctiveness of Machiavelli, F. Gilbert, 'The Humanist Concept of the Prince and "The Prince" of Machiavelli', *The Journal of Modern History*, vol. XI, 1939, pp. 449–83.

[9] N. Machiavelli, *The Prince*, p. 50.

[10] Ibid., p. 56.

[11] See Q. Skinner, *Machiavelli* (Oxford, Oxford University Press, 1981) and J.G.A Pocock, *The Machiavellian Moment: Florentine Political Thought and the Atlantic Republican Tradition*.

dykes and banks, so that when it rises it will either go into a canal or its rush will not be so wild and dangerous.'[12]

Machiavelli's *The Prince* is a realistic guide as to how princes might be enabled to secure power and provide political order and stability by displaying resourcefulness in their use of power and by responding flexibly and effectively to the impact of events. In his other major text on politics, *The Discourses*, which is based on Livy's *History of Rome*, and in contrast with *The Prince*, Machiavelli concentrates upon the republican form of government. He endorses republicanism while inquiring into the factors that enable it to survive and flourish. In doing so, he invokes and examines Livy's *History of Rome*. His resort to Livy and the example of classical Rome is of a piece with standard humanist scholarship.[13] Renaissance historians also imagined the past to be cyclical and so it was natural for Machiavelli, like contemporary scholars, to turn to the past to provide lessons for the present, as past and present were not taken to be distanced irretrievably from one another by the passage of time, because time was not figured in linear terms.[14] In the Introduction to *The Discourses* Machiavelli likens history to medicine due to its capacity to learn from the past in applying remedies for maladies of the present. Historical study of the politics of the Ancient world is more than of merely antiquarian interest as past and present are linked in a historical chain of events.[15] While all states are subject to change, Machiavelli imagines some states, notably the Republic of Rome, as achieving a stature, which enables them to survive and flourish.

In *The Discourses* fortune remains an important way of conceptualizing change and the contextual limits of human agency, but it is not an implacable force, subduing human resistance to its course. As in *The Prince*, virtue is the factor, which can operate with and exert an influence upon the course of a presumptive destiny. In *The Discourses* it is the collective virtue of engaged citizens rather than the outstanding talents of a virtuoso prince, which show how fortune is susceptible to a degree of control. Machiavelli reviews Livy's *History of Rome* in order to identify those features of the political constitution and practice of Ancient Rome, which enabled it to withstand the force of circumstances and degeneration. He identifies the vitality and resourcefulness of the Roman Republic to spring from the liberty of its people, which engenders a widespread patriotic virtue.

Machiavelli observes, 'For a people that governs and is well-regulated by laws will be stable, prudent, and grateful, as much so, and even more,

---

[12] N. Machiavelli, *The Prince*, p. 91.
[13] See Q. Skinner, 'Machiavelli's *Discorsi* and the Pre-humanist Origins of Republican Ideas', in G. Bock, Q. Skinner, and M. Viroli (eds), *Machiavelli and Republicanism*, pp. 121–42.
[14] P. Burke, *The Renaissance Sense of the Past* (London, Arnold, 1969).
[15] N. Machiavelli, *The Discourses*, pp. 103–5.

according to my opinion, than a prince, although he be esteemed wise; and, on the other hand, a prince freed from the restraints of the law, will be more ungrateful, inconstant, and imprudent than the people so situated.'[16] In *The Discourses* Machiavelli identifies the robustness of regimes to depend in part upon the work of founding fathers and restorers of civic institutions. His analysis of political forces is geared towards identifying institutional features that preserve and strengthen regimes and to this end he points to the role of mixed constitutions in providing energy and resources in political deliberation. He also offers instrumental advice on the exercise of war and the military establishment. Wars are to be short and decisive, for a prolonged war saps civic energy, and a decisive victory fosters patriotic morale, which in turn promotes the exercise of civic virtue.[17] He recommends that military commands are to be limited due to the prospect of political power tilting towards the holder of long-term command, and he urges the limitation of wealth, because he maintains that private interests should not dominate public issues and authority. He reviews the civic implications of religion, but shows little interest in its intrinsic value.[18] Anguish over personal salvation and reflection upon the ultimate destiny of the soul are conspicuous by their absence from his writings, and he values religion for its instrumental value in the prosecution of civic interests in war and peace. In the *Art of War* he expands upon his disinclination to employ mercenaries, which he had recorded in *The Prince*. Mercenaries cannot be relied upon, whereas a citizen army can harness and promote civic patriotism.[19]

THE CAMBRIDGE SCHOOL AND MACHIAVELLI: POCOCK, SKINNER, AND INTERPRETATION

Strauss and his followers interpret what they understand to be Machiavelli's instrumentalism to represent a fundamental shift between the pre-modern and modern forms of political discourse. On this reading Machiavelli is identified as breaking from a tradition of political thought, which frames politics in moral terms. Machiavelli is a teacher of evil.[20] This line of argument highlights Machiavelli's originality, where some rival commentators despair of

[16] Ibid., p. 263.

[17] The Second Book of *The Discourses* is devoted to a review of the role of war in Roman history and the lessons that can be derived from that history. See N. Machiavelli, 'The Discourses', p. 271–396.

[18] Ibid., pp. 149–58.

[19] See N. Machiavelli, *The Chief Works and Others*, ed. A. Gilbert (Durham NC, Duke University Press, 1989).

[20] L. Strauss, *Thoughts on Machiavelli*, pp. 10–12.

detecting coherence within the multiple ways in which Machiavelli apparently conceives of virtue, fortune, and political life.[21] In contrast Pocock and Skinner interpret Machiavelli as undertaking a coherent project in following intimations of a Florentine tradition. Rather than designating Machiavelli as operating outside traditional ways of thinking, they interpret him as practising political theory in a manner consonant with the traditions of Florentine humanism. The strength of their interpretations lies in how they relate Machiavelli to an historic language of political theory in which his thought is rendered intelligible by observing its relationship to current and past conventional discursive forms. The upshot is that Machiavelli emerges as operating with concepts that are aligned to a particular world of politics and political discourse, and his originality resides neither in his unique malignity nor in a disturbing singularity but in developing inherited concepts in particular ways.

In relating Machiavelli to the context of Italian humanism and Renaissance politics, Pocock and Skinner shift interpretive attention from a narrow concentration upon particular passages in his texts seemingly espousing a naked instrumentalism. They develop a wider contextual reading, in which he is occupied by standard questions of the time concerning how a prince might rule, how citizens might collectively constitute and display virtue, and how the political community might survive in time. A perspective on Machiavelli that allows for contrasting perceptions of his novelty and of his traditionalism is encapsulated in the following quotations from Plamenatz and Skinner. Plamenatz in volume 1 of *Man and Society* observes, 'He [Machiavelli] cares nothing for traditional arguments because he does not put traditional questions'.[22] In contrast, Skinner in his *Machiavelli*, observes how Machiavelli is to be interpreted as an exponent of a distinctive humanist tradition of classical republicanism.[23] This stylized dichotomy, between a theorist versed in tradition and an innovative maverick, derives from contrasting styles of interpretation. In his study of the transition from medieval to modern political thinking, *The Foundations of Modern Political Thought*, Skinner eschews a concentration on the major texts of successive philosophically oriented theorists in favour of a multidimensional review of a range of thinkers, whose texts share assumptions and concepts. In this interpretive frame, Machiavelli is related to a context of preceding traditions and contemporary figures, whose political ideas exhibit a common discourse.[24] In contrast, Plamenatz concentrates upon the texts of Machiavelli and in so doing

---

[21] See H. Mansfield, *Machiavelli's Virtue*. (Chicago, University of Chicago Press, 1996).
[22] J. Plamenatz, *Man and Society*, vol. 1, *Man and Society* (London, Longmans, 1963).
[23] Q. Skinner, *Machiavelli*, pp. 20–77.
[24] Q. Skinner, *The Foundations of Modern Political Thought*, vol. 1, *The Renaissance* (Cambridge, Cambridge University Press, 1978).

ignores links with other theorists pursuing related themes. The upshot is that Machiavelli's radical instrumentalism is emphasized along with his apparent departure from conventional forms of morality. Skinner's arguments for reviewing the context is that the character and degree of Machiavelli's originality cannot be assessed save by relating his standpoint to traditional notions. His difference from other theorists emerges against a background of shared assumptions.

The dichotomy between originality and tradition is itself problematic. Identifying originality turns upon recognizing how it differs from what has gone before. Condren urges that originality and influence are not inversely related.[25] Pure originality untouched by circumstance and convention is as miraculous and mythological as the Immaculate Conception. Skinner interprets Machiavelli's engagement with a discursive tradition as not detracting from his originality. His creative use of its conceptual resources allows for its more exact appreciation.[26] Recognizing the influences upon Machiavelli does not necessarily detract from his originality. Skinner and Pocock relate Machiavelli to prevailing conventions and ongoing traditions of thought in distinctive ways. Characteristically, Pocock in *The Machiavellian Moment* invokes a wider discourse of political thought to disclose an aspect of what a political theorist was concerned to achieve. *The Machiavellian Moment* is not devoted specifically to Machiavelli, but deals with a tradition of thinking, a discourse of inquiry. Its focus is upon a conceptual frame for understanding time and politics, though it is a discursive frame that is not identified by the historic theorists themselves. Indeed the phrase, 'the Machiavellian moment', was neither framed by Machiavelli, nor by any of the theorists, whom Pocock considers in his text. In the second edition of the book, we learn from Pocock that the term 'the Machiavellian moment' was actually coined by Skinner.[27]

What is indicated by the phrase, 'the Machiavellian moment', is a combination of elements. For a start, it captures the conceptual conditions underlying Machiavelli's project in theorizing how forms of polity can withstand and flourish in the face of constraining circumstances and unpredictable contingencies that combine to jeopardize the prospects of a republic surviving over time. Secondly it represents the more generic concern of Renaissance civic humanists in responding to the question of how a political association is situated in time and can negotiate temporality. This question is not one that is posed for all forms of political association and to all theorists of their constitution. It is an historic question that is posed when belief in God and

---

[25] C. Condren, *The Status and Appraisal of Classic Texts* (Princeton, New Jersey, University of Princeton Press, 1985), p. 132.

[26] Q. Skinner, *Machiavelli*, p. 2.

[27] See the afterword to the 2nd edition, particularly, J.G.A. Pocock, *The Machiavellian Moment: Florentine Political Thought and the Atlantic Republican Tradition* (with a new afterword by the author) (Princeton and London, Princeton University Press, 2003).

his imagined grace in interposing between the human world of politics and the infinite duration of time are no longer accepted. How can a political society in time be understood? This question is identified by Pocock as being posed in a novel way by Renaissance civic humanism. Augustinian Christianity had assumed the social world of time to be distinct from eternal time while medieval eschatological theorists and Savonarola, a religious leader in Renaissance Florence, had harmonized the two by relating apocalyptic thinking in the bible to political events so as to establish a linear development of the political world leading to the apocalypse.

What is at stake for Machiavelli and what engaged preceding and contemporary humanist theorists such as Bruni, Cavalcanti, and Guicciardini, in considering the social world in the context of time, is how to combine a non-providential secular conception of time, with the survival and flourishing of civic life that unites the individual with the universal value of the community. The dilemma facing Machiavelli and associated Florentine civic humanists is rehearsed by Pocock in the following way, 'After the advent of civic humanism, it was possible in addition [to preceding notions of time] for the individual to feel that only as citizen, as political animal involved in a *vivere civile* with his fellows, could he fulfil his nature, achieve virtue and find his world rational; while at the same time it might be that his conceptual means of understanding the particular and controlling the temporal, on which his ability to function as a citizen depended, had not increased to the degree commensurate with the new demands upon them.'[28] Another aspect of Pocock's study is to relate this conceptualization of time and politics, which is developed by Machiavelli and other Florentines, to successive forms of political thinking, notably to the seventeenth-century republican theories of Harrington and to the architects of the American constitution. In framing his conceptual history Pocock admits that his analysis of Machiavelli is selective in relating him to a particular discursive setting, rather than providing a broad analysis of Machiavelli's political thought. He observes, 'We are engaged in an attempt to isolate "the Machiavellian moment": that is to isolate the continuous process in the history of ideas which seems the most promising context in which to treat his contribution to that history; and the enterprise is selective in the sense that it does not commit us to interpreting the totality of his thought or the reality of its development.'[29]

Pocock's interpretation of the Machiavellian moment then is not a comprehensive reading of Machiavelli. Rather, it is a way of explaining the Machiavellian response to the temporal conditionality of politics, which is distinct from preceding Christian notions, but is akin to the Florentine civic humanist tradition and to theorists such as Guicciardini, Cavalcanti, and

---

[28] Ibid., p. 114.   [29] Ibid., p. 183.

Bruni, who responded to the crisis in Florentine politics that was generated by successive foreign invasions in the fifteenth century, the restoration of the Republic in 1494, and the subsequent return to power of the Medicis. Pocock identifies a particular context and a discursive focus for interpreting Machiavelli, which plays down his singularity. Machiavelli is associated with issues and questions that exercised fellow civic humanists. Pocock's interpretive framework constitutes the aspects of Machiavelli that are to be analysed, and thereby constructs its own object of explanation as well as the terms in which it is to be explained. Hence in his examination of *The Prince* Pocock accentuates Machiavelli's delimitation of the terms of his inquiry, observing how he specifies an interest in principalities, and yet more specifically, how he is to examine particular kinds of principality. Pocock observes how the principalities, upon which Machiavelli focuses, are those in which a prince has assumed power in parlous circumstances. He is interested in a prince acceding to power abruptly and adventitiously, by which preceding political traditions are disrupted, and in the light of which the prospects for a prince surviving and enabling his regime to stabilize over time are slim. Hence Pocock emphasizes how Machiavelli alerts his readers to the special qualities that will be needed by an innovative political leader, who is determined to tackle the contingencies of fortune by imposing political form on the vagaries of circumstances. It is within this specific interpretive context that Pocock minimizes the significance of Machiavelli's admission that a prince will resort in some circumstances to instrumental means that are violent and radically out of step with conventional morality. Pocock observes, 'The prince's moral and social, like his military and diplomatic behaviour, was carried on in a context dominated by *fortuna*, in which time brought with it good things and bad indifferently, and the greater part by far of his *virtu* was his ability to discern what time was bringing and what strategies were required to cope with it. Discussion of whether the prince should obey moral law becomes a question of when he should obey it, and this in turn blends into discussion of whether it is better to be loved or feared, to be audacious or prudent. The answer is always the same.'[30]

Pocock reads *The Prince* as showing how a virtuoso prince may survive hostility and the uncertainties of fortune. It represents a political achievement in resisting the force of intimidating circumstances in the present. But this achievement is only for the present, as the longer-term stability and the institutionalization of the regime are unfeasible. The longer-term project of securing a polity against the uncertainties of the future is held to be the focus of *The Discourses*.[31] In his account of *The Discourses* Pocock attends to how Machiavelli considers a republican regime might be able to survive in a situation where fortune militates against its durability. Hence he notes how

---

[30] Ibid., p. 177.   [31] Ibid., p. 179.

Machiavelli draws lessons from the record of classical Rome. Overall the most important insight is that it is the combined patriotism and virtue of the citizenry, which will allow for a regime to stabilize. He observes how Machiavelli imagines a militarization of citizenship so as to maximize patriotic civic virtue. In commenting on Machiavelli's preference for a republic over singular rule, Pocock observes, 'Republics mobilized more *virtu* than monarchies, and the multiplicity of their leadership made them more flexible and adaptable to the shifts of *fortuna* than could be expected of the single personality of the individual ruler.'[32] Pocock interprets Machiavelli's *Discourses* to represent a form of sustained reflection on how a regime can survive and prosper in time in the light of the uncertainties of fortune. Again, Pocock deflects from Machiavelli's instrumentalism by relating it to the project of securing a polity against the uncertainties of time. The strain of that project is indexed by the fact that no regime can supersede the vagaries of fortune even if a well-organized republic can secure a measure of stability before the inevitable cycle of historical decline. Pocock identifies Machiavelli's example in reviewing how a republic can sustain itself in the context of time to be relevant to the continuation of a particular language of politics and time in subsequent political thought. He traces its language in Harrington's republicanism in seventeenth-century England and in the founding of the republic of the United States in the eighteenth century.[33]

Skinner's reading of Machiavelli is akin to Pocock's in that he provides a contextual reading. Machiavelli develops a political theory that responds to a tradition of civic humanism and is compatible with a prevalent style of theorizing in Renaissance Italy. Skinner identifies Machiavelli's *The Prince* as a guidebook for a Medici prince, which adheres to the paradigm that had been established by similar advice books to princes written by other humanist scholars. Skinner observes how numerous humanist advice books to princes were published by the new medium of print. Distinguished authors such as Bartolomeo, Saachi, Giovanni, Pontano, and Fransceso Patrizi offered political advice to princes.[34] Hence, Machiavelli follows a convention and in following the convention he also invokes standard themes and concepts. Machiavelli, like other advice-givers, holds up a mirror to princes, offering them a reflective perspective on effective political practice. Moreover, like Pocock, Skinner observes the practical limits within which the advice is offered, observing how the advice pertains to particular circumstances and a delimited sphere. Skinner also notes that the content of Machiavelli's advice is for the most part conventional, in that he invokes standard concepts of the Renaissance humanists and their classical models of what is requisite in a political context.[35] Skinner perceives Machiavelli as resembling contemporary and

---

[32] Ibid., p. 212.   [33] Ibid.
[34] Q. Skinner, *Machiavelli*, p. 34.   [35] Ibid., p. 34.

classical humanists in insisting that the art of political leadership resides in the exercise of virtue, and in withstanding the uncertainties of fortune. Like Pocock, Skinner takes the Renaissance sense of the amenability of fortune to the exercise of virtue to inform Machiavelli's interpretation of the nature of politics. Again, Skinner identifies the objectives of Machiavelli's thought as conforming to a prevailing formula, which is to promote the order, stability, and glory of both the prince and his regime.

Unlike some other commentators, Skinner detects a consistency in Machiavelli's use of the concept of virtue. In framing the concept Machiavelli draws upon current conceptual readings of politics, while also signalling a departure from them. Machiavelli imagines virtue to consist in those qualities, which serve to resist the vagaries of fortune, but what enables a prince to withstand the instability of events does not consist in the practice of the traditional moral virtues of prudence, courage, wisdom, and temperance. Rather, it consists in resourcefulness, which will allow a prince to amend policies and attitudes to engage with changing circumstances. Skinner holds that it is this ability to adapt to situations that is the key to the coherence of Machiavelli's notion of virtue. It is also what renders Machiavelli's account of virtue and of politics original. Like traditionalist predecessors Machiavelli is keen to show how fortune may be negotiated, but Skinner emphasizes how Machiavelli imagines fortune is to be addressed by a radical and novel instrumentality rather than by a consistent application of morality. Yet Skinner insists that the intention of Machiavelli's text is not to turn princes into self-seeking fortune hunters even if they are to deal with fortune. To the contrary, they are to pursue stability and glory for their regimes. Agathocles, the Sicilian tyrant, who operated to maximize his own selfish goals, is critiqued by Machiavelli precisely for this trait. The upshot of Skinner's interpretation of *The Prince* is that it emerges as an original argument, in the course of which Machiavelli reworks concepts that were central to the humanist discourse of Renaissance Italy and conventions of current political theorizing.[36]

Skinner interprets *The Discourses* in the context of current and historical ideological debate. Machiavelli is seen as upholding the value of republicanism by drawing upon the example of classical Roman republicanism and classical notions of virtue, which rehearses the practice of humanist Renaissance scholars and the pre-humanist writers. Skinner's historical understanding of *The Discourses* recognizes its reflection of long-standing aspects of the Florentine tradition, which predate the humanist scholars of the Renaissance. In his essay, 'Machiavelli's *Discorsi* and Pre-humanist Origins of Republican Ideas' Skinner traces an ideology of self-governing republicanism to pre-humanist Italy.[37]

---

[36] Ibid., p. 2.
[37] Q. Skinner, 'Machiavelli's *Discorsi* and the Pre-humanist Origins of Republican Ideas', in G. Brock, Q. Skinner, and M. Viroli (eds), *Machiavelli and Republicanism* (Cambridge, Cambridge University Press, 1991), pp. 121–42.

This ideal of self-governing republicanism is the theme, which animates *The Discourses*. Skinner analyses the lineage of republican sentiments by reviewing the treatises on the *Ars dictamines*, which were composed by teachers of rhetoric and treatises on government. They were designed specifically for the guidance of magistrates. Skinner identifies how these treatises espoused the ideals of civic glory and greatness and attended to what contributes to the strength and endurance of regimes. They emphasize how there should be a general cultivation of the common good to counteract divisiveness. In identifying what preserves civic identity, pre-humanist authors, like their humanist successors, drew upon the ideas of classical Rome, notably the republican sentiments of Cicero and Sallust. Hence, Skinner perceives Machiavelli in *The Discourses* neither to be inventing a language of politics, nor operating with a unique political message and style. Rather, he is developing intimations of an ongoing tradition, which draw upon pre-humanist and humanist ideologues.

Like pre-humanists and humanist scholars, Machiavelli, in *The Discourses*, looks to classical Rome and notably to Cicero for the inspiration of his republicanism. Skinner differs from Pocock in minimizing the role of Aristotle and accentuating the influence of Cicero and Roman republicans in explaining the form of Machiavelli's political thought. He highlights Machiavelli's approach to liberty, which he takes to be a specifically republican notion of liberty. He interprets this notion of liberty to assume a negative form in that it does not prescribe what is to be done by citizens, but allows them to assume their own goals and pursuits, but within a frame whereby they partake in civil affairs. Republican citizens are free in that they engage in the collective freedom of citizens in the city, possessing the status of citizens, whereby they are free from the domination of others. Skinner sees this republican conception of freedom to constitute a significant conceptual feature in the history of political thought. It signifies a distinctive view of freedom, which is not captured in Berlin's famous mid-twentieth-century reading of the dichotomous nature of liberty, whereby liberty divides between the two classic forms of negative and positive liberty. Skinner observes how Machiavelli's republicanism is organized so as to withstand the uncertainties of fortune by providing for the collective energy of the citizens. Civil engagement is of the utmost importance, which is why Machiavelli insists on the utility of citizen militia against the evidence of history.[38]

Skinner's interpretation of Machiavelli is insightful. Machiavelli is revealed to be a theorist who is working within a discursive tradition and operating in a context in which his political thought is neither peculiar nor employs innovative concepts. Like others, he offers advice to a prince on how to secure

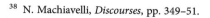

[38] N. Machiavelli, *Discourses*, pp. 349–51.

political stability and glory, reflects on political virtue, and subscribes to traditional arguments in favour of republicanism. In adhering to humanist notions on the role of virtue in offsetting the vagaries of fortune, Machiavelli engages with conventional notions of morality and reviews standard themes in the conduct of public life. Skinner, however, has been criticized for inflating Machiavelli's adherence to local languages of politics, and for abstracting overly from his political cynicism and immorality. Tarcov observes, 'Skinner interprets Machiavelli's statements as either contributions to or critiques of traditions which Skinner does not otherwise show were Machiavelli's major concerns.'[39] Del Lucchese reads Machiavelli as embracing a philosophical system that allows for the ontological integration of freedom and necessity, which is drawn from Lucretian metaphysics rather than from humanist sources.[40] Above all, and like Pocock, Skinner has been criticized for playing down striking aspects of Machiavelli's thought, notably his unflinching instrumentalism, so as to heighten his connections with local traditions. Indeed, the point of Machiavelli's employment of classical sources is not necessarily due to his adherence to classical traditions but, rather, due to his determination to press novel singular aims by means that will prove to be effective with his readership. For instance, Butterfield observes how Machiavelli is attracted to Ancient Roman republicanism not so much because of the inherent value of republicanism but because of its instrumental value in serving purposes such as political stability that he values for independent reasons.[41] Femia remarks, 'The *Discourses* may be a republican text, but it does not equate republicanism with sweetness and light.'[42]

MACHIAVELLI AND THE CAMBRIDGE SCHOOL

Pocock and Skinner are notable exponents of contextualist interpretation in the history of political thought. They relate discursive contexts to past theorists and trace connections between these discourses and political theories. They neither assume that theorists use concepts that are immediately accessible to later generations nor presume that past texts speak directly to political issues and questions of a later age. Their historical reconstruction of Machiavelli's ideas constitutes a revealing test case of their approach. It is a case study where the odds might be thought to be stacked against them. Machiavelli's reputation

[39] N. Tarcov, 'Quentin Skinner's Method and Machiavelli's Politics', in J. Tully (ed.), *Meaning and Context—Quentin Skinner and His Critics* (Cambridge, Polity Press, 1988), pp. 194–203.
[40] F. Del Lucchese, *The Political Philosophy of Niccolo Machiavelli* (Edinburgh, Edinburgh University Press, 2015), p. 40.
[41] H. Butterfield, *The Statecraft of Machiavelli* (London, G. Bell and Sons, 1940), pp. 14–56.
[42] J. Femia, *Machiavelli Revisited* (Cardiff, University of Wales Press, 2004), p. 115.

as an original and sinister figure, whose thought is a perennial example of the dangers of sacrificing morality on the altar of politics, does not lend itself easily to a contextualism that immerses him in historic and contemporary currents of thought. In constructing contextual readings of Machiavelli, which build upon the work of preceding historians, it is a measure of the achievement of Skinner and Pocock that they have altered the ways in which Machiavelli's political thought is understood and evaluated. Machiavelli's republicanism is now seen as relating to a tradition of republicanism and his realism is viewed by relating it to prevalent conceptual schemes that were applied to politics in the Florentine Renaissance. The upshot is that Machiavelli appears more attuned to contemporary and classical discursive paradigms in maintaining a form of republicanism that draws upon the past and is developed by subsequent theorists, and less of a maverick manipulative realist. Where Berlin and Plamenatz imagine Machiavelli to be compellingly original in breaking with commonplace moral assumptions in advancing forms of moral scepticism and pluralism, Skinner and Pocock trace the ways in which Machiavelli harnesses traditions of scholarship, literature, morality, and politics.[43] They succeed in rendering Machiavelli's originality credible and more nuanced by linking his undoubtedly original ideas to prevailing and historic currents of thought. The extent of Machiavelli's originality and his identity as a theorist, however, remain at issue. Skinner is insightful in interpreting *The Prince* as drawing upon standard forms of Renaissance political reasoning in its focus upon the role of virtue in guarding against the unpredictable contingencies of fortune. Yet, Machiavelli's analysis of virtue differs markedly from prevailing standpoints. Indeed, Machiavelli's willingness to see virtue in what contributes to political success in the context of a hostile political environment comes close to collapsing virtue into instrumentalism. Arguably its radicalism departs from the conceptualization of virtue in the classical republican tradition, and puts a strain on its connection to any moral tradition. Ascriptions of a past theorist to membership of a tradition are made by historians, and just like judgments on a thinker's radicalism or originality, do not inhere in an insulated past. To undertake intellectual history is to engage in construction of the past from the present and to make judgments that are underdetermined by forms of evidence, which are likewise constructed by the historian. What is identified and emphasized in framing the past reflects the historian's interests as well as their resourcefulness and skill in assembling and using evidence. Skinner and Pocock's focus upon Machiavelli's involvement with Renaissance republican and humanist frames of discourse tends to relieve his tracts of their eccentricity and striking features. However, a countervailing emphasis upon

---

[43] I. Berlin, 'The Originality of Machiavelli', in I. Berlin, *Against the Current: Essays in the History of Ideas* (London, Hogarth Press, 1979), p. 77; J. Plamenatz, *Man and Society*, vol. 1.

Machiavelli's radical instrumentality shifts the ways in which his texts and associated traditions are regarded.

Of course, Pocock and Skinner differ from one another as well as sharing a contextualist approach. Pocock's interpretation of Machiavelli is part of a bigger picture, a larger conceptual frame, in which he locates a series of thinkers, who imagine how political associations by their own constructive energy may sustain themselves in time. Hence, he interprets an aspect of Machiavelli's thought, in the light of a particular frame that relates him to preceding and succeeding thinkers and issues. It is a framing of Machiavelli, which is constructed by Pocock's interest in how a succession of theorists reflect on the character of politics in time and in the light of evidence pertaining to the ways in which they invoked this character in reflecting upon discontinuous political situations. In commenting upon this aspect of Pocock's methodology, Hampsher-Monk observes, 'The most scrupulous efforts to narrate a tradition in its own terms necessarily involve construction and selection.'[44] Pocock's Machiavelli is a constructed figure and the terms of the construction are shaped by his preoccupation with identifying how political theorists deal with time at a particular moment and how the Florentine humanist tradition related time to citizenship and virtue. In *The Machiavellian Moment* Pocock recognizes his own role in imagining Machiavelli and his texts in remarking, 'This study adopts a formal and analytical approach to *Il Principe*; it seeks to bring out certain of its implications by relating them to two schemes of ideas ... '.[45] Pocock's analysis is not directed at explaining Machiavelli's political theory in its entirety, yet he urges that there is room for his interpretive strategy in that its heuristics contributes to our understanding of Machiavelli's political thought.[46] While not ruling out other readings of Machiavelli he tends to disparage textual exegesis that concentrates rather more on individuating aspects of his thought.[47] Likewise, Skinner's interpretation of Machiavelli's republicanism is historically informed and links Machiavelli to preceding and ongoing theories of republicanism. In itself, however, his identification of Machiavelli's membership of a republican tradition does not preclude interpreting Machiavelli as maintaining a distinctive and extravagant instrumentalism.

If Skinner and Pocock both relate Machiavelli to wider contexts of political thought, and intimate his relevance to post-Renaissance political situations, then the thought occurs that Machiavelli might be construed in ways that abstract from his particular context and concerns in Renaissance Italy and that allow for a more general construal of his thought. Perhaps Machiavelli's

---

[44] I. Hampsher-Monk, 'Political Languages in Time—The Work of J.G.A. Pocock', *British Journal of Political Science*, vol. 14, no. 1, Jan. 1984, pp. 89–116.

[45] J.G.A. Pocock, *The Machiavellian Moment*, p. 157.

[46] Ibid., p. 158.   [47] Ibid., p. 157.

political thought might be read at a level of abstraction that connects it to more recent issues and styles of thought. Gramsci, the revisionist inter-war Marxist, reframes Marx's thought by relating it to contemporary contexts and by adopting a nuanced reading of the relations between material class interests, political strategies, and the role of ideas. The influence of Machiavelli and the clear impact of *The Prince* upon his thought are evidenced in Gramsci's use of the term 'the new prince' to designate the Communist Party. Gramsci takes the Jacobins to be an incarnation of Machiavelli's *Prince* and his projected mode of operation for the Communist Party was for it to attend closely to political realities and to engage in relevant and realistic political strategies. Gamsci recognized that political success did not depend on simply waiting for the inevitable collapse of capitalism.[48] More was demanded. Gramsci takes Machiavelli to be a guide in envisaging the virtue of the prince to be immanent within the historical process of time. The lesson for Marxist thought and the Communist Party is that theory is not to be conceived as operating outside the concrete world of practice.[49] Gramsci reads Machiavelli in the light of the present and abstracts from Renaissance circumstances and traditions with which he was engaging. Yet the relevance of Machiavelli to modern forms of class struggle is suggested and light is cast on what is distinctive and interesting in Machiavelli's reading of the inter-relations between theory and practice.

In the late twentieth century Bernard Williams invoked Machiavelli to represent a realist perspective to counter a prevailing moralistic liberalism. Williams was a distinguished exponent of the turn to realism against a Rawlsian and post-Rawlsian analysis of politics, which relates politics to moral principles. According to Williams, the Rawlsian approach abstracts from the actual world of politics in formulating principles that are dislocated from place and time in assuming a harmony between its general principles and an unspecified general audience. In 'The Liberalism of Fear', Williams observes how *The Prince* offers a more realistic alternative approach in addressing a presumptive and determinate audience when it considers what might be achieved in a principality and how the achievement might be enacted. Williams enlists Machiavellian realism in critiquing a moralized style of political philosophy that is overly general in its imagining of an audience that responds to generic ideals and principles rather than the particularities of political situations. He remarks, 'The relation between listener and audience (in moralistic political philosophy), which alienates politics from political philosophy rather involves this: that such political philosophy deals

---

[48] See A. Gramsci, *Prison Notebooks*, vols 1–3 trans. J. Buttigieg (Columbia, Columbia University Press, 2011).

[49] See the interesting discussion of Gramsci's interpretation of Machiavelli in F. Del Lucchese, *The Political Philosophy of Niccolo Machiavelli*, pp. 160–3.

in ideals, or natural rights, or virtue, and also addresses a listener who is supposedly empowered to enact just what such considerations enjoin.'[50]

CONCLUSION

The Cambridge School is to be credited with developing a contextually focused understanding of Machiavelli. In framing contextualist interpretations of Machiavelli, Pocock and Skinner have achieved at least two notable things. They have refined conceptions of Machiavelli, and located him in contexts whereby his ideas are neither simply to be dismissed, nor regarded as wildly singular. They identify his political theory by relating it to prevailing and preceding discourses, and they reveal Machiavelli to be a distinguished exponent of the style of political theory that was available to him. At the same time they have provoked a self-consciousness about how Machiavelli is to be understood. If he is to be labelled a maverick, an immoralist, or a political scientist then we need to be clear on how such judgments are to be made and by what criteria they can be justified. The other side of the coin is that Skinner and Pocock make interpretive judgments in focusing on aspects of Machiavelli and in accenting his continuity with Renaissance humanism and classical traditions. Their judgments in turn can be challenged by those who perceive Machiavelli as engaging with issues of politics in a more enduring and individual style. In looking to how a Marxist party might impact upon contingent historical developments or in reviewing the abstractions of current political philosophy in the light of the messiness of everyday life, Machiavelli appears as someone with the courage to face realities with appropriately negotiable concepts.

[50] B. Williams, 'The Liberalism of Fear', in B. Williams, *In the Beginning Was the Deed— Realism and Moralism in Political Argument* (Princeton and Oxford, Princeton University Press, 2005), p. 58.

9

Hobbes

The Politics of Absolutism

INTRODUCTION

Hobbes's *Leviathan* was published in 1651, and is a pre-eminent text of English political philosophy. It continues to attract critical comments from an array of commentators, including liberals, conservatives, Marxists, and post-structuralists. It was preceded by earlier versions of Hobbes's political theory, *The Elements of Law* and *De Cive* which were published in 1640 and 1642 respectively.[1] Hobbes's reputation owes much to the sharpness of his philosophical style, yet few commentators consider that his line of argument is either unproblematic or smoothly persuasive. Notwithstanding Hobbes's own confidence in the indisputable logic of his reasoning, many questions are raised by his political philosophy, which are answered in different ways by commentators.

Hobbes presents his arguments as if their explanatory force is logical and generic rather than relating to immediate contextual concerns, yet evidently he was influenced by the prevailing circumstances in which he developed his ideas.[2] He was born in Malmesbury, Wiltshire, in 1588, showing a decided intelligence at an early age, and became a gifted linguist at school, where, as Skinner observes, he studied a humanist syllabus, which was focused upon the

---

[1] T. Hobbes, *The Elements of Law, Natural and Politic*, ed. J.C.A. Gaskin (Oxford, Oxford University Press, 1994); T. Hobbes, *De Cive: The English Version entitled in the first edition Philosophical Rudiments Concerning Government and Society*, ed. Howard Warrender (Oxford, Clarendon Press, 1983); T. Hobbes, *Leviathan*, ed. M. Oakeshott (London, Macmillan, 1962).

[2] For a lively account of Hobbes and his life, see J. Aubrey, *Brief Lives*, ed. O.L. Dick (Harmondsworth, Penguin, 1972). For a full-length biography, see A. Rogow, *Thomas Hobbes—Radical in the Service of Reaction* (London and New York, W.W. Norton, 1986). The political and religious contexts within which Hobbes operated is set out in J.P. Sommerville, *Thomas Hobbes: Political Ideas in Historical Context* (Basingstoke, Macmillan, 1996); for Hobbes's letters, see N. Malcolm, *The Correspondence of Thomas Hobbes* (Oxford, Oxford University Press, 1994).

study of grammar and rhetoric.[3] Hobbes was impressed neither by this humanist syllabus nor by the University of Oxford, where he reacted against a curriculum of scholastic philosophy that rehearsed an antiquated Aristotelian worldview.[4] Hobbes himself was inspired by the logical rigour of Euclidean geometry and he followed contemporary developments in science, which were ignored in Oxford. Subsequent to Oxford, Hobbes was hired as a tutor for the son of Baron Cavendish (later the Earl of Devonshire). Political events in the years prior to his writing of the *Leviathan* (1651) impressed upon Hobbes the imperative need for security and for the establishment of unequivocal political authority. The English Civil War between Charles I and Parliament, between the years 1642 and 1649, highlighted how disputes over political and religious authority jeopardized the prospects for civil order. Notwithstanding his criticism of the claims of historical understanding, Hobbes himself wrote a history of the civil war, *Behemoth*, which was published in 1679, though he completed it earlier. In *Behemoth*, he identified the causes and consequences of a ruinous civil war.[5] Hobbes fled to France in 1640 and served as a tutor to the future Charles II at the exiled court. During this period of exile, Hobbes developed contacts with French philosophers. Following the Civil War Hobbes returned to England and made his peace with Cromwell's new regime. However, following the restoration of the monarchy in 1660 he enjoyed the patronage of Charles II.

While Hobbes developed his political ideas before the outbreak of civil war, the gathering tension between monarch and Parliament, and the consequential uncertainties of government throughout Charles I's reign contributed to his prioritizing of clear and undisputed sovereign authority. Hobbes was also impressed by the ideological and social tensions, which were generated by the prevailing religious discord and proliferation of religious sects.[6] Hobbes recognized the power of religion to move people's minds and passions. In particular Hobbes perceived the threat to social and political order that was posed by fanatical puritan sects and the Catholic Church, which maintained and proselytized for religious practices at variance with those sanctioned by the Church of England. Hobbes's recognition of the significance of religious doctrines in civil society is reflected in the extensive final part of the *Leviathan*, in which he sets out the conditions of state control over the promulgation and public practice of religious doctrine. This Erastian viewpoint is different from

---

[3] Q. Skinner, *Reason and Rhetoric in the Philosophy of Hobbes* (Cambridge, Cambridge University Press, 1996), pp. 19–66.

[4] A. Rogow, *Thomas Hobbes—Radical in the Service of Reaction*, pp. 42–57.

[5] T. Hobbes, *Behemoth*, ed. F. Tonnies (Chicago, Il, University of Chicago Press, 1990).

[6] See J.P. Sommerville, *Thomas Hobbes: Political Ideas in Historical Context* (Basingstoke and New York, Macmillan, 1920), pp. 1–28.

the authority that he accords the episcopy in the preceding *De Cive*.[7] Hobbes's own views on religion and God are by no means clear. The circumstances of the time militated against a declaration of atheism, and Hobbes's comments on the nature of God accommodated his philosophical determinism and materialism.[8] Commentators have lined up to maintain his atheism, and yet there are no conclusive grounds for considering him an atheist rather than a deist, who assumes God as a first but unknowable cause of nature.[9] What is uncontroversial, however, is that Hobbes aimed at circumscribing the potential for religious beliefs to undermine political authority. To minimize their potential for disruption, he urges that individuals should be prepared to maintain their personal religious convictions and practices in private but not to insist on their public display.[10] The issue of Hobbes's religious beliefs is significant in interpreting his argument for political authority and political obligation. Some interpreters take Hobbes to rely on a theistic conception of God's role in determining the principles underpinning political obligation, which is compromised if Hobbes is taken to be an atheist.[11]

FROM THE STATE OF NATURE TO THE COMMONWEALTH

Hobbes's avowed project in *Leviathan* is to set out the logic of political association, given the nature of individuals who are its members.[12] Hobbes explores the character of the individuals whom he takes to compose the essential components of civil association. Hence he adopts the resolutive-compositive method to analyse the commonwealth by examining its constituent parts and to consider the civil association as a whole by assessing these disassembled parts. He imagines individuals outside a political framework in the state of nature, where their conduct is determined by desires and aversions that arise from their contact with the world. Hobbes rejects an Aristotelian notion of a *telos* of political development, where a shared political life constitutes a common good. Hobbes's state of nature has been construed as anti-social, and

---

[7] For a focus upon differences between *Leviathan* and preceding works, including a note on its less egoistic reading of human nature, see D. Baumgold, 'Hobbes', in D. Boucher and P. Kelly, *Political Thinkers* (Oxford, Oxford University Press), p. 191.

[8] T. Hobbes, *Leviathan*, ed. M. Oakeshott, pp. 271–473.

[9] See R. Peters, *Hobbes* (London, Penguin, 1967), p. 246. See also A. Rogow, *Thomas Hobbes-Radical in the Service of Reaction*, pp. 236–7.

[10] T. Hobbes, *Leviathan*, ed. M. Oakeshott.

[11] See H. Warrender, *The Political Philosophy of Hobbes: The Theory of Obligation* (Oxford, Clarendon Press, 1957); F.C. Hood, *The Divine Politics of Thomas Hobbes: An Interpretation of 'Leviathan'* (Oxford, Clarendon Press, 1962).

[12] T. Hobbes, *Leviathan*, ed. M. Oakeshott, pp. 21–129.

yet it is by no means the case that Hobbes imagines a world of individuals, who exist outside of a social framework.[13] Again, Hobbes's state of nature lends itself to an image of individuals as being egoistic or selfish, but it is at least debatable that he is construing them in this way. Certainly, he takes individuals to lack a common frame of reference for moral life. There is no common good and individuals make sense of the world without resort to shared understandings of things. *Leviathan*, however, differs from earlier statements of Hobbes's political theory by employing a less egoistic perspective.[14] Hobbes depicts individuals as solipsistic in the state of nature, but solipsism does not necessarily imply egoism, and for Hobbes there is no common moral yardstick by which to measure their individual actions.

The logic of Hobbes's argument establishes that individuals in a state of nature experience a situation that is highly insecure and problematic. Hobbes observes the condition to be intolerable. In the state of nature individuals are in a state of uncertain competition with one another. Competition is intense because individuals are in a condition of equality with one another insofar as the differences between them are insufficient to guarantee victory in a conflict. Moreover, the rivalry is heightened as each aspires to glory in gaining renown over others and likewise fears an inglorious defeat at the hands of others.[15] The upshot is that each person is fearful of what will ensue, and the state of nature constitutes a state of war in which death, and the prospect of death are prominent features. Hobbes expounds upon the intolerable consequences of this condition, which entail that the amenities and constructive achievements of civilization are unavailable. He observes, 'In such a condition, there is no place for industry; because thereof is uncertain; and consequently no culture of the earth; no navigation, nor use of the commodities that may be imported by sea; no commodious building; no instruments of moving, and removing such things as require much force; no knowledge of the face of the earth; no account of time; no arts, no letters; no society; and which is worst of all, continual fear, and danger of violent death; and the life of man, solitary, poor, nasty, brutish and short.'[16] Hobbes concludes that the state of nature represents an intolerable predicament. The rough equality between individuals entails that all are subject to the insecurity consequent upon their individual pursuit of felicity, their overall capacity to satisfy desires. Individual felicity is endangered by the collective situation, in which there is a constant fear of violent death at the hands of others due to the generic risky pursuit of power over others.

The fear of death motivates individuals to seek the peace. They are imagined as heeding the logic of the laws of nature, which are prudential maxims,

---

[13] See D. Baumgold, 'Hobbes', in D. Boucher and P. Kelly, *Political Thinkers*, pp. 196–8.
[14] D. Baumgold, *Hobbes's Political Theory* (Cambridge, Cambridge University Press, 1988).
[15] T. Hobbes, *Leviathan*, ed. M. Oakeshott, p. 89.   [16] Ibid.

counselling peace and the adoption of the means to achieve peace. In the light of a rational consideration of their predicament Hobbes imagines that individuals will be willing to contract with one another to form a civil commonwealth under the political authority of a sovereign (preferably a single person). Hobbes imagines that sovereignty is to be absolute if its effectiveness is to be secured. Given the imperative of sovereignty, he allows for no impediments on its operation, save the logical one that individuals, who are motivated to establish the commonwealth to preserve life, will not risk their own lives in subscribing to it. Hobbes refers to the sovereign as '*that mortal god*, to which we owe under the *immortal God* our peace and defence' (emphasis in original).[17] The authority of the sovereign extends to control over religious doctrine and practice, disputes over which, had proved to be disruptive before the Civil War. If Hobbes's sovereign possesses absolute authority, however, the sovereign's rule is not presumed to be draconian in that the rule of law is the appropriate means to ensure civil peace.[18]

Notwithstanding the imperative of establishing conditions of peace and civil authority, there are multiple interpretations of how Hobbes imagines the transition to a civil condition is to be achieved. Is it a matter of individuals contracting to form a commonwealth and sticking to their agreement? Is it rather the mere de facto power of a ruler, which establishes political authority? Are the laws of nature, the prudential maxims guiding individuals to establish effective civil peace to be interpreted additionally as commands of God and thereby operate as morally binding instruments of God's will? The latter theistic interpretation of Hobbes's argument is urged by Hood, Warrender, and State and can be supported by passages from *Leviathan*.[19] However, countervailing theories point to features of Hobbes's argument that are at odds with a theistic reading. Gauthier favours a reading of the transition to civil society, which highlights the express agreement of self-interested rational actors. In so doing, he reads Hobbes in the light of the value attributed subsequently to rational actor contractualism in the present, and hence reads the past in the light of the present, which as Gadamer suggests is a condition of engaging in the history of ideas.[20] A subtle way of interpreting Hobbes is advanced by Oakeshott in a series of essays that show the historical and philosophical dimensions of Hobbes's political theory as well as revealing Oakeshott's style of interpreting the history of political thought.

---

[17] Ibid., p. 132.   [18] Ibid., p. 89.

[19] See H. Warrender, *The Political Philosophy of Hobbes: The Theory of Obligation*; F.C. Hood, *The Divine Politics of Thomas Hobbes: An Interpretation of 'Leviathan'*; S. State, *Thomas Hobbes and the Debate over Natural Law and Religion* (New York, Garland Publishing, 1991).

[20] D. Gauthier, *The Logic of Leviathan: The Moral and Political Theory of Thomas Hobbes* (Oxford, Clarendon Press, 1969).

OAKESHOTT'S HOBBES

Hobbes's political philosophy raises interpretive questions at every turn. How are we to understand Hobbes as a philosopher? How does his philosophy relate to his politics? Is Hobbes's conception of the state determined by analysis of asocial individuals? How does Hobbes understand natural law and natural rights? How, if at all, do Hobbes's texts relate to the wider history of political thought? These questions receive distinct if discordant answers from interpreters of Hobbes's texts. Oakeshott offers a distinctive reading of Hobbes as a philosopher and as an historic theorist of politics. Oakeshott's elegant essays envision Hobbes to be a commanding and systematic philosopher of politics, who imagines political conduct to be a creative enterprise on the part of reflective individuals. In what follows I review Oakeshott's interpretation of Hobbes, supplementing it by considering Collingwood's affiliated notion of Hobbes's constructivist construal of politics.

Oakeshott's Introduction for an edition of Hobbes's *Leviathan* (1946), which was subsequently revised and published as the lead essay in his collection of essays, *Hobbes on Civil Association*, sets out a reading of Hobbes in the context of the history of political philosophy.[21] In the essay Oakeshott reads Hobbes against the grain of established interpretations. He imagines Hobbes to be a systematic philosopher, who represents a distinctive place in a particular tradition of the history of political thought. Oakeshott's synoptic perspective offers a nuanced reading of Hobbes's systematic style. At the outset Oakeshott declares, '*Leviathan* is the greatest, perhaps the sole, masterpiece of political philosophy written in the English language.'[22] To substantiate this declaration he elaborates on the nature of political philosophy. It is characterized as the most abstract and general form of reflection about politics, differing from immediately practical or ideological forms of thinking and distinguished by its generic identification and assessment of political life. He observes, 'Political philosophy may be understood to be what occurs when this movement of reflection takes a certain direction and achieves a certain level of, its characteristic being the relation of political life, and the values and purposes pertaining to it, to the entire conception of the world that belongs to a civilization.'[23]

If political philosophy consists in highly general reflection on the nature of politics, then Hobbes is a philosopher, who reasons systematically on the constitution of political life and its location on the map of human experience. Oakeshott urges that Hobbes should be considered in a generic context of philosophical reflection about politics. Oakeshott associates Hobbes with the

---

[21] M. Oakeshott, 'Introduction to *Leviathan*', in M. Oakeshott, *Hobbes on Civil Association* (Oxford, Basil Blackwell, 1975), p. 3.
[22] Ibid.   [23] Ibid.

large-scale theorizing of other philosophers such as Plato and Hegel, rather than the piecemeal, immediate concerns that preoccupy the majority of his contemporaries. Oakeshott's reading neither implies that Hobbes is insensitive to immediate concerns nor that his thought cannot be related to specific historical contexts to clarify aspects of his thinking. Rather, it suggests a frame in which features of his political philosophy may be understood that might be neglected if Hobbes was to be absorbed by an immediate practical context. Oakeshott's interpretive strategy runs counter to the Cambridge School's tendency to focus upon local ideological contexts. He opens up the prospect of relating Hobbes to a wider context of political philosophy.

Oakeshott situates him in one of the three very broad traditions of political philosophy that he distinguishes.[24] Membership of these traditions is not a matter of self-identification upon the part of political philosophers. Rather, the traditions represent styles of political philosophy that are designated by the historian of political philosophy, whose perspective runs through past and present forms of its development. Oakeshott distinguishes three general traditions. The rational natural tradition is composed of theorists who maintain doctrines that assume the nature of human beings to be rational and that politics conforms to the given rational character of human nature. Plato in pursuing the analogy between the rational and just polis and the rational and just psyche represents the supreme representative of this tradition.[25] The tradition of will and artifice is the one in which Oakeshott locates Hobbes. It takes politics to represent creative work of artifice on the part of human beings, so that states are constructed by the creative agency of individuals, who transform the natural condition by their activities. Hegel is the paradigmatic representative of the rational will tradition that perceives political association as accommodating individual rational agency in collectively constructed political arrangements.[26]

Oakeshott's general analysis of traditions of political thought is elliptical and his identification of the tradition of will and artifice is lightly drawn. Yet his remarks are suggestive. The tradition takes individuals to be creative in their approach to politics and to operate freely in political activity. Political philosophers in this tradition do not assume that politics is a natural expression of a common human identity and that its rational form can be divorced from the free constructive agency of individuals. Seeing Hobbes's thought in the context of this tradition makes sense of the ways in which Hobbes employs the notions of natural law and natural rights. These are used in ways that are different from the predominant forms of the scholastic tradition, which in turn had drawn upon Aristotle and Plato in elaborating an order of

---

[24] Ibid., pp. 6–7.
[25] Plato, *The Republic of Plato* trans. F.M. Cornford (Oxford, Oxford University Press, 1945).
[26] M. Oakeshott, 'Introduction to *Leviathan*', pp. 6–7.

natural law.[27] Hobbes takes natural right to be an expression of an individual's assertiveness rather than an indication of the moral respect that is due to all human beings on account of their conformity to a natural order. Natural law is not a fixed and obligatory natural order to which individuals are aligned but represents the way in which individuals can reason prudentially. Oakeshott's specification of Hobbes's historical identity as a modern political philosopher aligns him with late medieval forms of nominalism and early modern scepticism, which is confirmed by Tuck's scholarly review of historical notions of natural law and right.[28]

If Oakeshott makes a case for perceiving Hobbes to relate to a distinctive tradition in political philosophy, his related interpretation of Hobbes's style of philosophizing focuses upon the power of his reasoning. Oakeshott connects Hobbes with Hegel and Plato by interpreting his philosophy to be systematic not so much due to the substantive content of his philosophy and its coverage of wide areas of reality but because of his unifying application of a systematic method. Oakeshott perceives that Hobbes's method of reasoning is affiliated to other systematic philosophers even if they adhere to differing traditions. The form of Hobbes's reasoning is systematic and dialectical, which resembles Hegel in connecting systemically its component parts. Oakeshott neither focuses upon Hobbes's materialism nor upon his ascription of universal motion to all bodies. Instead, he concentrates upon Hobbes's systemic logical reasoning, whereby causes are traced to their effects, and effects reciprocally are related to their causes.[29] Hobbes's constructive philosophical reasoning resumes the constructive activity of individuals in establishing a civil association. Civil association itself is a reasoned response to the predicament that is posed by the situation of individuals, lacking common bonds, who are driven by competitive desires. Will and artifice are key components of the repertoire of concepts that Hobbes invokes to show the constructive rational activity of individuals in framing an artificial political solution to the predicament of their situation.

Oakeshott's 'The Moral Life in the Writings of Thomas Hobbes,' was published in *Rationalism in Politics and Other Essays* (1962), and provides an analysis of Hobbes's moral thinking in the context of the history of philosophy. Oakeshott sets Hobbes in an historical context, which is different from but relates to the context of political philosophy that he had developed in his Introduction to *Leviathan*. In this essay, Oakeshott distinguishes between three traditions or idioms of moral thinking; the morality of communal ties,

---

[27] See A.P. D'Entreves, *Natural Law: Am Introduction to Legal Philosophy* (London, Transaction Publishers, 1994).

[28] R. Tuck, *Natural Rights Theories: Their Origins and Development* (Cambridge, Cambridge University Press, 1979).

[29] M. Oakeshott, 'Introduction to *Leviathan*', pp. 22–5.

the morality of individuality, and the morality of the common good.[30] All three idioms reflect on experience and moral obligations. The morality of common ties assigns moral obligations to the patterns of life prevalent in communities, while the morality of the common good imagines that members of a political association are related by their common commitment to an overall good. In contrast to these ways of conceiving of morality, Hobbes is taken to subscribe to the morality of individuality, which develops in response to the historical emergence of individualism in the seventeenth century. Oakeshott observes, 'And since the emergent human character of Western Europe in the seventeenth century was one in which a feeling for individuality was becoming pre-eminent—the independent, enterprising man out to seek his intellectual or material fortune, and the individual human soul responsible for its own destiny—this unavoidably became for Hobbes, as it was for his contemporaries, the subject matter for moral reflection.'[31]

Oakeshott reads Hobbes as a modern moralist of individuality, just as his political philosophy is distinguished from a pre-modern rational natural tradition. Hobbes's sense of individuality informs his philosophy in multiple and systemically related ways. In *Leviathan* the state of nature shows the constitutive features of individuals. They are distinct from one another and they recognize neither common ties nor a shared morality to order their conduct. They are animated by passions and by the pursuit of power to ensure individual felicity, which is the general capacity to satisfy their desires. This is not to say that Hobbesian individuals are conceived by Oakeshott to be isolated atoms. The predicament that is posed by the state of nature is perceived to be experienced most acutely by individuals as the frustration of their pride, which aims for glory over others, but faces the prospect of inglorious death at the hands of another individual.

Individuals, however, do not have to yield to the predicament that is constituted by their pride and the prospect of death. They are able to reason prudentially about their situation and they can see the advantage of seeking civil peace and of constructing an artificial political authority to enable the securing of peace. The processes of reasoning by which they are motivated to agree with others to give up their natural right to all things in their pursuit of felicity is encapsulated by natural laws that reason adduces to seek and maintain the peace. Oakeshott's interest in Hobbes's moral thinking leads him to focus upon what renders the conduct of Hobbesian individuals moral. Hobbesian individuals may see an instrumental value in seeking the peace, but how, if at all do they assume moral obligations? Oakeshott reviews three

---

[30] M. Oakeshott, 'The Moral Life in the Writings of Thomas Hobbes', in M. Oakeshott, *Rationalism in Politics and Other Essays* (London and New York, Methuen and Co Ltd, 1962), pp. 249–50.

[31] Ibid., pp. 250–1.

possible interpretations of the moral dimension in Hobbes's thought. In examining Hobbes's moral thinking, Oakeshott considers how individuals may be said to assume moral obligations. First he considers and rejects the assimilation of morality in Hobbes to prudential conduct. Oakeshott sees no justification in presuming that Hobbes imagines non-contradictory behaviour to be morally obligatory. He also disagrees with the thesis of Warrender and Hood, who identify natural law with God's command, which they take to provide the source of a moral obligation on the part of individuals to seek the peace and to accept the obligation of adhering to the laws of a commonwealth.

Oakeshott rejects a theistic interpretation of Hobbes's conception of natural law. He adduces textual evidence to indicate Hobbes's view of natural law as representing prudential maxims, which are not obligatory until they are sanctioned by civil law following the agreement of individuals to form a commonwealth.[32] Oakeshott admits that some passages of *Leviathan* lend themselves to Warrender's theistic reading of Hobbes's account of natural law. In so doing he acknowledges how critics must resist assuming that Hobbes's views are susceptible of a neat and coherent answer to a question that has been inspired by critical expectations that have been generated by subsequent developments.[33] His measured account of Hobbes's moral obligation as not to be seen as resting on theistic foundations is supported in differing ways by other commentators.[34]

While allowing for ambiguities in Hobbes' account of obligation, Oakeshott urges that interpretive emphasis should be placed on the general character of Hobbes's argument in *Leviathan* and his way of thinking.[35] If the thrust of Hobbes's *Leviathan* is to see political authority as deriving from the momentum of individual human agency and capacity for artifice, then it is unlikely that he will designate the defining aspect of political obligation to consist in the role of God, when Hobbes takes it that reason can only allow for a deistic conception of God.[36] Oakeshott recognizes that Hobbes is willing to augment political authority by allowing a role for divine sanction, but this is not primary for it does not reflect the mainspring of Hobbes's way of philosophizing. Hence Oakeshott accepts the line of reasoning about Hobbes's account of moral obligation that attributes its source to the acceptance of individuals of the consequences of the covenant constituting the commonwealth that they have entered into freely. Hence, Oakeshott perceives the emphasis in Hobbes's account of moral obligation is to be placed upon the

---

[32] M. Oakeshott, 'The Moral Life in the Writings of Thomas Hobbes', pp. 281–4.

[33] M. Oakeshott, 'Introduction to *Leviathan*', p. x.

[34] Skinner's early article on Hobbesian ideas noted how early followers of Hobbes were criticized for their alleged atheism. Q. Skinner, 'The Ideological Context of Hobbes's Political Thought', *Historical Journal*, vol. 9, 1966, pp. 286–317.

[35] M. Oakeshott, 'The Moral Life in the Writings of Thomas Hobbes', pp. 286–7.

[36] Ibid., pp. 286–7.

consent of individuals, who either form a commonwealth by institution or recognize sovereign political authority by acquisition or conquest.[37]

Oakeshott's interpretation of Hobbes's moral thinking goes further than recognizing the moral obligations to subscribe to the conditions of justice that are established in a commonwealth. He imagines that the impulse to set up a commonwealth might in some individuals be induced not by abandoning pride in aiming to triumph over others, 'and becoming [by covenant] tame man, but by moralization of pride itself.'[38] On this reading an individual may convert his pride into a sort of inner courage, a magnanimity in accepting the conditions that lead to peace rather than in aiming for peace as the prudential thing to do. It is a reading of individuality that Hobbes sees in the character of Sidney Godolphin.[39] Oakeshott sees its trace in Hobbes as attesting to his strong sense of individuality. The aristocratic aspect of this sense of pride does not deflect from Oakeshott's reading of Hobbes as decidedly modern in his focus upon individuality and creative agency. In his essay, 'Dr. Leo Strauss on Hobbes', Oakeshott endorses Strauss's recognition of Hobbes's specifically modern use of the language of natural rights and natural law.[40]

Oakeshott rehearses his reading of Hobbes as a pre-eminent theorist of a modern moral and political individualism in *On Human Conduct*, though he employs a new idiom by which to characterize Hobbes's enterprise. In *On Human Conduct* he connects Hobbes to Hegel as philosophers who develop an account of civil association, an ideal form of political association, which has been intimated in the development of a form of the modern European state, a *societas*. He imagines that Hobbes, like Hegel, conceptualizes a civil association, which frames the social and political conditions by which individuals, who pursue their own independent conceptions of the good, are associated. They see a political association as supplying a framework of laws by which social life between individuals is regulated so as to enable them to undertake self-chosen purposes. This framework of association differs from a *universitas*, a political association that is dedicated to the achievement of a common good, to which individuals are assimilated.[41] Oakeshott takes Hobbes to be a modern theorist, whose political philosophy represents a systematic analysis of a form of politics that allows for individualism and the capacity of individuals to frame a political association to enable them to live in association while pursuing their several and separate interests and purposes. Hobbes is seen to belong to a tradition of philosophizing whereby his affinity to philosophers who undertake general systematic accounts of the human condition and its political possibilities and his theorizing of modern social and political

---

[37] Ibid., p. 284. [38] Ibid., p. 289. [39] Ibid., p. 293.

[40] M. Oakeshott, 'Dr. Leo Strauss on Hobbes', in M. Oakeshott, *Hobbes on Civil Association* (Oxford, Basil Blackwell, 1975), pp. 134–5.

[41] M. Oakeshott, *On Human Conduct* (Oxford, Oxford University Press, 1975), pp. 185–327.

conditions are accented. Oakeshott also develops his own account of reflective agency and civil association, which draws upon his own reading of the modern state and the political philosophies of Hobbes and Hegel, notable theorists of civil association.

Collingwood, like Oakeshott, interprets Hobbes as a philosopher of a distinctively modern form of moral and political association. Again, like Oakeshott, Collingwood highlights what he takes to be the constructivist aspects of socially situated individual agency in Hobbes. Just as in *On Human Conduct* Oakeshott reads Hobbes as a sophisticated precursor to his own political theory, so Collingwood, in *The New Leviathan* imagines Hobbes as a forerunner to his own theory of a liberal polity within a liberal civilization. In *The New Leviathan* Collingwood frames his own political philosophy by theorizing the conceptual conditions of mind, politics, and civilization. He perceives them to be inter-linked in that the creative aspects of mind are developed in social conditions that are best organized in terms of a liberal political association, which in turn subscribes to wider notions of a liberal civilization. Collingwood imagines mind, state, and civilization to be historical creations in that it is in the nature of mind and political activity to develop freely and historically. This framework of *The New Leviathan* is modelled upon Hobbes's *Leviathan* in that the opening part of the text mirrors the *Leviathan* in specifying the aspects of the mind that contribute to the development and functioning of a liberal polity, namely its capacity to think freely and rationally and to undertake free actions.[42] This notion of mind is thereafter linked to frameworks of social practice and political association, to which it is dialectally related.

In elaborating a liberal form of politics Collingwood rehearses an historical account of how theorists have developed theories of mind and political associations by reflecting upon historic social and political practices. He urges that modern social contract theorists, such as Hobbes and Locke, have framed a classical account of politics, which turns upon its identification of the interplay between nature and free human activity.[43] Collingwood takes the concept of the social contract to represent the sense of creative political activity transforming merely natural relations into creative political conditions, which can sustain free human conduct. He understands Hobbes to be a pre-eminent theorist of a free political association, interpreting the contractual arrangements of Hobbes's *Leviathan*, which supersede merely natural relations, to serve as a metaphor for the creativity of human beings.[44] According to Collingwood, Hobbes recognizes how the social and political world is being recreated continually by ongoing formative activity that is symbolized by the idea of a social contract. Each generation for Collingwood, and on his reading,

---

[42] R.G. Collingwood, *The New Leviathan* (Oxford, Oxford University Press, 1992), pp. 1–130.
[43] Ibid., pp. 257–67.   [44] Ibid., pp. 262–3.

Hobbes, is to be inducted into a political order, whereby authoritative laws enable the freedom of those individuals who adhere to it. Collingwood interprets Hobbes's analysis of a free political association as an historical contribution to successive efforts to frame a conception of a liberal society within a wider form of liberal civilization, which he imagines as culminating at least temporarily in his own theory.

Collingwood's reading of Hobbes resembles Oakeshott's in accentuating the creativity of human agency in forming political associations. Like Oakeshott he downplays Hobbes's materialism and his reductive reading of human beings as so many bodies in motion. Likewise he identifies Hobbes in a modern tradition of political philosophizing, which culminates in his own approach to political philosophy. Collingwood's reading of Hobbes as a liberal inspiration for his own account of a liberal polity and civilization appears strange when in unpublished writings he had criticized Hobbes for lacking a properly conceptualized sense of human freedom.[45] Moreover, in *The New Leviathan* Collingwood himself develops an account of a liberal polity that contrasts markedly with the political order established by Hobbes in *Leviathan*. Hobbes's separation of the ruled from the sovereign gives way to a political order, the rules and policies of which are determined deliberatively by democratic representatives of all the members. Part of an explanation of the eminence attributed to Hobbes in *The New Leviathan* and the corresponding disparagement of German theorists such as Kant, Nietzsche, and Hegel, rests with the political context. Collingwood wrote *The New Leviathan* during the Second World War, and was at pains to appear patriotic in drawing upon an English philosopher, while denigrating the Germanic political tradition and German political philosophy.[46] The puzzle of Collingwood's denigration of Hegel, which goes against the grain of his own Hegelianism will be discussed in chapter 13 on Hegel. At this point it is enough to say that his reading of Hobbes is complicated by the political situation in which it was written.

Notwithstanding the complications arising out of wartime conditions, Collingwood, like Oakeshott, is insightful on Hobbes. If Hobbes does see politics as a creative activity in which individuals can manufacture a political association that is a testament to their own free powers of construction, then he is to be linked to subsequent theorists of freedom. As Oakeshott and Collingwood observe, Hobbes's philosophical review of the conditions composing a political association can be seen as a notable contribution to the ongoing philosophical tradition of Western civilization. Hobbes's project and the projects of traditional political philosophy and Western civilization,

---

[45] See R.G. Collingwood, 'Lectures on Moral Philosophy: For Michaelmas Term 1921', Collingwood Manuscripts, Bodleian Library Dep 4.
[46] See R.G. Collingwood, *The New Leviathan*, pp. lviii-lxi.

however, can be all be seen from a different perspective. And such a contrasting perspective is offered by Foucault, to whom we turn next.

FOUCAULT CONTRA OAKESHOTT?

Foucault, in his late Lectures at the College de France, addresses questions of politics and the history of political philosophy more expressly than in preceding works. His preceding archaeological and genealogical analyses of power are expressly critical of standard ways of conceiving of politics and the operations of power. Instead of seeing power as being concentrated in centralized political institutions, Foucault identifies power as operating in a multiplicity of sites and in uncircumscribed dynamic ways that shape the subjects over whom it is exercised. In *Discipline and Punish* he analyses power as circulating throughout society at local and regional levels and in a multitude of specific social structures and practices such as medicine, punishment, and education where forms of disciplinary power are institutionalized. His productive and relational sense of the dynamics of power challenges the idea of its concentration within the state so as to serve a determinate objective of public order. Foucault opposes the very idea of Hobbes's political philosophy. In contrast to Hobbes, Foucault designates his theoretical purpose as being 'to cut off the King's head'.[47] To imagine power as concentrated and determinate runs counter to the relational flows of power as a dynamic productive force in society. Foucault aims to dislodge the presumption of the state and state sovereignty by focusing on the microphysics of power.[48]

At the outset of his lectures of 1975–76, *Society Must Be Defended*, Foucault resumes his distinguishing perspective on power, recalling how his studies on genealogy show the dispersal and multiplicity of its operations in the organization and direction of punishment and prisons, of medicine and hospitals, and of madness and psychiatric institutions.[49] He recognizes how forms of knowledge accompany these operations of power so as to undermine the prospect of a summative understanding of their identities. He reviews his work over the previous ten to fifteen years, taking it to provide a productive impetus for contemporary practices of resistance to forms of power. In reflecting upon the status of his critical readings of diverse operations of power, he observes, 'I think that the essentially local character of the critique in fact indicates something resembling a sort of autonomous and noncentralized theoretical production, in other words a theoretical production that does

---

[47] See M. Foucault, *Society Must be Defended; Lectures at the College de France, 1975–76* (London, Penguin, 2003), p. 59.
[48] Ibid., p. 10.   [49] Ibid., pp. 1–6.

not need a visa from some common regime to establish its validity.'[50] Without abandoning his perspective on fragmentary and capillary operations of localized power, Foucault turns to opposing views of power and reviews the centralized unitary notions of power that are maintained by Marxism and liberalism. The liberal juridical conception sees liberalism as providing so many legal rights to serve as checks and balances to centralized power, whereas the Marxist version of power derives its operations uniformly from the interests of the dominant class in production. Foucault rejects both these models due to their centralizing circumscription on the operations of power. Power is to be held, used, passed on, delegated, or limited. It is objectified so that it resembles a commodity, which retains its identity in transactions but does not affect the identities of either power holders or its subjects.[51] Foucault frames a rival general conception of power, which contrasts with juridical and Marxist models by its relationality and by its dynamic illimitable presence in struggles between warring groups.

Hence in later lectures of *Society Must be Defended* Foucault contrasts two ways of considering political power. The juridico-political form presumes its centrality, and focuses upon kingly power, and is analysed as either constituting undiluted central authority or in its liberal guise it is limited by rights to protect individuals from its centralized operation. In contrast, a countervailing sense of historical power opposes this juridico-political form by imagining society to be subject to forms of domination, which are countered by rival historic forms of domination. The historical form of power takes war to be essential to its operations. It is relational and productive in its struggle for domination. Foucault interprets Hobbes as legitimating a juridico-political form of power, which he critiques on account of its misleading presentation of political power as unitary and subject to rationally considered purposes. He observes, 'In short we have to abandon the model of Leviathan, that model of an artificial man who is at once an automaton, a fabricated man, but also a unitary man who contains all real individuals, whose body is made up of citizens but whose soul is sovereignty.'[52]

In *Society Must Be Defended* Foucault contrasts a juridico-political image of a centralized power structure with an historico-political sense of power that maintains a contrasting dichotomous reading of power as consisting of warring groups, investing in its productive domination. In considering Hobbes's *Leviathan*, Foucault admits that on the face of things, Hobbes appears to view power in terms of war. He observes, 'It is the most general of all wars [for Hobbes], and it goes on at all times and in every dimension: "the war of every man against every man." '[53] However, in reviewing the structure of the state of war in the state of nature, Foucault identifies this Hobbesian war to represent

---

[50] Ibid., p. 6.   [51] Ibid., p. 14.   [52] Ibid., p. 34.   [53] Ibid., p. 89.

the imagined consequence of a rough equality between men rather than the result of concerted differences between antagonists. The propensity to war is not an actual war. What we are offered by Hobbes is a reading of the attitudes and calculations that underpin the imputed authority of the state and an avoidance of war instead of its enactment. Foucault points to a theatre of dissemblance and calculation in Hobbes's assessment of the human condition. He remarks, 'We are in a theatre where presentations are exchanged, in a relationship of fear in which there are no time limits; we are not really involved in war.'[54] Hobbes's apparent interest in the state of nature and the prospect of war is deceptive in that sovereignty by institution transforms the state of war between individuals into a transfer of right to a sovereign authority that assumes the right to represent them. An artificial person takes the place of real individuals in deciding upon public matters and a prospective state of war is invoked by philosophico-juridical analysis only to legitimate centralized authority and sovereignty. In Hobbes's conception of sovereignty by acquisition, what looks like a naked takeover of power by force of arms is taken to imply the consent of individuals to the transfer of authority to the victor. Relatedly, Foucault remarks upon Hobbes's interpretation of maternal authority over a child as arising out of the child's consent to the mother's authority.[55] Hence, Foucault emphasizes that the appearance of physical power and war in Hobbes masks a preoccupation with imagining centralized political authority as arising out of informed mutual consent rather than exhibiting naked struggle.

Hobbes may invoke war but only to deny its efficacy and Foucault sees Hobbes as maintaining a juridico-political notion of power in a theory of sovereignty, which traces its derivation to human agreement and ingenuity. While the insecurity of a state of war in the state of nature might induce a generalized fear, and victory in battle might bring a conqueror to power, Hobbes's aim is to legitimate authority by the consent of the fearful or the defeated to the authoritative operation of central power. In Foucault's words, 'Leviathan's invisible adversary is the Conquest.'[56] According to Foucault, what Hobbes is determined to avoid is chronic conflict, by which repression inexorably motivates counter-insurgency, and the ensuing lack of settled political authority excludes philosophical determination of the legitimation and delimitation of power. Hobbes is against a civil war of chronic struggle over who or what dominates. Foucault observes, 'It is this discourse of struggle and permanent civil war that Hobbes wards off by making all wars and conquests depend upon a contract, and by thus rescuing the theory of the State. And that of course is why the philosophy of right subsequently rewarded Hobbes with the senatorial title of "the father of political philosophy." When the State capitol was in danger, a goose woke up the sleeping philosophers.

---

[54] Ibid., p. 92.   [55] Ibid., pp. 95–6.   [56] Ibid., p. 98.

It was Hobbes.'[57] Foucault takes the Levellers and Diggers as breaking with the rhetoric of juridico-political discourse to level an attack upon the entire framework of domination by the propertied classes. They demanded its overthrow on historico-political grounds. They did not claim a right to provide a central and controllable delineation of power in a central legitimized authority. They waged war on repression and did not resort to generic theory on the state to neutralize the conflictual and conflicted nature of authority and power.

Paradoxically Oakeshott and Foucault interpret Hobbes in related ways. They differ in their assessments and review him according to differing categories, but they both see him as a pre-eminent philosopher of the state and centralized political authority. Moreover, they both see him as providing an analysis of political authority, whereby political power is viewed as an entity that can be dealt with by the creative energy of individuals, who agree on a centralized concentration of power to enable security. The state of nature on both their readings does not depict actual violence but is a thought experiment highlighting the insecurities to be experienced by socially situated competitive individuals who lack agreement on the framing of a concentrated central political power. Of course, they differ on their assessments of Hobbes and on juridical political power.

If Oakeshott and Foucault see Hobbes historically as representing a modern approach to representing the construction of centralized political power, they also both see him as advancing a political theory that bears upon their own theoretical schemes. Again they differ in what they take from Hobbes. In *On Human Conduct* Oakeshott presents an account of an ideal civil association, which draws upon Hobbes as a leading historic political theorist of civil association. Oakeshott incorporates Hobbes's understanding of an association, which eschews subordinating individuality and the self-chosen goals of an individual to a teleological state that aims at the common good. Conversely Foucault aims his assault on a juridical conception of power against Hobbes, who is taken to be a paradigmatic theorist of a commodified account of centralized power. Against the Hobbesian notion of political power, Hobbes sets himself to cut off the king's head by recognizing power to be decentralized and to be dynamic and insusceptible of delimitation in the struggles between rival forces.

CONCLUSION

Hobbes is taken by Oakeshott, Collingwood, and Foucault to be a major historic political theorist, who is intent on providing a philosophical

[57] Ibid., p. 99.

justification of the concentration of political power in the modern state. Oakeshott and Collingwood see him as advancing an image of political authority that derives from the creative energies of individuals and allows for their freedom. In contrast, Foucault takes Hobbes to be the arch-representative of a theoretical scheme that misperceives power to be susceptible to the negotiations of individuals. In viewing Hobbes historically, all three frame conceptual schemes or discourses by which to categorize Hobbes's thought. These discourses are imaginative constructions covering lengthy time periods to which Hobbes did not align himself self-consciously. They serve a purpose, however, in locating Hobbes's arguments historically and in allowing for connections with other historic theorists.

Oakeshott takes Hobbes to be a political philosopher, whose systematic approach to politics relates to other philosophers with similar systematic and comprehensive ambitions. More specifically Hobbes is identified as belonging to traditions of political and moral philosophy which allow for a more historically informed account of his theorizing. In different publications Oakeshott sees Hobbes as theorizing within the tradition of will and artifice, as subscribing to the morality of individuality, and as envisioning politics to allow for a form of civil association. In these categorizations of Hobbes's approach to moral and political philosophy, Oakeshott identifies Hobbes as adhering to modern styles of theorizing whereby the creativity and individuality of moral and political life are emphasized. Hobbes is not seen to reduce politics and human agency to what is merely given naturally; politics and morality is about individual agency. Likewise, Collingwood sees Hobbes as a theorist in the classical school of political thought, which is English and modern in taking politics as being about the agency and creativity of individuals in securing a polity that establishes conditions of freedom for individuals. Again, Foucault locates Hobbes in a broader discourse, namely a juridical political discourse whereby power is misconceived as being susceptible to the agency of individuals in creating a political structure that concentrates but limits the operations of power. They consider these traditions as stretching into a present in which their own theories reference Hobbes's political philosophy. Where Oakeshott and Collingwood build upon Hobbes's work in establishing their own conceptions of political regimes that allow for freedom of individuals, Foucault's own theory of power is pitched against Hobbes's theory.

Oakeshott, Collingwood, and Foucault review Hobbes in the light of their own theorizing on politics and power and employ their own discursive categories to identify Hobbes in terms of general discourses of political thought. On the face of things, the importation of their own ideas on historical development and the nature of political theory into their readings of Hobbes differs from the contextualism of Skinner. In contrast to their sense of the enduring reach and significance of Hobbes's political philosophy he puts a premium on identifying theorists as doing things in the light of their local particular contextual situations. Moreover while Skinner is appreciative of Collingwood's general approach to historical understanding he ignores *The New Leviathan* and has spoken of finding Oakeshott's writings on Hobbes to be unreadable and of his rejection of Oakeshott's anti-rationalism and conservatism.[58] Yet Skinner's interpretations of Hobbes are not completely at odds with those of Foucault, Collingwood, and Oakeshott. Just as Oakeshott interprets Hobbes on moral and political obligation in the light of an historical appreciation of Hobbes's ideas, so Skinner's early essays on Hobbes undermine theistic readings of his work by reviewing the historical reception of his ideas.[59] Again, Oakeshott's recognition of ambiguities in Hobbes that are traceable to his resort to rhetorical strategies that are at odds with his formal philosophy harmonizes with Skinner's reading of the contrary ways in which Hobbes conceives of and employs rhetoric in *Reason and Rhetoric in the Philosophy of Hobbes*.[60]

In *Hobbes and Republican Liberty* Skinner interprets the conception of freedom that is set out in *Leviathan* as responding to and countering republican advocates of a neo-Roman account of liberty. The impetus for this interpretation arises out of a contextual reading of Hobbes's perception of the dangers involved in the spread of republican views, and the need to provide an alternative account of liberty that is not linked to social or political status.[61] Yet its inspiration may also be seen as relating to debates about liberty past and present in which Skinner himself is involved, notably in Skinner's support for a conception of liberty as non-domination in preference to the notions of negative and positive liberty. Douglass observes, 'Questions concerning Hobbes's account of liberty are thus of more than mere historical interest, as they are increasingly intertwined with debates regarding the merits of the republican conception of liberty as non-domination'.[62] Skinner's argument that *Leviathan* introduces a negative conception of liberty as freedom from physical impediment to counter arguments of republican Parliamentarians has been disputed on a number of grounds.[63] Aside from its accuracy as

[58] Q. Skinner interview with P. Koikkalainen and S. Syrjamaki, 'Quentin Skinner On Encountering the Past', Finnish Yearbook of Political Thought [Redescriptions Yearbook of Political Thought Conceptual History and Feminist Theory] p. 45.

[59] Q. Skinner, 'The Ideological Context of Hobbes's Thought', *History*, vol. 9, 1966, pp. 286–317.

[60] Q. Skinner, *Reason and Rhetoric in the Philosophy of Hobbes* (Cambridge, Cambridge University Press, 1996).

[61] Q. Skinner, *Hobbes and Republican Liberty* (Cambridge, Cambridge University Press, 2008), pp. 124–77.

[62] R. Douglass, 'Thomas Hobbes's Changing Accounts of Liberty and Challenge to republicanism', *History of Political Thought*, vol. XXXVI, Summer 2015, p. 282.

[63] See A. Cromartie, 'Hobbes, History and Non-Domination', *Hobbes Studies*, vol. 22, 2004, pp. 171–77, in which the evidence for Hobbes's intentions is questioned. Douglass observes that

an historical account of Hobbes's intentions, however, it reveals how Skinner shares with Oakeshott, Collingwood, and Foucault a sense of the ongoing significance of Hobbes for contemporary debate in political philosophy. Like them he takes Hobbes to be a pivotal modern figure in setting out a liberal notion of freedom of the individual.

Skinner differs from Oakeshott and Collingwood in that he is critical of Hobbes's conceptualization of negative freedom and sees continuing merit in a republican form of argument. He laments the success that Hobbes enjoyed in countering republicanism and ends *Hobbes and Republican Liberty* by wondering rhetorically if he won the argument.[64] Where Collingwood and Oakeshott value Hobbes in articulating the social and political conditions of individual freedom, Skinner is critical of the enduring impact of his individualism. Skinner's critique of Hobbes shares something of Foucault's dismissal of the liberal notion of power that he detects and critiques in Hobbes. Of course, affinities between Skinner and Oakeshott, Collingwood, and Foucault on Hobbes are offset by differences.

In *Hobbes and Republican Liberty* characteristically Skinner undertakes a close analysis of the immediate context within which Hobbes operates. The closeness of this historical analysis distinguishes his analysis of Hobbes from Collingwood and Oakeshott as well as from Foucault. Skinner's interpretive style is also distinguished by his focus upon Hobbes's intentions. He does not identify Hobbes with discourses to which he did not align expressly. Skinner's focus upon the express intentions of Hobbes also sets him apart from a Marxist view of Hobbes, such as is developed by Macpherson in his account of the political thought of Hobbes and Locke in *The Political Theory of Possessive Individualism* which will be dealt with in the succeeding chapter on Locke.[65]

Hobbes is a controversial figure and the controversy that he excites is evident in the differing interpretations of his political philosophy that are offered by Collingwood, Oakeshott, Foucault, and Skinner. Oakeshott and Collingwood identify Hobbes to be an outstanding representative of a classic tradition of political philosophy. They also are at one in emphasizing Hobbes's recognition of the creative and constructive aspects of individuals, who determine the conditions of social and political life so as to protect individuality and freedom. They see Hobbes as a modern theorist, whose thought remains of relevance. Foucault agrees with much of this story but opposes rather than supports the project of establishing a legitimate central power to enable

---

the move towards a negative conception of liberty had been made in Hobbes's debate with Bramhall rather than in *Leviathan*.

[64] Q. Skinner, *Hobbes and Republican Liberty*, p. 216.

[65] C.B. Macpherson, *The Political Theory of Possessive Individualism* (Oxford, Oxford University Press, 1962).

individuals to pursue their own interests. The upshot is that Hobbes appears as a theorist, with whom subsequent generations can and do engage their own convictions and this engagement is evident too in the recent interpretation by Skinner even if he characteristically focuses upon the historical contexts in which Hobbes operated.

10

Locke

History and Political Thought

INTRODUCTION

John Locke was born in Wrington, Somerset in 1632. His parents came from Puritan trading families; his father was an attorney and clerk to the Justices of the Peace in Somerset. If his immediate family had a modest income, he benefited from the support of his uncle, Alexander Popham, a West Country Member of Parliament and an influential figure in national politics, who supported John Locke's education at Westminster School. After Westminster John Locke attended Christchurch College, Oxford, where he read medicine and philosophy, and became acquainted with Sydenham, the distinguished physician. Cranston observes how Locke, like Hobbes before him, was unimpressed by the scholastic philosophy that was dominant in Oxford, though he associated with members of the newly established experimental philosophy club.[1] In the 1660s Locke wrote, but did not publish, two works; *Two Tracts on Government*, a linked pair of essays arguing against religious toleration, and *Essays on the Law of Nature*, a set of lectures on the law of nature, which he gave as Censor of Moral Philosophy at Christchurch College in 1664. These works are conservative in their support for established authority and express standpoints at variance with his later views.[2] Following a meeting in Oxford with Anthony Ashley Cooper, later the Earl of Shaftesbury, Locke joined the latter's household having impressed the Earl by his conversation and medical expertise. Shaftesbury was the leader of a section of the Whig Party, which was opposed to Charles II, and critical of his perceived drift towards absolutism and Catholicism. While he was connected with the Shaftesbury household, Locke himself developed political views that were critical of the monarchy.

---

[1] M. Cranston, *John Locke: A Biography* (Oxford, Oxford University Press, 1985), pp. 29–46.
[2] P. Laslett, 'Introduction', John Locke, *Locke's Two Treatises of Government*, ed. P. Laslett (Cambridge, Cambridge University Press, 1970), pp. 1–20.

Between 1679 and 1683 political tensions came to a head when Shaftesbury's faction conspired to prevent Charles II's brother, James, an acknowledged Catholic, from ascending to the throne. This exclusion crisis culminated in the failure of the Rye House plot of 1683 and the aborted projected kidnapping of James, the Duke of York. In the aftermath of the plot and the implication of Shaftesbury and Locke in an act of treason, Locke followed the example of his patron Shaftesbury in leaving England for exile in Holland. In Holland he mixed with Dutch Armenian theologians and merchants, and Huguenot refugees. Louis XIV continued to exercise absolutist Catholic power in France, threatening Protestant states, and intensifying the disquiet amongst those in England who opposed absolutism and Catholicism.[3] Following the successful overthrow of James II in 1688, in the so-called Glorious Revolution, Locke returned to England and his *Two Treatises of Government* was published anonymously in 1689. Locke's *Letter on Toleration* was also published anonymously in the same year in Holland and England. Locke's *An Essay Concerning Human Understanding*, his most considered work of philosophy, also appeared in 1689, and its empiricist epistemology takes philosophy to be dependent upon observation and science.[4] Philosophy, for Locke, was assigned the role of conceptual clarification of first-order forms of knowledge, a role which it has largely retained in subsequent analytic and empirically minded forms of philosophy in the English-speaking world. In 1693 Locke published a disciplinarian tract on education, *Some Thoughts Concerning Education*, and two years later he composed the deistic *The Reasonableness of Christianity*.[5]

Interest in Locke's political thought has centred upon *Two Treatises of Government*. The *First Treatise* is a detailed refutation of Filmer's *Patriarcha*, a royalist tract, which was republished in 1680. Critical interest focuses upon *The Second Treatise*, which presents an independently formulated argument explaining the basis of government.[6] Interpretive controversy over the text ranges over a number of fields, not the least of which has been the dating and circumstances of its composition. It was published anonymously in 1689 and Locke took great care to protect his anonymity.[7] Laslett, an early exponent of an historically minded Cambridge approach to the history of political thought,

---

[3] On the exclusion crisis see J. Dunn, *Locke* (Oxford, Oxford University Press, 1984), pp. 31–3.

[4] J. Locke, *An Essay Concerning Human Understanding* (New York, Prometheus Book, 1995).

[5] J. Locke, *The Reasonableness of Christianity*, ed. J.C. Higgins-Biddle (Oxford, Oxford University Press, 1999); J. Locke, *Some Thoughts Concerning Education* (New York, Dover Publications, 2007).

[6] John Locke, *Locke's Two Treatises of Government*, ed. P. Laslett (Cambridge, Cambridge University Press, 1970); R. Filmer, *Patriarcha*, ed. P. Laslett (Oxford, Basil Blackwell, 1949).

[7] P. Laslett, 'Introduction', John Locke, *Locke's Two Treatises of Government*, ed. P. Laslett, pp. 10–20.

attends carefully to questions on the text's composition, invoking the evidence of Locke's diary, his engagement with contemporary texts, the circumstances of Locke's life, and the background contextual politics in the 1670s and 1680s. Although definitive evidence for the text's composition is lacking, Laslett makes a persuasive case for identifying its composition as taking place earlier than 1689. While Ashcraft has questioned his suggestion that a draft of some of *The Second Treatise* may be traced to 1679, the argument that the overall design and draft of the *Two Treatises of Government* follow the republication of Filmer's *Patriarcha* in January 1680 is generally accepted.[8] The dating of the composition of Locke's *Two Treatises of Government* is not of merely anti-quarian interest, because it relates to what Skinner would identify as its illocutionary force. What was Locke doing in writing the text? If it is to be seen as a response to the publication of Filmer's text and the politics of the exclusion crisis, then it is likely to have constituted a revolutionary interven-tion that was aimed at undermining the prevailing monarchy, rather than representing a retrospective endorsement of the Glorious Revolution.[9]

THE POLITICS OF LOCKE'S *SECOND TREATISE OF GOVERNMENT*

The Second Treatise begins by imagining men and women in a state of nature, a condition without express government. While it is a non-political condition it is a moral condition. Individuals in a state of nature are conceived as being equally free, rational, and independent. They can distinguish right from wrong and they can do so because they can discern natural law and its God-given moral obligations. These moral obligations entail that individuals are to respect one another's rights to life, liberty, and property, which in Locke's text tends to mean material property but can refer more broadly to entitle-ments.[10] Locke observes, 'The *State of Nature* has a Law of Nature to govern it, which obliges everyone: And Reason, which is that Law, teaches all Mankind, who will but consult it, that being all equal and independent, no-one ought to harm another in his Life, Health, Liberty or Possessions.'[11]

The rights to life, liberty, and property serve as constraints upon the conduct of government as well as restraints upon individual behaviour in a

---

[8] For details of Locke's reading of Filmer, see P. Laslett, 'Introduction', pp. 25–50; John Locke, *Locke's Two Treatises of Government*. See also R. Ashcraft, *Revolutionary Politics and Locke's Two Treatises of Government* (Princeton NJ, Princeton University Press, 1986), pp. 60–5.

[9] P. Laslett, 'Introduction', pp. 46–7.

[10] See J. Dunn, *Locke*, pp. 33–44.

[11] John Locke, *Locke's Two Treatises of Government*, p. 289.

state of nature. For Locke, individuals agree to form a political society because there are inconveniences in a state of nature, but they are not to sacrifice fundamental rights in the transition to government. These inconveniences arise out of the uncertain enforcement of the law of nature, which persuades individuals to establish a government, but the ensuing authority of government does not legitimate transgression against natural rights. Political authority for Locke is established by the consent of the people and it operates as a form of trust whereby each individual's right to interpret and enforce natural law is entrusted to government. Locke, however, was mindful of the possibility of a government abusing this trust, and he rests the legitimacy of government on the ongoing consent of the people. He notes, 'For all *Power given with trust* for the attaining an *end*, being limited by that end, whenever that *end is* manifestly neglected, or opposed, the *trust* must necessarily be *forfeited*, and the Power devolve into the hands of those who gave it, who may place it anew where they shall think best for their safety and security' (emphasis in original).[12]

While the general contours of Locke's enterprise in limiting the power of government are clear, the precise mechanisms of how the consent of the people is to be elicited are less clear. For instance, the manner in which the people are to be represented politically and the scope of the franchise are not specified in detail. If Locke's *Second Treatise* lacks detail on institutional arrangements and presumes rather than explains the operation of government by consent, it nevertheless expresses a cogent statement of limited government. The authority of government is limited by its hypothetical conditions of emergence, so that government functions legitimately only if it continues to recognize the law of nature and natural rights. Critical debate turns upon the extent to which *The Second Treatise* is to be seen either as an historical intervention into a particular political crisis, lacking the credentials to serve as a generic text for liberalism or as the formulation of a political philosophy that transcends its historical circumstances. Oakeshott in his posthumously published *Lectures in the History of Political Thought* contrasts Locke sharply with Hobbes by identifying Locke as a theorist who is primarily concerned with practical politics and the justification of political action, whereas Hobbes assumes a comprehensive and philosophical perspective on the political. Oakeshott imagines Locke to be an ideological thinker, whose arguments and rhetorical strategies relate to what is at hand rather than to systematic philosophical analysis.[13]

Laslett's scholarly studies on Locke and Filmer serve to identify Locke as operating in a specific historical context and review his thinking from an

---

[12] Ibid., p. 385.
[13] M. Oakeshott, *Lectures in the History of Political Thought*, ed. T. Nardin and L. O'Sullivan (Exeter, Imprint Academic, 2006), p. 393.

historical perspective. The illocutionary force of Locke's composition of *The Second Treatise* is reinterpreted in terms of his intention of influencing political events in the context of the exclusion crisis. Skinner, himself, highlights the ascription to Locke of historically situated ideological purposes by recalling how his turn to Hobbes, and to the challenge of a historical explanation of Hobbes's work, was motivated by his contrary response to Laslett's observation that Locke's more ideologically inspired writing was eminently susceptible to an historical perspective, whereas Hobbes's systemic standpoint was a very different proposition.[14] However, an historical perspective on Locke is not the only one that is in interpretive play. Waldron, amongst others, urges strongly that Locke offers a philosophical liberal perspective that remains of relevance to contemporary political thinking.[15] Moreover, a recent advocate of a tough-minded form of liberalism, Robert Nozick, draws expressly on Locke in framing a theory of rights and just property arrangements.[16] Nozick's Lockean ascription of rights to individuals in a state of nature and his justification of private property are modelled on Locke's theorizing. The evident relevance of Nozick's argument to the ideological context of late capitalist society intimates the continuing currency of Locke's ideas in their relation to subsequent economic and political conditions. This relevance of Locke's ideas, however, should not obscure how his express intentions reflect his contemporary circumstances and do not accommodate readily succeeding ideological debate, which is post-Keynesian and post-Marxist, as well as post-Lockean.

A productive way of examining interpretive issues surrounding Locke's *Second Treatise* is to review Dunn's argument in his *The Political Thought of John Locke*. Dunn's reading of Locke is expressly historical and is cited by Skinner as a notable example of the methodology of the Cambridge School, and so its review yields insight into the claims of this generic interpretive perspective.[17] Engagement with Dunn's emphatically historical reading of Locke provides a means of access into the historical context of Locke's political thought and affords us a perspective by which to review the status of Locke's theories of rights, consent, and property. Likewise, Dunn's critique of

---

[14] See Q. Skinner interview with Petri Koikkalainen and Sami Syrjamaki, 'Quentin Skinner On Encountering the Past', Finnish Yearbook of Political Thought [Redescriptions Yearbook of Political Thought Conceptual History and Feminist Theory] no. 6, p. 42.

[15] J. Waldron, 'Locke', in D. Boucher and P. Kelly, *Political Thinkers* (Oxford, Oxford University Press, 2004, pp. 207–24 and J. Waldron, *God, Locke and Equality: Christian Foundations of John Locke's Political Thought* (Cambridge, Cambridge University Press, 2002); see also J.A. Simmons, *The Lockean Theory of Rights* (Princeton NJ, Princeton University Press, 1992).

[16] On Nozick's use of Locke, see T. Kenyon, 'Locke', in A. Edwards and J. Townshend, *Interpreting Modern Political Philosophy* (Basingstoke and New York, Palgrave Macmillan, 2002), pp. 60–81.

[17] Q. Skinner interview with P. Koikkalainen and S. Syrjamaki, 'Quentin Skinner On Encountering the Past', p. 39.

Macpherson's Marxist analysis of Locke and property enables us to assess how an historical focus on a political thinker's express intentions and contextual assumptions bears upon a Marxist reading of a political thinker's alignment with emerging economic trends and structures.

In the Preface to *The Political Thought of John Locke* Dunn proclaims his commitment to an historical interpretation of Locke, which he takes to rule out imagining Locke's ideas as pertaining to present-day concerns. He observes, 'I simply cannot conceive of constructing an analysis of any issue in political theory around the affirmation or negation of anything which Locke says about political matters.'[18] This proclamation of an historical approach represents an emphatic commitment to the agenda of the Cambridge School in concentrating on explaining past political thought by reference to past contexts rather than invoking past ideas to serve current political agendas. Its challenging rhetoric, however, has been challenged, and not least by Dunn himself, who has been forthright in his self-criticism. He confesses subsequently, 'The sentence was intended, plainly enough as a challenge—perhaps even almost as a boast. It was certainly not intended as it now dispiritingly reads, as a ludicrous confession of intellectual myopia.'[19] In retracting the statement Dunn explains it to have been inspired by a legitimate yet misplaced concern to read texts holistically so as to avoid extracting doctrines for present purposes from an overall historical argument the general character of which is shaped by historical circumstances.[20]

In retrospect Dunn continues to maintain that much of Locke's theologically oriented argument remains of little relevance to a more secular society but he does allow that Locke's contractarian approach has something to offer, particularly in pointing to the role of trust in establishing viable political arrangements.[21] In his essay, '"Trust" in the Politics of John Locke', he urges the relevance of Locke's recognition of the rationality of trust in the operation of politics, though he specifies that this relevance is indirect in that his express arguments are related closely to contemporary circumstances. Dunn observes, 'To discuss Locke in this fashion is not to argue that today we should espouse all—or any—of Locke's own detailed conceptions, but it is implicitly to suggest that we have good reason to treat his political philosophy as exemplary...'.[22] Notwithstanding Dunn's subsequent repudiation of his hyperbolic defence of a purely historical reading of the *Two Treatises of Government* Dunn's

---

[18] J. Dunn, *The Political Thought of John Locke: An Historical Account of the Argument of the 'Two Treatises of Government'* (Cambridge, Cambridge University Press, 1969), p. x.

[19] J. Dunn, 'What is Living and What is Dead in the Political Theory of John Locke?', in J. Dunn, *Interpreting Political Responsibility* (Princeton NJ, Princeton University Press, 1999), p. 9.

[20] Ibid, pp. 9–12.

[21] Ibid., pp. 23–4.

[22] J. Dunn, '"Trust" in the Politics of John Locke', in J. Dunn, *Rethinking Modern Political Theory—Essays 1979–83* (Cambridge, Cambridge University Press, 1985), p. 34.

historical approach in *The Political Thought of John Locke* and interpretive strategy remains well-worth considering. It offers a perceptive reading of Locke and its approach and detailed analysis represents an outstanding historic example of the style of the Cambridge School. It remains a significant example of a contextual approach to the history of political thought and continues to stand out in providing an historical contextual approach to the history of political thought. A review of its arguments allows for understanding of what is involved in such an approach and its contextual reading of a past political philosophy continues to be supported in broad terms by Dunn and fellow contextualists.

DUNN ON LOCKE AND THE HISTORY OF POLITICAL THOUGHT

In *The Political Thought of John Locke* Dunn resists a Whig history whereby the past is read from the present. Historic theorists are to be understood as contributing to a specific context. Their ideas are not invoked to contribute to subsequent political debate or to a generalized conceptual analysis of an ideology or political argument. Theories and concepts are subsumable to particular ideological contexts. Hence Locke, commonly, if unreflectively, taken to be the founder of liberal thought, is not to be used as source material for a generic 'liberal' ideology. The separation of the past from the present is axiomatic for Dunn. Dunn maintains an historical reading, which excludes speculation about Locke's relevance to present circumstances. He makes this explicit in amplifying his sense of history, remarking, 'by "historical", then, is  meant an account of what Locke was talking about, not a doctrine written (perhaps unconsciously) by him on a sort of invisible ink which becomes apparent only when held up to the light (or heat) of the twentieth century mind.'[23] Dunn is unequivocal in interpreting Locke's thought to be precisely what Locke intended his ideas to mean. He observes, 'The claim that the account given here of Locke's argument in the *Two Treatises of Government* is "historical" implies that its status depends upon the adequacy of its identification of Locke's *own* meaning' (emphasis in original).[24]

Dunn's historical interpretive approach to Locke's thought neither assumes coherence nor comprehensiveness at the expense of contingent and local factors. Hence Locke's arguments are not pressed so as to demand details that would only be warranted if his intention were to provide comprehensive accounts of the nature of political representation, consent, and legitimacy. To

---

[23] Ibid., p. xl.   [24] Ibid., p. xli.

the contrary Dunn concludes that there is no evidence to justify interpreting Locke as aiming to deliver such comprehensive accounts. Similarly, if his ideas were to be reviewed generically as contributions to the clarification of generic political concepts and a justification of a theory that would be sustainable against all possible counter-arguments, then his political theory would have to be assessed by its perceived omissions and shortcomings. However, if Locke's *Second Treatise* is designed to achieve more specific objectives, namely under-mining absolutist arguments in favour of unlimited royal authority and providing grounds for opposing continued Stuart rule, then Locke's *Second Treatise* is to be understood and judged in the light of those goals rather than for its adequacy in pursuing more generic arguments. Dunn questions the assumption that Locke was attempting and failing to carry out a philosophical task when there is no evidence that he was so engaged.[25]

According to Dunn, the character of *The Second Treatise* should not be assumed in advance of analysis and interpretation of the text and its context. He maintains that Locke's particular use of concepts poses interpretive ques-tions at every turn about their provenance and purposes. While it might be tempting to distinguish a set of doctrines in Locke, on say political legitimacy, consent, rights, and property, it is misleading to imagine these doctrines as either determining the text or to operate as explanatory factors outside of their role in specific forms of argument. Hence Locke might highlight the role of consent in ruling, and its correlative absence may undermine legitimacy, but he is not overly concerned to spell out what is involved in consent, as his interest appears to be in highlighting the illegitimacy of absolutist rule, rather than in elaborating the generic conditions constituting legitimate rule.[26] More generally Dunn observes that the *Two Treatises of Government* requires an historical form of explanation rather than abstract speculation to identify exactly why Locke employs arguments in particular ways. The very project of invoking natural rights to set against the power of government demands explanation given the record of Locke's preceding beliefs. To discuss Locke in terms of the general acceptability of natural rights arguments begs the ques-tion of why Locke framed his argument in terms of natural rights.

Dunn sets out the above grounds for reading the *Two Treatises of Govern-ment* historically. In so doing he addresses the historical puzzle of how Locke, prior to the writing of the *Two Treatises of Government*, maintains a contrast-ing conservative political outlook and why Locke's views on natural law are so completely transformed by the time he wrote the *Two Treatises of Govern-ment*. Locke's preceding writings on natural law imagine that natural law is to be interpreted by authoritative, traditional channels, so his subsequent

---

[25] On this point note the arguments of I. Hampsher-Monk, 'John Locke', in *A History of Modern Political Thought* (Oxford, Blackwell, 1992), p. 101.

[26] J. Dunn, *The Political Thought of John Locke*, p. 9.

assumption that governments could be out of step with natural law, and that it might be legitimate to overturn governments poses historical questions over what led to Locke's radical change of mind. Like Laslett before him, Dunn observes how Locke's transformation of outlook coincides with his fifteen-year engagement with the household of Anthony Ashley Cooper, the first Earl of Shaftesbury, who was a critic of the government of the day. Locke's subsequent standpoint on natural law is aligned to Shaftesbury and more generally with the political opposition movement with which Shaftesbury was associated. To identify Locke's affiliation with the Shaftesbury household as bearing upon his political and ideological writings, as Laslett indicates, is clearly right. Laslett cites a reference in the Shaftesbury Papers from the Earl of Shaftesbury's grandson and Locke's pupil, the third Earl. Shaftesbury's grandson notes, 'Mr. Locke grew so much in esteem with my grandfather that as great as he had experienced him in physic, he looked upon this but as his least part. He encouraged him to turn his thoughts another way...He put him upon study of the religious and civil affairs of the nation...'.[27] Laslett also cites a reference to Locke in the Shaftesbury papers by F.C., who observes, 'My Lord imparted to him [Locke] from time to time all the secretest affairs then in agitation and by my Lord's frequent discourse of state affairs, religion, toleration and trade, Mr. Locke came to have a wonderful knowledge of these things...'.[28] In considering the impact of the Shaftesbury household on Locke's views and on *The Second Treatise*, Laslett concludes, 'We owe the *Two Treatises* to the wonderful knowledge of state affairs which Locke acquired from frequent discourse with the first earl of Shaftesbury; indeed the evidence suggests, as we shall see, that he actually wrote the book for Shaftesbury's purposes.'[29]

While the similarity of standpoint between Locke and the Earl of Shaftesbury suggests that engagement with the household was an important factor in the development of Locke's political thought, Laslett does not show in detail the nature and operation of the influence. He establishes that the composition of *The Second Treatise* is related to the exclusion crisis of 1679 until 1683. Shaftesbury and other Whig landowners opposed the monarch for a number of reasons including their determination to defend Protestantism, their concern to preserve their landed interests, and their dislike of arbitrary and absolutist government. They feared that the Stuart monarchy was heading in a direction that would endanger Protestantism, the landed interest, and limited, responsible government. Their resistance to the monarchy crystallized into a determination to exclude the brother of Charles II, the reigning monarch, from succeeding to the throne. James, Charles's brother, was next in line and likely to succeed to the throne given the absence of a legitimate heir. Minds amongst the opposition were duly concentrated, and Shaftesbury

---

[27] P. Laslett, 'Introduction', John Locke, *Locke's Two Treatises of Government*, pp. 27–8.
[28] Ibid., p. 27.   [29] Ibid.

orchestrated an opposition that was set against James' succession, given the likelihood that it would lead to everything that was most to be feared, absolutism, government by prerogative, the relegation of parliamentary government, and the ascendancy of Catholicism. This fractious political situation provides a context for Locke's thought, and informs Locke's critique of absolutist government. But, as Dunn points out, all this does not in itself explain particular and significant lines of Locke's political argument in the *Two Treatises of Government*. Moreover, as Dunn observes, we cannot be sure if Locke's assumption of anti-Stuart political ideas was a cause or effect of his joining the Shaftesbury household. In respect of this disarmingly simple but awkward question, he remarks, '[I]t is raised here in this simple-minded form because we do not at the moment apparently (and may never) know the answer to it.'[30]

An insistent aspect of Dunn's reading of Locke's political thought is his emphasis upon Locke's adoption of a theological line of argument, which he observes to be underdetermined by the contextual politics of the time. In fact, Locke's theological argument does not fit neatly with the goals of those who pressed the case for excluding James II. Locke's argument in *The Second Treatise* tends to focus on the individual rather than on the representative institutions, which were central to the argument of the anti-Stuart landed interest and of great moment to the Earl of Shaftesbury.[31] Dunn makes a good case for seeing the centrality of theological argument in Locke's *Two Treatises on Government*. The care with which Locke develops the argument suggests it is not a mere ploy in a strategy to achieve an otherwise unrelated outcome, the defence of an alternative political settlement.[32] As Dunn notes in his later book, *Locke*, 'Locke's arguments and Shaftesbury's tactics sometimes diverged.'[33] The theological line of argument is distinctive and does not fit with the standard rhetoric of those aligned with Shaftesbury against the Stuarts. It is a product of Locke's particular set of historical beliefs.

Dunn argues persuasively how Locke's puritanism and his use of theological argument are central to *The Second Treatise*. Theological arguments are not to be taken as merely instrumental in supporting independently specifiable conclusions. Dunn observes, 'Whenever he [Locke] began to sketch out the contours of an ethic and searched for the fundamental form which it must take, the touchstone which he set up was always the relation between the Creator and created.'[34] Locke's formulation of the state of nature at the outset of the text reveals the theological character of his argument. Locke's conceptualization of a state of nature argument is distinct from Hobbes's in *Leviathan*, due to its assertive incorporation of God-given rights. Locke

---

[30] J. Dunn, *The Political Thought of John Locke*, p. 8.   [31] Ibid., p. 27.
[32] Ibid., p. 24.   [33] J. Dunn, *Locke*, p. 31.
[34] J. Dunn, *The Political Thought of John Locke*, p. 28.

imagines the condition to be social but ahistorical. Moral rights derive from the natural law, which is authorized by God. They are imagined as pertaining to any human situation, given the ahistorical character that is imputed to the state of nature. Individuals owe a duty to God to discharge the duties of natural law by respecting the rights of all to life, liberty, and property. Natural theology and the authority of God demand that individuals maintain these rights in the state of nature. An individual's obligation to observe rights derives from God's command, hence individuals must respect their own right to life, irrespective of their own wishes. They have a duty to preserve their own life. These God-given rights and duties set the context for the obligations that individuals owe to the sovereign, whose duty, in turn, is to maintain these rights. If the sovereign fails to respect the rights of the citizen, individuals are endowed with a duty of resistance to oppose the failing political authority. Individuals remain empowered so to act notwithstanding the role that is allocated to the legislature in representing the people and in maintaining government by consent. Dunn observes how individual responsibility to God remains of significance throughout *The Second Treatise of Government*. It underlies its argument against absolutist government and hence its opposition to Stuart rule. The singularity of Locke's line of argument is disclosed in its discordance with standard arguments opposing absolutism that were presented during the exclusion crisis.[35]

Locke's argument in *The Second Treatise* does not replicate the priorities of elaborating representational government and of ending rule by prerogative, which are central to the views of those opposed to Stuart rule. Dunn makes a good case for aligning it to what Locke took to be demanded by an appropriately critical response to the publication of Filmer's work. If the *First Treatise* is an evident rejoinder to Filmer, then Locke's argument in the *Two Treatises of Government* can also be interpreted in the context of responding to Filmer. Dunn observes, 'When Filmer's *Patriarcha* was at last published in 1680 it became imperatively necessary to provide an ideological counterweight which could set out the rationale of the Exclusionist position in a way which assimilated it firmly to the solid continuous historical order of the English polity and protected it against the needling gibes of *Patriarcha*.'[36] To urge that Locke's *Two Treatises of Government* should be interpreted in the light of Filmer is to push at an open textualist door. After all, Locke's text advertises itself as a response to Filmer's *Patriarcha*. The context of frenzied political debate in which the publication of Filmer's text served as a provocative move in an ideological game underlines the point of Locke responding to Filmer. Locke devotes the *First Treatise* to a detailed and express response to Filmer's text, which had been published in its entirety in January 1680 by loyalist

---

[35] Ibid., p. 50.   [36] Ibid., p. 47.

royalists. Unlike, say Hobbes's *Leviathan*, Filmer's *Patriarcha* was clear-cut in its royalist sympathies and could be employed unambiguously as royalist propaganda. It had no truck with popular consent, because it located political authority directly in the monarchy, and did not conceive of consent arising out of those imagined to be in a primal state of nature. Nor did it raise the spectre of a multiplicity of forms of sovereign authority, which might include a representative body. Filmer urged that the authority of kings was derived naturally from God due to his granting of their patriarchal authority. While this argument from divine right in turn appears to raise difficulties given uncertain lines of succession in the past, at least it provides an unequivocal commitment to the rule of kings.

In line with other contextualist commentators, Dunn brings out the frenzy of dispute that attended the royalist publication of Filmer's text. Filmer constitutes the key element in the ideological strategy of royalist argument, to which critics are obliged to reply. The ebb and flow of the argument of Locke's *Second Treatise* is explained plausibly by Dunn as responding specifically to the arguments of Filmer. In setting himself against hereditary absolutist power that is sanctioned by divine right, Locke responds to the terms of Filmer's argument. In replying to Filmer, Locke highlights how the rights and duties of individuals derive directly from God. While the form of this argument is misaligned with standard critiques of absolutism, it furnishes an effective response to Filmer in bypassing the supposedly divinely ordained patriarchal authority of the king. Traditionalist patriarchal arrangements, for Locke, compromise the duty that each individual owes directly to God. Dunn observes, '[T]he *Two Treatises* is more individualist than can be explained by the Exclusion programme—But the individualism is more distinctively Lockean. The key appears to be the very intensive confrontation with the positions of Filmer.'[37] Whereas Shaftesbury and standard exclusionist arguments emphasize the role of Parliament and the right of legislative representation in the raising of revenue and in the pursuit of foreign policy or diplomacy, Locke pays only intermittent attention to the processes of government and legislation, opting instead to rely on the rights and duties of individuals. The right of resistance is squarely located in individuals, rather than in the mediated representative form of a Parliament. This specification of the rights of individuals makes sense if it is seen as serving Locke's strategy of responding directly and convincingly to the arguments of Filmer, but jars with the agenda of the landed interest. Dunn comments on this anomaly, 'There is no doubt that if the text of the *Two Treatises* as we have it now is exclusively or predominantly an Exclusion Tract it is often a notably ham-fisted one'.[38] The role of Locke's arguments in combating Filmer can also be detected in the right

[37] Ibid., p. 50.   [38] Ibid., p. 58.

of emigration that he grants to citizens. While irrelevant to the succession crisis, the right of emigration responds to Filmer's granting of a right of secession.[39] Again, the lack of details in Locke's account of parliamentary representation and his vagueness on how forms of express and tacit consent are to operate suggest that Locke is not overly concerned with these issues. In contrast to standard arguments against absolutism, Locke's priority is to highlight individual natural rights and to sideline or at least economize discussion of political arrangements.

DUNN, LOCKE, AND MACPHERSON

Dunn's interpretation of Locke incorporates a critique of a Marxist reading of Locke's *Second Treatise*. Marx made references to Locke and property in *Capital*, impugning Locke as a bourgeois apologist for the historical development of capital.[40] An elaborated Marxist critique of Locke is developed by Macpherson, a twentieth-century Marxist, in *The Political Theory of Possessive Individualism*, which sets out a concentrated reading of Hobbes and Locke as ideologues of the emerging form of capitalism. Macpherson distinguishes between a number of models of economy and society; customary or status society, a simple market society, and a possessive market society. He takes the latter to possess distinctive features of a modern competitive market society, notably due to its competitive market in products, differing levels of ability, possessions and desire, and the alienability of labour. Far from theorizing about individuals and society in the abstract, Hobbes and Locke are taken to theorize for the conditions of an emerging possessive market society. Macpherson's thesis, however, has been critiqued by many commentators, who observe the lack of evidence for taking Hobbes and Locke to conceive of society in the ways that are attributed to them.[41] Certainly, aspects of Hobbes's argument jar with an interpretation that aligns him with an emerging capitalist society. For example, Hobbes does not support laissez-faire, criticizes the growth of joint stock companies, accords authority over property to the sovereign, and shows a sympathy for aristocratic values. Macpherson's reading of Locke imagines him to be expressly supporting key features of a capitalist economy and a possessive market society.

---

[39] Ibid.

[40] K. Marx, *Capital* trans. S. Moore and E. Aveling and ed. F. Engels (Moscow, Progress Publishers, 1969), pp. 43–4.

[41] See I. Berlin, 'Hobbes, Locke and Professor Macpherson', *Political Quarterly*, vol. 35, no. 4, 1964, pp. 444–68; A. Ryan, 'Hobbes and Individualism', in G.A.J. Rogers and A. Ryan (eds), *Perspectives on Thomas Hobbes* (Oxford, Clarendon Press, 1988), pp. 81–105.

In support of his reading of Locke, Macpherson cites *The Second Treatise*'s wholesale endorsement of a money economy and the sale of commodities, including labour and property. Macpherson traces the stages of Locke's argument on property and money, observing how Locke assumes that God grants property to mankind in common, but that individuals establish the right of private property by working on and adding value to what is bequeathed to mankind. The assumed consent to the use of money enables the operation of a money economy, the acquisition of goods on a large scale, and a complex division of labour. These developments are justifiable, for Locke, if sufficient land resources remain available to all, as an increasing total level of productivity enhances general welfare. Affiliated to his reading of Locke as allowing for the unlimited accumulation of money and property, Macpherson observes Locke's intermittent references to differential forms of political consent, the development of the division of labour, and repression of the poor in the interests of generating a compliant and energetic labour force. Macpherson concludes that Locke promotes a two-tier society in which an emerging bourgeois class is accorded power so as to develop capital and to maximize their class interests.[42]

Laslett and Tully disagree with Macpherson by maintaining that Locke does not justify the operation of a fully-fledged capitalist economy. Against Macpherson, Laslett urges that Locke does not support a market in wage-labour. Locke's reference to the servant who cut the turfs of his master is interpreted as implying the supply of a service rather than labour. Laslett also observes how Locke advocated regulation of property and conceived of society to be subject to the laws of nature.[43] In a similar vein Tully identifies Locke as a Leveller rather than as an apologist for capital. He assigns Locke to a natural law tradition, which puts property rights on a communal basis, and subordinates property to the duties that subjects owe to God.[44] On this reading, far from setting out a market in property, Locke allows for the English Common, whereby the English yeoman is entitled to usufruct, which is the use of as much land as he could make use of. Accordingly, property is subject to regulation and distributive justice so that inheritance is to be regulated and charity is to provide for those who are needy. For Tully, Locke's reference to the servant performing a service for his master is not an endorsement of a free market in labour and property but represents a commitment to an artisanal model of economy.[45] On this reading, Locke presumes that a specific service might be sold but labour is not commodified generically and abstractly.

---

[42] C.B. Macpherson, *The Political Theory of Possessive Individualism* (Oxford, Oxford University Press, 1962).

[43] P. Laslett, 'Introduction', John Locke, *Locke's Two Treatises of Government*, pp. 105–6.

[44] J. Tully, *A Discourse on Property: John Locke and His Adversaries* (Cambridge, Cambridge University Press, 1980).

[45] Ibid., pp. 136–42.

If Macpherson reads Locke as expressly endorsing untrammelled market relations, Tully and Laslett follow Macpherson in endowing Locke's text with an equal precision, but in their case Locke is explicitly disavowing capitalist relations of production. All their assumptions are misplaced in that Locke's *Second Treatise* does not furnish precision, and the precision that is misattributed to Locke arises out of inattention to Locke's intentions. Townshend, a defender of the Macpherson thesis, observes how Locke's remarks about the regulation of property and his opposition to primogeniture reflect his opposition to Filmer rather than a positive commitment to a non-market economy.[46] Locke's treatment of property relations reinforces Dunn's identification of the contextual role that is played by his concern to rebut Filmer. Locke's imagining of God's grant of the earth to mankind as a whole while allowing for individuals to assume private property via their labour, is part of his strategy in undermining Filmer's patriarchal ideas. Property, for Locke, is to be divorced from the tight control of a patriarchal monarch. Dunn's contextual reading of Locke informs his critique of the Macpherson thesis, the force of which resides in his attention to Locke's historical intentions in *The Second Treatise*. In particular, he draws attention to the crucial roles played by Locke's theological arguments in framing individual rights and attitudes, which are directed at rebutting Filmer rather than providing wholesale endorsement of capital.

Dunn provides a considered response to Macpherson's overall reading of Locke, admitting the severity of the emerging hierarchical political economy but questioning the alleged role of Locke as an ideological apologist of capital.[47] He argues that Locke's Puritan theology does not serve the instrumental purpose of accommodating capital but rather constitutes a moral ahistorical reading of the human condition, by which 'natural' rights, including those of property, are distributed. On this reading, Locke takes theology seriously. Fundamentally, human beings are to be understood as oriented towards God, owing divinely sanctioned duties to themselves and to others. Hence, Locke's moral injunctions against laziness are not directed against the poor in the service of capital. Rather all have a duty to be industrious, which derives from their relationship to God. But this duty is conceived to be genuinely egalitarian, even if Locke does not prescribe an egalitarian organization of production and distribution.[48] Moreover, Dunn rebuts Macpherson's reading of Locke's references to differing forms of consent, express and tacit, as applying respectively to owners of property and propertyless labourers so as to exclude or minimize the political role of the poor. Locke's discussion of consent is opaque, but, for Dunn, this is most likely due

---

[46] J. Townshend, *C.B. Macpherson and the Problem of Liberal Democracy* (Edinburgh, Edinburgh University Press, 2000), p. 81.
[47] J. Dunn, *The Political Thought of John Locke*, p. 58.   [48] Ibid., p. 24.

to its primarily negative role in opposing Filmer and absolutist authority rather than because of its positive role in elaborating an operational political scheme. In any event Dunn observes how the likelihood of many opportunities for individuals to offer oaths of allegiance to the prevailing regime provided for possibilities of express consent. These possibilities suggest that tacit consent was designed most likely not to exclude the poor but to apply to resident aliens.[49]

Dunn's response to Macpherson and a Marxist reading of Locke is informed by his theological reading of *The Second Treatise* and his recognition that the relative lack of detail on consent and representation in the text is due to Locke's focus on rebutting Filmer rather than deriving from his support for an emerging bourgeois class. Locke is not to be taken as framing a text that is to promote the operations of capital and to secure an expressly bourgeois form of political rule. Rather, Locke's *Second Treatise* is pitched against a particular argument for absolutism and is animated by theological convictions. This is not to say that Locke, like Hobbes, cannot be read as presenting an ahistorical form of argument, which tacitly assumes and thereby legitimates aspects of developing forms of a money economy and individualist social orientations.[50] An intentionalist reading of a political theorist is not the only interpretive strategy in engaging with a past form of thinking.[51]

A growing interest in colonial and post-colonial aspects of the history of political thought is reflected in recent scholarly interest in recognizing Locke's arguments in *The Second Treatise* and elsewhere as supporting a differential treatment of European settlers and native American Indians and so as promoting the interests of colonization. The Earl of Shaftesbury was an energetic enthusiast for colonization in America and served as one of the Lords Proprietors of the Province of Carolina. Armitage argues plausibly for Locke's involvement in the writing of and revisions to the *Fundamental Constitutions of Carolina*.[52] In this constitutional document slavery is justified, which in supporting a differential treatment of individuals runs counter to the general tenor of Locke's natural rights argument of *The Second Treatise*.[53] Moreover, Arneil urges that references to the lack of cultivation of land on the part of the natives of America is highlighted in *The Second Treatise* and hence can be seen as justifying tacitly the expropriation of land from natives as long as the

---

[49] Ibid., p. 54.

[50] J. Townshend, *C.B. Macpherson and the Problem of Liberal Democracy*, p. 106.

[51] Dunn himself recognizes the potential for non-intentionalist readings of past political theory, including Marxist accounts of the structures of society in which theorizing took place. See J. Dunn, 'The History of Political Theory', in J. Dunn, *The History of Political Theory and Other Essays* (Cambridge, Cambridge University Press, 1996), p. 24.

[52] D. Armitage, 'John Locke, Carolina and the *Two Treatises of Government*', *Political Theory*, vol. 32, no. 5, October 2004, p. 615.

[53] Ibid., p. 632.

expropriated land can be anticipated to be developed more productively.[54] Again, Locke's references to the incapacity for rational thinking on the part of people with mental disabilities are taken by Arneil to signify the limits of Locke's support for rights. She understands Locke to exclude the mentally disabled from the terms of citizenship and from the enjoyment of natural rights.[55] While her arguments on land acquisition and differential citizenship do not show clearly Locke's intentions to operate restrictively in his conception of the application of rights, they certainly establish a case that his arguments align with colonialism and an exclusionary attitude towards disability. Intentionality is not the sole guide to the reading of a text.

CONCLUSION

Locke's political thought has yielded a disputed interpretive legacy. Dunn's *The Political Thought of John Locke* provides an astute reading of Locke, which relates texts to contexts and draws upon Locke's religious convictions to explain the force of his political thinking. To understand what Locke is doing in *The Second Treatise*, Dunn emphasizes Locke's intention of refuting Filmer's *Patriarcha*, so as to undermine contemporary royalist propaganda. To filter Locke's arguments through his engagement with Filmer is to allow for an appreciation of how they work. Locke's deployment of natural law and natural rights disturbs Filmer's identification of political authority with monarchical succession. Moreover, Locke's relative lack of engagement with determining the practicalities of consent and the operation of representative institutions in relation to civil and foreign affairs reflects how his argument concentrates on counterpointing the natural rights of individuals to unlimited political authority. Dunn's focus upon Locke's intentions in responding to countervailing arguments avoids extravagant and unwarranted speculation on what Locke may have meant by scattered references to express consent and Parliamentary representation. Dunn's focused historical interpretation of Locke's *Second Treatise* contrasts with Ashcraft's reading of Locke as a radical. Ashcraft's ascription of radical ideas on democracy to Locke rests upon speculation over indeterminate references by Locke to personal contacts with radicals, rather than drawing upon convincing evidence from Locke's texts or their historical contexts.[56]

[54] See B. Arneil, 'Liberal Colonialism, Domestic Colonies and Citizenship', *History of Political Thought*, vol. 13, no. 3, 2012, p. 496; B. Arneil, 'John Locke and Natural Law and Colonialism', *History of Political Thought*, vol. 13, no. 4, 1992, pp. 587–603.

[55] B. Arneil, 'Liberal Colonialism, Domestic Colonies and Citizenship', *History of Political Thought*, vol. 13, no. 3, 2012, p. 501.

[56] R. Ashcraft, *Revolutionary Politics and Locke's Two Treatises of Government* (Princeton NJ, University of Princeton Press, 1986), pp. 247–8.

Dunn's historical perspective on Locke and on *The Second Treatise* is enlightening and it demonstrates the general value of the Cambridge School in explaining political ideas by adopting an historical approach, which relates ideas to circumstances and the intentions of authors. Recent exploration of Locke's involvement with colonial enterprises and a related review of his references to native American Indians may be seen as continuing the enterprise of relating Locke's thought to his interests and purposes. Dunn's critique of Macpherson serves as a reminder that a particular context of socio-economic development does not in itself explain the specific ideas of a past political thinker. It might be reasonable to suppose that a theorist makes assumptions about contemporary economic conditions, but the specific character and force of her or his ideas is not reducible to generic economic and social conditions. However, to say that relating texts and contexts so that intentions are uncovered can yield understanding of a past thinker's ideas is not to say that past thinkers do not maintain unreflectively standard historic assumptions on the practices of social life. Arneil's attention to Locke's references to the mentally disabled highlights how Locke's theory of rights does not override standard contemporary assumptions concerning disability.

What is assumed by authors can be as significant as what is intended. Critics of Macpherson tend to assume that he was aiming to explain Locke's intentions and although there is an ambiguity over Macpherson's intentions, at least part of his project was to explain what Locke and Hobbes were assuming rather than intending in framing political arguments based on individualist natural rights.[57] Again, the perceptiveness of Dunn's historical study of Locke does not endorse that an historical focus upon contemporary historical contexts and the intentions of past authors captures everything of importance about past political thinkers. While Dunn himself has relaxed his contention that Locke's political thought has no bearing upon our own present-day issues of political theory, he continues to maintain that the theological orientation of his thinking rules out the direct ongoing relevance of his general political argument.[58] Many commentators dissent from this view. Waldron is a notable dissenter. He urges that Locke offers arguments, which contribute notably to ongoing liberal arguments for equality and rights.[59] What is at issue here is the viability of interpreting Locke's political thought at differing levels of abstraction. Dunn follows Locke's political thought closely, attending to the particularities of his argument so as to consider the reasons why he concentrated on specific aspects of a critique of absolutism. He highlights the singularity of Locke's argument in responding to historic arguments and circumstances. Locke maintains a particular adherence to a theology and focuses upon

---

[57] See J. Townshend, *C.B. Macpherson and the Problem of Liberal Democracy*, p. 156.
[58] J. Dunn, *The Political Thought of John Locke*, p. 98.
[59] J. Waldron, *God, Locke and Equality* (Cambridge, Cambridge University Press, 2002).

rebutting contemporary absolutist arguments. Waldron, however, steps back from the specifics of Locke's critique of absolutism to recognize how Locke may be seen to establish features of what subsequently appear as standard aspects of a distinctively liberal form of political argument. On this reading and at a high level of abstraction Locke is taken to frame the conditions of a credible form of political association, which accommodates individual rights, and which allows individuals to participate in the devising and maintenance of a political association that is committed to enabling the rights of individuals. Waldron's way of reading Locke reflects Bevir's identification of how past political theorists can provide enduring ways of conceiving politics.[60]

Dunn may well be right to point to the increasing irrelevance of Dunn's theological grounding of individual rights to later generations of readers. But the particular ways in which rights might be grounded are endlessly controversial and there is no contemporary agreement on specific formulas for justifying rights, whereas the general conception of a society in which individual rights are related to institutional contrivances to maintain and interpret them remains highly germane to the contemporary Western practice of politics. The ongoing relevance of Locke's political thought is registered in Nozick's subsequent employment of the language of rights, his analysis of property, and his critique of rival forms of political theory. Nozick's arguments rehearse Locke's conceptual language and the framework of his political theory, even if Nozick neither endorses nor employs the idiom of Locke's theological interpretation of rights.[61]

---

[60] M. Bevir, 'Are there Perennial Problems in Political Theory?', *Political Studies*, vol. 42, no. 4, 1995, pp. 662–75.

[61] R. Nozick, *Anarchy, State and Utopia* (New York, Basic Books, 1974).

11

Rousseau

Nature and Society

INTRODUCTION

Rousseau is an eighteenth-century theorist, whose successive publications deal in multiple ways with the question of modernity and what distinguishes modern civilization. He recognizes inequality and loss of identity to constitute defining features of the modern world, to which he counterposes an image of the state of nature as a simple and relatively untroubled form of existence. The self-contained life of natural man contrasts with the divided and alienated existence of his modern counterpart. In *The Social Contract* Rousseau offers a solution to the predicament that is posed by the prevailing alienation and inequality. His paradoxical solution is for individuals to subscribe to and participate within a radical popular democracy in which they can enjoy a form of civic, public freedom that resolves the divisiveness and inner discord disfiguring contemporary society.

Rousseau was born in 1712 in Geneva. His mother died shortly after his birth and his father, an eccentric romantic and watchmaker, was exiled from the city when Rousseau was ten years old. Having been apprenticed to an engraver and subjected to harsh discipline, he left Geneva when he was sixteen years old. Yet he remained fascinated by the city and its Calvinist disciplinarian republicanism figures prominently in his political imagination, notwithstanding his own subsequent denunciation by the city. In his imagination, the city represents an exemplary republican form of virtue, which along with the paradigms of Sparta and Rome, provides an exemplary contrast to the dissolute, centrifugal forces of modernity. In part, his *Letter to d'Alembert on the Theatre* and *Letters from the Mountain* (1764) are devoted to extolling the political culture of his native city.[1] On leaving Geneva, he was sent by neighbouring Catholic priests to Madame de Warrens, a Swiss baroness in

---

[1] See R. Wokler, *Rousseau* (Oxford, Oxford University Press, 1995), p. 3.

Annecy, with whom he found refuge. She was instrumental in Rousseau's conversion to Catholicism and guided his cultural development. In his *Confessions* he recounts how she was his lover as well as his patron.[2] Under her tutelage he read widely, if unsystematically, and developed an expertise in music and musicology. He visited Turin and Lyon, where he acted as a tutor in the house of M. de Mably, meeting the philosophers, the Abbe de Condillac and the Abbe de Mably. After moving to Paris in 1842, he befriended leading philosophes of the Enlightenment, including Diderot and d'Alembert, joint editors of the *Encyclopedie*. Rousseau composed entries for the *Encyclopedie* on music and political economy, and was influenced by the Enlightenment, absorbing its commitment to reason. He himself, however, develops a critical political sociology, which represents a Counter-Enlightenment critique of progress and an indictment of its uncritical reliance on reason.[3]

In Paris he met and later married Therese Le Vasseur, with whom he had five children. The children were despatched to a foundling home after their birth.[4] In 1750 Rousseau entered an essay competition of the Academy of Dijon, which posed the question of whether the revival of the arts and sciences had improved people's lives. Rousseau's prize-winning essay, *A Discourse on the Arts and Sciences* is polemical in its critique of cultural development and in its dismissal of the idea of progress. Sophistication, for Rousseau, cannot compensate for a loss of identity and the multiplication of needs that outstrips a capacity to satisfy them. Arts and sciences are embellishments, which obscure rather than enlighten us. They lend themselves to cultural pretension and to the fabrication of sophisticated desires, which supersede our powers to satisfy them.[5] His critique of modernity was a tour de force. It was awarded the prize, launching Rousseau on a path of cultural controversy. Rousseau's essay undertakes a critical sociological analysis of the present that informs his later writings. Progress, for Rousseau, is illusory and raises the question of whether or not the directionality of history can be reversed. For Rousseau regressive cultural development sets individuals at odds with one another and the ensuing alienation undermines social relations and the prospects of human happiness.

In 1755 Rousseau published *A Discourse on the Origin of Inequality*, which probes and challenges the capacity of modern political arrangements to provide an antidote to the alienation and inequality that poison modern society. In 1758 he critiqued Hobbes in the incomplete *L'État de Guerre*

[2] J.-J. Rousseau, *The Confessions* trans. J.M. Cohen (Harmondsworth, Penguin, 1976), pp. 52–129.

[3] For a succinct analysis of the French Enlightenment and Rousseau's attitude to it, see J. Schmidt, 'The Autocritique of Enlightenment: Rousseau and the Philosophes', *Journal of the History of Philosophy*, vol. 34, no. 3, 1996, pp. 465–6.

[4] J.-J. Rousseau, *Confessions*, pp. 326–492.

[5] See J.-J. Rousseau, *A Discourse on the Arts and Sciences*, in J.-J. Rousseau, *The Social Contract and Discourses* trans. G.D.H. Cole (London, J.M. Dent & Sons, 1973), pp. 4–5.

(*The State of War*), and in 1761 he published his popular novel, *Julie ou La Nouvelle Héloïse*. In 1762, his masterpiece, *The Social Contract* was published along with an educational treatise, *Émile*. In these latter texts, Rousseau responds to the social problems that he had diagnosed as afflicting modern society. He imagines new forms of political association and educational practice, which are designed to resolve the problems of modernity. *The Social Contract* sets out a formula by which individuals, taken as they appear in modern society, can achieve freedom. *Émile* frames a child-centred form of education for the eponymous Émile, which imagines how a new kind of person can be produced by a transformed and transformative educative process. Following publication of these books, Rousseau was denounced in both Geneva and France, due to his perceived atheism and in consequence he maintained a nomadic existence until his death in Ermenonville in 1782. In 1772 he published *The Government of Poland*, which proposed a series of constitutional reforms to establish republican civic virtue to secure Poland's independence. *Essay on the Origin of Languages*, which was written during the 1750s and 1760s and his *Confessions* and *Dreams of a Solitary Walker*, on which he was working towards the end of his life, were published posthumously. His *Confessions* is a well-crafted, highly wrought confessional account of his life. His frank yet stylish expression of thoughts and emotions that are concealed conventionally serves as a paradigm for the confessional modernist literature of Proust, Woolf, and Joyce.

The range of Rousseau's thinking bears the imprint of sundry and contrary influences. He is an Enlightenment thinker, whose thinking testifies to Enlightenment values of rationality and clarity, and yet he also disagrees sharply with what are taken to be its defining doctrines of rational and cultural progress. Wokler observes how the age of Enlightenment is a retrospective term that detracts from the openness and uncertainties of the period. The idea of a fixed and determinate Enlightenment project is a very recent invention that exaggerates the stability and unity of Enlightenment culture.[6] Rousseau's ideas are both related to yet distinct from those of contemporary figures such as Diderot. Like Diderot his egalitarian analyses of politics and society are undertaken in a critical rational spirit but at the same time they are suspicious of the claims and applications of reason. His intellectual identity is multi-faceted. Wokler observes how Rousseau's critical ambivalence anticipates Hegel's Counter-Enlightenment critique of reason's abstractions, or, alternatively, prefigures the post-modern critique of the Enlightenment project.[7]

---

[6] R. Wokler, 'Ancient Postmodernism in the Philosophy of Rousseau', in P. Riley (ed), *The Cambridge Companion to Rousseau* (Cambridge, Cambridge University Press, 2000), p. 419.
[7] See R. Wokler, 'Ancient Postmodernism in the Philosophy of Rousseau', and R. Wokler, 'Contextualizing Hegel's Phenomenology of the French Revolution and the Terror', *Political Theory*, vol. 4, 1998, p. 38.

Rousseau draws on aspects of modern political theory, but rejects many of its defining doctrines. While he assimilates the republicanism of Machiavelli, he reacts against the individualism of Hobbes and Locke. Rousseau's capacity to absorb multiple yet contrary influences is exhibited in his combination of opposing Augustinian and Stoic forms of thought. Brooke identifies how Rousseau adapts a natural rights discourse, which is drawn from the Stoic tradition, in establishing a critique of civil society that involves an Augustinian recognition of the necessary perversity of human willing in the context of the distortive effects of socialization.[8]

A DISCOURSE ON THE ORIGIN OF INEQUALITY AND THE SOCIAL CONTRACT

In *A Discourse on the Origin of Inequality* Rousseau suggestively imagines a history of civil society as a story of human sickness. A state of nature is contrasted with the distorted condition of contemporary, civilized mankind. In the state of nature human beings are stripped of the artifices and conventions that embellish but constrict society. Men and women are simple and free creatures at ease with themselves. Rousseau maintains that the natural condition is uncomplicated yet happy in that individuals have relatively straightforward and self-contained needs. These needs can be satisfied easily. Natural human beings may be self-centred, but their self-love (*amour-de-soi*) is neither contaminated by oppressive comparative engagement with others nor undermined by an overreaching desire for what cannot be attained. Natural individuals are not enmeshed in social relations that inculcate insatiable desires, and the self itself sets the limits on what is to be done. Desires do not outstrip the resources to satisfy them. Individuals establish contacts with one another informally, combining occasionally for pleasure and company, but fundamentally the social world is not a beckoning horizon, which entices individuals to venture beyond satisfying their own limited desires. While there are neither enduring ties of affection nor of hostility between individuals, if an individual encounters another in distress, natural pity supervenes so that assistance is given to the distressed individual. Yet Rousseau imagines that this relatively benign condition is unsustainable. Technological development provides a momentum for change. In particular the development of metallurgy and the application of agricultural techniques to the land, disturb

---

[8] See C. Brooke, 'Rousseau's Political Philosophy: Stoic and Augustinian Origins,' in P. Riley (ed), *The Cambridge Companion to Rousseau*, p. 94.

prevailing natural conditions of stability.[9] The dynamic of social change ensures that social distinctions of status and class become progressively pronounced. Benign self-love is transformed into the socially inflected and afflicted *amour propre*, a form of vanity in which individuals forego a sense of their own self-constituted identity and determine their status by comparing themselves with others. The movement away from a natural condition towards a more civilized state issues in a settled social life that is organized around the family. Inequality becomes progressively more pronounced in identifying and circumscribing individuals, who in comparing themselves with one another experience the alienation of divided identities.

A *Discourse on the Origin of Inequality* takes history to be the story of corruption. The onset of a settled social life entails that a healthy innocence gives way to a corrupt sophistication. A person's sense of self fragments as unattainable wants multiply in the context of an intensifying social condition in which happiness and self-regard are measured comparatively. Rousseau observes, 'It now became the interest of men to appear what they were not.'[10]At the centre of Rousseau's contrast between modernity and an imagined state of nature is his critique of the growth of inequality. The transformation of a rough and rude equality into a state of social inequality spells the ruin and fragmentation of mankind. <u>An individual becomes alien</u> to himself. Inequality fragments society from top to bottom, decentring individuals as well as constituting injustice in that there is an unjustifiable between those who lack resources and those who have acquired a countervailing surplus. Rousseau remarks, '[T]he destruction of equality was attended by the most terrible disorders. Usurpations by the rich, robbery by the poor, and the unbridled passions of both suppressed the cries of natural compassion and the still feeble voice of justice, and filled men with avarice, ambition and vice.'[11]

The sharp focus upon inequality and social divisions in A *Discourse on the Origin of Inequality* resonates with Marxist thought; notwithstanding that Marx himself did not show a great regard for Rousseau's thought. In *Karl Marx* Plamenatz observes how Marx's remarks on Rousseau are 'unflattering and unperceptive'.[12] Yet he goes on to argue a convincing case for identifying Rousseau as a precursor to Marx. Rousseau's diagnosis of the alienation that is constituted by the divided self of modern society, which is shaped by social forces that it cannot control, anticipates Marx's sense of the alienation of proletarian labour from its own products under a capitalist mode of production.[13] Moreover, the Marxist theorist Colletti sees Rousseau as exploring the

---

[9] J.-J. Rousseau, *A Discourse on the Origin of Inequality*, in J.-J. Rousseau, *The Social Contract and Discourses* trans. G.D.H. Cole (London, J. Dent & Sons, 1975), p. 83.

[10] Ibid., p. 86.

[11] Ibid., p. 87.

[12] J. Plamenatz, *Karl Marx's Philosophy of Man* (Oxford, Clarendon Press, 1975), p. 60.

[13] Ibid., 65.

conditions of a post-representative and post-bourgeois democratic society.[14] The modern world for Rousseau and Marx is limiting and the limits arise out of the very processes that appear to enhance possibilities. Rousseau focuses upon the intensifying demands of burgeoning recognitive social interaction, which are insatiable and destabilize personal identity and relations between individuals.[15] A glance at the contemporary Western social scene underlines the continuing relevance of Rousseau. In the UK parents compete to obtain either selective schooling or prestigious state schools for their children, and house prices reflect the designation of their locales as socially desirable or undesirable. The fashion industry creates labels of credibility, so that individual 'choices' are overdetermined by social factors beyond an individual's control.

Given the sharpness of Rousseau's critique of modern society it would seem that the prospects of renewal would be slim, but in 1762 Rousseau offered two ways of advancing matters. *Émile* and *The Social Contract* were both published in 1762 and can be seen as responses to the predicament posed by *A Discourse on the Origin of Inequality*. *Émile* takes for granted the existing political situation and outlines a form of education enabling its eponymous hero to live well. It sets out a child-centred education, whereby the reason of Émile, the pupil, is progressively enhanced by contriving situations for Émile to deploy it in tackling problems. At the same time the child is sheltered from the dangers of exposure to received and misleading ideas. He is educated so as to think for himself. Nonetheless, his socialization and learning are structured carefully by his educator in ways that have been diagnosed to be sinister and authoritarian.[16] Rousseau prescribes a radically different form of education for women. It is designed to refine their distinctive sensibility so as to prepare them for domestic tasks and child rearing. Feminists past and present have objected. Rousseau's imposition of sexually segregated education serves to highlight how his child-centred education reflects the controlling influence of the educator, who sets its goals and procedures.[17] The extent of the educator's control over Émile's development is evidenced in his careful framing of the love Émile is allowed to feel for his projected partner, Sophie. This disguised authoritarianism is an issue for all forms of child-centred

---

[14] L. Colletti, *From Rousseau to Lenin—Studies in Ideology and Society* trans J. White and P. Merrington (Los Angeles, California, Monthly Review Press, 1975).

[15] Berki, in his *History of Political Theory*, categorizes Rousseau as a thinker who adopts an expressly social rather than individualist frame for evaluating modern society: R. Berki, *History of Political Theory* (London, R.M. Dent, 1976), p. 114.

[16] See J. Charvet, *The Social Problem in the Philosophy of Rousseau* (London and New York, Cambridge University Press, 1974).

[17] See M. Wollstonecraft, *A Vindication of the Rights of Woman* (Harmondsworth, Penguin, 1982).

education, which structure styles of learning that are designed ostensibly to be libertarian.[18]

The Social Contract, Rousseau's major text of political theory, takes men as they are, and frames the logic of a form of political association which would enable men to be free and to resolve the problems that had been diagnosed in *A Discourse on the Origin of Inequality.* Its opening words are justly famous and establish the agenda for what follows, 'Man is born free and everywhere he is in chains.'[19] Rousseau imagines how a legitimate form of government can be established under present conditions, where a state of nature has given way to a form of society, in which an individual's freedom is constrained by intensive social interaction. Instead of reacting against the prospect of political association, Rousseau opts for a homeopathic remedy for its problems. *The Social Contract* sets out the terms of a legitimate and free form of political association, which establish the conditions of radical popular sovereignty. The natural independence of humanity in the state of nature is exchanged for the public freedom of citizenship. Rousseau envisages that individuals will grant public authority to the laws of the state in entering upon membership of a legitimate political community. Sovereignty is absolute, for Rousseau, because freedom is bound up with the public determination of the common good. He envisages that all men will participate in the ongoing process of determining public collective decisions for the common good. Women are assigned a private caring role, but their activity is seen as supportive of men's public engagement. The public world of the political association achieves moral freedom. In obeying laws men are held to achieve the freedom of adhering to the collective laws of rational public freedom. The people frame and adhere to the general will, rather than following their particular wills. The general will is distinguished from the will of all, which is the aggregated selfish wills of individuals rather than the rational disinterested common good. Rousseau remarks, 'There is often a great deal of difference between the will of all and the general will; the latter considers only the common interest, while the former takes private interest into account, and so is no more than the sum of particular wills ...'.[20]

The social contract represents a transformative social and political remedy for the problems of modern society. Individuals assume a public social identity rather than a divisive individualistic one, in which their desires are entangled by comparison with others. Men abandon their distortive form of self-love by participating in the collective achievement of a shared social freedom of a

---

[18] See J.-J. Rousseau, *Émile* trans. A. Bloom (New York, Basic Books, 1979).
[19] J.-J. Rousseau, *The Social Contract* trans. G.D.H. Cole, in J.-J. Rousseau, *The Social Contract and Discourses,* p. 165.
[20] J.-J. Rousseau, *The Social Contract,* p. 185.

shared morality, which is enacted in democratically determined laws. These laws are administered by an executive, which is not necessarily democratic, because its role is clearly separated from that of the law-making sovereign legislature. Rousseau refers to government in the following terms, 'An inter-mediate body set up between the subjects and the Sovereign, to secure their mutual correspondence, charged with the execution of the laws and the maintenance of liberty, both civil and political.'[21]

The role of government, the executive, is to execute the laws, which are determined by the legislature, and government has to respect the law. Rous-seau imagines the operation of the institutions of the state to be hugely significant in rectifying the problems of modern society. In its arduous task of framing laws advancing the common good, the work of the legislature is aided by the Educator, a person who possesses legal expertise and understand-ing of the nature of human beings. The legislature, on the advice of the Educator, will use education and civil religion to promote popular republican patriotic sentiments. These sentiments will direct opinion towards supporting the common good of the community. Rousseau maintains that a civil religion 'is good in that it unites the divine cult with the love of the laws, and, making country the object of the citizens' adoration, teaches them that service done to the State is service done to its tutelary god.'[22] The significance of civic patriotism is evidenced in his political texts, *The Government of Poland* and *Constitutional Project for Corsica*.[23] Rousseau's political recommendations include a stipulation that individuals should not belong to groups or associ-ations other than the state because of the divisiveness that these groups will foster. If associational groups are to persist, however, then they are to be as numerous as possible to dissipate the possibility of their concentration of sinister particular interests. Likewise, to advance its prospects of success, Rousseau imagines that his ideal state would be small, and composed of artisans and smallholders. The population is to be roughly equal so that individuals do not hold a concentration of wealth that enables them to exploit others. Given the record of discord and selfishness that has been generated by unequal conditions, Rousseau assigns significance to the maintenance of equality.[24] Overall Rousseau calls for a profound change in popular attitudes, whereby selfish, particular interests are to be sacrificed in favour of social solidarity. All will identify with the general will, and by so doing will achieve a public freedom.

---

[21] Ibid., pp. 208–9.   [22] Ibid., p. 272.
[23] See J.-J. Rousseau, *The Government of Poland* trans. W. Kendall (Indianapolis, Hackett, 1985); J.-J. Rousseau, *Constitutional Project for Corsica* trans. F. Watkins, in J.-J. Rousseau, *Political Writings* (Edinburgh, Thomas Nelson, 1953).
[24] J.-J. Rousseau, *The Social Contract*, p. 203.

INTERPRETATION AND THE PARADOXES
OF ROUSSEAU'S THOUGHT

Rousseau's political thought exhibits a number of paradoxes, which have elicited sharp critiques of his thinking. A major source of his paradoxical thinking arises out of his uncompromising radicalism in prescribing wholesale social change to counter the failings of modern civilized society. He sets out to overturn what he takes to be unacceptable social inequalities. Civilized, unequal individuals in modern society are wretched. They are divided against one another and within themselves. To counteract the fragmentation, Rousseau imagines dramatic change. His projection of a society of equality and public freedom has captured the imagination of subsequent radical theorists and activists. However, the scale of the proposed changes, when juxtaposed to prevailing conditions that entrench inequalities, exerts strains upon Rousseau's projected radical reform. How is political progress possible when conditions for the achievement of freedom and equality are conspicuously absent? Given that Rousseau's ideal state is projected to operate in ways that are radically at odds with standard procedures of a prevailing individualistic modern society, a number of its features appear paradoxical. For instance, central to Rousseau's image of a legitimate polity is the paradox that individuals will be forced to be free if they dissent from following the general will.[25] This paradox is focused upon by many of Rousseau's most trenchant critics. Commentators, who have critiqued Rousseau on this score, include Talmon and Berlin. Talmon's *The Origins of Totalitarian Democracy* indicts Rousseau as a totalitarian theorist, who anticipates the totalitarianism of Robespierre, Hitler, and Stalin. Rousseau is prepared to coerce individuals in the name of social justice or public freedom.[26] Berlin's interpretation of Rousseau emerges from his dichotomous analysis of the notion of liberty, by which he divides it into two distinct concepts, namely negative and positive liberty. While negative liberty is commonsensical in taking individuals in being free to act as they see fit, insofar as they are not prevented from doing so by constraints that are imposed on their conduct, positive liberty lends itself to political tyranny in imagining that individuals are to follow either prescribed courses of action or to develop in specific ways in order to be or to become free.[27] Rousseau is interpreted as holding the positive and problematic concept of positive liberty in maintaining the paradox that individuals are to

---

[25] Ibid., pp. 188–9.

[26] J. Talmon, *Rousseau and the Origins of Totalitarian Democracy* (London, Secker and Warburg, 1960).

[27] I. Berlin, 'Two Concepts of Liberty', in I. Berlin, *Four Essays on Liberty* (Oxford, Oxford University Press, 1969), pp. 118–73.

be forced to be free by being coerced into doing what is in the public good.[28] Berlin's focus upon Rousseau's willingness to use coercion to achieve freedom highlights the questionable character of Rousseau's political theory. Yet it is worth observing that Rousseau himself is aware of its paradoxical character. It arises from Rousseau's determination to deliver radical change, whereby individuals will no longer pursue their own welfare without regard for the general good. His social and political theory is predicated upon his sense that the common good cannot be reduced to the welfare of particular individuals. Hence Rousseau recognizes the split between public and private welfare, and if the public is to take precedence then the individual must respect the coercive force of law. Individuals are to identify with the public interest rather than continue to be divided by discordant private interests. His concern to guard against the intrusion of illegitimate private interests is reflected in the care he takes to eliminate the influence of particular interests upon the operations of state institutions. Wokler observes how Rousseau's specification of a division of powers between the executive and the legislature is expressly designed to avoid the law being used for particular purposes and to guard against the accretion of power in a particular office.[29]

Rousseau's thought is paradoxical precisely because he is a radical who is committed to radical change, which goes against the grain of standard assumptions and hence appears to be odd or contradictory. In imagining a radically different kind of society from that of the emerging modern liberal society, Rousseau anticipates subsequent thinkers and political actors who have broken from liberal norms. To align Rousseau with subsequent totalitarian forms of theory and practice, however, is questionable, because it assimilates Rousseau to succeeding standpoints that he could not have anticipated. To imagine Rousseau as a totalitarian is to relate Rousseau to contexts that postdate his reflections, and to reflect the assumptions of succeeding historians. Totalitarian states of the twentieth century were large-scale states that mobilized technology to secure their aims, while Rousseau imagined a small state that would be composed of independent farmers and artisans.[30]

DERRIDA, ROUSSEAU, AND DECONSTRUCTION

Rousseau is a paradoxical theorist and Derrida's reading of Rousseau examines Rousseau's paradoxical conceptions of language, politics, society, and the self.

---

[28] Ibid., p. 148.
[29] R. Wokler, 'Ancient Postmodernism in the Philosophy of Rousseau', p. 426.
[30] Note how Skinner is critical of Popper's reading of Plato in Q. Skinner, 'Meaning and Understanding in the History of Ideas', in J. Tully (ed.), *Meaning and Context: Quentin Skinner and His Critics* (Cambridge, Polity Press, 1988), p. 44.

Derrida imagines these paradoxes as intimating tensions within Rousseau's thought, which reflect his imposition of a rigid meaning upon terms that are insusceptible of such restriction. In *Of Grammatology* he perceives Rousseau's opposition of speech to writing to be symptomatic of his maintenance of a series of dichotomous oppositions. These oppositions underpin his critique of modernity and his remedial social and political prescriptions. Derrida observes, '*The Essay on the Origin of Languages* opposes speech to writing, presence to absence and liberty to servitude.'[31] In reviewing the tensions within his framing of writing as a corruption of speech, Derrida registers Rousseau's practical resort to the supplementary subtleties and intricacies of writing to convey his own innermost self along with the corruptions he associates with writing. He deconstructs Rousseau's natural man, which he identifies as a projection of and from civilized society, just as primitive speech coalesces with the written word. *Of Grammatology* concentrates on deconstructing Rousseau's *Essay on the Origin of Languages*, showing how its valorization of speech over writing and of the expressive South over the North is undermined by the articulation that is presumed in the operations of language, and by the series of accidents, which explain the increasing linguistic sophistication and articulation against which Rousseau fulminates.

Rousseau maintains that speech supersedes writing because it represents the pure expressive cry of primitive passion, and yet Derrida shows how expression is never pure as it requires mediation between sounds. Rousseau celebrates expressive pure cries of passion and deprecates the derivative and secondary expressions of need. Yet Rousseau himself mixes passion and need in remarks on love, which designate love as at the same time a need and a passion. Rousseau imagines language emerging in the passion of the South, and its decline is traced to the articulations of need in the North, but Derrida highlights the artificiality of the very distinction between North and South, as well as the mutual implication of need, passion, identity, and mediation. North is unimaginable without its contrary, the South. In music Rousseau privileges the simplicity of melody against the artificiality of harmony, but Derrida observes how melody, like harmony, operates as a form of imitation so that the distinction between the two is compromised. The supplementarity of harmony becomes indispensable for musical expression.

The upshot of Derrida's review of Rousseau's *Essay on the Origin of Languages* is that its series of oppositions dissolve under deconstructive examination. What ensues, amidst its resort to supplements and accidents, which subverts its argument, is a sense of language as a series of articulations, a mediating multiplicity of forms and styles without a founding or primitive truth. Writing, and its endless articulation, is what underlies the modalities

[31] J. Derrida, *Of Grammatology* trans. G. Spivak (Baltimore MD and London, Johns Hopkins University Press, 1976), p. 210.

and multiplicities of meaning. Rousseau's utopian primitivism is not to be divorced from the civilization that it is designed to denounce as a declination from its purity. It is a retrojection from the civilized present that is imagined by the very devices that it condemns.

Of Grammatology takes Rousseau's entire conceptual world as deriving from his critique of the present and his suspicion of the articulation of writing. The problematic nature of Rousseau's enterprise is evidenced by his resort to supplements that frame oppositions that cannot be sustained. Lines are drawn between the primitive and the sophisticated, between the past and the present, and between nature and society, but they represent projections from the present social world. The problems besetting Rousseau's metaphysical reduction of truth to the self-proclaimed truths reverberating within an inner sensibility are multiple and undermine his series of binary oppositions. Rousseau's very act of providing sophisticated textual commentary on the present via an imagined primitive past registers an uneasy and unsettling compromise with the art of writing. It is of a piece with the problematic supplementarity of his confessional writing, which serves as a means of expressing the inner truths of self-consciousness.[32]

Derrida's deconstruction of Rousseau's theory of language has implications for his political theory. Language and society do not lend themselves to the disruptive and utopian interventions which are engineered by Rousseau. Just as there is no outside to the ramifications of language, so there is no originary time beyond the temporal developments of social life. Natural man, like the revelatory presence of speech, is chimerical, because there is no independent bird's eye view of the social, complex, discursive world within which Rousseau is situated. Critique cannot operate outside the structures within which it emerges. There is no meaning beyond what is expressed in a multiplicity of discursive signs. Rousseau's artful separation of the natural from the social is designed to underscore the unacceptability of the present and to highlight its deformed character but the very sharpness of the separation undermines its value as critique. The assumption of an external and universal perspective on society is a piece of self-deception. Derrida identifies a reverse teleology in Rousseau's critique, whereby the present is related to a prelapsarian past.[33] Just as Levi-Strauss is indicted by Derrida, for imagining perversely a world without inequality, writing, and violence, so Rousseau is held to mythologize the natural so as to misidentify what he critiques in the present.[34] Derrida takes Rousseau's purported occupation of a metaphysical standpoint outside the flow of discourse to undermine his social and political critique of modern society. He observes how Rousseau's critique of inequality and alienation within modernity depends upon its identification of a mythical naturalism

---

[32] Ibid., p. 195.   [33] Ibid., p. 258.   [34] Ibid., p. 260.

outside of society that explains the shortcomings of contemporary culture and society. This mythological state of nature is held to be innocent of the corruption enveloping society, just as speech is speechless in regard to the onset of writing. In reviewing Rousseau's *Discourse on the Origin of Inequality*, Derrida comments, 'What we have called external teleology allows the stabilization of a sort of discourse on method: the question of origin involves neither event nor structure. The passage from one structure to the other—from the state of nature to the state of society for example—cannot be explained by any structural analysis: an external, irrational, catastrophic factum must burst in. Chance is not part of the system. And when history is incapable of determining this fact or facts of this order, philosophy must, by a sort of free and mythic invention, produce fatal hypotheses playing the same role, explaining the coming into being of a new structure.'[35]

Derrida's deconstruction of Rousseau's naturalistic reduction of society and modernity to a mythological point of origin is conducted in many idioms. Central to the deconstruction is his careful attention to the argument on language. In his analysis of *Essay on the Origin of Languages* Derrida shows how language is not to be subsumed under the rubric of Rousseau's restrictive scheme. At all stages of development it is complex and exhibits the articulations of writing. It is not to be reduced to originary and isolated cries of passion.[36] Writing, or the interplay of signs and the inter-mediation of expressions, constitute all forms of language. Likewise, Rousseau's two great projects for social and political reform, *Émile* and *The Social Contract*, profess to deliver what cannot be realized. Modern reflection on education and political association cannot dispense with the complications and adornments of modernity. Derrida questions *Émile*. If nature is the normative paradigm that is to be followed, and culture and society are to be abrogated, why is education necessary at all? Education is a supplement to nature. If nature were adequate in itself, there would be no recourse to an elaborated scheme of education. Supplements, such as writing and education, which feature in Rousseau's philosophical inventory of resources to resolve present predicaments, supersede the limits that are set by nature, and hence complicate Rousseau's adherence to the natural over the cultural. Émile's education is an example of Rousseau's problematic reliance upon a supplement. The prescribed educational scheme serves as a substitute for a mother, but its supplementary status is undertheorized. Supplements require explanation rather than provide solutions to the problems of modernity. Derrida notes, 'Here [in *Émile*] the problems of natural right, of the relationship between Nature and Society, the concepts of alienation, alterity, and corruption, are adapted most spontaneously to the pedagogic problem of the substitution of

---

[35] Ibid., p. 258.   [36] Ibid., p. 260.

mothers and children.'[37] Émile's education is to be controlled by an Educator, who directs his development so that its consonance with nature is secondary to the elaboration of the scheme. The complications of delivering expertise in science, a practical mastery of moral concepts, and an equilibrated emotional life, leave the supposed simplicities of nature far behind.

Just as the educational scheme in *Émile* is a problematic departure from nature rather than an exercise in its retrieval, so the elaborated political scheme of *The Social Contract* represents a sophisticated supplementary substitute for the supposed simplicity of nature and for the mythical independence of natural man. Rousseau's imagining of a small-scale community of artisans and individual farmers combining collectively to decide on the common good is powerful, but it represents Rousseau's reflective construction of a presumed harmonious society that is neither natural nor entirely removed from the divided and complex articulated society in which Rousseau is situated. It is a projection from the present. The upshot is a mismatch between the projected ideal society and its derivation from an imagined state of nature. There is an unrealizable distance between Rousseau's ideal community and the reality of contemporary society. These problems are not resolved by the series of dichotomies, which are constructed to highlight the elements of the social world, which require to be kept apart so as to fabricate a social purity that imitates imaginary innocence.

The dichotomies between the individual and the general will, between the inside and the outside of the ideal community, and between the imagination of the author and the developing individualism of modern society are constructions that Derrida deconstructs by showing their mutual dependence. Derrida identifies features of the argument of *The Social Contract*, which show the strains to which Rousseau's remedy for alienated modern society is subject. He observes how Rousseau's distrust of any form of political representation in his ideal community imposes an intolerable strain upon its projected operations. Just as the written word, for Rousseau, represents and so distorts reality unlike the directness of speech, so political decision-making and the exercise of sovereignty must be direct and enacted in speech. The law is only valid insofar as the people, or at least adult men collect together and decide on things directly without recourse to intermediary parties or political representatives. The pressure to avoid mediation is pressed to the extent that Rousseau refuses any reliance on a marker or recognition of decision-making. Derrida observes, 'The instance of writing must be effaced to the point where a sovereign people *must not even write to itself*, its assemblies must meet spontaneously, without "any formal summons". Which implies—and that is a writing that Rousseau does not wish to read—that there were "fixed and periodic" assemblies that

---

[37] Ibid., p. 146.

"cannot be abrogated or prorogued," and therefore a "marked day (jour marque)." That mark had to be made orally since the moment the possibility of writing was introduced into operation, it would insinuate usurpation into the body of society. But is not a mark, wherever it is introduced, the possibility of writing?' (emphasis in original).[38]

CONCLUSION

Rousseau was and remains a controversial figure. A representative figure of Enlightenment reason and a trenchant critic of modernity, he made enemies on the right and left. He was persecuted for atheism and shunned by the polite society. The suspicion in which he was held both reflected and aggravated the paranoia to which he was prone and which ruined relations between himself and David Hume.[39] Rousseau's fate at the hands of succeeding commentators has been equally perverse. Interpretations of Rousseau are multiple, but his work has frequently been subjected to sharp critique. Succeeding critiques often derive from theorists with a point to prove, who are not unduly troubled to specify either Rousseau's arguments or his context.

Reading the past from the perspective of the present is in some sense unavoidable given that historians are situated in the present, but this perspectival situation does not provide a licence for merely retrojecting ideas onto past thinkers.

Hegel is critical of Rousseau for identifying the general will with the aggregation of particular wills. Yet Wokler observes that the formulation of the general will is designed precisely to ensure that its operation cannot be assimilated to the logic of aggregating particular interests. Rousseau, in fact, resembles Hegel in critiquing Enlightenment reason.[40] Again, Hegel's identification of Rousseau's political thought with the fury of abstract reason that was unleashed in the French Revolution is at odds with Rousseau's careful demarcation of the work of the legislature from that of the executive and his distinguishing the process of framing general laws from that of executing particular legal decisions.[41] Likewise Marx is misleading in imagining Rousseau as accommodating to prevailing economic conditions by safeguarding the interests of small-scale property owners. Rousseau is a fierce critic of inequality,

[38] Ibid., p. 302.
[39] For an account of the complex relations between Hume and Rousseau, see R. Zaretsky and J. Scott, *The Philosopher's Quarrel: Rousseau, Hume and the Limits of Understanding* (New Haven, Yale University Press, 2009).
[40] See R. Wokler, 'Ancient Postmodernism in the Philosophy of Rousseau', p. 424.
[41] G.W.F. Hegel, *The Phenomenology of Mind* trans. J. Baillee (Oxford, Oxford University Press, 1970), pp. 599–610.

recognizing its psychological as well as material impact. He begins his manuscript, *State of War* by declaring an impassioned critique of inequality. He remarks, 'I open the books on Right and on ethics; I listen to the professors and jurists; and, my mind full of their seductive doctrines, I admire the peace and justice established by the civil order; I bless the wisdom of our political institutions and, knowing myself a citizen, cease to lament I am a man. Thoroughly instructed as to my duties and my happiness, I close the book, step out of the lecture room, and look around me. I see wretched nations groaning beneath a yoke of iron. I see mankind ground down by a handful of oppressors. I see a famished mob, worn down by sufferings and famine, while the rich drink the blood and tears of their victims at their ease. I see on every side the strong armed with the terrible powers of the Law against the weak.'[42]

The twentieth-century critics, Talmon, Cobban, and Berlin understand Rousseau's political theory to be highly authoritarian or totalitarian, which reflects their own preoccupation with the subsequent course of European political history rather more than their engagement with Rousseau's ideas. Rousseau constructs a utopian political community, which is at odds with contemporary norms, but he frames his political theory to accommodate difference as well as unity. His political theory does not specify individual rights, due to his commitment to popular sovereignty, but he imagines that the general will, if it is to achieve the common good, must take account of the interests of all.[43] Individuals are entitled to protection, but for Rousseau, there is no simple way of drawing lines to designate generically how individual and general interests are to be determined and protected.

Derrida's critique of Rousseau draws strength from its focused, careful reading of his texts. The contradictions to which Derrida draws attention are elicited from Rousseau's texts. While Rousseau's interpretation of modernity alerts readers to the unintended consequences of social engagement and misrecognition, Derrida attends to the problems that are associated with Rousseau's dichotomous opposition of the state of nature to civilization and modernity. Rousseau re-invokes face to face social and political relations that are derived from an image of an idealized primitive society. This image, however, is a fantasy that is retrojected from the present rather than constituting an anthropological truth, and as Carver observes, it is a particular male fantasy.[44] Deconstruction shows what is occluded in this discourse. Rousseau's political thought maintains many paradoxes but its underlying paradox derives from its apparent recourse to nature to critique civilized society.

---

[42] J.-J. Rousseau, *State of War*, in J-J. Rousseau, *Political Writings* trans. and ed. C.E. Vaughn (Cambridge, Cambridge University Press, 1915), p. 264.

[43] J.-J. Rousseau, *The Social Contract*, p. 60.

[44] T. Carver, *Men in Political Theory* (Manchester, Manchester University Press, 2009), pp. 177–205.

However, nature is only to be imagined and analysed by the very devices of the civilized world that are to be rejected. Rousseau is an elegant writer, whose artistry is shown by his eloquent testimony against the very devices at which he excels. Derrida's deconstructive method brings out the force of the divide between the author, his projections, and his idea of critique. A review of Rousseau's political thought which concentrated upon his intentions, and took him at his word in critiquing modernity, would be complicit in his misleading projection of nature as a distinct from of life from civilized society.

Yet Derrida's deconstruction does not dispose of Rousseau. The strain involved in Rousseau's invoking of a state of nature is mitigated if it is construed as hypothetical, and this might have been Rousseau's intention. At times his *A Discourse on the Origin of Inequality* appears to represent a hypothetical analysis of the state of nature, and at others as developing an historical account.[45] Simpson, in a balanced review, concludes, 'In general, the "hypothetical" interpretation is preferable to the "historical". It can account for more of the text because Rousseau himself often said that his work was hypothetical not historical.'[46] While Rousseau's naturalistic reading of contemporary society remains problematic whatever its construal, it nevertheless exposes issues facing contemporary society. The force of Rousseau's political thought lies in his recognition of how humanity is limited by its own powers of creativity, notably by the consequences of its transformation of the planet and of its intensification of modes of social interaction. Digital forms of communication now threaten to be used to control individuals and to be instruments in undermining individuality. The very agency of human beings can be costly as well as liberating, and Rousseau's confessional, introspective techniques capture this cost. Marx's affiliated critique of capital captures how capital is a Frankenstein figure that warps its creator, so that the energy of social creation assumes a demonic force that directs rather than responds to human beings. Rousseau is on to something in highlighting how social inequality becomes a central and distortive aspect of the human condition. Rawls might perceive social resentment of inequality as lacking normative force, but the modern world is one in which commodified desires are experienced in a common social setting. Rousseau is right to recognize the subversive role of inequality in distorting the self-images of individuals, who misrecognize themselves and their identities under its sway.[47]

Writers and critics clamour for recognition, just as parents compete in promoting the interests of their children. Recognitive goods depend on

---

[45] See J.-J. Rousseau, *A Discourse on The Origin of Inequality*, pp. 125, 128, 132.

[46] M. Simpson, *Rousseau—A Guide for the Perplexed* (London and New York, Continuum, 2007).

[47] In contrast to Rousseau, Rawls does not recognize material inequality as constituting a moral problem as envy is not to be respected as providing a moral motive for action. See J. Rawls, *A Theory of Justice* (Cambridge Mass., Harvard university Press, 1971).

some faring worse than others. The persistence and growth of inequality in a mediatized society where rich and poor share desires but experience unequal outcomes, establish the contours of individual and social identities.[48] Rousseau recognizes how the satisfaction of human wants cannot be determined individually, because individual wants and desires are created by social circumstances. Rousseau's mythological resort to nature serves a purpose in highlighting the hyper-sociality of modernity and its discourse. No doubt Rousseau's ideal society appears to be misaligned in its denial of the excesses of modernity and in its emulation of an unattainable primitivism. For instance, it insists on limiting its size and on disbarring mediated, representational forms of politics without regard to the feasibility and functionality of its arrangements. Yet it is by no means clear that Rousseau intended *The Social Contract* to serve as a practical political paradigm, just as it is unclear if he envisaged the general will to be operational. For instance, Shklar's *Men and Citizens* suggests that *The Social Contract* might not have been envisaged as a blueprint for practice.[49]

Rousseau's political thought is ambiguous and problematic, but it casts light on the troubled politics of modernity. Strong picks out two themes in Rousseau's thought that remain of relevance that are connected to his disturbing and paradoxical radicalism. He observes, 'Rousseau's work pursues two ends. The first is to make available to his readers what a human home would be. The second is to awaken in them the recognition that they are in fact, and all appearances to the contrary, homeless.'[50] Likewise, Honig draws upon Rousseau to highlight continuing issues facing radical forms of politics. Rousseau's distrust of representational democracy is echoed in the radical populism of Hardt and Negri.[51] If the disrepute of Rousseau's political thought might be receding in the light of the demise of Stalinism and Nazism, the vexations of modern society and politics remain. While Rousseau did not anticipate the intensification of a mediatized society, just as he did not envisage twentieth-century totalitarian movements, his thought remains of significance. The horizon of today can be related to Rousseau's in that he reckoned with the consequences of modern notions of identity, which emerge out of self-constitution and forms of social (mis)recognition.

Honig identifies the radical contrast between the projected egalitarian republican freedom of Rousseau's social theory, and his recognition of the

---

[48] On the persistence and growth of inequality, see T. Picketty, *Capital in the Twenty-First Century* (Cambridge Mass., Harvard University Press, 2014), pp. 237–471.

[49] J. Shklar, *Men and Citizens—A Study of Rousseau's Social Theory* (Cambridge, Cambridge University Press, 1969).

[50] T. Strong, *Jean-Jacques Rousseau—The Politics of the Ordinary* (London and Thousand Oaks, California, Sage Publications, 1994), p. 152.

[51] See M. Hardt and A. Negri, *Multitude—War and Democracy in the Age of Empire* (London, Penguin Books, 2005).

deep-seated divisiveness and inequality of the present as exhibiting the para-dox of politics.[52] Honig imagines Rousseau to be exemplary in recognizing the paradox, taking his recognition to inform his elaboration of the difficulties in advancing matters and his account of the multiplicity of steps to be taken.[53] This paradox of politics is not to be wished away; radical politics requires its confrontation.

Moreover Rousseau's paradoxical account of freedom reflects his stretching of the concept to recognize the sociality of modern individuals. He rejects a view of freedom that takes it to be a non-relational property that can be assigned to individuals. If individuals are to be understood as relational, and to be socially and politically motivated to work for a common good, then, of course, the concept of liberty will be different from standard liberal assump-tions. Rousseau urges that individuals and society are reciprocally related to one another, hence it is appropriate for individuals to see themselves as public citizens as well as private individuals. Underlying the various paradoxes which inform Rousseau's thought, is the paradox of his oppositional categories of nature and civilization. He employs the categories ambiguously to highlight the loss and distortion that has occurred via the process of civilization. If Rousseau's image of nature functions primarily as a hypothetical device to create a myth, which counterpoints simplicity to the sophisticated dishar-monies of modernity, it still begs questions. How do we decide what is nature from the vantage point of civilization? And if it cannot be retrieved, save by resort to techniques that reflect the very forces against which it is invoked, what is its point? This problematic paradoxical appeal to nature is the focus of Derrida's deconstruction.

[52] B. Honig, *Emergency Politics—Paradox, Law, Democracy* (Princeton NJ and Oxford, Princeton University Press, 2009), pp. 13–17.
[53] Ibid., pp. 17–39.

12

Kant

Morality, Politics, and Cosmopolitanism

INTRODUCTION

Kant was born in Konigsburg in 1724 and died there in 1804. He was an expressly critical thinker, whose philosophy is designed to determine the conditions and operations of reason. He published a number of works, including the *Critique of Pure Reason, Groundwork of the Metaphysics of Morals, Critique of Practical Reason, Critique of Judgment, Religion within the Boundaries of Mere Reason* and 'The Metaphysics of Morals'.[1] Kant developed his philosophical ideas in the context of the rise of modern science and of a growing scepticism over traditional metaphysics. In the spirit of the Enlightenment, of which he himself was a major figure, Kant appraised the grounds of knowledge. Kant's interest in philosophy ranged over epistemological questions, moral judgment, political theory, art, and religious belief. The social and political context of his political ideas was framed by the possibilities of enlightened absolutism in the eighteenth century, and towards the end of his life, by the impact of the French Revolution. Kant's critical perspective informs his analysis of the operation of reason and the limits of knowledge. He excludes religious belief from the sphere of knowledge but allows for faith. His philosophy endorses the rational content of morality, which is prescribed by reason, recognizes the intrinsic value of art, and looks to promote political progress by supporting republicanism and cosmopolitanism while eschewing

---

[1] I. Kant, *Critique of Pure Reason* trans. P. Guyer and A. Wood (Cambridge, Cambridge University Press, 1997); I. Kant, *Groundwork of the Metaphysics of Morals* trans. and ed. A. Wood (New York, Yale University Press, 2002); I. Kant, *Critique of Practical Reason* trans. and ed. L. Beck (Oxford, Maxwell Macmillan International, 1993); I. Kant, *Critique of Judgment* trans, J.C. Meredith (Oxford, Oxford University Press, 1969); I. Kant, *Religion within the Boundaries of Mere Reason and Other Writings* trans. and ed. A. Wood and D. Giovanni (Cambridge, Cambridge University Press, 1998); I. Kant, 'The Metaphysics of Morals', in *Kant's Political Writings*, ed. H. Reiss and trans. H.B. Nisbet (Cambridge, Cambridge University Press, 1991), pp. 131–75.

violence. Kant's scrupulousness in scrutinizing the grounds of knowledge while defending its objectivity is matched by his sensitivity to the realities of political power and circumstances, and by his commitment to advancing the progressive political goals of cosmopolitan peace and freedom.

Kant's politics are complicated by contextual considerations. In his *Critique of Pure Reason* Kant sets out the conditions and limits of our knowledge of the world. While the world in itself is inaccessible, the objectivity of our knowledge is provided by the categories with which we understand experiential phenomena. In morality we can prescribe freely to ourselves rules of rational conduct. Reason cannot provide demonstrable knowledge of political order but it can frame a conditional regulative idea of reason to exhibit ideal terms of association. Kant maintains that the rules of a rational political association constitute republicanism, which consists in the rule of law, representative government, and the maximization of the freedom of citizens. A rational approach to international politics demands that states forsake war to establish peace and freedom across borders. The question of how these conditions were to be achieved is raised by prevailing contextual circumstances. Notwithstanding Kant's view that political reflection is to establish universal rules, his own principles of political order accommodate historical contextual conditions. He favours a restricted franchise for his ideal republic, which excludes women and the propertyless.[2] Even though Rosen points out that Kant meant the capacity for establishing an independent means of living by property and Maliks observes that he did not rule out the propertyless developing so as to achieve independent livelihoods, the restrictions on the franchise show his acceptance of current conditions.[3] Again, Kant imagines that the prospect of a world-state is unfeasible, given its prospective power of such a state, so in practice he settles for a federation of like-minded republican states to serve as a vehicle for progressively achieving perpetual international peace.[4] Kant also considered that violent revolution to achieve radical change was unacceptable.[5] Moreover, the prospects for reform of international politics are limited by the prevailing self-serving conduct of nation states. Kant's own state, Prussia, an absolutist dynasty, prosecuted its own interests vigorously in the international arena.

To harmonize theory and practice in an imperfect context Kant maintains a theory of history that projects the realization of an ideal state of republicanism and international peace. This theory of history relies upon a regulative idea rather than a demonstrable truth, as assessing history as a whole does not

---

[2] See I. Kant, 'The Metaphysics of Morals', pp. 139–40.

[3] See A. Rosen, *Kant's Theory of Justice* (Ithaca and London, Cornell University Press, 1996), p. 36; R. Maliks, 'Revolutionary Epigones: Kant and his Radical Followers', *History of Political Thought* vol. 13, no. 4 Winter 2012, p. 659.

[4] I. Kant, 'Perpetual Peace: A Philosophical Sketch', in *Kant's Political Writings*, pp. 102–5.

[5] See H. Williams, *Kant's Critique of Hobbes—Sovereignty and Cosmopolitanism* (Cardiff, University of Wales Press, 2003), p. 30.

allow for determinate cognitive judgments but only a plausible scheme to regulate consideration of historical development.[6] In his essay, 'An Answer to the Question "What is Enlightenment?"' (1784) Kant imagines that the current and projected public use of reason supports his teleological reading of history, even if the subsequent reactionary turn in Prussia in the aftermath of the French Revolution diminishes his optimism.[7] Public reason is general reasoning about public affairs, which contrasts with reasoning that is attached to a particular office or civil duty.[8] Appreciation of Kant's understanding of the relations between theory and practice is complicated by the operation of censorship in Prussia. In correspondence, Kant acknowledges that he presents a truthful account of his beliefs, while not elaborating on what would be controversial and dangerous.[9] His own state, Prussia, under Frederick the Great's rule, was imperfect, though he is cautious in his express commentary on the regime. Cavallar is surely right to maintain that in relating politics to prevailing circumstances, 'Kant's judgment is extremely complex'.[10]

If the context in which Kant frames his international and political philosophy conditions its expression, then subsequent historical developments have shaped its interpretation. At the end of the twentieth century the renewal of academic and political enthusiasm for cosmopolitanism in response to perceived processes of globalization and the close of the Cold War revived interest in Kant's international political theory. Many current liberal theorists of politics and international relations recognize a kinship with Kant even if they modify aspects of his approach.[11] For instance Habermas and Held draw upon Kant's legacy to frame revised democratic versions of cosmopolitanism that dispense with his teleology. Their disavowal of Kant's theory of history and revision of his political norms are plausible in the light of changing circumstances, but the question of the relation between cosmopolitan theory and complex practical situations remains a thorny and largely unresolved issue. It is a question that was posed to Kant's cosmopolitanism by Hegel, just as current advocates of cosmopolitan theory face criticisms from realists, who recognize a continuing role for nation states.[12]

If Kant is a theorist with strong claims to remain of relevance, then he is also a figure whose moral and political thought has been subjected to radical

---

[6] I. Kant, *Critique of Judgment*, p. 94.

[7] See G. Cavallar, *Kant and the Theory and Practice of International Right* (Cardiff, University of Wales Press, 1999), p. 13.

[8] I. Kant, 'An Answer to the Question "What is Enlightenment?"', in *Kant's Political Writings*, p. 55.

[9] See G. Cavallar, *Kant and the Theory and Practice of International Right*, pp. 24–5.

[10] Ibid., p. 13.

[11] This is discussed and expressed in S. Anderson-Gold, *Cosmopolitanism and Human Rights* (Cardiff, University of Wales Press, 2001), p. 8.

[12] See G. Browning, *Global Theory from Kant to Hardt and Negri* (Basingstoke and New York, Palgrave Macmillan, 2011), chapters 2 and 6.

criticism. Hegel is an early and perhaps his most engaged critic, in that his own philosophy is constituted in part by sustained reflection on what he takes to be the strengths and weaknesses of Kant's philosophy. From the outset of his career Hegel sets his philosophical compass in response to the directions that were taken by Kant.[13] Hegel interprets Kant's philosophy to represent an exemplary philosophical expression of the Enlightenment. Hegel's practice of intellectual history is to locate theorists in their contexts so as to consider how their theories express the principles of and respond to tensions within their background public cultures. Hegel reflects critically on Enlightenment thought and the modern culture that supports it. On the one hand he respects the Enlightenment's wholesale commitment to reason in examining all aspects of life. On the other hand he recognizes how Enlightenment reason tends to split life into rational and non-rational parts in maintaining a dichotomy that threatens to stifle reason as well as to undermine integration in social and political life. The Kantian project of inspecting reason and analysing its operations aside from the conditions of social practice jeopardizes the unity and integrity of experience. Likewise, Kant's conception of morality's dependence on general rules of reason is countered by Hegel's insistence in *The Phenomenology* and in the *Philosophy of Right* on recognizing reason within social experience. Again Hegel takes Kant's cosmopolitanism to deflect from the actual role of states in maintaining ethical life. For Hegel the pros and cons of Kant's philosophy reflect divisions within the cultures of modernity in that there are cleavages and unresolved oppositions in modern societies that require dialectical integration.[14]

If Hegel's engagement with Kant is instructive for what it reveals about both Kant and Hegel, then the critiques of Kant that are offered by Foucault and Derrida are enlightening on how these post-structural theorists perceive problems within Kant's philosophy as an expression of Enlightenment thought as well as on the character of their own positions. Both Derrida and Foucault undertake their critiques of received notions of reason by way of a critical reading of Kant, and yet they also work with the grain of Kant's thought in developing their own readings of the present. Foucault and Derrida dispute the claims of reason to establish a rational framework to appraise our conceptualization of experience. Derrida deconstructs the project of establishing a fixed truth whereby the multiplicity of ways that meaning flows within language is arrested. Kant's critical project is read as aiming to inhibit the flow of signs and the motion of language, with the result that violence is committed against their possibilities. Yet Derrida considers how Kant's notion of an idea

[13] See G.W.F. Hegel, *Early Theological Writings* (Philadelphia, University of Pennsylvania Press, 1975).

[14] G.W.F. Hegel, *Lectures on the History of Philosophy*, vols. 1–3 trans. E.S. Haldane and F.H. Simpson (London, Paul, Trench and Trubner, 1892).

of reason that serves heuristically as an imaginative device to undertake holistic thinking can be adapted to stretch the horizon of possibilities in our thinking on ethical and political issues. Foucault is critical of Kant's abstraction of reason from the historicity of our conceptual worlds. From his earliest archaeological investigations into conceptual engagement with the world, Foucault is clear that the project of appraising concepts critically falls down if the historical dimension that registers conceptual change is not foregrounded. Foucault's turn to genealogical investigations into seemingly benign rational institutions highlights the dark side of the Enlightenment, which, ironically, is occluded in Kant's Enlightenment narrative of historical progress. Foucault, however, resembles Derrida in using an aspect of Kant's enterprise to develop a sense of how the present may be appraised critically.

REPUBLICANISM AND COSMOPOLITANISM

Kant's *Critique of Pure Reason* frames the epistemological limits of reason. These limits plot the contours of the necessary conceptual framework by which the world is experienced. Direct apprehension of things in themselves is ruled out. Cognition proceeds by categorial framing of sense experience. Generic reasoning about empirical phenomena that is not linked directly to observation is precluded. A combination of sense and reason is required to understand the phenomenal world of sense experience. Kant observes, 'Thoughts without content are empty, intuitions without concepts are blind.'[15] Reason of itself can and must be applied directly in establishing and maintaining moral laws in practical life. The moral law enacts reason in its application of universal rules to the conduct of human agents, prohibiting partiality and self-interestedness. While Kant recognizes the role of anthropological experience in suggesting the moral codes by which humanity lives, experience in itself does not supply either the motivation or the rationale of moral obligations.[16] The freedom of moral life is guaranteed by its autonomy and disengagement from the situated contexts and feelings of its agents; agents are moral insofar as they respect reason and hence the universal categorical demands of duty. Morality is insulated from self-interest and charity. It consists in treating all persons with the respect that arises from their status as rational agents. Moral duty obliges us to act rationally to others. Hence moral rules, which are universal in application, are categorically imperative. It is only by following rational rules that rational agents can be respected. It is neither relevant nor acceptable that I am moved to action by emotion.

---

[15] I. Kant, *Critique of Pure Reason*, p. 63.
[16] I. Kant, *Groundwork of the Metaphysics of Morals*, pp. 3–9.

Morality is to be motivated and endorsed by rational rules involving subscription to an order that can be universalized.

Politics, for Kant, resembles morality insofar as it is a disinterested normative practice, and is not merely instrumental in realizing the contingent purposes of particular sets of people. The formal universality of the conditions of a rightly ordered political association is encapsulated in its laws, which enable the reciprocal freedom of all by prohibiting coercive or violent conduct. Indeed, the principles of reciprocity and freedom determine the composition of the law. In 'The Metaphysics of Morals' Kant observes, 'In its "strict" Sense, Right can also be envisaged as the Possibility of a general and reciprocal Coercion consonant with the Freedom of Everyone in accordance with Universal Laws.'[17] Kant invokes the notion of a social contract to explain the basis of political association. Its terms establish the necessity for a curtailment of violence and coercion within the borders of particular states. The rubric of a social contract overseeing a political association prescribes a republican regime in which its members are to be treated equally under the law and male property owners are to be represented in the making of laws. Individuals, in being granted freedom from interference by others, recognize their mutual security and freedom, and can cultivate their moral respect for others by their adherence to the moral law. The social contract for Kant is neither historical nor contingent; rather it is a metaphorical register of the logical prerequisites of a rational community that allows its citizens the freedom to practise morality. It is an idea of reason, superseding empirical circumscription. It is not a demonstrable empirical proposition but serves as a paradigmatic device to convey the rationality of a political association.[18]

It is a misleading aspect of the metaphor of the social contract that it might appear to rest on contingent historical agreement preceding the formation of a state. Likewise it is not an instrumental device to achieve the determinate interests of particular agents, whose contingent insecure situation demands political order. The social contract is rational and moral rather than contingent and historical. It demands recognition and compliance due to its rationality rather than for its instrumentality. The status of the social contract is conveyed by Kant's construal of it as an 'idea of reason'. An idea of reason is a technical term in Kant's philosophy that stands for a process of pure reasoning, which does not refer to determinate empirical phenomena. Reason, for Kant, requires sense to enable it to furnish empirical knowledge of the world. However, an idea of reason is held to play a heuristic role in enabling our thinking on a subject without being strictly true or verifiable. Kant takes the social contract to represent a formal and helpful conception of what is required to ensure justice and freedom in the social world even if it cannot

---

[17] I. Kant, 'The Metaphysics of Morals', p. 135.   [18] Ibid., p. 137.

be verified. The social contract explains the formation of a civil association, without which all rights would be provisional, for a pre-political condition without public law would be 'a state devoid of justice'.[19]

Kant's republicanism answers to the demands of freedom and justice in allowing for the political representation, the provision of public law to protect individuals, and the freedom of its members. Citizenship, however, is limited to property owners, which in the contemporary circumstances excludes women and the poor.[20] If Kant's political arrangements reflect local conventions, his support for republican government was at odds with contemporary norms in absolutist monarchies. The disparity between the demands of reason and the empirical circumstances constituted a dilemma for Kant, as he eschewed violence due to his principled respect for persons as well as his doubts on the instrumental value of revolution. His moral philosophy is constructed by respecting each individual as a rational person, hence it would be immoral for Kant to propose a violent overthrow of an unjust regime.[21] Interpreting Kant on the relations between theory and practice has to recognize his deliberately ambiguous expression of his views in the light of censorship in Prussia.[22] For the most part Kant tolerated enlightened absolutist regimes such as Frederick the Great's insofar as they allowed for general expression of views on public matters. Indeed, Kant corresponded with reforming ministers of Frederick. Kant, however, takes the current international sphere to be a site of unjustifiable coercion and violence, which is fundamentally at odds with the values of peace and freedom to which he was committed. Reason, for Kant, demands that peace must be instituted at the expense of violence; hence the present practice of states must be superseded by the rational imperatives of universal respect for all persons. It was on its tendency to put its own interests first in foreign policy and to pursue war as an instrument of war that Kant is implicitly critical of Prussia and other contemporary states. Perhaps it was due to the prevailing censorship that he did not make specific charges against Frederick the Great's bellicose policies but concentrated on critiquing theorists who advocated *Realpolitik*.[23]

Kant is dismayed by the prevailing tendency for states to assert their interests by resorting to violence. Kant's response was to urge reform of present practice by institutionalizing cooperation and peace either through establishing a cosmopolitan state or by the creation and evolution of an enlarging federation of like-minded republics. Kant favours the development of cosmopolitanism by a gradually increasing federation of republics rather

---

[19] Ibid.

[20] For discussion of citizenship see the comments of A. Rosen, *Kant's Theory of Justice*, p. 36 and R. Maliks, 'Revolutionary Epigones: Kant and his Radical Followers', p. 659.

[21] See H. Williams, *Kant's Critique of Hobbes*, p. 30.

[22] See G. Cavallar, *Kant and the Theory and Practice of International Right*, pp. 24–5.

[23] I. Kant, 'Perpetual Peace: A Philosophical Sketch', in *Kant's Political Writings*, pp. 127–8.

than by a global state. The rationale for the former is not set out at great length but is motivated by his practical concern over the prospective concentrated force of a cosmopolitan state and the intuitive practicality of a developing federation.[24] Republican government and a concomitant cosmopolitan order constitute rational forms of politics superseding absolutist states and the conflictual pursuit of the interests of states in the international realm. Kant's perspective is rationalist in separating the pure form of republicanism and a supervening cosmopolitan republican international order from the preceding historical practice of actual states, including that of Prussia. War, violence, and *Realpolitik* were routine instruments of policy. Kant is aware of a dichotomy between the real and the ideal. The character of Kant's political philosophy reflects the formal priority of pure reason, but his estimate of actual practice calls into question the prospect of realizing a rational political order and the practical achievement of international peace, especially in the light of his disavowal of violence as a means to transform political order.

Kant's political thought raises taxing questions, which are a consequence of his principled ambitions and the realities of national and international politics. What will motivate individuals to develop republican and cosmopolitan institutions, given prevailing conventions? Granted the prevalence of war and the pursuit of particular interests, how will a cosmopolitan order be achieved? Kant resolves the tension between theory and practice by an optimistic reading of the prospective development of republicanism and of a harmonious peaceful international community. Kant's optimism informs his essay, 'An Answer to the Question: "What is Enlightenment?"', in which he interprets the present in the light of indicative signs of progress, notably the growth of enlightened thought and the progressive nature of the use of public reason in civil society, whereby even in absolutist regimes the prospect emerges of enlightened thinking changing the direction of policies.[25] In other texts Kant provides a more philosophical reading of history, which is expressly teleological. The normative requirements of a rational political regime and a peaceful international order furnish criteria for determining a summative narrative of historical progress. The end of history secures international peace and mutual respect for persons as ends in themselves. In turn this putative end of history explains the directionality of the historical process to consist in the progressive advance of the cause of reason. In his 'Idea for a Universal History with a Cosmopolitan Purpose' Kant faces squarely the most problematic issue of how his cosmopolitan reading of history allows for reconciliation with the messy particular events of history and also anticipates a forthcoming realization of reason. He observes, '[W]hat strikes us in the actions of individuals as confused and fortuitous may be recognised,

---

[24] Ibid., pp. 102–5.
[25] I. Kant, 'An Answer to the Question: "What is Enlightenment"', pp. 54–8.

in the history of the entire species, as a steadily advancing but slow development of man's original capacities.'[26]

Kant's historical perspective is as problematic as it is suggestive. To maintain radical cosmopolitan ideas against the grain of accepted practice is to suppose that its prospects are supported by past and present events. In framing a narrative of a universal history Kant provides a credible justification of why the current situation and its prospective development are conducive to cosmopolitanism notwithstanding the prevalent self-interested conduct of nation states. It is problematic, though, because like all general readings of histories it tends to perceive the past as if through a telescope, focusing upon events that are determined by present preoccupations and ignoring any intervening items that might obscure its vision. The history of humanity may be recounted in countless ways, and one single perspective is liable to misrepresent the variety of and relations between human activities. Universal histories abstract from the multiplicity of events and homogenize historical time, whereby stretches of time encompassing sundry cultures and activities are assessed according to the single criterion of their contribution towards achieving a stipulated form of progress towards an end state.

The underlying rationality of the historical process, for Kant, can be understood, if not definitively but at least heuristically by a regulative idea so that its multifarious events can be measured according to a rational formula. In Kant's reading of history, the end state defines the terms in which preceding states of affairs are to be interpreted, and licenses interpreting manifold events as conducive to the ultimate goals of republicanism and peace. On the one hand, notably in the *Critique of Judgement*, Kant takes the unsociability of humanity and its self-interested activities, including warfare, to enhance its rationality. In a situation of scarce resources, competitive conflictual behaviour between individuals and states has the unintended consequence of spurring technological progress, and so of promoting human reason.[27] On the other hand, he perceives the phenomenon of the Enlightenment and the related rational public discourse of philosophers, along with waves of popular and literary republican sympathy for the French Revolution, to constitute positive signs of impending progress.[28] This reading of signs in the present to intimate future progress, informs his seminal essay, 'An Answer to the Question: "What is Enlightenment."'[29] This very amenability of differing and

---

[26] I. Kant, 'Idea for a Universal History with a Cosmopolitan Purpose', in *Kant's Political Writings*, p. 41.

[27] I. Kant, *Critique of Judgment*, pp. 96–8.

[28] For the impact upon Kant of the enthusiasm for the French Revolution on the part of younger radical philosophers, see R. Maliks, 'Revolutionary Epigones: Kant and his Radical Followers'.

[29] I. Kant, 'An Answer to the Question: "What is Enlightenment"' in *Kant's Political Writings*, pp. 56–8.

contrary activities and opposing events and attitudes to the designated course of moral progress and universal peace in Kant's teleological framework, derogates from its plausibility. If sociability and unsociability are equally signs of progress, then it might appear that nothing can count against it.

Kant's teleological reading of history provides neither a demonstrable nor a clear-cut narrative of historical development. But if this much can be said against Kant's reading of history, then it must also be owned that Kant himself is alert to its uncertainties. Kant's critical philosophy is careful in scrutinizing the claims of reason. In his *Critique of Pure Reason*, Kant recognizes how causal explanations depend upon the categorial role of reason in framing empirical phenomena, but he understands holistic causal judgments such as a summative explanation of nature or history, where cause and effect do not qualify determinate phenomena, to be subject to the dialectical uncertainties of reason. The practice of holistic reasoning is only allocated a heuristic or regulative value in promoting the scientific project of tracing specific causal connections and in orienting reasoning and perception. In his *Critique of Judgement* Kant aims to provide a bridge between the limits of scientific knowledge that are outlined in thee *Critique of Pure Reason* and the practical claims of reason in determining the moral law.[30] In *Critique of Judgement* aesthetic judgment is conceptualized as developing categories alongside phenomena, rather than applying them. Phenomenon and judgment are worked through together to yield a feeling of appropriate judgment. Quasi-aesthetic judgment underlies the ways in which organisms are judged to act holistically and similarly in how history is conceived as exhibiting an overall purpose. Just as the beautiful is an indeterminate yet universal form of judgment so organisms can be taken to develop and history to show progress towards an end goal. Historical teleology, however, like the social contract, does not furnish determinate knowledge. It is a regulative idea, which is insusceptible of proof. Kant's *Critique of Judgment* provides a bridge between scientific knowledge and the practical realization of freedom and reason, but the bridge does not change the terrain; limits to reason remain and a teleological view of historical progress is a peculiar kind of judgment, lacking demonstrable criteria.[31]

PERSPECTIVES ON KANT

Hegel's approach to philosophy is historical. Philosophy, for Hegel, is situated and related to the social and political culture from which it emerges, but is not reducible to it.[32] Hegel sees his own philosophy as emerging from the

---

[30] I. Kant, *The Critique of Judgment*, pp. 15–18.   [31] Ibid., pp. 92–8.

[32] G.W.F. Hegel, *Lectures on the History of Philosophy*, vol. 1, 'Introduction', pp. 2–3.

vicissitudes of preceding philosophical and social and political developments. This way of reading philosophy and its history is decisive for appreciating Hegel's interpretation of Kant. Hegel reads Kant as a paradigmatic Enlightenment theorist, who articulates its tensions as well as its achievements, and he understands his own philosophy as surmounting the tensions that are exhibited in Kant's thought. Hegel, like Kant, respects the role of reason in understanding but he takes Kant, and the Enlightenment more generally, to divorce reason from the rest of life in a way that entrenches disunity and alienation. As Plant observes, in his early years, Hegel imagines the modern world to be in crisis, calling for processes of integration and social regeneration so as to overcome endemic fragmentation and divisiveness.[33] Kant's separation of reason from faith, of morality from the world, and international peace from the state is seen by Hegel to express a fragmentation, which requires ameliorative reconciliation. Hegel's reading of Kant as an historic philosopher is evidenced in his own practice as a philosopher, which was to respond to the abstractions and divisions of modernity that were expressed and legitimated in Enlightenment thought. In his *Early Theological Writings* he explores ways of interpreting Christianity as expressing discord and alienation while also considering ways in which it might play a role in reintegrating imagination, reason, and society in ways that were not entertained by Enlightenment thinkers. In one of the essays, 'The Spirit of Christianity and its Modern Fate' Hegel imagines Christ as preaching a doctrine of reconciliatory love, which supersedes mere adherence to law or principle. It is a message that is a critique of Enlightenment reason and Kant's separation of morality and reason from the wider spiritual and social life. Christ's message of love, however, is misinterpreted by the alienated Jewish people, who insist upon his divinity as they crave rescue from Roman domination.[34] Hegel's notion of the fate that Christianity suffers at the hands of misdirected social expectations, highlights his recognition of the way in which religious ideas can reflect and be shaped by social discord. In reviewing Hegel's fragment 'On Folk Religion', Harris observes, 'Folk Religion must satisfy the demands of pure reason in the end, but first it must meet the needs of the imagination and society.'[35] The task which Hegel sets a revived folk religion is one that integrates what Kant's philosophy keeps apart.

Hegel's *Phenomenology of Spirit* is an introduction to his philosophical system, and in doing so it reviews the historical possibility of its occurrence. Central to Hegel's historical analysis of his own systematic philosophical

---

[33] R. Plant, *Hegel* (London and New York, George, Allen and Unwin, 1973).

[34] G.W.F. Hegel, 'The Spirit of Christianity and its Modern Fate', in *Early Theological Writings*, p. 191.

[35] H.S. Harris, *Hegel's Development—Towards the Sunlight 1770–1800* (Oxford, Clarendon Press, 1972), p. 144.

perspective is a critique of preceding social divisions that are reflected in Enlightenment thought that reproduces divisions and tensions within its theoretical schemes. In the Introduction to *The Phenomenology of Spirit* Hegel criticizes an approach which retreats before truth by separating itself from the world and from absolute truth. He remarks, 'It [this fear of truth] starts with ideas of knowledge as an instrument, and as a medium; and presupposes a distinction of ourselves from this knowledge. More especially it takes for granted that the Absolute stands on one side, and that knowledge on the other side, by itself and cut off from the Absolute...'.[36] Although Kant is not specified, it is clear that Hegel has Kant in mind, and *The Phenomenology* serves as an extended critique of the divisions that are maintained in Kant's philosophy. It resolves the divisions that Kant observes between knowledge and reality, between part and whole, and between experience and truth. Far from abstracting reason from experience to examine its credentials as Kant undertakes in the *Critique of Pure Reason*, Hegel reviews an historical series of shapes of consciousness, which he designates 'a highway of despair.'[37] The 'highway of despair' signposts Hegel's separation from Kant and yet the way of despair involves multiple engagements with Kant and Enlightenment thought. In engaging with Kant's philosophy at crucial turns in its argument, *The Phenomenology* serves as a critical reading of key aspects of his thought.

In the section on *Spirit* in a late stage of *The Phenomenology* Hegel focuses upon Kantian morality, where he indicates how the modern moral attitude that is represented by Kant, separates itself from the world and is estranged by its inability to reconcile a rapprochement with the world. Stern observes how Hegel aims to show that the Kantian conception of freedom and moral goodness assumes a dualistic picture, which distinguishes sharply between the natural and moral order, between inclination and duty, and between happiness and morality in ways that are destructive for both sides of the dualities.[38] Hegel identifies conscience as the formal determination of the self to be true to itself but without opening to the world outside itself. Hegel remarks, 'But at the same time conscience is detached from every possible content. It absolves itself from every specific duty, which would try to pass for a law. In the strength of its certainty of itself, it has the majesty of absolute self-sufficiency...'[39] Conscience represents the Kantian ideal of the moral self obeying its own moral law rather than engaging with the world outside itself. In Hegel's phenomenological review of consciousness it is succeeded by another conflicted form of consciousness, that of the beautiful

[36] Ibid., p. 133.

[37] G.W.F. Hegel, *The Phenomenology of Mind* trans. with an Introduction by J.B. Bailee (London, George Allen and Unwin Ltd, 1971), p. 155.

[38] R. Stern, *Routledge Guidebook to Hegel's Phenomenology of Spirit* (London and New York, Routledge, 2001).

[39] G.W.F. Hegel, *The Phenomenology of Mind*, p. 658.

soul. A Kantian separation of the self from the world is also involved in the figure of the beautiful soul. The self-imposed isolation of the beautiful soul, which is intent upon preserving its purity by withdrawing from contact with others, reflects the alienation within the modern world that is rehearsed in Kantian philosophy.

In his *Lectures on the History of Philosophy*, which outline the successive philosophical developments reflecting historic forms of culture that lead on to his own philosophy, Hegel interprets Kant's philosophy to be a product of a modern world in expressing an Enlightenment commitment to reason that is entangled in a series of oppositions that reflect social divisions.[40] Hegel is critical of Kant's separation of reason from the world. Reason becomes purely formal and the world is divested of inherent meaning. He observes, 'Paul in speaking to the Athenians appeals to the altar, which they had dedicated to the unknown God and declares to them what God is, but the standpoint indicated here takes us back to the unknown God.'[41] Reason is imagined to serve as an instrument that is removed from the world to ensure its purity just as the moral impetus of humanity is to be encapsulated in the isolated endeavours of an individual. Hence, on this critical reading of Kant, the individual is withdrawn from a social setting to ensure the primacy of moral rational purpose and to avoid contamination by traditional and conventional factors. Hegel interprets Kant's critical perspective to be achieved at the cost of sacrificing the unity, integrity, and comprehension of the world.

In the *Philosophy of Right* Hegel outlines his own political philosophy, but it is established by reflection on historical experience and its standpoint involves a critique of Kant's moral and political philosophy even if Hegel does not trouble to cite Kant, whose philosophy was familiar to its readers. At its outset Hegel declares that political philosophy draws upon the actual political world, which is denied in the radical nationalist excesses of Fries. It is also a declaration that is directed against the separation of the formal from the actual in Kant.[42] Hegel also maintains that politics is to be seen holistically. A political association involves rights, individual freedom, and moral convictions that are to be related to social practices such as the family and civil society and political arrangements. If these elements are abstracted from the whole then they are rendered unsustainable. Hegel's holistic perspective contrasts pointedly with that of Kant. This stark contrast between Hegel and Kant is evident in Hegel's discussion of morality. Morality in itself is considered to be insufficient to provide a determinate content for social and ethical life of a community. Hegel argues that a morality that is taken to be external to the

---

[40] G.W.F. Hegel, *Lectures on the History of Philosophy*, vol. 3, p. 476.

[41] Ibid., p. 475.

[42] G.W.F. Hegel, *Hegel's Philosophy of Right* trans. T.M. Knox (Oxford, Oxford University Press, 1967), pp. 5–6.

social practices in which individuals are situated cannot legislate for a community's ethical life. Hegel imagines that a stylized Kantian formal view of morality is either abstract from or parasitic upon the social world. He observes, 'In morality self-determination is to be thought of as the pure restlessness and activity which can never arrive at anything that is.'[43] Moreover, morality's separation from the social world entails that it cannot guard against its corruption. He observes, 'Once self-consciousness has reduced all otherwise valid duties to emptiness and itself to the sheer inwardness of the will...it has become potentially evil.'[44] For Hegel, morality has to develop alongside a supportive social and political context.

In the *Philosophy of Right* Hegel also sets out a view of the international order that is distinguished by its contrast with Kant's. He is critical of a prospective cosmopolitan international order, where the promise of peace depends upon ignoring the claims of real social and political actors, nation states. These states of the modern world represent concrete particular ethical communities, which are not to be set aside or subsumed under wider, more abstract orders. Hegel observes, 'International Law springs from relations between autonomous states—its actuality depends on different wills, each of which is sovereign.'[45] While Hegel sees modern states as being constituted by their mutual recognition, as cooperating to achieve common aims, and to limit hostilities, the possibility of disorder and international conflict cannot be denied.[46] Unlike Kant, Hegel sees the unity of the world to be concrete rather than abstract and takes states to achieve integrated forms of ethical life, superseding the individualism and particularism of modern society that generates the abstractions of Enlightenment philosophy. The remedy for the divisions of contemporary society is neither to set the individual against the social order nor to elevate the abstraction of cosmopolitanism over actual states but to see individual and society as integrated within states that realize a concrete unity between individuals. While Hegel imagines that states aim to keep the peace, he acknowledges that a clash of interests can lead to wars. Where possible the devastation of war is to be avoided, but Hegel identifies the possibility of social breakdown in war as allowing individuals to appreciate the immense achievement of states in constructing social orders.[47] He sees the willingness of individuals to defend a state in war as a token of their recognition of what membership of a state means and demands. In commenting upon the individual's relation to the state, Hegel observes, 'This relation and the individual's recognition of it is therefore the individual's substantive

---

[43] Ibid., p. 76.   [44] Ibid., p. 92.   [45] Ibid., p. 212.

[46] For a discussion of Hegel and international relations, see A. Buchwalter (ed), *Hegel and Global Justice* (Dordrecht, Heidelberg, London and New York, Springer, 2012).

[47] For a good account of this aspect of war in Hegel's thought see I. Geiger, *The Founding Act of Modern Ethical Life—Hegel's Critique of Kant's Moral and Political Philosophy* (Stanford: California, Stanford University Press, 2007).

duty, the duty to maintain the substantive individuality, i.e. the independence and sovereignty of the state, at the risk and sacrifice of property and life.'[48]

Overall Hegel sees Kant as registering the positive and negative possibilities of the Enlightenment and as expressing the complex character of modernity in which individualism and reason develop in ways that endanger traditional forms of community and understanding. On the one hand, Kantian philosophy represents a commitment to critical reason and to the rationality of individuals which is symptomatic of the progress in freedom and reason of the modern world. On the other hand, Kant's adherence to an abstract conception of reason and abstracted moral and political principles shows the tensions and divisions in modernity. Hegel is critical of Kant's separation of theory from practice, which renders the practical realization of moral and political principles problematic and devalues social and ethical practices. Hegel himself locates his conceptions of ethics and politics within actual social and political practices. The upshot is that Hegel's social theory appears more realistic, but his realism exacts the price of complicity with war, violence, and conservatism against which Kant's commitments to the claims of reason and the aspirations of international peace and cosmopolitan right stand out.

KANT AND POST-MODERNISM

Foucault is a critic of Enlightenment critique, and so engages with Kant's philosophy. He identifies a dark side to the Enlightenment and in reviewing modern developments maintains its historical conditionality, observing the contingency of discourses and power relations underlying apparently enlightened regimes of medical provision for the insane and the delinquent.[49] His historical investigations are conducted in a different idiom from those of Kant and Hegel. Where Hegel looks for resolutions within his synoptic perspective and Kant projects rational progress, Foucault reveals discontinuities and dissonance. In early theoretical writings Foucault expressly imagines the modern world as being constituted by contingent discursive practices that establish particular horizons of understanding rather than an underlying unity to knowledge. The categories, for Foucault, are neither universal in form nor in application. They are historical and contingent.

---

[48] G.W.F. Hegel, *Hegel's Philosophy of Right*, p. 210.
[49] See M. Foucault, *Madness and Civilisation: A History of Insanity in the Age of Reason* trans. R. Howard (London, Routledge, 1999), pp. 279–91; M. Foucault, *Discipline and Punish: The Birth of the Prison* trans. A. Sheridan (Harmondsworth, Penguin, 1991), pp. 135–309.

Foucault's identification of the limits of reason simultaneously invokes and critiques Kant. In *The Order of Things*, Foucault is explicit in relating his project to Kant's. He takes Kant's transcendental project of establishing the limits of knowledge in critiquing metaphysics to represent the end of the episteme of representation of the Classical period. Foucault remarks, '[T]he Kantian critique, on the other hand, marks the threshold of our modernity; it questions representation, not in accordance with the endless movement that proceeds from the simple element to all its possible combinations, but on the basis of its rightful limits.'[50] While Foucault understands Kant as registering the limits of the discourse of representation, he himself differs from Kant in imagining discourses to be historical. Hence, unlike Kant, he plots the historical limits of discourses. In a reference to Kant he terms the ways in which discourses are maintained to depend upon an historical a priori. 'This *a priori* is what, in a given period, delimits in the totality of experience a field of knowledge, defines the mode of being of the objects that appear in that field, provides man's everyday perception with theoretical powers and defines the conditions in which he can sustain about things that is recognised to be true.'[51] Foucault differs from Kant in recognizing the historicity of perception and recognition, whereas Kant aims to establish the universal limits of knowledge.

Foucault's project of identifying the limits of knowledge, however, is ambiguous in that while critiquing Kant he acknowledges an affinity with his project. As Hutchings notes, '[A]lthough it is clearly the case that Kant would not have agreed with Foucault's historization of the a priori, it can be argued that Foucault's approach remains fundamentally Kantian.'[52] On this reading, Foucault is Kantian as he is motivated to plot the limits of knowledge so as to highlight the discursive conditionality of judgments, say on madness, at specific times. The divide between madness and sanity depends upon historical categorization; it is a way of seeing things that is constructed discursively. The difference between Kant and the early Foucault is that Kant universalizes the limits of knowledge, whereas Foucault takes them to be contingent. Indeed he understands Kant's project historically. Given their affinities, the question looms for both Kant and Foucault of how we are able to perceive the limits of knowledge. It is a vexing question for both of them. There is no supra-categorial or discursive perspective that can legitimate judgments on their limits. The limit is not to be known by the unlimited. The limits of the limits that are set by both Kant and Foucault turn upon this lack of unlimited knowledge. But how are the limits to be specified? Kant relies on transcendental argument to specify the limits, by which they can only be inferred rather than known directly. It is unclear how Foucault can establish the limits

[50] M. Foucault, *The Order of Things* (London and New York, Routledge, 1989), p. 263.
[51] Ibid., p. 10.
[52] K. Hutchings, *Kant, Critique and Politics* (London and New York, Routledge, 1996), p. 108.

of historical categories. He appears to rely on a sense of unease at the constrictiveness by which categories of historic discourses appear or are claimed to be universal when they can be shown to be contingent and historical. But he neither specifies nor justifies this way of thinking.

In *The Archaeology of Knowledge* Foucault identifies his own archaeological project by distinguishing it from philosophical forms of understanding history, which imagine historical development as conforming to a general scheme. Hence, for Foucault, the teleology of Kant is to be rejected along with the Hegelian and Marxist paradigms on which he concentrates his critical fire.[53] Foucault's use of genealogy to expose the power relations within apparently benign initiatives in social welfare and punishment contrasts with Kant's historical and moral rationalism. While Kant identifies determining rational aspects of humanity and its institutions that are removed from mechanistically determined features of conduct, Foucault perceives the interplay of power and knowledge in disciplinary operations.[54] Beneath Kant's universalizing logic and the abstractions of the Enlightenment the material conditions of knowledge show how power is intrinsic to the operations of knowledge. While humane forms of punishment are standardly taken to signify a more compassionate and rational world of modernity, Foucault identifies occluded disciplinary techniques that are used to modify and hence constitute the behaviour of rational subjects in the modern world. The body is ordered by repetitive techniques of manipulation to produce responsive subjects. Kant, for Foucault, ignores this world of discipline and subject formation to attend to the rational discourse of civil society and the anticipation of progress by rational discourse. In his later studies of sexuality and governmentality Foucault discloses how subjectivity that is taken by Kant to be the source of rational autonomy, is in fact constituted by contingent historic discursive formations.[55]

In a late essay, 'What is Enlightenment?' Foucault shows an altered appreciation of Kant recognizing his relevance. He is willing to see a trace of Kant in his own reflections on the present and on what it means to critique the present. In this essay Foucault reconsiders his own relationship to the critical spirit of the Enlightenment by reflecting upon how Kant's critical attitude to his time might bear upon his own sense of critiquing his time. He sees Kant's essay on the Enlightenment as representing an exercise in the ontological critique of the present, which does not claim to know its future directionality, but selects features of the present that seem to suggest its predominant

---

[53] M. Foucault, *The Archaeology of Knowledge*, pp. 203–4.

[54] See M. Foucault, *Discipline and Punish*, pp. 170–95. See also H.L. Dreyfus and P. Rabinow, *Beyond Structuralism and Linguistics* (Brighton, Harvester Press, 1982), pp. 126–42.

[55] See M. Foucault, 'What is Enlightenment?', in M. Foucault, *The Foucault Reader* (London and New York, Penguin books), p. 45.

character in relation to its past and imaginable future. Foucault draws the lesson that understanding the present focuses upon its contingency, and appreciation of its contingency might enable its transgression. Foucault observes, 'It seems to me that Kant's reflection is even a way of philosophizing that has not been without importance or effectiveness during the last two centuries. The critical ontology of ourselves has to be considered not certainly as a theory, a doctrine, nor even as a permanent body of knowledge that has been accumulating; it has to be conceived as an attitude, an ethos, a philosophical life in which the critique of what we are is at one and the same time the historical analysis of limits that are imposed on us and an experiment with the possibility of going beyond them.'[56]

Foucault's late, more benign reckoning with the spirit of the Enlightenment reflects Derrida's late and more sympathetic engagement with Kant. Derrida's project of disturbing metaphysical systems so as to deconstruct apparent authorial registers of stabilized meaning is at odds with the Kantian transcendental project of drawing the definitive limits of reason.[57] Kant's critique of metaphysics identifies the necessary limits of reason. Meaning remains fixed, rather than fluid and flowing in an endless chain of possibilities. Derrida's deconstructive techniques subvert definitive registers of meaning of this kind, but in his late, more political writings Derrida returns to Kant. He observes how something akin to an idea of reason, such as Kant operates within his philosophy of history, intimates how the possibilities of democracy and justice may be imagined. An idea of reason for Kant is regulative and non-demonstrable rather than a demonstrative empirical judgment. Likewise the notion of justice or democracy, for Derrida, is indeterminate, lacking fixity and completeness, because there is never to be a definitive summation of its meaning. There is always the possibility of a twist in the way terms operate. Even to set up a scheme of democratic decision-making to decide on a scheme of democracy presumes the operation of a scheme that lacks decisiveness. There is an undecidability over what and how we are to decide. Yet to intimate infinite possibilities Derrida invokes the notion of a democracy to come, by which the possibilities of developing and enhancing democracy are suggested.[58] In explaining this notion Derrida invokes its affinity to a Kantian idea of reason, if not an agreement with the terms of his critical project.[59]

---

[56] Ibid., p. 50.

[57] J. Derrida, *Of Grammatology* trans. G. Spivak (Baltimore and London, Johns Hopkins University Press, 1976), pp. 6–95.

[58] J. Derrida, *Rogues* trans. P.-A. Brault and M. Naas (Stanford, California, University of Stanford Press, 2005), pp. 28–42.

[59] Ibid., p. 37.

CONCLUSION

Kant is a critical theorist, who responds to and interrogates the critical spirit of modernity. After Kant, there is to be no assumption of an easy untroubled congruity between world and thought. Even Hegel's resort to actuality to identify ethical and political rationality recognizes how the world does not simply disclose its truths, but is to be examined critically. Kant challenges traditional metaphysics and his challenge reverberates in the deconstructive techniques of Derrida and Foucault. Kant's critical review of the alignment of knowledge with the world and his critical assessment of knowledge as an instrument to understand the world, are matched by his interrogation of the categories of politics and the inter-relations between states. His exploration of the possibilities of avoiding the destruction of war by establishing a cosmo-politan world of peace challenges the merely traditional autonomy that is granted to nation states in pursuing their own untrammelled interests. Kant's republicanism and cosmopolitanism are on the agenda of contemporary politics. Cosmopolitan adherents to the Enlightenment tradition such as Habermas, Held, Caney, and Pogge respond to processes of globalization that highlight global inequalities, accumulating possibilities of environmental disaster and continuing waves of political and economic migration by urging the imperatives of global governance and universal human rights.

If Kant's critical defence of universal rights and a cosmopolitan internation-al regime resonates in subsequent theory and practice, then criticism of Kant has been a continuing theme of political thought. Hegel is an early and trenchant critic, who identifies the problematic nature of a critique of reason, which relies uncritically on the very power of reason that is to be critiqued. The impetus of his *Phenomenology* is generated by the anti-Kantian insight that a wholesale and reflexive investigation of and by consciousness itself that includes the multifarious ways in which it has developed experientially should be the touchstone of a critical reading of knowledge and reality. Likewise Hegel resists the Kantian project of deploying reason in morality and politics in opposition historical and social circumstances. For Hegel, a formal moral procedure of reasoning is too abstract to be relied upon as a guide to ethical practices that can enable individuals to live and work with one another. Formal reason is powerless to produce an ethical community by which institutions can be justified; rather social institutions and practices are to provide the frames by which morality can be enacted. The dispute between Hegel and Kant is crystallized in their differing approaches to the state and international relations. Kant's cosmopolitanism is rejected by Hegel due to his ignoring of the positive ethical value of the state. Hegel sees the state as playing the crucial role in shaping and determining ethical life. Ethics for Hegel has to be determinate. Children have to be nurtured by institutions and practices, and while patriarchy and the allocation to women of the primary role in child care now appears problematic, alternative yet concrete forms of care and nurturing have to be developed to replace it. The persistence of the state in the modern world shows the limits of Kant's cosmopolitanism. His thinking informs contemporary debates and resonates with the movements of capital and labour beyond and between the borders of states but the debate on cosmopolitanism has not been finalized. Kant's international political theory is the object of critique as well as a source of inspiration, and populist forces demand more rather than less from states.

Kant's critical philosophy also exerts an ambiguous influence upon more recent and trenchant critics of Enlightenment thinking. Foucault and Derrida are critical of the rationalism of Kant's thinking, deprecating the universalism of his transcendental critique of reason. In singular ways, they reject a project that aims to set universal limits to knowledge. They deconstruct the Kantian form of philosophical construction, even if the terms of construction set its limits. They are also critical of Kant's formalism. Ethics and politics for Derrida are not susceptible of neat generic formal analysis. Concepts are susceptible of infinite variation and application so it is a mistake to imagine their formal specification. Kant's internationalism insofar as it inspires the new internationalism at the end of the Cold War is critiqued by Derrida in the name of Marx, who offers a form of internationalism that departs radically from Kant's formalism. Likewise Foucault identifies and critiques Kant's project of establishing extra-historical limits of knowledge at a point in history. Discourses are not fixed. The historicity of Kant's project undermines its message of universalism, and Foucault takes knowledge to be linked to power in successive discursive regimes. If Derrida and Foucault are critical of Kant, yet they also use and develop his ways of thinking. Derrida draws upon an idea of reason and Foucault re-invokes the notion of a critique of the present just as Hegel continues the Kantian project of critical thinking in a reformulated way.

13

Hegel

The Politics of Modernity

INTRODUCTION

Hegel is a dialectical theorist, whose aim was to deal inclusively with the empirical and conceptual world so as to achieve a coherent philosophical system, which would enable humanity to recognize itself in its concepts and practices. It was a heroic aim and Hegel was both heroic and painstaking in his dedication to this ambition. He surveyed empirical events in economic and political life, took account of scientific and cultural developments, and adopted a synoptic perspective in interpreting the history of philosophy. The upshot, however, is not exactly what Hegel anticipated. The continuity of critical engagement with Hegel by succeeding theorists testifies to the impact of Hegel's enterprise and yet at the same time it registers the ambiguities of Hegel's project. Post-Hegelian theorists have either aligned with or critiqued Hegel for a multiplicity of reasons. Hegel represents radically differing positions. Young Hegelians, Marxists, and French post-structuralists have critiqued his philosophical conservatism, Popper has branded him a totalitarian, Kierkegaard has denounced his holistic disregard for the individual and the existential, liberals have scorned his authoritarianism, while Hitler and the Nazis burnt his books. More positively there is hardly a subsequent theorist of the social world, who has not responded to Hegel and admitted his influence. Even Derrida, who is highly critical of Hegel's synthetic ambitions, recognizes the force of his dialectical critique of thought and practice.[1] Anglophone liberal political theorists, and philosophers who are intent upon minimizing metaphysical commitments, are now inclined to praise Hegel as a reasonable liberal offering a balanced review of the conceptual conditions of liberal society and

---

[1] See J. Derrida, 'Positions', in J. Derrida, *Positions* trans. A. Bass (Chicago, Il., University of Chicago Press, 1981), pp. 40–1.

how that society coheres with general features of practical life.[2] The upshot is that Hegel appears to be a man of many parts rather than the philosopher whom he aspired to be, the architect of a system which supersedes predecessors and resolves contemporary dispute. Hegel can and perhaps should be interpreted as a deeply ambiguous theorist, who provides a multifaceted understanding of social and political phenomena, without achieving the finalizing system to which he aspired.

Hegel's route to his mature philosophy can be described as a highway of despair. Indeed, that is the phrase that Hegel himself used to characterize his *Phenomenology of Spirit*, which serves as an introduction to his system.[3] *The Phenomenology of Spirit* is intended to serve as a generic examination of the conditions that make possible systematic reason, but Hegel's personal pathway in developing a philosophical system may equally be described as a way of despair, because his route to establishing a system incorporated his grappling with many issues and his resort to differing styles in expressing his thought. It was not always clear that he would succeed either in establishing a professional career or in achieving the synoptic perspective to which he was committed. He was born in the German city of Stuttgart in 1770 to parents of middle-class backgrounds. His father was a civil servant in the German state of Wurttemberg and, in an informative biography of Hegel, Pinkard points to the contextual significance of Hegel's familiarity with the home town politics of Wurttemberg and adverts to the impact upon Hegel of political reform and reformers in the state.[4] Hegel's mature political philosophy makes cautious use of the insights derived from this reform perspective. Certainly Hegel remained in contact with reformers in Swabia and was an ally of political reformers in Prussia.[5] Hegel studied at the Protestant seminary in Tubingen from 1778 along with fellow students Hölderlin and Schelling. All three reacted to the turbulent character of the post-Kantian philosophical context in Germany. Traditional metaphysics and religious faith had been disturbed by Kant's critical epistemology. Kant's epistemological revolution in framing limits to knowledge set a context for philosophy, in that successors explored ways in which these limits might be superseded.[6]

---

[2] The tendency of Anglophone scholarship over the last 50 years has been to downplay Hegel's metaphysics and his adherence to illiberal commitments such as primogeniture, estates, and war. Excellent commentary has been produced, see for instance, A. Wood, *Hegel's Ethical Thought* (Cambridge, Cambridge University Press, 1991); M. Hardimon, *Hegel's Social Philosophy: The Project of Reconciliation* (Cambridge, Cambridge University Press, 1994); A. Patten, *Hegel's Idea of Freedom* (Oxford, Oxford University Press, 1999).

[3] G.W.F. Hegel, *The Phenomenology of Mind* trans. J.B. Bailee (London, George Allen & Unwin, 1971), p. 135.

[4] T. Pinkard, *Hegel: A Biography* (Cambridge, Cambridge University Press, 2000), pp. 1–19.

[5] Ibid., pp. 418–69.

[6] See F. Beiser, *The Cambridge Companion to Hegel and Nineteenth Century Philosophy* (Cambridge, Cambridge University Press, 2008).

Kant's philosophy establishes divisions between what could be known and what was outside the province of knowledge. It also divides the freedom of moral duty from the causally determined phenomena of the empirical world. Hegel and Holderlin judged Kant's philosophy to be symptomatic of the fragmentation and disunity of modern culture and society. They diagnosed its divisions to be problematic, and in different ways looked to revive what they imagined to be the unity of the Ancient world.[7] Their imaginative endorsement of Ancient Greece reflects what Butler observes to constitute its magnetic attraction for early modern German intellectuals.[8] Subsequent to his studies in Tubingen, Hegel acted as a tutor to well-to-do families in Berne and Frankfurt and then held a non-stipendiary lectureship at the University of Jena. In this period Hegel composed a number of essays, which have become known collectively as early writings on theology, though they are rather more sceptical in orientation than implied by that designation.[9] The *Early Theological Writings* examines Christianity in historical and social terms, exploring how it reflects social circumstances and how it might allow for a reviving harmony in the contemporary world. In 'Religion ist Eine' Hegel invokes the notion of an integrative religious community to supply a coordinating force that modern life lacks.[10] In 'The Positivity of the Christian Religion' the hardening of Christian doctrine into external commands rather than a living morality is explained by the persecution suffered by the Jews.[11] In 'The Spirit of Christianity and its Modern Fate' Hegel develops a dialectical reading of Christ's life, message, reception, and subsequent interpretation. He explains the meaning of a Christian faith historically and sociologically, relating the appearance of a divine Christ to the sociological circumstances of the Jewish people, notably relating the expectation of the Jewish people for a Messiah to Christ's appearance. This expectation shapes how Christ's message of love is misinterpreted as a divine transcendent summons. It is the fate of Christianity that this Jewish reading of the Messiah distorts Christ's meaning, so that divine transcendence substitutes for his message of spiritual love and reconciliation.[12] This early essay signals the direction in which Hegel would travel. Throughout his career he reflects on the ways in which events and individuals are interpreted and recognized in historic social contexts. For Hegel the self

---

[7] See H.S. Harris, *Hegel's Development: Towards the Sunlight: 1770–1801* (Oxford, Oxford University Press, 1972), p. 75.

[8] E.M. Butler, *The Tyranny of Greece over Germany* (Cambridge, Cambridge University Press, 1935).

[9] See R. Kroner, 'Introduction: Hegel's Philosophical Development', in G.W.F. Hegel, *Early Theological Writings* trans T.M. Knox (Chicago, Chicago University Press, 1948), pp. 1–65.

[10] G.W.F. Hegel, 'Religion ist Eine, the Tubingen Essay of 1793' trans H.S. Harris, in H.S. Harris, *Hegel's Development Toward the Sunlight 1770–1801* (Oxford, Oxford University Press, 1972), pp. 482–507.

[11] G.W.F. Hegel, *Early Theological Writings*, pp. 68–83.   [12] Ibid., 182–301.

may be free intrinsically, but to realize freedom requires more than its abstract specification. It demands concrete recognition of an individual's freedom by others. Likewise the notion of fate anticipates Hegel's mature reading of history as a connected series of contingent developments, which impart a supervening meaning to the overall process so that individual agents contribute in ways that they neither foresee nor intend.

In early writings that he composed at the University of Jena while he was under the influence of Schelling, who had risen to a youthful academic eminence, Hegel labours to develop a metaphysics that accommodates a synoptic and realistic explanation of reality. These essays contain virtuoso readings of nature, imaginative explorations of social recognitive relations, and dense readings of contemporary economics and politics.[13] He is critical of contemporary politics in Germany, notably in his withering review in the *German Constitution* of the failure of German political arrangements to provide a unifying order.[14] Prior to the completion of *The Phenomenology of Spirit* (1807) Hegel had responded to contemporary social and political problems, and had drawn upon a wide-ranging expertise in religion, politics, science, and the history of philosophy in aspiring towards framing an integrative systematic philosophy. Perhaps most characteristically, he had displayed an historical cast of mind, reflecting on the form of history, the ways in which successive events develop out of but show the meaning of preceding ones, and how the past differed from what he diagnosed to be the fragmentation of the present.[15] *The Phenomenology* collects these themes and integrates them into a coherent if audacious narrative of the development of consciousness. It is a demanding yet incisive work. Its spiralling arguments draw together his historical perspective on the present, circling around notions of politics, morality, philosophy, and religion, and exhibiting a dense and intense engagement with philosophical and social issues.

HEGEL AND POLITICS: THE PHENOMENOLOGY OF SPIRIT AND THE PHILOSOPHY OF RIGHT

While *The Phenomenology of Spirit* is not dedicated to political philosophy, its analysis of consciousness bears upon politics in that it discloses, amongst

---

[13] G.W.F. Hegel, *System of Ethical Life (1802/3) and First Philosophy of Spirit (PART 111 of the System of Speculative Philosophy (1803/4)* trans. and ed. H.S. Harris and T.M. Knox (Albany, State University of New York Press, 1979).

[14] G.W.F. Hegel, *The German Constitution* trans. T.M. Knox, in G.W.F. Hegel, *Political Writings* (Oxford, Oxford at the Clarendon Press, 1964).

[15] See R. Plant, *Hegel* (London, George Allen &Unwin, 1971).

many other features, how consciousness is inherently social and experiences many forms of dissonance before realizing its unity in socially mediated engagement with the world. The multiplicity of ways in which it diagnoses the breaks within and fragmentation of experience indicates tensions within the political sphere. It represents a distinctive exploration of the conditions that are to be addressed by politics. As Jay Bernstein observes, its agenda 'is to provide its reader with "a ladder" to the standpoint of science, showing him "this standpoint within himself".'[16] The ladder is constitutive of absolute knowledge rather than a detachable instrument, and it begins with the most primitive expression of the claims of consciousness to express truth. The apparently economical presumption of sense certainty is set out in a Russell-esque form, yet Hegel shows how the certainty of sense experience, when abstracted from an informing conceptual designation of what is sensed, yields only a bare unrewarding 'this'. A mere 'this' is tantamount to saying nothing, as nothing determinate is conveyed by a bare ascription. So the demands of consciousness move on and we, the readers of the *Phenomenology*, acknow-ledge the movement to consist in the elaboration of ever more intricate conceptual claims, relating complex social interactions. Hegel's turn towards the social as Pinkard observes, highlights the sociality of reason.[17] It is misleading to imagine conceptual manoeuvres without countervailing real world developments in social life. Concepts imply language users, who are engaged in a multiplicity of interactions.

How do individuals relate to one another? Hegel constructs an imaginary frame of social interaction, which figures prominently in the subsequent imaginary of social and political thought. He imagines individuals as engaging in a life and death struggle, in which each asserts the claims of their own consciousness. They demand recognition of their own consciousness from the other and the contest between them is taken to the extreme in risking death.[18] Hegel's life and death struggle anticipates Heidegger's claims over the prim-ordial situation of embodied individuals facing the existential prospect of their own death.[19] The combatant who does not flinch in risking death overcomes their adversary, and the defeated combatant submits as a slave to the master. Yet submission to the victor does not guarantee the latter's satisfaction, for just

---

[16] J. Bernstein, 'Conscience and Transgression: The Exemplarity of Tragic Action', in G. Browning, *Hegel's Phenomenology: A Reappraisal* (Dordrecht the Netherlands, Kluwer, 1997), p. 79.

[17] T. Pinkard, *Hegel's Phenomenology: The Sociality of Reason* (Cambridge, Cambridge University Press, 1994).

[18] For a scholarly introduction to the master–slave relationship in Hegel, see R. Stern, *Routledge Guidebook to Hegel's Phenomenology of Spirit* (London and New York, Routledge, 2001).

[19] M. Heidegger, *Being and Time* trans. J. Macquarrie and E. Robinson (Oxford, Basil Blackwell, 1962), pp. 279–312.

as Groucho Marx will not join any club that will accept him as a member, so the master is not satisfied by the recognition of an abject defeated opponent. Given that the slave is not confirmed as a self, Hegel's analysis of the struggle for recognition does not yield an immediate textual resolution to the quest for confirmation of self-consciousness. What transpires is a case of misrecognition for both master and slave. Neither the master nor the slave is recognized by another self whom they can esteem. This scenario has been interpreted variously. French theorists, Hyppolyte and Kojeve have focused upon how the slave, working on nature at the behest of the master, develops self-awareness by transforming the world and his own skills in his work.[20] However, the express message of the struggle for recognition would appear to be its revelation of the negative possibilities of misrecognition. It implies more subtly that what is required is an equilibrated relationship between individuals in which their particularity and commonality are recognized.[21]

In *The Phenomenology of Spirit* authentic recognition of the underlying unity between individuals and of the individuality of distinct selves is intimated as being realized only in its late section on evil and forgiveness, where the ego accepts the other and the world, and opens to a religious perspective.[22] It is at this point that individuals can identify with unifying rational links and recognize their commonality in reason, which establishes a foundation for the succeeding absolute journey of philosophy and systematic reasoning. The *Phenomenology of Spirit* covers a lot of ground. It deals with many one-sided perspectives, including the unhappy consciousness that abases itself by surrendering autonomy to a transcendent religious belief, scepticism's withdrawal from confirmatory engagement, and the Kantian beautiful soul that holds itself aloof from the world. None of these standpoints can be sustained without a recognition of the unifying role of reason, which emerges at the end of its dialectical manoeuvres. It is a highway of despair that is susceptible of multiple and contrary interpretations. If the focus is upon the conclusion and its attainment of absolute reason, then what occurs along the way may be construed as detachable. However, Hegel can be interpreted more plausibly as maintaining that the processes of misrecognition are not to be dismissed but function as ongoing possibilities, which intimate reason and inter-subjective harmony, but also serve as reminders of the fallibility of reasoning and the

---

[20] J. Hyppolyte. *Studies on Marx and Hegel* trans. J. O'Neil (New York, Joanna Cotler Books, 1973); A. Kojeve, *An Introduction to the Reading of Hegel* trans. J.H. Nichols Jnr (New York, Cornell University Press, 1969).

[21] For a recognition of the significance of misrecognition, see G. Rose, 'The Comedy of Hegel and the *Trauerspiel* of Modern Philosophy', in G. Browning (ed.), *Hegel's Phenomenology: A Reappraisal* (Dordrecht, the Netherlands, Kluwer, 1997), p. 109.

[22] G.W.F. Hegel, *The Phenomenology of Mind*, pp. 642–79.

susceptibility of social life to breakdown and misrecognition.[23] The ambiguities in interpreting Hegel's *Phenomenology* recur in reading his political thought and in considering his system. Hegel can be interpreted as framing a frigid system, which supersedes the means by which it is achieved. Alternatively, he can be taken as offering a corrigible reading of social experience and history, the component parts of which are contingent and open to revisionary formulations.

Hegel's youthful writings disclose a recognition of social divisions, an awareness of modernity's problems, and an absorbing quest for an integrative, synoptic philosophy. His *Phenomenology* shows how a standpoint of reason can be accessed that can reconcile divergent claims and perspectives. Subsequently, Hegel provides a systematic account of the dynamics of reason, producing his *Science of Logic* and the *Encyclopedia of the Philosophical Sciences*, in which concepts are shown to be inter-related to the project of explaining the whole of reality.[24] The constitutive dynamic of concepts in Hegel's philosophy is provided by the incapacity of concepts when taken individually to justify their apparent meaning. They require to be related to one another dialectically and systematically. This entire project has been questioned by subsequent theorists. Kierkegaard famously objected to its exclusion of the existential individual. Why adhere to reason if one loses sight of what it means to exist? Marx was impressed by Hegel, but reacted against what he dismissed as his rationalism. He critiques how Hegel appears to dissolve social experience into conceptual questions and to deal with concrete social and political problems by resorting to an overarching system of abstractions.

Hegel undertakes two ways of understanding the modern state. On the one hand he sees it squarely as an historical product, and in his lectures on the philosophy of history he develops a history of the world by which there is a progressive development of freedom contrasting former types of state, such as the Ancient Greek polis, with the modern state, and observing how the modern world is distinguished by its exhibition of individual freedom.[25] On the other hand, the *Philosophy of Right* provides a systematic conceptual explanation of the characteristic features of a modern state. Hegel's *Philosophy of Right* analyses the conditions by which a rational political association is to be understood. Its conceptual scheme draws upon Hegel's wider philosophical

[23] See J. Flay, 'Rupture, Closure and Dialectic', in G. Browning, *Hegel's Phenomenology: A Reappraisal*, pp. 159–61.

[24] G.W.F. Hegel, *Science of Logic* trans. A.V. Miller (Oxford, Oxford University Press, 1969); G.W.F. Hegel, *The Encyclopedia Logic: Part 1 of the Encyclopedia of the Philosophical Sciences* trans. W. Wallace (Oxford, Oxford University Press, 1975); *Hegel's Philosophy of Nature* trans. A.V. Miller (Oxford, Clarendon Press, 1970); *Hegel's Philosophy of Mind* trans. W. Wallace with Zusatze in Baumann's text (1845) trans. A.V. Miller (Oxford, Clarendon Press, 1971).

[25] G.W.F. Hegel, *The Philosophy of History* trans. J. Sibree (London and New York, Dover Publications, 1956), p. 18.

system. It is a highly philosophical reading of politics, which frames a way of understanding the modern state as resolving the issues which the younger Hegel had perceived to be destructive of community. The modern state, for Hegel, possesses a deep and complex unity, which can allow for the potentially divisive individualism that characterizes the modern world, and a range of subordinate particular associations. In Hegel's *Philosophy of Right* individuals are conceptualized as possessing rights, and deriving individual satisfaction in the activities of civil society, notably in developing desires and needs while exercising particular skills in work. Family life and the practices and institutions of civil society and the political state provide forms of recognitive engagement that foster a sense of community and unify the diverse identities and interests of modern individuals, even if women are treated differently from men in merging their identities with the family. Hegel contrasts the freedom of the modern state with the imposed unity of Plato's ideal state. In a lecture on the *Philosophy of Right* he observes, 'Similarly, it might seem that universal ends would be more readily attainable if the universal absorbed the strength of the particulars in the way described for instance in Plato's *Republic*. But this too, is only an illusion since both universal and particular turn into one another. If I further my ends I further the ends of the universal.'[26]

In the Preface of the *Philosophy of Right* Hegel sets out a robust defence of a method that denounces utopian prescription in favour of drawing upon actual political experience. He is against fanciful unrealistic thinking. He remarks, 'When Philosophy paints its grey in grey the world then has a shape of life grown old. By philosophy's grey in grey, it cannot be rejuvenated but only understood. The owl of Minerva spreads its wings only with the falling of the dusk.'[27] In the Introduction he highlights his methodological focus upon actual experience in observing, 'What is actual is rational and what is rational is actual.'[28] What Hegel means precisely by these epigrams is not entirely clear, and arguably that is their point in that Hegel was mindful that his text was subject to censorship, and enigmatic if conservatively inclined epigrams helped to avoid charge of radicalism. In his Berlin lectures on political philosophy, when censorship was not so pronounced a consideration, he sounded a different note by referring to the rational becoming the actual.[29] However, in interpreting Hegel's political thought the role of censorship should not be exaggerated. It is central to the entire tenor of Hegel's philosophy that a philosopher is not to impose utopian schemes upon the world. To understand reality they are to reflect on actual experience, or at least on the

---

[26] G.W.F. Hegel, *Hegel's Philosophy of Right* trans. T.M. Knox (Oxford, Oxford University Press, 1967), p. 267.

[27] Ibid., p. 13.   [28] Ibid., p. 10.

[29] G.W.F. Hegel, *Die Philosophie des Rechts: Die Vorlesung von 1819/20*, ed. D. Henrich (Frankfurt, Suhrkamp Verlag, 1983).

essentials of what is occurring, as actuality for Hegel is what essentially underlies appearance. Hence Hegel in the *Philosophy of Right* deals with the rational essence of the modern state, conceptualizing the modern expression of human freedom and agency.

Hegel's methodological injunction to analyse what is essential in the practices of the modern state is not simply to endorse what has developed. He dissociates himself expressly from the historical school of law, maintaining that the school is mistaken in imagining that a rational polity can be justified by merely empirical historical considerations.[30] If he is opposed to unrealistic radicalism, then he is also against a mere empiricism. What is required is systematic justification, attuned to what may be discerned in social and political experience. Hegel's point is that philosophy is situated historically rather than wildly speculative in its reasoning about politics. A philosophical approach is not merely historical, because it treats its concepts systematically. Hegel begins the argument of the *Philosophy of Right* by focusing upon the master concept of freedom. Freedom is central because it is what essentially marks human beings. Moreover *The Phenomenology of Spirit* culminates in absolute reason, where the freedom of self-consciousness is realized in comprehensive reasoning. Hegel's prior conceptualization of logic and nature in his system underlies his philosophical analysis of the free and rational character of human beings, which is expressed in their activities by operating with and working on natural phenomena and engaging in social activities. His *Philosophy of Spirit* shows freedom to be integral to all human activities and his political philosophy sets out the specific ways in which freedom is developed in political life. In the *Philosophy of Right* Hegel relates systematically the concepts of politics to the central concept of freedom.[31] This systematic account is different from, though related to, his historical account of freedom in his lectures on the philosophy of history, in which he shows how the modern world operates by establishing freedom for all, whereas preceding political regimes had only allowed freedom for a minority of people.[32]

In the first section of the *Philosophy of Right* Hegel considers abstract right, which is a category arising out of an immediate consideration of freedom. Individuals are free and hence have a right to pursue their liberty, to assert their control over natural objects, and thereby to maintain private property. Notwithstanding the reasonableness of these rights, their abstract formulation does not guarantee that they will be respected. The insufficiency of this abstract specification of rights invokes the idea of a contract, whereby the

---

[30] G.W.F. Hegel, *Hegel's Philosophy of Right*, pp. 16–18.

[31] A recent emphasis upon the systematic approach of Hegel is developed in T. Brooks, *Hegel's Political Philosophy—A Systematic Reading of the Philosophy of Right*, 2nd edition (Edinburgh, Edinburgh University Press, 2013).

[32] G.W.F. Hegel, *Philosophy of History*, p. 18.

social practice of property rights is to be recognized by parties contracting with one another. But Hegel regards the status of contracts to be uncertain, because they can be broken. If the freedom and rights of individuals are to be explained comprehensively, the morality of maintaining contracts needs to be called upon to underpin contractual commitments. Hence Hegel proceeds to a review of morality, because claims about rights raise moral issues. Morality, for Hegel, is to be respected, but this respect does not entail that its operations are sufficient to secure ethical conditions. The problem with morality and the claims of conscience is that each individual is liable to press their own particular moral convictions at the cost of the general good. The right of conscience is part of the expectations of the modern world and is not to be dismissed; but conscientiousness on the part of the individual cannot generate the conditions of a stable social and political world.

To stabilize and secure social and political life, Hegel switches from a focus upon morality to that of ethical life, and an expressly social perspective. Family life constitutes a loving framework in which children can mature in an ethical context. This love grounds individuals, providing an experience of love and unity with others, which enables individuals to mature and express their own identities. Men and women are envisaged as developing differently. Women remain in family circles, in which marriage and care for their own children succeeds life with their parents. Male individuals participate in the turbulent social context of civil society, in which particular needs and individual ambitions are satisfied. Civil society allows for the expression of particularity and individuality. Commenting on its character, Hegel remarks, 'Particularity by itself, given free rein in every direction to satisfy its needs, accidental caprices and subjective desires.'[33] Hegel, however, draws upon the emerging science of political economy to identify the multiple ways in which the particular activities and interests of civil society at the same time constitute a unity of sorts in that individuals are connected by market mechanisms, which coordinate production and exchange. Hegel interprets the modern state as combining the freedom of individuals to pursue particular interests with a supervening sense of community identity. The dual character of civil society in allowing expressly for individual freedom, while connecting individuals by unplanned mechanisms intimates this complex identity of the modern state. The recognitive links between individuals are manifested expressly in institutions within civil society such as corporations and classes. The unifying recognition by which individuals identify themselves in terms of classes and corporate membership, however, is heightened by the representative institutions and the public laws of the state, and the focal point of sovereignty provided by a hereditary monarchy. Hegel's identification of the state's ethical role

[33] G.W.F. Hegel, *Hegel's Philosophy of Right*, p. 123.

underpins his scepticism over the prospects of an international order superseding the independence of states.[34] In itself civil society suffers from its
promotion of egoism that tends to result in each individual disregarding the
interests of others. The general interest, which is pursued by the state, and
which is evident in its laws and the policies of the executive, engenders a sense
of community that supersedes a merely selfish perspective on the part of
citizens.

Hegel's *Philosophy of Right* provides a synoptic reading of the modern state,
which observes its complexity in maintaining unifying recognitive links
between individuals while also allowing for the distinctively modern freedoms
that are developed in civil society. It exhibits Hegel's historical and philosophical sensitivity in framing a multivalent conception of the state, which embraces diverse features. It recognizes that the political thought of the past more
generally is superseded necessarily in a contemporary undertaking. It is
realistic in observing the problems of contemporary society, while imagining
that the modern state establishes an integrative framework for intricate patterns of particular activities. In his political philosophy Hegel highlights the
severity of the issues that he perceived to threaten the unity of society, notably
modern poverty, which is juxtaposed to manifest wealth, and is an involuntary
consequence of the very market mechanisms that promote wealth.[35] He
diagnoses structural and involuntary unemployment as liable to give rise to
an alienated rabble, with no stake in society.[36] The most general danger is that
individuals in society develop an egoism, which distracts them from their
connections to others. Hegel, however, imagines that the modern state harbours resources to deal with the excesses of individualism and failings of the
market in civil society. He entertains a variety of ways in which poverty and
periodic economic downturns might be addressed, which include charity, the
corporate activities of corporations, remedial interventions by the civil service,
and imperialism. Above all, the state can establish patterns of recognitive unity
by its institutions and activities. It can realize the conditions of an ethical
community, even if possibilities of misrecognition and market failure remain.
Hegel's focus upon actuality in his political philosophy, even if it receives
differing expressions in his lectures and in his publications, is not designed to
endorse existing phenomena but to discern an underlying rationality in
modern developments.[37]

[34] See A. Buchwalter (ed.), *Hegel and Global Justice* (Dordrecht, Heidelberg, London and New
York, Springer, 2012). Note the different representations of Hegel's position on international
relations in chapters by S. Hicks, 'Hegel on Cosmopolitanism, International relations and the
Challenge of Globalization', pp. 21–48; G. Browning, 'Hegel on War, Recognition and Justice',
pp. 193–210; and A. Buchwalter, 'Hegel, Global Justice and Mutual Recognition', pp. 211–32.
[35] G.W.F. Hegel, *Hegel's Philosophy of Right*, p. 149.
[36] Ibid., p. 150.   [37] See G.W.F. Hegel, *Science of Logic*, pp. 465–78.

CRITICS TO THE LEFT AND TO THE RIGHT

Hegel's philosophy is a heroic attempt to unite disparate elements. Formally it unites the individual and the universal, and in practice it aims to harmonize distinct and seemingly countervailing aspects of social and political experience. On Hegel's death, opposing camps of Left and Right Hegelians, or as they were alternatively styled Old and Young Hegelians, disputed the meaning of his system. Right Hegelians assumed that Hegel had captured the truth of historical development in schematizing a rational state, the fundamental truth of the Christian religion, and in devising a philosophical system that revealed the relative meaning of all its components. Left Hegelians urged that things were less clear-cut. They did not conclude that history had ended and they imagined that the task of Hegelianism was to continue its critical spirit. They sharpened their critique of the present to include criticism of Hegel's philosophy. Stirner set out an egoistic anarchism, in which the individual ego was set against any wider scheme of inclusive relations. Hegel's philosophy appeared as a systematic form of ghost-like spiritualism and the endpoint of history was revealed in his own untrammelled egoism.[38] Feuerbach urged a form of humanism that opposed transcendent forms of religion, and he focused upon deconstructing Christianity. In his *Essence of Christianity* he employed the transformative method to show how a transcendent God is in fact a projection of human beings, rather than the source of authority and direction.[39] In his *Principles of the Philosophy of the Future* he critiqued Hegel for an alleged transcendent rationalism and embraced humanistic materialism.

Marx's critique of Hegel is formulated within the context of a more general one that is undertaken by Young Hegelians. Marx's 'Critique of Hegel's Doctrine of the State (1843)' and his 'Economic and Philosophical Manuscripts' adopt a critical position, which draws upon the conceptual resources of Feuerbach. In the 'Critique of Hegel's Doctrine of the State (1843)' Marx criticizes Hegel's claim that the political institutions of the modern state can resolve the problems of civil society.[40] Marx conceives civil society to represent the defining social structure of the modern world and takes its interests to dominate the political sphere. Above all class is what matters. Power is unevenly distributed and the formal mechanisms of the state do not disturb the fundamentally unequal distribution of power. Moreover, Marx observes how Hegel himself perceives problems of poverty, unemployment, and

---

[38] See M. Stirner, *The Ego and Its Own* trans. S. Byington (Cambridge, Cambridge University Press, 1995).

[39] L. Feuerbach, *The Essence of Christianity* trans. G. Eliot (New York, Dover, 2008).

[40] K. Marx, 'Critique of Hegel's Doctrine of the State (1843)', in K. Marx, *Early Writings* trans. R. Livingstone and G. Benton (Harmondsworth, Penguin Books, 1975), pp. 157–98.

particularism as bedevilling civil society and, in the face of these realities, he rejects the idea that a hereditary monarchy will help achieve the public good. Moreover, Marx disparages the Hegelian conceit that a class of civil servants that is dedicated to the universal interest will enable the general interest to prevail over the particular interests of civil society. For Marx, bureaucracy creates its own tangled web of interests, which add to the congestion of particular interests rather than providing the means to secure the general good.[41] Marx maintains that the proletariat, the class which lacks capital and power, must take control of society by operating a democracy that is not restricted to the merely political form that is designated by Hegel, but opens up all of the aspects of civil society to social control.

If Marx's 'Critique of Hegel's Doctrine of the State (1843)' provides specific criticisms of Hegel's separation of the state from civil society and notes divisions of society that are not to be bridged by formal political arrangements, he also operates with a more general critique of Hegel's philosophy. Hegel justifies problematic empirical features of civil society by assuming that political arrangements can modify their impact. This is seen by Marx to be supported in turn by a way of seeing reality as conforming to abstractly specifiable requirements of reason. Marx adheres to the Feuerbachian transformative method in reversing the priority which Hegel assigns to the formal political state over civil society in exemplifying the rationality of formal reason, and he assigns a determinative social role to empirical phenomena within civil society. Hegel's reading of the rationality of the modern state in embodying conceptual inter-relations is denied by Marx. Marx imagines formal political relations of the state to be a source of alienation rather than a guide to citizenship. In his 'Economic and Philosophical Manuscripts' he frames an account of contemporary society as exemplifying alienation, due to the proletariat's lack of control over production and the products, for which it is responsible.[42] Just as God is imagined to be the author of the world rather than actual human beings, so the proletariat is controlled by the organization of the productive process, which depends upon their labour. Marx also provides a detailed critique of Hegel's *Phenomenology of Spirit*, which he imagines to be determined by its endpoint, the achievement of absolute reason. The goal of reason explains and justifies the contorted shapes of humanity that are reviewed along the highway of despair, but Marx disclaims the apparent reconciliation that is achieved by reason.[43] For Marx what is of moment is the disparity between classes in civil society and a productive system, capital, which controls those who produce under its rules.

---

[41] Ibid., pp. 162–3.
[42] K. Marx, 'Economic and Philosophical Manuscripts', in K. Marx, *Early Writings* trans. R Livingstone and G. Benton, p. 289.
[43] Ibid., pp. 383–96.

The general contours of Marx's critique of Hegel are set by these early direct confrontations and subsequent texts suggest that Marx continued to maintain a critique of Hegel along these lines despite the fact that his own theory can be seen to be Hegelian. In reacting to the sharpness of Stirner's critique of Hegelianism in *The German Ideology*, Marx disparages idealism and the resort to consciousness as a form of explanation. In a deliberate strategy of distancing himself from all shades of Hegelianism, he disparages the elaboration of ideas in Hegelianism to reflect the delayed development of German economy and society.[44] He also emphasizes how ideas more generally reflect material circumstances and class antagonisms. This critique of ideology fits with his criticisms of Hegel and his own privileging of economic forces, but his elaborate engagement with the form of Hegel's philosophy and the idiosyncrasies of Young Hegelian forms of ideological thought exerts a strain upon his own exaggerated materialism.[45]

In *Grundrisse* and *Capital* Marx maintains a critical perspective on Hegel. In *Capital* he observes famously how he stands Hegel on his head, so as to emphasize how his concentration upon material, social, and economic factors contrasts with Hegel's idealistic focus on ideas.[46] However, Marx's conceptualization of the operations of capital employs inter-related concepts to express a holistic reading of capitalism, which shows him to be conducting analysis in a Hegelian style. The style is Hegelian in that in the *Grundrisse* Marx urges that he is analysing capital in terms of social relations that are established under capitalism and adds that these relations are to be expressed and understood by employing concepts.[47] Marx is critical of Hegel, but the force of his critique should not deflect from his subscription to a form of Hegelian conceptual holism. Marx's interpretation of Hegel shows an ambivalence towards his predecessor and ambiguities in Hegel's philosophy. Marx is both an exponent of Hegelianism and a fierce critic of what he takes to be Hegel's reification of concepts. He perceives a sense of closure in Hegel's thought, whereby a nineteenth-century constitutional monarchy, which rests upon an uncertain set of representative institutions and a society divided by class, is held up to be decidedly rational. At the same time he assimilates Hegel's practice of dialectic whereby social relations are taken to be dynamic and holistic.

The British idealists, Oakeshott and Collingwood are ambiguous in the ways in which they formulate interpretations of Hegel. While they are

---

[44] K. Marx and F. Engels, *The German Ideology* trans. S. Ryazanskaya (Moscow, Progress Publishers, 1976).

[45] See G. Browning, 'The German Ideology, Stirner and Hegel', in G. Browning, *Hegel and the History of Philosophy* (Basingstoke and New York, Macmillan,1999), pp. 76–82.

[46] K. Marx, *Capital*, vol. 1 trans. S. Moore and E. Aveling and ed. F. Engels (Moscow, Progress Publishers 1969), p. 29.

[47] K. Marx, *Grundrisse* trans. M. Nicholas (Harmondsworth, Penguin, 1974), p. 102.

practising historians and appreciate the historicity of thought, and in considering Hegel recognize that he is to be understood as an historical figure
responding to historical developments, they draw upon him in framing their
own political theories. Oakeshott's most evocative and subtle consideration of
Hegel is offered in *On Human Conduct*, where Hegel's political thought is
related to an historic form of political association in European politics. He
imagines Hegel's political thought as arising out of the political context of the
development of a form of the modern state, a *societas*, which represents a
paradigmatic scheme of modern political association. In theorizing a *societas*,
Oakeshott takes Hegel to be operating within a developing tradition of European political thought, which imagines political society as a civil association.
Indeed, Oakeshott credits Hegel, alongside Hobbes, to be the supreme theorist
of a civil association. In so doing he maintains that Hegel takes individuals to
be the key actors in the social and political world and he does not imagine that
Hegel explains political association by resorting to the agency of an allegedly
supra-human Spirit or Reason.[48]

Oakeshott's identification of Hegel's political thought within the context of
a wider European tradition of political thinking has the merit of replicating
Hegel's own standpoint in that Hegel emphasizes how his thought depends
upon prior political and philosophical development. It also allows for Hegel to
be conceived as a less singular theorist, whose metaphysics should not obscure
his close attention to historical political developments and his engagement
with concrete issues. Oakeshott's interpretation of Hegel's *Philosophy of Right*
focuses upon Hegel's determination of the conditions whereby individuals can
undertake their multiple purposes within an association that is regulated by
general laws. *Geist,* for Oakeshott, represents individual subjects, who act in
terms of their rational understanding of themselves and of their situation and
on Oakeshott's reading Hegel's citizens do not submerge their identity into a
collective goal, but retain their individual identities and goals.[49] Oakeshott's
own conception of a civil association is in turn closely related to Hegel's and
demonstrates the inter-connections between history, philosophy, and politics
in Oakeshott's perspective.

Collingwood, like Oakeshott, engaged with Hegel's thought throughout his
life. His unpublished writings show a continuous reflection upon Hegel's
philosophy. For instance, Collingwood's appreciation of Hegel's dialectical
logic enables him to develop his own critique of the currently fashionable
propositional logic in Oxford, and also to frame a logic of question and
answer, which underpins his conception of historical understanding and his
later sense of metaphysics as a science of the absolute presuppositions of a

[48] M. Oakeshott, *On Human Conduct* (Oxford, Oxford University Press, 1975), pp. 257–63.
[49] Ibid., p. 262.

historical period.[50] Collingwood's understanding of nature and cosmology also owes much to Hegel, in that his posthumously published *The Idea of Nature* and *The Idea of History* testify to his appreciation of Hegel's reading of history and nature.[51] Collingwood also developed a first-order cosmology, which owed much to Hegel, though it remained unpublished in his lifetime. Hegel is read differently in his first-order cosmology and in his historical account of the subject. In *The Idea of Nature* Hegel's cosmology is viewed historically and Collingwood analyses Hegel's use of Plato's ideas in responding to Kant and the historic post-Kantian philosophical context testifies both to his historical insight into how influence operates and to Hegel's own sense of operating in the context of the history of philosophy.[52] In 'Notes towards a Metaphysic', which was unpublished in any form in his lifetime, Collingwood draws upon Hegel's cosmological ideas to frame his own first-order cosmology.[53] In his unpublished writings on moral philosophy and in his reflections on philosophical method, Collingwood takes Hegel's ideas to be paradigmatic for modern philosophizing and presents his own conceptions of morality and method in the light of Hegel's ideas.[54]

Collingwood's *The New Leviathan*, which represents his analysis of political thought and Western liberal civilization, strikes a contrary note from Collingwood's other writings in indicting Hegel. He takes Hegel, along with Kant, to constitute a paradigmatic German thinker, who in reflecting German political practice is an enemy of freedom.[55] Collingwood's critique of Hegel is frankly puzzling, given his general recognition of the value of Hegel's thought and his acknowledgement elsewhere that Hegel is a pre-eminent theorist of modern freedom and moral agency. It would appear that the context in which *The New Leviathan* was written explains its hyperbolic critique of Hegel. It was written during the war, when Collingwood aimed to support Englishness and freedom at the expense of contemporary German fascism. He presents his argument in a way that would appeal to his audience. His disparagement of Hegel is unfortunate in that it detracts and distracts from his argument. Nicholson and Vincent observe how the actual substantive argument of *The New Leviathan* bears affinities with Hegel's political thought.[56] It establishes an historical

---

[50] See the unpublished manuscript, R.G. Collingwood, 'Truth and Contradiction' (Collingwood Manuscripts, Bodleian Library, Dep. 16, 1917), p. 10.

[51] R.G. Collingwood, *The Idea of Nature* (Oxford, Clarendon Press, 1945), pp. 121–33.

[52] Ibid.

[53] See R.G. Collingwood, 'Notes Towards a Metaphysic' (Collingwood Manuscripts, Dep.18, 1933/4); R.G. Collingwood, *An Essay on Philosophical Method* (Oxford, Clarendon Press, 1933).

[54] R.G. Collingwood, 'Lectures on Moral Philosophy' (Collingwood Manuscripts, Dep. 8, 1933); R.G. Collingwood, *An Essay on Philosophical Method* (Oxford, Clarendon Press, 1933).

[55] R.G. Collingwood, *The New Leviathan* (Oxford, Clarendon Press, 1992), pp. 270–3.

[56] P. Nicholson, 'Collingwood's *New Leviathan*: Then and Now', *Collingwood Studies*, vol. 1, 1994; A. Vincent, 'Review Article: Social Contract in Retrospect', *Collingwood Studies*, vol. 2, 1995.

and social perspective for understanding politics and civilization and sees a free political association as an historical achievement, and situates individuals in the social contexts of family life and civil interactions. The argument of *The New Leviathan* recognizes that a liberal community draws upon historical traditions and social practices in ways that are highlighted by Hegel. The upshot is that Collingwood is an uneven guide to Hegel. The general tenor of his published and unpublished commentary on Hegel is informed and insightful. Yet his indictment of Hegel in *The New Leviathan* is problematic given that it follows an Hegelian style of doing political philosophy. Moreover, Collingwood's unpublished review of Foster's *The Political Philosophies of Plato and Hegel* represents a careful analysis of Foster's sympathetic interpretation of Hegel and goes further than Foster in emphasizing how Hegel's political philosophy is a paradigm of freedom in contrast with Plato's political philosophy.[57] Collingwood highlights how Hegel's fundamental concept of freedom informs his political philosophy and he traces how the *Philosophy of Right* allows for a range of particular freedoms including property rights and political representation.[58] The paradox in Collingwood's treatment of Hegel's political thought, is that at times he recognizes its insight, draws upon it, and yet at the end he indicts it.

Collingwood's *Principles of Art* is also puzzling in that it frames a theory of art by way of reviewing critically how sense experience and the imagination are conceived by philosophers in the British empirical tradition such as Berkeley and Locke. He shows the limits of this tradition before going on to develop his own expressive theory of art. He does not make use of Hegel and other idealist philosophers to whom he might have been expected to turn, and in a footnote he observes how the issues upon which he is writing have been solved by post-Kantian philosophy.[59] In his unpublished writings on moral philosophy he explains how, when using the term post-Kantian, he is referring primarily to Hegel. Hence in the margin of *Principles of Art* he recognizes Hegel's thought but does not draw upon it expressly, and this is most likely because Hegel and idealism would not have appealed to an English readership at the time. The complications in the ways in which Collingwood frames his thought and discusses Hegel highlights the difficulties in doing what Collingwood himself recommends in undertaking history, namely rethinking past thoughts. Collingwood's own presentation of his philosophy is evidently overdetermined by his reflections on presenting his views to audiences as well as in constructing ideas by drawing on past theorists.

---

[57] R.G. Collingwood, Report on M.B. Foster's *the Political Philosophies of Plato and Hegel*, Oxford, Clarendon Press Archives, PB/ED/002054, pp. 1–9.

[58] Ibid.

[59] R.G. Collingwood, *The Principles of Art* (Oxford, Clarendon Press, 1938), p. 201.

If Marx and Collingwood read Hegel critically while making use of his ideas, Gadamer recognizes Hegel's interpretive power, though he is also a critic of Hegel's absolutism. In *Truth and Method* Gadamer remarks intermittently upon Hegel's capacity to open up and explain cultural and historical texts and contexts. He also recognizes the positive possibilities of his self-proclaimed project of drawing upon their standpoints in developing his own. In his discussion of *Bildung*, Gadamer observes how the idea of education as assimilating a range of standpoints is shown to great effect in Hegel's work. He remarks, 'Thus every individual is always engaged in the process of *Bildung* and in getting beyond his naturalness, inasmuch as the world into which he is growing is one that is humanly constituted through language and custom. Hegel emphasizes that a people gives itself its existence in its world.'[60] Gadamer observes a kinship between his own hermeneutical method, which rests upon the reciprocity of past and present, and Hegel's sense of present understanding relying upon and assimilating past achievements. In *Hegel's Dialectic*, Gadamer reinforces this sympathetic reading of Hegel in that he imagines, plausibly, that Hegel is to be understood as reviving the spirit of Greek philosophy and in particular the dialectic of Plato. He remarks, 'With his own dialectical method Hegel claims to have vindicated Plato's way of justifying belief—dialectical scrutinizing of all assumptions.'[61] He sees Hegel's *Logic* as working with the tradition of Plato's later dialogues in following Plato's recognition of the inter dependence of forms of thought to inform the process of critical philosophizing.[62] Yet Gadamer maintains that we cannot follow Hegel as Hegel followed Plato. In *Truth and Method* he observes, 'Hegel's answer cannot satisfy us for Hegel sees *Bildung* as brought to completion through the movement of alienation and appropriation in a complete mastery of substance in the dissolution of all concretely being reached only in the absolute knowledge of philosophy.'[63] Gadamer rehearses Heidegger's critique of Hegel, which consists in Hegel's alleged collapse of difference into the linearity of time.[64] Ultimately, Gadamer is critical of the Hegelian project because he imagines that Hegel assimilates past thinkers into a single line of development and so imposes an illicit teleological unifying pattern onto diverse ideas. He contrasts his own interpretive hermeneutic procedure, which respects the differences between differing interpretive horizons, with Hegel's philosophy.[65] Hegel, on this critical reading, maintains

---

[60] H.-G. Gadamer, *Truth and Method* trans. J. Weinsheimer and D. Marshall (London, Sheed and Ward, 1960) p. 14.

[61] H.-G. Gadamer, *Hegel's Dialectic* (New Haven and London, Yale University Press, 1976), p. 6.

[62] Ibid., p. 10.

[63] Ibid., p. 15.

[64] See M. Heidegger, *Being and Time*, pp. 428–36.

[65] H.-G. Gadamer, *Truth and Method*, pp. 354–5.

a constrictive interpretive practice, which coerces past intellectual developments rather than interpreting them freely.

CONCLUSION

Hegel's political philosophy is a profound reflection on modern politics. It
engages with a number of specifically modern features of political life, notably
the centrality of freedom, property rights, and civil society within an analysis
of the relationship between the state and civil society that retains relevance in
the present. Its identification of politics by means of its historical development
also represents an insight into the undoubted historicity of political arrangements. Hegel is also an unrelenting philosophical thinker, who interprets
politics in the light of a comprehensive philosophical system, which identifies
the inter-relations between concepts that shape the political sphere. The
insight and influence of Hegel's political philosophy is reflected in its critical
reception. Hegel is critiqued and appreciated in multiple ways, which testify to
its ongoing and multidimensional impact. Marx provides a sharply critical
interpretation of Hegel's political philosophy in his critique of the *Philosophy
of Right*. Yet, the influence of Hegel upon Marx is evident in Marx's own social
and political theory, which takes off in a radical direction, but retains aspects
of Hegel's conceptual holism. Hegel's fundamental claim that reason is at work
in the social and political sphere is rebutted by Marx, who examines empirical
relations in civil society, and highlights inequalities and asymmetries of power.
For Marx, these imbalances are not to be redeemed by state intervention into
the operations of civil society. The argument between Hegel and Marx is
difficult to call, in that Hegel recognizes problems in civil society and takes
them to be deep-seated and insusceptible of neat solutions. They are to be
borne in the light of countervailing freedoms and the prospect of realizing an
integrative community. The strength of Marx's critique resides in its focus on
power relations and his identification of the ineffectuality of the state in
addressing profound structural failings in social and economic conditions.
The extent to which a liberal civil society is justifiable, given the ongoing
structural inequalities in power and market imperfections remains a live issue,
and Hegel's arguments continue to be relevant and plausible, given the risks
involved in radical alternatives.

Criticism of Hegel's philosophical system as being inimical to freedom and
contingency and a countervailing appreciation of his interpretive holism in
connecting past and present are two sides of Gadamer's interpretation of
Hegel. In another guise Collingwood is ambiguous in his interpretation
of Hegel, in that he combines overt critique with a recognition of the
power of Hegel's political ideas. A related ambivalence informs Derrida's

simultaneous critique of Hegel's absolutism and his endorsement of his critical stance towards particular conceptual forms.[66] Hegel is susceptible of multiple readings, but what stands out amidst all readings of Hegel is a respect for his capacity to engage critically with diverse theoretical positions and partial readings of the social world in presenting a synoptic perspective.

[66] H.-G. Gadamer, *Truth and Method*, pp. 354–5; J. Derrida, *Writing and Difference* trans. A. Bass (London, Routledge & Kegan Paul Ltd, 1978) pp. 251–78; R.G. Collingwood, *The New Leviathan*, pp. 270–3.

14

Karl Marx

One or Many?

INTRODUCTION

Karl Marx's influence has been profound. He wrote philosophical and historical texts, served as a radical activist, composed a concentrated critique of capital, and gave his name to a global political movement. Marx's ideas have inspired countless theorists, who have adopted, revised, and reacted against them in responding to the modern world. Hence Marxists and post-Marxists, ideological sympathizers, and theoretical opponents offer distinctive and multiple interpretations of Marx's social and political thought. The possibilities of interpretation are heightened by the range of Marx's publications. He composed dense philosophical works, which are enveloped in a highly wrought Hegelian vocabulary, intensive scholarly studies of the operations of capitalism, which depend upon his expertise in philosophy, economics, and history, and many occasional pieces, including journal writings, newspaper articles, and manifestos. Marx scholarship and schemes of interpretation also reflect the impact of subsequent theoretical and social developments. Marx has been subject to continual re-imagining in the light of events and issues of which he was necessarily ignorant.

A shorthand formula to indicate the intellectual context of Marx's ideas is the celebrated notion of Lenin's that he combines German philosophy with English (Scottish) economics and French politics. His reading of German philosophy, which is reflected in his early critique of Hegel, bestows a holistic yet critical conceptual framework to his theoretical style, by which rival positions are critiqued and assimilated rather than merely rejected.[1] His detailed study of classical political economists, such as Smith and Ricardo,

---

[1] See D. McLellan, *The Young Hegelians and Karl Marx* (London and New York, Macmillan, 1969) and M. McIvor, 'The Young Marx and German Idealism: Revisiting the Doctoral Thesis', *Journal of the History of Philosophy*, vol. 46, no. 3, July 2008, pp. 315–419.

reflects his close analysis and critique of the economic system. French political thought and practice, which he experienced at first hand during his stay in Paris in 1844, inspires the revolutionary aspect of his thinking. Marx was also energized by his direct experience of social injustice when writing articles on the poverty of wine-growers in the Moselle valley for the *Rheinische Zeitung*.[2] Marx's combination of these elements shapes a perspective that separates him from related Young Hegelian theorists, who reacted to Hegel by accentuating the critical and reformist aspects of his thought in contrast to Old or Right Hegelians, who imagined the end of history had been achieved. Rival Young Hegelian theorists presented dense and abstract theories of history, which highlight critical readings of the present, which are inflected by conceptions of humanism, egoism, or perpetual criticism. Without ditching Hegel's holistic conceptualizing by which he linked civil society and the state, the past and the present, the economy, politics, and ideology, Marx is distinguished from other Young Hegelians by his concentrated analyses of social and economic practices, and by his radical contextualization of political and philosophical ideas.

Marx was born in Trier in the Prussian Rhineland in May 1818, studying law at Bonn University before moving to Berlin, where he switched to philosophy and came under the sway of Hegelianism. He completed a thesis on the philosophies of Democritus and Epicurus, under the Young Hegelian theorist, Bruno Bauer, in which he observes affinities between social and political circumstances of post-Aristotelian Greek philosophy and the current circumstances pertaining to the development of post-Hegelian philosophy. It exhibits a readiness to situate ideas in society and to engage in comparative history.[3] Marx's 'Critique of Hegel's Doctrine of the State' (1843) criticizes Hegel's political ideas by maintaining how Hegel's abstraction of reason from the empirical world misconstrues the role of reason and the determinative features of social and economic life.[4] In the same year, Marx published 'On the Jewish Question', which relates legal and political discrimination against Jews to the wider social and economic structure that produces notions of Jewishness. It is a text which remains of interest in showing how ethnic prejudice is rooted in socio-economic conditions.[5] During his exile in Paris in 1844, Marx drafted the 'Economic and Philosophical Manuscripts', in which he framed a radical critique of modern society that is focused upon the notion of humanity's alienation under capitalism. Marx's recourse to the language of alienation

---

[2] See F. Mehring *Karl Marx, The Story of his Life* (London and New York, Routledge, 2003).

[3] See G. Browning, 'Marx's Doctoral Dissertation: The Development of a Hegelian Thesis', in T. Burns and I. Fraser (eds), *The Hegel–Marx Connection* (Basingstoke and New York, Palgrave Macmillan, 2000), pp. 131–45.

[4] K. Marx, 'Critique of Hegel's Doctrine of the State (1843)', in K. Marx, *Early Writings* trans. R. Livingstone and G. Benton (Harmondsworth, Penguin Books, 1975), pp. 57–198.

[5] K. Marx, 'On the Jewish Question', in K. Marx, *Early Writings* trans. R. Livingstone and G. Benton (Harmondsworth, Penguin Books, 1975), pp. 211–43.

draws upon Hegel's critique of estranged forms of consciousness and owes much to Feuerbach's critique of religion as an alienated expression of humanity's identity.[6] Shortly after completing the manuscript, Marx began a friendship with Friedrich Engels, the revolutionary socialist son of a German industrialist, which continued throughout his life. They shared ideas and co-authored several significant volumes, including *The Communist Manifesto* (1848).[7]

From the mid-1840s Marx develops a materialist theory of history, by which he assigns a primary determining to the productive process, and sets out specific and more general analyses of class. Marx breaks with fellow Young Hegelians and sets out more determinately how social and political practices and ideas are to be seen as changing historical forms in the manuscripts that form *The German Ideology*, which he composed with Engels in 1845–46.[8] In these essays, *The Communist Manifesto* (1848) and the 'Preface to a Contribution to a Critique of Political Economy' (1859) Marx, in collaboration with Engels, set out the principles of a general theory of history, alternative interpretations of which reflect their ambiguous formulations.[9] Class conflict is central to their understanding of historical development, and in *The Communist Manifesto* and in occasional texts responding to events, such as 'The Class Struggles in France: 1848–1850' and 'The Civil War in France', political organization and change are explained by class interest and alignments.[10] Alongside major theoretical works, Marx contributed articles in newspapers on political events, and he participated in the activities of revolutionary political parties, which were advancing the interests of the proletariat. Along with Engels, he joined *The Communist League* in 1847 and later in 1864 he helped to found the *International Working Man's Association*, which was known subsequently as *The First International*. In 1867 he published the first volume of *Capital*, which consists in his most assiduously researched and elaborated critique of capitalism that incorporates a rigorous analysis of its form of production and affiliated economic exploitation. Throughout his life and amidst his several activities Marx's theoretical energy was focused upon producing a comprehensive critique of capital and capitalism. *Capital* and the *Grundrisse*, a rough draft

---

[6] See K. Marx, 'Economic and Philosophical Manuscripts', in K. Marx, *Early Writings* trans. R. Livingstone and G. Benton, pp. 57–198.

[7] K. Marx and F. Engels, *The Communist Manifesto* trans. S. Moore, in *The Revolutions of 1848* ed. D. Fernbach (Harmondsworth, Penguin Books, 1973).

[8] See the comments in chapter 2 on the status of the manuscripts of *The German Ideology*. See also T. Carver and D. Blank, *Marx's 'German Ideology' Manuscripts—Presentation and Analysis of the 'Feuerbach Chapter'* (Basingstoke and New York, Palgrave Macmillan, 2014).

[9] See K. Marx and F. Engels, *The German Ideology* trans. S. Ryazanskaya (Moscow, Progress Publishers, 1976); K. Marx and F. Engels, *The Communist Manifesto*, pp. 67–87; and K. Marx and F. Engels, *'Preface' to a Contribution to A Critique of Political Economy*, in K. Marx and F. Engels, *Selected Works* (Moscow, Progress Publishers, 1970).

[10] K. Marx, 'The Class Struggles in France: 1848–1850' trans. P. Jackson, in K. Marx, *Surveys From Exile* (Harmondsworth, Penguin Books, 1973), pp. 35–145.

of *Capital*, show the care that he devoted to the analysis of the operations of capital.[11] Just as in his early critical philosophical critique of capitalism, in his late economic writings Marx establishes a systematic and critical reading of capital by examining the assumptions of political economists.

MARX: POLITICS, CLASS, AND COMMUNISM

Marx is a radical theorist, who provides a comprehensive critique of capitalism and its emerging liberal forms of politics. His radicalism is exemplified in his early writings. In his 'Critique of Hegel's Doctrine of the State' Marx counterposes a radical form of democracy to Hegel's constitutional monarchy. True democracy, for Marx, differs markedly from preceding and alternative political regimes in that it stands for the self-rule of civil society and so aims to abolish the division of society into economic and political spheres.[12] In a companion article, 'A Contribution to the Critique of Hegel's *Philosophy of Right*; Introduction', Marx critiques ideological mystification of the realities of economic and social oppression, observing notably, 'Religion is the sigh of the oppressed creature, the feeling of a heartless world and the soul of soulless circumstances. It is the opium of the people.'[13] The project of achieving revolutionary change, whereby society and social interests are to be brought under democratic popular control is assigned to the proletariat. Marx identifies the revolutionary potential of the proletariat, which resides in its exploitation under prevailing social conditions and its interest in securing the general interest over particular and divisive ones. He identifies the force for emancipation in contemporary Germany to reside 'in the formation of a class with radical chains, a class that is the dissolution of all social groups, of a sphere that has a universal character because of its universal sufferings, and lays claim to no particular right, because it is the object of no particular injustice but of injustice in general.'[14] Throughout his career, Marx demands more than palliative reform of capitalism and takes the proletariat to represent the engine of radical, revolutionary change. He maintains consistently that the state and traditional forms of politics are to be overturned by the proletariat, so that all aspects of society will be directed by democratic organization.

[11] K. Marx, *Capital*, vol. 1 trans. S. Moore and E. Aveling, ed. F. Engels (Moscow, Progress Publishers, 1969); K. Marx, *Grundrisse* trans. M. Nicholas (Harmondsworth, Penguin, 1974).
[12] K. Marx, 'Critique of Hegel's Doctrine of the State' (1843), p. 87.
[13] K. Marx, 'A Contribution to the Critique of Hegel's *Philosophy of Right*. Introduction. trans. G. Benton, in K. Marx, *Early Writings*, p. 244.
[14] Ibid., p. 256.

In the 'Economic and Philosophical Manuscripts' of 1844 Marx develops a systematic and radical critique of capitalism, which provides a foundation for his revolutionary condemnation of class society. Marx diagnoses society to be beset by contradictions, which demand its revolutionary overthrow. Whereas many theories of modernity criticize specific aspects of society, objecting to its inequalities or its materialism, Marx is both more radical and more systematic in his critique. Capital is viewed as structuring activities without regard to social actors. Those responsible for producing wealth are not only denied appropriate reward but more fundamentally are denied control of the processes of production. Capitalism is not to be ameliorated, because its entire structure misaligns producers with their productive activities and demands wholesale change. Revolutionary change is necessitated by the force of radical social misalignment under capital. The 'Economic and Philosophical Manuscripts' is powerful precisely because of its systematic critique of capital and the force of the critique emanates from a holistic analysis of the interconnected ways in which the creative powers of humanity are systemically frustrated by the conditions under which production takes place.

In this early work the starting points for critique are the assumptions of political economists on the nature of capital and capitalism. Marx works with the political economists' sense of the generative role that is played by labour in establishing value, but critiques an historic system of production that is organized on behalf of private property. Marx's critique of capital highlights how its processes of production constitute conditions of alienation for labour. While production depends on labour, workers are denied control over what happens in production and to the products of their labour. Marx remarks, 'Political economy starts out from labour as the real soul of production, and yet gives nothing to labour and everything to private property. Proudhon has dealt with this contradiction by deciding for labour and against private property. But we have seen that this apparent contradiction is the contradiction of *estranged labour* with itself and that political economy has merely formulated the laws of estranged labour.'[15] Under capital Marx highlights four inter-related forms of alienation. Given that production is organized so that its forces are owned by the capitalist class, the producers, that is the proletariat, are thereby alienated from the products they produce, which are owned and sold by capitalists. The conditions of production, under which the proletariat produces commodities, are alienating because the proletariat is denied the freedom to produce freely. Members of the proletariat are alienated from one another because they are competitors in a market for labour that is constituted by capital. Again and relatedly, human beings under capitalism are alienated from their species' powers, which consist in their capacities to produce freely,

---

[15] K. Marx, 'Economic and Philosophical Manuscripts', p. 332.

socially, and universally. Under capital, production is turned against those who are the producers in that the latter determine neither what is produced nor how it is produced. This alienation is an historical condition and its resolution resides in a prospective historical communist revolution that will break with the very conceptual world of capital.

The 'Economic and Philosophical Manuscripts' take communism to be radically distinct from capitalism even if the prospect of communism is shaped by its historical formation under capitalism. Marx neither takes the human species to be defined nor to be confined by supposedly enduring characteristics. Rather, humanity develops as its productive capacity increases and capitalism contributes to human development by enabling a sharp increase in productive techniques. But capitalism limits the capacity of human beings to express themselves in free and cooperative ways. A revolutionary break from capitalism is required because a competitive, unequal system, in which producers do not exert control over production has to be overturned in favour of a new cooperative system in which production is planned and coordinated on a cooperative basis under communism. Marx declares, 'It [socialism] is the *positive* self-consciousness of man, no longer mediated through the abolition of religion, just as *real life* is positive reality no longer mediated through the abolition of private property, through *communism*. Communism is the act of positing as the negation of the negation and is therefore a real phase, necessary for the next period of historical development, in the emancipation and recovery of mankind.'[16] Communism is not to be conceived as an authoritarian and restrictive system, as Marx imagines that a free and equal relationship between men and women will be an index of social progress under communism.[17] Marx insists that capitalism is insusceptible of piecemeal reform, because its problems are not to be ameliorated. For instance, increasing the share of wealth that is distributed to the poor or to workers is inadequate, because of the endemic alienation of the entire system of relationships and operations under capitalism. Conditions of production determine the producers in ways that have to be reversed. Hence Marx's politics are revolutionary in that relations of production have to be overturned and an entirely new system of productive social relations established.

After 1844 Marx frames a more determinate historical perspective on capitalism, the development of production, and the practice of politics. *The German Ideology* is taken standardly to be seminal in Marx's development of a theory of history.[18] Its essays on Young Hegelians highlight the role of the mode of production as the site for incubating historical change and identify large-scale historical change as arising out of the contradictions obtaining at critical conjunctures between the forces and relations of production. Hence

---

[16] Ibid., p. 358.   [17] Ibid., p. 347.   [18] But see the comments in chapter 2.

they provide a set of conceptual terms to identify specific historic forms of production and general analysis of the human species is largely jettisoned. Marx and Engels provide a synoptic account of historical development in *The Communist Manifesto*, and both texts highlight the role of technology in causing tensions in modes of production, but they also point to the role of class and the tensions between classes in providing the impetus for revolutionary change. In theory and practice Marx recognizes how class conflict shapes political behaviour and the dynamics of historical change. In his generic surveys of the sociology of capitalism and of the prospect of revolution he abstracts from the specificity of particular situations to designate class conflict a straightforward struggle between capitalists and the proletariat. This designation is of a piece with the language of his more general theoretical statements on history, which tend to portray change as occurring due to very general causes that abstract from particular circumstances. In his occasional writings on politics, class and historical circumstances are specified more closely, and class conflict appears to be expressed in particular and divergent ways.

In 'The Class Struggles in France: 1848–1850' and 'The Eighteenth Brumaire of Louis Bonaparte', conflicts between classes and political institutions and leaders receive more complex and individuated forms of analysis.[19] While class interests derive from the generic role of class in production, classes are specified in more detail and their activities are taken to allow for a degree of independence from structural determination. In 'The Class Struggles in France: 1848–1850' financial capital organizes itself separately from industrial capital, and classes and fractions of classes are taken to operate politically in coalition with other interests to form power blocs. In 'The Eighteenth Brumaire of Louis Bonaparte', the peasantry plays a significant political role and Louis Napoleon is shown to operate independently from the class interests of civil society. Marx allows for him to play a tragi-comic role that is somewhat independent even from the interests of the peasantry. Marx observes, 'Driven by the contradictory demands of his situation and being at the same time, like a conjurer, under the necessity of keeping the public gaze fixed on himself, as Napoleon's substitute, by springing constant surprises, that is to say, under the necessity of executing a *coup d'etat en miniature* every day, Bonaparte throws the entire bourgeois economy into confusion . . .'.[20] What remains constant is the fundamental role that is played by class in politics and the directionality of radical political activity. In his late *Critique of the Gotha Programme*, Marx critiques reformist socialists for contemplating accommodation to capital and existing political organization. He remains firm in his resolve to achieve

---

[19] K. Marx, 'The Class Struggles in France: 1848–1850' and 'The Eighteenth Brumaire of Louis Bonaparte' trans. B. Fawkes, in K. Marx, *Surveys from Exile* (Harmondsworth, Penguin Books, 1973).
[20] K. Marx, 'The Eighteenth Brumaire of Louis Bonaparte', p. 248.

communism and securing a radically different system of production, which will render traditional distributional schemes, and their proposed modifications, redundant.[21]

Marx's later systematic analysis of capital rehearses the radical and holistic critique of capitalism that is expressed in the 'Economic and Philosophical Manuscripts'. It provides for a wholesale rejection of capital, as well as identifying and indicting inter-related forms of alienation. Marx's mature economics establishes the constitutive patterns of social and economic activity under capital that determine forms of exploitation and the coercive regulation of behaviour. Marx conceives of the social practices associated with capital and its productive relations as constraining conduct, so that it is not open to individual capitalists or even social and political movements to campaign for piecemeal changes to alter the conditions of social and economic life. Rather, Marx sees the systemic operations of capital as defining and regulating how the system operates, which in turn demands its wholesale overthrow. In the *Grundrisse* Marx offers a systemic account of how money circulates and how its reproduction enables its further expansion, which in turn establishes the conditions for the development and further deployment of capital.[22] Money is understood as forming an infinite system. Marx remarks, 'The circulation of money like that of commodities, begins at an infinity of different points, and to an infinity of different points it returns.'[23] Capital is conceived as self-determining, and unlike money forms an infinitely expansionary process as the redeployment of an expanded fund of money yields a further increase on its return, which in turn furnishes the conditions for further expansion. There is no limit on this activity, it is continuous and provides no terminus or telos for its activity, because the deployment of capital is a move that adheres neither to an end nor to a limit, save that of its own maintenance. Just as thinking for Hegel is a freely developing expansionary activity so, for Marx, the processes that produce capital entail its continuous self-expansion, and yet just as forms of thinking, such as purely quantitative procedures are incoherent in themselves, so capital depends crucially upon the exploitation of the use-value of labour. Labour is at once integral to the creative conditions of the production and reproduction of capital, and yet is exploited, subject to commodified processes of misrecognition, and declines as a proportion of capital in its processes of expansion.[24] The *Grundrisse* rehearses the language of alienation that Marx had used in his early writings to portray the use and

---

[21] K. Marx, *Critique of the Gotha Programme* trans. T. Carver, in K. Marx, *Marx's Later Political Writings* (Cambridge, Cambridge University Press, 1998).

[22] K. Marx, *Grundrisse*, p. 186.

[23] K. Marx, *Grundrisse*, p. 261. See also G. Browning, 'Good and Bad Infinites in Hegel and Marx', in G. Browning, *Hegel and the History of Philosophy* (Basingstoke and New York, 1999), pp. 93–106.

[24] See K. Marx, *Capital*, vol. 1, pp. 76–88.

misuse of labour, invoking also Hegel's master–slave relationship to express labour's alienation. He observes, 'It [the master–slave relation] is represented—in mediated form—in capital, and thus likewise forms a ferment of its dissolution and is an emblem of its limitation.'[25]

In his later writings Marx reads the operations of capital to be comprehensive and intensive. He analyses the prodigious expansion of capital and capitalism and highlights the manifest and destructive effects of capital on labour and on forms of social recognition. Landscapes and townscapes are transformed literally by capital, as capital exploits intensifying opportunities for its employment, and tightens its grip on activities. These processes are exemplified by subsequent developments such as the commodification of sport and the commercial exploitation of human affective relations. Marx's elaborated dissection of the political economy of capital in the *Grundrisse* and *Capital* provides a holistic critique of capital and its operations. *Capital* imagines commodification as a process of mystification just as commodities are totems of alienation in the 'Economic and Philosophical Manuscripts'. The systematic analysis of the conditions of capital entail a revolutionary break with capitalism the projected achievement of communism and the continuity of Marx's critique of capitalism.

INTERPRETING MARX

Marx's social and political theory has proved to be a continuous influence on subsequent theorists and a source of continual reinterpretation, not least by those who consider themselves Marxist or post-Marxist. The continuing process of reinterpretation is a feature of the history of political thought. The study of Marx's ideas provides a concentrated case study in the processes of interpretation and reinterpretation, because there have been multiple and divergent interpretations by supporters and sympathetic interpreters. The divergences between Marxist interpretations of Marx reflect back interestingly on the doctrines of Marx. They pose the questions of if and why Marx's theory lends itself to the process of continuing reinterpretation. In the following survey of particular Marxist and post-Marxist interpretations of Marx, the plausibility of several differing interpretations of Marx will be reviewed in the light of the character of Marx's theory and the changing standpoints of its interpreters.

The continuing reinterpretation of Marx's social and political theory reflects the truth of Gadamer's contention that interpretation constitutes an ongoing

---

[25] K. Marx, *Grundrisse*, p. 501.

dialogue between past and present. Hence no interpretation of a past doctrine is ever fixed definitively. The present is continually changing and its perspectives on the past are transformed accordingly. There are many reasons why interpretations of Marx have changed over time. Interpretations reflect different horizons of the present, which in turn affect horizons of the past. The process of interpreting Marx is influenced by changing perceptions on the present and past. These perceptions alter due to changes in the availability and knowledge of Marx's publications and to developments in the way in which the contexts in which he operated are understood as well as reflecting the changing circumstances of interpreters that include socio-economic developments and philosophical and ideological affiliations that bear upon Marx's theory. Of course the altered circumstances in which interpreters are situated may be interpreted by their proponents in Marxist terms that reflect back on their interpretations of Marx. The very variety of interpretations of Marx raises questions over how Marx is to be read. The interpretive ambiguities to which they draw attention deflects from a deterministic or scientific way of reading Marx.

Karl Kautsky, editor of the journal of the German Social Democratic Party (SPD), *Neuve Zeit,* played a leading role in interpreting Marx for the party and became an authoritative figure in the Second International (1889–1916). The SPD became a mass party in the latter half of the nineteenth century and gained widespread popular support, but at the same time was denied access to power by the authoritarian German monarchy. It pursued moderate reforms and built up its membership while Kautsky framed an interpretation of Marx that anticipated the demise of capitalism, due to its growing and necessary contradictions. Kautsky's interpretation of Marx concentrates upon *Capital* in highlighting the destructive tendencies internal to capital, and does not reference the earlier philosophical writings, which were published in the twentieth century. In his Introduction to the English publication of Marx's *Early Writings* Colletti observes, '[T]he Marxism of the Second International was constituted in almost total ignorance of the difficult and intricate process through which Marx had passed in the years from 1843 to 1845, as he formulated historical materialism for the first time.'[26] Kautsky's Marxism is formulated before Marx's key early writings, 'Critique of Hegel's Doctrine of the State' and 'Economic and Philosophical Manuscripts' were published, in 1928 and 1932 respectively. *The German Ideology* was first published in 1932. If Kautsky's interpretation of Marx did not take account of unpublished early writings, it also reflects the circumstances of contemporary Germany and Europe. Bernstein a fellow leader of the SPD broke with Kautsky and the Party by developing revisionist views. Bernstein considered that material

[26] A. Colletti, 'Introduction', in K. Marx, *Early Writings*, p. 9.

progress under capitalism had allowed the working class to improve its situation and he cast doubt on the breakdown of capitalism and questioned the necessity of revolution if workers could benefit from increasing wealth under capitalism.[27] While Kautsky countered by denying that he maintained the sheer inevitability of revolution, in the Erfurt Programme of 1893 he had observed, 'We consider the breakdown (*Zusammenbruch*) of existing society as inevitable.'[28] Moreover, the emphasis of his interpretation of Marx was on the internal destructive crises of capital and the necessity of revolution, while concentrating on developing mass support for the Party. This debate between Bernstein and Kautsky reflects events subsequent to Marx's death and shows how interpretations arise out of new circumstances in which orthodox and revisionist analyses of the current economic situation impacted upon interpretations of Marx.

Gadamer's insistence that interpretation of past texts is conditioned by changing interpretive horizons is borne out by this debate. Kautsky's deterministic reading of Marx and Marxism is shaped by the situation of a Party, which is motivated by a sense of an impending necessary victory for a mass party that is growing in strength and can come to power without the complications of revolutionary activity. Likewise, Bernstein's revisionism arises out of reflection on developments after the death of Marx, notably in his perception of an improvement in the position of the working class that casts doubt on the claims and the directionality of Marx's theory.[29] Again, Lenin's innovative Marxist reading of how a Marxist Party is to operate in an absolutist state and to prepare for an international revolution reflects local Russian circumstances and wider international developments since Marx's death. He imposes tight central organization on the Bolsheviks and perceives capitalism's survival to be due in part to heightened imperial exploitation of colonies, which at the same time presage the collapse of capitalism because of the competition between imperial powers.[30] The confluence of changing theoretical and political circumstances and the accessibility of recently published texts explains the rise of a more philosophical interpretation of Marx after the Second World War in the West. Anglo-American scholars such as McLellan, Avineri, and Ollman, drawing upon preceding Hegelian interpretations by Lukacs, Marcuse, and the Frankfurt School, interpreted Marx as maintaining a philosophical theoretical perspective. The post-war prosperity and increasing popular indifference to

[27] R. Bernstein, *Evolutionary Socialism* trans. E. Harvey (New York, Random House Publications, 1961).

[28] See G. Lichtheim, 'Karl Kautsky', in G. Lichtheim, *Marxism* (London, Routledge and Kegan Paul, 1961), pp. 259–78.

[29] R. Bernstein, *Evolutionary Socialism*.

[30] V. Lenin, *What is To Be Done*, vol. 1, pp. 119–271 and V. Lenin, *Imperialism the Highest Stage of Capitalism,* vol. 2, pp. 187–310, in V. Lenin, *Lenin's Selected Works* (Moscow, Progress Publishers, 1963).

ideology disturbed optimistic estimates of the necessary demise of capital and of the inevitability of proletarian revolution. Added to these contextual considerations, accessibility to the Hegelian early works encouraged a more philosophical and humanistic reading of Marx.

Hegelian and philosophical Marxism was countered in turn by Marxist scholars, including Althusser, who drew upon the French twentieth-century structuralism and a determination to support a specifically communist form of politics by maintaining a line of interpretation that demarcated Marxist science from normative social democratic standpoints.[31] Towards the end of the twentieth century Anglophone Marx scholars, such as Elster and Cohen, interpreted Marx's thought by deploying current analytical methods of philosophy and social science. They disavowed Marx's Hegelian language as so much nineteenth-century baggage and applied functionalist and rational choice concepts to reinvigorate Marx studies. They ditched Marx's teleology along with his philosophical holism to concentrate upon what they took to be his formulation of causal explanations of historical change. They privileged Marx's later writings, because of their perceived departure from the more Hegelian language of the early writings and their intimation of a form of rational choice technological determinism, though they disagreed on the latter's plausibility.[32] Cohen takes the 'Preface to A Contribution to the Critique of Political Economy' to encapsulate a programme of causal explanation, where causal priority is assigned to productive forces, which are separated from relations of production and the economic structure or economic base of society that is constituted by the sum total of productive forces.[33] Cohen argues that the technological development of forces of production is the determining rational explanation of the affiliated functional development of production relations and of the superstructural arrangements of politics and culture. While Elster agrees that Marx develops this form of causal historical explanation, he is sceptical of the explanatory force of a theory that does not supply a mechanism for instituting the development of forces of production.[34] In retrospectively attributing to Marx a form of rational choice theory that was developed after Marx's death, Cohen observes how continuous technological innovation harmonizes with the rationality of human beings and the priority humanity must assign to improving total productive capacity so as to satisfy human needs. The theory allows for the impact of the unintended consequences of large-scale technological change.

---

[31] See L. Althusser, *For Marx* trans. B. Brewster (Harmondsworth, Penguin, 1969).

[32] G. Cohen, *Karl Marx's Theory of History: A Defence* (Oxford, Clarendon Press, 1978), pp. 1–35; J. Elster, *Making Sense of Marx* (Cambridge, Cambridge University Press, 1985), pp. 1–30.

[33] K. Marx, '"Preface"' to A Contribution to the Critique of Political Economy.

[34] See G. Cohen, *Karl Marx's Theory of History: A Defence*, pp. 138–75; J. Elster, *Making Sense of Marx*, pp. 235–511.

The argument for attributing to Marx a causal theory of history is supported by some of Marx's express comments, notably his highlighting of the impact on history of industrial machinery and of new forms of transportation. However, Marx neither argues decisively for such a theory, nor assumes the individualistic premises of rational choice theory. Moreover a structural, functional explanation does not provide a sufficiently supple account of social agency to explain historical change. From time to time Marx uses the language of determinism and of general theorizing on history, but he qualifies these commitments by maintaining that historical developments require empirical explanations rather than deriving them from general formulas.[35] The impetus for rethinking Marx in an analytic guise sprang from the ossification of Soviet communism, the continued effectiveness of capitalism, and a fashionable preference for current analytic methods over holistic Hegelianism. The upshot is that Cohen and Elster appear more post-Marxist than Marxist in interpreting Marx. Yet their focus upon causal explanation allows for a reading of Marx which recognizes technological and functionalist dimensions of his thought.

The influential texts of Hardt and Negri, *Empire*, *Multitude*, and *Commonwealth*, are assumed to be post-Marxist due to their engagement with events and developments post-dating Marx, and because they break with the Hegelian teleology of Marx.[36] Hardt and Negri imagine the world to be globalized, with power stretching across and beyond borders, and with the possibilities of revolt no longer concentrated in an industrial and male proletariat. Prospective agents of revolution are located across the confines of class, gender, and ethnicity. Hardt and Negri also theorize production anew in imagining positive possibilities in what is common and beyond demonstrable quantification. Workers are seen as sharing affective and innovative activities, which are not designated aspects of their labour but which contribute to production and presage a new social order. Their disruption of standard Marxist arguments is motivated by their reading of developments since Marx and their application of post-Marxist Foucauldian and De Leuzean arguments to supersede what they take to be a monolithic Hegelian-Marxist conceptualization of society. Like analytical Marxists, their reading of Marx is shaped by post-Marxist assumptions that tend to misidentify aspects of Marx. Like Hegel, Marx is aware of the risks that a teleological approach can misconstrue the past, and again like Hegel, his holism is designed to be inclusive rather than exclusionary. Yet Marx's Hegelianism runs counter to post-Marxist assumptions of what Hegelianism might offer. Ironically, Hardt and Negri rely on a highly generic conceptualization of empire and the multitude, which displays the very features of an

---

[35] Both kinds of statement are evident in K. Marx and F. Engels, *The German Ideology*. For Marx's methodology more generally see K. Marx, *Grundrisse*, pp. 1–101.

[36] M. Hardt and A. Negri, *Empire* (Cambridge, Boston and London, Harvard University Press, 2000), p. 49.

essentialized conceptual holism and supervening teleology that they impute to Marx and Hegel.[37]

Marx is interpreted in many guises by Marxists and post-Marxists, and these changing permutations lend support to Gadamer's hermeneutical sense of interpretation representing a fusion of horizons between past and present. A past thinker's theories are viewed differently from differing horizons. The malleability of interpretive practice indicates the role that is played by subsequent developments and changing interpretive strategies in formulating a past thinker's ideas. Marxist and post-Marxist theories of Marx read the past world of Marx in the light of their situations so that Marx appears as a Hegelian critic of cultural commodification, a prophet of an inevitable proletarian victory, a New Left liberationist, a proto French structuralist, an analytical theorist of social change, or a relic of a nineteenth-century form of emancipation that has been post-dated by globalization. The differences between these appearances of Marx reflect the changing intellectual and political contexts of interpretation. They also draw upon different texts of Marx, showing how the past is constructed according to the available evidence. The changing interpretations of Marx's political thought do admit of critical evaluation. The influence of changing circumstances on the interpretation of ideas does not entail that interpretations are to be reduced to the circumstances in which they were produced. Interpretations can be evaluated. For instance, reading Marx in the light of all his available texts suggest that interpretation of Marx should include his early writings as they convey a powerful critique of modern capitalist society. Moreover, connections can be made between the early and later texts so that a continuity between Marx's early and later thought makes sense of all the texts rather than imagining many discrete forms of Marx's thought. The very range of interpretations of Marx, which often turn upon differing conceptualizations of Marx's theoretical strategy, points to the irreducibility of ideas to non-ideational factors. To appreciate the significance of theory and its formulations militates against reading Marx as a reductive theorist, who embraces economic or technological determinism and excludes the efficacy of ideas. An interpretive history of Marx interpretation highlights the role of ideas and interpretation.

Interpreting Marx in the light of present ideas and interests is the express focus of Derrida's *Specters of Marx* (1993). This reading of Marx is an example of Derrida's late turn towards the political and represents a productive way of re-imagining the present by turning to the past.[38] Derrida uses Marx to interrogate the contemporary new internationalism, by which Western powers assert a global political agenda that privileges human rights and

---

[37] See G. Browning, *Global Theory from Kant to Hardt and Negri* (Basingstoke and New York, Palgrave Macmillan, 2012), pp. 139–54.

[38] J. Derrida, *Specters of Marx* trans. P. Kamuf (London and New York, Routledge, 1994).

economic freedom. Derrida takes this agenda to be partial. It represents a partisan position masquerading as the truth. Its closure of debate and its construction of a definitive normative route to the future persuades Derrida to call up a contrary spirit, a spectre that can play upon the prejudices of the present like Banquo's ghost. Marx is summoned to offer an alternative reading of global development, which is challenging in its departure from a neo-liberal agenda. The ideological identification of freedom with acquisitiveness, commodification, and human rights as individual possessions constitute a form of injustice to which Marx's focus upon production and the exploitation of labour provides a timely counter-move. Derrida's reading of Marx exhibits the timeliness of reading Marx out of his immediate context so that he contributes to a future context of debate that is shorn of radical alternatives to the language of individualism. It is a demonstration that the past may serve as a vantage point to interrogate the present by unsettling present contextual assumptions. Derrida remarks, 'At a time when a new world disorder is attempting to install its neo-capitalism and neo-liberalism, no disavowal has managed to rid itself of all Marx's ghosts.'[39] Marx's own internationalism renders his thought strikingly apposite to the contemporary admission of a global perspective. He observes, 'And communism was essentially distinguished from other labor movements by its *international* character. No organized political movement in the history of humanity had ever yet presented itself as *geo-political*, thereby inaugurating the space that is now ours and that today is reaching its limits, the limits of the earth and the limits of the political' (emphasis in original).[40]

For Derrida, Marx is to be re-addressed in the spirit of critique, which is not to be trammelled by Marxism as an ontology, a philosophical doctrine, or a metaphysical system. Marx is to be distinguished from the trajectory of Marxism as instituted in the apparatus of party, state, or workers' international.[41] Derrida invokes a Marx that is severed from Marxism to counter the universalization of liberal democracy and to question a formal conception of law and rights that ignores socio-economic injustices.[42] Above all, what Marx offers is the promise of communism, the messianism of a 'democracy to come', in which the limits and partiality of the neo-liberal economic and political global order are exposed as being partial and limited.[43] Derrida's interpretive procedure is deconstructive. He is alert to the multiplicity of meaning in Marx's texts and to the unacknowledged limits of the neo-liberal discursive global order. He revives an irregular form of Marx to disconcert the regularity of the new world order. His reading of Marx accentuates what is marginal in Marx, namely his preoccupation with ghosts. In *The Communist Manifesto* a spectre is held to be haunting Europe, the spectre of communism, which conveys Marx's preoccupation with

---

[39] Ibid., p. 46.   [40] Ibid., p. 47.   [41] Ibid., pp. 86–7.
[42] Ibid., p. 97.   [43] Ibid., p. 91.

the ghostly and unreal. What appears as ghostly plays a role in shaping perceptions of the present and future.[44] Derrida suggests that the figure of the spectre serves as a metaphor for what lies between presence and non-presence. He likens a spectre to a reading of a legacy, such as Marx's thought, which calls upon us to work through its meaning, and to open the present to its interpretive penetration by the past.[45] He observes, 'A masterpiece always moves, by definition, in the manner of a ghost.'[46] If Derrida conjures up Marx as a ghost to disrupt the binary divide between the real and the unreal and so to exert pressure on the restrictions of contemporary thought and practice, he also detects in Marx an obsession with ghosts. While the beginning of *The Communist Manifesto* announces communism as a spectre, *The German Ideology* reveals an obsession with ghosts and the spectral. Derrida notes, 'It was a Hegelian neo-evangelism that Marx denounced with great verve and vehemence in the Stirnerian theory of ghosts.'[47] The predominant concern of the manuscripts of *The German Ideology* is to critique Stirner, and Stirner had been obsessed by his self-appointed task of destroying the ghosts of Hegelian philosophy. Stirner is caricatured by Marx as Saint Max, who trails the ghosts of Hegel's philosophy and who identifies the multiplicity of ghosts that haunt the texts of his immediate Hegelian successors, Feuerbach and Bauer. Certainly Hegel and Young Hegelian theorists are condemned by Stirner for postulating abstract essentialized entities that absorb the material living being that is the ego, the individual, who is at the centre of Stirner's own philosophy. *Geist*, the Hegelian Spirit is dismissed as a ghost to whom individuals are subordinated and Feuerbach's philosophy is denounced because his substitution of humanity for Hegel's *Geist* does not exorcize spiritual possession of the individual. Individuals, in Feuerbach's philosophy, are neither free nor real in that they are taken to adhere to an essentialized humanity.

Marx's critique of Stirner consists in exposing Stirner's obsessive compulsive fixation upon ghosts and abstractions. Derrida observes, 'Marx denounces a hyperbolic surplus of spectrality.'[48] Moreover, Marx turns Stirner's critique of Hegel and the Young Hegelians against Stirner's own philosophy. He highlights how Stirner's use of abstract concepts such as self-consciousness and man are themselves religious or spectral and he condemns the elaborated teleological history of humanity that Stirner deploys to justify the culmination of egoism in his own, *The Ego and Its Own*.[49] Marx pours scorn on Stirner by contrasting his grandiose claims of historical development, climaxing in egoism, with his exclusion of actual social and economic phenomena from its consummation. The individual ego, for Marx, is restricted and abstract outside of a supporting and informing social context. Derrida rehearses Marx's critique of Stirner and observes its affinity with Stirner's own preceding

---

[44] K. Marx and F. Engels, *The Communist Manifesto*, p. 67.
[45] J. Derrida, *Specters of Marx*, pp. 13–14.   [46] Ibid., p. 20.
[47] Ibid., p. 83.   [48] Ibid., p. 161.   [49] Ibid., p. 153.

critique of the Young Hegelians. Marx, like Stirner, is obsessed with ghosts and tracks Stirner's exorcism of Hegelian thought. Yet Marx's obsession with ghosts in *The German Ideology*, as Derrida observes, is never explained.

If *The German Ideology* reveals Marx to be a theorist who resembles Stirner in his obsession with ghosts, Derrida goes on to show how *Capital* resumes a preoccupation with the spectral. He highlights how Marx's analysis of exchange-value and of the fetishism of commodities ascribes ghost-like qualities in capitalism. The fetishism of commodities consists in their apparent autonomy from the actual conditions of production. Marx maintains, 'A commodity is therefore a mysterious thing, simply because in it the social character of men's labour appears to them as an objective character stamped upon the product of their labour; because the relation of the producers to the sum total of their own labour is presented to them as a social relation, not between them, but between the products of their labour.'[50] Marx interprets commodities to be ghost-like in their apparent determining of production, which is an inversion of the actual social world and the actual production of commodities by workers. Derrida concludes, 'In other words, as soon as there is production, there is fetishism: idealization, autonomization and automatization, dematerialization and spectral incorporation, mourning work coextensive with all work, and so forth.'[51] Derrida's recognition of Marx's reliance upon the language of ghosts and the spectral leads him to question *Capital*'s separation of the real from the ghost-like. Derrida reconsiders the opening chapters of *Capital* and their specification of the contradictions between use-value, exchange-value, and hence the exploitation of surplus-value. Marx imagines that use-value is specifiable outside of any reference to the spectral inverted world of exchange-value in that the use of an object is assumed to be clear-cut and demonstrable without reference to the mysteries of exchange. In contrast Derrida maintains that use-value implies exchange-value, because meaning is infinite and inter-relational rather than determinate and restricted. Signs do not operate outside of their mutual relations. Use-value is not to be conceived as a determinate code of reference by which calculations of value and surplus-value can be conducted, but like all concepts it is to be interpreted. The upshot is that Derrida is critical of Marx's critique of capital. His work of deconstruction recognizes that the interplay of concepts is not to be interrupted by a privileging of a particular conceptual framework. The real does not trump the ghostly because the spectral implies the indeterminacy of the real.

While *Specters of Marx* is critical of Marxist theory, it testifies to its force by invoking it as a spectre to subvert current orthodoxies that determine what are

---

[50] K. Marx, *Capital*, p. 77.   [51] J. Derrida, *Specters of Marx*, p. 209.

to count as realities. Derrida interprets Marx in the light of the prevailing situation, and refuses to read Marx as being absorbed by subsequent communist state practice. His conjuration of ghosts sets the scene for a review of the present in the light of a shade from the past. Derrida's Marx is not simply Marx, for Derrida interprets him in the light of the present time being out of joint and he undertakes a very particular interpretation of Marx. It is one that reflects Derrida's interpretive practice. It invokes selective themes in Marx, notably the promise of communism in ways that Marx himself would not have highlighted, to serve as a reminder of the possibility of the impossible and the openness of the present to voices from the past, which can provide alternative futures possibilities. Derrida succeeds in showing the relevance of Marx's focus on production and economic domination, which contrasts with the formulaic rhetoric of a new internationalism that maintains a legal civil formalism. Moreover, the very distinctness of the goal of communism from the present agenda also serves to challenge current expectations. His reading of Marx is partial and questions can be raised over his ignoring of Marx's large-scale reading of history, as well as his materialism. For instance, Derrida does not question how Marx's interrogation of Stirner relates to his professed assertion of materialism and a materialist theory of history, which are announced at the outset of the essays in *The German Ideology*. Doubtless Derrida would not claim to provide the last or only word on Marx and might well settle for providing precisely an interpretation that is unsettling in leaving questions unanswered.

CONCLUSION

Marx's political theory offers a sharp critique of liberalism that remains of continuing relevance in the current century. Its relevance is brought out by Derrida, who turns to Marx to question assumptions of a neo-liberal order, which has dominated global politics into the twenty-first century. Derrida's turn to Marx reflects how a past political theorist is not to be imprisoned in the context in which their theories are formulated. Readings of theorists are never final because meaning is never to be finalized for the present and for the past. The present can be disturbed by ghost-like interventions from the past while the past remains open to being interpreted in new ways. Gadamer's hermeneutical insight into the inter-relations between past and present horizons of understanding allows for multiple readings of Marx and for multiple readings of the present. Contemporary global theory aspires to replace preceding modern theories, such as Marxism, yet in the light of the present, Marx himself is to be seen as a global theorist. Certainly radical theorists of globalization, such as Hardt and Negri, owe much to Marxist language and Marx's insight into the illimitable character of the operations of capital.[52] Marx's identification of the dynamic power of capital to transform the world contributes to an understanding of how global relations are constituted. The relentless production of commodities and their continual conversion into money that supplies flows of capital, intensifying and extending the reach of commodity production throughout the globe and in every sector of social life provide an explanation for the radical transformation of global social and economic life. Recognition of the power of global capital lies at the heart of a Marxist message to the planet, which indicts liberalism's commitment to equality by highlighting the role of oppressive structures of economic power.

The interplay between past and present in interpreting Marx is evident in the history of Marxist interpretation of Marx. Evidently Marx's political project of communism and the subsequent history of Marxist parties and regimes have influenced the ways in which his texts have been read. The Stalinist regime used his texts blatantly to sanction its own status. But more objective interpretations of Marx's work by Marxist scholars have reflected their intellectual and political contexts. Theorists of the Second International offered a deterministic reading of the prospective achievement of communism, at least in part to confirm support amongst mass working class parties. The philosophically sophisticated versions of Marxism that have been formulated by Frankfurt School theorists reflect their own philosophical engagement with predecessors and the dark times of inter-war Germany, where philosophical or aesthetic resistance to the status quo offered relief amidst burgeoning pessimism. Post-war Anglo-American readings of Marx as a philosophical humanist are consonant with a prevailing prosperity, and a decline in working class radicalism. More recent rational choice versions of Marx reflect changes in academic fashion that appear distant from Marx's own engagement with Hegel and Hegelian philosophy. The varieties of interpretation disclose changing interpretive contexts but also reflect critical concentration upon certain texts. The early philosophical writings were unavailable to theorists of the Second International and were ignored by recent analytical theorists. The possibilities of Marx interpretation should also recognize contextual influences upon Marx's intentions and interests and rhetoric. An undertheorized aspect of Marx scholarship is the interpretation of Marx's intentions. While Skinner and the Cambridge School have tended to ignore Marx, their interpretive style would be suited to examining important issues relating to the circumstances in which his texts were composed and the purposes for which they were written. *The German Ideology* is a

---

[52] M. Hardt and A. Negri, *Empire*, p. 65; M. Hardt and A. Negri, *Multitude—War and Democracy in the Age of Empire* ((New York, The Penguin Press, 2004), p. 225; M. Hardt and A. Negri, *Commonwealth* (Cambridge Mass, Belknapp Press of Harvard University Press, 2009), p. 172.

case in point in that its very claim to be a text is under suspicion.[53] Moreover, the rhetoric of Marx in the manuscripts of *The German ideology* and in related texts such as *The Holy Family* derives from the force of Marx's polemical opposition to fellow Young Hegelian theorists.[54] Marx's texts are shaped by the occasions and purposes for which they are written. *Capital* might appear as a comprehensive analysis of capital and capitalism and yet its composition reflects Marx's decisions on what to prioritize, for instance in his raising the question of the nature of class without providing a detailed account of its character.[55]

[53] See T. Carver and D. Blank, *Marx's 'German Ideology' Manuscripts—Presentation and Analysis of the 'Feuerbach Chapter'*.

[54] See G. Browning, '*The German Ideology*: The Theory of History and the History of Theory', *History of Political Thought*, vol. 14, no. 3, 1993, pp. 75–92.

[55] K. Marx, *Capital*, vol. 1, p. 267.

15

Jeremy Bentham

Enlightenment Politics

INTRODUCTION

Understanding in the history of political thought involves the interplay between texts and contexts. The devil, of course, is in the detail, in that texts, as Derrida's deconstructive manoeuvres insinuate, cannot be read innocently as the mere instruments of authors' purposes. Again, the Cambridge School shows how texts relate to contexts in ways that require historical research, linking the themes and rhetoric of texts to contemporary assumptions and discourses. Amidst interpretive controversies the actual physical identification of texts tends to be taken for granted, even if interpretation raises questions about their character and the intentions of their authors.[1] With Bentham, fundamental questions about what constitutes a text cannot be avoided. As the Director of the Bentham Project that is dedicated to producing an authoritative *The Collective Works of Jeremy Bentham*, Schofield observes, 'In relation to the Bentham "canon" the aggregate of texts that have been attributed to Bentham has changed radically in the past, is changing now and will certainly change in the future.'[2] The identity of Bentham's texts, and hence the very materiality of his thought, is by no means straightforward. He is most well known for a handful of writings that he published in his lifetime, which elaborate a general conception of utilitarianism and set out his moral and political ideas. These texts include *An Introduction to the Principles of Morals and Legislation* and *A Fragment on Government*.[3] Outside the UK Bentham's

---

[1] Marx is a case in point. His collaboration with Engels, the status of his occasional writings, and the questions over the nature of *The German Ideology* remain controversial.

[2] P. Schofield, *Bentham: A Guide for the Perplexed* (London, Continuum, 2009), p. 20.

[3] J. Bentham, *An Introduction to the Principles of Morals and Government* (London, Athlone Press, 1970) and J. Bentham, *A Fragment on Government*, in J. Bentham, *A Comment on the Commentaries and a Fragment on Government*, ed. J.H. Burns and H.L.A. Hart (London, Athlone Press, 1977), pp. 393–553.

ideas were made available through a number of recensions of his works that were produced by Etienne Dumont, which in turn were translated back into English. These works, along with texts that Bentham himself published, and selected unpublished writings were collected together in a standard edition of works, which was published between the years 1838–43.[4] However, this Bowring edition of Bentham's works only included a fraction of his unpublished writings, which, in turn, were not always presented in ways consonant with Bentham's apparent intentions. The Bentham Project, which was established in the twentieth century at University College, London is dedicated to producing an authoritative collection of his works, including his voluminous hitherto unpublished works, which are produced in ways that aim to reflect Bentham's own intentions.[5]

The shifting character of Bentham's texts and the status that is to be accorded to those works published in his lifetime, and for which he became famous, raise questions beyond those that are called for by interpreting the intricacies and ambiguities of what is said in the texts. Hampsher-Monk, in reviewing Bentham scholarship, makes the case for continued concentration upon those texts which have traditionally been taken to be the core of Bentham's political thought.[6] This standpoint is plausible though the subsequent and continued publication of texts that bear upon issues of Bentham interpretation entail that attention requires to be paid to recently published material that has not figured in hitherto influential interpretations of Bentham. An example of how recent Bentham scholarship and editions of his work revise perceptions of Bentham is exemplified in the publishing history of the so-called 'Book of Fallacies', in which Bentham sets out a series of fallacious arguments that are seen to serve political ends. Some of Bentham's work on fallacies first appeared in 'Traite de sophisms politiques' in *Tactiques des assemblees legislatives,* a two-volume recension that was translated and published by Dumont in 1816. A two-volume work that was also based on Bentham's manuscripts, *The Book of Fallacies,* was edited and published by Bingham in 1816. *Bentham's Handbook of Political Fallacies,* which was based upon the Bingham edition, was published in 1952.[7] These editions of Bentham's work on fallacious arguments frame the arguments in abstract mode, highlighting how they commit the various fallacies for which they are condemned. In fact, Bentham intended his work on fallacies to be distinctly

---

[4] J. Bowring (ed.), *The Works of Jeremy Bentham* (Edinburgh, William Tait, 1843).

[5] See P. Schofield, *Bentham: A Guide For the Perplexed,* p. 20 and F. Rosen 'The Bentham Edition', *Politics,* vol. 16, 1996, pp. 127–32.

[6] I. Hampsher-Monk, *A History of Modern Political Thought* (Oxford, Blackwell, 1992), p. 306.

[7] See J. Bentham, *The Book of Fallacies* (Oxford, Oxford University Press, 2015); J. Bentham trans. E. Dumont, *Tactiques des assemblees legislatives* (Las Vegas, Nevada, Nabu Press, 2012); J. Bentham, *The Handbook of Political Fallacies,* ed. H. Larrabee (London, Octagon Books, 1980).

political in that he grouped the fallacies according to how they favoured political groups. Hence, he associated certain fallacies as 'ins' according to their use by government; others were deemed 'outs' because they were favoured by the opposition. Fallacies that were used by government and opposition were termed 'eithersides'. This distinctive way of organizing political arguments is followed in the latest edition of the fallacies, Schofield's *The Book of Fallacies,* which was published in 2015 as part of the Collected Works of Bentham.[8]

Schofield justifies following Bentham's original design for his argument on fallacies in terms of its historical authenticity in representing Bentham's original intentions.[9] The argument for publishing works in the form that their author intended is a strong one on historical grounds. It makes sense to present a work so that it reflects how an author intended it to be presented. The upshot of reading Bentham's work on fallacies in the way he intended highlights how Bentham is attuned to what may be termed the ideological dimensions of political argument. For instance, the fallacy of ancestor worship, which Bentham derives from a justification of a political practice by its following precedence, is deemed irrational insofar as a link to the past is not justificatory, but it serves a political purpose in promoting a political interest. The point behind, say, the maintenance of an undemocratic voting system does not reside in its consonance with past experience but with its 'fallacious' support for the interests of those who benefit from the present system. Bentham understood the source of much political argument to be the special and sinister interests of the few, namely politicians and their supporters, rather than the inherent reasonableness of the arguments. His exposure of fallacies is engaging in itself, but his recognition of the ideological character of political rhetoric becomes clearer when the original contextual frame of his analysis of fallacies is revealed.

What texts should be invoked in discussing Bentham's ideas? There is certainly a case for considering closely those works that Bentham himself published, and which served to promote his reputation. They constitute what Bentham and Benthamism have been taken to mean. Likewise the scholarly edition of Bowring contains material that remains of relevance to an assessment of Bentham. However, preceding works have been superseded if not altogether replaced by the latest scholarly editions, emanating from the Bentham Project at University College, London. They are designed to be comprehensive and historically accurate in reflecting the intentions of Bentham himself. The current publishing project of producing a comprehensive set of Bentham's writings is far from being realized, however, and is not without critics. *Of Sexual*

---

[8] See P. Schofield, 'Introduction' in J. Bentham, *The Book of Fallacies.* See also P. Schofield, *Bentham: A Guide for the Perplexed,* chapter 5.

[9] See P. Schofield, 'Introduction', in J. Bentham, *The Book of Fallacies,* pp. 1–35.

Irregularities and Other Writings on Sexual Morality (2014) collects multiple writings of Bentham on sex and sexuality, which were unpublished in his lifetime.[10] A former Director of the Bentham Project, Fred Rosen had observed that it would be wrong to publish a volume specifically devoted to sexual matters as it would not have been entertained as a publishing project by Bentham, given the prevailing climate of opinion in his lifetime.[11] However, Schofield, Pease-Watkin, and Quinn have put together such a book. Its essays show Bentham to be radical in ways not previously appreciated in that he expresses his tolerance of homosexuality and of diverse sexual practices. Utility is taken to be the determining criterion by which sexual activities are to be judged and hence abnormal forms of sex are to be permitted if happiness can thereby be increased. However, this edition does not include all of Bentham's essays pertaining to sexuality and has been criticized on that score.[12]

LIFE AND WORKS

While the publication of Bentham's texts continue to develop his profile, the figure of Bentham and his place in the history of political thought allows for multiple interpretations and excites controversy. On the face of things Bentham appears to be a very English theorist. He reacts against a disciplinary father, attends a public school, studies at Oxford University, and begins a projected career in law before devoting his life to applying clear thinking to the project of reforming English law, and its social and political practices. He values empirical observation, and suspected metaphysical language. He and his followers have exerted an impact upon British institutions and policies notably in public health, welfare provision, education, and the law. Yet things can be looked at differently. Bentham read continental European thinkers and influenced developments in the wider continent of Europe. Hence, he can be seen as a figure in a wider tradition of European Enlightenment, and his rationalism in promoting social change clashes with traditionalist elements of English thought and practice. Bentham was a radical who critiqued custom, the common law, and reliance upon tradition. He deprecated muddled thinking and traditional ways of doing things, and maintained a distinctly critical, rationalist edge to his thinking. Bentham's radicalism in shaping public policy divides critical opinion. His influence as a reformer has been immense and his

---

[10] J. Bentham, *Of Sexual Irregularities and Other Writings on Sexual Morality*, ed. P. Schofield, C. Pease-Watkin, and M. Quinn (Oxford, Oxford University Press, 2014).

[11] F. Rosen, 'The Bentham Edition', p. 16.

[12] See F. Dabholwala, Review of *Of Sexual Irregularities and Other Writings on Sexual Morality*, in the *Guardian*, 28 June 2015.

thinking has affected subsequent developments in many disciplines. While neo-classical economists and contemporary moral and legal philosophers acknowledge his example, critics of the Enlightenment and rationalism tend to set their sights against Bentham and his brand of utilitarianism. Hence, the force of Hegel's Counter-Enlightenment thinking is brought out in his critique of utility in a crucial section of his *Phenomenology of Spirit*.[13] English idealists Oakeshott and Collingwood react against what they take to be Bentham's one-dimensional rationalism.[14] Most famously, Foucault's deconstruction of Enlightenment assumptions imagines Bentham to be an emblematic figure of the disciplinary society, which he detects as operating underneath the surface of ostensibly liberal and humane developments in Enlightenment society.[15]

Bentham was born in 1748, the son of a London attorney, Jeremiah Bentham, whose ambitions for his son led to the latter attending Westminster School and then Queen's College, Oxford from the age of twelve. If Jeremiah Bentham's ambitions for his son included the latter becoming a distinguished lawyer, then Jeremy reacted against his father's wishes. Notwithstanding being called to the Bar, Jeremy Bentham developed an antipathy to the practice of law. Bentham imagined the law to be in urgent need of reform. Reform was necessitated because law was failing to perform its social role. There was a lack of clarity in the content of law and irrationality in the scheme of punishments that were assigned to crimes. Traditional legal practice allowed for the development of an assortment of offences which did not reflect current concerns. Confusion and partiality were prevalent and fallacies required correcting. The partiality of particular interests, notably amongst lawyers who benefited from using their expertise in dealing with unnecessary arcane forms of law, needed to be swept away. This work of reform is signalled in his first book, *A Fragment on Government*, which is a sustained critique of Blackstone's defence of the common law. Blackstone symbolized what was wrong with the current practice of law by his reliance on common law and in his resort to metaphorical and misleading language as was evidenced in his support for the doctrines of social contract and natural law. Common law was neither clear nor rational and hence did not set a principled system of law and punishment that would deter would-be criminals and guide the conduct of citizens. Bentham took the social contract to be a fiction, which masqueraded as a principled explanation of government. Natural law was another piece of obfuscation, mixing up

---

[13] G.W.F. Hegel, *The Phenomenology of Mind* trans. J. Bailee (London, George, Allen and Unwin, 1971), pp. 500–8.

[14] See R.G. Collingwood, *The New Leviathan* (Oxford, Oxford University Press, 1992), p. 415; Oakeshott's views on Bentham are reflected in S. Letwin, *The Pursuit of Certainty* (Cambridge, Cambridge University Press, 1965), pp. 110–65.

[15] M. Foucault, *Discipline and Punish—The Birth of the Prison* trans. A. Sheridan (London, Penguin Books, 1991), pp. 135–231.

positive and normative ways of understanding law.[16] Bentham's critique of Blackstone in *A Fragment on Government* informs his longer critical review of Blackstone's *Commentaries on the Laws of England*, which has been published subsequently as *A Comment on the Commentaries*.[17] Bentham prioritized clarity in legal matters and *An Introduction to the Principles of Morals and Legislation* was motivated by this ambition. Legal reform and the criticism of muddled thinking in law and associated aspects of government are central to Bentham's concerns throughout his career. Further criticisms of social contract and natural rights are contained in his *Book of Fallacies*. By 1782 he had also produced a lengthy manuscript on the nature of law that has been published since his death as *Of Laws in General*.[18] His work on legal evidence and judicial procedure *Rationale of Judicial Evidence* was edited and published by J.S. Mill.[19]

In *A Comment on the Commentaries* and in other writings Bentham takes the confusions in the practice of law to arise out of obtuse legal language and the law's reliance on common law precedents that confuse the descriptive with the prescriptive. His proposed revision of law was aimed at rendering its provisions useful to the needs of society and to establish a rational scheme of punishment. Punishment was to be arranged so as to reflect the seriousness of crimes and to enable deterrence of crime and the reform of delinquents. Bentham took exception to fictions or fallacies which undermined the prospect of rational government and administration. For Bentham the social contract is a fictive account of the formation of government. Its historicity is a fiction and its plausibility in explaining the legitimacy of government is dubious.[20] Historically states have not been formed by social contracts and even if states were so established the nature and legitimacy of promise-making would still require justification. Hence the social contract fails to justify government and its putative explanatory role is redundant. For Bentham, it makes more sense to justify government by reference to the interests that it serves. After all, an imaginary social contract could only justify government if contractors held that it serves their interest. The explanatory role that is assigned to a social contract depends upon the underlying rationale of interest. Interests are what individuals know themselves to possess and so it is realistic to link the justification of political association to individual interests. Just as Bentham was a critic of the social contract, so he was critical of natural

---

[16] J. Bentham, *A Fragment on Government*.

[17] J. Bentham, *A Comment on the Commentaries*, in J. Bentham, *A Comment on the Commentaries and a Fragment on Government*, ed. J.H. Burns and H.L.A. Hart (London, Athlone Press, 1977), pp. 8–392.

[18] J. Bentham, *Of Laws in General*, ed. H.L.A. Hart (London, Athlone Press, 1970).

[19] J. Bentham, *Rationale of Judicial Evidence*, in J. Bowring (ed.), *The Works of Jeremy Bentham*, vols.VI and VII (Edinburgh, William Tait, 1843).

[20] J. Bentham, *A Fragment on Government*, pp. 30–40.

law and natural rights theory.[21] Natural law, for Bentham, lacks meaningful verification. How is the natural to be determined or specified? There is no straightforward way to establish or verify what is natural, because it implies a fundamental standard or value that is not accessible to or verifiable by sense experience. Rather it relies on unreliable intuition. It is a fiction that Bentham opts to discard.

Central to Bentham's reputation as a moral and political theorist is his commitment to the principle of utility. The doctrine of utility predates Bentham's formulations of it. For instance, Helvetius, the Enlightenment theorist, refers to the utility principle. Bentham's use of the principle, however, became symbolic of the Benthamite commitment to establish rational thinking about morality and public policy, even if Bentham himself did not expressly invoke it in his writings between 1776 and the 1820s.[22] A renowned formulation of the principle is presented at the outset of *The Introduction to the Principles of Morals and Legislation* where Bentham remarks, 'Nature has placed man under the governance of two sovereign masters, *pain* and *pleasure*. It is for them alone to point to what we ought to do, as well as to determine what we shall do. On the one hand the standard of right and wrong, on the other the chain of causes and effects, are fastened to their throne... The principle of utility recognises this subjection... By the principle of utility is meant that principle which approves or disapproves every action whatsoever, according to the tendency which it appears to have to augment or diminish the happiness of the party whose interest is in question, or what is the same thing in other words, to promote or oppose that happiness' (emphasis in original).[23] In *A Fragment on Government*, Bentham expresses the doctrine in a succinct and memorable form, 'It is the happiness of the greatest number that is the measure of right and wrong.'[24] The utility of the utility principle lies in its disavowal of metaphysical and intuitionist notions of right and wrong, which are removed from empirical observation and which depend upon controversial assumptions. The principle of utility, however, does not resolve controversy because the presumed commensurability of pleasures and pains is disputable and its focus upon maximizing the interests of the greatest number raises issues of fairness relating to the rights and interests of individuals and minorities. Bentham himself is aware of problematic aspects of the principle and his final considered formulation of the principle accommodates issues relating to the aggregation of interests. In a pamphlet of 1831, *A Parliamentary Candidate's Proposed Declaration of Principles*, the end of government is

[21] Ibid., p. 45.

[22] See J. Dinwiddy, *Bentham* (Oxford, Oxford University Press, 1989), p. 25.

[23] J. Bentham, *An Introduction to the Principles of Morals and Legislation Government* (London, Athlone Press, 1970), p. 1.

[24] J. Bentham, *A Fragment on Government*, p. 1.

presented as, 'the greatest happiness of the members of the community in question: greatest number of all of them, without exception, in so far as possible: the greatest happiness of the greatest number of them, on every occasion on which the nature of the case renders the provision of an equal quantity of happiness for every one of them impossible, by its being a matter of necessity, to make sacrifice of a portion of the happiness of a few, to the greatest happiness of the rest.'[25] Dinwiddy, Rosen, and Schofield, past and present Directors of the Bentham Project, highlight aspects of Bentham's work that mitigate the apparent neglect of individuals in the doctrine of utility.[26] Rosen observes how the iterative formulations of the principle of utility in *A Parliamentary Candidate's Proposed Declaration of Principles* goes some way towards meeting the objection that the doctrine does not provide for the welfare of individuals.[27] Collectively, they argue that while Bentham denies natural rights, he is not indifferent to the provision of rights. For instance, Schofield adverts to the priority that Bentham assigns to security, which is to be provided for by legal rights.[28] He notes that Bentham takes security, abundance, subsistence, and equality to serve as subordinate principles that conduce to establishing utility in public policy. For Bentham, security is pre-eminent amongst these subordinate principles, because a lack of security of the person and of property inflicts significant pain, and avoidance of pain takes precedence over pleasure in the Benthamite calculus of welfare.[29] Hence, for Bentham, the public protection of an individual's person, property, and reputation is a crucial aspect of security even if it does not constitute a 'natural' obligation. Schofield is right to point out Bentham's concern to provide for individual security; nonetheless his doctrine of utility does not allow the right of an individual to counter the operation of the general interest. Likewise, his moral thought considers principles and actions to be commensurable, which means that tensions between the pursuit of knowledge and welfare, and between freedom and equality tend to be underplayed.

In the mid-1780s Bentham visited his brother Samuel, an architect working in Russia, who had designed a circular building, which allowed him, when situated at the centre of operations, to inspect the totality of his workforce. Jeremy Bentham recognized the potential for such a design to serve as a model

[25] J. Bentham, *Constitutional Code*, ed. F. Rosen and J. Burns (Oxford, Oxford University Press, 1983), p. 114.

[26] See F. Rosen, *Jeremy Bentham and Representative Democracy* (Oxford, Oxford University Press, 1983); J. Dinwiddy, *Bentham*; P. Schofield, *Utility and Democracy: The Political Thought of Jeremy Bentham* (Oxford, Oxford University Press, 2006).

[27] F. Rosen, *Jeremy Bentham and Representative Democracy*, pp. 10–35.

[28] P. Schofield, *Bentham: A Guide For the Perplexed*, chapter 3.

[29] For analysis of the principles of security, equality, abundance, and subsistence, see the writings on law and policy in the recently published J. Bentham, *'Legislator of the World': Writings on Codification, Law, and Education*, ed. P. Schofield and J. Harris (Oxford, Clarendon Press, 1998).

for the construction of prisons, asylums, schools, and work houses. He developed a plan to build a Panopticon prison in London, which was based upon his brother's architectural innovation. The projected prison building was to be circular, with singular cells positioned at different levels, which would be situated around the centre, where a single inspector could inspect activity in all the cells while remaining invisible to the inmates. For Bentham, the projected construction represented an advance upon preceding forms of custodial confinement. It would maximize effective supervision, reduce costs, and allow scope for the reformation of prisoners. Bentham's original 'Letters' on the Panopticon scheme were supplemented by 'Postscripts', which refined their design. For instance, they allowed for multiple occupancy cells instead of the projected atomization of prisoners.[30] Bentham also proposed to adopt the Panopticon architectural style in responding to a gathering crisis of the poor laws. A rise in the price of bread had led to an increase in the number of paupers, which, in turn, exerted a strain on the costs of supporting poor law relief. In 1797–98 Bentham framed proposals to resolve the problems. He proposed a nationwide scheme of Panopticon-style industry houses for the indigent, who were those paupers unable to work. Save for beggars and criminals, residence in the industry houses was to be voluntary, and selective provision would be provided according to the status of inmates so that, for instance, criminals would be separated from law-abiding paupers. A National Charity Company was to be set up, which would reduce costs and establish profits by employing inmates in schemes of profitable work. Paupers in the industry houses were to be subject to conditions which would not be more eligible than those experienced outside of them.[31] Bentham, however, abandoned his plan for industry houses due to his inability to calculate costs and profits, given uncertainties in determining the numbers of paupers. The subsequent Poor Law Amendment Act of 1834, however, incorporated aspects of Bentham's scheme. Likewise, Bentham's plans to build a Panopticon prison were thwarted. Potential sites for the construction of Panopticon prisons were identified, but could not be developed because of objections by private landowners and by the withdrawal of the government's initial permission for a Panopticon prison to be constructed on its land at Millbank.

The failure of Bentham's plans for a Panopticon impacted upon his political, constitutional views and he became disillusioned with the present political system, interpreting the failure of the Panopticon scheme as being due to self-interested political representatives and leaders obstructing the public interest. His initial enthusiasm for democracy had waned in the wake of the excesses of the French Revolution. However, his disillusionment with the political elite in the aftermath of their indifference or hostility to his reforming plans, revived

---

[30] J. Bentham, *Panopticon Writings* (London, Verso, 2010).
[31] See P. Schofield, *Bentham: A Guide for the Perplexed*, p. 87.

his interest in democratic reform. He reasoned that elites tend to favour their own 'sinister' interests and hence fail to support the public good; the happiness of the greatest number. Like his close colleague James Mill, Bentham was attracted to democracy for instrumental reasons, for it represented a way of ensuring that elites and their selfish or 'sinister' interests were kept in check. Hence Bentham came to support a radical form of representative democracy, which would combine competence and expertise with democratic accountability as the people would provide an effective instrumental check on the elite that represented them. In the last years of his life, notably in *The Constitutional Code* and affiliated writings, his radical democratic views are articulated.[32] In *The Constitutional Code* Bentham argues for a republican unicameral system, in which sovereignty is to be exercised by the people, who elect a one-chamber legislature that exerts authority over the administration and judiciary, which are composed of experts who devise and implement legislation. Bentham urges that the unicameral legislature should be controlled by the electors and he provides a number of instruments to determine this control. The democratic voting system would serve as a check on the power of the legislature, and deputies were to be elected annually by manhood suffrage by secret ballot to ensure accountability. Bentham recognizes the force of arguments for female emancipation, but judges that contemporary opinion would not support its implementation.[33] These democratic checks on the power of the legislature are to be supplemented by the electors having the power to dismiss representatives between elections. Likewise, members of the administration and judiciary are to be subject to dismissal following a petition of electors. More generally, democratic supervision over the legislature and executive is to be exercised by the force of public opinion. 'The Public Opinion Tribunal' is to be organized as a body operating through the press and public meetings, by which transgressions by political actors could be exposed and subjected to critique. The Public Opinion Tribunal receives architectural form in *The Constitutional Code* in a kind of reverse Panopticon. It is to be housed in a minister's audience chamber, in which the minister would occupy the centre, and would thereby be exposed to the full view of the public who would occupy boxes on the periphery of the building.[34]

THE DISCIPLINE OF UTILITY

Foucault invokes Bentham's Panopticon to serve as the centrepiece of his critique of Enlightenment disciplinary thought and practice in *Discipline and*

---

[32] J. Bentham, *The Constitutional Code.* [33] Ibid., pp. 80–130.
[34] Ibid., pp. 156–80.

Punish. Bentham's mission was to reform society in a wholesale way, critiquing the irrationality of society and public life, and in particular challenging and reforming the framework of law and punishment. His critique was radical and egalitarian insofar as he proposed to overturn the rule of an elite and to render society subject to rational analysis, which substitutes the general good for the pursuit of particular interests. Foucault recognizes the egalitarian and reforming side of the Enlightenment that is expressed in Bentham's commitment to reform, and that is epitomized in his plans to establish a rational calculation of law and appropriate punishments. *Discipline and Punish* is centrally concerned to track the transition from the infliction of gross, physical forms of punishment to modern forms where punishment is determined by scientific, calculating procedures so as to deter crime and reform criminals through less draconian techniques. However, Foucault imagines this transition does not constitute an unqualified amelioration in the treatment of human beings.

The discourse and practice of law and correlative forms of punishment change as modern Western social regimes move away from a dynastic hierarchical ordering society to a disciplinary regime, in which power is dispersed in organizational structures that operate with a range of affiliated techniques that are calculated to discipline individuals. In this context Foucault remarks, 'Historically, the process by which the bourgeoisie became in the course of the eighteenth century the politically dominant class was masked by the establishment of an explicit, coded and formally egalitarian juridical framework, made possible by the organization of a parliamentary, representative regime. But the development and generalization of disciplinary mechanisms constituted the other dark side of these processes.'[35]

Foucault's comment on the dark side of the Enlightenment appears within the chapter of *Discipline and Punish* that is entitled, 'Panopticism', where Foucault observes, 'The "Enlightenment", which discovered the liberties, also invented the disciplines.'[36] Foucault takes the Panopticon to symbolize a novel regime of power relations, whereby the establishment of a series of disciplinary mechanisms constitute a set of techniques of control that departs from what had gone before. He observes, 'Panopticism is the general principle of a new "political anatomy" whose object and end are not the relations of sovereignty but of discipline... The celebrated, transparent, circular cage, with its high tower, powerful and knowing, may have been for Bentham a project of a disciplinary institution; but he also set out to show how one may "unlock" the disciplines and get them to function in a diffused, multiple, polyvalent way throughout the whole social body.'[37] For Bentham, the Panopticon is a design that could be adapted for multiple purposes in that it might serve, for instance,

---

[35] M. Foucault, *Discipline and Punish—The Birth of the Prison*, p. 222.
[36] Ibid.   [37] Ibid., pp. 208–9.

to deal with criminality and to handle pauperism. Its utility consists in maximizing the public good by improving the operation of punishment while minimizing public expenditure. Its concentration of rational expertise and clarity in addressing pressing issues of public policy exemplifies the wide ambition of Bentham's reforming energy. For Foucault, however, the Panopticon and panopticism constitute a new form of power circulating within society, which exerts control that is all the more exacting for being applied scientifically by insidious techniques. Foucault's conception of the Panopticon highlights its efficiency in exerting power. He remarks, '[I]ts strength is that it never intervenes, it is exercised spontaneously and without noise, it constitutes a mechanism whose effects follow from one another. Because, without any physical instrument other than architecture and geometry, it acts directly on individuals; it gives "power of mind over mind".'[38]

Foucault considers the Panopticon to combine an economy of expenditure with an effectivity of outcome, which establishes a regime of control that is disturbing in the power that it marshals and exerts. Prisoners will be controlled and disciplined into normalized behaviour without a manifest display of power. He imagines it to be paradigmatic for the development of the modern disciplinary society, which is composed of a multitude of institutions operating mechanisms of power without an overall hierarchized command structure as in preceding forms of statist power. He takes this disciplinary regime to be one which establishes docile bodies receptive to the ordering regimes in which individuals in schools, hospitals, workhouses, and prisons are embedded. Whatever rights and freedoms might be enshrined in political constitutions, the disciplinary mechanisms of society coerce individuals into forms of 'normal' conduct rather than allow freedom and autonomy. Foucault's critique of Bentham's Panopticon and its associated disciplinary regime has been criticized, not least by critics who are sympathetic to Bentham. For instance, after referencing Foucault's condemnatory reading of the Panopticon, Schofield observes, 'All this would have seemed very odd to Bentham, who regarded his panopticon prison scheme as humane, and an enormous improvement on the practices of the criminal justice system of his time.'[39] Schofield maintains that Foucault appears uninterested in Bentham's intentions, but Foucault's critique of Bentham and the Panopticon does not depend on a reading of Bentham's intentions. Rather, Foucault identifies the disciplinary regime that is symbolized by the Panopticon to be intensive and novel and is thereby incommensurable with preceding regimes of punishment. Bentham's Panopticon might have reduced the exaction of bodily forms of punishment, but its disciplinary regime is not thereby justified. Foucault is aware of its economy in producing submissiveness, but raises questions over

---

[38] Ibid., p. 206.   [39] P. Schofield, *Bentham: A Guide for the Perplexed*, p. 70.

the systemic character of its surveillance and control. Dinwiddy's objection to Foucault's critique of Bentham is that the latter's most overtly disciplinary regimes are to be applied only to paupers and criminals. But the restriction of application does not in itself justify the schemes.[40] Foucault is aware of Bentham's selective focus upon certain categories of individual in the application of his project, but he maintains its repressive and generalizable character.[41]

If Foucault draws attention to repressive aspects of the Panopticon and the darker side of the Enlightenment, his reading of panopticism in *Discipline and Punish* is tendentious. In recent years, French scholars, investigating the relationship between Foucault and Bentham, have sought to correct presumptions of a merely negative Foucauldian assessment of Bentham. For instance, Anne Brunon-Ernst has produced two influential books, *Beyond Foucault: New Perspectives on Bentham's Panopticon* and *Utilitarian Biopolitics— Bentham and Foucault on Modern Power*.[42] In the Introduction to *Beyond Foucault: New Perspectives on Bentham's Panopticon*, she calls for a revised conception of the relation between Foucault and Bentham in the light of the additional sources of their thought that are now available. She urges the relevance of Bentham's writings that have been made available by the London-based Bentham Project and of the posthumous publication of Foucault's College de France lectures.[43] She makes use of this additional material to register how it is possible to perceive affinities between Foucault and Bentham and to appreciate how Foucault's own reading of Bentham was not entirely negative.

In *Utilitarian Biopolitics—Bentham and Foucault on Modern Power*, Brunon-Ernst observes how Foucault's reading of Bentham is shaped by how he makes use of Bentham's ideas. She notes, 'Foucault read some of Bentham's works, but he is not a Bentham scholar. When quoting Bentham in his writings Foucault's aim is not to interpret Bentham's thought, but to use his theories, projects and concepts to feed into his own strategic discourse.'[44] While this reading of Foucault's Bentham assumes a debatable dichotomy between interpretation and strategic use, it remains true that Foucault was not centrally concerned to explicate a preceding author's views. Characteristically he is concerned to highlight the specificity of historic discourses, to which historic texts might be aligned. Hence, for Foucault in *Discipline and Punish*, Bentham and the Panopticon can be assimilated to a pervasive panopticism,

---

[40] J. Dinwiddy, *Bentham*, p. 96.

[41] M. Foucault, *Discipline and Punish—The Birth of the Prison*, p. 200.

[42] A. Brunon-Ernst (ed.), *Beyond Foucault: New Perspectives on Bentham's Panopticon* (Aldershot, Ashgate, 2012) and A. Brunon-Ernst, *Utilitarian Biopolitics—Bentham and Foucault on Modern Power* (London, Chatto and Windus, 2012).

[43] A. Brunon-Ernst (ed.), *Beyond Foucault: New Perspectives on Bentham's Panopticon*, p. 4.

[44] A. Brunon-Ernst, *Utilitarian Biopolitics—Bentham and Foucault on Modern Power*.

which characterizes disciplinary society. This focus upon panopticism abstracts from the particular fate of Bentham's project. In particular it abstracts from the resistance to the Panopticon and to Bentham. Bentham himself was well aware of the opposition to his ideas on the part of the British Establishment. This resistance is worth noting in that it flags the context in which Bentham operated and disturbs Foucault's sense that panopticism can be used to show the nature of an emerging disciplinary society. Panopticism is a category that is constructed by Foucault to highlight disciplinary society, but, given that it is not a clear-cut historic category, it is not susceptible of evidential historical assessment in the way that Bentham's projects may be assessed in terms of establishing the extent to which they were put into practice. We can review the history of the Panopticon project and perhaps conclude that Bentham's ambitions for it were not realized. But how are we to assess the extent to which panopticism was put into practice? Opposition to Bentham and the Panopticon project came from many quarters and the extent of the opposition casts doubt on the efficacy of the term panopticism to capture the nature of a new disciplinary society. On the other hand, Foucault's invention of the term panopticism points to the emergence of a style of thinking and disciplinary practice in the late eighteenth century that differs markedly from what had gone before and is neither humane nor progressive.

A central element of the contemporary revision of the Foucault–Bentham relationship is a reading of Foucault's College de France Lectures, *the Birth of Biopolitics*.[45] Laval, in a chapter of *Beyond Foucault—New Perspectives on Bentham's Panopticon* highlights how Foucault shows a more considered reading of Bentham in these lectures than is demonstrated in *Discipline and Punish*.[46] The recent publication of previously unpublished writings by Bentham is also held to deflect from an undue concentration upon the Panopticon.[47] In *Utilitarian Biopolitics—Bentham and Foucault on Modern Power*, Brunon-Ernst investigates the relationship between Foucault and Bentham in the light of their posthumously published writings. She points to affinities, observing, for example, how they both emphasize the value of pleasure though she considers that Bentham offers a more considered calculus of its possibilities. Yet she concludes that Foucault's reading of monstrous acts as arising out of an instinctual force is more convincing that Bentham's unilateral reading of acts in terms of pleasure and pain.[48] Her comparison of Foucault and Bentham minimizes significant differences between their perspectives. For instance, Bentham's account of pleasure, given the complexity

---

[45] M. Foucault, *The Birth of Biopolitics—Lectures at the College de France 1978–1979* trans. G. Burchell, ed. M. Senellart (London and New York, Palgrave Macmillan, 2008), pp. 248–55.

[46] A. Brunon-Ernst (ed.), *Beyond Foucault: New Perspectives on Bentham's Panopticon*, chapter 2.

[47] Ibid., chapters 4 and 5.

[48] See A. Brunon-Ernst, *Utilitarian Biopolitics—Bentham and Foucault on Modern Power*, chapters 2 and 3.

of measuring and comparing pleasures, is not manifestly superior to Foucault's ethics and their views are not combined easily. Misgivings over Brunon-Ernst's analysis are heightened by her assessment of the overall affinity between their ethical standpoints. She concludes, 'Bentham and Foucault share a common goal in their ethical writings: that of challenging established ethical standards in order to create an ethics based on the conduct of conducts.'[49] This similarity between Foucault and Bentham operates at a level of abstraction such that Plato and Heidegger might be taken to share a perspective. Differences tend to be unduly minimized in such an operation and calls to mind Skinner's observation that attending to influences between theorists across time and context is akin to betting and guessing.[50]

Brunon-Ernst is on stronger ground in reassessing Foucault and Bentham when she is reviewing the relevance of Foucault's *The Birth of Biopolitics*. She highlights how Foucault imagines the emerging liberal form of governmentality in the mid-eighteenth century to reflect and to promote utilitarian thinking. She remarks, 'Hence Foucault's theorization of biopolitics was based on a practice of liberalism defined by utilitarian principles. Bentham's philosophy, especially with his concept of "frugal government", his *agenda/ non agenda divide* [of governmental activity], lies at the roots of the concept of biopolitics and shapes our understanding of the world in which we live. Foucault encapsulates this idea when he writes: Utilitarianism is a technology of government' (emphasis in original).[51] In *The Birth of Biopolitics* Foucault traces the rise of the discourse of political economy and the notion of a conceptual separation of the economic sphere from the social and political spheres. This separation is not to be conceived as 'natural' or fundamental, but as a way of conceiving the operation of society and the conceptual divide develops along with the notion of a market. Foucault observes how this allows for the emergence of a new form of governmentality, namely liberalism, which rests upon this separation of the government from the operations of the economy. Foucault highlights two forms of liberalism. One form invokes a pre-existing juridico-political analysis of politics, whereby a liberal limited form of central political authority is assumed, and justified, as it is in Locke's proto-liberal argument.[52] The utilitarian form is different from the Lockean one. It imagines distinct social interests, which set the direction government should follow. Government, in this light, maximizes social utility, which is constituted by the aggregation of social interests. Liberal governmentality, for Foucault, fits with a utilitarian perspective in enabling individuals to maximize their interests, and in allowing society as a whole to maximize the aggregate

---

[49] Ibid., p. 105.
[50] Q. Skinner, 'The Limits of Historical Explanation', *Philosophy*, vol. 41, 1966, p. 211.
[51] A. Brunon-Ernst, *Utilitarian Biopolitics—Bentham and Foucault on Modern Power*, p. 113.
[52] M. Foucault, *The Birth of Biopolitics*, pp. 27–51.

social interest. Foucault maintains that utilitarianism and the art of governing by maximizing interests harmonizes with the development of technologies of power to provide discipline to organize society, and to supplement the market in maximizing interests.[53] Brunon-Ernst and Laval are right to point to the impact that Bentham exerts upon Foucault's narrative of the development of liberalism. Foucault takes Bentham to be a crucial figure and frames his conception of liberalism and its contribution to a developing biopolitics upon the Benthamite idea of maximizing the welfare of populations. He observes, 'Don't think that English radicalism is no more than the projection of utilitarian ideology on the level of politics. It is rather an attempt to define the sphere of competence of government in terms of utility on the basis of an internal elaboration of governmental practice which is nevertheless fully thought through and always endowed and permeated with philosophical, theoretical, and juridical elements.'[54]

Foucault draws upon Bentham in a more nuanced way than might be imagined by relying solely on *Discipline and Punish*. He recognizes how utilitarianism expresses the liberal art of government and how it allows for maximizing social interests. He perceives how utilitarianism takes the art of government to consist in the devising and implementation of public policy, allowing for the market but monitoring its operations and surveying society so as to remove obstacles to social progress. Nonetheless, Foucault continues to critique an unacknowledged repressive aspect to the disciplinary processes unleashed by the consolidation of liberal and 'enlightened' interests. Social and scientific discipline that is administered to maximize social welfare constitutes a controlling force, which is all the more sinister for being insidious. Hegel and the British idealists also critique Bentham due to his Enlightenment commitment to a formulaic rationality. Hegel's *Phenomenology of Spirit* serves as a spirited introduction to his system and outlines a series of shapes of *Geist*, which are entangled in contradictions as the unity and self-relatedness of Spirit is dispersed and at odds with itself. The section on the Enlightenment sees reason asserting its claims against religion and tradition. However, reason is engulfed in contradictions. Its form as utility sees Spirit presuming that the subject of reason is distinct from the object of reason and the ongoing and unending task of reason is to assimilate the world to the utilitarian scheme of reason. Hegel observes, 'The process, which thus puts itself outside that unity thereby constitutes, however, the shifting change—a change that does not return into itself—of the moments of being-in-itself; of being-for-another, and of being-for-self: is actual reality in the way this is object and for the concrete consciousness of pure Insight—viz. Utility.'[55] Utility leads to an endless process of treating what lies before one as a means and while

---

[53] Ibid., pp. 27–71.   [54] Ibid., pp. 40–1.
[55] G.W.F. Hegel, *The Phenomenology of Mind*, p. 594.

determining objects to serve as instruments renders them continually useful, objects are by this process always set apart from the subject that uses them. Hegel's philosophy is dedicated to exploring and explaining the claims that are made by subjects and Bentham's utilitarianism is taken to be a form of thought that does not explore the relation between subject and object.

The British idealist Collingwood critiques utility in a similar manner to Hegel. In his discussion of the presuppositions of mind, morality, society, and civilization in *The New Leviathan*, Collingwood points up defects of utilitarianism and, by implication, Bentham. While recognizing the force of utility as a principle of action, he dismisses it as a complete explanation of morality, which demands analysis of right and duty. He observes, 'This is the negative characteristic of utility. It explains nothing except the abstract conformity of the means-plan with the abstract specifications of the end-plan. Each of these plans is an indefinite individual.'[56] Oakeshott likewise is a critic of Bentham and utility. He condemns it for betraying an Enlightenment prejudice in favour of scientific analysis and organization of society, which abstracts from an individual's capacity to act in self-chosen ways, which do not require scientific explanation to render them intelligible. In *On Human Conduct*, Oakeshott refers disparagingly to Bentham's plan to theorize human behaviour in terms of axioms, specifying its functional rationality. For Oakeshott such a project is a disturbing dream, 'The dream of a science of "human nature", a dynamics of human character, has long beckoned those concerned with the theoretical understanding of agents, their actions and utterances.'[57] Shirley Letwin's *The Pursuit of Certainty* is written under Oakeshott's influence and she is critical of Bentham for his scientific treatment of human conduct that lends itself to a one-dimensional analysis of how political organization is to be aligned so as to promote human happiness.[58]

CONCLUSION

Bentham was a radical, whose radicalism stirred contemporary politics. He challenged conventional thinking on law, morals, social policy, and politics, by asking questions of the common law and he prioritized clear logical thinking over custom, tradition, and sentiment. He was an Enlightenment thinker who valued the systematic application of reason to human activity, and worked with concepts that could be related to empirical phenomena. He argued

---

[56] R.G. Collingwood, *The New Leviathan or Man, Society, Civilization and Barbarism* (Oxford, Oxford University Press, 1992), p. 110.
[57] M. Oakeshott, *On Human Conduct* (Oxford, Clarendon Press, 1975), p. 4.
[58] S. Letwin, *The Pursuit of Certainty*, chapters 11–15.

against the intuitive in favour of supporting what could manifestly contribute to happiness. If Bentham's rationalism is clear, then the details of his political philosophy are less familiar. They lack familiarity because a steady stream of Bentham's previously unpublished writings continue to be published. They change details of a conventional understanding of Bentham. The famous formula of utility, in fact, is specified differently in different manuscripts, and his thinking on law, political fallacies, democracy, and sexuality are to be understood differently in the light of increased evidence of his thinking. He remains a radical, entertaining ideas that break with conventions and contemporary norms. He embraces female emancipation and unconventional forms of sex and sexuality. He remains a rationalist in that he set himself against what was merely the status quo, just as he opposed intuitions without empirical support and campaigned against the substitution of interests for the general good in public policy. The virtue of his political style is that he is unimpressed by adventitious and self-interested argument and focuses resolutely on what can be decided on rational grounds.

Suspicion of Bentham remains, and it remains focused upon his rationalism. Can one single frame of thought, which is derived from a utilitarian calculation of pleasure and pain, determine the public good? Does a utilitarian perspective supersede the multiple ways in which conceptions of the good are formulated and acted upon? Are the means to achieve utility susceptible of calculation when some activities and qualities might be seen as incommensurable? Alternative conceptions of ends might be formulated, such as awareness of self and others, individuality, rights of minorities, and respect for the humanity of persons. Critics of the Enlightenment such as Hegel and Marx and Collingwood and Oakeshott warn against the over-reliance on rational formulas within Bentham's philosophy. Foucault, a late critic of the Enlightenment, now appears as a prime critic of Bentham. The Panopticon project encapsulates the problematic character of Bentham's thought and practical philosophy. However, contemporary French theorists, conversant with Foucault and Bentham, raise questions over Foucault's conception of Bentham, and scholars, sympathetic to Bentham, who have edited his recently published works, question the legitimacy of Foucault's critique of Bentham. Foucault's Bentham is more complicated than has been maintained in the past. Foucault's *The Birth of Biopolitics* draws upon Bentham in specifying how the development of the ideology of liberalism allows for a form of governmentality that supports and shapes an individualist market-based society. Bentham is taken to be an acute theorist, who understands the ways in which society frames doctrines that allow for the recognition and development of social interests.[59] Yet Foucault's identification of Bentham's Panopticon project as epitomizing a new form of

---

[59] M. Foucault, *The Birth of Biopolitics*, p. 67.

disciplinary society overstates its symbolic and practical significance. He does not attend to its various formulations, and its fate. The Panopticon cannot be seen as symbolizing an entire social ethos, when the project failed to be implemented and its lack of support prompted Bentham to turn to radical democracy. If Foucault overstates his case, defenders of Bentham are wrong to overlook the severity of the disciplinarity of the Panopticon project. While Bentham might have imagined the Panopticon to represent a less severe regime of punishment than what had gone before, the project aims to control individuals by machinery and surveillance so that they perform in required ways. It is an exercise in behaviour modification, which assumes that rational ends justify the objectification of individuals. Insofar as it represents a rationalist scheme that abstracts from concerns over the humanity of inmates, it shows Bentham's indifference to individuals and their humanity and casts a shadow over the Enlightenment and the goal of a rational society.

16

John Stuart Mill

Then and Now

INTRODUCTION

John Stuart Mill is a central figure in the history of British radicalism and liberalism. His texts, *On Liberty* (1859) and *Considerations on Representative Government* (1861), are classic expressions of liberal notions of the freedom of the individual and of representative democracy.[1] Mill writes on many topics, providing authoritative analyses on political economy, logic, utilitarianism, and feminism amongst other subjects. His texts have acquired classic status as paradigms of liberal political theory, yet to contemporaries, he was a controversial figure, who canvassed challenging radical ideas. In the article, 'Changing Reputations and Interpretations in the History of Political Thought: J.S. Mill', Geraint Williams contrasts the esteem with which Mill is regarded in the late twentieth century to the controversy his views generated amongst contemporaries that led to a critical obituary in *The Times*.[2] This disjunction between the contemporary perception of Mill and subsequent readings of him is taken up by Collini in *Public Moralists—Political Thought and Intellectual Life in Britain 1850–1930*. The passage of time changes perspectives and renders Gadamer's ideal of achieving a fusion of horizons in interpreting past texts a demanding undertaking in that changing perceptions can lead to a mere assimilation of the past into the present.

Williams observes how in the context of the mid- to late nineteenth century Mill appeared to be an unsettling figure. He propounded radical causes such as cooperativism, secular education, feminism, atheism, contraception, and

---

[1] J.S. Mill, *On Liberty*, in J.S. Mill, *On Liberty and Other Writings* (Cambridge, Cambridge University Press, 1989), pp. 1–116; J.S. Mill, *Considerations on Representative Government*, in J.S. Mill, *Three Essays: On Liberty, Representative Government, The Subjection of Women* (Oxford, Oxford University Press, 1978).

[2] G. Williams, 'Changing Reputations and Interpretations in the History of Political Thought: J.S. Mill', *Politics*, vol. 15, no. 3, September 1995, pp. 183–9.

democracy in ways which disturbed the Establishment. His private life courted controversy, in that he maintained a platonic relationship with a married woman. His status as a controversial figure is reflected in his critical obituary in *The Times* which was penned by Abraham Hayward, a reactionary political opponent.[3] By the latter part of the twentieth century however, many of Mill's ideas were seen as highly acceptable and consonant with mainstream society. Rights for women, freedom of the individual, contraception, and representative democracy had all been achieved. Mill was assimilated safely into the orthodoxies of the Establishment. Collini observes how changing circumstances and cultural and political preoccupations continually reframe the ways in which Mill is perceived.[4]

Mill himself relates his political philosophy to a peculiar education and upbringing. In his *Autobiography* he recounts how his father, James Mill, a close friend and intellectual associate of Bentham, supervised his education.[5] James Mill imposed a hothouse education upon his son to maximize his rational powers so that he could exercise them on behalf of the community and the general welfare. From an early age, J.S. Mill, the eldest son of James, studied Greek and Latin. He read the dialogues of Plato and other classic texts in the original Greek, progressed to the study of advanced mathematics, natural sciences, and logic, and to working alongside his father on political economy. Mill's *Autobiography* is moving in its disclosure of the impact of his education and of his recognition of its partiality. At the age of twenty, J.S. Mill suffered a mental crisis, which he puts down to his reaction against the unrelieved rationalism of his upbringing, which had failed to nurture his emotions.[6] In the wake of his lapse into depression, Mill resolved to widen his education by reading more broadly so as to take in poetry and the emotional side of experience. He opened up to influences outside of the Benthamism to which his father had subscribed, reading Romantic poetry and reviewing ideas that counterpointed Benthamite rationalism.[7] J.S. Mill's project of self-invention led him to absorb an eclectic set of influences that extended beyond utilitarianism. He drew upon the works of Counter-Enlightenment theorists, whose holistic perspectives incorporated emotion and tradition as well as reason. He also read critics of modernity such as Tocqueville and tested the utilitarianism with which he had been imbued by reviewing the arguments of its critics, notably Macaulay. Mill enlarged his sensibility by reading Romantic poets and drawing upon writers of history and culture to re-imagine individuality and social development. Tocqueville's

---

[3] For a discussion of Hayward, see S. Collini, *Public Moralists—Political Thought and Intellectual Life in Britain 1850–1930* (Oxford, Clarendon Press, 1991), p. 323.

[4] Ibid., p. 324.

[5] J.S. Mill, *Autobiography* (Harmondsworth, Penguin Books, 1989), pp. 25–65.

[6] Ibid., pp. 65–112.   [7] Ibid., pp. 112–45.

critique of the French revolution and his analysis of the experimental egalitarian society of the USA alerted Mill to the impact of rapid cultural and political change and to the cultural currency of a mass society. Tocqueville, along with Humboldt, raised questions about individual identity in the context of increasingly one-dimensional mass societies, which influenced Mill's mature expression of liberalism.

Mill, however, neither rejected his rationalist upbringing nor abandoned the formulas of utilitarianism. Throughout his life, he retained his father's commitment to applying reason to social issues and to scrutinizing the utility of social conventions and laws. His academic reputation was established by the publication of *A System of Logic* (1843) and *The Principles of Political Economy* (1848), which he had developed by a systematic reading of texts that had been guided by his father.[8] In the former, Mill examines the operations of induction and deduction, connecting experiential phenomena of reality by their associations with one another. Induction tracks the associations of cause and effect, and scientific knowledge is established by framing deductive chains of reasoning so that experiential phenomena are deduced from foundational principles. Mill's aspirational social science constitutes a development of classical utilitarianism, in that it aspires to establish large-scale historical explanations of social phenomena. *The Principles of Political Economy* subscribes to the rationale for scientific explanation that is established in his *Logic*. It provides a clear account of Ricardo's doctrines as constituting a deductive and hypothetical system that explains the logic of economic behaviour. For the most part, in *Political Economy* Mill supports the logic of laissez-faire, though he calls for a redistribution of income by inheritance taxation so that inequities of inherited wealth are moderated. Subsequent editions of his *Principles of Political Economy* reveal sympathy for the ideals of socialism in that he contemplates the introduction of cooperative forms of industry. In his later *Chapters on Socialism*, which was unpublished in his lifetime, he is sympathetic to the egalitarian ideals and the cooperative ethic of socialism, but is critical of its revolutionary and statist forms.[9]

UTILITARIANISM

J.S. Mill was educated so that he would be useful to society. The inspiration for his education was utilitarian in that it was designed so that he would assimilate

[8] J.S. Mill, *A System of Logic: Ratiocinative and Inductive*; and J.S. Mill, *The Principles of Political Economy, with some of their Applications to Social Philosophy*, in J.S. Mill, *Works*, ed. J. Robson et al. (Toronto, University of Toronto Press, 1963), pp. 1–70.

[9] See J.S. Mill, *Chapters on Socialism*, in J.S.Mill, *On Liberty and Other Writings*, pp. 219–80.

the Benthamite doctrine of utilitarianism to which his father subscribed in order that he would be in a position to contribute significantly to the general welfare. J.S. Mill duly absorbed the doctrine and from about the age of fourteen he employed its arguments to argue for radical change. However, the impact of his mental crisis and his subsequent engagement with a critical literature induced J.S. Mill to consider alternative doctrines on society and culture and to question the doctrine of utility.[10] He was careful not to break clearly and decisively from his father's utilitarianism, though he was prepared to develop a more open and critical position after his father's death in 1836. Thereafter, he develops a more refined, critical form of utilitarianism, which informs his arguments in *On Liberty* and his *Considerations on Representative Government*. His essay, 'Utilitarianism' was finally published in instalments in 1861 but its critical and qualified adherence to utilitarianism supports all his mature writings. In this essay Mill defends utilitarianism, which he continues to do throughout his life, but he adopts a revisionary reformulation of the doctrine.

In 'Utilitarianism' Mill takes pleasure to be the aim of human activity. Pleasure constitutes what is desired and hence it is what is desirable. Consequently happiness, which is realized in pleasure, is the end that should be promoted. This line of reasoning incorporates a move from descriptive to evaluative language and has been criticized subsequently by logical positivists and like-minded analytical philosophers for perpetrating the naturalistic fallacy, whereby an 'ought' is derived illicitly from an 'is.' The manoeuvre continues to exercise cautious moral philosophers. Mill qualifies classical utilitarianism by maintaining that different pleasures are not to be seen as commensurable. Some pleasures are inherently superior to others. Mill argues that mental pleasures, such as those associated with imagination, the emotions, and the intellect, are superior to bodily pleasures. His argument to this effect rehearses that of Plato in the *Republic*, whereby a person, who experiences both intellectual and non-intellectual pleasures, constitutes a qualified judge who is capable of assessing their relative merits. Like Plato, Mill assumes that a qualified judge will rank intellectual pleasures above merely physical ones.[11] Someone unversed in intellectual pleasures cannot be trusted to assess their merits. Mill emphasizes the superiority of intellectual pleasures and the role of a qualified judge in the following observation. He maintains, 'It is better to be a human being dissatisfied than a pig satisfied; better to be Socrates dissatisfied than a pig satisfied. And if the fool or the pig, are of a different opinion, it is because they only know their own side of the question. The other

---

[10] See W. Thomas, *Mill* (Oxford and New York, Oxford University Press, 1985), pp. 10–13.

[11] J.S. Mill, 'Utilitarianism', together with 'On Liberty' and 'Essay on Bentham', in J.S. Mill, *Utilitarianism* (London and Glasgow, Fontana Books, 1970), pp. 158–61.

party to the comparison knows both sides.'[12] Socrates' life is not merely more valuable, it is also happier given the discount that Mill attaches to what are taken to be higher pleasures. Mill's argument refines utilitarianism by allowing for qualitative distinctions between pleasures. A moment's reflection on the experience of life suggests that we face difficult choices, and their difficulty is not to be resolved by reducing them to a procedure that calculates a quantitative balance sheet of pleasures and pains. The distinction between intellectual and non-intellectual pleasures introduces experiential subtleties, whereby we have to decide between qualitatively distinct activities that resist merely quantitative commensuration. At the same time, however, distinguishing between higher and lower pleasures and invoking the arbitration of a suitably qualified judge, allows for the charges of elitism and paternalism to be levelled against Mill. Indeed, Cowling's critical reading of Mill is focused precisely on what he identifies as Mill's illiberal paternalism.[13] The radicalism of Bentham's classical doctrine of utilitarianism consists squarely in its fundamental critique of traditional forms of elitism. To reduce the analysis of action to a uniform pleasure though risks coercing analysis to commensurate what cannot be commensurated. Yet to hold that intellectual pleasures are superior to non-intellectual pursuits is to invite the prospect of valuing elite pleasures such as opera and art-house cinema over a populist taste for football and box-office film hits. It is by no means clear that Wagnerian opera is superior to Brazilian football or that French new wave films supersede the James Bond brand, let alone Hitchcock and John Ford movies.

Mill qualifies the doctrine of utilitarianism to avoid the rigidities of a narrow theoretical scheme of thought to embrace the complexities of experience. His revisionism, however, poses questions. Are his later texts utilitarian? Is his express revision of the doctrine of utilitarianism a sign of an altered perspective, which means that *On Liberty* is not to be assimilated neatly to utilitarianism? *On Liberty* addresses the question of 'the nature and limits of the power which can be legitimately exercised by society over the individual.'[14] Against the force of class and hierarchy, the strength of religious convictions and custom, and the growing influence of mass society, Mill concludes that the principle informing legislation should be to allow individuals freedom insofar as their actions do not harm others. He observes, 'The object of this essay is to assert one very simple principle, as entitled to govern absolutely the dealings of society with the individual in the way of compulsion and control, whether the means used be physical force in the form of legal penalties or the moral coercion of public opinion. That principle is that the sole end of which mankind are warranted individually or collectively, in interfering with the

---

[12] Ibid., p. 260.
[13] See M. Cowling, *Mill and Liberalism* (Cambridge, Cambridge University Press, 1963).
[14] J.S. Mill, *On Liberty*, in J.S. Mill, *On Liberty and Other Writings*, p. 5.

liberty of action of any of their number is self-protection. That the only purpose for which power can be rightfully exercised over any member of a civilised community against his will is to prevent harm to others. His own good, either physical or moral, is not a sufficient warrant.'[15] Mill extols individual freedom, recognizing the value of autonomy by which an individual determines their own conduct by rational deliberation. Above all, he argues vigorously for the right of individuals to express their opinions. Debate enhances understanding of a subject, even where there is not much room for doubt over what is in question. Discussion permits discrimination and consideration of all aspects of a question. He remarks, 'There is the greatest difference between presuming an opinion to be true, because, with every opportunity for contesting it, it has not been refuted, and assuming its truth for the purpose of not permitting its refutation.'[16]

On Liberty provides a succinct but robust case for individual liberty and for limiting the grounds whereby an individual's liberty may be restricted legitimately. Individuals are to enjoy freedom, save where their actions manifestly harm others. Yet the precise grounds on which Mill defends what is known as the 'harm principle' are questionable, and have been disputed by a succession of commentators. Questions arise over what constitutes harm and over how self-regarding actions, that is actions that do not affect others, are to be distinguished from other-regarding actions when social factors are implicated in ostensibly private activities. These questions are complicated by Mill's dual commitments to the value of individual liberty and to the theoretical primacy of utilitarianism. Mill justifies the 'harm principle' expressly by the theory of utility. Regulation of individual conduct is to be decided by what conduces to human happiness, though Mill stipulates that happiness is to be calculated by taking into account the progressively rational character of humanity.[17]

On Liberty appears concise and clear and yet it is by no means clear how Mill understands either harm or what constitutes self-regarding actions. How is Mill's utilitarianism compatible with individual liberty if, in principle, happiness might be maximized by extensive regulation of individual conduct? The notion of a self-regarding sphere of action is problematic given that language itself is social and that nominally private actions depend upon the operation of linguistic rules. All forms of action can be seen as social so the idea of a private sphere, in which individuals cannot be held to impinge upon others, is liable to the objection that the self cannot be separated easily from a social context.[18] Anyone who has experienced the suicide of a family member would acknowledge how we cannot divorce this seemingly aberrant personal act from its

---

[15] Ibid., p. 13.   [16] Ibid., p. 22.   [17] Ibid., p. 14.

[18] Wittgenstein's notion of the impossibility of a private language may be seen as pointing to this conclusion. See L. Wittgenstein, *Philosophical Investigations* (Oxford, Basil Blackwell, 1976). See the remarks on sensations and on lying, pp. 88–93.

social causes and consequences, even if suicide is to be recognized as a justifiable act. Again, drug addiction affects immediate family and friends of the addict but also society more generally. In considering practical examples of his harm principle, Mill shows a readiness to allow regulation of individuals that harmonizes neither with subsequent opinion nor with an implacable individualism that is opposed to state activity. Mill allows for regulation where an individual owes an assignable moral duty to others. Hence Mill considers that the illiterate and the indigent should be excluded from having children if it can be shown that they would not constitute responsible parents.[19] What appears a clear criterion for regulating the conduct of individuals is less transparent under inspection.

Commentators have resorted to a number of strategies in specifying more precisely Mill's harm principle. Ten identifies morality-dependent harms which are not to be subject to legislation because they consist in harms that cause offence to the moral beliefs of others rather than from harms that do not depend on moral judgments.[20] Rees urges regulation of individual conduct is to be undertaken only if harm is to be inflicted on the interests of others.[21] On this reading, which draws upon Mill's express reference to interests, individual action is to be unconstrained and hence judged to be self-regarding action if it does not impinge on the interests of others. This refinement transfers the problem of deciding what constitutes harm to the question of what constitutes the interests of others. Rees maintains that interests are to be determined by current social and political values, which results in the harm criterion reflecting rather than determining political judgments. Perhaps this transformation of the harm principle into a reflection of current norms is a plausible manoeuvre, as it allows for the important distinction between private and public without committing to a universal principle, which might endorse temporary prejudices on issues such as a woman's role in society. But its plausibility does not certify its credibility as an interpretation of Mill's view. Mill's harm principle is insightful without providing a convincing account of how it is to be determined. Its continuing political relevance, however, is indisputable. Ultimately, the line between the private and the public might be undecidable on general or logical grounds, but its consideration cannot be neglected. Recent controversy over state and corporate access to electronic data raises issues over the sphere of individual liberty. Constant surveillance and monitoring of an individual's correspondence might be justified by a threat of terrorism but it is susceptible to a counter-argument over the

---

[19] J.S. Mill, *On Liberty*, in J.S. Mill, *On Liberty and Other Writings*, p. 14.

[20] C.L. Ten, *Mill On Liberty* (Oxford, Clarendon Press, 1980). See also T. Honderich, '"On Liberty" and Morality-Dependent Harms', *Political Studies*, vol. 30, 1982, pp. 504–14.

[21] J. Rees, 'A Re-Reading of Mill on Liberty', in J. Gray and G.W. Smith (eds), *Mill On Liberty: In Focus* (London, Routledge, 1991), pp. 169–89.

countervailing priority of individual liberty. The hacking of an individual's phone by a newspaper that is bent on a salacious story or on ascertaining evidence of a criminal victim's state of mind appears to lack justification. Why is this so? Its unacceptability might be argued to derive from a lack of support for its practice by a countervailing public interest such as the prevention of harm to others.

Mill's concern for identifying the grounds by which an individual's conduct might be regulated remains of continuing interest, but his argument for restriction on an individual's conduct is neither clear nor convincing. Perhaps interpretive tensions arise out of the combination of Mill's impassioned defence of individual liberty with his subscription to utilitarianism. Berlin observes how Mill's enthusiastic support for the value of individual autonomy approximates to an intrinsic endorsement of the principle.[22] Certainly Mill's celebration of an individual, who employs their reason to deliberate on how they should act, appears to be unqualified and to be independent of utilitarian justification. Moreover, even Mill's ostensibly utilitarian arguments for individual liberty are derived from a qualified notion of utility, which imagines humanity as a progressive species that develops its rationality over time. Hence Gray urges that Mill accommodates rational autonomy as a goal of human development in that it constitutes a developing feature of happiness. Mill was acutely aware of the problem of Chinese stationariness, the alarming situation of a culture that fails to develop because ideas are neither canvassed nor debated freely. Mill's own career and personal history disclosed to him the constitutive role of rational autonomy in the achievement of happiness. Social and political progress could also be seen to arise out of free debate and rational deliberation. Mill identified persisting inequalities and moral blackspots in his own society that required the moral commitment of free individuals. Individuals, for Mill, should resist the pressures of mass society and conformism, and commit to improving their society by supporting what as yet were unpopular causes, such as recognizing the claims of women. There is a tension in Mill's argument in *On Liberty* between his recognition of the value of individual liberty and the potential for utilitarianism to override individual liberty in its focus upon general happiness. Mill's qualified notion of utility goes some way to relieve that tension but there is no unequivocal expression of either how the principle of individual freedom is to be conceived or how the regulation of individual conduct is to be enacted.[23] O'Rourke maintains that Mill operates with a cohesive anti-paternalist view of utilitarianism

[22] See I. Berlin, 'John Stuart Mill and the Ends of Life', in I. Berlin, *Four Essays on Liberty* (Oxford, Oxford University Press, 1969), pp. 182–3.

[23] See, for instance, J. Riley, *Mill on Liberty* (London, Routledge, 1998), where the argument is put forward that Mill reserves the notion of other-regarding actions for certain sorts of harm.

that entails a commitment to individuality and freedom but he abstracts from the tensions that are evident in Mill's account.[24]

In *Considerations on Representative Government*, Mill reviews citizenship, democracy, and the role of political representatives. He urges popular civic participation in democratic life by citizens, while defending the freedom of representatives to deliberate independently on public issues when representing their electors. The executive sphere of governance is taken to be separate from the activity of framing laws, which is the responsibility of elected representatives. Mill recognizes the civic responsibilities of electors, and in the light of the burden of these responsibilities he recommends the franchise is to be limited to those who are literate and numerate. The rationale for the restriction of the franchise turns upon the premium he places upon reasonable deliberation on the part of electors, which is to be enhanced by provisions for plural voting, whereby those in professions are to be awarded additional votes. Rational deliberation over the merits of prospective public representatives will ensure that they possess the requisite capacities for deliberation and rational decision-making. He favours proportional representation on account of the opportunities it affords for the election of public-spirited and independently minded candidates.

Mill assumes representative government to be best suited to expressing and nurturing the public-spiritedness of citizens while allowing for rational deliberation on the part of representatives. Participation in local government allows scope for wider civic activity and an increasing provision of education will qualify more of the population for voting and for engaging reasonably in public life. His views on political participation are thereby qualified by the requirements of historical progress in England and more emphatically in the colonies. Mill's views on the colonies reflect a contemporary imperialism that has been critiqued subsequently for its complicity in a despotism that is paradoxically justified by a commitment to future freedom.[25] His views on democracy are balanced between a commitment to public engagement and a concern to protect and nurture individuality and reason, which imposes limits on its inclusivity. The idea is that paternalism prepares the way for a more inclusive civic engagement. Civic engagement, for Mill, is itself educative and constitutive of the self-realization and hence happiness of individuals. The rationale for his advocacy of open voting resides in its promotion of reason and responsibility. He observes, 'The bare fact of having to give an account of

---

[24] K.C. O'Rourke, *John Stuart Mill and Freedom of Expression—The Genesis of a Theory* (London and New York, Routledge, 2001), p. 125.

[25] See B. Parekh, 'Liberalism and Colonialism: A Critique of Locke and Mill', in J. Pieterse and B. Parekh (eds), *The Decolonization of the Imagination* (London and Atlantic Highlands, Zed Books, 1995), p. 90; B. Arneil, 'Liberal Colonialism, Domestic Colonies and Citizenship', *History of Political Thought*, vol. 33, no. 3, Autumn 2012, p. 503.

their conduct, is a powerful inducement [for electors] to adhere to conduct of which at least some decent account can be given.'[26]

In 1869 Mill published *The Subjection of Women*, a project which he had shared with his companion Harriet Taylor. The text registers Mill's whole-hearted support for equality and in particular for sexual equality. He justifies female equality on utilitarian criteria, because he imagines that the emancipation of women will contribute to the general happiness of society by enrolling the capabilities of a section of the population that has been denied access to education and employment possibilities. He maintains that men will benefit from the emancipation of women, because a prospective companionate marriage between equals will be more rewarding and satisfying for men as well as for women. The repressive domination hitherto exercised by men is harmful to men as well as to women, because it denies reciprocal respect to both parties. Mill urges that women are entitled to political representation and to an education that will enable them to play their part in the social world. To the reactionary complaint that women are not men's equals, Mill observes that the status of women cannot be assessed until their social situation is equal to that of men. He notes, 'Until conditions of equality exist, no one can possibly assess the natural differences between women and men, distorted as they have been.'[27] Subsequent feminists have critiqued Mill, for his limiting assumption that emancipated women will tend to concentrate on family life and the rearing of children. Mill's feminism may have reflected contemporary conventions but it is opposed in principle to dominant patriarchal assumptions and it contributed to his contemporary reputation as a disturbing radical.

COLLINI, MILL, AND VICTORIAN MORALITY

Collini is a contextualist historian, whose interpretive strategy resembles the Cambridge School in attending to what he terms 'the recovery of intentions, the reconstruction of conventions and the restoration of contexts'.[28] He has published a number of pieces on Mill, notably, *Public Moralists: Political Thought and Intellectual Life in Britain 1850–1930* but also the Introduction to the influential Cambridge University Press collection of essays, *J.S. Mill On Liberty and Other Writings* and an essay on Mill, 'The Tendencies of Things: J.S. Mill and the Philosophic Method' in the edited collection of essays by

[26] J.S. Mill, *Three Essays: On Liberty, Representative Government, The Subjection of Women*, p. 300.

[27] J.S. Mill, *The Subjection of Women*, in J.S. Mill, *On Liberty and Other Writings*, p. 130.

[28] See S. Collini, *Liberalism and Sociology—L.T. Hobhouse and Political Argument in England 1880–1914* (Cambridge, Cambridge University Press, 1979), p. 7. A footnote contains an express recognition of a debt to Skinner.

Collini, Winch, and Burrow, *That Noble Science of Politics—A Study in Nineteenth Century Intellectual History.*[29] In *Public Moralists: Political Thought and Intellectual Life in Britain 1850-1930*, Collini reads Mill contextually, observing what Mill shares and disputes with contemporary figures and how he anticipates specific audiences for his texts. Collini sets himself against the view that Mill's political thought can be gleaned simply by reading his texts. His interpretation of Mill is related expressly to a wider sense of how the history of political thought of Mill's time should be conducted. He observes, 'The conventional explanatory relation tends to suggest that the political attitudes widely encountered in the records left by the educated class should be seen as evidence of the "influence" of the most prominent theories of the period, such as Utilitarianism and Social Darwinism or philosophical idealism. My initial assumption has been, rather, that those theories acquired their prominence partly because they gave a coherent form and foundation to attitudes and beliefs already widely if unselfconsciously entertained. In this sense political theories are parasitic upon the less explicit habits of response and evaluation that are embedded in the culture.'[30] Hence Collini interprets Mill as a thinker who reflects the cultural milieu in which he is situated and whose moral sensibility is of a piece with the prevailing historical culture. Mill is not taken to be an author whose doctrines are formulated in ways that do not fit with contemporary assumptions.

Collini reads Mill in the light of a prevailing political culture. Mill is shown to react against, and to act so as to influence, that culture. In this light Mill looks rather different from standard ways of reading him. First, Mill's texts are not taken primarily to represent vehicles for logically articulated arrangements of ideas, which advance theoretical standpoints. Rather than elaborating sets of abstract, timeless ideas, Mill's texts appear as instruments of communication that respond to and aim to modify a climate of opinion. Mill appears polemical rather than serene, and Collini highlights the moral and instrumental force of Mill's rhetoric. For instance, he identifies how Mill's call for the emancipation of women is charged by references to slavery in the American South.[31] Collini recognizes how Mill's texts reflect moral imperatives, which in turn mirror a contemporary preoccupation, namely an urgent agenda to ameliorate the moral health of society. The educated classes of the period are observed to be preoccupied with morality and the moral temper of society. Collini identifies this moralism and more specifically a commitment to

---

[29] See S. Collini, *Public Moralists—Political Thought and Intellectual Life in Britain 1850-1930*; S. Collini, 'Introduction', in J.S. Mill, *On Liberty and Other Writings*, pp. vii–xxvi; and S. Collini, 'The Tendencies of Things—J.S. Mill and the Philosophic Method', in S. Collini, D. Winch, and J. Burrow, *That Noble Science of Politics—A Study in Nineteenth Century Intellectual History* (Cambridge, Cambridge University Press, 1983), pp. 127–60.

[30] S. Collini, *Public Moralists—Political Thought and Intellectual Life in Britain 1850-1930*, p. 4.

[31] Ibid., pp. 141–4.

promote altruism to be central to Mill's work. While Mill's later texts might concentrate upon particular themes such as individual liberty, the status of women, and the nature of democracy, they are taken to exhibit a common moralism in their inspiration and tone. Collini observes, 'Behind the particular issues to which the topical pieces of this last period [of Mill's life] were addressed there runs a common theme; the moral health of society is the highest good.'[32]

Collini is alert to changing perspectives on Mill, which he traces to the particularities of the contexts, cultures, and standpoints of his interpreters. He situates succeeding readings of Mill within a general typology that is devised to indicate how an author is likely to be interpreted by successive generations. Contemporary readings of an author are taken to be liable to reflect the partisan nature of contemporary debate. Thereafter the author is likely to be interpreted as manifesting paradigmatic standpoints that are associated with the preoccupations of the succeeding generation, before he or she fades from direct relevance only to be revived by a more distant generation as a classic, magisterial authority. Collini notes how on his death the treatment of Mill is quite removed from a respectful honouring of his place in the great tradition of English political thought, which must await a suitable lapse of time when polemical skirmishes are forgotten. The immediate response is partisan and Mill is represented as a partisan figure. His obituary in *The Times* by Abraham Hayward, a reactionary opponent of Mill's liberalism, is a case in point. *The Times* obituary was neither detached nor respectful. It is a reminder that at the time of his death Mill was a controversial figure, who had dealt polemically with issues such as the status of women, atheism, and contraception. For Hayward, Mill was doctrinaire and un-English.[33] Thereafter Mill's reputation was entangled in the subsequent divide between theorists and ideologues who lined up either in favour of individualism or of collectivism.[34] Collini observes the partiality and restrictiveness of this framework of interpretation, 'In the 1880s and 1890s Mill was increasingly treated as an "old-fashioned" Liberal and *On Liberty*, his protest against the intolerance and bigotry of some of the most active forces in Victorian public life and public opinion was conscripted retrospectively to serve as a canonical statement of the Individualist doctrine of the State.'[35]

Collini's sensitivity to issues of interpretation informs his incisive Introduction to the volume, *On Liberty and Other Writings*. In the Introduction he recognizes the partiality of a construal of Mill that is shaped by subsequent preoccupations. He is at pains to warn readers of the dangers of schematic interpretations, which misleadingly consider Mill's thought without reference to his historical context. In analysing *On Liberty*'s discussion of the question of

---

[32] Ibid., p. 132.   [33] Ibid., p. 323.   [34] Ibid.   [35] Ibid., p. 324.

the desirability of state intervention on social and economic issues, he remarks pointedly on the text's propensity to be misinterpreted. 'It is worth drawing attention to Mill's explicit insistence that this set of issues has not been the subject of his essay, because one of the most frequent misreadings of *On Liberty* [encouraged by the use made of the book in the late nineteenth-century debate between Individualists and Collectivists] sees it as recommending a policy of laissez-faire or non-interference by the state in the economy. In fact, Mill held a far more complex position on the social and economic role of the state than is often recognised, recommending considerably more "interference" in some areas than was common in Victorian Britain, and rather less in others.'[36] This common misconstrual of Mill is traced to the interpretive fallacy by which an interpreter projects anachronistically assumptions of their own context on to the subject of interpretation. Likewise, Collini takes it to be misleading to interpret Mill as imagining a sphere of private life to be sealed off from the social world. To presume that Mill might separate individuals from their social context is to impute to Mill assumptions about individualism that are drawn from a subsequent and different era. Collini interprets Mill's reference to self-regarding actions to constitute a rhetorical way of making a normative point about the legitimacy of state interference upon the conduct of individuals, rather than expressing a substantive commitment to the separation of the private from the public.[37]

Collini's Mill reflects a reading of the public culture of the Victorian society in which Mill was situated. Like other public intellectuals of the period, Mill is a moralist and a determined altruist, who deploys his rhetorical and polemical skills to argue for moral improvement in the individual and in society. Collini's selective focus upon a Victorian Mill succeeds in altering the way in which Mill is to be perceived. If Mill is portrayed standardly as an individualist combating collectivism, or as an ideological adherent of classic or new liberalism, he is absorbed by general theoretical or ideological doctrines, which abstract from the thicker moral attitudes that stirred the educated classes in the mid-nineteenth century.[38] Collini is perceptive in observing the rhetorical urgency and moral commitment of Mill's writings. *On Liberty* is infused with a moral passion. Mill enthuses over the possibilities of autonomy, whereby individuals might express and achieve moral enlightenment. Likewise Mill is appalled by the prospect of 'Chinese stationariness', and to avert moral indifference he canvasses vigorously for freedom of expression to promote the moral and political improvement of the condition of England.[39]

---

[36] S. Collini, 'Introduction', in J.S. Mill, *On Liberty and Other Writings*, p. xvi.
[37] Ibid., p. xvi.
[38] For an interpretation that imagines Mill as a utilitarian, whose thought can be read as expressing a particular doctrine, see K.C. O'Rourke, *John Stuart Mill and Freedom of Expression—The Genesis of a Theory*.
[39] See J.S. Mill, *On Liberty and Other Writings*, pp. 19–55.

Collini's 'The Tendencies of Things: John Stuart Mill and the Philosophic Method', a chapter that he contributes to the volume, *That Noble Science of Politics* that he co-edited with Winch and Burrow, is underpinned by his contextualist reading of Mill. The object of the text is to investigate a range of approaches to the science of politics in the nineteenth century. Collini's analysis of Mill takes its bearings from the avowed aim in Mill's *Logic* to develop a comprehensive science of politics by relating politics to large-scale laws of social development. If Mill's grand intellectual ambitions run counter to his father's more specific focus upon politics, Mill's actual engagement with the study of politics is taken to undercut the announced ambition. Instead, Collini presents a morally engaged Mill, who reflects upon the idiosyncrasies of English history and engages with its contemporary political culture to urge the moral case for liberty and timely reforms.[40] Mill is shown to have turned against an intellectualist view of collective and individual conduct after his 'mental crisis', and to have looked to the force of emotions and the roles of habit and convention. In practice, however, Collini notes that Mill's change in perspective, 'issued only in the highly conventional practice of making "character" and "national character" his central explanatory concepts. By contrast to the Universalist prescriptions of deductive Utilitarianism this does have a certain relativizing tendency, but unless it is resolved into some more fundamental set of determinants (which Mill never saw his way of doing), it remains within a strongly traditional-moral-political vocabulary.'[41] Collini remarks on how, in his later writings, Mill turns to the notion of character rather than to the grand scientific laws to which his *Logic* had appealed. In combating the great evils of the age, conformity and stationariness, Mill relies upon the countervailing moral qualities of character and virtue.[42] Collini concludes by observing how Mill's political texts attest to the significance of politics, and a circumstantial engagement with particular events and episodes in the light of perceived issues and problems. He remarks, 'Diversity and individuality were the most constant features of Mill's dreams; uniformity and stagnation stalked his nightmares. In Mill's ideal, the clash of contending powers, and the conflict of opinions, the pursuit of principles and the exercise of judgment, the actions of individuals and the mastering of circumstances—politics, in short—were ineliminable.'[43]

In assessing Collini's overall interpretation of Mill, it is instructive to bear in mind his interpretive strategy. The Mill that constitutes the subject of Collini's inquiry is a construction. There are multiple ways of inquiring into Mill's thought. There are general and theoretical contexts, more immediate cultural factors, and personal issues. Just as Pocock does not establish a monopoly on explaining Machiavelli by way of his construction of the Machiavellian

---

[40] S. Collini, 'The Tendencies of Things—J.S. Mill and the Philosophic Method', p. 129.
[41] Ibid., p. 151.   [42] Ibid.   [43] Ibid., p. 159.

moment, so Collini abstracts from sundry influences upon Mill's thought to offer a productive analysis of aspects of Mill that reflect his participation in contemporary currents of the moral and political culture. In *Public Moralists—Political Thought and Intellectual Life in Britain 1850–1930*, Collini observes, 'I am dealing with an aspect—or more precisely, a set of characteristics together with their implied assumptions—of the moral sensibility of the Victorian educated classes.'[44] Hence Collini selects from Victorian public culture and sifts the multiple aspects of Mill's to focus upon those features that he takes to be symptomatic of a particular mindset. Collini understands public intellectuals of the period to be preoccupied by morality, altruism, and character in ways that are evidenced in Mill's writings. These preoccupations tend to be neglected in subsequent interpretations of his thought that are formulated by later generations of critics operating with alien assumptions. The upshot is that Collini recognizes distinctive aspects of Mill's political thought that tend to be overlooked. Mill is neither to be neatly categorized as an individualist or as a utilitarian, nor is he to be venerated as a classic English liberal.

If the sharpness of Collini's perception of Mill is to be respected, then what he tends to underplay or overlook should also be recognized. Mill emerges from his analysis as an engaged moralist, who is fired by encounters with contrary intellectuals. Yet the assimilation of Mill to cultural norms tends to downplay the force of Mill's enduring reflective theoretical commitments. After all, Mill was a utilitarian, albeit a qualified one, and the arguments of his key works, such as *On Liberty* and *The Subjection of Women*, are framed in utilitarian terms. Collini is quite explicit in subordinating the role of theory to moral sensibility in Mill's thought. He observes, 'My initial assumption has been, rather, that those theories acquired their prominence partly because they gave a coherent form and foundation to attitudes and beliefs already widely if unselfconsciously entertained... In this sense political theories are parasitic upon the less explicit habits of response and evaluation that are embedded in the culture.'[45] This express assumption of Collini's, that theory is subordinate to less explicit and formulated cultural beliefs and attitudes, begs questions. What does it mean to suggest that political theories are parasitic on less explicit habits of thinking and evaluating? How can this claim be established? The relationship between differing styles and levels of thinking are difficult to specify. It is tempting to reduce more elaborate and reflectively intricate forms of thinking to more basic and rudimentary sources. A provocatively 'materialist' Marx, for instance, in polemical mode, imagines ideas to constitute mere reflections of electrical activity in the brain. Freud understands unconscious

---

[44] S. Collini, *Public Moralists—Political Thought and Intellectual Life in Britain 1850–1930*, p. 64.
[45] Ibid., p. 4.

drives to underlie forms of conscious reflection and purposeful behaviour. But such moves are problematic as well as interestingly provocative. Relations between levels of thinking and between express thought and less explicit attitude are more likely to be interactive and dialectical than to be reductively causal. For instance, a commitment to utilitarianism might not be dependent upon more primitive ways of seeing and experiencing things. In Mill's case he was educated to be a utilitarian and from the outset he sees acting in the world as reflecting the assignable values of pleasure and pain. It is true that Mill reacts sharply against his upbringing, and his modification of utilitarianism is to be seen in that light. This reaction, however, takes place at a variety of levels including a theoretical engagement with utilitarianism and is not to be construed as representing a determination of his ideas by sub-theoretical phenomena. It is not enough to dismiss Mill's commitment to utilitarianism as an abstract and remote theoretical activity that is detached from real world engagement with politics and morality. Rosen casts doubt on Collini's perspective precisely because he takes Mill to be doing more than merely reflecting Victorian prejudices in developing his conception of social science.[46] Mill's *Autobiography* reveals a complex thinker, who frames a continuous and deliberate strategy to widen theoretical horizons by reading texts that work against the grain of his intellectual inheritance. Hence his theoretical commitment to broaden the range of his utilitarianism, to examine the historic conditions of individuality, to deepen his conception of social science, and to intensify his engagement in rational criticism are neither to be ignored nor declared to be necessarily subordinate to less reflexively constituted attitudes.

Collini distinguishes his own historical reconstruction of Mill's moral sensibility from his paradigmatic typology of generational readings of past thinkers. This typology is schematic in presuming that generational interpretations conform to a general pattern that is not affected by the particularities of the contexts in which it is displayed. Hence Collini's own avowedly contextual interpretation of Mill is set apart from the purview of the generic interpretive scheme that he outlines. The relationship between past and present is integral to interpretative understanding but is not to be explained by a generic standardized formula. In his own interpretation of Mill, Collini aims to recover the moral and intellectual context in which Mill operated and he warns against the intrusion of anachronistic assumptions into an historical contextual explanation. Yet he offers a generic acontextual formula for understanding successive interpretations of past thought. The upshot is that he wavers uneasily between allowing past or present perspectives to dominate interpretive horizons. In contrast, Gadamer insists that interpretation is to be achieved by achieving a fusion of horizons, which is realized through a

---

[46] F. Rosen, *Mill* (Oxford, Oxford University Press, 2013).

dialogue between past and present. Present horizons frame the questions that are asked of past texts, and recovered past attitudes reshape present convictions. Yet in undertaking a hermeneutical fusion of past and present the devil is in the detail. Much depends upon the ways in which questions are posed and upon the ways in which the past is allowed to be constituted. How, if at all, can Mill's political thought be related to the present in ways which provide mutual interpretive understanding of past and present? The question of Mill's relationship to the present and hence the possibilities of fusing past and present informs Skorupski's interpretation of Mill in his *Why Read Mill Today?* Hence, we will review Skorupski's argument to consider if and how Mill's thought might be construed so as to bear upon the present.[47]

Skorupski takes Mill to be a political thinker, who elaborates a liberal response to the questions of how to live and how to live with others. His response to those questions are seen to be of continuing relevance to readers in the twenty-first century. Mill's assimilation of multiple perspectives, including Enlightenment and Counter-Enlightenment ideas tempers the rationalism of his inherited utilitarianism to allow for the ideal of individual self-realization. Mill's eclecticism is held to equip him with a synoptic perspective that renders his thought relevant to distinctively modern problems. Skorupski sets out salient aspects of modernity and post-modernity that constitute contemporary conditions to which he then relates Mill's liberalism. He imagines modern Western society to be confronted by political tensions arising out of a rise of individualism that runs counter to wider social responsibilities and to traditional and revived ideals of community and collectivism.

Skorupski expands upon his reading of these tensions of modernity, which are identified as preoccupying Hegel and Comte, and as inspiring Marx's critique of capital and related commitment to communism. On the one hand, Hegel's synthesis of currents of modernity combines individualism with a reassertion of conservative corporatism. On the other hand, Skorupski takes Marx to support the idea of an immanent and imminent revolutionary break with a divisive capitalism. These responses to social divisiveness are held to contrast with Mill's more balanced engagement with modernity's tensions. Mill combines an appreciation of the ideal of individual self-realization with a commitment to democratic citizenship whereby individuals undertake civic engagement for the public good. Skorupski considers Mill's balanced alignment of individualism with democratic citizenship to constitute a productive way of dealing with the contrary currents of modernity, while avoiding the excesses of reaction and revolution. Mill avoids forms of conservative and radical collectivism and is valued for steering a path between liberty and equality. In advocating Mill's relevance to current questions of individual

---

[47] J. Skorupski, *Why Read Mill Today?* (Abingdon and New York, Routledge, 2006), p. 1.

and social life, Skorupski concludes, 'Certainly Mill sets out a real option. It is not a set of high-minded platitudes that no-one could dispute nor is it an outlook that we might find interestingly strange but could not think of adopting. It is close enough but different enough, to be challenging. He develops a liberal humanistic and civic ideal which stands in distinct contrast to other visions, such as the soul-saving ascetic ideal provided by communitarian ideals of society, and strange as it may seem to pick out a single thinker in this context, the anti-political aesthetic perfectionism of Nietzsche.'[48]

As well as assessing Mill's relevance to individual and collective values, Skorupski considers how Mill's thought relates to a post-modern questioning of objectivity in social and political thought. On this reading of the epistemological status of social and political analysis, post-modern questioning of foundations has combined with the waning of religious belief and a concomitant popularity of scientific forms of explanation to issue in a prevailing relativization of values in our contemporary world.[49] Mill's determination to think freely and critically about empirical and theoretical issues offers a reasonable alternative to Nietzsche and to his denial of the objectivity of thought.[50] In the context of a decline in ethical objectivism Skorupski takes contemporary liberalism to trade upon and reinforce a relaxed but unsatisfactory subjectivism, which harmonizes with a prevailing commodification and disputability of values. Rawls's later formulation of liberalism in *Political Liberalism* is taken as paradigmatic in justifying a form of liberalism that minimizes comprehensive commitments to liberal values. It relies upon the commitments that participants in liberal democracies make to the rules of the political game. This limited defence of liberal values is at odds with Mill's strong support for individuality and a comprehensive justification of liberal values. On this admittedly contentious reading of the present, Mill appears to be distinct from contemporary frames of argument, but also shows a continuing relevance in providing a more robust and persuasive defence of liberalism than that currently on offer.[51] Skorupski sees Mill's strategy for defending liberalism to retain value for a world in which liberal politics are practised but lack theoretical justification of its values that motivates liberal citizens.

Past and present can be related together in multiple ways. Skorupski's study of Mill may well rely upon his own contentious reading of the present and yet it succeeds in providing a context whereby Mill's liberalism is at once removed from present preoccupations and yet at the same time contributes to contemporary liberal values. In fact Skorupski might have pressed the point that Mill is relevant to the contemporary situation precisely because of the distinctiveness of his Victorian context and moral sensibility. Collini might deny the continuing relevance of Mill given the latter's highly wrought and

---

[48] Ibid., p. 92.   [49] Ibid., pp. 65–91.
[50] Ibid., pp. 92–107.   [51] Ibid., pp. 106–7.

high-minded moralism that is at odds with our contemporary situation. However, Mill's very high-mindedness allows him to urge the moral case for liberty of the individual and for participative citizenship that represents a more rhetorically persuasive case for liberalism than is provided by Rawls and post-Rawlsian liberalism. *On Liberty* may not be a dry text of classic liberal thought and a rhapsody for old-fashioned individualistic liberalism, and it might be animated by a variety of unfamiliar Victorian moral themes, but its theoretical precision, its recognition of modern problems, and its high-minded and rhetorically persuasive commitment to the value of liberty render it of relevance to debates about how individuals are to live when citizens are looking for direction and public purpose.

CONCLUSION

Estimates of Mill and his political theory have changed over time. Whereas the status of Mill in the history of political thought now appears unquestionable, Collini shows that this status is itself the product of historical development. Mill's controversial status at the time of his death has receded as the emotions unleashed in political struggles over the emancipation of women, contraception, and atheism have quietened. Nonetheless, Mill's thought is not to be treated as a museum piece. It remains vibrant in a way that resists the fate of a sedate and respected afterlife that Collini imagines is reserved for political theorists. Mill's unique education and his reaction against his upbringing motivated him to assume an eclectic perspective that enabled him to incorporate a range of viewpoints in his thought. The breadth of his thought in combination with his moral commitment to improve society ensures his nineteenth-century attitude to public affairs remains pertinent to contemporary political issues. He develops a liberal politics that deals with aspects of modern life that continue to exercise the citizens of today.

Mill confronts the issue of liberty of the individual directly in a measured way that commands respect even if the precise terms of his argument are contentious. He recognizes how a developing mass society places a premium on individuality and autonomous self-development. In a context of ever increasing commodification and the production of cultural products for a mass market, the ideal of a self-governed life in which plans are deliberated and individual ideas are canvassed resonates. If Mill's 'harm' principle can be questioned, his recognition of the political point in drawing a line between private and public conduct remains of significance. In societies where the possibilities of surveillance and concerted intervention into the lives of individuals have increased immeasurably along with the capabilities of communications technology, the need to strike a balance between popular control over public concerns and the protection of individual liberties must remain on the political agenda. The contemporary security agenda in Western countries struggling to extirpate terrorist activities entail that pressures are placed on individual liberties, while distrust of public agencies and cultural conformity ensure that individual liberty is a valued ideal.

If Mill is a political theorist who remains relevant to present-day politics, he is also a remote figure, whose thought is rooted in a public culture with a different moral sensibility. Collini provides a convincing account of Mill that accentuates the distinctiveness of his milieu, which is a past world in which altruism and moral fervour were commonplace amongst public intellectuals. His assumptions and characteristic moralism differ sharply from more subjectivist and undemanding attitudes of the contemporary public scene. Yet the differences between his age and our own do not render his thought of merely academic interest to today's world. Consideration of Mill supports Gadamer's way of understanding the history of ideas that envisages past and present perspectives to be constituted reciprocally. Historical scholarship can reveal the differences of Mill's thought and context from subsequent developments. His acceptance of colonialism and restrictions on the franchise reveal complicity with recessive attitudes, yet his distinctive moral commitments to public life render his thought of decided interest to a contemporary world in which political direction and moral commitments appear to be waning.

17

Nietzsche

Politics, Power, and Philosophy

INTRODUCTION

From the outset to the end of his career and beyond, Nietzsche appears as a polemical stylist, who courts controversy. He quarrels with the academic establishment and with Wagner while dismissing conventional moral and political attitudes. His most significant quarrel was with God, and in breaking with God Nietzsche also disputes the notion that there can be any transcendence of life. Culturally, Nietzsche was a destructive force, who trained his sights on the remainders of traditional beliefs in transcendent deities and principles. But he intended his destructiveness to be creative. He disavowed a merely reactive attitude that did not break decisively from preceding impediments so as to release creativity. He was acutely aware of how *ressentiment*, festering resentment, tends to reinforce what is being resisted, so that, for instance, moral crusades on behalf of the poor or the suffering tend to register a special pleading on behalf of nominated victims, who then have to bear with the corrosive effects of assuming the label of 'victims'.

If Nietzsche's life was a force of polemical controversy, engendering enmity and incredulity, then his subsequent fate has been to excite feverish mythologizing either of partisan endorsement or of passionate rejection. He has been worshipped and crucified by those who have succeeded him. His life and thought have been subjected to the metaphorical rehearsal of the Christian mythology, which Nietzsche rejected in part precisely because of its rhetorical departure from material embodied existence. His sister Elisabeth, who cared for him after he had collapsed into insanity, reconstructed his life and thought so that Nietzsche would appear as a philosophical guru and serve as a cult figure for Nazism. If Nietzsche was taken up by the radical right, he has also been feted by the radical left. His destruction of God, truth, and transcendence appealed to the mood of post-war French post-structuralism.[1] Derrida

---

[1] See M. Foucault, 'Nietzsche, Genealogy, History', trans. D. Bouchard and S. Sherry, in M. Foucault, *The Foucault Reader* (London and New York, Penguin Books, 1984); G. Deleuze, *Nietzsche and Philosophy* trans. H. Tomlinson (New York, Columbia University Press, 1983).

identifies with and continues Nietzsche's critique of metaphysics, Foucault takes Nietzsche to anticipate the collapse of the modern episteme and adapts Nietzsche's genealogical exposure of the contingencies and power relations that shape conceptual history, while Deleuze sees Nietzsche as exposing the shortcomings of Hegelian dialectics.

LIFE AND WORK

Nietzsche was born in Röcken, Saxony in 1844, the son of a Lutheran pastor. His paternal grandfather was a superintendent of the Lutheran Church. If Nietzsche appears to emerge out of nowhere in declaring war on conventional wisdom, it is worth bearing in mind that he emerged from a particular place, and was subject to a determinate set of influences. His family Lutheranism alerted him to issues of faith, transcendence, and a Protestant insistence on questioning the centralized religious authority of the papacy.[2] Nietzsche's father died when he was five years old, which doubtless contributed to his early exhibition of a melancholy if ostensibly courteous disposition. From 1858–64 he attended Schulpforta School, responding positively to its expertise in classical education. Thereafter he enrolled at the Universities of Bonn and Leipzig, studying philology in Leipzig, having initially read Theology and Philology at Bonn. His philological talent was recognized and at the age of twenty-four he was offered a Chair in Philology at the University of Basel. Nietzsche developed his philosophical career outside the frame of German university circles, even if he read widely and was influenced by major and minor public figures in German intellectual and cultural life.[3]

Nietzsche's influences were multiple. He drew on major cultural and intellectual figures such as Darwin, Wagner, and Schopenhauer, as well as minor figures, who contributed to cultural discussion in fields that included biology, philosophy, and psychology. In all cases, the influences were refracted through intensive critical engagement. Nietzsche regarded it as a badge of honour to incite enemies and the fiercer the argument between himself and others, and the stronger the opponents, the more satisfaction that he derived from the conflicts.[4] The influence of fellow intellectuals on the character of Nietzsche's thought is mediated by Nietzsche's own style, which ensured that differences

[2] See R.J. Hollingdale, *Nietzsche* (London and New York, Routledge and Kegan Paul, 1973), pp. 71–90.
[3] See R.J. Hollingdale, 'The Hero as Outsider', in B. Magnus and K.M. Higgins (eds), *The Cambridge Companion to Nietzsche* (Cambridge, Cambridge University Press, 1996), pp. 73–6; see also R. Small, *Nietzsche in Context* (Aldershot and Burlington, USA, 2001), pp. 5–30.
[4] F. Nietzsche, *Ecce Homo*, in F. Nietzsche, *The Anti-Christ, Ecce Homo, Twilight of the Idols*, ed. A. Ridley and J. Norman (Cambridge, Cambridge University Press, 2005), p. 82.

would disrupt debts to others. This pattern is exemplified by his adoption of a distinctive genealogical conception of morality and punishment. Nietzsche is notable in assuming a thoroughly historical approach to morality, whereby the origins of punishment are seen to lie in practices that are removed from contemporary notions. Similarly, his friend, the psychologist Paul Rée, highlights the historicity of forms of punishment. Unlike Nietzsche, however, he attributes notions of guilt and retribution to an underlying and originary utility, which he imagines as determining the rationality of punishment.[5] Nietzsche regarded the derivation of punishment from utility to be overly rationalist. Likewise, he objected to the ideas of Dühring, the materialist and positivist, who identified the source of punishment as primitive expressions of natural feeling, *ressentiment*. Nietzsche acknowledged the force of such feelings but understood feelings, like ideas, to be historical, and hence lacking the universality to furnish the generic causal capacity that Dühring attributed to them.[6] In his analysis of the modifications and agonistic struggles to which humanity is subject Nietzsche engages with Darwin and a host of German and European public intellectuals, who embraced the doctrine of evolutionary change at the level of the species. Nietzsche reacts against what he conceived as a teleological dimension in Darwin's thought that sees particular local changes in terms of an overall narrative of effective species development.[7] Nietzsche also denies that there is a survival instinct operating in human beings, and draws upon the contemporary Anglo-German zoologist, Rolph, in recognizing an expansive rather than a survivalist underpinning to life.[8] Nietzsche, however, at least in his later thought, takes this creative expansive feature of humanity to represent the non-mechanical operation of a will to power. In framing his notion of the will to power Nietzsche draws upon the work of the embryologist Roux, who conceived organisms to be self-regulating hierarchies. However, Nietzsche's formulation of the creative urge for self-mastery in human development is distinctive. Likewise his notion of the internal struggle between contending corporal elements is not derived from Roux and other scientists, who embraced non-Darwinist notions of evolution.[9]

In his early texts Nietzsche draws upon Schopenhauer and Wagner in framing an aestheticized approach to life and philosophy. Nietzsche appreciated Schopenhauer's tragic aesthetic acceptance of life as art, which harmonized with his own abandonment of Christianity and his related ambition to break with all traces of idealism. Nietzsche interpreted Wagner's music as re-awakening the spirit of Greek tragedy in establishing a form of art that

---

[5] See R. Small, *Nietzsche in Context* (Aldershot and Burlington, USA, Ashgate, 2001), pp. 72–4.

[6] Ibid., pp. 21–40.

[7] See G. Moore, *Nietzsche, Biology and Metaphor* (Cambridge, Cambridge University Press, 2002), pp. 21–115.

[8] Ibid.   [9] Ibid.

embraced the inconsolable conditions of life. Nietzsche perceived the essence of classical Greek tragedy to consist in its acceptance of reality and its refusal to claim redemption in imaginary flights from the actual world in which life and death were experienced. Greek tragedy's combination of realism and engagement with the actual conditions of experience appealed to him, and contrasted with what he took to be the abstractions of Kant's critical categorial examination of the limits of reason.

For Schopenhauer, music was a way of directly experiencing the tragic aspects of life. Tragedy is celebrated in Nietzsche's polemical and controversial study of the aesthetics of Classical Greece, *The Birth of Tragedy* (1872), which invokes Wagner, whom he had befriended in 1868 as a source of inspiration in interpreting classical art. Subsequently, Nietzsche broke with Wagner on account of the latter's racism and strident German nationalism. Thereafter he concentrated upon disturbing conventional formulations of truth and the standpoints of everyday morality by inventing coruscating aphorisms to counterpoint standard formulas and inherited traditions. Nietzsche took aim against Establishment views but also critiqued ordinary cultural assumptions, which shielded mankind from confronting the reality of life. Working with the grain of lived experience entails a lack of transcendent meaning and teleological redemption. His meandering work, *Thus Spoke Zarathrustra* (1873) offers insights from a secluded life that are designed to provoke individuals to develop their own way of embracing and affirming the contingencies and pain of experience. Nietzsche's determination to recognize the consequences of the destruction of religion runs with reflection upon how an elite may be enabled to flourish. His thought is powerful but unsettling for those who take the West and its associated liberal values to be paradigmatic for the modern world. In his latter writings Nietzsche undertakes a transvaluation of values, whereby the creative and realistic acceptance of experiential conditions are to supplant failing and misguided Christian and idealist notions, which claim an objectivism that they cannot sustain. Nietzsche's political thought concentrates upon delivering a critique of modernity and its optimistic and conventional ideological nostrums of liberalism, socialism, and nationalism, as well as exploring aristocratic political forms that are attuned to positive achievement.

THE DEATH OF GOD AND THE END
OF TRANSCENDENCE

A recurring theme in Nietzsche's texts is the death of God. It is asserted and re-asserted as if to underline that it is not enough to say that God is dead. It must be repeated so that its ultimate meaning seeps into all aspects of life, because belief in God blocks creative forms of theory and practice. For Nietzsche the death of God is more than a contingent event in the ongoing life of humanity. It transforms or should transform everything. The parable of the madman in *The Gay Science* dramatizes God's demise. The madman enters the market place apparently seeking God, and he is laughed at by the assembled crowd. The madman is deadly serious, proclaiming, 'Whither is God? I will tell you. We have killed him.'[10] He continues, 'Is not the greatness of this deed too great for us? Must we ourselves not become gods simply to appear worthy of it? There has never been a greater deed; and whoever is born after us—and for the sake of this deed he will belong to a higher history than all history hitherto?'[11] For Nietzsche, belief in God and the death of God are not forms of abstract speculation. Human beings are not defined by an abstract humanity. What human beings do and become historically matters because their activities shape their very identity. Humanity is not a trans-historical universal form that allows actual human beings to disown responsibility. Nietzsche's rejection of God entails an injunction for human beings to accept responsibility, to 'become what you are.'[12]

For Nietzsche, the invention of God in its Judeo/Christian formulation distorts moral life and the subsequent killing of this God requires a commitment to deal with its consequences. Nietzsche maintains that the array of terms signifying 'beyond', in ethics, in epistemology, and in metaphysics, need to be destroyed in the wake of God's demise. The end of transcendence is signalled by the death of a presumed transcendent Supreme Being, which held in place the architecture of truth and the foundations of morality. In *Daybreak*, Nietzsche urges that humanity must bear the uncomfortable condition of accepting honestly a reality without God. He observes, 'How many there are who still conclude: "life could not be endured if there were no God!" (or as it's put amongst the idealists): "life could not be endured if its foundation lacked an ethical significance!"—therefore there *must* be a God (or existence must have an ethical significance). The truth, however, is merely that he who is accustomed to these notions does not desire a life without them.'[13] Human beings must accept responsibility for what remains, the ebb and flow of life, which is to be embraced in the spirit of tragedy without resort either to alibis or to modulation. Nietzsche comes to see his project as a transvaluation of all values whereby transcendence is abandoned and in its stead a realistic engagement with the actual world is to be embraced. The project of composing a book with a specific title spelling out this theme might have been abandoned, but

---

[10] F. Nietzsche, *The Gay Science* trans. W. Kaufmann (New York, Vintage Books, 1974), p. 180.

[11] Ibid., p. 181.   [12] Ibid., p. 270.

[13] F. Nietzsche, *Daybreak—Thoughts on the Prejudices of Morality* trans. R.G. Hollingdale (Cambridge, Cambridge University Press, 1982), p. 90.

Nietzsche's commitment to transforming the cultural and moral values that are associated with belief in God informs his writings from *Daybreak* onwards.

The contingency and historicity of values are dealt with emphatically in Nietzsche's *On The Genealogy of Morals*. In a sense all Nietzsche's writings tend to be genealogical in that they deal with historical contingencies where other philosophers might identify foundations and essences. Yet *On The Genealogy of Morals* stands apart by focusing expressly on tracing the contingently changing forms of morality, and in framing a methodology that is devoted specifically to dismantling essences and foundations. History for Nietzsche is related necessarily to present perspectives and genealogy answers practical questions of the moment. What appears to be foundational in the present is shown by Nietzsche's genealogical examination to have in fact emerged contingently in the past. The contemporary value of moral value is opened for questioning by genealogical exploration. Nietzsche observes, 'So let us give voice to this *new demand*. We need a *critique* of moral values, *the value of these values* should for once be and so we need to know about the conditions and circumstances under which the values grew up, developed and changed (morality as result, as symptom, as mask, as tartuffery, as sickness, as misunderstanding; but also morality as cause, remedy, stimulant, inhibition, poison) ...' (emphasis in original).[14] Nietzsche's historical study invokes and challenges the commonplaces of the present by showing how morality is not to be taken as a constant and unwavering guide or as a fixed law of conduct but is a mutable invention, whose character changes over time. Nietzsche's genealogy is neither continuous nor exhaustive as history but it identifies key historical moments and is suggestive in dislodging supposed universal truths. In *On the Genealogy of Morals*, Nietzsche shows how the configuration of morality has changed over time. In pre-Christian Homeric Greece, morality is encompassed by a warrior elite of masters, who contend agonistically amongst themselves, and establish a moral code in which positive achievements are recognized as emblems of heroic conduct. The revolt of the slaves transforms the contours of social life and alters the language of morals. Morality switches from being a positive code highlighting admirable conduct to a relational framework, which aims to curtail the powerful. The slave revolt is directed against those who rule, the masters, who depend upon slaves to supply the means of existence that enables them to assert their power and style in competition with one another. The slaves revolt and set themselves and the law against the masters. Good, which was a term directed towards the achievement of great deeds, now becomes a relational concept that is employed to combat the force of the masters. The social contract is not the triumph of egalitarian

---

[14] F. Nietzsche, *On the Genealogy of Morals* trans. Carol Diethe (Cambridge, Cambridge University Press, 1994), p. 8.

liberalism that is envisaged in Enlightenment theory, but represents the revenge of the slaves against masters that renders the resulting resentful language of morality barren of positive achievement.

The genealogical narrative that Nietzsche relates resembles Hegel's story of the master–slave struggle for recognition. It incorporates historical developments but constitutes a constructed paradigm that is distilled from complex historical events to point up aspects of the present. Nietzsche's genealogy of morality does not culminate in relating how slaves transform morality by disempowering masters. The resentment that is inflamed in the process of transformation is taken up by a priesthood that canvasses the notion of evil as a ubiquitous threat against which the good must guard themselves in all of its possible manifestations.[15] Extending the reach of moral *ressentiment* beyond antagonism to the strong and powerful, the evil against which a struggle ensues is identified as lurking within the psyche and the task is to monitor and expunge inner possibilities of evil. Christianity and its priesthoods serve the slaves by idealizing the meek and the indigent as incarnating virtue by their downtrodden status. They conduct a relentless critique of intimations of evil that are presented in self-interested conduct. Hence sexual indulgence and the formulation of evil thoughts are to be subject to constant surveillance so as to be expunged in favour of a manageable docility.

If truth and morality are not to be seen as timeless but are viewed as so many historic expressions that include fabrications of God and the cultural production of evil, a clear register of progress is withdrawn and a departure from standard Enlightenment accounts of modernity is declared. Whereas Enlightenment thinkers celebrate technological, scientific, moral, and political progress, Nietzsche sees the frigid maintenance of an unacknowledged other-worldliness and an increasingly enervated recognition of an emasculated God and lingering transcendent moral principles. God may be dead but an unacknowledged belief in transcendent values and truth remains. Science undermines traditional beliefs in God and humanity and yet an unjustified belief in a unifying identity of the subject and an objective truth remains. Yet what supports the notion of an underlying essential human identity? What can support the notion of truth, when God and essentialisms are abandoned? Modernity is not to be admired. Material development and scientific precision compromise but do not supplant traditional formulas of truth and morality. Indeed, what is promised by the present is a future in which beliefs falter and lose their force in the wake of diminishing respect for a transcendent God. A transformed and reinvigorated morality is not created. Instead, modernity offers the prospect of a withering nihilism, in which a lack of energy and a corrosive cynicism are all that will remain.

---

[15] Ibid., pp. 100–2.

Nietzsche offers an alternative, a transvaluation of values, which is a response to the death of God that takes the residue of experience seriously. Experience that arises out of life is replete with hardship and dissonance. Yet there should be no resort either to the magical or transcendent to justify or assuage the dissonance of what is to be experienced. Nietzsche invokes a form of philosophy, a perspective, which is courageous and artful in accepting experience. In *Thus Spoke Zarathrustra* he enlists the notion of the eternal recurrence to suggest what is demanded experientially by living without God and without transcendence. In Part 3 of the text Zarathustra's animals exhort him to become the teacher of eternal recurrence, which is an appeal to which he eventually responds. They declare, 'For your animals well know, O Zarathrustra, who you are and must become: behold *you are the teacher of the eternal recurrence* that is now your destiny! That you should be the first to teach this doctrine—how should this great destiny not also be your greatest danger and sickness! Behold, we know what you teach: that all things recur eternally and we ourselves with them, and that we have already existed an infinite number of times before and all things with us.'[16] Eternal recurrence is a disputed item in the repertoire of Nietzschean concepts, but at the least it serves as a metaphor for experiencing the actual material moment without recourse to fantasy or palliatives. If we are to live as if each moment is recurring eternally, then we must be prepared to live within the moment and to avoid the fantasy of escaping towards heaven or a principled beyond.

POLITICS

Like all aspects of his thought, Nietzsche's politics are controversial, though they can be approached negatively by specifying what he rejects. This negativity that is constituted by Nietzsche's rejection of conventional political forms is potent in dismissing what is conventionally taken for granted. Nietzsche's negativity forces attention to be paid to the values entrenching dominant styles of Western political thought. Nietzsche is a critic of modernity and the self-image of Enlightenment thought as the harbinger of progress and critical analysis. Where others identify rational progress, Nietzsche sees contradictions and loss. Above all Nietzsche signposts and disturbs the ongoing legacy of religion and transcendence. The Enlightenment commitment to truth is deprecated by Nietzsche, and his critique of the independence of 'scientific' truth informs his disdain for conventional ideological forms of modern Western political thought, such as nationalism, socialism, and

---

[16] F. Nietzsche, *Thus Spoke Zarathrustra* trans. R.G. Hollingdale (Harmondsworth and Baltimore, Penguin, 1961), p. 237.

liberalism. He is critical of the egalitarianism of liberal and socialist political theory because they offer a bland brand of levelling down that deflates aspirational engagement. Their focus upon protecting the individual from the assertiveness of the powerful, and redistributing wealth from the rich to the poor, is inspired by a politics of *ressentiment*, in which individuals shrink from positive engagement and responsibility and expect collective organization to provide a form of public protection. Whereas liberals imagine the law as providing a means to allow individuals to fulfil their potential, Nietzsche sees it as an instrument of resentful coercion whereby the powerful are limited by a collective enforcement of norms.[17] Likewise, socialism is an insipid doctrine, which imposes egalitarian norms to establish the common welfare without reference to what the community might achieve if it focused upon enhancing life rather than providing social insurance. For Nietzsche a political community is to be judged by the strength of purpose that is exhibited by its individuals and not by its re-allocation of resources so that uneven distributions of wealth and power are reduced in the interests of a supposed common good. Nietzsche suspects that moralistic appeals to protect individual liberty and general welfare mask an impulse to secure conformity, whereby the creativity of the species is endangered.

Nietzsche's critique of the politics of modernity serves to problematize the question of what is to be achieved in a political community. For Nietzsche it is not enough that the rules of the game, its laws of association, are to be arranged fairly so that all citizens associate on equal conditions. This modern preoccupation with the fairness of the terms of association deflects from asking substantive questions about the character of the association and the nature of the individuals who compose it. Radical socialists, as well as their neo-liberal critics in Europe after the Second World War recognize ways in which the welfare state erodes identities and freedoms. In *Beyond Good and Evil* Nietzsche urges that politics should be directed towards enhancing the condition of life.[18] Conway, in his analysis of Nietzsche's political thought, offers the following observation, 'Humankind is best enhanced, he believes, not through the Whiggish reforms and liberal ideals favoured by modernity, but through the cultivation of those rare individuals who body forth an expanded complement of human powers and perfections. He consequently recommends that social resources should be reserved and mobilized for the production of great human beings.'[19] What is disconcerting in Nietzsche's thought is his contention that a political association should be aristocratic, and that a pathos of distance should be established between the best, the elite that presses forward to achieve greatness and the rest, the herd that furnishes the

---

[17] See F. Nietzsche, *On the Genealogy of Morals*, pp. 54–5.
[18] F. Nietzsche, *Beyond Good and Evil*, p. 257.
[19] D. Conway, *Nietzsche and the Political* (London and New York, Routledge, 1997), p. 6.

elite with the resources by which they can live. Achieving a political aristocracy is a recurring theme in Nietzsche's work. At times it is recessive, and then Nietzsche appears to appeal to an individualism whereby the best, the *Übermensch*, might avoid the shackles of social conformity by concentrating upon fostering their individuality. In a number of early and late works, however, he favours an aristocratic community.[20] Nietzsche's aristocratic political ideas are removed from what have constituted central elements in fascist and Nazi regimes, namely a single leader, radical nationalism, racism, and corporatism.[21] Yet Nietzsche valorizes discrimination between an elite, who are to be privileged, and the remainder who are designated subordinate and incapable of the creativity that is required to enhance experience.

NIETZSCHE INTERPRETATION

Nietzsche has been interpreted variously and appropriated indiscriminately since his death at the turn of the twentieth century. Notably, at the instigation of his sister Elisabeth he was taken up by the Nazis. The Nazis stressed assertively if unconvincingly the continuity of Nietzsche's ideas of the *Übermensch* and the will to power with their own radical nationalism, commitment to hierarchy, and racism.[22] In less discordant ways, Nietzsche has been enlisted as a precursor to many currents of thought on the right and left. Feminists have been drawn to his conception of the embodied character of thought and truth, which challenges abstract notions of the individual that ignore embodied experiential standpoints that testify to gendered aspects of personal and public life. Like the Nazi assimilation of Nietzsche, which ignores his antipathy to nationalism, feminists have contrived either to ignore or to explain away his express views on the dependence of women and their incapacity to bear the vicissitudes of self-development.[23]

After the Second World War Kaufmann pioneered a re-reading of Nietzsche that was oriented towards rehabilitating Nietzsche as a respectable philosopher, innocent of entanglement with Nazi credos. Nietzsche was taken

---

[20] See F. Nietzsche, 'The Greek State', in F. Nietzsche, *The Nietzsche Reader*, ed. K. Ansell Pearson and D. Large (Oxford, Malden MA and Victoria Australia, Blackwell, 2006), pp. 88–94; F. Nietzsche, *Beyond Good and Evil*; F. Nietzsche, 'The Anti-Christ', in F. Nietzsche, *The Anti-Christ, Ecce Homo, Twilight of the Idols* ed. A. Ridley and J. Norman, p. 155.

[21] See R. Griffin, *The Nature of Fascism* (Abingdon, Routledge, 2003).

[22] For observations which are diametrically opposed to racism and nationalism, see, amongst many instances, F. Nietzsche, 'Twilight of the Idols', in F. Nietzsche, *The Anti-Christ, Ecce Homo, Twilight of the Idols* ed. A. Ridley and J. Norman, pp. 188–90.

[23] See C. Diethe, 'Nietzsche and the Woman Question', *History of European Ideas*, vol. 11 (1989), pp. 865–76.

as maintaining acceptable philosophical doctrines that did not espouse disturbing political views. He allowed Nietzsche a safe passage into post-war theoretical literature but misleadingly underplayed the radicalism of his philosophy.[24] In post-war France, post-structuralists embraced Nietzsche with some plausibility as a precursor of their own views on the end of metaphysics, on the ubiquity of power, and on the historicity of truth. Occasionally, these theorists foisted onto Nietzsche ideas and perspectives that reflected their own concerns. For instance, Deleuze's admittedly engaging study of Nietzsche reads him as contending with Hegel and his system, whereas, for the most part, Nietzsche neither references Hegel nor assumes Hegel as a target for critique.[25]

Foucault's reading of Nietzsche is worth reviewing for at least two reasons. First, Foucault evidently reads Nietzsche carefully and productively. Second, his interpretation of Nietzsche bears upon the formulation of his own influential ideas. The trajectory of Foucault's intellectual and political development shows a persisting but discontinuous engagement with Nietzsche. Foucault himself frames a series of historical interventions by which he identifies changing discursive forms and in doing so he takes Nietzsche to be a precursor of his own determination to break with essentialisms and to think without recourse to transcendent and teleological categories. The upshot is that Foucault is a persuasive guide to Nietzsche and the consequences of Nietzsche. A feature of his interpretation in the differing idioms that he employs in early and late texts is that he reads Nietzsche differently from how he interprets other thinkers. While Marx, Hegel, Kant, and Bentham are read as issuing from prevailing discursive schemes, Nietzsche is taken as superseding preceding and contemporary discursive regimes by affirming the historicity and contingency of truth. Foucault's reading of Nietzsche is insightful but the capacity of Nietzsche to grasp the implications of discourse and its history are not explained. Just as the possibility of Foucault's own perspective is never convincingly justified, so Foucault's interpretation of Nietzsche is not to be explained by his characteristic historical methods.

In *The Order of Things* Foucault takes truth to be a series of historical productions, which he terms *epistemes*. They are determined locally and historically, and can be recovered subsequently by historical excavation. Like Nietzsche, Foucault assumes truth, science, and ethics to represent a series of evolving discourses, embracing discontinuous features. The metaphorical *episteme* of the Renaissance is succeeded by the representational scheme of the classical period, which, in turn, is followed by modernity's turn to history

---

[24] W. Kaufmann, *Nietzsche: Philosopher, Psychologist, Antichrist* (New York, Vintage, 1974).
[25] See G. Deleuze, *Nietzsche and Philosophy* (New York, Columbia University Press, 1983); see also S. Houlgate, *Hegel, Nietzsche and the Criticism of Metaphysics* (Cambridge, Cambridge University Press, 2004).

and humanism. The Nietzschean notion of discontinuity is exemplified by the disorderly succession of epistemological schemes, which jars with the Kantian notion that the conditions of knowledge can be captured by transcendental analysis. The modern episteme is intimated to be coming towards a close. In the conclusion of *The Order of Things* Foucault observes, 'As the archaeology of our thought easily shows, man is an invention of recent date. And one perhaps nearing its end.'[26] Foucault anticipates the imminent collapse of the humanism of the modern age, but this anticipation itself has been anticipated by Nietzsche. Foucault invokes and supports Nietzsche's dismantling of redundant transcendent notions of humanity. According to Foucault, 'Nietzsche rediscovered the point at which man and God belong to one another, at which the death of the second is synonymous with the disappearance of the first...'.[27] Foucault highlights Nietzsche's relevance to his deconstructive project by observing how his destruction of transcendent principles must inform contemporary and future philosophy. He remarks, 'In this, Nietzsche offering this future to us as both promise and task, marks the threshold beyond which contemporary philosophy can begin thinking again; and he will no doubt continue for a long while to dominate its advance.'[28] Foucault captures the force of Nietzsche's critique of modernity and embodies its ongoing relevance in his own thinking, but his respect for Nietzsche is not supported by an explanation of how Nietzsche is enabled to critique his own discursive context. Foucault's relative silence on explaining the formation and capacity of his own theoretical standpoint is mirrored in his seeming acceptance of Nietzsche's inherent capacity to critique the discursive assumptions of his age.

Foucault's turn towards a more central engagement with power in his disciplinary studies and studies on governmentality rehearses Nietzsche's identification of truth with power. Foucault expressly invokes Nietzsche as a guide in his genealogical investigations by which he traces historical ways in which regimes of truth and power operate Moreover, Foucault's affinity with Nietzsche is marked by their shared critique of the Enlightenment's occlusion of power in abstracting reason and moral and political schemes from the operations of power. Schrift observes, 'Foucault engaged in a highly sophisticated analysis of power which, following Nietzsche's example, focused not on the subjects of power but power relations, the relations of forces that operate within social practices and systems.'[29] Foucault takes Nietzsche to be a kindred spirit in disturbing the alleged objectivism of the Enlightenment project,

---

[26] M. Foucault, *The Order of Things* (London and New York, Routledge, 1989), p. 422.
[27] Ibid., p. 373.   [28] Ibid.
[29] A.D. Schrift, 'Nietzsche's French Legacy', in B. Magnus and K. Higgins (eds), *The Cambridge Companion to Nietzsche* (Cambridge, Cambridge University Press, 1996), p. 340.

which Habermas maintains in the face of post-structural critique.[30] Foucault's rehearsal of Nietzschean themes highlights their radicalism by showing how they are both at odds with prevailing orthodoxies of knowledge and morality.

Foucault's genealogical explorations of contingent discursive regimes are modelled expressly on Nietzsche's practice. In his essay, 'Nietzsche, Genealogy, History', Foucault highlights his connection with Nietzsche.[31] Foucault's endorsement of Nietzsche and his genealogical method also serves as a justification of his own methodological practice. At its outset, Foucault emphasizes how the genealogist steers clear of imposing a scheme of supra-historical coordination upon the singularity of events with which he or she is concerned. Like Nietzsche he distinguishes this genealogical attitude from that of Paul Rée, Nietzsche's friend, who aimed to reduce the variety amongst moral principles to the rational operations of utility.[32] Foucault reads Nietzsche as eschewing all meta-historical readings of history. There is to be no reduction of the plurality of historical events. Above all, there is to be neither an imposed teleology, where a projected end state simplifies the narrative of multitudinous events, nor a corresponding quest for origins, which will only reduce the past to the requirements of a narrative of the present. Foucault testifies to his own determination to avoid the philosophical crutch of a meta-narrative, but it is an attitude that he recognizes in Nietzsche.

Foucault conducts a close reading of Nietzsche in which he distinguishes his use of *Ursprung* from *Herkunft* and *Entstehung*. These terms can all be translated as origin, but Foucault insists that they are not interchangeable. He detects two uses of *Ursprung* in Nietzsche's work, one of which is merely a synonym for the other terms. In one use of *Ursprung*, for instance in *On the Genealogy of Morals*, it denotes a search for metaphysical origins purporting to furnish fundamental truths. It is a use, which Nietzsche, and Foucault in his commentary, condemn due to its refusal to accept discontinuity and dispersion in history. There are no ultimate metaphysical truths to serve as ends of inquiries. Foucault takes *Herkunft* and *Entstehung* to be more exact than *Ursprung* in conveying what genealogy is undertaking. *Herkunft* denotes the tracing of descent, which is not to be conceived as the quest for a single or unifying set of traits but the pursuit of an assemblage of features that allow for diversity and disqualify reading past and present as continuous. Likewise *Entstehung* denotes the emergence or development of phenomena that does not lead to a predetermined end. It is not even the realization of a potential that lies behind the sinuous and excessive events that are to be traced. There is no unifying theme or metaphysical explanation of the sheer plurality of events. Forces emerge, clash, reconstitute. There is no underlying or overriding plan.

---

[30] J. Habermas, *The Philosophical Discourse of Modernity* trans. F.G. Lawrence (Mass., USA, MIT Press, 1990).

[31] M. Foucault, 'Nietzsche, Genealogy, History', pp. 76–100.   [32] Ibid., p. 77.

Foucault observes, 'The isolation of different points of emergence does not conform to the successive configurations of an identical meaning; rather they result from substitutions, displacements, disguised conquests and systematic reversals.'[33]

Foucault highlights the radical disassociation or deconstruction of identities in Nietzsche's genealogical practice. The self is no more stable and unified than a people or a concept. The conflicted character of the creative struggle is exemplified in the self where differing elements vie for pre-eminence and the residues of conflicts can be detected in the investigations of the past. Genealogical study does not focus upon a cerebral being, whose body is irrelevant to the changing modulations of practical life. For Nietzsche, and also for Foucault, everything is subject to change, and the instability of identities is radical in that emotions, feelings, and instincts cannot be reduced to primordial revelations. They change along with all aspects of the human identity. Likewise historical study should not be directed to the intentions and rational purposes of individuals. Historical truth is not the sum of these rational components. Rather, unplanned happenings, conflicts in which unintended outcomes and bodily skirmishes all play a part in a whole that lacks both unity and a formal rational structure. The genealogist, in Foucault's Nietzschean guise, is not to act like a prim historian, who subtracts their own embodied nature from their analysis. The genealogist brings to the study of phenomena his or her own tumultuous sets of forces, which work on the evidence that they bring to light, suggesting particular lines of inquiry. There is no detached disengaged rational mode of scholarship.

Foucault concludes his article on Nietzsche and genealogy by reflecting upon its uses. Foucault draws upon what Nietzsche designates valuable from the historical sense, which he takes to be worthwhile in contrast to the frigid supervening truths of standard historians. He identifies three uses of this notion. One is its value in demystifying the objects of historical analysis by parodying inflated notions of identity. Another is the radical disassociation of identities that an historical sense can convey. Instead of imagining a single form of morality or a unifying line of development, Nietzsche registers the thoroughly conflicted and dissonant series of forms that morality assumes. Another valuable aspect of the historical sense is that it destroys the fiction of an overall or supervening truth. History, in this Nietzschean sense, is useful in disrupting the assumptions of everyday experience by which concepts, values, and objects are held up for generic analysis or for dispassionate identification of underlying truths. Nietzsche, for Foucault, performs the valuable task of exposing the radical contingency of existence, which is at odds with a Platonic world of forms and essences. These essences, the purportedly unifying

---

[33] Ibid., p. 86.

character of transient phenomena are mythical, and in detracting from the malleability of the present, impede radical change. Nietzsche aimed to transform assumptions and values. Likewise Foucault undertakes genealogical surveys to disrupt contemporary practice and break free from supposed eternal essences. Foucault respects the intentions of Nietzsche, which he perceives to be realized in his texts, just as he imagines his own affiliated project to be warranted. Foucault's commentary on Nietzsche is valuable precisely because he values him and yet his analysis of Nietzsche's texts takes Nietzsche at his word in a way that is at odds with his standard deconstructive historical practice.

Like Foucault, Derrida identifies with Nietzsche. Again, like Foucault, Derrida is a critic of univocal conceptions of meaning. Texts, for Derrida, are not to be interpreted as expressing a single line of thought, which can be traced to an author. A text is more than an author's intended meaning. Meaning, for Derrida, is multiple and cannot be restricted. Metaphysics, for Derrida, epitomizes the misleading assumption of a univocal meaning. Platonic forms, the Cartesian ego, and Rousseau's sensibility are so many expressions of the metaphysical impulse to identify meaning as constant. Derrida's deconstructive techniques disturb apparent universal frames of meaning. *Of Grammatology* sets out a reading of the history of philosophy in which he challenges this prioritizing of speech over writing and the essential over the marginal. Derrida recognizes a turning point in the history of metaphysics to occur in Nietzsche's destructive aphoristic critique of preceding forms of philosophy. Nietzsche is a fierce critic of religion and metaphysics in that he is suspicious of all forms of transcendence whereby the particularity of experience is sacrificed to what is taken to be the essential and universal. Experience is thereby sacrificed on the altar of abstraction. Derrida recognizes the force of Nietzsche's critique, remarking, 'Nietzsche, far from remaining simply (with Hegel and as Heidegger wished) within metaphysics, contributed a great deal to the liberation of the signifier from its dependence or derivation with respect to the *logos* and the related concept of truth...'.[34]

While recognizing Nietzsche's break from inherited styles of philosophy, Derrida also observes how the unmediated stridency of Nietzsche's language lends itself to an interpretation of his style as blunt assertiveness in the service of a new metaphysics. Indeed, Derrida notes how Heidegger, in focusing on the late notebooks, invests Nietzsche plausibly with a metaphysical frame of thought.[35] Derrida intimates that this reading is not to be simply denied, but takes it to complement rather than to undermine an anti-metaphysical

---

[34] J. Derrida, *Of Grammatology* trans. G. Spivak (Baltimore and London, Johns Hopkins University Press, 1976), p. 19.

[35] For Heidegger's reading of Nietzsche see M. Heidegger, *Nietzsche* (4 vols) trans. D. Krell (New York, Harper Row, 1979–86).

conception of Nietzsche.[36] In 'Interpreting Signatures (Nietzsche/Heidegger): Two Questions' Derrida notes, 'Heidegger directs this whole interpretation of Nietzsche's essential and singular thinking to the following argument: this thinking has not really gone beyond the end of metaphysics; it is still itself a great metaphysics...'.[37] Derrida contends that it is a mistake to impose on Nietzsche the essentialism of either a metaphysics or an anti-metaphysics. He takes issue with Heidegger's interest in how Nietzsche names his thinking, protesting that Nietzsche is a thinker who defies definition and naming. He maintains, 'Next to Kierkegaard, was not Nietzsche one of the few great thinkers who multiplied his names and played with signatures, identities and masks?'[38] Derrida reads Nietzsche as anticipating his own project of deconstruction, just as Foucault's reading of Nietzsche is affiliated to his own practice of genealogy. The upshot is that Derrida's reading of Nietzsche, like Foucault's, is empathetic and productive, and yet it operates in a way which is distinct from his general practice of deconstruction. His reading of Nietzsche offers a way of understanding how Derrida sees his own critical style, which is related to Nietzsche's characteristic style of philosophizing.

Derrida recognizes Nietzsche's styles, and this is an express theme of his *Spurs: Nietzsche's Styles*, the title of which conveys the many-sidedness of Nietzsche. It is a many-sidedness which is assumed by Derrida in his own writing. This reading of Nietzsche is not straightforward, and that is because Derrida takes Nietzsche to be far from straightforward. Derrida intimates that it is intrinsic to Nietzsche's style to possess multiple styles, which aim to show how truth is neither clear-cut nor susceptible of a one-dimensional statement. There are differing questions and differing sides to questions so that truth is not to be configured as closure, or as a statement of what is the case. Language is not an instrument to represent an external objective truth, even if traditional Western metaphysics might assume that truth is susceptible of such verification in conforming to an objective order of things. Western metaphysics might assume a project whereby truth can be conveyed explicitly so that it does not depend upon the indirection of a style that rehearses multiple forms. But Nietzsche, at least in Derrida's eyes, is not doing traditional metaphysics. Heidegger's metaphysical reading of Nietzsche is misplaced, because Nietzsche declared against such a project while avoiding the performative perils of declaring against metaphysics. Derrida attributes to Nietzsche, with some plausibility, his own suspicions of a presumed universality of truth. Nietzsche takes truth to be an operation of power, and its form must

---

[36] J. Derrida, *Of Grammatology*, p. 19.

[37] J. Derrida, 'Interpreting Signatures (Nietzsche/Heidegger): Two Questions' trans D. Michelfelder and R. Palmer, in D. Michelfelder and R. Palmer (eds), *Dialogue and Deconstruction—The Gadamer-Derrida Encounter* (New York, State University of New York Press, 1989), p. 65.

[38] Ibid., p. 67.

accommodate to its operational perspectival terms. Derrida aims to show how Nietzsche conveys the indirectionality and perspectivalism of truth.

In so doing, Derrida invokes how Nietzsche conceives of woman. Questions concerning women are a theme of Nietzsche scholarship. On the face of things, Nietzsche is dogmatic, proclaiming conventional patriarchal views. Women are to be subordinate, lacking power and creativity. He observed, 'Women are considered deep. Why? Because there is no bottom to them. They are not even shallow.'[39] Yet Nietzsche's brutal dismissal of women is not the only or last word of and on Nietzsche's treatment of women and gender issues. Contemporary German feminists were divided on how they understood Nietzsche, but for the most part, they were enthused by his radicalism.[40] Subsequent feminists have been attracted to aspects of Nietzsche's thought, appreciating his reading of the historicity of morality and his insistence on the embodied character of thinking.[41] Nietzsche appears to offer more fertile possibilities for conceptualizing thought, the body, and gender than is standard in Enlightenment notions of reason, which take the body to be removed from reason, while tacitly assuming that men are best placed to operate in a rational manner.[42] Derrida's analysis of the ways in which Nietzsche imagines women complicates matters further by intimating ambiguities in Nietzsche's attitudes to women that track his multiple perspectives on truth. Derrida reflects upon entries in Nietzsche's notebooks, commenting on one of his entries in the following way. He considers Nietzsche's reflection on the progressive elaboration of ideas, observing how Nietzsche maintains '[T]he progress of the Ideas becoming more subtle, insidious, incomprehensible, it *becomes female*' (emphasis in original).[43] Derrida remarks, 'All the emblems, all the shafts and allurements that Nietzsche found in woman, her seductive distance, her captivating inaccessibility, the ever-veiled promise of her provocative transcendence, the *Entfernung*, these all belong properly to a history of truth by way of the history of an error.'[44] Derrida takes Nietzsche to eschew a simple and singular way of regarding truth. If truth were so simple then the traditional metaphysics, which he subjected to sustained critique, would not be so evidently mistaken. Derrida does not envisage truth to be susceptible to

---

[39] F. Nietzsche, 'Twilight of the Idols', in F. Nietzsche, *The Anti-Christ, Ecce Homo, Twilight of the Idols* ed. A. Ridley and J. Norman, p. 159.

[40] See B. Helm, 'Combating Misogyny—Responses to Nietzsche by Turn-Of-The-Century German Feminists', *Journal of Nietzsche Studies*, no. 27, Spring 2004, pp. 64–84.

[41] See M.J. Bertram, 'God's Second Blunder—Serpent Woman and the Gestalt in Nietzsche's Thought', *Southern Journal of Philosophy*, vol. 19, Fall 1981, pp. 259–77.

[42] As an example of Enlightenment rationalism and gendered readings of experience, see J. Locke, *Locke's Two Treatises of Government* ed. P. Laslett (Cambridge, Cambridge University Press, 1970).

[43] J. Derrida, *Spurs Nietzsche's Styles* trans. B. Harlow (Chicago, University of Chicago Press), p. 89.

[44] Ibid.

singular formulations, hence he himself takes truth to be elaborated circuitously. Hence, the multiplicity of ways in which women and truth are configured in Derrida's reading of Nietzsche insinuates Derrida's own sense of the multiplicities of meaning. Woman and truth are reciprocally revealing and dissembling in that they neither close nor disclose their meaning, because they are open and multiple.

Derrida imagines Nietzsche to anticipate his own determination to break with metaphysics and with a counter-metaphysics, which would merely rehearse the language of traditional metaphysics. Hence, Derrida is insistent that Nietzsche's seemingly dogmatic statements on women, truth, and ethics are not to be taken at face value. Meanings are multiple in Derrida and in Derrida's Nietzsche, because truth is not susceptible of a universalizing discourse, by which oracular statements reveal the truth in singular ways. On this reading Nietzsche, like Derrida, prioritizes writing and the nuances of style by which a plurality of meanings are to be explored.[45] In *Spurs Nietzsche's Styles* Derrida's reflections on the indeterminacy of language and the impossibility of a single univocal expression of truth culminate in his interrogation of Nietzsche's words, 'I have forgotten my umbrella.'[46] These words, in quotation marks, were found in Nietzsche's unpublished manuscripts. They are isolated and apparently disconnected from other entries. Derrida raises questions over their meaning and concludes that they are indeterminable. He remarks, 'There is no infallible way of knowing the occasion of this sample or what it could have been later grafted onto. We never will know *for sure* what Nietzsche wanted to say or do when ne noted these words, not even that he actually *wanted* anything.'[47] In 'Interpretation and the Understanding of Speech Acts', Skinner responds to Derrida's commentary. He concurs with Derrida that there is no infallible guide to meaning and agrees that intellectual historians might lack the evidence to provide convincing interpretations in particular cases. But Skinner observes that fallibilism should not preclude interpretive explanations of intentions, so that plausible explanations of texts and actions can be offered if there is sufficient evidence even if infallibility is never to be attained.[48]

Skinner's response to Derrida is to the point and offers a plausible defence of the commitment to explain social actions and texts by interpretation of intentions and contexts. The issues between Skinner and Derrida are hard to pin down. Both admit fallibility, and recognize how multiple interpretations of texts and actions are possible so that there is no indefeasible way of deciding between them. However, Derrida recognizes how texts and actions might resist intentional explanation in that they might not operate as vehicles of

---

[45] Ibid., pp. 123–43.   [46] Ibid., p. 123.   [47] Ibid.
[48] Q. Skinner, 'Interpretation and the Understanding of Speech Acts', in Q. Skinner, *Visions of Politics*, vol. 1, *Regarding Method* (Cambridge, Cambridge University Press, 2002), pp. 121–2.

determinate intentions of authors. They might be either overdetermined by a plurality of causal factors or radically underdetermined. In relation to the words 'I have forgotten my umbrella' Derrida speculates on the possibilities of interpreting them by applying a Freudian theory of unconscious associations, by speculating on as yet unknown contextual links, and finally by recognizing the possibility that there is no express meaning to be attached to the words at all.[49] Words after all may be uttered or written with no determinate purpose in mind. Derrida takes the comment about the umbrella to serve as an unlikely inspiration for speculating on how Nietzsche's writing as a whole might be interpreted. He observes, 'If Nietzsche had indeed meant to say something, might it not be just that limit to the will to mean, which, much as a necessarily differential will to power, is forever divided, folded and manifolded. To whatever lengths one might carry a contentious interpretation, the hypothesis that the totality of Nietzsche's text, in some monstrous way, might well be of the type "I have forgotten my umbrella" cannot be denied.'[50] Derrida muses that Nietzsche's texts might have multiple layers of meaning, in which part or the whole might be parody. He concludes that 'truth' and 'woman' for Nietzsche are multiple and should not be read as if they are terms standing in for traditional metaphysical longings to encapsulate the truth.[51]

CONCLUSION

Nietzsche has been interpreted in multiple ways. The multiplicity reflects the preoccupations of subsequent thinkers as much as the density and richness of his texts. The vigour and apparent clarity of Nietzsche's texts paradoxically impose difficulties on interpreters. What if the clarity does not serve to express truths directly but instead to register thoughts and counter-thoughts that challenge readers to engage in their own thinking? Derrida is insightful in imagining how the apparent dogmatism of Nietzsche's declarations on 'woman' and 'truth' might not be taken at face value as if they are formulations of a new if dogmatic form of metaphysics. On this reading Nietzsche aims to break with God and associated metaphysical and moral principles to establish a distinctly novel and form-breaking perspectival way of thinking and writing.

The interests and styles of French post-structuralism are suited to evoking the form-breaking aspects of Nietzsche's thought. Nietzsche's break with Enlightenment ideology fits with the iconoclastic anti-essentialism and anti-humanism of Derrida and Foucault. Nietzsche's genealogical deconstruction of naturalistic and essentialist moral and political principles coheres with

---

[49] Ibid., p. 123.   [50] Ibid., p. 133.   [51] J. Derrida, *Spurs Nietzsche's Styles*, p. 135.

Foucault's exposure of the changing and power-charged disciplinary mechanisms underpinning apparently benevolent developments in punishment and social organization. Likewise, Derrida's deconstruction of metaphysical frames of thinking, which abstract from the endless possibilities of linguistic meaning in positing an essential and universal truth, is akin to Nietzsche's artful destruction of supposed transcendent truths. On the other hand, the Nazi assimilation of Nietzsche relies upon using isolated phrases from his texts, which allows for the misconstrual of texts and their author and clearly is generated by subsequent interests rather than an openness to Nietzsche's words. Yet, while French post-structuralist thinkers might be held to offer productive and plausible interpretations of Nietzsche, their readings raise interpretive questions. The influence of their own preoccupations and styles of thinking evidently bear upon their interpretations of Nietzsche, and these influences might be construed as benign in that they capture deconstructive possibilities of Nietzsche's enterprise. However, both Foucault and Derrida offer interpretations of Nietzsche that are at odds with their general interpretive practice. Nietzsche is taken at his word in challenging transcendent principles and metaphysical systems, whereas characteristically Derrida and Foucault deconstruct the theories of preceding theorists, aligning them with discursive orders and textual implications that are not recognized by the authors that are the objects of analysis. We are left wondering why we should take Nietzsche at his word just as we are not enlightened about their deployment of a hermeneutics of recovery in this instance. Questions about the rationale of the interpretation of Nietzsche by Derrida and Foucault relate to unanswered questions about the justification of their own deconstructive projects. These appear to rest upon uncorroborated intentions to undermine universalistic modes of thought and to rehabilitate the destructiveness of Nietzsche.

18

Simone de Beauvoir

The Politics of Sex

INTRODUCTION

Beauvoir is a controversial twentieth-century figure. Notably, she raises the question of what it means to be a woman, and assesses the impact of sexual identity on politics. She poses questions for politics by observing how social practices constitute a subordinate female identity. Single-handedly she did much to project the notion of sex and 'woman' into the field of academic study and into the sphere of public debate. Inevitably she stirred emotions and shocked sensibilities, because femininity and masculinity had not figured in standard ways of conceptualizing public life and philosophical analysis. Raising the very question of the identity of 'woman' inevitably compromised Beauvoir's status as a philosopher and ostracized her from café society. Her legacy speaks for itself. Questions of sexual identity are now routine items of public and academic discourse on politics and culture. Yet controversy continues in several ways. Recent feminists question the feminist credentials of her relationship to her partner Sartre.[1] As Angela Carter once observed, 'Why is a nice girl like Simone wasting her time sucking up to a boring old fart like J-P?'[2] Wider critical questions are asked about her brand of feminism. Critique is directed at her dismissal of the merits of motherhood, her focus upon Western white women, and her apparent prioritizing of masculine values.[3] If Beauvoir's feminism is now subject to critique it exerts a sustained impact on the way the public world is to be understood and assessed. Her thought is rich;

[1] See, for instance, M. Evans, *Simone de Beauvoir—A Feminist Mandarin* (London, Tavistock, 1985).
[2] A. Carter, 'Colette', in M. Mason (ed.), *London Review of Books Anthology* (London, Junction Books, 1981), p. 135; cited in T. Moi, *Simone de Beauvoir—The Making of an Intellectual Woman* (Oxford and Cambridge Mass., Blackwell, 1994).
[3] For a considered discussion of these issues see T. Moi, 'Afterword', in T. Moi, *Simone de Beauvoir—The Making of an Intellectual Woman*, pp. 270–5.

bearing upon modern political thought and practice in multiple ways. She remains a subject of continued if critical interest.

Beauvoir was an existentialist, who maintained an enduring relationship with Jean-Paul Sartre. In the aftermath of the Second World War Sartre was the pre-eminent existentialist philosopher, exploring and endorsing freedom and existential commitment in the wake of a war that had stripped life and society of the assurance of essentialized truth and historical destiny. Beauvoir shares Sartre's existentialist perspective and applies it to her analysis of the condition of women. Women are challenged to refuse their subordinate role in the social world. Existentialism and Sartre no longer have the currency that they enjoyed in the immediate post-war world of the 1950s. Yet existentialism continues to ask questions of philosophy and of the individual, and Beauvoir's formulation of it is distinctive. She situates individuals in social contexts and conceptualizes social situations as shaping the possibilities of individual existential action. This is highlighted in her analysis of the situation of women. They are socialized to behave in conventional ways that thwart authentic existential choices.

In *The Second Sex* Beauvoir draws on Hegel to frame the social conditions in which women find themselves. Her use of Hegelian language and concepts has been recognized by recent commentators, who interpret her work as operating within a Hegelian or Hegelian-Marxist frame.[4] Beauvoir uses Hegelian themes and her engagement with historical and social practice and preceding historical forms of thought can also be interpreted in Hegelian terms. Beauvoir re-reads myths and past theories in the light of her own understanding of the 'othering' of women, so that Ancient religions, medieval myths, and modern psychoanalytic and Marxist theories are critiqued by focusing upon their depiction of women as subordinate and dependent. Ostensible universal theories are shown to be partial and androcentric by their interrogation from a subsequent feminist standpoint, just as Hegel engages with sundry preceding forms of thought to establish the dialectical achievement of his own perspective. A Hegelian reading of Beauvoir will be explored in this chapter along with a hermeneutical perspective on how her analysis of the sexual framing of social and political practices allows for a re-reading of past political theorists, who apply gendered notions of public and private forms of social life.[5] Relatedly, Beauvoir's own exploration of the

---

[4] See K. Hutchings, *Hegel and Feminist Philosophy* (Cambridge, Polity, 1993); S. Sandford, *Beauvoir* (London, Granta Books, 2006); E. Lundgren-Gothlin, *Sex and Existence—Simone de Beauvoir's 'The Second Sex'* trans. L. Schenck (Hanover and London, Wesleyan University Press, 1996); N. Bauer, 'Must We Read Simone de Beauvoir?', in E. Grosholz (ed.), *The Legacy of Simone de Beauvoir* (Oxford, Clarendon Press, 2004), pp. 115–37.

[5] A Hegelian reading of Beauvoir is offered in K. Hutchings, *Hegel and Feminist Philosophy*.

situation of women is situated historically in reflecting affluent European mid-twentieth-century assumptions.[6]

LIFE AND WORKS

Beauvoir wrote many kinds of text. Autobiographical explorations of her life, novels that draw upon her experience, essays addressing political and social themes of the moment, and more considered abstract philosophical works. Students of Beauvoir have a variety of literary sources to consider in establishing the trajectory of her thinking and in assessing the value of her ideas. Of course, Beauvoir did not express an unvarnished truth in her autobiographical and experiential writings. A commitment to existential authenticity might incline an author to be candid, and there is no reason to think that she lies or falsifies experience either in her novels or in her autobiographical accounts. But she views things from a particular point of view and an existential perspectivalism is consonant with her philosophy. In her autobiographical writings she is silent about her lesbian sexual relationships and refrains from criticizing Sartre when it would appear that she differs from Sartre emotionally and philosophically.[7] So the autobiographical and experiential writings have to be interpreted, for they do not reveal all aspects of her situation and thought. Beauvoir's recourse to experiential commentary in essays and autobiographical writings in itself is revealing. It is not an accidental feature of her thought. It reflects her sense of how reflection on experience operates. Metaphysics informs judgments and perspectives in ordinary life as well as in abstract philosophical treatises. She allows expressly for a metaphysics of lived experience, which is undertaken by reflection upon social practices and personal and social relationships.[8] She undertakes to access and reflect upon this metaphysics of lived experience in sociological essays and imaginative literature. *The Second Sex* constitutes a way of analysing lived experience. It reviews how women are oriented towards the world in mundane activities such as daydreaming, doing the housework, gossiping with one another about house decorations, and fussing over a son or admonishing a daughter. Hence there

---

[6] See C. Imbert 'Simone de Beauvoir: A Woman Philosopher in the Context of Her Generation' trans. E. Grosholz, in E. Grosholz, *The Legacy of Simone de Beauvoir* (Oxford, Clarendon Press, 2004), pp. 3–21.

[7] See K. Fullbrook and E. Fullbrook, 'Sartre's Secret Key', in M. Simons (ed.), *Feminist Interpretations of Simone de Beauvoir* (Pennsylvania, Pennsylvania State University Press, 1995), pp. 97–111.

[8] S. de Beauvoir, 'Literature and Metaphysics (1946)', in S. de Beauvoir, *Philosophical Writings*, ed. M.A. Simons with M. Timmerman and M. Mader (Urbana and Chicago, University of Illinois Press, 2004) trans. V. Zaytzeff and F. Morrison.

are sound reasons for drawing critically upon Beauvoir's autobiographical writings and sociological essays in considering her philosophy, because philosophy, for her, is not divorced from everyday experience.

Beauvoir was born into a bourgeois family soon after the turn of the century, yet the comfortable lifestyle of her parents suffered when their wealth diminished in the wake of an economic downturn. The ensuing financial strain on the household was matched by a deterioration in the relationship between her parents. Hard times exerted an emotional strain. Quarrels ensued and Beauvoir's father often absented himself from the family home to frequent local cafés and bars, and having occasional sex with local prostitutes.[9] Beauvoir's mother shrank from facing reality, maintaining the fiction that things were as they should be. Beauvoir's recollection of her mother is unsympathetic, reflecting her sense of her mother's bad faith in refusing to recognize the manifest problems in her domestic situation. Beauvoir's autobiographical study, *A Very Easy Death*, reflects her unease with her mother. From an early age her own sense of self was oriented to academic work and she flourished in achieving academic success when studying philosophy at the Sorbonne, where she took one of the first cohort of places that were made available for women. She enjoyed studying philosophy and performed well in her graduating examination, coming second to Sartre.[10] The collegiality of university life and a mutual devotion to philosophy embedded her relationship with Sartre. They also afforded Beauvoir a way of flourishing in the world, without suffering undue discrimination due to her sex. Her relationship with Sartre was defining for her emotional, sexual, political, and intellectual life. She shared ideas with Sartre and a sense of how life should be experienced. They conducted a relationship that aspired to be authentic in that they sought to refuse deceit and compromise to accommodate infidelity and low points. They allowed one another sexual freedom to engage in other sexual relationships while maintaining their own bond. Beauvoir's novel, *She Came to Stay* deals with a woman in an open sexual relationship, who experiences dislocating jealousy when her partner engages emotionally as well as sexually with another woman. The plot mirrors her own experience, for Sartre developed a strong relationship with another woman.[11] The novel shows Beauvoir working through the complications of lived experience.

Intellectually, Beauvoir and Sartre shared a commitment to existentialism and Beauvoir respected the authority of Sartre's metaphysical analysis of the

---

[9] See S. de Beauvoir, *A Very Easy Death* trans. P. O'Brien (Harmondsworth, Penguin, 1983).

[10] It is worth observing that Sartre was repeating the examination. On the examination see T. Moi, 'Second Only to Sartre', in T. Moi, *Simone de Beauvoir—The Making of An Intellectual Woman*, pp. 37–58.

[11] S. de Beauvoir, *She Came to Stay* trans. Y. Moyse and R. Senhouse (London, Fontana, 1984).

human condition in *Being and Nothingness*.[12] Although Sartre's *Being and Nothingness* is currently as unfashionable as existentialism, it represents a philosophical exploration that harmonized with the existentially charged conditions of war and its aftermath. Iris Murdoch, in a letter to Queneau at the end of the war, comments on the 'kick' of French philosophy and discusses existentialism animatedly.[13] The conditions of the Second World War and its aftermath put a strain upon faith in God and upon subscribing to philosophical systems that imagine the universe to be rational or for history to be the story of progress. The Nazis and concentration camps undermine the view of history as a redemptive process.[14] Existentialism in its various guises, but notably in Sartre's *Being and Nothingness*, undermines the notion of an underlying essence to human beings that could anchor their beliefs and conduct. Sartre insists that existence precedes essence and the distinguishing feature of human beings is held to be their capacity for freedom, an ability to transcend or go beyond the given, the facticity of experience. Like Heidegger, Sartre understands human beings to be unique in imagining themselves to be beings for whom being is an issue.[15] Freedom matters because there is no essential route that individuals are to follow. They have to choose, and authenticity consists in choosing freely without deferring to pressures or subscribing unreflectively to prescribed social roles.[16]

For Sartre, bad faith occurs when individuals repress their freedom or opt out of choosing by failing to recognize that they are beings for whom being is in question. Individuals are agents who can choose and undertake projects. In *Being and Nothingness* Sartre explains 'bad faith' by citing what now seems the odd example of a 'frigid' woman, who affects that a man's advances to her are not in fact sexual. She takes what he says and does at merely face value when it is clear he is making a sexual advance.[17] The abstraction of this example from a sexist social practice for which a woman cannot be assigned responsibility is neither noticed by Sartre nor critiqued by Beauvoir. She accepts and testifies to Sartre as a philosophical guide.[18] However, subsequent feminists have drawn attention to differences of emphasis in Beauvoir's presentation of existentialism from that of Sartre's.[19]

---

[12] J.-P. Sartre, *Being and Nothingness* trans. H.E. Barnes (New York, Washington Square Press, 1966), pp. 617–29.

[13] I. Murdoch, Letters to R. Queneau in Iris Murdoch Archive, Kingston University.

[14] T. Adorno, *Minima Moralia—Reflections on a Damaged Life* trans. E.F.N. Jephcott (London and New York, Verso, 1995).

[15] M. Heidegger, *Being and Time* trans. J. Macquarie and E. Robinson (Oxford, Basil Blackwell, 1962), pp. 28–35.

[16] J.-P. Sartre, *Being and Nothingness*, pp. 73–107.

[17] Ibid., pp. 55–6.

[18] S. de Beauvoir, *Letters to Sartre* trans. and ed. Q. Hoare (New York, Arcade, 1991).

[19] See for instance, M. Evans, *Simone de Beauvoir: A Feminist Mandarin*.

Differences between Sartre and Beauvoir surface in Beauvoir's *The Ethics of Ambiguity* in which she provides an ethics for existentialism, which appears to be an individualist philosophy that is not overly concerned by a moral concern for others.[20] Beauvoir declares that an existentialist ethics cannot rely on what is taken to transcend individuals. The source of ethics must be located in an individual's capacity to choose. In this sense Beauvoir is at one with Sartre's formulation of existentialism in *Being and Nothingness*. *The Ethics of Ambiguity* proceeds by setting up a series of dichotomies that frame existence and render the human situation ambiguous. Individuals are situated between life and death, between nature and freedom, between subject and object, between the individuality and society, and between being and existence.[21] It is because of the ambiguities of the human situation that individuals must choose and determine their own ethics. Yet Beauvoir's very interest in ethics highlights her interest in the social situation of individuals and her concern for an individual's relations with others. This perspective distinguishes her formulation of existentialism from the narrow focus upon the individual and his freedom in Sartre's *Being and Nothingness*. The social aspect of Beauvoir's thought is revealed clearly in the conclusion of *The Ethics of Ambiguity*. It insists on the social character of individualism and an individualist ethic. Beauvoir observes, 'It is individualism...But it is not solipsistic, since the individual is defined only by his relationship to the world and to other individuals...'.[22] Moreover, she also acknowledges the social pressures on women, recognizing how their potential for freedom is compromised by their status in society. Beauvoir is mindful of the dependent status of women in society. She remarks, 'To the extent that they respected the world of the whites the situation of the black slaves was exactly an infantile situation. This is also the situation of women in many civilizations; they can only submit to the laws, the gods, the customs, and the truths created by the males. Even today in western countries, among women who have not had in their work an apprenticeship of freedom, there are still many who take shelter in the shadow of men; they adopt without discussion the opinions and values recognized by their husband or lover, and that allows them to develop childish qualities which are forbidden to adults because they are based on a feeling of irresponsibility.'[23]

If the situation of women is intimated in *The Ethics of Ambiguity*, it is highlighted in the succeeding *The Second Sex* (1949). *The Second Sex* proclaims its existentialism and cites Sartre as its exemplary theorist, but it follows its own path in tracing women's subservience. It is radical in emphasizing the subordinate situation of women and in clearing a path for a second wave of feminism to contest male supremacy. *The Second Sex* expresses a metaphysics

---

[20] S. de Beauvoir, *The Ethics of Ambiguity* trans B. Frechtman (New York, The Citadel Press, 1948), p. 9.
[21] Ibid., pp. 7–35.   [22] Ibid., p. 156.   [23] Ibid., p. 37.

of lived experience in providing a comprehensive analysis of how the social world is structured for women and how it appears to them.[24] *The Second Sex* begins by facing squarely the issue of the status of women. Beauvoir recognizes how the very raising of the question of women's specific identity signifies that women are being identified in terms of their sex, whereas the identity of men is assumed to consist in general human qualities. Questions about the nature of men tend not to be posed, so that men can operate without a focus upon their sex. She observes, 'And she is simply what man decrees; thus she is called "the sex", by which is meant that she appears essentially to the male as a sexual being. For him she is sex—absolute sex, no less. She is defined and differentiated with reference to man and not he with reference to her; she is incidental, the inessential as opposed to the essential. He is the Subject, he is the Absolute—she is the Other.'[25]

The Introduction to *The Second Sex* sets out an agenda. The dependent status of women is to be examined in its existential, historical, and sociological ramifications. The sex of women matters in a way that the sex of men does not. Women are Other. Beauvoir accepts Sartre's notion of existential freedom as defining the individual. But the self, which is for itself and capable of expressing itself is the male individual. Man determines his existential freedom but woman has to contend with being Other. Beauvoir's relational analysis of the situation of women and men identifies men as oppressing women so as to enhance their own status. Her recognitive conceptualization of relations between women and men draws upon Hegel and his dialectical review of self-consciousness. She observes, 'Things become clear, on the contrary, if following Hegel, we find in consciousness itself a fundamental hostility towards every other consciousness; the subject can be posed in only being opposed—he sets himself up as the essential, as opposed to the other, the inessential, the object.'[26] Beauvoir imagines women to be potentially free and self-determining individuals. Their dependence is not to be explained causally by biological or psychoanalytical factors. Rather, their relations with men provide the context in which women fail to realize their freedom. The struggle for self-consciousness in Hegel's *Phenomenology of Spirit* is a dialectical analysis of the character of self-consciousness as it is put to the test in the form of a life and death conflict between two individuals. The struggle exemplifies what is at stake in social relations. Without sociality there is no prospect of individuals realizing their identities as self-conscious beings.[27] However, Hegel diagnoses the immediate

---

[24] For this notion of lived experience, see S. de Beauvoir, 'Literature and Metaphysics' (1946), pp. 261–78.

[25] S. de Beauvoir, *The Second Sex* trans. H.M. Parshley (London, Jonathan Cape Ltd, 1953), p. 16.

[26] Ibid., p. 17.

[27] See T. Pinkard, *Hegel's Phenomenology* (Cambridge, Cambridge University Press, 1994), chapter 3.

outcome of the struggle to be self-defeating because it yields a master and a slave. The slave is in fear of his life and so submits to the master, but the areciprocal relations between the two of them undermines the prospect of recognition for the master as well as for the slave. Recognition by a defeated slave is not affirmative. A truly reciprocal recognition that can establish the freedom of individuals is only to be realized in an organized and equilibrated society, where individuals can achieve ethical freedom. In analysing the situation of women, Beauvoir draws upon Hegel's perception of how status, recognition, and individuality are at stake in socially engaged relations. She sees the objectification of women by men to be the outcome of a relational struggle in which the stakes are their freedom and status. In prevailing social relations men operate as subjects, and women serve as the collective Other.

Beauvoir reworks Hegel's dialectic of recognition in framing her analysis of how men dominate women. Women serve as objects to enhance male status, though their dependent status entails that men do not value the recognition that they receive from them. Men cannot value recognition from those whom they do not respect. For Beauvoir, the dependence of women is social and existential rather than causal. She rejects a move to explain dependence by appealing to a biological determination that takes women to be naturally inferior to and dependent on men. She acknowledges biological differences between men and women and allows that their reproductive function affects women's lives. Motherhood is not to be dismissed lightly, because it puts a strain upon a woman's capacity to act as an individual agent. Likewise women's bodies operate to a different rhythm from those of men, and she concedes that women are less physically strong than men. Yet Beauvoir concludes that biological differences do not entail that women are to be less free and independent than men. Physical differences contribute to the situation of men and women, but how they respond to these differences is shaped culturally and existentially rather than by biological causes. Men oppress women in socially constructed ways, and it is up to women and men to change the social conditions. Likewise, Beauvoir recognizes how the lives of women are susceptible to psychoanalytic interpretation but refuses to imagine that the status of women is to be causally explained by or reduced to the terms of psychoanalysis. The explanation of the female psyche by unconscious drives does not capture the freedom of an individual's capacity to choose, whereas existentialist analysis respects this capacity to choose. She also rejects Engels's reading of the dependence of women upon men as it is set out in *The Origins of the Family, Private Property and the State*.[28] While she acknowledges that male insistence on the patrilineal line of inheritance to ensure control over property plays its part in sexual oppression, she concludes that it does not

---

[28] F. Engels, *The Origins of the Family, Private Property and the State* trans. E. Untermann (London and New York, Penguin, 2010).

capture the sheer will to exercise domination that is at play in relations between the sexes. Instead, she turns to a Hegelian existential framework, in which agonistic engagement and the assertion of male subjectivity constitute the underlying rationale of male dominance.

Beauvoir's rejection of Engels's explanation of sexual inequality does not entail a wholesale rejection of Marxism. Beauvoir follows Marx in identifying a potential for social change in historical developments in work and technology. The development of effective forms of contraception and the growing work opportunities for women admit of a prospect of change. Changes in employment and control over the reproductive process provide a context in which women can be empowered to assert equality, and men might come to accept egalitarian socialism.[29] Beauvoir's discussion of the historical conditions for female emancipation follows on from her analyses of historic forms of inequality, and preceding mythological representations of women. Her account of historic inequalities between men and women includes a review of primitive nomadic societies, where physical differences and the primacy of women in reproductive and nurturing roles structures demarcated unequal roles for men and women. Even where women receive a privileged status as symbols of fertility or as incarnations of virtue, they are objectivized and deprived of an equal status with men. Beauvoir discusses a series of literary images of women that are gleaned from the works of Stendhal, Montherlant, Claudel, and Lawrence to highlight how women are figured as the dependent sex. The modern world, however, harbours the prospect of women gaining a greater equality of status given the changes in work and reproductive patterns.

In Book Two of *The Second Sex* Beauvoir turns to an analysis of the nature and meaning of women's lives in the contemporary world, covering their formative years, their roles as wives, mothers, and their experience in old age. Her analysis of the situation of contemporary women is notable on a number of scores. It highlights the ways in which women live lives that do not allow for subjectivity or freedom. The narrative of women's lives reveals the social construction as well as the restriction of their identities. She begins the Second Book of *The Second Sex* with the following words, 'One is not born, but becomes a woman.'[30] She goes on to draw out the implications of this statement, 'No biological, psychological or economic fate determines the figure that the human female presents in society; it is civilization as a whole that produces this intermediate between male and eunuch which is described as feminine.'[31] Femininity is the product of socialization and Beauvoir is contemptuous of the product.

The processes of socialization begin with childhood and Beauvoir identifies how boys and girls are labelled and nurtured in contrasting ways, and with

---

[29] S. de Beauvoir, *The Second Sex*, pp. 139–69.   [30] Ibid., p. 295.   [31] Ibid.

contrasting consequences. Girls are treated differently from boys. A girl is encouraged to be sensitive, to show affection, and tellingly to attend to and respond to the moods and inclinations of the father. A boy is allowed more freedom and is not expected to register sensitivity on the same scale. The young girl, unlike her male counterpart, is discouraged from being active and physical in the way she plays. Fights are reserved for boys and the control that the young girl is expected to exert over her physical appearance and activities has implications for her developing mindset. She becomes and is encouraged to become, more restrained and less assertive. She is less boisterous, more circumspect, and hence less free than a boy. The boy is allowed and even encouraged to experiment sexually. Sex is not something to be avoided or endured passively but is to be pursued and practised assertively. Ideals of chastity and virginity are held up before the girl and contribute to an unworldly and eunuchic aspect of the female persona, which will be picked up and critiqued later by second wave feminists such as Germaine Greer.[32] Beauvoir discusses the possibility of lesbianism in a young woman's sexual experience, but notices its tendency to assume exaggerated expressions that reflects and confirms its marginalization.

The socialization of girls and young women prepares them for the roles that are performed by adult women. It produces women who prioritize marriage. Women succumb to the dependence of married life. A young woman is groomed for marriage. Marriage provides the defining life role for women. Married life also comes with an expectation of motherhood. Motherhood, for Beauvoir, is not a life-enhancing or expansive experience. It is a restriction on a woman's liberty and life opportunities. It belongs to the sphere of immanence rather than transcendence. Adhering to Sartre's conceptualization of freedom Beauvoir imagines it to be a matter of going beyond the given, a movement of transcendence, whereas motherhood in its passivity is the reverse. It happens to women and constrains their possibilities so that they do not transcend the given. They are merely carrying on the conditions of species life as an immanent activity. The roles of wife and mother are critical in restricting the lives of women. They tend to rule out work, whereas men, in working, extend the range of their activities and possibilities. Women, in their restrictive roles, are constrained to focus their emotional lives on aligning to their husbands and children. In consequence, they neither develop practical skills nor express their own emotional possibilities. Ironically, the very restrictiveness of their emotional range limits their attractiveness to both husband and children. The husband is inclined to become bored by the confines of home and like Beauvoir's own father seeks sex and emotional comfort in alternative settings, outside the home. The children are also

---

[32] G. Greer, *The Female Eunuch* (London, New York, and Sydney, Harper Perennial, 2002).

constrained by home and the mother's presence. They are motivated to move on and set their sights on what lies beyond the family home. Young men look to the public activities of civil society, while young women look for a husband to begin their own family. If women tend to outlive husbands by surviving into old age, then their fate is to become increasingly unattractive and isolated. They appear as strange and marginal figures.

Beauvoir's review of women's lives is a narrative of their dependence. Her depiction of the unassertive restrictiveness of women's lives appears misogynistic. The image of a married woman, stranded in an unaccommodating marriage, gossiping with other alienated wives, and tending to children, who strain against her controlling ministrations is an unappealing vision. In summing up the situation Beauvoir concludes, 'Woman wears herself out in haughty scenes, and in the end gathers up the crumbs that the male tosses to her. But what can be done without masculine support by a woman for whom man is at once the sole means and the sole reason for living. She is bound to suffer every humiliation; a slave cannot have the sense of human dignity; it is enough if a slave gets out of it with a whole skin.'[33]

The solution to the problem of women's lives is disarmingly simple. Women are to become equal with men. The abstract right of equality must be realized in practice. Beauvoir ends *The Second Sex* by citing Marx's 'Economic and Philosophical Manuscripts', which identifies the realization of communism with the achievement of meaningful equality between men and women.[34] Female emancipation demands that women exchange immanence for transcendence and participate in the world of work on equal terms with men. They are no longer to be prisoners of serial childbirths and the preoccupation of motherhood. Technology is currently enabling women to be capable of working on equal terms with men and innovations in contraception allow motherhood to be regulated so that women are not at the mercy of maternity. Here and there in *The Second Sex* Beauvoir suggests how men and women can both assume responsibility in parenting and make use of nurseries and crèches to relieve themselves of its burdens.[35]

BEAUVOIR AND PHILOSOPHY: PAST AND PRESENT

Beauvoir's *The Second Sex* exerted an immediate and prolonged impact in opening up the relevance of sexual identity to social and ethical questioning.[36]

---

[33] Simone de Beauvoir, *The Second Sex*, p. 615.   [34] Ibid., p. 741.
[35] Ibid., pp. 690–714.
[36] A female friend of mine in the 1980s always carried a copy of *The Second Sex* wherever she went.

It continues to exert an impact. On its publication, and with some justice, Beauvoir could be seen as an existentialist who simply follows Sartre in making individualism and choice the central features of her philosophical concerns. She was certainly read as an ally of Sartre, who did not herself develop a distinctive philosophy.[37] It is true that she puts individual freedom at the forefront of her reasoning about humanity. However, Beauvoir and *The Second Sex* can be read productively as contributing to the history of philosophy and political theory in ways which are not identical with Sartre. A Hegelian reading of *The Second Sex* can highlight its engagement with Hegel and Marx as much as with Sartre in framing its commentary on a developing social context. A number of commentators on Beauvoir, notably Hutchings, Lundgren-Gothlin, Sandford, Simons, and Le Doeff, observe how Beauvoir uses Hegelian ideas in developing an understanding of the social construction of femininity and the power that is exerted by men.[38]

In *The Ethics of Ambiguity* Beauvoir sets out her position by demarcating it from Hegel and Marx. She testifies to her admiration for Hegelian philosophy and its systematic character. It proved to be an intellectual comfort amidst the uncertainties of individual life during the occupation of France by the Nazis.[39] However, she explains how she reacts against the intellectual certainties of Hegel to embrace the ambiguities of an existentialist ethic that is committed to individual freedom. She abandons an holistic account of the development of history in favour of a situated and contingent existential engagement with existence. Likewise she discounts Marxism because of its totalizing historical narrative, whereby individuals are merely assigned places in the wider scheme of history.[40] Where she differs from Sartre, however, is in insisting on how ethics demands that individuals align themselves with others, rather than pursuing lone choices.[41] Moreover, she alludes to Hegel in imagining a festival by which individuals are joined with one another in an ebb and flow of celebratory movement. The image suggests an engagement of individuals with one another even if the unity is fleeting and cannot be sustained. Hutchings recognizes perceptively how Beauvoir's reference to a festival alludes to Hegel's depiction of self-consciousness as a Bacchanalian revel in *The Phenomenology of Spirit*.[42]

---

[37] See M. Simons, 'Introduction', in M. Simons (ed.), *Feminist Interpretations of Simone de Beauvoir* pp. 7–9.

[38] See K. Hutchings, *Hegel and Feminist Philosophy*; E. Lundgren-Gothlin, *Sex and Existence*; S. Sandford, *Beauvoir*; M. Simons (ed.), *Feminist Interpretations of Simone de Beauvoir*; M. Le Doeff, 'Simone de Beauvoir: Falling (Ambiguously) into Line', in M. Simons (ed.), *Feminist Interpretations of Simone de Beauvoir*, pp. 22–36.

[39] S. de Beauvoir, *The Ethics of Ambiguity*, pp. 8–9.

[40] Ibid., pp. 22–3.   [41] Ibid., pp. 60–73.

[42] See K. Hutchings, *Hegel and Feminist Philosophy*, pp. 62–3.

The Second Sex reflects Beauvoir's continued engagement with Hegel. She highlights the sociality of experience in ways that depart from Sartre. Her fundamental analysis of the status of women draws expressly upon Hegel's identification of a struggle for recognition in *The Phenomenology of Spirit*.[43] Women are dependent on men and this dependence is neither natural nor open-ended. It arises out of men's determination to elevate themselves and their status by abasing women, just as slavery and mastery are the outcomes of the struggle for recognition in *The Phenomenology*. Beauvoir's critical use of Hegel, however, is at odds with *The Phenomenology of Spirit*, because in *The Phenomenology* women are not seen as competing over status and recognition, even though Hegel recognizes Antigone's historic challenge to Creon in the name of the family.[44] Women do not take part in a life and death struggle that Hegel outlines in *The Phenomenology*. Hegel depicts women as representing the merely natural in his generalized account of the sexes.[45] Moreover, Beauvoir's use of Hegel to highlight social and cultural conflict goes against the grain of the dominant interpretation of Hegel in France. Butler observes how post-war French interpretations of *The Phenomenology* were mediated by the reading of Hegel by Kojeve, who developed a psychological reading of the life and death struggle that did not envisage its completion in social cooperation and an equilibrated society.[46] Hence Beauvoir transforms Hegel by using his ideas to infuse a particular social dimension to the travails of consciousness. She provides a dramatic interpretation of the social situation of women by invoking a Hegelian style of argument. She shows how the conflict between men and women issues in women being consigned to subordination. Beauvoir's explanation of women's dependent position in society, however, imagines oppression to be so pervasive as to threaten to undermine the prospect of radical change. Women must assert their freedom or men and women jointly must acknowledge their reciprocal freedom. The prospects for either of these eventualities are not good in that women are currently oppressed by men and appear spiritless and seemingly incapable of rebelling.[47] What offers some hope for the future is her reading of the forces at work in modernity, which are changing the situation of women, notably changes at work and over the control of reproduction. In locating her analysis of sexual politics and its future possibilities in the actual social and the course of history, Beauvoir is again linked with Hegel.

---

[43] See E. Lundgren-Gothlin, *Sex and Existence*.

[44] G.W.F. Hegel, *The Phenomenology of Mind* trans. J. Bailee (London, George, Allen and Unwin, 1971), pp. 464–96.

[45] See K. Hutchings, *Hegel and Feminist Philosophy*, pp. 82–94.

[46] J. Butler, *Subjects of Desire* (New York, Columbia University Press, 1987), pp. 61–79. See also E. Lundgren-Gothlin, 'Hegel and Kojeve', in E. Lundgren-Gothlin, *Sex and Existence*, chapter 3.

[47] S. de Beauvoir, *The Second Sex*, pp. 725–43.

While Beauvoir uses Hegel's ideas, she also draws upon Marx. In *The Ethics of Ambiguity* she deprecates Marxism's narrative of human emancipation due to its underplaying of individuality.[48] *The Second Sex* takes Marxism to provide a large-scale social theory that offers a possible but one-sided explanation of female oppression. Beauvoir recognizes the force of Engels's alignment of sexual oppression to the maintenance of property interests that enable male control over property and women.[49] Yet Beauvoir argues that the identification of sexual oppression with property interests misses out on the fundamental motivation for sexual domination on the part of men. She highlights the desire of men to dominate women and female acquiescence in their subordination. In particular she explains male oppression of women by observing how men identify woman as the Other, and subject women, as mere others, to their rule. Beauvoir also recognizes how Marx offers hope to women in that his vision of communist society includes a commitment to equality between the sexes. Communism serves as a utopian goal that both men and women can respect. It represents a future society in which there is no longer to be oppression on either class or sexual grounds. Beauvoir observes how actual communist regimes have not realized this aim of sexual equality, because they have not recognized the scale of the demands that are placed upon women in their role in reproducing the species. But Moi points out how Beauvoir envisages socialism and a socialist form of society to be constitutive of a future society that is free of sexual oppression.[50] In the context of the Cold War, Beauvoir deepened her commitment to Marxism. For instance, in her article for *Les Temps Modernes*, 'Right-Wing Thought Today', she affirms her Marxism by concluding witheringly, 'Today the expression "bourgeois ideology" no longer refers to anything positive. The bourgeoisie still exists, but its catastrophist and empty thought is nothing but a counter-thought.'[51]

Beauvoir engages with Hegel and Marx in developing her ideas on the status of women in society and in envisaging radical social change. Reading her thought in the light of a Hegelian-Marxist framework highlights her focus upon the actual social world and historical developments. It also allows for an appreciation of the way in which she reworks preceding ideas, such as the dialectic of recognition by relating them to her own reading of society. Her thought can also be assessed in the light of Gadamer's interpretive framework. Gadamer understands how the horizon of the present reconfigures the ways in which past thought is to be constituted and analysed. Beauvoir is radical and innovative in identifying the role of women in society. She attends to the

---

[48] S. de Beauvoir, *The Ethics of Ambiguity*, pp. 20–4.

[49] S. de Beauvoir, *The Second Sex*, pp. 84–92.

[50] T. Moi, *Simone de Beauvoir—The Making of An Intellectual Woman*.

[51] S de Beauvoir, 'Right-Wing Thought Today', trans. V. Zayteff and F. Morrison, in S. de Beauvoir, *Political Writings*, ed. M. Simons and M. Timmerman (Chicago, University of Illinois Press, 2012), p. 183.

multiple ways in which women do not so much act in society but rather receive dependent private roles by which men are enabled to act and to dominate. Beauvoir's rethinking of what it means to be a woman in society sets her thought apart from preceding political theories. Preceding theorists tend to be uninterested in sexual identities and interpret politics as a public activity in which men merely happen to be conspicuous. Beauvoir's refusal to accept sexual identities and standard formulas of what constitutes public and political spheres raises questions about the identity of political theory as well as preconceptions of sexual identity. Preceding political theorists separate the public from the private, whereas Beauvoir's *The Second Sex* challenges traditional divisions and condemns the consignment of women to a private sphere, in which their actions are immanent rather than transcendent. Beauvoir's formulation of how a contemporary independent woman contrasts with what went before presumes that this style of woman will operate in the public sphere. In the conception of the future that Beauvoir allows herself she imagines a socialist world in which women operate with men in the public world on equal terms. There is a clear division between traditional political theory and Beauvoir's sociology of the lived experience of women's lives. She observes how the public and private spheres are constructed to establish sexual identities that are unequal and must be transformed. Is there a chasm between her thought and predecessors that cannot be bridged?

Gadamer's perspective allows for a constant readjustment between past and present, by which changing interpretive horizons reconsider forms of past thought. From this perspective, preceding political theory can be revisited in the light of Beauvoir's re-evaluation of the sexually charged identity of the public sphere. Beauvoir's thought allows for multiple re-readings of preceding theories, and a focus upon aspects of their thinking that otherwise might be overlooked. Central to any re-reading is a focus upon how preceding political theories divide public from private activities. Although a dividing line might be drawn differently by different theorists, they are united in reserving political analysis for a distinguishable and male sphere of public activity. For Hobbes, the achievement of public security might include any action the sovereign determines as pertaining to it, so that the public is to be equated with the province of the sovereign.[52] For Locke, individual rights are secured by a public authority, which is constituted by the consent of citizens, who entrench rights to protect a private sphere, to which women are consigned. Rousseau diagnoses the problems of modernity to require democratic sovereignty, which operates to achieve the common good. The common good is to be defined by the general will, but women are external to the process of its determination and are designated as attending to the private emotional needs

---

[52] For an interesting account of Hobbes, women, and the public sphere see G. Slomp, 'Hobbes and The Equality of Women', *Political Studies*, vol. 42, no. 3, 1994, pp. 441–52.

of the family that lie outside the scope of public activity.[53] Pateman observes how social contract theory in its various guises presupposes a prior sexual contract, whereby women are subordinated to men, and the plausibility of her standpoint is confirmed by Beauvoir's evaluation of the situation of women.[54]

Hegel sets out a scheme for a rational political association, which conceives of the private and public as being intertwined, but he insists upon the restriction of women to the private sphere of the family and their exclusion from the activities of civil society and the state. Hegel's patriarchal viewpoint appears one-sided and repressive in the light of Beauvoir's critique of the restrictedness of women's lives in prevailing forms of social and political life. However, Hegel's dialectical reading of the inter-relations of the private and public spheres recognizes how the nurturing of individuals in family life allows for their development as agents, who are capable of exercising agency and contributing to private and public ends. He is akin to Beauvoir in identifying the public significance of the private sphere. Marx is not an exponent of patriarchy and Engels's *The Origins of the Family, Private Property and the State* critiques male domination. Marx himself in his 'Economic and Philosophical Manuscripts' emphasizes how equality between the sexes is a mark of an authentically free and equal society, and in *The Communist Manifesto* he and Engels are scornful of bourgeois sexual oppression.[55] However, Marx, in *Capital*, cites the onerous working conditions of women as a manifest example of the inhumanity of capital, which appears to be motivated by a paternalistic concern for women's welfare rather than a commitment to equal conditions for both sexes.[56] Marx, unlike Beauvoir, does not emphasize inequality between the sexes to constitute a major feature of capitalist oppression. Beauvoir's radical critique of the status of woman in the past and in the present offers a perspective which allows for a revisionist re-reading of Marx, which might imagine sexual identity and class as inter-sectional components of social oppression.

CONCLUSION

Reading from within and from a Hegelian perspective serves to underline Beauvoir's socially inflected existential critique of the oppression of women in

---

[53] See D.H. Coole, *Women in Political Theory—From Ancient Misogyny to Contemporary Feminism* (Sussex, Harvester Wheatsheaf, 1993).

[54] C. Pateman, *The Sexual Contract* (Cambridge, Polity, 1988).

[55] K. Marx, 'Economic and Philosophical Manuscripts', in K. Marx, 'Early Writings' trans. R Livingstone and G. Benton (Harmondsworth, Penguin, 1975), p. 289; K. Marx and F. Engels, *The Communist Manifesto*, in K. Marx, *Political Writings*, vol. 1, *The Revolutions of 1848* (Harmondsworth, Penguin, 1973), pp. 435–75.

[56] K. Marx, *Capital*, vol. 1 trans. S. Moore and E. Aveling and ed. F. Engels (Moscow, Progress Publishers, 1969).

past and present societies. She is not to be read as merely employing Sartre's perspective in considering the situation of women. She draws expressly upon Hegel in establishing a fundamental critique of the conflicted character of sexual conditions of the present. Just as in Hegel's *Phenomenology* the freedom and truth of self-consciousness demands a struggle for recognition, so men and women conflict in establishing their identities. Men impose their mastery and dominate women, and women acquiesce in this oppression. Beauvoir invokes Hegel's conceptualization of recognition to highlight the existential and social dimensions of sexual oppression. Her account of the sociological forms of dependence that women experience in contemporary and past social conditions provide phenomenological evidence of the scale of the social domination of women by men in ways that depart from Sartre's individualistic perspective.

The innovative and radical character of Beauvoir's analysis of the oppression of women can be seen by comparing her perspective on social and political power with preceding political theories, which tend to ignore the dependent status of women and to assume that public issues can be divorced from a private sector in unproblematic terms. Beauvoir recognizes how women are excluded from the public sphere and are restricted to a subordinate role in the private sphere. She challenges contemporary social attitudes and an entire tradition of imagining the social and political world. She takes the dependence of women to constitute a question for politics, because it is not a natural condition, but is one which can be altered by radical action. The demand for political change raises the question of how Beauvoir imagines the political world in the wake of female emancipation. She does not specify a set of rights and institutions of government that would underpin an equal regime in the way that Locke or Rousseau have specified political arrangements. Beauvoir also does not elaborate upon how child care would operate in a future equal society. Her lack of specificity in imagining the future might be seen to detract from her vision, but she is clear that an equal socialist society is to be achieved and that the lives of men and women are not to be demarcated by being assigned to distinct spheres. Child care will have to be non-discriminatory, in that it will not be left as a private activity to be undertaken exclusively by women.

If Beauvoir's radical conception of sexual equality constitutes a provocative challenge to past and present political theories, in the aftermath of her death feminists have offered revisionist readings of her thought. While Beauvoir's role in advancing a critique of sexual oppression and in inspiring second wave feminism is universally acknowledged, her attitude to women and to traditional female qualities and activities has been subjected to critique. Third wave feminism, in one of its manifestations, identifies distinguishing and positive aspects of female identity to provide paradigms for the self-realization of women. In this light, Beauvoir's faithfulness to Sartre's intellectual leadership and the priority she assigns to her relationship with Sartre have been questioned.

Feminist writers have wondered if her deflection to Sartre's moral and philo-sophical authority betrays a patriarchal respect for a man of authority.[57] Likewise, Beauvoir's critique of maternity and the receptive aspects of the traditional female persona has been diagnosed to be misogynistic rather than emancipatory.[58] Moreover, in the light of post-modern awareness of differ-ences in society and forms of thinking, Beauvoir's focus upon the narrow concerns of middle-class European women has been critiqued.[59] Again, it has been urged that Beauvoir's deployment of Sartre's theories and language is problematic in that it subordinates feminine to masculine ways of thinking and acting. The rhetoric of Beauvoir in adhering to Sartrean language, for instance, in taking transcendence and commitment to projects to be emblem-atic of existential self-realization may be seen as privileging male attitudes to sex and personal achievement.[60]

The passage of time and the further development of feminism affords a perspective whereby Beauvoir's feminism can be judged to reflect the horizon of its time rather than epitomizing a progressive doctrine of emancipation. However, critique of Beauvoir should not neglect its own historicity as a form of critique in its critical appraisal of the historical character of Beauvoir's ideas. Beauvoir was silent on her lesbian relationships in her autobiographical writings. Silence, however, can be interpreted in many ways.[61] It may be construed as a betrayal of women's sexuality in deflecting to contemporary norms of heterosexuality. Perhaps, however, it was occasioned by the priority Beauvoir gave to protecting her 'private' identity at a time when she would have been subject to fierce intrusion. Indeed, she did suffer severe criticism on account of her assertive feminism.[62] Again, her focus on a narrow section of European middle-class women might be excused or at least understood if the severity of the subordination facing women in France at the time of her writing is appreciated.[63] Subsequent forms of post-modern feminism can be

---

[57] M.Evans, *Simone de Beauvoir—A Feminist Mandarin*, p. 58.

[58] See J. Leighton, 'Simone de Beauvoir on Motherhood and "Le Devouement"', in J. Leighton, *Simone de Beauvoir on Woman* (London and Cranbury New Jersey, Associated University Presses, 1975), pp. 185–208.

[59] See E. Holveck, 'Introduction to Political Reporting from Spain, Portugal and the U.S.', in S. de Beauvoir, *Political Writings*, pp. 9-16. Beauvoir's political writings do review politics in a colonial and post-colonial context, and refer to the situation of women in non-Western coun-tries, see notably 'Preface to Djamila Boupacha' and 'Political Reporting from Spain, Portugal and the United States'.

[60] M. Evans, *Simone de Beauvoir—A Feminist Mandarin*, p. 108.

[61] On silence and its many meanings see J.-F. Lyotard, *The Differend—Phrases in Dispute* trans. G. Van Den Abbeele (Manchester, Manchester University Press, 1988), p. 15.

[62] See M. Le Doeuff, 'Towards a Friendly Transatlantic Critique of the Second Sex', trans. E. Grosholz, in E. Grosholz (ed.), *The Legacy of Simone de Beauvoir* (Oxford, Clarendon Press, 2004), pp. 22–36.

[63] See C. Imbert, 'Simone de Beauvoir: A Woman Philosopher in the Context of her Generation', pp. 3–21.

seen as reflecting a particular expression of identity politics and the cultural turn. Their response to proliferating identity claims on behalf of multiple claimants marks a cultural transition, which can be seen as detracting from the combinatory power of a generic feminist message. The historicity and partiality of Beauvoir's thought must be recognized along with the positive aspects of her subscription to a form of existentialism that is mediated by Hegelianism and Marxism. Existentialism tends to be neglected or disparaged in recent philosophical and cultural contexts, yet it focuses an appeal to respond to the challenges of the human condition. This appeal, while no longer fashionable, is powerful particularly in Beauvoir's formulation that draws upon Hegel and Marx in framing it within a social and historical context.

19

Conclusion

Political Thought and History

A PLURALITY OF INTERPRETIVE PERSPECTIVES

The preceding analysis shows how past political thinkers are to be understood in multiple and divergent ways. In this chapter interpretive pluralism will be defended alongside the construction of a holistic dialectical interpretation of interpretation, which explains the interplay of the conditions composing this pluralism. Interpretive pluralism aligns with the phenomenon of reinterpretation. Instead of bemoaning the seemingly endless interpretive revisions of classic texts, the processes by which revisions take place can be endorsed. A plurality of interpretive styles invites new forms of evidence and perceptions of thinkers so as to disturb prevailing formulas. Hence, Machiavelli's thought is rendered less strange and less diabolical by seeing what he was trying to do and how he used concepts and strategies that were available to him. Skinner and Pocock contextualize his purposes to show the point of his enterprise, which is not to be reduced to a mere denial of moral principle. Again, and to the contrary, Locke is rendered rather less familiar but more interesting by our recognizing, along with Dunn, how his arguments are framed in terms of a theology with which we are less comfortable and are pitched against opponents whose identities are no longer familiar. While it may be tempting to see Locke as contributing to an onward march of liberalism, the theological frame of his political thought separates him from a modern ideology that defines itself against theological politics.[1] Instead of reading Rousseau's texts as Romantic masterpieces or as precursors to a terrible totalitarianism, Derrida allows us to recognize the tensions within his texts, which, in turn, enable us to wonder about how texts formulate and express their meanings. Foucault

---

[1] For an account of liberal democracy as constituting the ongoing directionality of history encompassing a number of issues and writings, see F. Fukuyama, *The End of History and the Last Man* (London and New York, Penguin, 1992), pp. xii–xxiii.

re-imagines Enlightenment social reforms so that we see their apparent rationality and humanity as occluding forms of insidious repression.

Refocusing the contexts by which we perceive thinkers allows for their reconsideration. While Mill may be imagined to represent the inspiration behind commonplace liberal doctrines, Collini reframes him in a neglected context, and adduces evidence of Mill's distinct but remote moral sensibility. Likewise Hobbes's hard-edged support for absolutist sovereignty is not so much overturned as re-envisioned by Oakeshott's recognition of his contribution to a tradition of radical but morally inflected individualism. Nietzsche is re-aligned to post-structuralist forms of thought by his assimilation to the deconstructive projects of Foucault and Derrida. Marx's critique of Hegel is destructive but does not destroy Hegel's continuing relevance to Marxist traditions of thought, which rework conceptions of Hegel and Marx. Beauvoir's re-imagining of contemporary society allows for a systemic hermeneutic revisiting of past politics that revises gendered readings of civil society and political participation. Again, Marx might seem old hat in using convoluted Hegelian language and in bemoaning the spiritualism of obscure marginalized figures in German intellectual circles. Yet his ghost can be conjured to haunt the apparent certainties of subsequent ideologies. Gadamer's hermeneutics allows us to perceive the senselessness of decrying the history of Marxism as so many betrayals of an originary source of enlightenment. The originary moment itself is subject to reinterpretation. There is no singular Marx awaiting resurrection at the hands of a self-denying disciple, who attends ceremonially to the savant's words and relishes his sacred texts. The past does not exist without reference to present and future horizons of interpretation. In his unpublished papers, Collingwood observes, 'The past is the explanation of the present, but the past is only known by analyzing its traces [evidence] in the present. To discover what the evidence is, is already to interpret it.'[2]

Political texts can be interpreted in multiple ways and our preceding survey of interpretations of texts establishes a collective rationale for going beyond Plamenatz and the mantra of reading and reflecting on texts again and again.[3] There is nothing wrong with reading texts again, and for reflecting upon them, but past texts are not to be assimilated by a process of osmosis. They demand a concentration upon how they are to be read and interpreted. To ignore theory is to invite misinterpretation, because to read past texts as if they rehearse present styles is to manifest a reckless optimism over the accessibility of their purposes, and forms of argument. A reflexive interpretive strategy avoids assimilating a past thinker to a present context without remainder. Interpretive schemes differ from one another, yet they all raise the question of

---

[2] R.G. Collingwood, 'Philosophy of History', Collingwood Manuscripts, Bodleian Library, Dep. 15. 2, 1 (1932).

[3] J. Plamenatz, *Man and Society* (London, Longmans, 1963).

interpretation in investigating the past. For instance, Foucault and Skinner differ over how contexts are to be conceptualized, but they share something in common, namely the need to conceptualize discursive contexts. They recognize that to understand Bentham or Hobbes depends upon reconstituting the languages or discourses within which they operated. Likewise Derrida and Gadamer agree on the need for an interpretive strategy. They might disagree on the degree to which texts reveal authorial intentions, but they concur in imagining that past theorists, such as Marx or Hegel, are to be interpreted in the light of theoretical and political considerations of the past and present. Marx himself diverges from Hegel, perhaps even standing him on his head, but he remains tied to Hegel in interpreting the past in the light of a theory of the directionality of history, which imparts a conditional meaning to particular historical conditions and texts.[4] Again, Oakeshott and Collingwood may employ divergent vocabularies but they invoke traditions and styles of thought which identify continuities and discontinuities in past forms of political thought.

This study of the history of modern political thought exhibits a plurality of interpretive techniques of inquiry that yield dividends in providing divergent but productive ways of conceiving of texts and contexts. To decry interpretive variety is to misconstrue the history of political thought as if it were an exercise in retrieving pre-constituted objects that are fixed rather than fluid and constructed. The identity of past political thought is open to interpretation and none of its component aspects are either definitive or fixed. While Collini attends to the contextual public morality in which Mill develops his thought and sees him to be essentially Victorian, Mill's continuity with the present can be accentuated by framing his conceptualization of liberty in the light of current concerns. Raising the question of which perspective is true is to misconceive the relativity of our concepts to the questions that we ask and to abstract from perspectival orientation. Rethinking past thinkers is neither an alibi for failing to think for ourselves nor a process of atonement for the sins of the past. It is how the history of political thought is to be conducted. A general history of modern political thought cannot consist in the rehearsal of a settled set of opinions on a series of past texts. If it is to capture the spirit of interpretive inquiry it has to reflect the changing ways in which past thinkers are continually reconstituted and reconsidered in the light of interpretive perspectives. Past thought is coeval with its continuing interpretation and reinterpretation.

If interpretive pluralism yields dividends then these dividends are not to be distributed to their owners without qualification. Each interpretive perspective claims an exclusive monopoly of interpretive insight, whereas multiple

---

[4] K. Marx, 'Afterword to the Second German Edition', *Capital*, vol. 1 trans. S. Moore and E. Aveling and ed. F. Engels (Moscow, Progress Publishers, 1969), p. 29.

interpretive trails, exhibiting opposing methods, and reflecting quite contrary assumptions, can be followed. The very collective success of interpretive schemes counts against the individual ways in which they aim to exclude rival accounts. They emphasize interpretive features that differentiate their explanations from rival perspectives. While these emphases demarcate their standpoints, the upshot is that they underplay important constituents of interpretive explanation and fail to account for their own standpoints. A more inclusive relational approach to interpretation is required, which allows for interpretive pluralism and explains the character of and relations between its constitutive features. This interpretation of interpretation does not supersede or replace the several interpretive perspectives that have been examined previously. It is dialectical in developing by means of their critical examination an integral holistic framework, which explains their interpretive value while reworking the conceptualization of interpretive explanation so as to show their limits. It highlights the reciprocal inter-dependence of the constitutive elements of interpretation and in so doing shows a way in which individual interpretations of political thinkers can be criticized even though their perspectival differences do not render them strictly commensurable. Particular interpretations of past thinkers can be criticized by recognizing omissions and limits that derive from the one-sidedness of the styles of interpretation to which they subscribe. The dialectical integral perspective on interpretation that is to be set out emerges from recognition of the explanatory deficiencies of the forms of interpretation that have been considered in preceding chapters. These deficiencies are highlighted by their confrontations with one another. These confrontations demonstrate the reciprocal limits of their limited alternative styles of interpretation and point to the explanatory edge that might be offered by a more inclusive relational perspective. The interpretive conflict between rival schemes will be reviewed in succeeding sections, in which the conflict between styles of construction and deconstruction and critiques of contextualism and teleology will be considered.

INTERPRETIVE CONFLICT: CONSTRUCTION AND DECONSTRUCTION

The several interpretive schemes that have been reviewed in this book yield positive but conflicting results. The countervailing critiques that they offer on one another's perspectives betoken the problems that each of the perspectives faces in explaining their identity. Interpretive explanation is often construed in terms of alternative hermeneutic strategies; a hermeneutics of recovery and a hermeneutics of suspicion. While some of the schemes follow a strategy of hermeneutic recovery, they are all equally suspicious of rival theories. Indeed, all schemes succeed in undermining aspects of the ways in which alternative standpoints explain things. It is worth looking at the ways in which they challenge one another's strategies to show how these challenges point to deficiencies that warrant a more inclusive dialectical account of how they relate to one another and to how the history of political thought is to be best understood.

A clear example of the way in which countervailing interpretive perspectives pose questions for one another is provided by the encounter between Gadamer and Derrida, which took place in Paris in 1981.[5] The encounter demonstrates a conflict between construction and deconstruction as forms of interpretive operation. In the encounter Gadamer's paper, 'Text and Interpretation', takes interpretation to be dialogical. Interpretation resembles a conversation in which participants develop their understanding of a subject by discussing one another's views.[6] Gadamer aims to reach out to Derrida and to French post-structuralist thought more generally. To accommodate post-structuralist presumptions, he denies that he privileges authors and the subjectivity of individuals. He observes, 'The dialogical character of language, which I tried to work out, leaves behind it any starting point in the subjectivity of the subject, and especially in the meaning-directed intentions of the speaker. What we find happening in speaking is not a mere reification of intended meaning, but an endeavour that continually modifies itself...'[7]

Gadamer maintains that dialogue is integral to interpretive achievement in speech and that texts are affiliated to speech in assuming virtual horizons of interpretive understanding, which replicate the attitude and positions of interlocutors in a conversation.[8] However, certain types of text do not operate as express objects of interpretive interplay on the part of authors and readers. Ideological texts reflect social interests; dreams and the psychopathological devices of everyday life reveal unconscious interruptions to the flow of conscious expression. Gadamer holds these forms of expression to be susceptible to a hermeneutics of suspicion rather than to the standard operation of a hermeneutics of recovery. They are outside the frame of ordinary linguistic transactions, and are not to be analysed by the paradigmatic form of textual interpretation. For the most part texts serve as vehicles for intended communication, which require to be interpreted by readers. Readers as interpreters,

---

[5] The contributions of Derrida and Gadamer to this encounter are collected in D. Michelfelder and R. Palmer (eds), *Dialogue and Deconstruction—The Gadamer–Derrida Encounter* (Albany, State University of New York Press, 1989), pp. 21–74.

[6] H.-G. Gadamer, 'Text and Interpretation' trans. D. Schmidt and R. Palmer, in D. Michelfelder and R. Palmer (eds), *Dialogue and Deconstruction—The Gadamer–Derrida Encounter*, p. 26.

[7] Ibid.　　　[8] Ibid., p. 35.

however, do not passively receive the intended meaning of an author. An author of a text does not dictate its reception, but as in an oral conversation, there is a 'process of reaching agreement in understanding.'[9] Gadamer highlights the specificity of literary, poetic texts, which require interpreters to respect the form of a text in all its particularity. Notwithstanding the specificities of literary interpretation, in this encounter with Derrida, Gadamer sees meaning as a process of interpretation in which understanding is not to be achieved solely by a speaker or by an author. Likewise the listener or reader is not to impose upon a conversation or a text. Rather, hermeneutical understanding is a joint achievement on the part of participants in communication. This applies to texts and readers as much as to interlocutors in a conversation. Authors and interpreters are to interrogate their situations and to accommodate one another's standpoints in a mutual process of interpretation. Interpretation is a process of reciprocal adjustment on the part of participants in a shared enterprise.

Derrida's response to Gadamer goes against the grain of the latter's expectations. It is a retort reflecting interpretive suspicion rather than a move in a shared enterprise. In challenging Gadamer, Derrida inquires, 'The first question concerns what he said to us last evening about "good will", about the appeal to good will and to the absolute commitment to the desire for consensus in understanding...Doesn't this unconditional axiom nevertheless presuppose that the will is the form of this unconditionality, its last resort, its ultimate determination.'[10] Derrida questions the presupposition of communicative good will on the part of participants in conversation and of authors and readers. He is sceptical of Gadamer's absorption of a psychoanalytic perspective into a wider scheme of interpretation and wonders to himself if disturbing assumptions rather than sharing understanding is what is demanded. Crucially, Derrida's response to Gadamer jars with the expectations that inform Gadamer's paper. While Gadamer aims to build bridges between himself and French post-structuralist heirs of Heidegger, Derrida strikes out without engaging directly with what has been said.

Gadamer's response to Derrida's retort reiterates his viewpoint. He presents an *ad hominem* plea, 'Even immoral beings try to understand one another. I cannot believe that Derrida would actually disagree with me about this. Whoever opens his mouth wants to be understood. And finally I have an exceptionally good piece of evidence for this: Derrida directs questions to me and therefore he must assume that I am willing to understand them. Certainly this is completely unrelated to Kant's "good will," but it does have a lot to do

[9] Ibid., p. 40.
[10] J. Derrida, 'Three Questions to Has-Georg Gadamer' trans. D. Michelfelder and R. Palmer, in D. Michelfelder and R. Palmer (eds), *Dialogue and Deconstruction—The Gadamer–Derrida Encounter*, p. 52.

with the difference between dialectic and the sophists.'[11] Gadamer and Derrida talk past one another and so demonstrate interpretive conflict. Gadamer assumes that the presuppositions of discourse allow for an interpretive fusion of horizons between one interlocutor and another, between past and present, and between text and reader. Derrida, on the other hand, is suspicious of authors and of speakers who proclaim a truth that is set on mediating between alternative formulations and assuaging disruption. His deconstructive probing of a text's language is not designed to align with the author but is pitched against an author's intentions to establish a truth beyond the ebb and flow of linguistic signs.

Derrida's practice of deconstruction works. He deconstructs a series of theoretical frameworks from those of Plato to Levi-Strauss that essentialize meanings and privilege the ideal, the natural, the rational, or the primitive over their designated and disparaged opposites. Likewise, Gadamer's analysis of interpretation makes sense of the changing perspectives on past texts in the light of changing horizons of interpretations. If the interpretive perspectives of Gadamer and Derrida are individually productive in examining past texts, the debate between them exposes their interpretive blind spots. The pros and cons of constructive and deconstructive forms of interpretation imply reciprocal strengths and weaknesses. Derrida disturbs the unintended contradictions that entangle texts. Gadamer identifies the ways in which texts transmit meanings to attentive engaged readers. Yet they mutually sideline the possibilities of alternative forms of interpretation. Their conflict shows the limits of their interpretive strategies.

Derrida might expose Rousseau's unacknowledged resort to the very forms of modernity that he disparages but equally he does not recognize the interpretive power of Rousseau's mythological imaginary. Rousseau's critique of modernity may well be constructed by a series of supplements that transgress against his own arguments, but nonetheless he succeeds in conveying a current homelessness and in framing an ideal of a political home for the alienated individuals of modernity.[12] In deconstructing Rousseau's linguistic transgressions Derrida fails to recognize Rousseau's constructive achievement. Likewise in *Of Grammatology* he performs a series of textual deconstructions that disturb the truth claims of Western metaphysics from its manifestations in Platonic forms to structuralist anthropology. Yet he does not register how he himself constructs a narrative of the end of metaphysics to frame his own deconstructive enterprise. In setting the scene for deconstruction he provides a

---

[11] H.-G. Gadamer, 'Reply to Jacques Derrida' trans. D. Michelfelder and R. Palmer, in D. Michelfelder and R. Palmer (eds), *Dialogue and Deconstruction—The Gadamer–Derrida Encounter*, p. 55.

[12] See T. Strong, *Jean-Jacques Rousseau—The Politics of the Ordinary* (London and Thousand Oaks, California, Sage Publications, 1994).

narrative of the unilinear directionality of history that runs counter to the usual course of his thought. The narrative is neither justified nor explained. As Gadamer complains, Derrida wants to be understood and yet he refrains from conveying the terms by which he solicits understanding. The constructive aspect of his deconstructive project is unacknowledged.[13] This lack of reflexivity underlies his sympathetic reading of Nietzsche. Whereas Heidegger, to whom Gadamer is sympathetic, reads Nietzsche as constructing a metaphysics of sorts, Derrida takes Nietzsche to conduct a critique of metaphysics that does not fall back into metaphysics.[14] Hence, for Derrida, Nietzsche is to be understood on his own terms by a careful non-deconstructive reading of his texts.[15] While Derrida's practice of deconstruction does not imply a complete dismissal of intentionality and apparent authorial meaning, his evocation of Nietzsche's intended philosophical achievement and his presentation of the emergence of deconstruction run counter to his standard deconstructive practice.[16] His account of the emergence of deconstruction and his reading of Nietzsche's challenge to traditional metaphysics is unsupported by reflexive interpretive argument and is at odds with deconstructive procedures. The tensions in Derrida's practice allow for the possibilities of other contrary forms of interpretation that allow more readily for authorial construction and invite the formulation of a more integral and supervening account of interpretation.

Gadamer insists upon interpretive possibilities, which arise out of the constructive interpretive interplay between participants in a conversation and between authors and their readers. Yet he is insensitive to the ways in which texts and speech convey unintended meanings. He imagines that critical engagement with texts is to be oriented by the traditions within which interpreters are operating. His understanding of tradition, however, does not allow for its conflicted character, for its contradictory strains, and for its critique. As Eagleton observes, '[H]is theory holds only on the enormous assumption that there is indeed a single "mainstream" tradition: that all "valid" works participate in it; that history forms an unbroken continuum, free of decisive rupture, conflict and contradiction...'.[17] Gadamer examines Hegel imaginatively and productively, observing the Socratic aspects of the dialectical operations of his *Logic*, but he does not interrogate the patriarchy

---

[13] Ibid., p. 55.

[14] J. Derrida, 'Three Questions to Has-Georg Gadamer', p. 68.

[15] Ibid., p. 69. See also J. Derrida, *Of Grammatology* trans. G. Spivak (Baltimore, Maryland, Johns Hopkins University Press, 1974), p. 19; for an expansive non-metaphysical reading of Nietzsche see J. Derrida, *Spurs: Nietzsche's Styles* trans. B. Harlow (Chicago and London, University of Chicago Press, 1979).

[16] For reference of Derrida's working with intentionality and authorial meanings, see C. Norris, *Derrida* (London, Fontana Press, 1979), p. 14.

[17] T. Eagleton, *Literary Theory: An Introduction* (Oxford, Blackwell, 1996), p. 72.

and overt conservatism of Hegel's political thought.[18] While Derrida subjects Hegel's endorsement of a gendered distribution of freedom in civil society and of a theologically transfigured social and political settlement to its radical critique by way of juxtaposing it to Genet's subversive texts, Gadamer neither questions nor disturbs Hegel's conventionalism.[19]

Gadamer's hermeneutics are countered expressly in Foucault's deconstructive critique of hermeneutical readings of ideas that privilege the role of authors and an engagement with intended meanings.[20] Authors take a backseat in Foucault's enterprise. Discourses on madness, reason, discipline, and punishment determine rather than convey intended meanings. Foucault takes power and truth to represent not so much what is constructed and intended but as conditions underlying express forms of construction. They are discerned within discursive practice by historians, who uncover what is covered up in formulations that take authors and agents at their word. Foucault identifies the operations of power in multiple sites, extending the range of politics beyond a circumscribed public sphere. Hence he disconcerts Gadamer's aspiration for a shared horizon of understanding between speakers and between authors and readers. Foucault's undermining of agency, authors, and truth, however, is at odds with his later lectures on governmentality and care of the self. It is subversive of his own interpretive practice.[21] As with Derrida, a problematic feature of Foucault's deconstructive enterprise is that his standard deconstructive way of operating is neither applied to his own standpoint nor to that of affiliated past thinkers, whom he privileges.

Foucault's *Order of Things* is a dense study of the historical conditionality of a modern episteme, which stretches across academic disciplines in its maintenance of an inexpressible inner force that defies the schemes of representation, which constitute standard styles of discourse in the preceding Classical period. Foucault takes Nietzsche at his word in his delivery of a deconstructive critique of prevailing values, his destruction of humanism and supra-empirical qualities. Nietzsche's critical perspective resonates with Foucault's own critique of his present, and Foucault rehearses Nietzsche's disturbance of conventional essentialisms in a hermeneutical ritual of recovery that ordinarily he disparages. Foucault offers no discursive explanation of what enables or accounts for Nietzsche's critique other than that of a respectful reader acknowledging the

[18] See L. Code (ed.), *Feminist Interpretations of Hans-Georg Gadamer* (Pennsylvania, Pennsylvania State University Press, 2003).

[19] See G.W.F. Hegel, *Hegel's Philosophy of Right* trans. T.M. Knox (Oxford, Oxford University Press, 1967), pp. 117–26 and 179–88; and J. Derrida, *Glas* trans. J.P. Leavey and R. Rand (Lincoln and London, University of Nebraska Press, 1986).

[20] See M. Foucault, *The Archaeology of Knowledge* (London, Tavistock Publications, 1995), p. 162.

[21] See Q. Skinner, 'Motives, Intentions and Interpretation', in Q. Skinner, *Visions of Politics*, vol. 1, *Regarding Method* (Cambridge, Cambridge University Press, 1992), p. 90.

incisiveness of a fellow author. The question of what enables Nietzsche to supersede discursive limits is neither asked nor answered. Likewise, Nietzsche anticipates Foucault's genealogical method, but we are not told what historical conditions enable Nietzsche to originate such a strategy. Nietzsche assumes the role of the traditional author that is deprecated in Foucault's interpretive strategy.[22]

Foucault's reading of Nietzsche poses the more reflexive question of what enables Foucault to break free from discursive conventions? How can Foucault perceive the logic of Nietzsche and envisage the end of the modern episteme or even the layers of neo-liberalism? Why is Foucault himself to be privileged as an author of ideas? Derrida and Foucault deliver telling deconstructive readings of texts and discourses, which are directed against the claims of hermeneutics to encapsulate interpretation within its framework. Their own perspectives, however, depend upon their unrecognized and unexplained construction of ideas that furnish a truth that is held to constitute more than a local discursive phenomenon. The upshot is that their emphasis upon deconstruction is compromised by an unreconstructed reading of Nietzsche and an unwarranted privileging of their own authorial credentials. The deficiencies in their reflexive interpretations of interpretation intimates the need for a more inclusive and integral account of deconstruction and construction.

In the essay, 'Cogito and the History of Madness' in *Writing and Difference* Derrida raises the question of the viability of Foucault's discursive intervention into the history of madness. Derrida highlights Foucault's determination to avoid the trap of writing about the intrinsic character of madness from an external perspective. How can the rationality of discourse capture the irrationality of madness? To employ standard categories of reason would be to determine madness from the outside and to replicate a psychotic adherence to external voices. Derrida remarks, 'It [this trap] is the most audacious and seductive aspect of his venture, producing its tension. But it is also, with all seriousness, the maddest aspect of his project.'[23] Derrida disputes the position from which Foucault speaks. What can justify his critical history of madness, which aspires to write in a way that is uncontaminated by the history of which it itself is a part? This question can be adapted and posed more generally to the perspectives of both Foucault and Derrida. How do they construct deconstructive projects? How is Foucault's perspective to be explained? Likewise, *Of Grammatology*, a deconstructive project, is predicated without explanation upon a constructive teleological reading of the projected end of metaphysics. What justifies Derrida's critical use of Marx in *Specters of Marx*? The text itself is

---

[22] M. Foucault, 'What is an Author?' trans. J.V. Harari, in M. Foucault, *The Foucault Reader*, ed. P. Rabinow (London and New York, Penguin, 1984), pp. 118–19.

[23] J. Derrida, 'Cogito and the History of Madness', in J. Derrida, *Writing and Difference* (London and New York, Routledge and Kegan Paul Ltd, 1978), p. 34.

coruscating in what it enacts, but why turn to Marx? What justifies Derrida's constructive use of Marx for the purposes of deconstruction? In these examples, the project of deconstruction presupposes a prior construction that requires justification. Deconstruction requires a more relational framing of its relations with construction so that its explanatory reach can be explained, just as Gadamer's hermeneutical readings of the past are susceptible to multiple forms of deconstruction that are unrecognized by his focus on overt intended meaning.

CONTEXTUALIZING CONTEXTUALISM

Contextualism as an interpretive strategy derives its force from the historical context in which its most celebrated expressions were formulated.[24] Skinner's article, 'Meaning and Understanding in the History of Ideas' (1969) announces a more critical and historical perspective on the history of political thought. Skinner's original article is decidedly critical in its polemical challenge to ahistorical interpretations. Dunn's *Political Thought of John Locke* of the same year is equally challenging in its forthright declaration of a resolutely historical approach to the history of ideas. In preceding chapters, the work of Skinner, and of like-minded colleagues Pocock, Dunn, and Collini, has been shown to enhance understanding of Machiavelli, Locke, and Mill. The value of their commentaries resides in their recovery of past contexts by historical scholarship. They recognize the distinctive historical contexts in which past contributions to political thought were situated and were designed to achieve determinate historical purposes.

Contextualists focus upon the retrieval of past contexts to explain what thinkers were intending in constructing ideas relating to past political issues and debates. Gadamer, however, counters this emphasis upon retrieving the past by maintaining that past texts are constituted as much by the questions that are posed as by the answers that are delivered. Thinking about past thought is not a matter of uncomplicated receptivity; it is reflexive as well as oriented towards what is past. To understand a past political thinker demands attention to the reflexive recognition of the interpreter's own contextually inflected thinking. Gadamer denies that there is a commanding position in either the past or the present, whereby authoritative interpretive judgments can be declared.[25]

[24] See Q. Skinner, 'Meaning and Understanding in the History of Ideas', *History and Theory*, vol. 8, 1969 and J. Dunn, *The Political Thought of John Locke: An Historical Account of the Argument of the 'Two Treatises of Government'* (Cambridge, Cambridge University Press, 1969).
[25] H.-G. Gadamer, *Truth and Method* trans. J. Weinsheimer and D.G. Marshall (London, Sheed and Ward, 1960), pp. 265–311.

Perspectives on the past alter because they are shaped by continually changing interpretive contexts. Present interests frame the questions that are asked about the past, just as past answers are received and assessed differently in the light of changing perspectives. Questions and answers are constituted reciprocally. Gadamer is critical of Collingwood's evocative characterization of history as a rethinking of past thought if that is to imply that the past is impervious to the questions and interests of the present.[26]

In the course of their careers Skinner and Dunn have acknowledged the truth of Gadamer's critique of historical realism. Their practice bears out their recognition of the inter-relations between past and present. Skinner's reading of Machiavelli and latterly of Hobbes relates republicanism to enduring conceptualizations of freedom. Likewise Dunn has ditched his extravagant commitment to an absolute separation of Locke from issues of the present. Yet contextualism continues to emphasize the recovery of past contexts by historical scholarship and to highlight the imperative of excluding anachronistic assumptions that are drawn from the present in accounts of the past. Skinner has referred to anachronism as a sin.[27] In his defence of a Collingwoodian approach to the history of political thought that focuses upon the retrieval of past authorial intentions, Skinner counters the anti-intentionalist arguments of Foucault, Gadamer, and Derrida by explaining, 'I have been arguing that texts are acts, so that the process of understanding them requires us, as in the case of all voluntary acts, to recover the intentions embodied in their performance.'[28] Relatedly, Collini disparages a Foucauldian dismissal of agency in remarking, 'The work of Michel Foucault and his followers has encouraged a rather different form of engagement with the "discourses" dominant in past societies—one which often displaces purposive agency from the scene altogether...'.[29] While contextualists are right to argue that intentions of past agents are not to be dismissed, intentional forms of explanation do not dictate the terms of interpretation. The intentions of past authors are not susceptible of neat and unambiguous reference. Derrida and Foucault disturb the intentionality of past theory by subsuming it within discourses and practices that carry meanings that are not attributable to authorial agency.[30]

---

[26] Ibid., p. 372.

[27] Q. Skinner, Interview with Tersa Bejan, 'Quentin Skinner on Meaning and Method', *The Art of Theory—Conversations in Political Philosophy*, November 2011, www.artoftheory.com, p. 57.

[28] Q. Skinner, 'Interpretation and the Understanding of Speech Acts', in Q. Skinner, *Visions of Politics*, vol. 1, *Regarding Method*, p. 120.

[29] S. Collini, 'Introduction', in S. Collini, R. Whatmore, and B. Young (eds), *Economy, Polity and Society—British Intellectual History 1750–1950* (Cambridge, Cambridge University Press, 2000), p. 3.

[30] J. Derrida, *Of Grammatology*; M. Foucault, 'What is an Author?', pp. 118–19.

Contextualism underplays the impact of present contexts and judgments upon explanations of the past. Interest in the past is generated by interests in the present and so it makes sense to reflect upon the interpretive reciprocity of past and present perceptions. If Derrida and Foucault do not explain the construction of their own perspectives, they are clear that their interests in the past derive from their perceptions of the impact of the past upon present intellectual and political practices that they aim to disrupt. The determination of contextualists to avoid anachronism and to reject the mythology of perennial issues and questions, which reduces the contingency of the past to a mere manifestation of the eternal, restricts their interrogation of the philosophical and political claims of the past. The assumptions and purposes of past theorists are not subjected to a critique of their theoretical and political ambitions that is motivated by a present philosophical or political argument. Contextualists tend to adhere to a division of labour between history and philosophy that rules out theoretical critique of past arguments.[31] Past theorists, however, do not subscribe to the self-denying ordinances of contemporary contextualists, who stipulate limits within which past thinkers are to be scrutinized. If past political theorists imagine that their arguments are aimed at persuading readers of a universal truth, then what is inappropriate in appraising their historical arguments? In 'Rescuing Political Theory from the Tyranny of History', Kelly critiques contextualism in part because he questions whether a strict divide between past and present can be maintained. He invokes Gadamer's hermeneutics to suggest that interpretation connects forms of meaning in ways that allow for interpreting the past in the light of subsequent developments. He observes, 'To recognise and understand others is to assume overlaps of schemes of interpretation which make possible trans-generational communication. This precludes the possibility of identifying fixed and discrete contexts within which the meaning of others is locked.'[32]

If Gadamer's hermeneutics lends itself to a philosophical engagement with past arguments, then the impetus for Derrida's deconstruction derives from his questioning of theorists, past and present, who presume an essentialized set of truths by resorting to what he shows to be unrealizable arguments that spring from unreliable assumptions. The anti-foundationalism of contextualists, who now tend to deny a foundational reality to the past, would seem to demand rather than preclude their questioning of the philosophical viability of past arguments.[33] Contextualists develop sophisticated historical accounts of

---

[31] See the remark of Klosko referred to at the outset of this book: G. Klosko 'Introduction', in G. Klosko (ed.), *The Oxford Handbook of the History of Political Philosophy* (Oxford, Oxford University Press, 2011), p. 1.

[32] P. Kelly, 'Rescuing Political Theory from the Tyranny of History', in J. Floyd and M. Stears (eds), *Political Philosophy versus History?* (Cambridge, Cambridge University Press, 2011), p. 31.

[33] See Q. Skinner, Interview with Tersa Bejan, 'Quentin Skinner on Meaning and Method', *The Art of Theory—Conversations in Political Philosophy*, p. 52.

past political thinkers by relating their thought to determinate past contexts but philosophy cannot be segregated from history. Hegel's conception of the reciprocity of philosophy and the history of philosophy remains a valuable guide. To engage in the history of philosophy is to engage in philosophy.[34]

The idea of judging the past on its own terms and in distinction from the present is problematic.[35] It smacks of maintaining an externality of relations between aspects of the interpretive process, which are best conceived as relational and holistic rather than as discrete and separate. Collini's reading of Collingwood's *The New Leviathan* is a case in point. He concentrates upon interpreting the text in terms of its historic context but then assumes rather quickly that the severity of its abstract formulation of a political philosophy undermines its credentials as a contribution to public policy.[36] Likewise, he dismisses the relevance of Collingwood's *An Essay on Metaphysics* to his professed project of public engagement because of what he takes to be the manifest irrelevance of its conception of metaphysics as the analysis of absolute presuppositions to the political conditions of inter-war Europe.[37] Collini may be right in his elliptical judgments on the merits of Collingwood's texts, but it is far from clear that they reflect contextual considerations rather than his own unmediated present-day opinions. Collingwood claims that a civilization can be judged in the light of its artistic expression, its metaphysical analysis, and the lucidity of its political debate, and he perceives an interconnected contemporary decline in the practice of all three. His judgment is debatable yet his sense of the historic connections between a commodified form of art, a philosophy that is reduced in scope by its homage to positivism, and a political culture in which liberalism is on the defensive due to a weakening in its emotional resolve is not implausible.[38] Collini does not attend to the historical specificities of Collingwood's arguments in deprecating the content and style of his public engagement. Ironically, in so doing, he appears to judge the past in the light of the present and hence to demonstrate interdependence of past and present, which runs counter to his own determination to avoid anachronistic judgments at all costs. Judging the past in the light of the present is not to be discredited but self-awareness of the practice allows for its reflective consideration. Derrida's practice of deconstruction is

---

[34] G.W.F. Hegel, *Lectures on The History of Philosophy*, vol. 1 trans. E.S. Haldane and F.H. Simpson (London, Paul, Trench and Trubner, 1892), pp. 1–10.

[35] I take it this sentiment lies behind Skinner's retrospective summary of his position: Q. Skinner, 'Introduction: Seeing Things their Way', in Q. Skinner, *Visions of Politics, vol. 1, Regarding Method*.

[36] S. Collini, 'Professorial Cacking: R.G. Collingwood', in S. Collini, *Absent Minds—Intellectuals in Britain* (Oxford, Oxford University Press, 2006), pp. 342–3.

[37] Ibid., pp. 341–2.

[38] R.G. Collingwood, *An Essay on Metaphysics* (Oxford, Clarendon Press, 1948), p. 343.

a productive theoretical device precisely because it is directed reflectively and explicitly.

The contextualist emphasis upon recovering the intentions of past thinkers in establishing explanations of the past is contestable, just as a deconstructionist denial of the efficacy of attending to the purposes and constructionist intentions of past authors is problematic. Problems are not resolved by construing deconstruction and contextualism as two different activities that do not bear upon one another. For instance, in 'Interpreting and Appropriating Texts in the History of Political Thought: Quentin Skinner and Poststructuralism', Burns suggests that post-structuralist and contextualist approaches can be accommodated by seeing them as two quite separate ways of reading texts.[39] To distinguish appropriations from interpretations, however, is to deny the impact of present theoretical and political ideas upon any interpretations of the past and to minimize the interpretive claims of poststructuralists. Both interpretive styles are valuable but they require to be reconfigured dialectically if their distinctive styles are to be appreciated and to be rendered compatible with one another. Things are brought into focus by Skinner's objection to Derrida's reading of a phrase in Nietzsche's notebooks, which has been looked at previously. Derrida takes the phrase, 'I have forgotten my umbrella' to be inherently undecidable. For Skinner, Derrida's response is a hyperbolic expression of interpretive scepticism, whereas the phrase calls for a scrutiny of the available contextual evidence to throw light on what Nietzsche might have intended by the phrase.[40] For Derrida, however, interpretation is not to be circumscribed by the availability of evidence and its reference to context and intentions. He concentrates upon the text because texts are not to be reduced to factors that are imagined as subsisting outside the flow of words and the possibilities of multiple interpretation. Texts can call into question the very possibility of definitive interpretation. Interpretation in this light is more a matter of how we take words and meaning rather than how we piece together historical evidence of immediate contexts. For Derrida, philosophical questions cannot be reduced to narrowly historical ones. What constitutes a text and its meanings are not reducible to evidential formulas. A phrase might incite us to interpret it so as to question its amenability to intentional interpretability.

---

[39] A. Burns, 'Interpreting and Appropriating Texts in the History of Political Thought: Quentin Skinner and Poststructuralism', *Contemporary Political Theory*, vol. 10, 2011, pp. 313–31.

[40] Q. Skinner, 'Interpretation and the Understanding of Speech Acts' in Q. Skinner, *Visions of Politics: Regarding Method* (Cambridge, Cambridge University Press, 1992) pp. 103–7; J. Derrida, *Spurs—Nietzsche's Styles*.

THE TELEOLOGY OF ENDS AND
THE END OF TELEOLOGY

Marx and Hegel register dialectical continuities between past and present by imagining past events and ideas as contributing to a purpose or end. These continuities do not exclude discontinuities. The past is connected reciprocally to the present in that past events and ideas are taken to be linked continuously to the development of the present and the past is imagined to be susceptible of explanation by means of the theoretical understanding that has been developed in the light of reflection on the past. Their interpretations of the history of political thought recognize an internality of the relations between its explanatory features. Hegel reads each historical epoch as exhibiting a unity that informs the sundry activities of its public culture, imagining the end of history to be achieved when the public culture of the state recognizes all its members to be free. Marx imagines class conflict to disrupt apparent unity amongst social formations until the end goal of communism allows production to operate freely and socially. Of course, the answers that Hegel and Marx provide to the interpretation of the meaning of history suffer from being responses to a misleading question. There is neither a single question nor a single answer that can be applied to historical events. There is no single end to the historical process, whether or not the end is construed as either communism or political freedom within a state. The very differences between the theories of Hegel and Marx alert us to their limitations. The unity that they confer upon the project of interpreting the history of political thought comes at a price. The dialectical interplay between the component parts of their explanations is imposed upon the plurality of ways in which these parts interact. The unity that is bestowed is a closure rather than an opening to events and possibilities; their theories do not allow for forms of deconstruction and contextual specificities that highlight discontinuities in historical developments.

The endism of teleological narratives compromises the contingency and openness of historical change. Oakeshott and Collingwood recognize a countervailing historical contingency. They theorize the disciplinary practice of historians, and take contingency and discontinuity to constitute defining postulates of historical knowledge. Collingwood's *The Idea of History* recognizes the originality of Hegel and Marx in their respective specialisms of philosophical and economic history but insists there is no supervening end to be ascribed to the historical process.[41] Oakeshott does not engage with Hegel and Marx on history but takes contingency and discontinuities between

---

[41] R.G. Collingwood, *The Idea of History* (Oxford, Clarendon Press, 1946); revised edition, edited by W.J. van der Dussen (Oxford, Clarendon Press, 1993), pp. 113–26.

past and present to constitute a quite contrary view. For Oakeshott and Collingwood historical knowledge is not to be directed by philosophical speculation. The particularity of historical events is not to be sacrificed to a supervening unity. The objective of historical understanding is to understand the past on its own terms. Yet in undertaking histories of political thought Collingwood and Oakeshott exhibit their Hegelian heritage in that they relate past and present in framing political theories that draw upon and relate to past ways of thinking Their absorption of features of preceding theory within their own substantive political theories is dialectical in that it is motivated by their sense of an interplay between past and present and of connections between apparently disconnected theories. Yet their use of the past is questionable in that it is neither fully explained nor justified in the light of their insistence on the autonomy of history as a discipline of inquiry.

The dialectical relations between past and present that are established in the interpretive schemes of Hegel and Marx, and Oakeshott and Collingwood intimate ways in which the history of political thought might be conceived relationally so as to bridge apparent differences between past and present and the object and form of interpretation. If a dialectical overcoming of opposition and externality is signalled by their interpretive practice, then note must also be taken of the problems that are evident in their practice. Their use of dialectical reasoning suggests how schemes of interpretation might be drawn upon critically to furnish a synoptic integrative perspective on interpretation in the history of political thought. But the process of integration should neither override interpretive pluralism nor impose a unity on the features of interpretive explanation that is external to the processes that are to be explained.

THE DIALECTIC OF THE HISTORY
OF POLITICAL THOUGHT

How are we to understand the history of political thought? How is interpretation to be assessed in the light of conflicting styles of interpretation? The several interpretive styles that have been examined in this book yield insights when applied to past political thought, but an interpretation of interpretation needs to be developed that harnesses their explanatory powers while modifying their accounts of interpretation to accommodate rival perspectives. The blind spots in their analytical frameworks by which they overplay their own favoured forms of inquiry while excluding others require to be superseded by an integral perspective that recognizes the interplay between constituent features of interpretation and the collective value of diverse styles of interpretation. An interpretive pluralism is called for, which respects the interpretive possibilities of individual schemes while critiquing their claims to provide exclusive and comprehensive forms of interpretation. In developing a dialectical integral interpretation of interpretation this book draws upon the reciprocal critiques of the individual schemes that it has examined. Its value will be shown in two ways. It indicates how specific interpretations of historic political thinkers can be criticized productively. It also allows for a coordinated and coherent explanation of component aspects of the interpretive process in the history of political thought. It recognizes the interplay between construction and deconstruction, between the form and object of explanation, between continuity and discontinuity, and between past and present.

Deconstruction and construction are productive ways of undertaking the history of political thought and neither should be discarded at the expense of the other. Indeed, deconstruction depends upon construction because the practice of deconstruction is a constructed practice and the deconstruction of texts does not undermine the credibility of all past constructions. Likewise, construction demands a critical engagement with its own situation and with that of past thinkers to incorporate deconstruction of assumptions and traditions. Past authors frame political theories for determinate purposes, which can be reconstructed from available evidence in the present. Yet what past theories express and what its authors intend are not to be accepted at face value. Both contextualism and deconstruction are legitimate forms of inquiry. Bentham offers a radical critical review of political and legal practice, recommending innovative schemes and radical democratic procedures in an express strategy of delivering rational government and economical schemes to promote the general welfare. His thought is susceptible to an interpretation that tracks his intentions in rethinking public policy in the light of a commitment to a radical social theory. On the other hand, his thought can be interpreted as relating to a discourse of liberal governmentality and to the development of disciplinary techniques that mould subjects in ways that are not reflected in his express formulations.

The deconstructive practice of Foucault and Derrida is effective in undermining the professed universal logic of past discourses and philosophies but their own critical practice requires constructive explanation just as their sympathetic accounts of like-minded theorists presume a constructivist style of explanation. Again contextualism's focus upon historical scholarship and the reconstruction of the intentions of past theorists abstracts from the processes by which their own intellectual ambitions are constructed and past philosophical and political ideas might be deconstructed. While the interpretive emphases of deconstruction, contextualism, and hermeneutics support insightful analyses of past thinkers, their tendency to overplay aspects of explanation at the expense of others points to partialities in their interpretive practices. Hence while a focus upon the local political contexts of thinkers can enrich understanding of the political thought of Machiavelli or Locke, the question of the logic and acceptability of their arguments is not to be dismissed. Likewise, recognition of the historical discourse to which *Capital* might be assigned does not explain all of its dimensions, just as a deconstruction of Plato's essentialism does not explain how Plato intended his essentialism to be taken. The interdependence of construction and deconstruction requires express recognition if the possibilities of interpretation are to be appreciated.

A dialectical integrative interpretation of interpretation conceptualizes an interplay between the form and object of explanation, so that past political thought is not to be considered as something outside the frame of interpretation but as connected to its processes. The objects of political thought are themselves the product of interpretive activity in that political associations are reflective as well as material entities and their institutions and practices are reflected upon in multiple ways that issue in a plurality of forms of political thinking. These forms are then reviewed interpretively in the history of political thought and can be construed in multiple ways. An inclusive dialectical approach recognizes that what is interpreted is shaped by the preoccupations and assumptions of the interpreter. Hence Bentham's political thought is recorded in writings, most of which were not published in his lifetime. Subsequent interpreters have to judge whether or not his thoughts on sexual irregularities, which he himself judged to be out of step with contemporary thinking, are now to be included as constituent parts of his political thought. Likewise, interpretive judgments have to be made on whether Bentham's texts and his express intentions should be focused upon or if his thinking is to be located in a wider context of an emerging disciplinary society. These judgments are not easy and an inclusive dialectical interpretive perspective allows for both narrow and wider forms of assessment of his thought, though his intentions should not be allowed to supersede the actual effects of his doctrines and disciplinary schemes. Likewise, Mill can be construed from a particular historical perspective but his thought should not be read to exclude a recognition of how this persepctive relates to subsequent perceptions and practices of liberalism.

A dialectical way of proceeding in the history of political thought recognizes continuities and discontinuities, and an interpretive reciprocity that entwines them. At times and in particular interpretations of a political thinker or doctrine, discontinuities are registered but if the interpretive frame is widened then underlying continuities can be recognized. Hence a plurality of perspectives is legitimated but this prospect is only to be appreciated if the constitutive inter-related dimensions of interpretation are forefronted. This constitutive dimension is evidenced in the multiplicity of interpretations of past political thinkers. Marx takes Hegel to task for endowing the nineteenth-century political state with a rationality, which he sees to be fundamentally flawed. Yet in *Capital* and the *Grundrisse* he recognizes his own general categories of social and economic explanation to follow a Hegelian dialectical form that he now takes to possess a continuing currency. Oakeshott and Collingwood identify Hobbes as a political philosopher in an ongoing and enduring political tradition, while Skinner takes Hobbes to be responding to specific historical arguments even if he takes that historical debate to bear upon current conceptions of freedom. Dunn's focus on the historical specificities of Locke's arguments led him to deny any ongoing relevance of Locke to political and philosophical argument and yet in the wake of his reconsideration of the concept of political trust he identifies Locke's thought as maintaining persisting if indirect relevance. Dunn's alteration in his view on the historical relevance of Locke amounts to a recantation of a perspective that would preclude interpretive interplay allowing for persisting continuities. The process of interpretation itself determines what interpretive emphasis is to be placed upon continuity or discontinuity and a dialectical integral perspective on interpretation, which acknowledges an interplay between aspects of interpretation, recognizes this determining role that is played by interpretation.

The interplay between explanatory features of interpretation in the history of political thought involves a reciprocity between past and present. Past and present forms of political thought are neither united by theorists adhering to common conventions nor by their fixing upon the same designated objects. There are differences between past and present styles of political thought and between past and present political objects and purposes. Yet the impetus for undertaking a history of past political thought derives from present concerns, which, in turn, reflect the impact of past forms of thinking. Present and past intersect in multiple ways that are registered in interpretive schemes and multiple studies of particular past thinkers. They are best captured in a dialectical perspective. Past thought is of interest to the present in multiple ways. Past metaphysical analyses purporting to establish universal accounts of justice or freedom can be deconstructed so as to deflect their ongoing and disturbing influence on the present. Derrida's deconstruction of the philosophies of Hegel and Plato exemplify this project. Yet, as Skinner has demonstrated, past and apparently discredited conceptions of freedom can be recovered so as to reconsider the current conceptual scene. A dialogue with the past might raise questions about past patriarchal assumptions, and the meaning of the exclusion of women from public life might be interrogated so as to shed light on private and public worlds and on the conceptualization of men and women. Questioning the implications of past patriarchal forms might raise doubts over what currently counts as an individual in political debate. If women have been excluded from political activity how are they now included? Have the disabled, the displaced, or the non-human been excluded as Foucault and Derrida maintain?[42] How, if at all, are they now included? The

---

[42] See Foucault's path-breaking study of the treatment of the mentally ill, M. Foucault, *Madness and Civilisation: A History of Insanity in the Age of Reason* trans. R. Howard (London,

questions that are posed to the past are framed in the context of what is perceived to matter in the present and perceptions of the present are shaped by inherited traditions and practices. It is a problematic feature of Gadamer's hermeneutics that he does not interrogate sufficiently sharply those traditions and practices. Likewise, Skinner's revisiting of past debates about freedom might impact upon the present, but his investigation of the past is not prefaced by an analysis of what political features of the present demand historical investigation. Again, Derrida's invocation of Marx to probe the new internationalism of the post-Cold War world is a critical tour de force but his focus on the nature of the new internationalism and his decision to interrogate it via Marx is neither explained nor justified by constructive argument.

A dialectical holistic perspective on the history of political thought takes account of the interplay between its constitutive conditions and provides a comprehensive interpretive framework that encompasses differing features and styles of interpretation. It shows the interpretive utility of a range of approaches but frames an interpretation of their styles of interpretation that is critical and inclusive. It accommodates features of interpretation that are denied by individual schemes due to their one-sided concentration upon aspects of interpretation that exclude rival approaches. A critical and dialectical interpretation of interpretation evidently owes much to the example of Hegel and Marx, who interpreted the history of political thought in relational terms so that past and present were united in their own synoptic dialectical standpoints. But they subsumed preceding and alternative positions within a supervening unity that imposed upon the plurality of ways in which political thought is practised. The dialectical approach that is advocated here is one that does not impose a unity upon phenomena but rather is constructed by reflection upon the several schemes that are reviewed in preceding chapters and hence includes a plurality of interpretive styles. It does not claim to be the last word on the history of political thought. There are interpretive schemes that have not been considered in detail and its interpretive pluralism re-envisions features of interpretation in the light of an integral interpretation of interpretive perspectives.

The dialectical interpretive standpoint expressed here makes sense of the various elements that contribute to interpretation. Its value is indicated in its accommodation of differing productive interpretations of Hegel and Marx. Foucault and Derrida deconstruct the supervening interpretive unities that are maintained in their dialectical schemes. Hegel's uncompromising patriarchy is compromised by Derrida's deconstruction and Marx is seen by Foucault as

---

Routledge, 1999); and for Derrida's discussion of the contingency of democracy and the possibility of non-human political representation see J. Derrida, *Rogues—Two Essays on Reason* trans. P.-A. Brault and M. Naas (Stanford, California, Stanford University Press, 2005), pp. 28–42.

adhering to a discourse that frames his thought in ways that are not captured in his own formulations.[43] If deconstruction can show the problematic character of the forms of explanation that are offered by Hegel and Marx, then careful contextual studies of the development of their thought reveals the utility of the constructionist dimension of interpretation.[44] In addition to constructionist and deconstructionist readings that are sanctioned by a dialectical interpretation of interpretation, the interplay between past and present allows for imaginative readings. Derrida's use of Marx to critique subsequent neo-liberal forms of internationalism shows how Marx is not to be imprisoned by a narrow reading of his context. While the thought of Hegel and Marx is discontinuous with the present, continuities can be identified. For instance, they can be seen as crucial figures in an ongoing tradition of critical theory, which can be directed against ideological notions of globalization in the twenty-first century.[45] A dialectical overview of interpretation allows for an interpretive pluralism, whereby theorists such as Hegel and Marx can be interpreted in multiple ways. Its recognition of the inter-relations between past and present in the framing of interpretation intimates that the most productive interpretations of past thought will be those that speak most urgently to the present without sacrificing textual and contextual recognition of the distinctiveness of the past. This task calls for a critical engagement with the history of political thought, so that its interpretation is to be seen as at once engendering and arising out of its own critical practice. The history of political thought relates to the present as well as to the past, hence a review of its implications for contemporary political theory is conducted in the succeeding section.

POLITICAL THOUGHT: PAST AND PRESENT

A common feature of many interpretive approaches to the history of political thought is their anti-foundationalism, whereby an essential or foundational view of politics or of political thought is denied.[46] Understanding past thought is not seen to be a matter of relating theories either to the underlying or real

---

[43] See, for instance, J. Derrida, *Glas* trans. J.P. Leavey and R. Rand (Lincoln and London, University of Nebraska Press, 1986) and M. Foucault, *The Order of Things* (London and New York, Routledge, 2002).

[44] See T. Pinkard, *Hegel: A Biography* (Cambridge, Cambridge University Press, 2000) and D. McLellan, *The Young Hegelians and Karl Marx* (London and New York, Macmillan, 1969).

[45] See, for instance, this author's own reading of global theory, G. Browning, *Global Theory from Kant to Hardt and Negri* (Basingstoke and New York, Palgrave, 2006).

[46] This feature distinguishes the interpretive styles that are analysed in this book from that of Strauss.

character of the past or to that of a standard form of politics. This anti-foundationalism extends to some of the guises of Hegelianism and Marxism in that both Hegel and Marx take the conditions of politics to develop over time and some adherents to Hegelianism or Marxism question whether their teleological narratives either constitute or presuppose essences.[47] The anti-foundationalism of contextualism and deconstruction is expressed idiomatically but each idiom opposes the idea that political questions are susceptible of universal answers. Derrida's deconstruction takes off from its critique of logocentrism and from hostility to metaphysical closure.[48] Contextualists imagine the contingency of contexts and discourses to undermine the presumption that past thinkers are answering the same essential questions.[49] Foucault substitutes an historical for a transcendental a priori of knowledge and Gadamer imagines interpretation to be creative because past realities change along with their horizons. The political ideals of Collingwood and Oakeshott arise out of contingent changing historical developments that preclude a universal response to political predicaments. Hegel and Marx are committed to absolute rather than relative judgments yet recognize that the nature of politics changes over time. These interpreters of past political thought deny definitive answers to past political questions, even if they might acknowledge that present horizons owe debts to past traditions. They are at one in recognizing that the differences between past and present are not reducible to a conceptual sameness. Likewise, a dialectical interpretation of the interpretation of the history of political thought denies a conceptual identity between past and present in its reading of a non-reductive interplay between them.

If the history of political thought allows for discontinuities between past and present, then the character of political thought in the present must reflect this historical character. Political thought is necessarily situated and historical in its present as well as in its past forms, just as the present necessarily becomes past in the passage of time. Past forms of political thought are multiple and interpretive. They lack a foundational essence to justify a privileged conceptualization that might transcend the contingency and interpretive corrigibility of their formulation. Political thought as a present activity resembles its past forms in reflecting a diversity of styles and assumptions. Political thought in all of its manifestations, past or present, is interpretive in reflecting upon

---

[47] See G. Rose, *Hegel Contra Sociology* (London and New York, Continuum, 2000); J. McCarney, *Hegel on History* (London and New York, Routledge, 2000); and B. Ollman *Alienation—Marx's Conception of Man in Capitalist Society* (Cambridge, Cambridge University Press, 1971).

[48] J. Derrida, *Of Grammatology*, pp. 8–26.

[49] See Skinner's remarks on anti-foundationalism in Q. Skinner, Interview with Tersa Bejan,'Quentin Skinner on Meaning and Method', *The Art of Theory—Conversations In Political Philosophy*, pp. 52–3.

changing forms of political association. In recent years, there has been a discernible shift in the organizational frames of political activity, and this shift in turn reflects differences in the ways in which individuals and groups interpret their situation. Whereas the notion of modernity presumes the development of the nation state, which duly informs the thinking of modern political theorists such as Hobbes, Locke, and Hegel, global dispositions of power are now in the picture.[50] The picture and its frame matter. For instance, migration looks different when viewed from the perspective of a nation state than if it is conceived as global flows of population that are determined by supra-national patterns of trade, wealth, and political interest. The contemporary turn to cosmopolitanism reflects changes in the ways in which allegiances to states and responsibilities in the wider world are imagined. Texts on political philosophy mark perspectival changes in reflection upon frames of political thought. In a former period political philosophy might take the state for granted, now its status is questioned. It is located on a wider topographical map of politics.[51] Of course, contemporary reconsideration of the frame of political association entails neither essentialized conceptions of cosmopolitanism nor standardly conceived global structures. There are weak and strong cosmopolitanisms just as there are radical and liberal forms of global theory.[52]

Just as differences between city states, medieval realms, and modern nation states altered political perceptions so supra-national developments are changing contemporary ways of viewing politics. Likewise, changing perceptions of individual and collective identity, reflecting changeable conceptions of what constitutes the maturity of an individual, disability, and nationality impact upon how citizenship is conceived. Essentialist responses run counter to the evidence of conceptual contingency.[53] Current interpretations of politics are affected by changing ideas that reflect changing circumstances, and these changes alter perceptions of past thought, which in turn influence the ongoing development of ideas. Hence Kant and Hegel continue their quarrels in the light of present attitudes so that they are now assigned differing roles in debates about cosmopolitanism, and reconstituted conceptions of their thinking on political and international relations in turn influences current notions of national, international, and supra-national identity.[54]

---

[50] For an account of how modern political thought reflects the development of the state, see R. Berki, *History of Political Theory* (London, R.M. Dent, 1976); for the impact of perceptions of globalization on political thought, see G. Browning, *Global Theory from Kant to Hardt and Negri*.

[51] But note the subsequent comments on A. Swift, *Political Philosophy—A Beginner's Guide for Students and Politicians* (Cambridge and Malden MA, Polity, 2001).

[52] See G. Browning, *Global Theory from Kant to Hardt and Negri*.

[53] For an interesting account of how disability has been a neglected aspect of political thinking, see A. MacIntyre, *Dependent Rational Animals* (Illinois, Duckworth, 1999).

[54] See G. Browning, *Global Theory from Kant to Hardt and Negri*.

Hegel maintains that to engage in the history of philosophy is to engage in philosophy, and the reciprocity between philosophy and its history is evident in the interplay between contemporary political theory and preceding traditions.[55] While the preceding pages review the past by examining continental forms of deconstruction and Anglophone traditions of idealism and contextualism, contemporary political theory exhibits a related interpretive pluralism. Occasionally the impact of the history of political theory upon its current practice is denied, just as the prevalence of interpretive pluralism is ignored by texts that minimize interpretive conflicts and the influence of history upon political concepts. For instance at the outset of the twenty-first century, in a text on political philosophy, Swift proclaims that it 'is not a guide to the history of political philosophy.'[56] He follows this declaration by maintaining that he is interested in the truth of arguments rather than their provenance and pronounces that his study 'sees the political as concerned specifically with the state.'[57] Of course, his focus upon the state is a product of the history that he disparages and represents a particular and problematic focus of interpretive analysis in the light of current developments. Indeed by the close of the book and his discussion of community he mentions different attitudes to the state, citizenship, and the possibility of cosmopolitanism and in doing so he cites but does not explore the role of war and the welfare state in the twentieth century.[58] By 2014 and the third edition of the text, Swift adds discussions on global justice and gender equality. Yet there is no reflection on what has happened in history to change the focus of analysis, simply a reference to students talking about global justice.[59] Miller, in *Political Philosophy—A Very Short Introduction*, recognizes that things change and in particular that the claims of women and cultural minorities appear to alter the very nature of politics.[60] Yet he maintains these claims are exaggerated and that they can be accommodated by traditional ways of conducting political philosophy, which focus upon the authority of the state and the nature of democracy, freedom, and justice. He appears to consider that the very normative commitments to freedom and equality that have been critiqued by women and cultural minorities enable their claims to surface, thereby limiting the relevance of political struggle and uneven historical developments to questions of political philosophy.[61] On this reading, historical change is reduced to the conceptual

---

[55] G.W.F. Hegel, *Lectures on the History of Philosophy*.
[56] A. Swift, *Political Philosophy: A Beginner's Guide for Students and Politicians*, p. 4.
[57] Ibid., p. 5.   [58] Ibid., pp. 168–74.
[59] A. Swift, *Political Philosophy: A Beginner's Guide for Students and Politicians*, 3rd edition, (Cambridge and Malden, MA, Polity Press, 2014). Note the comments in the Preface, p. xii and on pp. 48–9.
[60] D. Miller, *Political Philosophy—A Very Short Introduction* (Oxford, Oxford University Press, 2003), p. 92.
[61] Ibid., p. 93.

reach and causal priority that is assigned to essential political norms, whereas political struggle would appear to have caused a change in identifying the reach and operation of politics.

What the analytical texts of Swift and Miller underplay is the historical character of political philosophy whereby its content and form change, just as they do not recognize the extent to which political philosophy is conducted in a plurality of idioms. Hence, they deal with analytical constructs of freedom, justice, authority, and democracy that are formulated in a particular idiom. These constructs, however, are liable to the deconstruction of post-structuralist forms of thought that draw upon continental traditions of thought that deploy differing idioms of analysis. Derrida objects to a new internationalism that conceives of rights in a formulaic and determinate way that is highlighted by Marx's countervailing emphasis upon economic structures and which runs counter to an inexorable plurality of interpretive forms.[62] The history of political thought demands an interpretation of interpretation to integrate holistically a variety of interpretive possibilities. Likewise, contemporary political thought, if it is to be comprehensive, must deal with a variety of idioms, criticizing and integrating a plurality of styles that demand respect and considered review. If it is to be reflexive contemporary political thought must take account of its emergence from past traditions and must engage with changing practices and interpretations of politics.[63]

Political thought must be dialectical. The theoretical ambitions of Hegel and Marx tend to override openness and interpretive pluralism, yet their dialectical style offers a paradigm for recognizing the reciprocity of past and present and for the integration of apparently opposing styles and developments within an holistic perspective. A critical dialectical standpoint must respect alternative perspectives in an interpretive pluralism, whereby arguments of texts and theorists may be reconstructed or deconstructed and political ideas are to be constructed in the present that are tested by deconstruction. The resources for undertaking the history of political thought are the plurality of interpretive schemes that can be brought to bear upon the past. Similarly, current political thought emerges from critical interpretation of past and present forms of political thought, in which interpretation is taken to determine all elements of the process. As Honig and Stears observe in their defence of a related agonistic realism, '[H]ere we have the final element of an agonistic realism;

---

[62] See J. Derrida, *Rogues* pp. 28–42; J. Derrida, *Specters of Marx: The State of the Debt, the Work of Mourning and the New International* trans. P. Kamuf (London, Routledge, 1994), pp. 96–118.

[63] It is this lack of interpretive reflexivity on the subject that marks the analytical texts referred to above. See D. Miller, *Political Philosophy–A Short Introduction* and A. Swift, *Political Philosophy—Beginner's Guide*.

it takes nothing for granted, not even the "real".[64] The questions of interpretation are answered by recognizing that interpreting past political thought depends upon present perceptions of significance, which in turn are shaped by the interpretation of seminal modern political thinkers. Interpretation itself is to be interpreted in the processes of interpretation.

[64] B. Honig and M. Stears, 'The Challenge of Realism', in J. Floyd and M. Stears (eds), *Political Philosophy versus History* (Cambridge, Cambridge University Press, 2011), p. 204.

Bibliography

T. Adorno, *Minima Moralia—Reflections on a Damaged Life* trans. E.F.N. Jephcott (London and New York, Verso, 1995).

T. Adorno, *Can We Live After Auschwitz—A Philosophical Reader* trans. R. Livingstone and others, ed. R. Tiedemann (Stanford, California, Stanford University Press, 2003).

G. Almond and S. Verba, *The Civic Culture: Political Attitudes and Democracy in Five Nations* (Princeton, Princeton University Press, 1963).

L. Althusser, *For Marx* trans. B. Brewster (Harmondsworth, Penguin, 1969).

S. Anderson–Gold, *Cosmopolitanism and Human Rights* (Cardiff, University of Wales Press, 2001).

D. Armitage, 'John Locke, Carolina and the *Two Treatises of Government*', *Political Theory*, vol. 32, no. 5, October 2004, pp. 602–7.

B. Arneil, 'John Locke and Natural Law and Colonialism', *History of Political Thought*, vol. 13, no. 4, 1992, pp. 587–603.

B. Arneil, 'Liberal Colonialism, Domestic Colonies and Citizenship', *History of Political Thought*, vol. 13, no. 3, 2012, pp. 491–523.

C. Arthur, Review of T. Carver and D. Blank, *Marx's 'German Ideology' Manuscripts—Presentation and Analysis of the 'Feuerbach Chapter'* and T. Carver and D. Blank, *A Political History of the Editions of Marx and Engels's 'German Ideology' Manuscripts, Marx and Philosophy: Review of Books,* 22 May 2015.

R. Ashcraft, *Revolutionary Politics and Locke's Two Treatises of Government* (Princeton NJ, University of Princeton Press, 1986).

J. Aubrey, *Brief Lives*, ed. O.L. Dick (Harmondsworth, Penguin, 1972).

S. Avineri, *The Social and Political Thought of Karl Marx* (Cambridge, Cambridge University Press, 1968).

T. Ball, *Reappraisals in Political Theory* (Oxford, Oxford University Press, 1995).

T. Ball, 'The Value of the History of Political Philosophy', in G. Klosko (ed.) *The Oxford Handbook of the History of Political Philosophy* (Oxford, Oxford University Press, 2011), pp. 759.

N. Bauer, 'Must We Read Simone de Beauvoir?', in E. Grosholz (ed.), *The Legacy of Simone de Beauvoir* (Oxford, Clarendon Press, 2004), pp. 115–37.

D. Baumgold, *Hobbes's Political Theory* (Cambridge, Cambridge University Press, 1988).

D. Baumgold, 'Hobbes', in D. Boucher and P. Kelly (eds), *Political Thinkers* (Oxford, Oxford University Press, 2009), pp. 189–206.

S. de Beauvoir, *The Ethics of Ambiguity* trans. B. Frechtman (New York, The Citadel Press, 1948).

S. de Beauvoir, *The Second Sex* trans. H.M. Parshley (London, Jonathan Cape Ltd, 1953).

S. de Beauvoir, *A Very Easy Death* trans. P. O'Brien (Harmondsworth, Penguin, 1983).

S. de Beauvoir, *She Came to Stay* trans. Y. Moyse and R. Senhouse (London, Fontana, 1984).

S. de Beauvoir, *Letters to Sartre* trans. and ed. Q. Hoare (New York, Arcade, 1991).

S. de Beauvoir, 'Literature and Metaphysics (1946)', in S. de Beauvoir, *Philosophical Writings* trans. V. Zayteff and F. Morrison, ed. M.A. Simons with M. Timmerman and M. Mader (Urbana and Chicago, University of Illinois Press, 2004), pp. 261–78.

S. de Beauvoir, *Political Writings* (Chicago, University of Illinois Press, 2012).

S. de Beauvoir, 'Right-Wing Thought Today' trans. V. Zayteff and F. Morrison, in S. de Beauvoir, *Political Writings* (Chicago, University of Illinois Press, 2012), pp. 103–12.

F. Beiser, *The Cambridge Companion to Hegel and Nineteenth Century Philosophy* (Cambridge, Cambridge University Press, 2008).

W. Benjamin, 'The Critique of Violence', in W. Benjamin, *Reflections, Essays, Aphorisms* trans. E. Jephcott (New York, Schocken Books, 1985).

J. Bentham, *Rationale of Judicial Evidence*, in J. Bowring (ed.), *The Works of Jeremy Bentham*, vols. 6 and 7 (Edinburgh, William Tait, 1843).

J. Bentham, *The Works of Jeremy Bentham*, ed. J. Bowring (Edinburgh, William Tait, 1843).

J. Bentham, *An Introduction to the Principles of Morals and Legislation Government* (London, Athlone Press, 1970).

J. Bentham, *Of Laws in General*, ed. H.L.A. Hart (London, Athlone Press, 1970).

J. Bentham, *A Comment on the Commentaries*, in J. Bentham, *A Comment on the Commentaries and a Fragment on Government*, ed. J.H. Burns and H.L.A. Hart (London, Athlone Press, 1977), pp. 8–392.

J. Bentham, *A Fragment on Government*, in J. Bentham, *A Comment on the Commentaries and a Fragment on Government*, ed. J.H. Burns and H.L.A. Hart (London, Athlone Press, 1977), pp. 393–553.

J. Bentham, *The Handbook of Political Fallacies*, ed. H. Larrabee (London, Octagon Books, 1980).

J. Bentham, *Constitutional Code*, ed. F. Rosen and J. Burns (Oxford, Oxford University Press, 1983).

J. Bentham, *'Legislator of the World': Writings on Codification, Law, and Education*, ed. P. Schofield and J. Harris (Oxford, Clarendon Press, 1998).

J. Bentham, *Panopticon Writings* (London, Verso, 2010).

J. Bentham, *Tactiques des assemblees legislatives* trans. E. Dumont (Las Vegas, Nevada, Nabu Press, 2012).

J. Bentham, *Of Sexual Irregularities and Other Writings on Sexual Morality*, ed. P. Schofield, C. Pease-Watkin, and M. Quinn (Oxford, Oxford University Press, 2014).

J. Bentham, *The Book of Fallacies*, ed. P. Bingham, (Oxford, Oxford University Press, 2015).

R. Berki, *History of Political Theory* (London, R.M. Dent, 1976).

I. Berlin, 'Hobbes, Locke and Professor Macpherson', *Political Quarterly*, vol. 35, no. 4, 1964, pp. 444–68.

I. Berlin, 'Historical Inevitability', in I. Berlin, *Four Essays on Liberty* (Oxford and New York, Oxford University Press, 1969), pp. 41–117.

I. Berlin, 'John Stuart Mill and the Ends of Life', in I. Berlin, *Four Essays on Liberty* (Oxford, Oxford University Press, 1969), pp. 173–206.

I. Berlin, 'Two Concepts of Liberty', in I. Berlin, *Four Essays on Liberty* (Oxford, Oxford University Press, 1969), pp. 118–92.

I. Berlin, 'The Originality of Machiavelli', in I. Berlin, *Against the Current: Essays in the History of Ideas* (London, Hogarth Press, 1979), pp. 33–100.

J. Bernstein, 'Conscience and Transgression: The Exemplarity of Tragic Action', in G. Browning, *Hegel's Phenomenology: A Reappraisal* (Dordrecht, the Netherlands, Kluwer, 1997), pp. 79–98.

R. Bernstein, *Evolutionary Socialism* trans. E. Harvey (New York, Random House Publications, 1961).

M.J. Bertram, 'God's Second Blunder—Serpent Woman and the Gestalt in Nietzsche's Thought', *Southern Journal of Philosophy*, vol. 19, Fall 1981, pp. 259–77.

M. Bevir, 'Are there Perennial Problems in Political Theory?', *Political Studies*, vol. 42, no. 4, 1995, pp. 662–75.

M. Bevir, *The Logic of the History of Ideas* (Cambridge, Cambridge University Press, 1999).

M. Bevir, 'Contextualism', in G. Klosko (ed.), *The Oxford Handbook of the History of Political Thought* (Oxford, Oxford University Press, 2011), pp. 11–23.

A. Black, 'Skinner on the "Foundations of Modern Political Thought"', *Political Studies*, vol. 28, no. 3, 1980, pp. 451–7.

C. Blum, 'Rousseau and Feminist Revisionism', *Eighteenth Century Life*, vol. 34, no. 3, Fall 2010, pp. 51–6.

D. Boucher, *Texts in Context: Revisionist Methods for Studying the History of Ideas* (Dordrecht, D. Reidel, 1985).

D. Boucher and P. Kelly, 'Introduction', in D. Boucher and P. Kelly, *Political Thinkers* (Oxford, Oxford University Press, 2009), pp. 1–24.

A. Bradley, *Derrida's 'Of Grammatology'* (Edinburgh, Edinburgh University Press, 2008).

C. Brooke, 'Rousseau's Political Philosophy: Stoic and Augustinian Origins,' in P. Riley (ed.), *The Cambridge Companion to Rousseau* (Cambridge, Cambridge University Press, 2000).

T. Brooks, *Hegel's Political Philosophy—A Systematic Reading of the Philosophy of Right* 2nd edn.(Edinburgh, Edinburgh University Press, 2013).

G. Browning, 'Plato and Hegel: Reason, Redemption and Political Theory', *History of Political Thought*, vol. 8, no. 3, 1987, pp. 377–93.

G. Browning, 'Hegel's Plato: The Owl of Minerva and a Fading Political Tradition', *Political Studies*, vol. 36, 1988, pp. 476–85.

G. Browning, 'The German Ideology: The Theory of History and the History of Theory, History of Political Thought, vol. 14, no. 3, 1992, pp. 455–73.

G. Browning, '*The German Ideology*, Stirner and Hegel', in G. Browning, *Hegel and the History of Philosophy* (Basingstoke and New York, Macmillan, 1999), pp. 75–92.

G. Browning, 'Good and Bad Infinites in Hegel and Marx', in G. Browning, *Hegel and the History of Philosophy* (Basingstoke and New York, Macmillan, 1999), pp. 93–105.

G. Browning, *Hegel and the History of Philosophy* (Basingstoke and New York, Macmillan, 1999).

G. Browning, 'Marx's Doctoral Dissertation: The Development of a Hegelian Thesis', in T. Burns and I. Fraser, *The Hegel–Marx Connection* (Basingstoke and New York, Palgrave Macmillan, 2000), pp. 131–45.

G. Browning, 'What is Wrong with Modernity and What is Right with the *Philosophy of Right*', *History of European Ideas*, vol. 29, no. 2, 2003, pp. 223–39.

G. Browning, *Rethinking R.G. Collingwood—Philosophy, Politics and the Unity of Theory and Practice* (Basingstoke, Palgrave Macmillan, 2004).

G. Browning, *Global Theory from Kant to Hardt and Negri* (Basingstoke and New York, Palgrave, 2006).

G. Browning, 'Agency and Influence in the History of Political Thought: The Agency of Influence and the Influence of Agency', *History of Political Thought*, vol. 31, no. 2, 2010, pp. 345–66.

G. Browning, 'Hegel on War, Recognition and Justice', in A. Buchwalter (ed.), *Hegel and Global Justice* (Dordrecht, Heidelberg, London, and New York, Springer, 2012), pp. 193–210.

G.A. Brucker, *Renaissance Florence* (New York, John Wiley and Sons, 1969).

A. Brunon-Ernst (ed.), *Beyond Foucault: New Perspectives on Bentham's Panopticon* (Aldershot, Ashgate, 2012).

A. Brunon-Ernst, *Utilitarian Biopolitics—Bentham and Foucault on Modern Power* (London, Chatto and Windus, 2012).

A. Buchwalter (ed.), *Hegel and Global Justice* (Dordrecht, Heidelberg, London and New York, Springer, 2012).

P. Burke, *The Renaissance Sense of the Past* (London, Arnold, 1969).

A. Burns, 'Interpreting and Appropriating Texts in the History of Political Thought: Quentin Skinner and Poststructuralism', *Contemporary Political Theory*, no. 10, 2011, pp. 313–31.

E.M. Butler, *The Tyranny of Greece over Germany* (Cambridge, Cambridge University Press, 1935).

J. Butler, *Subjects of Desire—Hegelian Reflections in Twentieth Century France* (New York, Columbia University Press, 1987).

H. Butterfield, *The Statecraft of Machiavelli* (London, G. Bell and Sons, 1940).

A. Carter, 'Colette', in M. Mason (ed.), *London Review of Books Anthology* (London, Junction Books, 1981), pp. 15–17.

T. Carver, *Men in Political Theory* (Manchester, Manchester University Press, 2009).

T. Carver, '*The German Ideology* Never Took Place', *History of Political Thought*, vol. 31, no. 1, 2010, pp. 107–27.

T. Carver and D. Blank, *Marx's 'German Ideology' Manuscripts—Presentation and Analysis of the 'Feuerbach Chapter'* (Basingstoke and New York, Palgrave Macmillan, 2014).

T. Carver and D. Blank, *A Political History of the Editions of Marx and Engels's 'German Ideology' Manuscripts* (Basingstoke and New York, Palgrave, 2015).

F. Chabod, *Machiavelli and the Renaissance* (New York, Harper and Row, 1958).

J. Charvet, *The Social Problem in the Philosophy of Rousseau* (London and New York, Cambridge University Press, 1974).

L. Code (ed.), *Feminist Interpretations of Hans-Georg Gadamer* (Pennsylvania, Pennsylvania State University Press, 2003).

G. Cohen, *Karl Marx's Theory of History: A Defence* (Oxford, Clarendon Press, 1978).

L. Colletti, *From Rousseau to Lenin—Studies in Ideology and Society* trans. J. White and P.Merrington (Los Angeles, California, Monthly Review Press, 1975).

L. Colletti, 'Introduction', in K. Marx, *Early Writings* trans. R. Livingstone and G. Benton (Harmondsworth, Penguin Books, 1975), pp. 7–56.

R.G. Collingwood, 'Truth and Contradiction', Collingwood Manuscripts, Bodleian Library, Dep. 16 (1917).

R.G. Collingwood, 'Lectures on Moral Philosophy: For Michaelmas Term 1921', Collingwood Manuscripts, Bodleian Library Dep 4 (1921).

R.G. Collingwood, 'Lectures on Moral Philosophy: 1929,' Collingwood Manuscripts, Bodleian Library, Dep. 10 (1929).

R.G. Collingwood, 'Philosophy of History', Collingwood Manuscripts, Bodleian Library, Dep. 15.2, 1 (1932).

R.G. Collingwood, *An Essay on Philosophical Method* (Oxford, Clarendon Press, 1933).

R.G. Collingwood, 'Lectures on Moral Philosophy', Collingwood Manuscripts, Dep. 8 (1933).

R.G. Collingwood, 'Notes Towards a Metaphysic', Collingwood Manuscripts, Dep. 18 (1933/4).

R.G. Collingwood, *The Principles of Art* (Oxford, Clarendon Press, 1938).

R.G. Collingwood, *The Idea of Nature* (Oxford, Clarendon Press, 1945).

R.G. Collingwood, *The Idea of History* (Oxford, Clarendon Press, 1946); revised edition, ed. W.J. van der Dussen (Oxford, Clarendon Press, 1993).

R.G. Collingwood, 'Progress As Created by Historical Thinking', in R.G. Collingwood, *The Idea of History* (Oxford, Clarendon Press, 1946).

R.G. Collingwood, *An Autobiography* (Oxford, Clarendon Press, 1978).

R.G. Collingwood, 'Political Action', in R.G. Collingwood *Essays in Political Philosophy* (Oxford, Clarendon Press, 1989).

R.G. Collingwood, *The New Leviathan or Man Society, Civilization and Barbarism Essay,* revised edition ed., with an Introduction, D. Boucher (Oxford, Clarendon Press, 1992).

R.G. Collingwood, *An Essay on Metaphysics,* revised edition ed. with an Introduction, R. Martin (Oxford, Clarendon Press, 1998).

R.G. Collingwood, *The Principles of History and Other Writings in Philosophy of History* (Oxford, Oxford University Press, 1999).

R.G. Collingwood, Report on M.B. Foster's *The Political Philosophies of Plato and Hegel,* Oxford, Clarendon Press Archives, PB/ED/002054, 1929, pp. 1–9.

S. Collini, *Liberalism and Sociology—L.T. Hobhouse and Political Argument in England 1880–1914* (Cambridge, Cambridge University Press, 1970).

S. Collini, 'The Tendencies of Things—J.S. Mill and the Philosophic Method', in S. Collini, D. Winch, and J. Burrow, *That Noble Science of Politics—A Study in Nineteenth Century Intellectual History* (Cambridge, Cambridge University Press, 1983), pp. 127–60.

S. Collini, 'Introduction', in J.S. Mill, *On Liberty and Other Writings* (Cambridge, Cambridge University Press, 1989), pp. vii–xxvi.

S. Collini, *Public Moralists—Political Thought and Intellectual Life in Britain 1850–1930* (Oxford, Clarendon Press, 1991).

S. Collini, 'Introduction', in S. Collini, R. Whatmore, and B. Young (eds), *Economy, Polity and Society—British Intellectual History 1750-1950* (Cambridge, Cambridge University Press, 2000), pp. 1–30.

S. Collini, *Absent Minds—Intellectuals in Britain* (Oxford, Oxford University Press, 2006).

S. Collini, 'Professorial Cacking: R.G. Collingwood', in S. Collini, *Absent Minds—Intellectuals in Britain* (Oxford, Oxford University Press, 2006), pp. 331–49.

C. Condren, *The Status and Appraisal of Classic Texts* (Princeton, NJ, University of Princeton Press, 1985).

W. Conkin, *Hegel's Laws—The Legitimacy of a Modern Legal Order* (Stanford, California, Stanford University Press, 2008).

D. Conway, *Nietzsche and the Political* (London and New York, Routledge, 1997).

D. Coole, *Women in Political Theory: From Ancient Misogyny to Contemporary Feminism* (London, Harvester/Wheatsheaf, 1993).

M. Cowling, *Mill and Liberalism* (Cambridge, Cambridge University Press, 1963).

M. Cranston, *John Locke: A Biography* (Oxford, Oxford University Press, 1985).

A. Cromartie, 'Hobbes, History and Non-Domination', *Hobbes Studies*, vol. 22, 2004, pp. 171–7.

A.P. D'Entreves, *Natural Law: Am Introduction to Legal Philosophy* (London, Transaction Publishers, 1994).

F. Dabholwala, Review of *Of Sexual Irregularities and Other Writings on Sexual Morality* in the *Guardian* 28 June 2015.

W. Davies, 'A Response to Nick Gane's "Emergence of Neoliberalism"', *Theory, Culture and Society*, vol. 31, no. 4, 2014, pp. 299–302.

F. Del Lucchese, *The Political Philosophy of Niccolo Machiavelli* (Edinburgh, Edinburgh University Press, 2015).

G. Deleuze, *Nietzsche and Philosophy* (New York, Columbia University Press, 1983).

J. Derrida, *Of Grammatology* trans. G.C. Spivak (Baltimore, Maryland, Johns Hopkins University Press, 1974).

J. Derrida, 'Cogito and the History of Madness', in J. Derrida, *Writing and Difference* (London and New York, Routledge and Kegan Paul Ltd, 1978), pp. 31–63.

J. Derrida, 'Structure, Sign and Discourse in the Human Sciences', in J. Derrida, *Writing and Difference* trans. A. Bass (London, Routledge & Kegan Paul Ltd, 1978), pp. 278–94.

J. Derrida, *Writing and Difference* trans. A. Bass (London, Routledge & Kegan Paul Ltd, 1978).

J. Derrida, *Spurs Nietzsche's Styles* trans. B. Harlow (Chicago, Il., University of Chicago Press, 1979).

J. Derrida, 'Plato's Pharmacy', in J. Derrida, *Dissemination* (Chicago, Chicago University Press, 1981), pp. 67–186.

J. Derrida, *Positions* trans. A. Bass (Chicago, Il., University of Chicago Press, 1981).

J. Derrida, *Glas* trans. J.P. Leavey and R. Rand (Lincoln and London, University of Nebraska Press, 1986).

J. Derrida, 'Interpreting Signatures (Nietzsche/Heidegger): Two Questions' trans. D. Michelfelder and R. Palmer, in D. Michelfelder and R. Palmer (eds), *Dialogue and Deconstruction—The Gadamer-Derrida Encounter* (New York, State University of New York Press, 1989), pp. 58–74.

J. Derrida, 'Three Questions to Hans-Georg Gadamer', in D. Michelfelder and R. Palmer (eds), *Dialogue and Deconstruction—The Gadamer–Derrida Encounter* (New York, State University of New York Press, 1989), pp. 52–4.

J. Derrida, 'Force of Law: The "Mystical Foundation of Authority"' trans. M. Quaintance, in D. Cornell, M. Rodenfield, and D. Gray Carlson (eds), *Deconstruction and the Possibility of Justice* (London, Routledge, 1992), pp. 1–67.

J. Derrida, *Specters of Marx: The State of the Debt, the Work of Mourning and the New International* trans.P.Kamuf (London, Routledge, 1994).

J. Derrida, 'Positions: Interview with Jean–Louis Houdebine and Guy Scarpetta' trans. A. Bass, in J. Derrida, *Positions* (London, Continuum, 2004).

J. Derrida, 'Autoimmunity: Real and Symbolic Suicides—A Dialogue with Jacques Derrida', 'Deconstructing Terrorism', in G. Borradori (ed.), *Philosophy in a Time of Terror—Dialogues with J. Habermas and J. Derrida* (Chicago and London, University of Chicago Press, 2005).

J. Derrida, *Rogues* (Stanford, California, University of Stanford Press, 2005).

J.F. Dienstag, 'Postmodern Approaches to the History of Political Thought', in G. Klosko (ed.), *The Oxford Handbook of the History of Political Philosophy* (Oxford, Oxford University Press, 2011), pp. 36–46.

C. Diethe, 'Nietzsche and the Woman Question', *History of European Ideas*, vol. 11, no. 6, 1989, pp. 865–76.

J. Dinwiddy, *Bentham* (Oxford, Oxford University Press, 1989).

R.J. Dostal (ed.), *The Cambridge Companion to Gadamer* (Cambridge, Cambridge University Press, 2002).

R. Douglass, 'Thomas Hobbes's Changing Accounts of Liberty and Challenge to Republicanism', *History of Political Thought*, vol. 36, Summer 2015, pp. 281–309.

W. Dray, 'R.G. Collingwood and the Understanding of Actions in History', in W. Dray, *Perspectives on History* (London and Boston, Routledge and Kegan Paul, 1980), pp. 9–26.

H.L. Dreyfus and P. Rabinow, *Beyond Structuralism and Linguistics* (Brighton, Harvester Press, 1982).

J. Dunn, 'The Identity of the History of Ideas', *Philosophy*, vol. 43, no. 164, 1968, pp. 85–104.

J. Dunn, *The Political Thought of John Locke: An Historical Account of the Argument of the 'Two Treatises of Government'* (Cambridge, Cambridge University Press, 1969).

J. Dunn, 'Introduction', in J. Dunn, *Political Obligation in Its Historical Context—Essays in Political Theory* (Cambridge, Cambridge University Press, 1980), pp. 1–12.

J. Dunn, *Locke* (Oxford, Oxford University Press, 1984).

J. Dunn, *Rethinking Modern Political Theory—Essays 1979–83* (Cambridge, Cambridge University Press, 1985).

J. Dunn, '"Trust" in the Politics of John Locke', in J. Dunn, *Rethinking Modern Political Theory—Essays 1979–83* (Cambridge, Cambridge University Press, 1985), pp. 34–54.

J. Dunn, 'The History of Political Theory', in J. Dunn, *The History of Political Theory and Other Essays* (Cambridge, Cambridge University Press, 1996), pp. 11–38.

J. Dunn, 'What is Living and What is Dead in the Political Theory of John Locke?', in J. Dunn, *Interpreting Political Responsibility* (Princeton, NJ, Princeton University Press, 1999), pp. 9–25.

406 Bibliography

T. Eagleton, *Literary Theory: An Introduction* (Oxford, Basil Blackwell, 1981).

J. Elster, *Making Sense of Marx* (Cambridge, Cambridge University Press, 1985).

F. Engels, *The Origins of the Family, Private Property and the State* trans. E. Untermann (London and New York, Penguin books, 2010).

M. Evans, *Simone de Beauvoir—A Feminist Mandarin* (London, Tavistock, 1985).

J. Farr, 'The History of Political Thought', in J. Dryzek, B. Honig, and A. Phillips (eds), *The Oxford Handbook of Political Theory* (Oxford, Oxford University Press, 2006), pp. 225–45.

J. Femia, *Machiavelli Revisited* (Cardiff, University of Wales Press, 2004).

L. Feuerbach, *The Essence of Christianity* trans. G. Eliot (New York, Dover, 2008).

R. Filmer, *Patriarcha*, ed. P. Laslett (Oxford, Basil Blackwell, 1949).

J. Findlay, 'Hegel and Platonism', in J.J. O'Malley, K.W. Algozin, and F.G. Weiss (eds), *Hegel and the History of Philosophy* (The Hague, Martinus Nijhoff, 1974), pp. 62–76.

J. Flay, 'Rupture, Closure and Dialectic', in G. Browning (ed.), *Hegel's Phenomenology: A Reappraisal* (Dordrecht, the Netherlands, Kluwer, 1997), pp. 149–64.

J. Floyd and M. Stears, *Political Philosophy versus History?* (Cambridge, Cambridge University Press, 2000).

M. Foucault, *The Birth of the Clinic* trans. A. Sheridan Smith (New York, Vintage, 1975).

M. Foucault, *Discipline and Punish: The Birth of the Prison* trans. A. Sheridan Smith (Harmondsworth, Penguin, 1977).

M. Foucault, *The History of Sexuality vol. 1 The Will to Knowledge* (London, Penguin, 1978).

M. Foucault, 'Prison Talk', trans. C. Gordon, in C. Gordon (ed.), *Power/Knowledge* (Brighton, Harvester, 1980), pp. 42–58.

M. Foucault, 'Nietzsche, Genealogy, History', in M. Foucault, *The Foucault Reader*, ed. P. Rabinow (London and New York, Penguin, 1984), pp. 76–100.

M. Foucault, 'What is an Author?' trans. J.V. Harari, in M. Foucault, *The Foucault Reader*, ed. P. Rabinow (London and New York, Penguin, 1984), pp. 101–20.

M. Foucault, 'What is Enlightenment?' trans. M. Henson, in M. Foucault, *The Foucault Reader*, ed. P. Rabinow (London and New York, Penguin, 1984), pp. 32–50.

M. Foucault, *Technologies of the Self: A Seminar with Michel Foucault*, ed. L. Martin, H. Gutman, and P. Hutton (Amherst MA., University of Massachusetts Press, 1989).

M. Foucault, *The Care of the Self, History of Sexuality vol. 3* trans. R. Hurley (Harmondsworth, Penguin, 1990).

M. Foucault, *The Use of Pleasure, The History of Sexuality vol. 2* trans. R. Hurley (Harmondsworth, Penguin, 1990).

M. Foucault, *The Archaeology of Knowledge* trans. A.M. Sheridan Smith (London, Tavistock Publications, 1995).

M. Foucault, *Madness and Civilisation: A History of Insanity in the Age of Reason* trans. R. Howard (London, Routledge, 1999).

M. Foucault, *The Order of Things* (London and New York, Routledge, 2002).

M. Foucault, *Society Must be Defended: Lectures at the College de France 1975/6* trans. D. Macey, ed. M. Bertani and A. Fontana (London, Allen Lane, 2003).

M. Foucault, *The Birth of Biopolitics—Lectures at the College de France 1978–1979* trans. G. Burchell, ed. M. Senellart (London and New York, Palgrave Macmillan, 2008).

M. Foucault, *Security, Territory, Population: Lectures at the College de France 1977–1978* trans. G. Burchell, ed. M. Senellart (London and New York, Palgrave Macmillan, 2009).

F. Fukuyama, *The End of History and the Last Man* (London and New York, Penguin, 1992).

K. Fullbrook and E. Fullbrook, 'Sartre's Secret Key', in M. Simons (ed.), *Feminist Interpretations of Simone de Beauvoir* (Pennsylvania, Pennsylvania State University Press, 1995), pp. 97–112.

H.–G. Gadamer, 'Hermeneutics and Historicism', in H–G. Gadamer, *Truth and Method* trans. revised by J. Weinsheimer and D.G. Marshall (London, Sheed and Ward, 1960), pp. 505–41.

H.–G. Gadamer, *Truth and Method* trans. revised by J. Weinsheimer and D.G. Marshall (London, Sheed and Ward, 1960).

H.–G. Gadamer, *Hegel's Dialectic* (New Haven and London, Yale University Press, 1976).

H.–G. Gadamer, 'On the Scope and Function of Hermeneutics', trans. G. Hers and R. Palmer, in H.–G. Gadamer, *Philosophical Hermeneutics*, ed. D.E. Linge (Berkeley, University of California Press, 1976), pp. 18–43.

H.–G. Gadamer, *Philosophical Hermeneutics*, ed. D.E. Linge (Berkeley, University of California Press, 1976).

H.–G. Gadamer, *The Idea of the Good in Platonic–Aristotelian Philosophy* (New Haven, Yale University Press, 1986).

H.–G. Gadamer, 'The Relevance of the Beautiful', in H.–G. Gadamer, *The Relevance of the Beautiful and Other Essays* (Cambridge, Cambridge University Press, 1986), pp. 1–56.

H.–G. Gadamer, *The Relevance of the Beautiful and Other Essays* (Cambridge, Cambridge University Press, 1986).

H.–G. Gadamer, 'Reply to Jacques Derrida' trans. D. Michelfelder and R. Palmer, in D. Michelfelder and R. Palmer (eds), *Dialogue and Deconstruction—The Gadamer–Derrida Encounter* (New York, State University of New York Press, 1989), pp. 55–8.

H.–G. Gadamer, 'Text and Interpretation' trans. D. Schmidt and R. Palmer, in D.P Michelfelder and R.E. Palmer (eds), *Dialogues and Deconstruction—The Gadamer–Derrida Encounter* (New York, State University of New York Press, 1989), pp. 21–51.

H.–G. Gadamer, *Plato's Dialectical Ethics: Phenomenological Interpretations relating to the Philebus* (New Haven, Yale University Press, 1991).

R. Gall, 'Between Tradition and Critique: The Gadamer–Habermas Debate', *Gelgung*, vol. 8, no. 1, 1981, pp. 4–18.

N. Gane, 'The Emergence of Neoliberalism: Thinking Through and Beyond Michel Foucault's Lectures on Biopolitics', *Theory Culture and Society*, vol. 31, no. 3, 2014, pp. 3–27.

D. Gauthier, *The Logic of Leviathan: The Moral and Political Theory of Thomas Hobbes* (Oxford, Clarendon Press, 1969).

I. Geiger, *The Founding Act of Modern Ethical Life—Hegel's Critique of Kant's Moral and Political Philosophy* (Stanford, California, Stanford University Press, 2007).

Bibliography

A.H. Gilbert, *Machiavelli's 'Prince' and its Forerunners: 'The Prince' as a Typical Book de regimine principium* (Durham, NC, Duke University Press, 1938).

F. Gilbert, 'The Humanist Concept of the Prince and "The Prince" of Machiavelli', *The Journal of Modern History*, vol. 11, 1939, pp. 449–83.

A. Gramsci, *Prison Notebooks*, vols 1–3 trans. J. Buttigieg (Columbia, Columbia University Press, 2011).

G. Greer, *The Female Eunuch* (London, New York, and Sydney, Harper Perennial, 2002).

R. Griffin, *The Nature of Fascism* (Abingdon, Routledge, 2003).

J. Grimshaw, 'Practices of Freedom', in C. Ramazanoglu (ed.), *Up Against Foucault: Exploration of Some Tensions Between Foucault and Feminism* (London and New York, Routledge 1993), pp. 51–73.

E. Grosholz, *The Legacy of Simone de Beauvoir* (Oxford, Clarendon Press, 2004).

J. Gunnell, 'History of Political Philosophy as a Discipline', in G. Klosko (ed.), *The Oxford Handbook of the History of Political Philosophy* (Oxford, Oxford University Press, 2011), pp. 60–74.

G. Gutting, *The Cambridge Companion to Foucault* (Cambridge, Cambridge University Press, 2003).

G. Gutting, 'Foucault and the History of Madness', in G. Gutting, *The Cambridge Companion to Foucault* (Cambridge, Cambridge University Press, 2003), pp. 49–73.

G. Gutting, *Foucault: A Very Short Introduction* (Oxford, Oxford University Press, 2005).

J. Habermas, 'Summation and Response' trans. M. Matesich, *Continuum*, vol. 8, 1970, pp. 124–8.

J. Habermas, 'On Systematically Distorted Communication', *Inquiry*, vol. 1, no. 13, 1970, pp. 205–18.

J. Habermas, 'A Review of Gadamer's Truth and Method', in J. Habermas, *Understanding and Social Inquiry*, ed. F. Dallmayr and T. McCarthy (South Bend, Notre Dame University Press, 1977), pp. 335–63.

J. Habermas, *The Philosophical Discourse of Modernity* trans. F.G. Lawrence (Cambridge, USA, MIT Press, 1990).

J. Habermas, *Between Facts and Norms: Contributions to a Discourse Theory of Law* (Cambridge, MIT Press, 1996).

J. Habermas and D. Heinrich (eds), *Theorie Diskussion: Hermeneutic und Ideologiekritik*. Mit beitragen von K–O A.C. v. Bormann, R. Bubner, H.–G. Gadamer, H.J. Giegel, J. Habermas (Frankfurt, Surhkamp, 1973).

J.R. Hale, *Machiavelli and Renaissance Italy* (London, English Universities Press, 1961).

I. Hampsher-Monk, *A History of Modern Political Thought* (Oxford, Blackwell, 1992).

I. Hampsher-Monk, 'John Locke', in I. Hampsher-Monk, *A History of Modern Political Thought* (Oxford, Blackwell, 1992).

I. Hampsher-Monk, 'Political Languages in Time—The Work of J.G.A. Pocock', *British Journal of Political Science*, vol. 1, Jan. 1984, pp. 89–116.

M. Hardimon, *Hegel's Social Philosophy: The Project of Reconciliation* (Cambridge, Cambridge University Press, 1994).

M. Hardt and A. Negri, *Empire* (Cambridge, Boston, and London, Harvard University Press, 2000).

M. Hardt and A. Negri, *Multitude—War and Democracy in the Age of Empire* (New York, Penguin Press, 2004).

M. Hardt and A. Negri, *Commonwealth* (Cambridge MA, Belknapp Press of Harvard University Press, 2009).

H.S. Harris, *Hegel's Development: Towards the Sunlight: 1770–1801* (Oxford, Oxford University Press, 1972).

G.W.F. Hegel, *Lectures on the History of Philosophy*, vols 1–3 trans. E.S. Haldane and F.H. Simpson (London, Paul, Trench and Trubner, 1892).

G.W.F. Hegel, *Early Theological Writings* trans T.M. Knox (Chicago, Chicago University Press, 1948).

G.W.F. Hegel, 'The Spirit of Christianity and its Modern Fate', in G.W.F. Hegel, *Early Theological Writings* trans. T.M. Knox (Chicago, Chicago University Press, 1948), pp. 182–301.

G.W.F. Hegel, *The Philosophy of History* trans. J. Sibree (London and New York, Dover Publications, 1956).

G.W.F. Hegel, *Political Writings* trans. T.M. Knox (Oxford, Clarendon Press, 1964).

G.W.F. Hegel, 'The German Constitution', in G.W.F. Hegel, *Political Writings* (Oxford, Clarendon Press, 1964), pp. 56–126.

G.W.F. Hegel, *Hegel's Philosophy of Right* trans. T.M. Knox (Oxford, Oxford University Press, 1967).

G.W.F. Hegel, *Science of Logic* trans. A.V. Miller (Oxford, Oxford University Press, 1969).

G.W.F. Hegel, *Hegel's Philosophy of Nature* trans. A.V. Miller (Oxford, Clarendon Press, 1970).

G.W.F. Hegel. *Hegel's Philosophy of Mind* trans. W. Wallace with Zusatze in Baumann's text (1845) trans. A.V. Miller (Oxford, Clarendon Press, 1971).

G.W.F. Hegel, *Phenomenology of Mind* trans. J.B. Bailee (London, George Allen & Unwin, 1971).

G.W.F. Hegel, 'Religion ist Eine, the Tubingen Essay of 1793' trans. H.S. Harris, in H.S. Harris, *Hegel's Development Toward the Sunlight 1770–1801* (Oxford, Oxford University Press, 1972), pp. 482–507.

G.W.F. Hegel, *The Encyclopedia Logic: Part 1 of the Encyclopedia of the Philosophical Sciences* trans. W. Wallace (Oxford, Oxford University Press, 1975).

G.W.F. Hegel, *Lectures on the Philosophy of World History. Introduction: Reason in History* trans. H.B. Nisbet (Cambridge, Cambridge University Press, 1975).

G.W.F. Hegel, *System of Ethical Life (1802/3) and First Philosophy of Spirit (PART 111 of the System of Speculative Philosophy (1803/4)* trans. and ed. H.S. Harris and T.M. Knox (Albany, State University of New York Press, 1979).

G.W.F. Hegel, *Die Philosophie des Rechts: Die Vorlesung von 1819/20*, ed. D. Heinrich (Frankfurt, Shurkamp Verlag, 1983).

M. Heidegger, *Being and Time* trans. J. Macquarrie and E. Robinson (Oxford and Malden MA, Blackwell, 1962).

M. Heidegger, 'The Origin of the Work of Art', in D. Krell (ed.), *Martin Heidegger: Basic Writings* (London, Routledge, 1978), pp. 83–140.

M. Heidegger, *Nietzsche*, 4 vols trans. D. Krell (New York, Harper Row, 1979–86).

S. Hekman, 'The Ontology of Change', in L. Code (ed.), *Feminist Interpretations of Hans-Georg Gadamer* (Pennsylvania, Pennsylvania State University Press, 2003), pp. 181–202.

B. Helm, 'Combating Misogyny—Responses to Nietzsche by Turn-Of-The-Century German Feminists', *Journal of Nietzsche Studies*, no. 27, Spring 2004, pp. 64–84.

S. Hicks, 'Hegel on Cosmopolitanism, International relations and the Challenge of Globalization', in A. Buchwalter (ed.), *Hegel and Global Justice* (Dordrecht, Heidelberg, London, and New York, Springer, 2012), pp. 21–48.

T. Hobbes, *Leviathan,* ed. M. Oakeshott (London, Macmillan, 1962).

T. Hobbes, *De Cive: The English Version entitled in the first edition Philosophical Rudiments Concerning Government and Society,* ed. Howard Warrender (Oxford, Clarendon Press, 1983).

T. Hobbes, *Behemoth,* ed. F. Tonnies (Chicago, Il., University of Chicago Press, 1990).

T. Hobbes, *The Elements of Law, Natural and Politic,* ed. J.C.A. Gaskin (Oxford, Oxford University Press, 1994).

R.J. Hollingdale, *Nietzsche* (London and New York, Routledge and Kegan Paul, 1973).

R.J. Hollingdale, 'The Hero as Outsider', in B. Magnus and K.M. Higgins (eds), *The Cambridge Companion to Nietzsche* (Cambridge, Cambridge University Press, 1996), pp. 71–89.

E. Holveck, 'Introduction to Political Reporting from Spain, Portugal and the U. S.', in S. de Beauvoir, *Political Writings* (Chicago, University of Illinois Press, 2012), pp. 1–9.

T. Honderich, '*On Liberty* and Morality-Dependent Harms', *Political Studies*, vol. 30, 1982, pp. 504–14.

B. Honig, *Emergency Politics—Paradox, Law, Democracy* (Princeton NJ and Oxford, Princeton University Press, 2009).

A. Honneth, *The Struggle for Recognition* trans. J. Anderson (Cambridge MA, MIT Press, 1996).

F.C. Hood, *The Divine Politics of Thomas Hobbes: An Interpretation of 'Leviathan'* (Oxford, Clarendon Press, 1962).

S. Houlgate, *Hegel, Nietzsche and the Criticism of Metaphysics* (Cambridge, Cambridge University Press, 2004).

K. Hutchings, *Hegel and Feminist Philosophy* (Cambridge, Polity, 1993).

K. Hutchings, *Kant, Critique and Politics* (London and New York, Routledge, 1996).

J. Hyppolyte, *Studies on Marx and Hegel* trans. J. O'Neil (New York, Joanna Cotler Books, 1973).

C. Imbert, 'Simone de Beauvoir: A Woman Philosopher in the Context of Her Generation' trans. E. Grosholz, in E. Grosholz (ed.), *The Legacy of Simone de Beauvoir* (Oxford, Clarendon Press, 2004), pp. 3–21.

P. Johnson, *The Renaissance: A Short History* (New York, Modern Library, 2000).

I. Kant, *Critique of Judgment* trans. J.C. Meredith (Oxford, Oxford University Press, 1969).

I. Kant, 'An Answer to the Question "What is Enlightenment?"', in *Kant's Political Writings* trans. H.B. Nisbet and ed. H. Reiss (Cambridge, Cambridge University Press, 1991), pp. 54–60.

I. Kant, 'Idea for a Universal History with a Cosmopolitan Purpose', in *Kant's Political Writings* ed. H. Reiss (Cambridge, Cambridge University Press, 1991), pp. 41–53.

I. Kant, 'The Metaphysics of Morals' in *Kant's Political Writings*, trans. H.B. Nisbet and ed. H. Reiss (Cambridge, Cambridge University Press, 1991), pp. 131–75.

I. Kant, 'Perpetual Peace: A Philosophical Sketch', in *Kant's Political Writings* trans. H.B. Nisbet and ed. H. Reiss (Cambridge, Cambridge University Press, 1991).

I. Kant, *Critique of Practical Reason* trans. and ed. L. Beck (Oxford, Maxwell Macmillan International, 1993).

I. Kant, *Critique of Pure Reason* trans. P. Guyer and A. Wood (Cambridge, Cambridge University Press, 1997).

I. Kant, *Religion within the Boundaries of Mere Reason* trans. and ed. A. Wood and D. Giovanni (Cambridge, Cambridge University Press, 1998).

I. Kant, *Groundwork of the Metaphysics of Morals* trans. and ed. A. Wood (New York, Yale University Press, 2002).

W. Kaufmann, *Nietzsche: Philosopher, Psychologist, Antichrist* (New York, Vintage, 1974).

P. Kelly, 'Rescuing Political Theory from the Tyranny of History', in J. Floyd and M. Stears (eds), *Political Philosophy versus History?* (Cambridge, Cambridge University Press, 2011), pp. 13–37.

T. Kenyon, 'Locke', in A. Edwards and J. Townshend, *Interpreting Modern Political Philosophy* (Basingstoke and New York, Palgrave Macmillan, 2002), pp. 60–80.

P. King, 'Historical Contextualism Revisited' in P. King, *Thinking Past a Problem* (London, Routledge, 2000), pp. 213–27.

G. Klosko, 'Introduction', in G. Klosko (ed.), *The Oxford Handbook of the History of Political Philosophy* (Oxford, Oxford University Press, 2011), pp. 1–10.

G. Klosko, *The Oxford Handbook of the History of Political Philosophy* (Oxford, Oxford University Press, 2011).

T.M. Knox, 'Editor's Preface', *The Idea of History* (Oxford, Clarendon Press, 1946), pp. x–xxv.

A. Kojeve, *An Introduction to the Reading of Hegel* trans. J.H. Nichols Jnr (New York, Cornell University Press, 1969).

P. Laslett, 'Introduction', in J. Locke, *Locke's Two Treatises of Government*, ed. P. Laslett (Cambridge, Cambridge University Press, 1970), pp. 3–65.

C. Lawn, *Gadamer: A Guide for the Perplexed* (London and New York, Continuum, 2006).

M. Le Doeff, 'Simone de Beauvoir: Falling (Ambiguously) into Line', in M. Simons (ed.), *Feminist Interpretations of Simone de Beauvoir* (Pennsylvania, Pennsylvania State Press, 1995), pp. 59–66.

M. Le Doeuff, 'Towards a Friendly Transatlantic Critique of the Second Sex', trans. E. Grosholz, in E. Grosholz, *The Legacy of Simone de Beauvoir* (Oxford, Clarendon Press, 2004), pp. 22–36.

J. Leighton, 'Simone de Beauvoir on Motherhood and "Le Devouement"', in J. Leighton, *Simone de Beauvoir on Woman* (London and Cranbury New Jersey, Associated University Presses, 1975), pp. 185–208.

V. Lenin, *Imperialism the Highest Stage of Capitalism*, in V. Lenin, *Lenin's Selected Works: vol. 1* (Moscow, Progress Publishers, 1963), pp. 187–315.

V. Lenin, *What is To Be Done*, in V. Lenin, *Lenin's Selected Works: vol. 2* (Moscow, Progress Publishers, 1963), pp. 119–271.

S. Letwin, *The Pursuit of Certainty* (Cambridge, Cambridge University Press, 1965).

G. Lichtheim, 'Karl Kautsky', in G. Lichtheim, *Marxism* (London, Routledge and Kegan Paul, 1961), pp. 259–77.

J. Locke, *An Essay Concerning Human Understanding* (New York, Prometheus Book, 1995).

J. Locke, *The Reasonableness of Christianity*, ed. J.C. Higgins-Biddle (Oxford, Oxford University Press, 1999).

J. Locke, *Some Thoughts Concerning Education* (New York, Dover Publications, 2007).

John Locke, *Locke's Two Treatises of Government*, ed. P. Laslett (Cambridge, Cambridge University Press, 1970).

A. Lovejoy, *The Great Chain of Being: A Study of the History of An Idea* (New York, Touchday, 1960).

E. Lundgren-Gothlin, *Sex and Existence—Simone de Beauvoir's 'The Second Sex'* trans. L. Schenck (Hanover and London, Wesleyan University Press, 1996).

J.-F. Lyotard, *The Condition of Postmodernity* trans. J. Van Den Abbeele (Manchester, University of Manchester Press, 1979).

J.-F. Lyotard, *The Differend—Phrases in Dispute* trans. G. Van Den Abbeele (Manchester, Manchester University Press, 1988).

N. Machiavelli, *The History of Florence* (London, Routledge and Sons, 1891).

N. Machiavelli, *Discourses on the First Ten Books of Livy* trans. C. Detmold, in N. Machiavelli *The Prince and The Discourses* (New York, The Modern Library, 1950), pp. 103–540.

N. Machiavelli, *The Prince* trans. L. Ricci, in N. Machiavelli *The Prince and The Discourses* (New York, The Modern Library, 1950), pp. 4–102.

N. Machiavelli, *The Literary Works of Machiavelli*, ed. and trans. J. Hale (Oxford, Oxford University Press, 1961).

N. Machiavelli, 'Mandragola', in N. Machiavelli, *The Literary Works of Machiavelli*, ed. and trans. J. Hale (Oxford, Oxford University Press, 1961), pp. 1–81.

N. Machiavelli, *The Chief Works and Others*, ed. A. Gilbert (Durham NC, Duke University Press, 1989).

N. Machiavelli, 'Legations', in N. Machiavelli, *The Chief Works and Others* ed. A. Gilbert (Durham NC, Duke University Press, 1989), pp. 1–161.

A. MacIntyre, *A Short History of Ethics* (London, Routledge and Kegan Paul, 1967).

A. MacIntyre, *Dependent Rational Animals* (Chicago, Illinois, Duckworth, 1999).

C.B. Macpherson, *The Political Theory of Possessive Individualism* (Oxford, Oxford University Press, 1962).

N. Malcolm, *The Correspondence of Thomas Hobbes* (Oxford, Oxford University Press, 1994).

R. Maliks, 'Hermeneutics and the History of Political Thought', in Herman Paul and Madeleine Kasten (eds), *Gadamer's Influence on the Humanities* (Leiden, Leiden University Press, 2012), pp. 173–85.

R. Maliks, 'Revolutionary Epigones: Kant and his Radical Followers', *History of Political Thought*, vol. 33, no. 4, Winter 2012, pp. 647–67.

H. Mansfield, *Machiavelli's Virtue* (Chicago, University of Chicago Press, 1996).

H. Marcuse, *Reason and Revolution: Hegel and the Rise of Social Theory* (London, Routledge, 1955).

K. Marx, *Capital*, vol. 1 trans. S. Moore and E. Aveling and ed. F. Engels (Moscow, Progress Publishers, 1969).

K. Marx, 'The Class Struggles in France: 1848–1850' trans. P. Jackson, in K. Marx, *Surveys From Exile* (Harmondsworth, Penguin, 1973), pp. 35–142.

K. Marx, 'The Eighteenth Brumaire of Louis Bonaparte' trans. B. Fawkes, in K. Marx, *Surveys from Exile* (Harmondsworth, Penguin, 1973), pp. 143–250.

K. Marx, *Grundrisse* trans. M. Nicholas (Harmondsworth, Penguin, 1974).

K. Marx, 'A Contribution to the Critique of Hegel's *Philosophy of Right*', in K. Marx, *Early Writings* trans. R. Livingstone and G. Benton (Harmondsworth, Penguin, 1975), pp. 243–58.

K. Marx, 'Critique of Hegel's *Doctrine of the State (1843)*', in K. Marx, *Early Writings* trans. R. Livingstone and G. Benton (Harmondsworth, Penguin, 1975), pp. 57–198.

K. Marx, *Early Writings* trans. R. Livingstone and G. Benton (Harmondsworth, Penguin, 1975).

K. Marx, 'Economic and Philosophical Manuscripts', in K. Marx, *Early Writings* trans. R. Livingstone and G. Benton (Harmondsworth, Penguin, 1975), pp. 279–400.

K. Marx, 'On the Jewish Question', in K. Marx, *Early Writings* trans. R. Livingstone and G. Benton (Harmondsworth, Penguin, 1975), pp. 211–42.

K. Marx, 'Critique of the Gotha Programme' trans. T. Carver, in K. Marx, *Marx's Later Political Writings* (Cambridge, Cambridge University Press, 1998), pp. 208–27.

K. Marx, *The Poverty of Philosophy* trans. H. Squelch (New York, Cosimo, Inc., 2008).

K. Marx and F. Engels, 'Preface to a Contribution to A Critique of Political Economy', in K. Marx and F. Engels, *Selected Works* (Moscow, Progress Publishers, 1970).

K. Marx and F. Engels, *Selected Works* (Moscow, Progress Publishers, 1970).

K. Marx and F. Engels, *The Communist Manifesto* trans. S. Moore, in K. Marx, *Political Writings*, vol. 1, *The Revolutions of 1848* (Harmondsworth, Penguin, 1973), pp. 46–112.

K. Marx and F. Engels, *The German Ideology* trans. S. Ryazanskaya (Moscow, Progress Publishers, 1976).

J. McCarney, *Hegel on History* (London, Routledge, 2010).

M. McIvor, 'The Young Marx and German Idealism: Revisiting the Doctoral Thesis', *Journal of the History of Ideas*, vol. 46, no. 3, July 2008, pp. 395–419.

D. McLellan, *The Young Hegelians and Karl Marx* (London and New York, Macmillan, 1969).

L. McNay, *Foucault and Feminism: Power, Gender and the Self* (Cambridge, Polity, 1992).

L. McNay, *Foucault: A Critical Introduction* (Cambridge, Polity Press, 1994).

F. Mehring, *Karl Marx, The Story of his Life* (London and New York, Routledge, 2003).

J. Mendelsen, 'The Habermas–Gadamer Debate', *New German Critique*, no. 18, 1979, pp. 44–73.

D.P. Michelfelder and R.E. Palmer (eds), *Dialogues and Deconstruction: The Gadamer–Derrida Encounter* (New York, SUNY Press, 1989).

J.S. Mill, *A System of Logic: Ratiocinative and Inductive*, in J.S. Mill, *Works*, ed. J. Robson et al. (Toronto, University of Toronto Press, 1963).

J.S. Mill, *The Principles of Political Economy, with some of their Applications to Social Philosophy*, in J.S. Mill, *Works*, ed. J. Robson et al. (Toronto, University of Toronto Press, 1963).

J.S. Mill, 'Utilitarianism', in J.S. Mill, *Utilitarianism,* together with 'On Liberty' and 'Essay on Bentham' (London and Glasgow, Fontana Books, 1970).

J.S. Mill, *Considerations on Representative Government*, in J.S. Mill, *Three Essays: On Liberty, Representative Government, The Subjection of Women* (Oxford, Oxford University Press, 1978), pp. 145–401.

J.S. Mill, *Autobiography* (Harmondsworth, Clarendon Press, Penguin Books, 1989).

J.S. Mill, *Chapters on Socialism*, in J.S. Mill, *On Liberty and Other Writings* (Cambridge, Cambridge University Press, 1989), pp. 219–80.

J.S. Mill, *On Liberty*, in J.S. Mill, *On Liberty and Other Writings* (Cambridge, Cambridge University Press, 1989), pp. 1–116.

D. Miller (ed.), *Liberty* (Oxford, Oxford University Press, 1991).

D. Miller, *Political Philosophy—A Very Short Introduction* (Oxford, Oxford University Press, 2003).

K. Minogue, 'Method in Intellectual History: Quentin Skinner's *Foundations*', in J. Tully (ed.), *Meaning and Context: Quentin Skinner and his Critics* (Cambridge, Polity Press, 1988), pp. 176–93.

T. Moi, 'Afterword', in T. Moi *Simone de Beauvoir—The Making of an Intellectual Woman* (Oxford and Cambridge, MA, Blackwell, 1994), pp. 270–5.

T. Moi, 'Second Only to Sartre', in T. Moi, *Simone de Beauvoir—The Making of An Intellectual Woman* (Oxford and Cambridge, MA, Blackwell, 1994), pp. 37–48.

T. Moi, *Simone de Beauvoir—The Making of an Intellectual Woman* (Oxford and Cambridge, MA, Blackwell, 1994).

G. Moore, *Nietzsche, Biology and Metaphor* (Cambridge, Cambridge University Press, 2002).

I. Murdoch, *The Fire and the Sun: Why Plato Banished the Artists* (Oxford, Oxford University Press, 1977).

I. Murdoch, Letters to R. Queneau in Iris Murdoch Archive, Kingston University.

P. Nicholson, 'Collingwood's *New Leviathan*: Then and Now', *Collingwood Studies*, vol. 1, 1994, pp. 163–81.

F. Nietzsche, *Thus Spoke Zarathrustra* trans. R.G. Hollingdale (Harmondsworth and Baltimore, Penguin, 1961).

F. Nietzsche, *The Gay Science* trans. W. Kaufmann (New York, Vintage Books, 1974).

F. Nietzsche, *Daybreak—Thoughts on the Prejudices of Morality* trans. R.G. Hollingdale (Cambridge, Cambridge University Press, 1982).

F. Nietzsche, *On the Genealogy of Morals* trans. C. Diethe (Cambridge, Cambridge University Press, 1994).

F. Nietzsche, *The Anti-Christ*, in F. Nietzsche *The Anti-Christ, Ecce Homo, Twilight of the Idols*, ed. A. Ridley and J. Norman (Cambridge, Cambridge University Press, 2005), pp. 1–68.

F. Nietzsche, *Ecce Homo*, in F. Nietzsche, *The Anti-Christ, Ecce Homo, Twilight of the Idols*, ed. A. Ridley and J. Norman (Cambridge, Cambridge University Press, 2005), pp. 19–152.

F. Nietzsche, *Twilight of the Idols*, in F. Nietzsche, *The Anti-Christ, Ecce Homo, Twilight of the Idols*, ed. A. Ridley and J. Norman (Cambridge, Cambridge University Press, 2005), pp. 153–230.

F. Nietzsche, 'The Greek State', in F. Nietzsche *The Nietzsche Reader*, ed. K. Ansell Pearson and D. Large (Oxford, Malden MA and Victoria Australia, Blackwell, 2006), pp. 88–95.

F. Nietzsche, *The Nietzsche Reader*, ed. K. Ansell Pearson and D. Large (Oxford, Malden MA and Victoria Australia, Blackwell, 2006).

C. Norris, *Derrida* (London, Fontana Press, 1987).

R. Nozick, *Anarchy, State and Utopia* (New York, Basic Books, 1974).

K.C. O'Rourke, *John Stuart Mill and Freedom of Expression—The Genesis of a Theory* (London and New York, Routledge, 2001).

M. Oakeshott, *Experience and Its Modes* (Cambridge, Cambridge University Press, 1933).

M. Oakeshott, 'The Activity of Being an Historian', in M. Oakeshott, *Rationalism in Politics and Other Essays* (London and New York, Methuen & Co, Barnes and Noble Books, 1962), pp. 137–67.

M. Oakeshott, 'The Moral Life in the Writings of Thomas Hobbes', in M. Oakeshott, *Rationalism in Politics and Other Essays* (London and New York, Methuen and Co Ltd, 1962), pp. 248–300.

M. Oakeshott, 'The Voice of Poetry in the Conversation of Mankind', in M. Oakeshott, *Rationalism in Politics and Other Essays* (London and New York, Methuen & Co, 1962), pp. 197–247.

M. Oakeshott, 'Dr. Leo Strauss on Hobbes', in M. Oakeshott, *Hobbes on Civil Association* (Oxford, Basil Blackwell, 1975), pp. 137–149.

M. Oakeshott, 'Introduction to *Leviathan*', in M. Oakeshott, *Hobbes on Civil Association* (Oxford, Basil Blackwell, 1975), pp. 1–74.

M. Oakeshott, *On Human Conduct* (Oxford, Oxford University Press, 1975).

M. Oakeshott, 'Present, Future and Past' in M. Oakeshott, *On History and Other Essays* (Totowa, New Jersey, Barnes and Noble Books, 1983), pp. 1–44.

M. Oakeshott, 'Political Philosophy', in M. Oakeshott, *Religion, Politics and the Moral Life*, ed. T. Fuller (New Haven and London, Yale University Press, 1993), pp. 138–55.

M. Oakeshott, *Lectures in the History of Political Thought*, ed. T. Nardin and L. O'Sullivan (Exeter, Imprint Academic, 2006).

M. Oakeshott, 'Review of R.G. Collingwood, *The Idea of History* (1947)', in M. Oakeshott, *Selected Writings*, vol. 3, *The Concept of Philosophical Jurisprudence* (Exeter, Imprint Academic, 2007), pp. 197–199.

M. Oakeshott, *Selected Writings*, vol. 3, *The Concept of Philosophical Jurisprudence* ed. L. O'Sullivan (Exeter, Imprint Academic, 2007).

M. Oakeshott, *Notebooks: 1922–86*, ed. L. O'Sullivan (Exeter, Imprint Academic, 2014).

B. Ollman, *Alienation—Marx's Conception of Man in Capitalist Society* (Cambridge, Cambridge University Press, 1971).

B. Ollman, *Dialectical Investigations* (London, Routledge, 1993).

K. Palonen, *Quentin Skinner: History, Politics, Rhetoric* (Cambridge, Polity Press, 2003).

B. Parekh, 'Liberalism and Colonialism: A Critique of Locke and Mill', in J. Pieterse and B. Parekh (eds), *The Decolonization of the Imagination* (London and Atlantic Highlands, Zed Books, 1995), pp. 81–90.

B. Parekh and R.N. Berki, 'The History of Political Ideas: A Critique of Quentin Skinner's Methodology', *Journal of the History of Ideas*, vol. 34, no. 2 (April–June 1973), pp. 163–84.

C. Pateman, *The Sexual Contract* (Cambridge, Polity Press, 1988).

A. Patten, *Hegel's Idea of Freedom* (Oxford, Oxford University Press, 1999).

M. Philp, 'Introduction', in J. Plamenatz, *Machiavelli, Hobbes and Rousseau*, eds. M. Philp and Z.A. Pelczynski (Oxford, Oxford University Press, 2012).

T. Picketty, *Capital in the Twenty-First Century* (Cambridge MA, Harvard University Press, 2014).

T. Pinkard, *Hegel's Phenomenology: The Sociality of Reason* (Cambridge, Cambridge University Press, 1994).

T. Pinkard, *Hegel: A Biography* (Cambridge, Cambridge University Press, 2000).

J. Plamenatz, 'The Use of Political Theory', *Political Studies*, vol. VIII, no. 1, 1960, pp. 37–47.

J. Plamenatz, 'Introduction', in J. Plamenatz, *Man and Society* (London, Longmans, 1963).

J. Plamenatz, *Man and Society* (London, Longmans, 1963).

J. Plamenatz, *Karl Marx's Philosophy of Man* (Oxford, Clarendon Press, 1975).

J. Plamenatz, M.E. Plamenatz and R. Wokler, *Man and Society: Political and Social Theories from Machiavelli to Marx*: 3 volumes. Revised edition (London, Longmans Group, 1992).

J. Plamenatz, *Machiavelli, Hobbes and Rousseau*, eds. M. Philp and Z.A. Pelczynski (Oxford, Oxford University Press, 2012).

R. Plant, *Hegel* (London, George Allen &Unwin, 1971).

Plato, *The Republic of Plato* trans. F.M. Cornford (Oxford, Oxford University Press, 1945, 2006).

Plato, *Parmenides* trans. F.M. Cornford, in E. Hamilton and H. Cairns (eds), *The Collected Dialogues of Plato, including the Letters* (Princeton, Princeton University Press, 1961), pp. 920–56.

J.H. Plumb, *The Italian Renaissance* (New York, American Heritage Library, 1989).

J.G.A. Pocock, 'Theory and History: Problems of Context and Narrative', in J. Dryzek, B. Honig, and A. Phillips (eds), *The Oxford Handbook of Political Theory* (Oxford, Oxford University Press, 2006), pp. 163–74.

J.G.A. Pocock, 'The History of Political Thought: Methodological Enquiry', in P. Laslett and W.G. Runciman (eds), *Philosophy, Politics and Society* (2nd Series) (Oxford, Blackwell, 1969), pp. 183–202.

J.G.A. Pocock, 'The Concept of a Language', in J.G.A. Pocock, *Political Thought and History— Essays on Theory and Method* (Cambridge, Cambridge University Press, 2009), pp. 87–105.

J.G.A. Pocock, 'Custom and Grace, Form and Matter, an Approach to Machiavelli's Concept of Innovation', in M. Fleischer (ed.), *Machiavelli and the Nature of Political Thought* (New York, Croom Helm, 1973), pp. 153–74.

J.G.A. Pocock, *The Ancient Constitution and the Feudal Law: A Study of English Historical Thought in the Seventeenth Century: A Reissue with Retrospect* (Cambridge, Cambridge University Press, 1987).

J.G.A. Pocock, *The Machiavellian Moment: Florentine Political Thought and the Atlantic Republican Tradition* (Princeton, NJ, Princeton University Press, 1987).

J.G.A. Pocock, 'Present at the Creation: With Laslett in the Lost Worlds', *International Journal of Public Affairs* vol. 2, 2006, pp. 7–17.

J.G.A. Pocock, *Political Thought and History—Essays on Theory and Method* (Cambridge, Cambridge University Press, 2009).

J.G.A. Pocock, 'Preface', in J.G.A. Pocock, *Political Thought and History—Essays on Theory and Method* (Cambridge, Cambridge University Press, 2009), pp. vii–xvi.

J.G.A. Pocock, *Quentin Skinner: The History of Politics and the Politics of History* (Cambridge, Cambridge University Press, 2009), pp. 123–44.

J.G.A. Pocock, 'Time, Institutions and Action: An Essay on Traditions and their Understanding', in J.G.A. Pocock, *Political Thought and History—Essays on Theory and Method* (Cambridge, Cambridge University Press, 2009), pp. 187–216.

K. Popper, *The Open Society and Its Enemies*, vol. 1 (London, Routledge, Kegan & Paul, 1945).

K. Popper, *The Poverty of Historicism* (London, Routledge, 1996).

J. Rawls, *A Theory of Justice* (Cambridge, MA, Harvard University Press, 1971).

B. Redhead (ed.), *From Plato To Nato* (London, BBC Books, 1985).

J. Rees, 'A Re-Reading of Mill on Liberty', in J. Gray and G.W. Smith (eds), *Mill On Liberty: In Focus* (London, Routledge, 1991), pp. 169–89.

J. Riley, *Mill on Liberty* (London, Routledge, 1998).

A. Rogow, *Thomas Hobbes—Radical in the Service of Reaction* (London and New York, W.W. Norton, 1986).

G. Rose, 'The Comedy of Hegel and the *Trauerspiel* of Modern Philosophy', in G. Browning (ed.), *Hegel's Phenomenology: A Reappraisal* (Dordrecht, the Netherlands, Kluwer, 1997), pp. 105–12.

G. Rose, *Hegel Contra Sociology* (London and New York, Continuum, 2000).

A. Rosen, *Kant's Theory of Justice* (Ithaca and London, Cornell University Press, 1996).

F. Rosen, *Jeremy Bentham and Representative Democracy* (Oxford, Oxford University Press, 1983).

F. Rosen, 'The Bentham Edition', *Politics*, vol. 16, 1996, pp. 127–32.

F. Rosen, *Mill* (Oxford, Oxford University Press, 2013).

J.-J. Rousseau, *State of War*, in J.-J. Rousseau, *Political Writings* trans. and ed. C.E. Vaughn (Cambridge, Cambridge University Press, 1915), pp. 298–306.

J.-J. Rousseau, *Constitutional Project for Corsica* trans. F. Watkins, in J.-J. Rousseau, *Political Writings* (Edinburgh, Thomas Nelson, 1953), pp. 277–356.

J.-J. Rousseau, *The Discourses and Other Early Political Writings*, ed. V. Gourevitch (Cambridge, Cambridge University Press, 1971).

J.-J. Rousseau, *Essay on the Origin of Languages* trans. J. Moran and A. Gode, in J.-J. Rousseau, *The Discourses and Other Early Political Writings* ed. V. Gourevitch (Cambridge, Cambridge University Press, 1971), pp. 247–99.

J.-J. Rousseau, *A Discourse on the Arts and Sciences*, in J.-J. Rousseau, *The Social Contract and Discourses* trans. G.D.H. Cole (London, J.M. Dent & Sons, 1973), pp. 1–26.

J.-J. Rousseau, *A Discourse on the Origin of Inequality*, in J.-J. Rousseau, *The Social Contract and Discourses* trans. G.D.H. Cole (London, J.M. Dent & Sons, 1975), pp. 28–114.

J.-J. Rousseau, *The Social Contract*, in J.-J. Rousseau, *The Social Contract and Discourses* trans. G.D.H. Cole (London, J.M. Dent & Sons, 1975), pp. 164–278.

J.-J. Rousseau, *Confessions* trans. J.M. Cohen (Harmondsworth, Penguin, 1976).

J.-J. Rousseau, *Émile* trans. A. Bloom (New York, Basic Books, 1979).

J.-J. Rousseau, *The Government of Poland* trans. W. Kendall (Indianapolis, Hackett, 1985).

A. Ryan, 'Hobbes and Individualism', in G.A.J. Rogers and A. Ryan (eds), *Perspectives on Thomas Hobbes* (Oxford, Clarendon Press, 1988), pp. 81–105.

S. Sandford, *Beauvoir* (London, Granta Books, 2006).

J. Sartre, *Being and Nothingness* trans. H.E. Barnes (New York, Washington Square Press, 1966).

J. Schmidt, 'The Autocritique of Enlightenment: Rousseau and the Philosophes', *Journal of the History of Philosophy*, vol. 34, no. 3, 1996, pp. 465–6.

P. Schofield, *Utility and Democracy: The Political Thought of Jeremy Bentham* (Oxford, Oxford University Press, 2006).

P. Schofield, *Bentham: A Guide for the Perplexed* (London, Continuum, 2009).

P. Schofield, 'Introduction', in J. Bentham, *The Book of Fallacies* (Oxford, Oxford University Press, 2015), pp. 1–35.

A.D. Schrift, 'Nietzsche's French Legacy', in B. Magnus and K. Higgins (eds), *The Cambridge Companion to Nietzsche* (Cambridge, Cambridge University Press, 1996), pp. 323–55.

J. Shklar, *Men and Citizens—A Study of Rousseau's Social Theory* (Cambridge, Cambridge University Press, 1969).

R. Shorten, 'How to Study Ideas in Politics and "Influence": A Typology', *Contemporary Politics*, vol. 19, no. 4, 2013, pp. 361–78.

J.A. Simmons, *The Lockean Theory of Rights* (Princeton NJ, Princeton University Press, 1992).

J. Simons, *Foucault and the Political* (London and New York, Routledge, 1995).

M. Simons, 'Introduction', in M. Simons (ed.), *Feminist Interpretations of Simone de Beauvoir* (University Park, Pennsylvania, Pennsylvania State University Press, 1995), pp. 1–28.

M. Simpson, *Rousseau—A Guide for the Perplexed* (London and New York, Continuum, 2007).

Q. Skinner, 'The Ideological Context of Hobbes's Political Thought', *Historical Journal*, vol. 9, 1966, pp. 286–317.

Q. Skinner, 'The Limits of Historical Explanation', *Philosophy*, vol. 41, 1966, pp. 199–215.

Q. Skinner, 'Meaning and Understanding in the History of Ideas', *History and Theory*, vol. 8, 1969, pp. 29–67.

Q. Skinner, 'Conquest and Consent: Thomas Hobbes and the Engagement Controversy', in *The Interregnum: The Quest for a Settlement, 1646–1660*, ed. E.G. Aylmer (London, Macmillan, 1972), pp. 79–98.

Q. Skinner, *The Foundations of Modern Political Thought*, vol. 1, *The Renaissance* (Cambridge, Cambridge University Press, 1978).

Q. Skinner, *Machiavelli* (Oxford, Oxford University Press, 1981).

Q. Skinner, 'Meaning and Understanding in the History of Ideas', in J. Tully (ed.), *Meaning and Context—Quentin Skinner and His Critics* (Cambridge, Polity Press, 1988) (reprinted from the original article in *History and Theory* (1969)).

Q. Skinner, 'Machiavelli's *Discorsi* and the Pre-humanist Origins of Republican Ideas', in G. Brock, Q. Skinner, and M. Viroli, *Machiavelli and Republicanism* (Cambridge, Cambridge University Press, 1991), pp. 121–42.

Q. Skinner, 'The Paradoxes of Political Liberty', in D. Miller (ed.), *Liberty* (Oxford, Oxford University Press, 1991), pp. 183–205.

Q. Skinner, *Reason and Rhetoric in Hobbes's Leviathan* (Cambridge, Cambridge University Press, 1996).

Q. Skinner, 'The Rise of, Challenge to and Prospects for a Collingwoodian Approach to the History of Political Thought', in D. Castiglione and I. Hampsher-Monk (eds), *The History of Political Thought in a National Context* (Cambridge, Cambridge University Press, 2001), pp. 175–87.

Q. Skinner, 'Introduction: Seeing Things their Way', in Q. Skinner, *Visions of Politics: Regarding Method* (Cambridge, Cambridge University Press, 1992), pp. 1–7.

Q. Skinner, *Visions of Politics: Regarding Method* (Cambridge, Cambridge University Press, 1992).

Q. Skinner, 'Interpretation and the Understanding of Speech Acts', in Q. Skinner, *Visions of Politics Regarding Method* (Cambridge, Cambridge University Press, 2002), pp. 103–27.

Q. Skinner, 'Meaning and Understanding in the History of Ideas', in Q. Skinner, *Visions of Politics*, vol. 1, *Regarding Method* (Cambridge, Cambridge University Press, 2002) (revised version), pp. 57–89.

Q. Skinner, 'Motives, Intentions and Interpretation', in Q. Skinner, *Visions of Politics*, vol. 1, *Regarding Method* (Cambridge, Cambridge University Press, 2002), pp. 90–102.

Q. Skinner, 'Retrospect: Studying Rhetoric and Conceptual Change', in *Visions of Politics*, vol. 1, *Regarding Method* (Cambridge, Cambridge University Press, 2002), pp. 175–87.

Q. Skinner, 'A Third Concept of Liberty', *Proceedings of the British Academy*, vol. 87, 2002, pp. 237–68.

Q. Skinner, *Hobbes and Republican Liberty* (Cambridge, Cambridge University Press, 2008).

Q. Skinner, interview with P. Koikkalainen and S. Syrjamaki, 'Quentin Skinner on Encountering the Past', Finnish Yearbook of Political Thought [Redescriptions Yearbook of Political Thought Conceptual History and Feminist Theory], no. 6, 2002, pp. 32–65.

Q. Skinner, interview with Tersa Bejan, 'Quentin Skinner on Meaning and Method', *The Art of Theory—Conversations in Political Philosophy*, November and December 2014, www.artoftheory.com.

J. Skorupski, *Why Read Mill Today?* (Abingdon and New York, Routledge, 2006).

G. Slomp, 'Hobbes and The Equality of and The Equality of Women', *Political Studies*, vol. 42, issue 3, 1994.

M.R. Small, *Nietzsche in Context* (Aldershot and Burlington, USA, Ashgate, 2001).

S. Smith, 'Practical Life and the Critique of Rationalism', in E. Podoksik (ed.), *The Cambridge Companion to Oakeshott* (Cambridge, Cambridge University Press, 2012), pp. 131–52.

T. Smith, *Dialectical Social Theory and Its Critics* (New York, State University of New York Press, 1993).

J. Somerville, *Thomas Hobbes: Political Ideas in Historical Context* (Basingstoke, Macmillan, 1996).

S. State, *Thomas Hobbes and the Debate over Natural Law and Religion* (New York, Garland Publishing, 1991).

C. de Stefano, *Configurations of Masculinity: A Feminist Perspective on Modern Political Theory* (Ithaca New York, Cornell University Press, 1991).

R. Stern, *Routledge Guidebook to Hegel's Phenomenology of Spirit* (London and New York, Routledge, 2001).

L. Strauss, *Thoughts on Machiavelli* (Chicago Il. and London, University of Chicago Press, 1958).

L. Strauss, *What is Political Philosophy? And Other Studies* (Glencoe Il., Free Press, 1959).

L. Strauss, *The City and Man* (Chicago, Il., University of Chicago Press, 1964).

L. Strauss, *Persecution and the Art of Writing* (Chicago, Il., University of Chicago Press, 1988).

T. Strong, *Jean-Jacques Rousseau—The Politics of the Ordinary* (London and Thousand Oaks, California, Sage Publications, 1994).

A. Swift, *Political Philosophy—A Beginner's Guide for Students and Politicians* (Cambridge and Malden MA, Polity, 2001).

A. Swift, *Political Philosophy—A Beginner's Guide for Students and Politicians*, 3rd Edition (Cambridge and Malden MA, Polity, 2014).

J. Talmon, *Rousseau and The Origins of Totalitarian Democracy* (London, Secker and Warburg, 1960).

N. Tarcov, 'Quentin Skinner's Method and Machiavelli's Politics', in J. Tully (ed.), *Meaning and Context—Quentin Skinner and his Critics* (Cambridge, Polity Press, 1988), pp. 194–203.

C. Taylor, 'Self–Interpreting Animals,' in C. Taylor, *Human Agency and Language: Philosophical Papers 1* (Cambridge, Cambridge University Press, 1985), pp. 45–76.

C. Taylor, *Sources of the Self—The Making of the Modern Identity* (Cambridge MA, Harvard University Press, 1989).

C. Taylor, 'The Politics of Recognition', in A. Gutmann (ed.), *Multiculturalism: Examining the Politics of Recognition* (Princeton, NJ, Princeton University Press, 1994), pp. 25–74.

C. Taylor, 'Gadamer on the Human Sciences', in R.J. Dostal (ed.), *The Cambridge Companion to Gadamer* (Cambridge, Cambridge University Press, 2002), pp. 126–42.

C.L. Ten, *Mill on Liberty* (Oxford, Clarendon Press, 1980).

W. Thomas, *Mill* (Oxford and New York, Oxford University Press, 1985).

J. Townshend, *C.B. Macpherson and the Problem of Liberal Democracy* (Edinburgh, Edinburgh University Press, 2000).

R. Tseng, 'Scepticism in Politics: A Dialogue Between Michael Oakeshott and John Dunn', *History of Political Thought*, vol. 34, no. 1, Spring 2013, pp. 143–70.

R. Tuck, *Natural Rights Theories: Their Origins and Development* (Cambridge, Cambridge University Press, 1979).

J. Tully, *A Discourse on Property: John Locke and His Adversaries* (Cambridge, Cambridge University Press, 1980).

J. Tully (ed), *Meaning and Context–Quentin Skinner and His Critics* (Cambridge, Polity Press, 1988).

A. Vincent, 'Review Article: Social Contract in Retrospect', *Collingwood Studies*, vol. 2, 1995, pp. 134–5.

B. Wachterhauser, 'Getting It Right: Relativism, Realism and Truth', in R.J. Dostal (ed.), *The Cambridge Companion to Gadamer*, (Cambridge, Cambridge University Press, 2002), pp. 52–78.

J. Waldron, *God, Locke and Equality: Christian Foundations of John Locke's Political Thought* (Cambridge, Cambridge University Press, 2002).

J. Waldron, 'Locke', in D. Boucher and P. Kelly (eds), *Political Thinkers* (Oxford, Oxford University Press, 2004), pp. 207–24.

R. Ware, 'Hegel's Metaphilosophy and Historical Metamorphosis', *History of Political Thought*, vol. 17, no. 2, 1996, pp. 253–79.

H. Warrender, *The Political Philosophy of Hobbes: The Theory of Obligation* (Oxford, Clarendon Press, 1957).

B. Williams, *Ethics and the Limits of Philosophy* (Glasgow, Fontana Press/Collins, 1985).

B. Williams, 'The Liberalism of Fear', in B. Williams, *In the Beginning Was the Deed—Realism and Moralism in Political Argument* (Princeton and Oxford, Princeton University Press, 2005), pp. 52–61.

G. Williams, *Political Theory in Retrospect: From the Ancient Greeks to the Twentieth Century* (London, Edward Elgar, 1992).

G. Williams, 'Changing Reputations and Interpretations in the History of Political Thought: J.S. Mill', *Politics*, vol. 15, no. 3, September 1995, pp. 183–9.

H. Williams, *Kant's Critique of Hobbes—Sovereignty and Cosmopolitanism* (Cardiff, University of Wales Press, 2003).

L. Wittgenstein, *Philosophical Investigations* (Oxford, Basil Blackwell, 1976).

R. Wokler, *Rousseau* (Oxford, Oxford University Press, 1995).

R. Wokler, 'Contextualizing Hegel's Phenomenology of the French Revolution and the Terror', *Political Theory*, vol. 26, no. 1, 1998, pp. 33–55.

R. Wokler, 'Ancient Postmodernism in the Philosophy of Rousseau', in P. Riley (ed.), *The Cambridge Companion to Rousseau* (Cambridge, Cambridge University Press, 2000), pp. 418–44.

R. Wokler, 'Introduction', *Man and Society*, in J. Plamenatz *Man and Society: Political and Social Theories from Machiavelli to Marx: Hegel, Marx and Engels and the Idea of Progress*. Revised edition (London, Longmans Group, 1992), pp. i–xxv.

M. Wollstonecraft, *A Vindication of the Rights of Woman* (Harmondsworth, Penguin, 1994).

A. Wood, *Hegel's Ethical Thought* (Cambridge, Cambridge University Press, 1991).

R. Zaretsky and J. Scott, *The Philosopher's Quarrel: Rousseau, Hume and the Limits of Understanding* (New Haven, Yale University Press, 2009).

Catherine H. Zuckert, 'Hermeneutics in Practice: Gadamer on Ancient Philosophy', in R.J. Dostal (ed.), *The Cambridge Companion to Gadamer* (Cambridge, Cambridge University Press, 2002), pp. 201–24.

Index